perspectives

Industrial and
Organizational
Psychology

perspectives

Industrial and Organizational Psychology

Academic Editor
Karl N. Kelley
North Central College

coursewise
publishing
inc.

Bellevue • Boulder • Dubuque • Madison • St. Paul

Our mission at **Coursewise** is to help students make connections—linking theory to practice and the classroom to the outside world. Learners are motivated to synthesize ideas when course materials are placed in a context they recognize. By providing gateways to contemporary and enduring issues, **Coursewise** publications will expand students' awareness of and context for the course subject.

For more information on **Coursewise,** visit us at our web site: http://www.coursewise.com

To order an examination copy, contact: Houghton Mifflin Sixth Floor Media: 800-565-6247 (voice); 800-565-6236 (fax).

Coursewise Publishing Editorial Staff

Thomas Doran, ceo/publisher: Environmental Science/Geography/Journalism/Marketing/Speech
Edgar Laube, publisher: Political Science/Psychology/Sociology
Linda Meehan Avenarius, publisher: **Courselinks**™
Sue Pulvermacher-Alt, publisher: Education/Health/Gender Studies
Victoria Putman, publisher: Anthropology/Philosophy/Religion
Tom Romaniak, publisher: Business/Criminal Justice/Economics
Kathleen Schmitt, publishing assistant
Gail Hodge, executive producer

Coursewise Publishing Production Staff

Lori A. Blosch, permissions coordinator
Mary Monner, production coordinator
Victoria Putman, production manager

Note: Readings in this book appear exactly as they were published. Thus, inconsistencies in style and usage among the different readings are likely.

Cover photo: Copyright © 1997 T. Teshigawara/Panoramic Images, Chicago, IL. All Rights Reserved.

Interior design and cover design by Jeff Storm

Copyright © 2000 by Coursewise Publishing, Inc. All Rights Reserved.

Library of Congress Catalog Card Number: 99-62982

ISBN 0-395-97204-3

No part of this publication may be reproduced, stored in a retrieval system, or transmitted, in any form or by any means, electronic, mechanical, photocopying, recording, or otherwise, without the prior written permission of the publisher.

Printed in the United States of America by Coursewise Publishing, Inc.
7 North Pinckney Street, Suite 346, Madison, WI 53703

from the
Publisher

Edgar Laube
Coursewise Publishing

Instead of counting sheep the other night, I counted the number of jobs I've had. The number was over thirty before I got to sleep, and no doubt I missed some. Most of it's a blur now, but taking the time to remember individual jobs usually leads me to a memory of something really stupid about the job—some rule or norm about how to behave, how to dress, what tools I could use, or who was considered a "secretary" on Secretary's Day. Sometimes it was a company rule, sometimes a union rule, sometimes a norm that no one challenged, or sometimes it was an outgrowth of the boss's personality.

The problem is that work is not optional for most of us. So, over a period of years, we can find ourselves in these environments where irrational rules or pressure become a source of irritation. In thinking about the jobs I didn't like, I realized that it usually wasn't the work itself but rather the environment surrounding the work that made things difficult. It's one thing to have to dig a ditch or write a report—but if you're digging the ditch with shovels because the backhoe is broken or if you're writing a report that you know won't be read—that's when the aggravation starts.

What does an employer owe you? A wage, maybe some benefits, a safe and clean working environment, and so on. What do you owe the employer in exchange? An honest effort, adherence to rules and procedures, maybe clean fingernails, and a smile for customers. Obviously, the ideal is for the organization to meet the needs of the workers and for the workers to achieve the goals of the organization. Working toward the ideal takes an understanding of the issues on both sides. This is the domain of the industrial/organizational (I/O) psychologist.

Students, I commend you for your interest in I/O psychology. Work often occupies the intersection where our individual selves mesh with—or collide with—the larger society. What you learn here will certainly help you make better decisions about your own work, and may well help you contribute to the work satisfaction of others.

Karl Kelley has done a fine job of selecting readings that illustrate the major themes of industrial/organizational psychology. I'd like to thank him for his conscientiousness and attention to detail. I'm especially heartened by the fact that these readings are drawn from over thirty source periodicals, reflecting the many aspects of work and the many ways in which they affect us.

Please make a point of logging on to the **Courselinks**™ site for Industrial and Organizational Psychology and checking out the rich resources there. You can also contact Karl or me via the site. We want to know what you think. In return I may have some further thoughts about alternatives to counting sheep.

from the
Academic Editor

Karl N. Kelley
North Central College

Dr. Karl N. Kelley graduated from Virginia Commonwealth University and is currently an associate professor and chair of the Psychology Department at North Central College in Naperville, Illinois. For the past twelve years, he has been teaching courses in industrial psychology, organizational behavior, statistics, tests and measurements, and personality. His primary area of research involves examining how individuals respond to success and failure feedback in industrial and academic settings. He has supervised student projects addressing the assessment of self-concept and the effects of procrastination on performance. Apart from his interests in psychology, Karl enjoys reading about early American history, riding his bike, playing with his dog Maddy Egon, and spending time with his wife Jai'neen and 5-year-old daughter Mary Emma (see photo above).

I like my job. Although there are some bad days, on the whole, I am convinced I am doing something important. I have a reason to get up in the morning and genuinely look forward to walking into my classroom or meeting with my colleagues. As a teacher, I still experience some anxiety before every lecture or presentation, but it is a positive feeling, rather than one to avoid. I am constantly exposed to exciting, innovative ideas and new ways of thinking. I work with a group of individuals who are passionate about what they do, and I am fortunate to be a part of all that goes on around me.

Some may say that this sounds too good to be true, and maybe, as I sit here writing this introduction, I am focusing primarily on the positive aspects of my work. However, the fact is that there are many positive parts to my job. I am not sure if everyone can say that about his or her job, but wouldn't it be nice if they could? Imagine a world where everyone believed they were accomplishing important tasks and their organizations encouraged and supported personal/professional growth. Imagine if all organizations were able to attract and maintain a passionate, dedicated workforce. I think that these are good things to imagine and as an industrial/organizational psychologist, I also think that these are goals worth working for.

These are some of the reasons that I became interested in industrial/organizational psychology as a profession and why I wanted to serve as the Academic Editor for this reader. Individuals in industrial/organizational psychology are in a unique position to address issues related to the human element of work by employing sound, scientific strategies in understanding people at work. As I hope it comes through in the readings in this text, our mission is to help organizations become more productive and profitable while addressing the needs and desires of all individuals in the workplace.

In teaching industrial/organizational psychology, I try to bring this perspective to the classroom. I want students to understand the complex nature of work by accounting for the numerous issues that have a direct impact on individuals. I have worked with the Editorial Board to present a balanced view of the workplace, addressing both organizational and individual perspectives. I believe we have achieved that balance in this reader.

This was an exciting project for me. I had the opportunity to read some papers relevant to my field that I probably would not have otherwise read, and I thought about what I do in some different ways. I also had the opportunity to begin strategically exploring the Internet. This emphasis on connected learning was one of the primary reasons I wanted to work for **Coursewise.** The Internet is an amazing resource, but it can also present a confusing and tangled web that can lead to a lot of misinformation and some outright garbage. I hope that those who use this reader and visit the **Courselinks**™ site will benefit from some of my explorations and will be able to use their time more productively by visiting sites that have R.E.A.L (relevant, enhanced, approved, and linked) characteristics.

Before closing, I want to acknowledge all those who played an important role in helping this book come into being. I extend my thanks and appreciation to the members of the Editorial Board for their constructive comments and suggestions, and also to the many professionals at **Coursewise** who worked to make this book a quality publication. In particular, I want to thank Ed Laube for encouragement and support during the entire process. Finally, to my wife, partner, and friend Jai'neen and to my daughter, Mary Emma, I want to express my love and gratitude for your support and patience as I worked on this project.

To all of the students and teachers who use this book, I trust you will enjoy and learn from the readings and web sites that are in this volume. Since I view this as a work in progress, I encourage you to visit with me on the **Courselinks** web site for Industrial and Organizational Psychology and offer your suggestions and feedback. My hope is that you will find the field of industrial/organizational psychology as exciting and intriguing as I do.

Editorial Board

We wish to thank the following instructors for their assistance. Their many suggestions not only contributed to the construction of this volume, but also to the ongoing development of our Industrial and Organizational Psychology web site.

Dr. Nancy Gussett
Baldwin-Wallace College

Nancy Gussett is an assistant professor of psychology at Baldwin-Wallace College. She teaches courses in industrial/organizational psychology, human relations, group dynamics, and tests and measurements. Her primary scholarly interests are in testing and selection.

Dr. Jack Hartnett
Virginia Commonwealth University

Jack Hartnett is an associate professor at Virginia Commonwealth University, where he has taught since 1968. He has considerable consulting experience in both the private and public sectors, particularly in the areas of job satisfaction, selection, assessment, and organizational development.

Elizabeth Johnson
North Central College

Elizabeth Johnson holds a master's degree in human resources and industrial relations from Loyola University. She has worked in the human resources field since 1982, focusing on discipline counseling, performance evaluation, job analysis, and training. She is also a Girl Scout Leader and Pioneer Club Program Coordinator. Currently, she is an instructor of psychology at North Central College.

Heather LaCost
Northern Illinois University

Heather LaCost holds a master's degree in psychology and is a doctoral student in the social/organizational psychology program at Northern Illinois University. She has interned with organizations such as United Airlines and McDonald's Corporation. Her primary research areas include organizational politics, organizational climate, office romance, and sexual harassment.

Dr. Larry Penwell
Mary Washington College

Larry Penwell is currently an associate professor in the Departments of Business Administration and Psychology at Mary Washington College. He specializes in organizational development and change.

Dr. Nora Reilly
Radford University

Nora Reilly teaches industrial/organizational psychology at Radford University. Her research focuses on the social psychology of organizations, with special interests in the development and behavioral expression of commitment and applied stigma research related to the Americans with Disabilities Act.

Dr. Cathy Riordan
University of Missouri-Rolla

Cathy Riordan is a professor of psychology and the director of management systems (an interdisciplinary undergraduate degree program) at the University of Missouri-Rolla. Her research interests focus on the impact of technologies — particularly computer technologies—in the workplace.

Dr. Lisa Scherer
University of Nebraska

Lisa Scherer is an associate professor of psychology at the University of Nebraska. Her areas of interest include organizational problem solving and decision making, self-efficacy, work-family issues, and emotions in the workplace.

Dr. Dennis Stewart
Benedictine University

Dennis Stewart is an assistant professor at Benedictine University. He has a Ph.D. in social psychology from Miami University. His primary research interests are small-group discussion and decision making.

WiseGuide Introduction

Critical Thinking and Bumper Stickers

The bumper sticker said: Question Authority. This is a simple directive that goes straight to the heart of critical thinking. The issue is not whether the authority is right or wrong; it's the questioning process that's important. Questioning helps you develop awareness and a clearer sense of what you think. That's critical thinking.

Critical thinking is a new label for an old approach to learning—that of challenging all ideas, hypotheses, and assumptions. In the physical and life sciences, systematic questioning and testing methods (known as the scientific method) help verify information, and objectivity is the benchmark on which all knowledge is pursued. In the social sciences, however, where the goal is to study people and their behavior, things get fuzzy. It's one thing for the chemistry experiment to work out as predicted, or for the petri dish to yield a certain result. It's quite another matter, however, in the social sciences, where the subject is ourselves. Objectivity is harder to achieve.

Although you'll hear critical thinking defined in many different ways, it really boils down to analyzing the ideas and messages that you receive. What are you being asked to think or believe? Does it make sense, objectively? Using the same facts and considerations, could you reasonably come up with a different conclusion? And, why does this matter in the first place? As the bumper sticker urged, question authority. Authority can be a textbook, a politician, a boss, a big sister, or an ad on television. Whatever the message, learning to question it appropriately is a habit that will serve you well for a lifetime. And in the meantime, thinking critically will certainly help you be course wise.

> Question Authority

Getting Connected

This reader is a tool for connected learning. This means that the readings and other learning aids explained here will help you to link classroom theory to real-world issues. They will help you to think critically and to make long-lasting learning connections. Feedback from both instructors and students has helped us to develop some suggestions on how you can wisely use this connected learning tool.

WiseGuide Pedagogy

A wise reader is better able to be a critical reader. Therefore, we want to help you get wise about the articles in this reader. Each section of *Perspectives* has three tools to help you: the WiseGuide Intro, the WiseGuide Wrap-Up, and the Putting It in *Perspectives* review form.

WiseGuide Intro

In the WiseGuide Intro, the Academic Editor introduces the section, gives you an overview of the topics covered, and explains why particular articles were selected and what's important about them.

Also in the WiseGuide Intro, you'll find several key points or learning objectives that highlight the most important things to remember from this section. These will help you to focus your study of section topics.

> WiseGuide Intro

At the end of the WiseGuide Intro, you'll find questions designed to stimulate critical thinking. Wise students will keep these questions in mind as they read an article (we repeat the questions at the start of the articles as a reminder). When you finish each article, check your understanding. Can you answer the questions? If not, go back and reread the article. The Academic Editor has written sample responses for many of the questions, and you'll find these online at the **Courselinks**™ site for this course. More about **Courselinks** in a minute. . . .

WiseGuide Wrap-Up

Be course wise and develop a thorough understanding of the topics covered in this course. The WiseGuide Wrap-Up at the end of each section will help you do just that with concluding comments or summary points that repeat what's most important to understand from the section you just read.

In addition, we try to get you wired up by providing a list of select Internet resources—what we call R.E.A.L. web sites because they're **R**elevant, **E**nhanced, **A**pproved, and **L**inked. The information at these web sites will enhance your understanding of a topic. (Remember to use your Passport and start at http://www.courselinks.com so that if any of these sites have changed, you'll have the latest link.)

Putting It in *Perspectives* Review Form

At the end of the book is the Putting It in *Perspectives* review form. Your instructor may ask you to complete this form as an assignment or for extra credit. If nothing else, consider doing it on your own to help you critically think about the reading.

Prompts at the end of each article encourage you to complete this review form. Feel free to copy the form and use it as needed.

The Courselinks™ Site

The **Courselinks** Passport is your ticket to a wonderful world of integrated web resources designed to help you with your course work. These resources are found at the **Courselinks** site for your course area. This is where the readings in this book and the key topics of your course are linked to an exciting array of online learning tools. Here you will find carefully selected readings, web links, quizzes, worksheets, and more, tailored to your course and approved as connected learning tools. The ever-changing, always interesting **Courselinks** site features a number of carefully integrated resources designed to help you be course wise. These include:

- **R.E.A.L. Sites** At the core of a **Courselinks** site is the list of R.E.A.L. sites. This is a select group of web sites for studying, not surfing. Like the readings in this book, these sites have been selected, reviewed, and approved by the Academic Editor and the Editorial Board. The R.E.A.L. sites are arranged by topic and are annotated with short descriptions and key words to make them easier for you to use for reference or research. With R.E.A.L. sites, you're studying approved resources within seconds—and not wasting precious time surfing unproven sites.

- **Editor's Choice** Here you'll find updates on news related to your course, with links to the actual online sources. This is also where we'll tell you about changes to the site and about online events.

http://www.courselinks.com

- **Course Overview** This is a general description of the typical course in this area of study. While your instructor will provide specific course objectives, this overview helps you place the course in a generic context and offers you an additional reference point.

- **www.orksheet** Focus your trip to a R.E.A.L. site with the www.orksheet. Each of the 10 to 15 questions will prompt you to take in the best that site has to offer. Use this tool for self-study, or if required, email it to your instructor.

- **Course Quiz** The questions on this self-scoring quiz are related to articles in the reader, information at R.E.A.L. sites, and other course topics, and will help you pinpoint areas you need to study. Only you will know your score—it's an easy, risk-free way to keep pace!

- **Topic Key** The online Topic Key is a listing of the main topics in your course, and it correlates with the Topic Key that appears in this reader. This handy reference tool also links directly to those R.E.A.L. sites that are especially appropriate to each topic, bringing you integrated online resources within seconds!

- **Web Savvy Student Site** If you're new to the Internet or want to brush up, stop by the Web Savvy Student site. This unique supplement is a complete **Courselinks** site unto itself. Here, you'll find basic information on using the Internet, creating a web page, communicating on the web, and more. Quizzes and Web Savvy Worksheets test your web knowledge, and the R.E.A.L. sites listed here will further enhance your understanding of the web.

- **Student Lounge** Drop by the Student Lounge to chat with other students taking the same course or to learn more about careers in your major. You'll find links to resources for scholarships, financial aid, internships, professional associations, and jobs. Take a look around the Student Lounge and give us your feedback. We're open to remodeling the Lounge per your suggestions.

Building Better Perspectives!

Please tell us what you think of this *Perspectives* volume so we can improve the next one. Here's how you can help:

1. Visit our **Coursewise** site at: http://www.coursewise.com

2. Click on *Perspectives*. Then select the Building Better *Perspectives* Form for your book.

3. Forms and instructions for submission are available online.

Tell us what you think—did the readings and online materials help you make some learning connections? Were some materials more helpful than others? Thanks in advance for helping us build better *Perspectives*.

Student Internships

If you enjoy evaluating these articles or would like to help us evaluate the **Courselinks** site for this course, check out the **Coursewise** Student Internship Program. For more information, visit:

http://www.coursewise.com/intern.html

Brief Contents

section 1 Introduction to Industrial/Organizational Psychology 1

section 2 Perspectives on Work 52

section 3 The Legal Environment 73

section 4 Recruitment and Selection 94

section 5 Training and Development 125

section 6 Evaluation and Compensation 158

section 7 Motivation 175

section 8 Satisfaction and Attitudes 194

section 9 Leadership 211

section 10 Stress, Health, and Safety 233

Contents

At **Coursewise,** we're publishing *connected learning tools.* That means that the book you are holding is only a part of this publication. You'll also want to harness the integrated resources that **Coursewise** has developed at the fun and highly useful **Courselinks**™ web site for *Perspectives: Industrial and Organizational Psychology.* If you purchased this book new, use the Passport that was shrink-wrapped to this volume to obtain site access. If you purchased a used copy of this book, then you need to buy a stand-alone Passport. If your bookstore doesn't stock Passports to **Courselinks** sites, visit http://www.courselinks.com for ordering information.

section 1

Introduction to Industrial/ Organizational Psychology

WiseGuide Intro 1

1. **Whither Industrial and Organizational Psychology in a Changing World of Work?,** W. F. Cascio. *The American Psychologist,* November 1995.
   This reading examines some of the dramatic changes occurring in the world of work and the role of industrial/organizational psychologists. Specifically, Cascio addresses how work is being redefined and the impact these changes are having on individuals in the workplace. **3**

2. **Survey Shows HR in Transition,** A. Halcrow. *Workforce,* June 1998.
   As the nature of work has changed over the last few years, so has the role of human resource professionals. This reading discusses some of these changes and gives you a sense of the daily life of someone working in this profession. Would you find this type of work appealing? **15**

3. **Early Influences on the Development of Industrial and Organizational Psychology,** F. J. Landy. *Journal of Applied Psychology,* August 1997.
   Our past influences who we are today. In this reading, Landy describes the history of industrial/organizational psychology and how early events in the field influence what industrial/organizational psychologists do today. **21**

4. **American Female Pioneers of Industrial and Organizational Psychology during the Early Years,** L. L. Koppes. *Journal of Applied Psychology,* August 1997.
   This reading discusses the important contributions of female psychologists to the development of industrial/organizational psychology. These early pioneers blended research, application, and service in ways that foreshadowed current issues in the field. **31**

5. **Why I'm Proud to Be an I/O Psychologist,** M. Campion. *The Industrial Organizational Psychologist,* Vol. 34, No. 1, 1996.
   Why would someone want to become an industrial/organizational psychologist? After reading Campion's lists, how would you answer that question? **45**

6. **I-O Psychology: What's Your Line?,** M. Gasser, D. Whitsett, N. Mosley, K. Sullivan, T. Rogers, and R. Tan. *The Industrial Organizational Psychologist,* April 1998.
   So what exactly do industrial/organizational psychologists do? A good starting point might be to describe what they do not do, and that is part of the purpose of this reading. Do you find it surprising that people are confused about the roles of industrial/organizational psychologists? **47**

WiseGuide Wrap-Up 51

section 2

Perspectives on Work

WiseGuide Intro 52

7 **Employment and Employability: Foundation of the New Social Contract,** B. R. Ellig. *Human Resource Management,* Summer 1998.
Are employees assets or expenses? Ellig suggests that how we answer this question can profoundly affect the organization and its workers. **54**

8 **The Moral Obligations of Workers,** J. Tucker. *The Freeman,* May 1997.
Do you believe that we have a moral obligation to work? Be sure to read the six virtues of labor in this article and think about them as they pertain to your life. **57**

9 **The Abusive Organization,** G. N. Powell. *Academy of Management Executive,* May 1998.
According to this reading, organizations can become abusive. What are some of the reasons why this can happen? **61**

10 **An Inside Look at Making the Grade,** M. N. Martinez. *HR Magazine,* March 1998.
This reading addresses how work/life programs can boost employee satisfaction, which can translate into happier customers and more profits. Keep this reading in mind as you read the articles in Section 8. **63**

11 **Downsizing in the Past,** S. Jacoby. *Challenge,* May/June 1998.
This reading examines the important issue of downsizing by focusing on the partnership formed between the employee and the corporation. As you read this article, think about what is meant by welfare capitalism and about what you think is the appropriate role for unions. **66**

12 **A Shorter Week? Hell, No,** A. Gumbel. *World Press Review,* January 1998.
This reading focuses on France's attempt to create and enforce a national 35-hour work week. What do you see as the practical benefits and problems with such a policy? **71**

WiseGuide Wrap-Up 72

section 3

The Legal Environment

WiseGuide Intro 73

13 **Life at the EEOC,** B. Leonard. *HR Magazine,* January 1998.
Gilbert Casellas served as the Equal Employment Opportunity Commission (EEOC) chairman for three years, and in this reading, he describes his work at the EEOC and some current trends in employment law. **75**

14 **Ending the Culture of Corporate Discrimination,** H. J. Van Buren III. *Business & Society Review,* Fall 1996.
Does unfair discrimination still exist? Do we need the Equal Employment Opportunity Commission? These are the main questions addressed in this reading. Based on your experiences, do you agree with Van Buren's arguments? **79**

15 **What Would *You* Do? It's (Still) a Man's World,** D. Wallace. *Business Ethics,* July/August 1998.
This case study examines the problem of sexual discrimination. What would you do in this situation? **82**

16 **Are the ADA Guidelines on Mental Disabilities Fair to Business?,** T. Gore. *The Washington Post,* May 12, 1997.
This reading presents the case for the Americans with Disabilites Act. Do you agree with this position? **84**

17 **Kafka Wasn't Kidding,** D. A. Price. *Forbes,* June 2, 1997.
Can following one law cause you to break another? Have we created a situation where, no matter what you do, you can get into legal trouble? After reading this article, what do you think? **86**

18 **Troubled at Work,** H. Wray. *U.S. News and World Report,* February 9, 1998.
How should organizations address issues related to mental disorders? How should organizations and our legal system respond to the topics raised in this reading? **87**

19 **The Americans with Minor Disabilities Act,** J. P. Shapiro. *U.S. News and World Report,* July 6, 1998.
Has the Americans with Disabilities Act gone too far in defining the term *disability?* Where do you think we should draw the line? **89**

20 **Finally, a Corporate Tip Sheet on Sexual Harassment,** S. B. Garland. *Business Week,* July 13, 1998.
Here are some suggestions on developing a proactive affirmative defense plan to reduce sexual harassment in the workplace. The author recommends establishing a zero-tolerance policy. **91**

WiseGuide Wrap-Up   93

section 4: Recruitment and Selection

WiseGuide Intro   94

21 **Wanted: Workers with Flexibility for 21st Century Jobs,** P. A. McGuire. *APA Monitor,* Vol. 29, No. 7, 1998.
With recent changes in the workplace, organizations are increasingly turning to psychologists to help understand employee reactions and to build an effective workforce. **96**

22 **Employee Selection: Will Intelligence and Conscientiousness Do the Job?,** O. Behling. *Academy of Management Executive,* February 1998.
Should organizations hire for general intelligence and conscientiousness, or focus more on specific skills? This reading presents an important challenge to industrial/organizational psychologists and to human resource professionals. **99**

23 **Personality Measurement and Employment Decisions: Questions and Answers,** R. Hogan, J. Hogan, and B. W. Roberts. *American Psychologist,* May 1996.
Should organizations consider personality characteristics when making hiring decisions? The authors argue that the appropriate use of personality measures can promote social justice and increase organizational productivity. **107**

24 **The Boundaryless Organization: Implications for Job Analysis, Recruitment, and Selection,** J. B. Nelson. *Human Resource Planning,* Vol. 20, No. 4, 1997.
As organizations become more integrated, they need to recruit and hire people with skills and traits congruent with those of the company. In this process, we should address both organizational and individual value systems. **115**

WiseGuide Wrap-Up   124

section 5: Training and Development

WiseGuide Intro   125

25 **Psychologists Needed to Retain Employees,** B. Murray. *APA Monitor,* March 1997.
A common theme you may have noticed is that jobs are becoming increasingly dynamic. This reading addresses issues related to the necessity of constantly retraining employees and the unique role of industrial/organizational psychologists in this process. **127**

26 **The Six Components of Successful Ethics Training,** S. B. Knouse and R. A. Giacalone. *Business and Society Review,* Fall 1996.
Can and should we train employees in ethical decision making? These authors say yes and present a method for accomplishing this goal. **129**

27 **Using Outdoor Training to Develop and Accomplish Organizational Vision,** G. M. McEvoy, J. R. Cragun, and M. Appleby. *Human Resource Planning,* Vol. 20, No. 3, 1997.
This reading is a detailed case study relating training to organizational strategy. An outdoor training program provides the context for the development of an organization's strategic vision. **133**

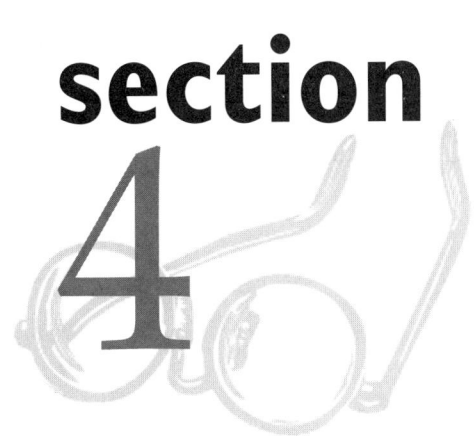

28 **Workstation Meets Playstation,** J. J. Salopek. *Training and Development,* August 1998.
Technology is changing everything, including how we train employees. This reading presents several examples of how computer simulations can be used to develop employees. **141**

29 **Effect of Cognitive-Behavioural Training on Job-Finding among Long-Term Unemployed People,** J. Proudfoot, D. Guest, J. Carson, G. Dunn, and J. Gray. *The Lancet,* July 12, 1997.
Cognitive-behavioral training (CBT) attempts to modify attributional styles (how we explain why events occur). This reading explains the differences between effective and ineffective styles, and presents an application of the theory. Can you think of other applications for CBT? **150**

WiseGuide Wrap-Up   157

section 6

Evaluation and Compensation

WiseGuide Intro   158

30 **Following a Few Simple Rules Can Ease the Pain of Employee Reviews,** B. D. Jaffe. *InfoWorld,* January 26, 1998.
Why would someone hate doing performance reviews? Do you think that the seven guidelines presented here are realistic? **160**

31 **Just What Is a Competency (And Why Should You Care?),** S. B. Parry. *Training,* June 1998.
This reading operationally defines job competencies and describes their application in evaluation programs. **162**

32 **High-Tech 360,** D. W. Bracken, L. Summers, and J. Fleenor. *Training and Development,* August 1998.
One of the more recent developments in evaluation has been called the 360-degree feedback process. This reading takes this process a step further by incorporating technology into the process. **165**

33 **Accountability in 360-Degree Feedback,** L. Atwater and D. Waldman. *HR Magazine,* May 1998.
This reading addresses the general process of 360-degree feedback and describes methods used to introduce it to an organization. **170**

WiseGuide Wrap-Up   174

section 7

Motivation

WiseGuide Intro   175

34 **Actions Speak Louder than Posters,** J. Laurinaitis. *Psychology Today,* May 1997.
This reading discusses the effectiveness of motivational posters. **177**

35 **Employee Motivation: Creating a Motivated Workforce,** D. J. McNerney. *HRFocus,* August 1996.
This reading examines three organizations that have been successful at creating a motivated workforce. Do you notice any common themes among these companies? **178**

36 **How Starbucks Impassions Workers to Drive Growth,** N. Weiss. *Workforce,* August 1998.
To address turnover and low motivation, Starbucks instituted a liberal benefit package and a unique work/life program for its employees. Do you think that this would be a practical solution for other organizations? **181**

37 **The Importance of Future Time Perspective in Theories of Work Motivation,** G. H. Seijts. *Journal of Psychology,* Vol. 132, No. 2, 1998.
　　This reading suggests that how an individual perceives the future is an important component in understanding an individual's motivation to succeed.   **185**

WiseGuide Wrap-Up   193

section 8
Satisfaction and Attitudes

WiseGuide Intro   194

38 **A Philosopher's Dream of Making Work Fun,** P. C. Newman. *Maclean's,* October 7, 1996.
　　Can work be fun? Should work be fun? Read the article and decide for yourself.   **196**

39 **We Want You to Stay. Really,** A. Bernstein. *Business Week,* June 22, 1998.
　　Turnover is becoming an increasingly important issue for organizations. This reading presents some strategies organizations can use to keep valued workers.   **198**

40 **What Makes Companies Well-Loved?** A. Perle. *Workforce,* April 1998.
　　Employees with a positive attitude toward a company can keep turnover low and productivity high. This reading reviews several case studies in which organizations have become well-loved.   **202**

41 **The Search for Community in the Workplace,** T. H. Naylor, W. H. Willimon, and R. Osterberg. *Business & Society Review,* Summer 1996.
　　Some organizations are trying to build a sense of community in the workplace. The authors of this reading suggest that, to accomplish this goal, organizations must address ten critical issues. These issues are presented and discussed.   **205**

WiseGuide Wrap-Up   210

section 9
Leadership

WiseGuide Intro   211

42 **Leadership: Seven Behaviors for Muddling Through,** J. R. Houghton. *Vital Speeches of the Day,* July 1, 1996.
　　This speech was presented at the senior leadership/corporate transformation conference and discusses what leaders need to do to address the paradigm shift occurring in organizations today.   **213**

43 **The Slight Edge: Valuing and Managing Diversity,** G. Fraser. *Vital Speeches of the Day,* February 1, 1998.
　　In this reading, Fraser suggests that we must move from a position of accepting and understanding individual differences to one of valuing and using diversity in the workplace. Organizations that accomplish this task will have a competitive advantage over those that do not.   **217**

44 **Teaching Leadership at the U.S. Military Academy at West Point,** J. A. McNally, S. J. Gerras, and R. C. Bullis. *Journal of Applied Behavioral Science,* June 1996.
　　Have you ever wondered how our military leaders are developed? This reading presents an intellectual procedure for developing leaders at West Point. Note the similarities between this model and the scientific method.   **224**

WiseGuide Wrap-Up   232

> **Questions**
>
> **Reading 1.** If jobs are no longer a bundle of tasks, what are they? How does this affect workers and organizations?
>
> **Reading 2.** Why is HR intervention sometimes considered to be crisis management? Why does HR have the attention of most CEOs?
>
> **Reading 3.** Describe the links early industrial/organizational psychologists made between the academic discipline and the marketplace (both private industry and government). Why are these relationships important to the field today?
>
> **Reading 4.** What were the unique contributions of the female pioneers of industrial/organizational psychology? Was their perspective truly unique?
>
> **Reading 5.** Try to organize Campion's items into themes or factors. What patterns emerge? Did he miss any items identified by the other authors? Do you see any potential conflicts in what we do?
>
> **Reading 6.** Why are people confused about industrial/organizational psychology? Why is it important for industrial/organizational psychologists to respond to this confusion?

increasingly diverse in culture, values, and motivations. There are new organizational structures designed to empower workers and reduce management. As Cascio illustrates, a job is no longer a fixed bundle of tasks; rather, it is a dynamic process. What you do on the job today may not be what you will be doing three months from now.

As mentioned before, within this changing world of work, industrial/organizational psychologists try to balance the needs of the organization with those of the workers. We accomplish this by helping organizations redesign jobs to maximize efficiency. We help select appropriate individuals, train and develop them, monitor their performance, and help motivate them. Thus, we are directly affecting individuals and shaping organizations for the future.

The second reading in this section examines changes within human resource (HR) departments (sometimes still called personnel departments). Employees in these departments perform duties directly related to industrial/organizational psychology. As you can see from this reading, the issues facing these departments are the same as Cascio discussed in his paper. You can also see from this article the dynamic and sometimes frustrating aspects of this type of work. People working in this area must often address issues ranging from an employee's constant tardiness because of daycare problems to racial tension (see the box "Before We've Even Had Coffee: HR's Worst Morning Crises"). Again, this article highlights both the excitement and the challenges facing this area.

The next two readings are important, because they provide a brief history of industrial/organizational psychology. As both Landy and Koppes argue, it is important to know our past in order to understand our present and future. This argument makes sense, because, in order to understand who you are now, you need to know something about your past. In this brief historical overview, Landy focuses on the early influence of four influential figures in industrial/organizational psychology; Münsterberg, Cattell, Scott, and Bingham. In many ways, their works defined the scope of the field. Koppes highlights the unique contributions of several female psychologists in her article. Together, these early industrial/organizational psychologists have had a profound effect on what we do today.

In Reading 5, Mike Campion identifies some of the reasons why he is proud to be an industrial/organizational psychologist. In these lists, he captures both the tasks and the values that most individuals in this area share.

In the final reading, Gasser, Whitsett, Mosley, Sullivan, Rogers, and Tan suggest that, for a variety of reasons, many people outside the field of psychology do not understand what industrial/organizational psychologists actually do. Often, when people outside the discipline hear that someone is a "psychologist," they assume that person is a therapist. In fact, according to the authors' survey, most of the general public have never even heard of industrial/organizational psychology. This lack of understanding can cause problems. If people do not understand the differences between industrial/organizational psychologists and therapists or "business consultants" (a generic term that anyone can use), they will not seek industrial/organizational psychologists or use information in the field. Thus, part of the job of industrial/organizational psychologists should be to educate others about the discipline—explaining what they do and what they can offer.

If jobs are no longer a bundle of tasks, what are they? How does this affect workers and organizations?

Whither Industrial and Organizational Psychology in a Changing World of Work?

Wayne F. Cascio
University of Colorado at Denver

Dramatic changes are affecting the world of work. Examples include increased global competition, the impact of information technology, the re-engineering of business processes, smaller companies that employ fewer people, the shift from making a product to providing a service, and the growing disappearance of "the job" as a fixed bundle of tasks. These trends are producing a redefinition of work itself. They provide great opportunities for industrial and organizational psychologists to contribute to the betterment of human welfare. This article identifies 6 key areas in which to start: job analysis, employee selection, training and development, performance appraisal, compensation (including incentives), and organizational development. Relevant research in these areas can provide substantial payoffs for individuals, organizations, and society as psychology moves into the 21st century.

As citizens of the 20th century, we have witnessed more change in our daily existence and in our environment than anyone else who ever walked the planet. But if you think the pace of change was fast in this century, expect it to accelerate in the next one. The 21st century will be even more complex, fast paced, and turbulent. It will also be very different. Industrial and organizational psychology potentially has much to contribute to this new world of work. It has the potential to lead change rather than to simply react to it, but to do so it must seize opportunities to provide research-based answers to pressing organizational problems. This article is organized into two parts. The first part describes some of the dramatic changes that are affecting the world of work; the second proposes a research agenda in six key areas in which applied psychologists often practice. I begin by considering the changing nature of economic competition.

Changing Nature of Economic Competition

Just as wars—two World Wars, the Korean conflict, Vietnam, and Desert Storm—dominated the geopolitical map of the 20th century, economics will rule over the 21st. The competition that is normal and inevitable among nations increasingly will be played out, not in aggression or war but in the economic sphere. The weapons used will be those of commerce: growth rates, investments, trade blocs, and imports and exports (Nelan, 1992).

These changes reflect the impact of globalized product and service markets, coupled with increased domestic competition (largely fueled by deregulation in telecommunications, airlines, and banking) and new business start-ups. By a wide margin, however, global competition is the single most powerful economic fact of life in the 1990s. In the relatively sheltered era of the 1960s, only 7% of the U.S. economy was exposed to international competition. In the 1980s, that number zoomed past 70%, and it will keep climbing (Gwynne, 1992). Today, one in five American jobs is tied directly or indirectly to international trade. Merchandise exports are up more than 40% since 1986, and every $1 billion in U.S. merchandise exports generates approximately

20,000 new jobs. For the most part these are good jobs that pay about 22% more than average ("Investing in people," 1994).

The results of accelerated global competition have been almost beyond comprehension—free political debate throughout the former Soviet empire, democratic reforms in Central and South America, the integration of the European community, the North American Free Trade Agreement, and an explosion of free market entrepreneurship in Southern China. In short, the free markets and free labor markets that we in the United States have enjoyed throughout our national history have now become a global passion (Doyle, 1992).

There is no going back. Today, firms and workers in America must compete for business with firms and workers in the same industries in England, France, and Germany; in Poland, Hungary, and the former Russian republics; in Mexico, Brazil, Argentina, and Chile; and in Japan, Korea, Malaysia, Taiwan, Singapore, Hong Kong, and China, just to name a few of our competitors. However, it takes more than trade agreements, technology, capital investment, and infrastructure to deliver world-class products and services. It also takes the skills, ingenuity, and creativity of a competent, well-trained workforce. Our competitors know this, and they are spending unstintingly to create one.

The *World Competitiveness Report* (1994) provides a ranking of countries that combines the quality of public education, levels of secondary schooling and on-the-job training, computer literacy, and worker motivation. The United States ranks sixth, behind (in descending order) Singapore, Denmark, Germany, Japan, and Norway. Although none of the higher-ranking countries is as heterogeneous as the United States, the lesson for decision makers is clear: The race to create a broad, technically literate labor pool has no finish line!

Impact on Jobs in the United States

As nations around the world move from wartime to peacetime economies, from industrial societies to information societies, we are witnessing wrenching structural changes in our economy. These changes have impacted most profoundly in terms of jobs (Cascio, 1993). In the United States, more than 7 million permanent layoffs have been announced since 1987. That number includes 6 million between 1987 and 1992 (Baumohl, 1993), 615,000 in 1993 (Byrne, 1994), and 516,000 in 1994 (Murray, 1995).

Companies are not downsizing because they are losing money. Fully 81% of companies that downsize in a given year were profitable in that year. Major reasons, according to the American Management Association's 1994 survey on downsizing, were strategic or structural in nature: to improve productivity, transfers of location, new technological processes, mergers and acquisitions, or plant obsolescence ("1994 AMA").

Laid-off workers who must return to the job market often must take huge pay cuts. Downward mobility is the rule rather than the exception ("Downside," 1994). Of roughly 2,000 workers let go by RJR Nabisco, for example, 72% found jobs subsequently but at wages that averaged only 47% of their previous pay ("Jobs," 1993). Surprisingly, older, higher-paid workers may fare better. A recent study of 311 workers (285 men and 26 women) whose average age and salary were 57 and $75,000, respectively, took an average of 5.6 months to land jobs that paid an average of $61,500 (Drake, Beam, Morin, Inc., 1994). Whether young or old, however, the bottom line for most reemployed workers is that both their spending power and their standards of living have dropped.

What's happening here? In a nutshell, as an executive in the pharmaceutical industry noted, we're moving from an economy where there are a lot of hard-working people to one where there are fewer, smarter-working people (Pilon, 1993). Jobs aren't being lost temporarily because of a recession; rather, they are being wiped out permanently as a result of new technology, improved machinery, and new ways of organizing work. In the following sections, I briefly examine the impact of these changes and then discuss how organizations are responding, particularly to the changes affecting managers and workers.

Effects of Technology on Organizations and People

Fifty million workers use computers every day along with other products of the digital age—faxes, modems, cellular phones, and E-mail. This is breaking down departmental barriers, enhancing the sharing of vast amounts of information, creating "virtual offices" for workers on the go, collapsing product development cycles, and changing the ways that organizations service customers and relate to their suppliers and to their employees. To succeed and prosper in the changing world of work, companies need motivated, technically literate workers.

A caveat is in order here, however. It relates to the common assumption that because production processes have become more sophisticated, high technology can substitute for skill in managing a workforce. Beware of such a "logic trap." On the contrary, high technology actually makes the workforce even more important for success, as Pfeffer (1994) has noted,

This is because more skill may be necessary to operate the more sophisticated and advanced equipment, and with a higher level of investment per employee, interruptions in the process are increasingly expensive. This means that the ability to effectively operate, maintain, and repair equipment—tasks all done by first-line employees—become even more critical. (p. 8)

Ideally, therefore, technology will help workers make decisions in organizations that encourage them to do so ("Workplace of the Future," 1993). However, organizations of the future will look very different from organizations of the past, as the next section illustrates.

Changes in the Structure and Design of Organizations

In today's world of fast-moving global markets and fierce competition, the windows of opportunity are often frustratingly brief (Byrne, 1993). The features that dominated industrial society's approach to designing organizations throughout the 19th and 20th centuries—mass production and large organizations—are disappearing. Trends such as the following are accelerating the shift toward new forms of organization for the 21st century (Kiechel, 1993): (a) smaller companies that employ fewer people; (b) the shift from vertically integrated hierarchies to networks of specialists; (c) technicians, ranging from computer repair persons to radiation therapists, replacing manufacturing operatives as the worker elite (see Barley, 1991); (d) pay tied less to a person's position or tenure in an organization and more to the market value of his or her skills; (e) the change in the paradigm of doing business from making a product to providing a service; and (f) the redefinition of work itself—growing disappearance of "the job" as a fixed bundle of tasks (see Bridges, 1994) and increased emphasis on constantly changing work required to fulfill the ever-increasing demands of customers. This will require constant learning, more higher order thinking, and the availability to work outside the standard hours of 9 A.M. to 5 P.M.

In this emerging world of work, more and more organizations will focus carefully on their core competencies and outsource everything else. They will be characterized by terms such as *virtual, boundary-less,* and *flexible,* with no guarantees to workers or managers. Hundreds of big companies have outsourced non-core operations: Continental Bank Corporation has contracted its legal, audit, cafeteria, and mailroom operations to outside companies. American Airlines is doing the same with customer service jobs at 30 airports.

This approach to organizing is no short-term fad. The fact is, organizations are becoming leaner and leaner, with better and better trained "multispecialists"—those who have in-depth knowledge about a number of different aspects of the business. Eschewing narrow specialists or broad generalists, organizations of the future will come to rely on cross-trained multispecialists to get things done. One such group whose roles are changing dramatically is that of managers.

The Changing Role of the Manager

In the traditional hierarchy that used to comprise most bureaucratic organizations, rules were simple. Managers ruled by command from the top (essentially one-way communication), used rigid controls to ensure that fragmented tasks (grouped into clearly defined jobs) could be coordinated effectively, and partitioned information into neat compartments—departments, units, and functions. Information was (and is) power, and, at least in some cases, managers clung to power by hoarding information. This approach to organizing, that is, 3-C (command, control, and compartmentalization) logic, was geared to achieve three objectives: stability, predictability, and efficiency.

In today's reengineered, hyper-competitive work environments, the autocratic, top-down command-and-control approach is out of step with the competitive realities that many organizations face. To survive, organizations have to be able to respond quickly to shifting market conditions. In this kind of an environment, a key job for all managers, especially top managers, is to articulate a vision of what the organization stands for and what it is trying to accomplish. The next step is to translate that vision into everything that is done and to use the vision as a benchmark to assess progress over time.

A large and growing number of organizations now recognize that they need to emphasize workplace democracy to achieve the vision. This involves breaking down barriers, sharing information, using a collaborative approach to problem solving, and an orientation toward continuous learning and improvement. For many managers, these kinds of skills simply weren't needed in organizations designed and structured under 3-C logic.

Does this imply that we are moving toward a universal model of organizational and leadership effectiveness? Hardly. Contingency theories of leadership such as path-goal theory (House, 1971), normative decision theory (Vroom & Yetton, 1973), or least-preferred coworker (LPC) contingency theory (Fiedler, 1967) suggest that an autocratic style is appropriate in some situations. In recent years many organizations (e.g., Eaton Corporation and Levi Strauss & Co.) have instituted formal information-sharing and workplace education programs that reduce or eliminate a key condition that makes autocratic leadership appropriate—workers who lack the information or knowledge needed to make meaningful suggestions or decisions. More often, today's networked, interdependent, culturally diverse organizations require transformational leadership (Bass, 1985). The ability of leaders to transform followers to bring out their creativity, imagination, and best efforts requires well-developed interpersonal skills, founded on an understanding of human behavior in organizations. Industrial and organizational psychologists are well-positioned to help managers develop these kinds of skills.

In addition, although by no means universal, much of the work that results in a product, service, or decision is now done in teams—intact, identifiable social systems (even if small or temporary) whose members have the authority to manage their own task and interpersonal processes as they carry out their work. Such teams go by a variety of names—autonomous work groups, process teams, and self-managing work teams. All of this implies a radical reorientation from the traditional view of a manager's work.

In this kind of an environment, workers are acting more like managers, and managers more like workers. The managerial roles of controllers, planners, and inspectors are being replaced by coaches, facilitators, and mentors (Wellins, Byham, & Wilson, 1991). This doesn't just happen—it requires good interpersonal skills, continuous learning, and an organizational culture that supports and encourages both.

Flattened hierarchies also mean that there are fewer managers in the first place. The empowered worker will be a defining feature of such organizations.

The Empowered Worker— No Passing Fad

It should be clear by now that we are in the midst of a revolution—a revolution at work. Change isn't coming only from large, high-profile companies doing high-technology work. It has also permeated unglamorous, low-tech work. As an example, consider Toronto-based Cadet Uniform

Services, which outfits the employees of some of North America's leading corporations (Henkoff, 1994).

Cadet doesn't just hire people to drive trucks, deliver clean uniforms, and pick up dirty ones. Rather, its concept of customer service representatives (CSRs) extends much further. They are mini-entrepreneurs who design their own routes, manage their own accounts, and, to a large extent, determine the size of their paychecks.

Cadet ties compensation almost entirely to measures of customer satisfaction. Lose a customer on your watch and your salary sinks. CSR pay is about $40,000 a year, nearly twice the industry average. In practice, Cadet rarely loses a customer; its annual defection rate is less than 1%. Employees don't leave either; turnover is a low 7%. To a large extent this is because Cadet spends considerable time and effort on selecting employees—who take pride in their work, are exceedingly neat, and are outgoing. In all, 46 ethnic groups are represented at Cadet.

How has the company done? Its annual growth has averaged 22% for the past 20 years, and it boasts double-digit profit margins that exceed the industry norm. Says Quentin Wahl, chief executive officer, "The jobs we do aren't so special—the pay is good, but it's not great. The main thing we have to sell to employees is the culture of the organization" (Henkoff, 1994, p. 122).

Organizations of the 1990s, both large and small, differ dramatically in structure, design, and demographics from those of even a decade ago. Demographically, they are far more diverse. They comprise more women at all levels, more multiethnic, multicultural workers, more older workers, workers with disabilities, robots, and contingent workers. Paternalism is out; self-reliance is in. There's constant pressure to do more with less and steady emphasis on empowerment, cross-training, personal flexibility, self-managed work teams, and continuous learning. Workers today have to be able to adapt to changing circumstances and be prepared for multiple careers. Industrial and organizational psychologists are helping to educate prospective, current, and former workers to these new realities. In the future, they will be expected to do much more, as I describe later, but first I consider some organizational responses to these new realities.

Implications for Organizations and Their People

What do these trends imply for the ways that organizations will compete for business? In a world where virtually every factor that affects the production of goods or the delivery of services—capital, equipment, technology, and information—is available to every player in the global economy, the one factor that doesn't routinely move across national borders is a nation's workforce. In the years to come, the quality of the American workforce will be a crucial determinant of America's ability to compete and win in world markets.

Human resources can be sources of sustained competitive advantage as long as they meet three basic requirements: (a) They add positive economic benefits to the process of producing goods or delivering services; (b) the skills of the workforce are distinguishable from those of competitors (e.g., through education and workplace learning); and (c) such skills are not easily duplicated (Barney, 1991). Human resource systems (the set of interrelated processes designed to attract, develop, and maintain human resources) can either enhance or destroy this potential competitive advantage (Lado & Wilson, 1994).

Perhaps a quote attributed to Albert Einstein, the famous physicist, best captures the position of this article. After the first atomic reaction in 1942, Einstein remarked, "Everything has changed, except our way of thinking" ("Workplace of the Future," 1993, p. 2). As psychology in general, and industrial and organizational psychology in particular, stands poised on the brink of the 21st century, I believe that our greatest challenge will be to change the way we as a field think about organizations and their people. The first part of this article addressed some key changes in the world of work; the remainder identifies some pressing research questions that must be addressed if our science is to remain relevant to 21st-century organizations.

A Research Agenda for Industrial and Organizational Psychologists

Each of the following sections identifies traditional practices, new developments, and research questions that require attention if the field is to lead organizational change rather than react to it. These sections are job analysis, employee selection, training and development, performance appraisal, compensation (including incentives), and organization development. Admittedly, these areas represent only some of the broad range of activities that psychologists are engaged in and that relate to the management of people in work settings. In total, however, they comprise much of the work in this area.

Job Analysis: Identifying the Work to Be Done and the Personal Characteristics Necessary to Do the Work

Traditional task-based "jobs" were once packaged into clusters of similar tasks and assigned to specialist workers. Today, many firms have no reason to package work that way. Instead, they are unbundling tasks into broader chunks of work that change over time. Such shifting clusters of tasks make it difficult to define a job, at least in the traditional sense. Practices such as flex time, job sharing, and telecommuting, not to mention temporary workers, part-timers, and consultants, have compounded the definitional problem.

Job analysis is a common activity of industrial and organizational psychologists, and there exists a well-defined technology for doing such analysis (Gael, 1988; Harvey, 1991; Ilgen & Hollenbeck, 1991; McCormick, 1979). Terms such as *job element, task, duty, position, job, job description,* and *job family* are well-understood parts of the lexicon of industrial and organizational psychologists everywhere.

Today, however, there is a detectable shift away from a task-based toward a process-based organization of work. A *process* is a collection of activities (such as procurement, order fulfillment, product development, or credit issuance) that takes one or more kinds of input and creates an output that is of value to a customer (M. Hammer & Champy, 1993). Customers may be internal or external. Individual tasks are important parts of the process, but the process itself cuts across organizational boundaries and traditional functions, such as engineering, production, marketing, and finance.

Consider credit issuance as an example. Instead of the separate jobs of credit checker and pricer, the two may be combined into one "deal structurer." Such integrated processes cut response time and increase efficiency and productivity. Bell Atlantic created a "case team"—a group of people who have among them all of the skills necessary to handle an installation order. Members of the team—who previously were located in different departments and in different geographical areas—were brought together into a single unit and given total responsibility for installing the equipment. Such a process operates, on average, ten times faster than the assembly line version it replaces. Bell Atlantic, for example, reduced the time it takes to install a high-speed digital service link from 30 days to 3 (M. Hammer & Champy, 1993).

Employees involved in the process are responsible for ensuring that customers' requirements are met on time and with no defects, and they are empowered to experiment in ways that will cut cycle time and reduce costs. Result: Less supervision is needed, while workers take on broader responsibilities and a wider purview of activities. Moreover, the kinds of activities that each worker does are likely to shift over time.

In terms of traditional job analysis, this leaves many unanswered questions and a number of challenges. Some of these questions follow.

What will be the future of traditional task-based descriptions of jobs and job activities? Should other types of descriptors replace task statements that describe what a worker does, to what or whom, why, and how? Will "task cluster" statements or "subprocess" statements become the basic building blocks for describing work? What does a job description look like in a process-based organization of work? Will job specifications (which identify the personal characteristics—knowledge, skills, abilities, and other characteristics—necessary to do the work) supersede job descriptions? Does identification of the environmental, contextual, and social dimensions of work become more important in a process-based structure? Will emphasis shift from describing jobs to describing roles?

Managers often look to industrial and organizational psychologists to help them analyze jobs and describe work processes as a foundation for other human resource management activities, such as employee selection, training, compensation, work and organization design, and performance appraisal. In the next section, I discuss the implications of the new organization of work for employee selection.

Selecting Employees

In the traditional paradigm, so-called "one-shot" selection–placement programs worked as follows: analyze the job, identify relevant job performance criteria, identify job-related predictors of performance, validate predictors, and then select candidates who score highest on the set of validated predictors. As with job analysis, the technology for working within this paradigm is also well developed (see, e.g., Cascio, 1991; Guion, 1991; Schmitt & Borman, 1993).

I just described the problems associated with analyzing jobs under a process-based organization of work. To compound those problems, consider that relatively few jobs in today's economy are performed independently of others and that most are interdependent or coordinate in nature— that is, they are a function of group efforts, not just the sum of individual talents. For example, both Xerox Corporation and General Electric (GE) now develop new products through multidisciplinary teams that work in a single process, instead of vertical functions or departments. At GE a senior team of 9–12 people oversees nearly 100 processes or programs worldwide, from new product design to improvement of the yield on production machinery. The senior team—consisting of managers with multiple competencies rather than narrow specialists—exists to allocate resources and ensure coordination of the processes and programs. "They stay away from the day-to-day activities, which are managed by the teams themselves," explains Harold Giles, manager of human resources in GE's lighting business ("The Horizontal Corporation," 1993, p. 79). That's quite a change from the traditional role of a supervisor.

Let us add just one more complicating factor to this mix: In some cases workers will join intact work teams that stay together to perform different kinds of work, such as assembly of different models of an automobile, or different products entirely, as under a flexible manufacturing system. In project-based work, such as research and development, consulting, legal defense, or movie production, "virtual" teams consisting of multidisciplinary players are created to work on a project and then are disbanded when the project is finished. In these cases, the nature of the work changes, as does the composition of the teams that do the work.

From the point of view of industrial and organizational psychology, the challenge is to move beyond valid, job-based predictors because the work to be done changes constantly. This raises a number of research issues relevant to the selection of employees (including managers): How does the selection process influence team effectiveness? As Klimoski and Jones (1995) noted, selecting the right mix of individuals to comprise a team implies attention to worker requirements on at least three dimensions: ability, values and personality, and politics (a team member's future role in making things happen once a decision is reached).

Will the role of tests of cognitive abilities focus on identifying candidates with general (as opposed to specific) abilities, such as basic verbal and numeracy skills, the ability to think critically, to reason logically, and to draw conclusions from a body of facts? If so, this would comport with recent findings that general cognitive ability is an efficient predictor in terms of job performance (Ree & Earles, 1992; Ree, Earles, & Teachout, 1994) and training performance (Ree & Earles, 1991).

How can psychology contribute to the optimal use of people with lower levels of cognitive abilities? Because not all jobs require high levels of cognitive ability (e.g., many types of service jobs), what other types of predictors of work performance will validly forecast success in such jobs? Services, which now account for 74% of the gross domestic product, and 79% of all employment in the United States, are expected to account for all of the net growth in jobs in the next decade. Will measures of personality characteristics—for example, adaptability, empathy, and ability to work under stress—receive relatively more attention than cognitive ability tests in jobs whose primary objective is customer service? To be sure, the ability to select, train, and retain front-line, customer-contact workers will be a top priority for many organizations. Companies such as Marriott and Disney now require the same skills of workers that they once demanded of managers—"people who are resilient and resourceful, empathetic and enterprising, competent and creative" (Henkoff, 1994, p. 110).

There is no question that well-developed measures of personality characteristics can account for additional variance in the prediction of behavior on the job (Hogan, 1991; Ones, Mount, Barrick, & Hunter, 1994; Tett, Jackson, Rothstein, & Reddon, 1994). Although a wide variety of such measures exists, they have not been used routinely to select employees. However, given the emphasis on effective interpersonal interaction in the new forms of work organization, more and more managers insist that such characteristics be taken into account. This poses another question of interest to industrial and organizational psychologists, namely the following:

Do alternative modes of pre-hire personality assessment—paper-and-pencil measures, interactive video, computer-based, structured individual or group interviews, or situational tests, for example—provide equivalent psychometric properties? Do they measure the same constructs? As Campbell and Fiske (1959) noted, any test or other measurement procedure is really a trait–method unit—that is, a test measures a given trait by a single method. Hence if one wants to know the relative contribution of trait and method variance to test scores, one must study more than one trait (e.g., dominance and affiliation) and use more than one method (e.g., paper and pencil and interactive video). Second-order confirmatory factor analysis (Marsh & Hocevar, 1988) may be especially helpful in this context.

To probe personality characteristics, pre-hire assessment procedures, especially those used by large organizations, often include patterned behavior description interviews, in which candidates are asked to provide detailed accounts of actual situations (Alderman, 1995). For example, instead of asking, "How would you reprimand an employee?" now it's "Give me a specific example of a time you had to reprimand an employee. What action did you take, and what was the result?" Answers tend to be remarkably consistent with actual (i.e., subsequent) job behavior (Dipboye & Gaugler, 1993; Weekley & Gier, 1987).

Alternatively, interviewers may pose "What would you do if . . . ?" questions. Such questions compose the situational interview, which is based on the assumption that a person's expressed behavioral intentions are related to subsequent behavior. In the situational interview, candidates are asked to describe how they think they would respond in certain job-related situations. Validities for both types of interviews vary from about 0.22 to 0.28 (Motowidlo et al., 1992). This brings up the following questions. (a) Does it matter whether patterned behavior description interview questions or situational interview questions are administered face-to-face or by computer? (b) Do they (interview questions) measure the same constructs and yield equivalent validities? (c) Will work samples or situational tests be used more frequently to assess the compatibility of potential team members, especially members of self-managed work teams? Such procedures measure the ability to do, not just the ability to know. Group-based situational tests (e.g., the leaderless group discussion) have long been used in management selection (e.g., Bass, 1954). How should they be designed to fit the context of a self-managed team—whether intact or virtual?

"Why is it that I always get a whole person when what I really want is a pair of hands?" Henry Ford lamented (Labich, 1994, p. 64). In today's (and tomorrow's) world of work, characteristics of the whole person—cognitive as well as personality—are required to improve continuously the business processes that satisfy the needs of internal and external customers. Managers know this, and increasingly they are turning to industrial and organizational psychologists for answers.

Training and Development

The old Chinese proverb, "Give a man a fish and you feed him for a day; teach a man to fish and you feed him for life," fits neatly into today's emphasis on self-reliance and career resiliency. Career-resilient workers are dedicated to continuous learning. They stand ready to reinvent themselves to keep pace with change, they take responsibility for their own career management, and they are committed to their company's success (Waterman, Waterman, & Collard, 1994). This implies two things: (a) Companies must make it easy for employees to learn and to become flexible, and (b) workers should have the right to obtain ongoing training.

For example, at Sun Microsystems, a core value is "We acknowledge the essential link between company growth and the development of individuals" ("Career," 1994). To make this link a reality, Sun supports training and development activities in three areas: (a) assessment of interests, values, and temperament (to help employees understand who they are and where they are going); (b) assessment and development of technical and functional work skills (to help employees benchmark and improve their work performance); and (c) assessment and development of work strategies (to help employees understand and improve their performance in areas such as problem-solving and conflict resolution).

Compelling as the idea of training may seem, there are strong disincentives for implementing it. To illustrate, consider just three macrolevel structural issues in the design and delivery of training (Cascio, 1994b):

1. Corporate commitment is lacking and uneven. Most companies spend nothing at all

on training. Those that do spend tend to concentrate on managers, technicians, and professionals, not rank-and-file workers. Fully 89% of American workers never receive any formal training from their employers ("Labor Letter," 1991).

2. Poaching trained workers is a major problem for U.S. business and provides a strong disincentive for training. Unlike in Germany, where local business groups pressure companies not to steal one another's employees, there is no such system in the United States (Salwen, 1993). This has profound consequences for "selling" senior managers on the value of training in the United States.

3. Despite the rhetoric about training being viewed as an investment, current accounting rules require that it be treated as an expense. Business might spend more on training if accounting rules were revised. Unlike investments in plant and equipment, which show up on the books as an asset, training expenditures are seen merely as expenses to be deducted in the year they are incurred ("Labor Letter," 1991).

Industrial and organizational psychologists have little control over these macrolevel problems. However, there is much that they can contribute. For example, with respect to the poaching problem, it is important to point out the "training paradox," as described by Robert Waterman (Filipczak, 1995). The paradox runs both ways. That is, if employees take charge of their own employability by keeping their skills updated and varied so they can work for anyone, de facto they build more job security with their current employer—assuming the employer values highly skilled, motivated employees. Similarly, the company that provides lots of training and learning opportunities is more likely to retain workers because it creates an interesting and challenging environment. In theory, therefore, increasing an individual's employability outside a company simultaneously increases his or her job security and desire to stay with the current employer.

A related area in which psychologists can contribute on the basis of strong inferences from data is that of training evaluation. The literature on training evaluation shows that whereas the potential returns from well-conducted training programs can be substantial, there is often considerable variability in the effectiveness with which any given training method or content area is implemented (Cascio, 1994a). Considerable planning (through needs analysis) and follow-up program evaluation efforts are necessary to realize these returns. Both needs analysis and program evaluation are well-developed areas in industrial and organizational psychology (Goldstein, 1989, 1994; Kraiger, Ford, & Salas, 1993).

For example, one issue that often vexes employers is whether to spend money on reskilling programs for older workers with shorter payback periods. Another is whether to invest in training for the hard-core unemployed or for workers who lack basic literacy skills. In both cases, business sees lower payback probabilities. Utility analyses can play an important role in dispelling myths about the costs of training relative to its benefits. The technology is available now to do such analyses (Cascio, 1989), and a number of them already have been reported in the personnel psychology literature (Cascio, 1994a). However, what generally has not been reported, and that will be essential in the future, is objective evidence of the extent to which the financial returns forecasted by utility analyses actually do materialize.

One area in which objective evidence does indicate positive payoffs for individual and organizational performance is that of high-performance work practices (HPWPs), of which training is an integral component. Such practices provide workers with the information, skills, incentives, and responsibility to make decisions essential for innovation, quality improvement, and rapid response to change (U.S. Department of Labor, 1993). A recent study based on a national sample of nearly 1,000 publicly-traded firms found that HPWPs have an economically and statistically significant impact both on employee turnover and productivity on short-term and long-term measures of corporate financial performance (Huselid, 1995).

Earlier I showed how the roles of workers and managers are changing dramatically, from controlled to empowered, from boss to mentor. Both groups will require extensive training and support to change entrenched attitudes and beliefs to function effectively in the new world of work. For example, empowered employees need to develop the kind of understanding of business and financial issues that no one but an owner or an executive used to be concerned with (Bridges, 1994). Moreover, several studies have supported the novel proposition that the "skills gap" is really about attitudes (Cappelli, 1992). Thus a 1989 employer survey by Towers Perrin found that the most common reasons for firing new employees were absenteeism and failure to adapt to the work environment; only 9% of the workers were dismissed because of difficulties in learning how to perform their jobs. A 1990 survey by the National Association of Manufacturers found that the belief that applicants would not have the work attitudes and behaviors needed to adapt to the work environment was almost twice as common a reason for rejecting applicants as the next most important factor. This raises several intriguing research questions:

If attitudes play such an important role in work performance, then constructs such as adaptability, consistency, and prosocial behavior become particularly important components of workplace learning programs. To what extent can such characteristics be taught? How should they be taught? To what extent can research findings in applied social psychology, cognitive psychology, and instructional technology inform training practices in these areas?

In designing training systems to promote team development and workplace learning, what are the most effective methods for developing skill, knowledge, and attitudinal competencies (Cannon-Bowers, Tannenbaum, Salas, & Volpe, 1995)? Do results hold up when teams must operate in stable as opposed to rapidly changing environments?

Senior managers are looking for evidence of the extent to which workers and managers can change their attitudes and behavior to fit new organizational designs. Research is needed to identify methods and activities that will facilitate and maintain such change. The relapse prevention model, a cognitive-behavioral model of self-control strategies designed to reduce the likelihood of relapse, is a good place to start (Marx, 1982).

Performance Appraisal

Performance appraisal refers to the systematic description of the job-relevant strengths and weaknesses of an individual or group. In recent years, one issue that has generated considerable debate is the relevance and appropriateness of performance appraisal in work contexts that emphasize total quality management (TQM).

TQM emphasizes the continuous improvement of products and processes to ensure long-term customer satisfaction. Its group problem-solving focus encourages employee empowerment by using the job-related expertise and ingenuity of the workforce. Cross-functional teams develop solutions to complex problems, often shortening the time taken to design, develop, or produce products and services. Because a team may not include a representative of management, the dividing line between labor and management often becomes blurred in practice, as workers themselves begin to solve organizational problems. Thus adoption of TQM generally requires cultural change within the organization as management reexamines its past methods and practices in light of the demands of the new philosophy (Wiedman, 1993).

If the "father of TQM," W. Edwards Deming, had his way, appraisal systems that tie individual performance to salary adjustments would be eliminated. In his view, such systems hinder teamwork, create fear and mistrust, and discourage risk-taking behavior, thereby stifling innovation. Worse yet, Deming believes, most appraisal systems are based on the faulty assumption that individuals have significant control over their own performance—that is, that most individuals can improve if they choose to do so by putting forth the necessary effort (Deming, 1986).

Most industrial and organizational psychologists would agree that as a basis for implementing a "pay-for-performance" philosophy, performance appraisal is a meaningful tool only if workers have significant control over the variables that impact their individual performance. If not, then it is true, as Deming (1986) believes, that appraisals only measure random statistical variation within a particular system. Here are three suggestions for harmonizing these two processes (Wiedman, 1993): Let customer expectations (a) generate individual or team performance expectations, (b) include results expectations that identify actions to meet or exceed those expectations, and (c) include behavioral skills that make the real difference in achieving quality performance and total customer satisfaction.

Here are several other pressing research issues in appraisal:

1. Traditionally, the immediate supervisor is responsible for rating subordinates (Bernardin & Beatty, 1984; Murphy & Cleveland, 1991). New organizational designs that incorporate self-managed work teams or manufacturing "cells" (small teams of workers) may not have an immediate supervisor. Research is needed to provide answers to questions such as Who should rate performance under these circumstances and on what criteria? What should be the relative role (if any) of customers or suppliers? McIntyre and Salas (1995) have identified a number of behavioral indicators of team performance, and their work can help guide future research in this area.

2. To create greater allegiance to a process, rather than to a boss, GE has begun to put in place so-called "360-degree appraisals" in which peers and others above and below the employee evaluate the performance of an individual in a process ("The Horizontal Corporation," 1993; see also Tornow, 1993). Research is needed to identify the relative weights of the various raters as well as optimal means for combining information. Moreover, given that multiple perspectives are represented (e.g., peers, subordinates, and supervisors), and that each is best able to rate different aspects of performance (Borman, 1974; Mabe & West, 1982), what should each rater rate?

3. In work that is highly coordinate in nature (e.g., grant proposal writing and process reengineering), it is simply not possible to disaggregate individual from team performance. Although individual behaviors can be rated (e.g., initiative, flexibility, and effort), individual outcomes cannot. As McIntyre and Salas (1995) pointed out, teamwork and task work are distinct. Research is needed to identify the components and mechanics of team-based performance appraisal.

4. What is the most appropriate format and method for communicating performance feedback when multiple perspectives are represented? Should a single individual serve as the conduit for such feedback? Who is responsible for following up to ensure that goals are set and progress is monitored? What is the long-term impact of such feedback on behavior and work outcomes (Smither et al., 1995)?

Answers to these kinds of questions are particularly relevant to the changing world of work. Industrial and organizational psychologists have the tools and know-how to advance cumulative knowledge in this area while making genuine contributions to better management of human resources.

Compensation and Incentives

Traditionally, pay systems were job-based. That is, each job had an intrinsic worth (identified through the process of job evaluation) so that, in theory at least, pay stayed relatively constant regardless of who performed the job. Individual contributions were rewarded, as was position in the hierarchy and tenure on the job. Base salaries tended to increase year after year, as percentage increases yielded larger and larger amounts of money added to the base.

In today's flatter, less hierarchical organizations, the old assumptions about pay systems are being questioned. Some organizations are rewarding employees not just for individual performance but also for the development of their skills and for team or organizational performance (Ost, 1995). Others are asking employees to put more of their pay at risk. Consider each of these trends.

In a skill- or knowledge-based pay system, workers are not paid on the basis of the job they currently are doing but rather on the basis of the number of jobs they are capable of doing, or on their depth of knowledge. In such a "learning environment," the more workers learn, the more they earn. Workers at American Steel & Wire can boost their annual salaries by up to $12,480 by acquiring as many as 10 skills. Is there any impact on productivity or morale? A recent survey of 27 companies with such programs revealed that 70% to 88% reported higher job satisfaction, product quality, or productivity. Some 70% to 75% reported lower operating costs or reduced turnover ("Skill-Based Pay," 1992).

Such systems cannot work in all situations. They seem to work best when the following conditions exist (Gomez-Mejia & Balkin, 1992): (a) A supportive human resource management (HRM) philosophy underpins all employment activities (such a philosophy is characterized by mutual trust and the conviction that employees have the ability and motivation to perform well); (b) HRM programs such as profit sharing, participative management, empowerment, and job enrichment complement the skill- or knowledge-based pay system; (c) technology and organization structure change frequently; (d) employee exchanges (i.e., assignment and rotation) are common; (e) there are opportunities to learn new skills; (f) employee turnover is relatively high; and (g) workers value teamwork and the opportunity to participate.

A second trend among many firms is to increase the proportion of pay that is at risk or variable, thereby reducing fixed costs. A third trend is to use team or organization-wide incentives, such as profit sharing or productivity gain sharing, to provide broader motivation than is furnished by incentive plans geared to individual employees. Their aim is twofold: to increase productivity and to improve morale by giving employees a feeling of participation in and identification with the company (Florkowski, 1987).

It is important to distinguish *gain sharing* from *profit sharing*. The two approaches differ in three important ways (T. H. Hammer, 1988): (a) Gain sharing is based on a measure of productivity. Profit sharing is based on a global profitability measure. (b) Gain sharing, productivity measurement, and bonus payments are frequent events, distributed monthly or quarterly, whereas the measures and rewards of profit-sharing plans are annual. (c) Gain-sharing plans are current distribution plans, in contrast to most profit-sharing plans, which have deferred payments. Hence gain-sharing plans are true incentive plans rather than employee benefits. As such, they are more directly related to individual behavior and therefore can motivate worker productivity.

Does profit sharing improve productivity? One review of 27 econometric studies found that profit sharing was positively related to productivity in better than 9 of every 10 instances. Productivity was generally 3% to 5% higher in firms with profit-sharing plans than in those without plans (U.S. Department of Labor, 1993).

Does gain sharing improve productivity? Of 72 companies using Improshare (Fein, 1982)—production standards based on time-and-motion studies, plus a sharing of productivity gains 50–50 between employees and the company—38 companies were nonunion and 34 were represented by 18 international unions. The average gain in productivity over all companies using the plan after one year was 22.4%. Productivity gains tended to be larger if workers were provided with training and information; gains tended to be smaller, none, or negative (i.e., productivity deteriorated) if workers perceived that there was "nothing in it" for them.

Such changes in compensation and incentive systems raise several important research questions:

1. American culture emphasizes "rugged individualism" rather than a group orientation. What specific contextual issues are relevant when team or organization-wide incentives are applied in such a culture?

2. Empowerment emphasizes an active role for employees in determining outcomes. Yet employees sometimes feel powerless to influence profits, as under a profit-sharing program. How can firms deal with this inconsistency?

3. Logically, team-based performance appraisals should form the basis for team-based incentives. However, there is almost no extant research on team-based appraisals (an exception is Norman & Zawacki, 1991), with respect either to process or to format.

4. Although firms such as General Foods, General Motors, Procter and Gamble, and Anheuser-Busch have been experimenting with skill- or knowledge-based pay (Tosi & Tosi, 1987), job evaluation methods remain more popular. Why? What employee or work-related factors might enhance the applicability of such systems in a changing world of work?

Organizational Development

Organizational development (OD) can be described broadly as the use of planned, behavioral science-based interventions in work settings for the purpose of improving organizational functioning and individual development (Porras & Robertson, 1992). At its core, OD is about change, and in the future world of work, "the core competitive advantage for companies will be their capacity for mastering revolutionary change at all levels of the organization" (Tichy, 1994).

For many organizations, this will require a metamorphosis into a "learning organization." Yet as compelling a notion as that is, in-depth interviews with 350 executives in 14 industries found that in attempting to implement change, from work redesign to organization culture, many firms had not learned from their past mistakes, or else somehow felt doomed to repeat them (Arthur D. Little, Inc., 1994). As many as 70%–80% of change initiatives had failed; 40% of the executives surveyed were very unhappy, finding change too slow or patchy; there were no significant benefits from the change initiatives; and 80% of the companies expected to be going through other major changes within a few years.

These results are not encouraging, but they certainly increase opportunities and raise some important research issues for industrial and organizational psychologists. These issues span two broad areas: planning for change (based on theory) and implementing change (based on practice). With respect to planning, the most pressing need is to develop a well-specified theory about the process of organizational change. Indeed, a comprehensive review of literature in the field of OD concluded, "It is a major weakness of the field that; as a group, the theories supposed to define the dynamics of the planned change process are so vague" (Porras & Robertson, 1992, p. 760). Specifically, two types of research are needed:

1. Identification and specification of alternative models of organizations on which to base change process theories. As has been shown, both the structure and variety of organizational forms are changing dramatically as organizations strive to meet the ever-changing demands of the marketplace. Change process theory is not keeping pace.

2. More comprehensive frameworks, categorization schemes, or models that will allow industrial and organizational psychologists to make sense of the theory and knowledge that already exists (Woodman, 1989).

In the Arthur D. Little (1994) survey, those who were successful in implementing change were able to help managers and employees fundamentally change the way they think about and approach change. This can be done in a number of ways. From the perspective of implementing change, a variety of OD intervention techniques exists, from simple to complex, from short-term to long-term, from affecting one individual to affecting an entire organization, and from affecting only one organizational variable (e.g., social factors) to affecting several (e.g., organizing arrangements, technology, and physical setting; Porras & Robertson, 1992).

If OD interventions are to be maximally effective, however, practitioners must identify the best change technique or combination of techniques to apply to a given situation, while at the same time addressing fundamental characteristics such as underlying assumptions, beliefs, and attitudes. Unfortunately, present OD theory does not provide sufficient guidance for determining the best techniques to use in particular situations. As a result, practice is leading theory, instead of the other way around (Mirvis, 1988).

What Can Be Done?

Perhaps the greatest need in this area today, as in the past, is for methodologically sound evaluations of the relative impact of alternative OD interventions. Problems such as the unit of analysis and random assignment of individuals to groups make classic experimental designs difficult to implement in field settings. This should not be cause for abandonment of efforts to evaluate the relative impact of alternative interventions. Application of quasi-experimental designs, qualitative research methods (Van Maanen, 1979), and assessment of the agreement of laboratory and field results (Gersick, 1989) all can contribute to the advancement of knowledge and practice.

Thousands of change efforts are initiated every year. If the field is to maintain a scientific basis for its continued existence, then it is essential to evaluate change efforts to determine which interventions have the greatest impact on which organizational variables. The ultimate objective is to develop cumulative knowledge that can be translated into a science-based practice of OD that is directly useful to organizations. Such knowledge will be critical to mastering change at all levels and ensuring a sustained competitive advantage for organizations that rely on behavioral science-based change interventions to do so.

Summary and Conclusions

Dramatic changes are affecting the world of work. Some of these include increased global competition, the impact of information technology, the reengineering of business processes, the shift from vertically integrated hierarchies to networks of specialists, smaller companies that employ fewer people, and the change in the paradigm of doing business from making a product to providing a service. Beyond those, there is an emerging redefinition of work itself: growing disappearance of the job as a fixed bundle of tasks, along with an emphasis on constantly changing work required to fulfill the ever-increasing demands of customers.

There are great opportunities for industrial and organizational psychologists to contribute to the betterment of human welfare in the context of these changes. To lead change rather than to follow it, however, will require a break with traditional practices and a focus on rigorous research that addresses emerging trends. This article identified six key areas in which to start: job analysis, employee selection, training and development, performance appraisal, compensation (including incentives), and organizational development. These challenges provide an exciting agenda with large potential payoffs for individuals, organizations, and society as psychology moves into the 21st century.

References

Alderman, L. (1995, April). What you need to ace today's rough-and-tough job interviews. *Money*, pp. 35, 36, 38.

Arthur D. Little, Inc. (1994, September). *Managing organizational change: How leading organizations are meeting the challenge.* Cambridge, MA: Author.

Barley, S. (1991). *The new crafts: The rise of the technical labor force and its implications for the organization of work.* Philadelphia: National Center on the Educational Quality of the Workforce, University of Pennsylvania.

Barney, J. (1991). Firm resources and sustained competitive advantage. *Journal of Management, 17,* 99–120.

Bass, B. M. (1954). The leaderless group discussion. *Psychological Bulletin, 51,* 465–492.

Bass, B. M. (1985). *Leadership and performance beyond expectations.* New York: Free Press.

Baumohl, B. (1993, March 15). When downsizing becomes "dumbsizing." *Time,* p. 55.

Bernardin, H. J., & Beatty, R. W. (1984). *Performance appraisal: Assessing human behavior at work.* Boston: Kent.

Borman, W. C. (1974). The rating of individuals in organizations: An alternative approach. *Organizational Behavior and Human Performance, 12,* 105–124.

Bridges, W. (1994, September 19). The end of the job. *Fortune,* pp. 62–64, 68, 72, 74.

Byrne, J. A. (1993, February 8). The virtual corporation. *Business Week,* pp. 98–103.

Byrne, J. A. (1994, May 9). The pain of downsizing. *Business Week,* pp. 60–69.

Campbell, D. T., & Fiske, D. W. (1959). Convergent and discriminant validation by the multitrait–multimethod matrix. *Psychological Bulletin, 56,* 81–105.

Cannon-Bowers, J. A., Tannenbaum, S. I., Salas, E., & Volpe, C. E. (1995). Defining competencies and establishing team training requirements. In R. A. Guzzo & E. Salas (Eds.), *Team effectiveness and decision making in organizations* (pp. 333–380). San Francisco: Jossey-Bass.

Cappelli, P. (1992). *Is the "skills gap" really about attitudes?* Philadelphia: National Center on the Educational Quality of the Workforce. (Educational Quality of the Workforce Catalog No. WP01)

Career management services @ Sun. (1994). Milipitas, CA: Author.

Cascio, W. F. (1989). Using utility analysis to assess training outcomes. In I. Goldstein (Ed), *Training and development in organizations* (pp. 63–88). San Francisco: Jossey-Bass.

Cascio, W. F. (1991). *Applied psychology in personnel management* (4th ed.). Englewood Cliffs, NJ: Prentice Hall.

Cascio, W. F. (1993, February). Downsizing: What do we know? What have we learned? *Academy of Management Executive, 7(1),* 95–104.

Cascio, W. F. (1994a). *Documenting training effectiveness in terms of worker performance and adaptability* (Educational Quality of the Workforce Catalog No. WP23). Philadelphia: University of Pennsylvania, National Center for the Educational Quality of the Workforce.

Cascio, W. F. (1994b). *Public investments in training: Perspectives on macro-level structural issues and micro-level delivery systems* (Educational Quality of the Workforce Catalog No. WP24). Philadelphia: University of Pennsylvania, National Center for the Educational Quality of the Workforce.

Deming, W. E. (1986). *Out of the crisis.* Cambridge, MA: MIT Center for Advanced Engineering Study.

Dipboye, R. L., & Gaugler, B. B. (1993). Cognitive and behavioral processes in the selection interview. In N. Schmitt & W. C. Borman (Eds.), *Personnel selection in organizations* (pp. 135–170). San Francisco: Jossey-Bass.

Downside to the jobs upturn. (1994, November 14). *Business Week,* p. 26.

Doyle, F. P. (1992, June). Unpublished keynote address, National Academy of Human Resources, Santa Fe, NM.

Drake, Beam, Morin, Inc. (1994). *Career transition study, November 1993 to August 1994.* Washington, DC: Author.

Fein, M. (1982, August). *Improved productivity through worker involvement.* Paper presented at the annual meeting of the Academy of Management, New York.

Fiedler, F. E. (1967). *A theory of leadership effectiveness.* New York: McGraw-Hill.

Filipczak, B. (1995, January). You're on your own: Training, employability, and the new employment contract. *Training,* pp. 29–36.

Florkowski, G. W. (1987). The organizational impact of profit sharing. *Academy of Management Review, 12,* 622–636.

Gael, S. (Ed.). (1988). *The job analysis handbook for business, industry, and government.* New York: Wiley.

Gersick, C. J. G. (1989). Marking time: Predictable transitions in task groups. *Academy of Management Journal, 32,* 274–309.

Goldstein, I. L. (Ed.). (1989). *Training and development in work organizations.* San Francisco: Jossey-Bass.

Goldstein, I. L. (1994). *Training in organizations: Needs assessment, development and evaluation* (4th ed.). Monterey, CA: Brooks/Cole.

Gomez-Mejia, L. R., & Balkin, D. B. (1992). *Compensation, organizational strategy, and firm performance.* Cincinnati, OH: Southwestern.

Guion, R. M. (1991). Personnel assessment, selection, and placement. In M. D. Dunnette & L. M. Hough (Eds.), *Handbook of industrial and organizational psychology* (2nd ed., Vol. 2, pp. 327–397). Palo Alto, CA: Consulting Psychologists Press.

Gwynne, S. C. (1992, September 28). The long haul. *Time,* pp. 34–38.

Hammer, M., & Champy, J. (1993). *Reengineering the corporation.* New York: Harper Business, p. 90.

Hammer, T. H. (1988). New developments in profit sharing, gainsharing, and employee ownership. In J. P. Campbell & R. J. Campbell (Eds.), *Productivity in organizations* (pp. 328–366). San Francisco: Jossey-Bass.

Harvey, R. J. (1991). Job analysis. In M. D. Dunnette & L. M. Hough (Eds.), *Handbook of industrial and organizational psychology* (2nd ed., Vol. 2, pp. 71–163). Palo Alto, CA: Consulting Psychologists Press.

Henkoff, R. (1994, October 3). Finding, training, and keeping the best service workers. *Fortune,* pp. 110–122.

Hogan, R. T. (1991). Personality and personality measurement. In M. D. Dunnette & L. M. Hough (Eds.), *Handbook of industrial and organizational psychology* (2nd ed., Vol. 2, pp. 873–919). Palo Alto, CA: Consulting Psychologists Press.

House, R. J. (1971). A path-goal theory of leader effectiveness. *Administrative Science Quarterly, 16,* 321–339.

Huselid, M. A. (1995). The impact of human resource management practices on turnover, productivity, and corporate financial performance. *Academy of Management Journal, 38,* 635–672.

Ilgen, D. R., & Hollenbeck, J. R. (1991). The structure of work: Job design and roles. In M. D. Dunnette & L. M. Hough (Eds.), *Handbook of industrial and organizational psychology* (2nd ed., Vol. 2, pp. 165–207). Palo Alto, CA: Consulting Psychologists Press.

Investing in people and prosperity. (1994, May). U.S. Department of Labor, Washington, DC, p. 7.

Jobs in an age of insecurity. (1993, November 22). *Time,* p. 35.

Kiechel,, W., III. (1993, May 17). How we will work in the year 2000. *Fortune,* pp. 38–52.

Klimoski, R., & Jones, R. G. (1995). Staffing for effective group decision making: Key issues in matching people and teams. In R. A. Guzzo & E. Salas (Eds.), *Team effectiveness and decision making in organizations* (pp. 291–332). San Francisco: Jossey-Bass.

Kraiger, K., Ford, J. K., & Salas, E. (1993). Application of cognitive, skill-based, and affective theories of learning outcomes to new methods of training evaluation. *Journal of Applied Psychology, 78,* 311–328.

Labich, K. (1994, November 14). Why companies fail. *Fortune,* pp. 52–54, 58, 60, 64, 68.

Labor letter. (1991, October 22). *The Wall Street Journal,* p. A1.

Lado, A. A., & Wilson, M. C. (1994). Human resource systems and sustained competitive advantage: A competency-based perspective. *Academy of Management Review, 19,* 699–727.

Mabe, P. A., & West, S. G. (1982). Validity of self-evaluation of ability: A review and meta-analysis. *Journal of Applied Psychology, 67,* 280–296.

Marsh, H. W., & Hocevar, D. (1988). A new, more powerful approach to multitrait–multimethod analyses: Application of second-order confirmatory factor analysis. *Journal of Applied Psychology, 73,* 107–117.

Marx, R. D. (1982). Relapse prevention for managerial training: A model for maintenance of behavior change. *Academy of Management Review, 7,* 433–441.

McCormick, E. J. (1979). *Job analysis: Methods and applications.* New York: AMACOM.

McIntyre, R. M., & Salas, E. (1995). Measuring and managing for team performance: Emerging principles from complex environments. In R. A. Guzzo & E. Salas (Eds.), *Team effectiveness and decision making in organizations* (pp. 9–45). San Francisco: Jossey-Bass.

Mirvis, P. H. (1988). Organization development: Part 1: An evolutionary perspective. In W. A. Passmore & R. W. Woodman (Eds.), *Research in organizational change and development* (Vol. 2). Greenwich, CT: JAI Press.

Motowidlo, S. J., Carter, G. W., Dunnette, M. D., Tippins, N., Werner, S., Burnett, J. R., & Vaughan, M. J. (1992). Studies of the structured behavioral interview. *Journal of Applied Psychology, 77,* 571–587.

Murphy, K. R., & Cleveland, J. N. (1991). *Performance appraisal: An organizational perspective.* Boston: Allyn & Bacon.

Murray, M. (1995, May 4). Thanks, goodbye: Amid record profits, companies continue to lay off employees. *The Wall Street Journal,* pp. A1, A5.

Nelan, B. W. (1992, Fall). How the world will look in 50 years (Special issue: Beyond the Year 2000). *Time*, pp. 36–38.

1994 AMA survey on downsizing and assistance to displaced workers. New York: American Management Association.

Norman, C. A., & Zawacki, R. A. (1991, September). Team appraisals—team approach. *Personnel Journal*, pp. 101–104.

Ones, D. S., Mount, M. K., Barrick, M. R., & Hunter, J. E. (1994). Personality and job performance: A critique of the Tett, Jackson, and Rothstein (1991) meta-analysis. *Personnel Psychology, 47*, 147–156.

Ost, E. J. (1995). Team-based pay: New wave strategic initiatives. In J. B. Miner & D. P. Crane (Eds.), *Advances in the practice, theory, and research of strategic human resource management* (pp. 353–366). New York: Harper Collins.

Pffefer, J. (1994). *Competitive advantage through people*. Boston: Harvard Business School Press, p. 8.

Pilon, L. J. (1993, February 22). Quoted in "Jobs, Jobs." *Business Week*, p. 74.

Porras, J. I., & Robertson, P. J. (1992). Organizational development: Theory, practice, and research. In M. D. Dunnette & L. M. Hough (Eds.), *Handbook of industrial and organizational psychology* (2nd ed., Vol. 3, pp. 719–822). Palo Alto, CA: Consulting Psychologists Press.

Ree, M. J., & Earles, J. A. (1991). Predicting training success: Not much more than *g*. *Personnel Psychology, 44*, 321–332.

Ree, M. J., & Earles, J. A. (1992). Intelligence is the best predictor of job performance. *Current Directions in Psychological Science, 1*, 86–89.

Ree, M. J., Earles, J. A., & Teachout, M. S. (1994). Predicting job performance: Not much more than *g*. *Journal of Applied Psychology, 79*, 518–524.

Salwen, K. G. (1993, April 19). The cutting edge: German-owned maker of power tools finds job training pays off. *The Wall Street Journal*, pp. A1, A7.

Schmitt, N., & Borman, W. C. (Eds.). (1993). *Personnel selection in organizations*. San Francisco: Jossey-Bass.

Skill-based pay boosts worker productivity and morale. (1992, April 18). *The Wall Street Journal*, p. A1.

Smither, J. W., London, M., Vasilopoulos, N. L., Reilly, R. R., Millsap, R. E., & Salvemini, N. (1995). An examination of the effects of an upward feedback program over time. *Personnel Psychology, 48*, 1–34.

Tett, R. P., Jackson, D. N., Rothstein, M., & Reddon, J. R. (1994). Metanalysis of personality–job performance relations: A reply to Ones, Mount, Barrick, & Hunter (1994). *Personnel Psychology, 47*, 157–172.

The horizontal corporation. (1993, December 20). *Business Week*, pp. 77–81.

Tichy, N. (1994, May). The future of workplace learning and performance. *Training and Development*, p. S46.

Tornow, W. W. (1993). Perceptions or reality: Is multi-perspective measurement a means or an end? *Human Resource Management, 32*, 221–230.

Tosi, H., & Tosi, L. (1987). What managers need to know about knowledge-based pay. In D. A. Balkin & L. R. Gomez-Mejia (Eds.), *New perspectives on compensation* (pp. 43–48). Englewood Cliffs, NJ: Prentice Hall.

U.S. Department of Labor. (1993, August). *High performance work practices and firm performance*. Washington, DC: U.S. Government Printing Office.

Van Maanen, J. (Ed.). (1979). Qualitative methodology [Special issue]. *Administrative Science Quarterly*, 24(4).

Vroom, V. H., & Yetton, P. W. (1973). *Leadership and decision making*. Pittsburgh, PA: University of Pittsburgh Press.

Waterman, R. H., Jr., Waterman, J. A., & Collard, B. A. (1994, July–August). Toward a career-resilient workforce. *Harvard Business Review*, pp. 87–95.

Weekley, J. A., & Gier, J. A. (1987). Reliability and validity of the situational interview for a sales position. *Journal of Applied Psychology, 72*, 484–487.

Wellins, R. S., Byham, W. C., & Wilson, J. M. (1991). *Empowered teams: Creating self-directed work groups that improve quality, productivity, and participation*. San Francisco: Jossey-Bass.

Wiedman, T. G. (1993, October). Performance appraisal in a total quality management environment. *The Industrial–Organizational Psychologist, 31(2)*, pp. 64–66.

Woodman, R. W. (1989). Organizational change and development: New arenas for inquiry and action. *Journal of Management, 15*, 205–228.

Workplace of the future: A Report of the Conference on the Future of the American Workplace. (1993). New York: U.S. Departments of Commerce and Labor.

World Competitiveness Report. (1994). Lausanne, Switzerland: World Economic Forum and Institute for Management Development.

Article Review Form at end of book.

Why is HR intervention sometimes considered to be crisis management? Why does HR have the attention of most CEOs?

Survey Shows HR in Transition

Allan Halcrow

Allan Halcrow is publisher and editor-in-chief of Workforce. *E-mail halcrow@workforcemag.com to comment.*

If you're at work when you're reading this, be prepared for anything. On this day, you might have to fire an employee who came to work drunk because his girlfriend died of cancer last night. On the other hand, you might receive a letter from Nigeria offering a $350,000,000 bribe. You will interact with others in your department, employees, line managers, vendors and consultants. Someone may ask you how late Disneyland is open, though it's more likely someone will ask you when payday is. That might be followed by the CEO asking you to identify the biggest impediment to your corporate success. You may get thanks for the work you do directly or indirectly ("Are you really a mean person? You seem nice"), but don't count on it. If you aren't careful, you might deliver a performance appraisal to the wrong employee. Through it all, you will deal with the reality that HR is still in the midst of a transition from administrative support function to strategic partner. Perhaps this is the day to launch the new equity-based pay system that you designed for 600 clerical employees—or something equally accomplished—that will leave a lasting impact on your organization and prove that HR is making that transition successfully.

All that—and much more—is drawn from the results of a *Workforce* survey, "A Day in the Life of HR." Almost 900 HR professionals answered more than 70 questions about their workdays. The survey began by asking what time respondents wake up in the morning, and followed them through the day until they went to bed at night. Some questions were lighthearted ("How deep is the stack of papers in your in-box right now?") and others were more serious ("What percentage of your day is spent on consultative or developmental projects?"). Collectively, the questions were designed to offer readers the chance to compare their average day with that of their peers and to offer some insight into the state of the profession.

The hard numbers yield some statistics that are so trivial they'll never even make it into an edition of Trivial Pursuit™ (13 percent of you have vacation souvenirs in your offices), and others that offer more insight (32 percent of you meet with the CEO at least twice a week). But it's the anecdotal data, provided in response to open-ended questions, that's ultimately more compelling. The stories show the breadth of issues faced by HR better than any statistics could. They show a side of HR rarely seen by anyone except those living it. And they make it clear that because HR is about people, it will always be an unpredictable, frustrating and demanding—yet finally rewarding—job. A day in the life of HR may be many things, but boring will never be among them.

Often, HR Is Crisis Management

One person's crisis ("someone stole my favorite pen") may be another person's minor annoyance, but responding to crises is a given in HR management. The time lost to crises, in fact, was one of the biggest surprises of the survey. Only 2 percent of you spend no time responding to crises. A majority—40 percent—spends less than 10 percent of time in crisis. But 8 percent spend more than half their time responding to crises, and another 17 percent spend at least 25 percent of their time that way. One respondent concluded, "My job is a crisis in the making all the time."

Those numbers mean that thousands of work hours are being lost to crises every day, hours that might have been spent on long-range planning or project consultation. And the impact is felt in organizations of all sizes. The statistics in this case, however, don't begin to tell the story. When asked to name the worst crisis they ever faced in the morning, a few of you mentioned computer glitches and two or three mentioned a natural disaster. All the rest of the crises mentioned were, one way or another, about people. One respondent answered the question by stating, "There have been so many over the years, and they have been so horrifying, that I have chosen to black them out." Could HR really be that bad? On some days, it could.

"Survey Shows HR in Transition," by Allan Halcrow, copyright June 1998. Used with permission of ACC Communications Inc./*Workforce*, Costa Mesa, CA. All rights reserved.

HR at the Table: Best Questions Posed to HR by CEOs

Some CEOs may be clueless, but many are working hand in hand with HR to make businesses better. For evidence that HR is playing a strategic role in organizations, look no further than some of the provocative, challenging questions that CEOs have posed to HR professionals. How could you answer these questions?

1. What makes an employee want to stay at our company?
2. Can you develop an HR strategy that will get the business from point A to point B?
3. If the company were yours, what changes would you make?
4. What are you doing to provide value-added services to your internal clients?
5. What are the three most important things we could do to improve employee morale?
6. How are you going to invest in HR this year so that we have a better HR department than our competitors?
7. In the eyes of HR, what should we be doing to improve our marketplace position?
8. What can the HR department do to add to the bottom line?
9. Five years from now, how will cultural diversity affect our business?
10. Which do you consider more important: customers or employees?
11. How are you measuring the effectiveness of HR?
12. What's the best change we can make to prepare for the future?
13. What do you see as the biggest impediment to our performance?
14. How can we reinvest in employees?
15. What can the company do to develop and promote women?

—AH

What are the employee-related crises that demand attention? Some respondents told stories of sudden terminations and sexual harassment complaints, but most often—and by a wide margin—you told tales of violence and death. "An ex-employee showed up with a gun, looking for his former supervisor," cited one respondent. Another said, "A psychiatric patient had taken a staff member hostage. A SWAT team and a hostage-negotiating team had surrounded the building." Sometimes the mayhem was accidental ("An employee had cut off a finger in a machine") and sometimes very deliberate ("An employee hit another over the head with a tire iron").

You have had to deal with the deaths of employees and their family members. You've faced murders, suicides, plane crashes and car accidents. All of it has taken a heavy toll. The stories speak for themselves:

"An employee on vacation with his family was in an auto accident. His wife was killed, his children were hospitalized and he was in a coma. The plant manager instructed me to do what we could to help the family . . ."

"I found out that a co-worker and friend had committed suicide the evening before. I had to deal with the pain of the loss of a friend while maintaining my role to communicate the incident to everyone and arrange for employee counseling."

"One of our staff members was unusually late for work. I had the manager of her apartment complex go to her apartment. She was found murdered . . ."

"An employee had a heart attack and died in the office. I had to call his spouse . . ."

"An employee in HR came to work for approximately an hour, left abruptly, and drove to the Golden Gate Bridge and jumped off."

"The death of an employee [was the worst thing I encountered in the morning]. Her son was in my office to take care of some business the morning after her death, and while he met with me he finally broke down and cried . . ."

"[The worst thing I encountered was] the sudden death of the Vice President of Sales, who was in New York City on business at the time. He died in a woman's apartment. He was married. What do you tell the wife, a woman you know well?"

There were dozens more such stories, all heartbreaking. Happily, not all the stories ended so tragically. One respondent made a 911 telephone call that saved an employee's life; another "intervened to prevent the suicide of a staff member who was found with her head in the oven."

Other crises cited that weren't literally matters of life or death were still traumatic. Among the incidents shared were a bomb threat; a tuberculosis scare; a hazardous chemical scare forcing the evacuation of an entire facility; an employee's psychotic break; and several requests to bail employees out of jail. (For other examples, please see "Before We've Even Had Coffee: HR's Worst Morning Crises," p. 18.)

The point here is not to dwell on the macabre or bizarre. Instead, it's important to recognize that some sort of crisis happens often enough to make crisis management an ongoing and time-consuming part of HR's job. That reality is rarely noted when HR is discussed. Furthermore, the nature of most crises faced by HR makes them emotional and complicated. They are imperfect situations without easy answers. Their resolution is difficult to measure. Nonetheless, managing crises well has substantial impact on the business and potentially incalculable impact on individuals.

The responsibility for dealing with such crises might be unendurable if it weren't for a sense of humor. One respondent advised, "no matter what, laugh a lot," and most of you seem quite happy to comply. Sometimes the laughs are at our own expense ("I forgot it was the weekend, and wondered why I was the only person in the office," one respondent cited as the worst-ever crisis) and sometimes they are in recognition of other people's foibles. You are privy to every quirk of human nature there is, apparently, and sometimes you just have to smile. If you have any doubts, consider another worst-ever "crisis":

"It was brought to my attention that one of our associates, thought to be a female, was in a stall in the ladies' restroom with `her' feet pointed in the `wrong' direction. Several female associates witnessed this and came to me to complain about it. I had to speak to the associate. She admitted that she was genetically a male, but that she had been living as a woman for two years . . ."

Time Spent on Administrivia Is Diminishing

Beyond the crises, your work may not be so fraught with drama. It is, however, of equal or even greater impact. After all, HR is still a business function, albeit an atypical one. To maximize its contribution, HR has been evolving into a more active business partner. Your typical day shows that the transition to strategic partner is not complete, but it also shows that HR professionals are not the paper-pushing, picnic-planning policy police that they used to be. Evidence for the shift to more big-picture thinking can be found in how you spend your day, your relationship with the CEO and your reputation in the organization.

Respondents were asked to divide the time spent on a typical day into four broad activities: routine or administrative tasks, strategic or big-picture thinking, consultative or development projects and responding to a crisis. Although one respondent asserted that, "I'm not paid by my employer to think," most of you are paid to think and spend your time fairly evenly divided among the four activities.

That division makes it clear that administrative tasks no longer dominate the profession. Only 20 percent of you spend half your time or more on routine tasks, and only 5 percent spend 75 percent of the time on such work. In contrast, almost half (45 percent) of you spend one-quarter of your day or less on the routine, and for 11 percent of you it's 10 percent of the day or less. A very strategic 1 percent of you spends no time on administrivia at all.

So, how are you spending the time that was once spent on the routine? A big part of the day is spent on consultative or developmental projects. Twenty-eight percent of you spend at least one-quarter of the time on such work, and 9 percent spend more than half the day consulting. More than a third of you (34 percent) spend somewhere between 10 percent and 25 percent of the time in consulting or developing.

Big-picture planning also constitutes a significant portion of your day. Seventeen percent of you spend at least one-fourth of your day on strategic planning, which amounts to the equivalent of more than one full day each week. One in five of you spends more than half your time on the big picture.

Still, for those who believe that the future of HR lies in strategic planning and consulting, the news is not all good. Almost one-third of you (30 percent) spends 10 percent or less of your day on consultative or developmental projects. An even greater proportion—40 percent—spends less than 10 percent of the time on strategic planning.

Those numbers make it easy for cynics to say that the glass is half empty and HR still is not the strategic partner that it wants to be. There is ample evidence, however, that the glass is half full. For one thing, the shift away from administrivia extends through all levels of the HR function.

Almost one-third (32 percent) of respondents report directly to the CEO. Another 21 percent report to another top title, such as the COO or a site manager. A total of 54 percent respondents, then, are the senior HR officers in their organizations. Exactly one-third of respondents report to the senior HR officer, and have less responsible positions. Yet those at lower levels of the HR function are just as likely to spend time on consultative work or big-picture thinking as their executive counterparts.

In fact, how time is spent is determined more by the size of your organization than your title. Those of you with the top title in smaller organizations, where the HR function is smaller, spend more time on the routine than do those who have lower-level titles at larger organizations where there's more depth in the department. For example, when all 874 responses are considered, almost half of you (48 percent) spend at least 25 percent of your day on administrative tasks. Yet when the responses of those in organizations with 5,000 employees or more are broken out, the percentage drops to just 20 percent. On the flip side, 18 percent of the total respondents spend one-fourth of the time or more on strategic issues. But when those in the largest organizations are broken out, the figure jumps to 34 percent.

Focusing on the numbers for too long is enough to make all but the most fanatic statistician get cross-eyed. What's important to note is that HR, overall, is spending less time on administrivia and more time impacting the business in broader strokes—and that's true even in organizations with limited resources.

HR Has the CEO's Attention

It may be a chicken-or-egg question whether you have the CEO's attention because you're focusing on

---

Hindsight Is 20/20: Career Advice from Your Peers

When asked "What was the smartest thing you ever did in the course of doing your job?," some respondents identified specific accomplishments. The majority, however, offered more general wisdom. Here's the wisdom shared most often; consider it priceless career advice:

1. Stay visible to employees, and to the boss.
2. Stand by your values.
3. Make time for personal development.
4. Unilaterally administer policies consistently—without exception.
5. Think about what you would want from HR if you were the boss.
6. Plan ahead.
7. Document everything.
8. Keep confidential matters confidential.
9. Be respectful of everyone always.
10. Be honest.
11. Delegate!
12. Read. Read. Read.
13. Ignore the cynical people and maintain a positive, enthusiastic attitude.
14. Surround yourself with good people.
15. No matter what, laugh a lot.

—AH

Before We've Even Had Coffee: HR's Worst Morning Crises

No question in the survey prompted more response than number 20: "What's the worst work-related problem you ever had to face first thing in the morning?" You answered with hundreds of examples, ranging from the gruesome to the hilarious. Sadly, violence and death were cited most often, with surprise terminations next. We found it impossible to pick the worst crisis, but these examples show the range of problems faced by HR:

1. The discovery that union officials had been reporting inflated earnings for pension benefit credit. The inflated reporting resulted in the tripling of retirement benefits for certain union officials.
2. An HR employee had stayed late and instigated a racial uprising.
3. A medical emergency when we had just switched to a new carrier. We had to convince the new insurance company that we had coverage.
4. An employee was found naked and unconscious in a motel room with a prostitute. I had to determine what disciplinary action to take and how.
5. I found out my boss was sexually harassing my peers. I had to confront her with the policy against harassment and the complaints.
6. I gave someone feedback about how the person performed on a personality test. We then had a psychiatrist sedate the person, and the individual willingly decided to seek inpatient status.
7. An employee crashed her car into the side of the building.
8. A manager and two employees were caught smoking marijuana.
9. FBI agents arrived with a search warrant to remove all company documents and computer files.
10. I had to climb in the window and restart the computer. The computer system was tied to the security system, so the doors were locked and 225 people were waiting to get in.
11. On my first day, I had the Department of Labor at my door for an audit.
12. A surprise raid by the immigration department.
13. It's a toss-up between the narcoleptic forklift driver who almost hit a pedestrian and the nurse in our Mexico plant who was modeling lingerie for male hourly employees.
14. An employee suicide in the building the previous evening.
15. An employee was caught "pleasing himself" on company property during work hours.

—AH

---

strategic issues or the other way around. Either way, you do have support from the top.

A third of you report directly to the CEO, and another 9 percent report to a CEO-equivalent, such as plant manager. The reporting relationship is more than a formality. Three-fourths of you meet with the CEO at least monthly, and some considerably more often than that. Sixteen percent of you meet with the CEO every day.

When asked to name the best question ever posed to HR by the CEO, a few naysayers sneered that the CEO only focuses on trivia ("Pretty good Danish, huh?" was one respondent's best-question evidence) or that the CEO only surfaces when there are problems. As one respondent put it, "When I see him, it's always about a situation that someone has blamed us for." Most of you, however, volunteered that you're regularly asked your opinion about business issues, and many offered specific evidence that CEOs challenge you with serious, thought-provoking issues.

The topics for discussion ran the gamut from employee turnover to marketing challenges. Among the other issues that HR was invited to help address:

- Employee retirement planning
- Learning organizations
- Legal issues
- HR's internal clients
- Employee morale
- Competitors to the business
- Financial issues
- Diversity

There isn't an employee picnic on the list, which is perhaps why HR's reputation is improving. (Judge the CEOs best questions yourself; please see "HR at the Table: Best Questions Posed to HR by CEOs," p. 16.)

Despite What You Might Think, Catbert Is Not the HR Norm

Observers point to Scott Adams' comic strip character Catbert, or to the lead character of TV's "The Drew Carey Show" for evidence of HR's image problem. Fortunately, from where you're sitting, the situation isn't nearly so bleak.

True, there was one respondent who lamented that "even my boss calls me Catbert, the Evil HR Director." At the other extreme was the 1 percent who reported that HR in their organizations is "universally loved and admired."

In between was the majority. When asked to select the phrase that best described how HR is perceived in their organization, more than half (54 percent) say that "some people in the organization see our contribution and others don't." That's a long way from being universally ridiculed, as DILBERT™ would suggest is the case. The best news is that almost one in five respondents say, "we're seen as allies and partners." A mere 5 percent say that HR in their companies is seen as "obstacles and enforcers."

These perceptions are based on more than blind optimism or denial. Despite stereotypes to the contrary, HR is appreciated by at least some people. When asked when they last heard someone in the organization (outside HR itself) say something nice about HR, 14 percent cited the current day and another 14 percent cited the previous day. A total of 74 percent, in fact, had heard something nice as recently as the last month. And only 11 percent had to go back to the Bush administration to find an example.

The Addams Family at Work: The Weirdest Questions Posed to HR

Some questions are dumb, but others are just plain peculiar. When you get them, you often don't know whether to laugh or cry. And sometimes you can't help but wonder what prompted them. But chances are, when you get questions like these, you won't forget them. Here are our favorites, along with some thoughts on how we might answer them.

1. Do employees have to wear underwear? *Only during work hours.*
2. Is testing for arsenic poisoning covered under our health plan? *No, but we do address it in our funeral plan.*
3. If I were interested in killing my boss, would I be violating any company policy? Which one? *Technically, no company policy prohibits that. However, the government frowns upon such action.*
4. What happens to an employee who's caught having oral sex on company time? *Memo to self: contact Kenneth Starr.*
5. Do you want to see the boil on my butt? *Not until the next show-and-tell day.*
6. Do I have to dress as a man every day? *No, Saturday, Sunday and national holidays are exempt.*
7. How much time can I spend going to the bathroom? *As long as it takes.*
8. What are we going to do about the homosexual, draft-dodging good ol' boys running the building? *That's just what we've been wondering.*
9. Can I hang bath mats on the walls in my office to insulate against outside noise? *Yes, provided they match the décor in your office.*
10. What do you think of Victoria's Secret for employee incentives? *Incentives to do what?*
11. What's my astrological sign? *I'd say it's the dodo bird.*
12. Do employees have to be able to sing? *Yes, please check in the employee manual under "whistleblowing."*
13. Can I claim dental benefits if I don't have any teeth? *Hmmm . . . Let me chew on that a bit.*
14. When I leave, can I take my cubicle walls? *Take them where?*
15. Do you hire athletes? *Yes. The CEO is a big athletic supporter.*

—AH

Oops! HR's Biggest Mistakes

OK, even HR isn't perfect. We asked you to identify the biggest mistake you ever made in the course of doing your job. Although one respondent asked hopefully, "HR people don't make mistakes, right?" most of you 'fessed up. There were a lot of mistakes to choose from, but these were the ones that struck us as best justifying the universal complaint, "Man, I've had a bad day":

1. Forgot to process raises for an entire department.
2. Spelled the CEO's name wrong on a letter going to all employees about a major change in their compensation. The letter was signed "Rat Smith" instead of "Rod Smith."
3. Accidentally deleted the entire HRIS database.
4. Delivered a training program designed for Asians to a group of Germans.
5. Had our health insurance canceled because I forgot to pay the bill.
6. Developed a proposal for the CEO with a cost estimate of $300,000. After his approval, I plugged in the real numbers and found the cost to be $688,000.
7. Ignored an IRS request.
8. Didn't have employees complete I-9 forms.
9. Put my home telephone number in the employee directory.
10. When revising the employee handbook, forgot to include the sexual harassment policy.
11. Signed a contract that put my budget in jeopardy.
12. Incorrectly calculated exchange rates on insurance premiums for employees overseas.
13. Gave myself a raise.
14. Hung up on the CEO.
15. Sold stocks of an employee who didn't want to sell.
16. Assumed that one of our employees was sane. She wasn't.
17. Signed a contract before a formal decision was agreed upon.

—AH

An even larger percentage of respondents have been thanked by someone in the organization for something they did in the course of doing their job. Forty-eight percent of respondents heard "thank you" on the current day or the day before. All but 7 percent of respondents have received thanks within the last month.

Unfortunately, the number of respondents who have heard HR criticized recently is almost as high as the number who have heard praise. Whether that reflects the transition state HR is in or an inevitability built into the function remains to be seen. In the meantime, you are working hard to demonstrate your value.

To begin with, you're spending a lot of time interacting with your constituencies. Thirty-eight percent of you spend most of your time with employees on the average day, and 29 percent spend the most time with line managers. During that time, both groups are seen as customers. When asked to name the smartest thing you've ever done in the course of doing your job, several of you cited examples of work intended directly or indirectly to prove HR's value.

One person took pride in "being visible to employees and the boss." Another got an assignment in operations and "newfound respect was established on both sides." Indeed, you are making a lot of effort to link your work more directly to the business. "I job-shadow hourly production workers to better understand our manufacturing process and day-to-day work issues," said one respondent. And one brave HR professional imperiled any sense of a personal life when he or she "met individually with managers to see what they needed from HR and then made myself available any time of the day or night."

HR Is Making an Impact

It may come as a shock, but even HR professionals aren't perfect (to see how imperfect you can be, please see "Oops! HR's Biggest Mistakes" on this page). Still, imperfections and all, HR is making a substantial positive impact on business.

When identifying the smartest thing they've ever done, respondents offered numerous examples showing the impact they have. Sometimes the impact is on only a single person ("I helped an employee get help for a drug problem"), but more often the impact is broader. Respondents cited issues ranging from flexible compensation to grievance procedures in identifying their contributions. Among the other successes cited:

"I saved my organization $250,000 by responding promptly and thoroughly to an FLSA audit."

"I put together a personal career path for each employee."

"I produced a product that brought national recognition to our CEO."

"I implemented an attendance management program that drastically reduced absenteeism."

"I headed off a class-action sexual-harassment suit involving 40 women."

"I was lead negotiator and returned a three-year union contract with a 0-0-0 wage increase."

"I put together a key retention program before turnover rose above 10 percent."

"I completely developed and implemented a new compensation program in six months without the use of outside consultants."

The accomplishments speak for themselves.

HR is about people, so it will always be an unpredictable, frustrating and demanding—yet finally rewarding—job. But it's also about business. So the next time someone asks what HR (or the "human remains" department as one employee dubbed it) does, you can tell them, "HR makes business better—in spite of everything."

Article Review Form at end of book.

Describe the links early industrial organizational psychologists made between the academic discipline and the marketplace (both private industry and government). Why are these relationships important to the field today?

Early Influences on the Development of Industrial and Organizational Psychology

Frank J. Landy

Landy, Jacobs and Associates

The subdiscipline of industrial and organizational (I/O) psychology is almost as old as the parent discipline, psychology. Psychology had its start in the rooms of William James at Harvard and in the laboratory of Wilhelm Wundt in Leipzig, Germany, in the late 1870s. The first American journal devoted to psychology did not appear until 1892, the same year the American Psychological Association (APA) was formed. The first text applying psychological principles to problems of business and commerce appeared in 1903, and the first text in industrial psychology appeared in 1910. Thus, it would appear that I/O psychology existed at the beginning. In fact, the core of psychology was experimental psychology, and all other "specialties" or subdisciplines were extensions or outgrowths of those first basic principles.

This article covers the period from 1876 through World War I (WWI). In an attempt to present a coherent description of those early years, consideration is limited to the contributions of four leading figures in the early days of I/O psychology: Hugo Münsterberg, James McKeen Cattell, Walter Dill Scott, and Walter VanDyke Bingham. In his own way, each contributed significantly, but uniquely, to the development of the field. It was through their efforts that other names began to emerge during that period, including Harold Burtt, E. K. Strong, Donald Paterson, and Bruce V. Moore. Although others began to contribute to the growing body of I/O knowledge by the end of WWI, the tone and structure of the field had been developed by these four men. As a result, by concentrating on them, we have a rather complete view of the early days of the field.

One might reasonably ask why is the consideration limited to only American (although Münsterberg was adamant about being seen as a German American) psychologists?

Industrial and organizational psychology was peculiarly American at its inception. That is not to say that psychologists in other countries were irrelevant. In fact, there was substantial interaction between American and non-American applied psychologists both before and after WWI. But certainly during the period from 1895 to 1920, special attention was being paid to American scientists and practitioners. This was understandable because America had spawned alternatives to the rather formal and restrained European structuralist paradigm. These alternatives were differential psychology and functionalism. Both of these influences, individual differences and functionalism, are cornerstones of I/O psychology, so it is not surprising that the subdiscipline arose in America rather than in Europe. Thus, for all practical purposes, I/O psychology was peculiarly American during the period in question.

Finally, consideration is limited to I/O psychology rather than to the broader topic of applied psychology.

The emergence of the broader arena of applied psychology has been addressed by others (Kuna, 1976; Napoli, 1975) in substantial detail, and although there may be some disagreement (cf. Kuna, 1976) regarding the founders of applied psychology, there is less disagreement about the earliest I/O psychologists.

In keeping with a goal of making this early history both coherent and interesting, I have kept references to a minimum. Other sources provide substantial detail and documentation for the material presented here (Landy, 1992b; 1993). Rather than simply reproduce those early treatments, I have extended those earlier discussions to include new material and inferences. Many of these extensions are deconstructionist in temper, but I believe that they are reasonable expansions and not at odds with earlier work. Those interested in the details and primary sources might examine a recent treatment of Münsterberg (Landy, 1992a) and a recent chapter on the early influences in the development of I/O psychology (Landy, 1993), as well as smaller pieces that have appeared in *The Industrial–Organizational Psychologist* over the past decade (e.g., Landy, 1991a, 1991b).

An Overview

In 1879, Wilhelm Wundt formed a new discipline from an older one: Philosophy gave way to psychology. The transformation had been a long and careful one and was almost inevitable because philosophy alone could not handle the mind–body debate. In addition, philosophy was increasingly influenced by the writings of the positivists and empiricists. By 1879, the time had come to create more room and new tools for the debate, and as a result, the discipline of psychology emerged. The discipline appeared almost simultaneously in both Europe, in the laboratory of Wundt, and America, in the experimental rooms of William James at Harvard. This might have been expected, because both James and Wundt were both philosophers and physicians. Both were fascinated by the interplay of the mind and the body, and both were familiar with the same philosophical writings.

There was an interesting symbiosis between the two initiatives. Because the German branch of the discipline developed relatively quickly, with specific methods and instrumentation, budding psychologists truly interested in learning about the new discipline would spend 1 or more years with Wundt learning technique. After such an internship, they would then return to their home country and either teach what they had learned or use that foundation to develop a paradigm of their own. Three of the four persons we consider (Münsterberg, Cattell, and Scott) did much more than serve an internship. They spent extended periods of time working under Wundt and completed a dissertation under his direction. The fourth of our figures of interest, Bingham, began his graduate career when American universities were fully established with well-developed psychology programs. As a result, it was not necessary for Bingham to travel abroad to receive his training. In some senses, Germany was to developing psychologists what France was to developing painters. Painters from all over the world converged on France in the latter part of the 19th century and used impressionism as a foundation for developing individual styles and schools of painting. Psychologists went to Germany to learn structuralism and would use that knowledge base as a point of departure for developing new paradigms.

There was some tension between Wundt and his American colleagues, however. Wundt and his associates intended to build the new science of psychology on a protocol intended to identify the underlying elements or building blocks of behavior, a protocol he called *structuralism*. In forming this new science, Wundt believed that its legitimacy would be furthered by developing general laws of behavior rather than a multiplicity of principles, theories, and exceptions. Such an approach was compatible with the existing natural and physical sciences. As a result, he tended to diminish the fact and the importance of individual differences. There would be time for exceptions and modifications later. At its inception, psychology needed to appear as much like existing sciences as possible. This desire to conform to "normal science" also explains, to some extent, the devotion to the brass instruments of the early experimental laboratories. Wundt and his colleagues developed very precise devices for measuring reaction time, the loudness of noises, the brilliance of colors, the variety of smells, and the intensity of pressure applied to various portions of the body. They concentrated on understanding how sensation became perception. Chemists, biologists, and physiologists would be more accepting of a science based on the observable measurements taken to the second decimal place using scientific-looking devices. These precise brass instruments might have also served to make the technique of introspection, a defining parameter of the new experimental psychology, less objectionable.

In contrast, William James and his colleagues had a different foundation and protocol in mind. They believed that the solution to the riddle of behavior could be found in understanding the *function* of behavior and articulated the precepts of *functionalism* or *pragmatism*. They had less interest in brass instruments and the method of introspection and greater interest in individual differences and teleology. They were not so radical as to cast out the instruments of the structuralist laboratory, but they were inclined less to use those instruments to study themselves, as did the structuralists through introspection, and more to study variations in "subjects" as a way of mapping the mind. James had never studied with or under Wundt. In fact, James was largely intolerant of the constraints of German experimental psychology and expended considerable effort to develop a paradigm that was different from structuralism.

Even though three of the four leading figures in the formation of I/O psychology—Münsterberg, Cattell, and Scott—had studied with Wundt, each departed significantly from the structuralist paradigm. Münsterberg and Cattell acknowledged the importance of individual differences early in their graduate training and developed research programs around differential phenomena and the functionalist paradigm. Scott also acknowledged the importance of individual differences and incorporated this interest into the study of persuasion and eventually motivation. But in each of the three cases, there appears to be an external event or force that strengthened this move away from structuralism. Cattell encountered Sir Francis Galton and was greatly influenced by Galton's attempts to verify the evolutionary principles of his cousin, Charles Darwin. Münsterberg appears to have simply given up his efforts at classic experimentation and theory building because of a lack of acceptance by his American colleagues at Harvard. Instead, he turned his creative efforts toward application. Walter Dill Scott seemed destined to become an academic who would train others in the new discipline of psychology until he was asked to apply these new principles to advertising. Each had an encounter that changes the direction of their lives. The fourth leading figure, Bingham, also experienced an event that changed the course of his professional life. Shortly after Münsterberg underwent his applied transformation, Bingham spent a year at Harvard, initially to study philosophy but, instead, to become one of the first converts of Münsterberg to application. By the time Bingham had received his doctor of philosophy degree (PhD) from the University of Chicago in 1908, he was already in the third generation of I/O psychology. Münsterberg, Cattell, and Scott were already well established in the new science. Nevertheless, Bingham was a product of the foremost functionalist training program in existence and had spent time at Harvard, receiving the influence of both William James and Hugo Münsterberg.

From 1908 until 1915, these four emerging I/O psychologists worked relatively independently. They were certainly well known to each other and, on the occasion of a conference or a university visit, would talk with each other about various developments in the field. Their correspondence files document a keen interest in the work of their fellow practitioners. But they did not collaborate with each other in any palpable way. Geography may have played a role: Münsterberg was in Cambridge, MA, Cattell in New York City, Bingham at Dartmouth, NH, and Scott in Evanston, IL. But more significantly, each had the temperament of a lone wolf—a single contributor.

By 1915, the four leading figures in I/O psychology were well established with national reputations, the respect of their colleagues, and a bright future. Although they did not collaborate with each other on theory building, research, practice, or writing, they did share an appreciation for the two primary building blocks of this new science: individual differences and the functionalist perspective. World War I presented a dramatic opportunity to collaborate in further establishing the foundation of this new science, but two of the four would not participate in the war effort. Cattell was an isolationist–pacifist and would have nothing to do with applying the new science to the art and practice of war, and Münsterberg died on the eve of America's involvement in the "great war," and, thus, played no role in this grand experiment. It was left to Scott and Bingham to demonstrate what I/O psychology could accomplish in the "real world." Before we consider the role of WWI in the development of I/O psychology, it is best to consider, one at a time, the individuals who had brought the field to this point.

Hugo Münsterberg

Münsterberg's early personal and professional years have been well documented elsewhere (Hale, 1990; Landy, 1992a) and are not repeated here. Instead, I cover the period leading up to his conversion to applied psychology in 1907, until his sudden and untimely death at the age of 53 in 1916.

Hugo Münsterberg was brought to Harvard in 1892 by William James for two reasons. First, James had no interest in teaching or running a laboratory. In addition, he was opposed to much of the work of Wundt and was pleased to have a well-respected critic of Wundt on the faculty. However, Münsterberg was a German and was seldom permitted to forget that fact. He was constantly chided because he was not a "Yankee" and did not possess American sensibilities. His English writing was also often ridiculed by reviewers. As a result of this latter handicap, Münsterberg chose to publish his more significant work in German, a language increasingly inaccessible to American scholars as the exodus to the labs of Wundt slowed to a trickle at the turn of the century. He did not help his cause any by his bombastic manner, his tendency to pontificate, or his loyalty to his fatherland and his proselytizing efforts on behalf of that country. Nevertheless, Münsterberg was appointed chair of the Department of Psychology at Harvard in 1900, a short 8 years after first setting foot on American soil, and he remained chair for almost a decade and director of the psychology laboratory until his death. Even though he could see the possibilities of an applied psychology through the work of his colleagues in Germany (e.g., William Stern and Sigmund Freud), before 1907, he had little interest in application himself. Furthermore, Münsterberg regularly admonished those who would seek such application. He conceded that a classically trained psychologist might have some impact on pedagogy but warned that psychology in the hands of a teacher would wreak havoc.

In 1907, Münsterberg took a dramatic turn toward application. In the course of less than 1 year, he moved from a critic to a cheerleader. From 1907 until his death in 1916, his applied exhortations were everywhere. He published applied books in clinical, industrial, educational, and forensic psychology. He prepared articles for magazines like *Harper's Monthly*, extolling the virtues of the new science for everyday problems. He lobbied presidents, congressional leaders, cabinet heads, and men of influence to consider the potential contributions of psychology. He was a favorite contributor to influential newspapers both in the form of columns and letters to the editor and was always available for a quote. At the time of his death, he was preparing a series of short mental tests to be administered to moviegoers before the feature film that would demonstrate the importance of psychological assessment to well-being.

How can one account for this radical transformation? After reviewing all the available documentation, I can conclude only that his frustration at not being accorded the status he believed he deserved at Harvard led to his abandonment of orthodox experimental psychology in favor of its application. If he could not get attention and respect from his colleagues, he would get it from a broader domestic and international audience. There are indications of earlier dissatisfaction with his colleagues. He resigned the chairmanship of the department in 1905 because of a letter from James that he considered insulting. Münsterberg was the driving force in establishing the new psychology building and believed that those efforts were not given suitable recognition. In his letter, James scolded Münsterberg for playing too great a role in the public ceremonies held for the dedication of the new building, Emerson Hall. Later, James persuaded him to reconsider his resignation, and Münsterberg returned to his post. George Santayana, one of Münsterberg's colleagues in the philosophy department, had taken to openly ridiculing Münsterberg's mannerisms in his letters to colleagues. Münsterberg had long developed a sensitivity for detecting such signals. Even William James's literary brother, Henry, took advantage of opportunities to embarrass Münsterberg. Münsterberg had taken great pains to debunk seances and other supernatural events that were of interest to William James. Henry James made a contribution to Harvard of $10,000 with the stipulation that it must be used to study paranormal events. Münsterberg lobbied (unsuccessfully) to have Harvard reject the donation. No one could misunderstand the message in that donation. Were such a situation to develop today, the target of scorn might simply leave for another university. But Münsterberg could not leave Harvard. It was the premier program in the country, and he would not stoop to join a lesser faculty. So he simply abandoned that faculty intellectually and devoted himself and his considerable talent and enthusiasm to application.

During the period 1907–1916, Münsterberg was a constant lobbyist for the contributions of psychology. He worked tirelessly to develop the notion of a National Institute of Industrial Psychology, an idea already gaining momentum in several European countries. He was in great demand as a consultant and entrepreneur of psychological practice, and he was not alone in this effort. Scott was establishing a substantial reputation in the business community. Cattell had gathered an impressive group of applied statisticians and differential psychologists at Columbia, and Bingham was beginning to attract considerable attention for his college testing program at Dartmouth. Nevertheless, it was Münsterberg who had best access to influential national leaders, both politicians and captains of industry.

It is likely that Münsterberg's efforts on behalf of applied psychology created the environment that embraced the potential contribution of psychology for the classification of inductees into the armed services in WWI. Münsterberg published the first modern book in industrial psychology, *Psychology and Industrial Efficiency*, first in German (1910) and then in English (1913). This book was the bible for the application of differential psychology in industry and established the concepts of validity and utility. There was no rival for this book until well after his death. Harold Burtt published a revision and extension of Münsterberg's text in 1926. Morris Viteles published his landmark comprehensive text in 1932, more than two decades after the appearance of Münsterberg's text. As one might expect, these later publications greatly enhanced the coverage and methods of the field. But they did not replace the structure that Münsterberg had put in place; rather, they built on it.

It is somewhat unsettling to conclude that a mainstay of applied psychology was in that subdiscipline by caprice. But perhaps it is not without precedent. Freud turned to clinical practice because as a Jew, he was not permitted to hold a position in the university. Skinner discovered intermittent schedules of reinforcement because he preferred to spend time with his new child rather than forming food pellets and filling food trays on weekends. The important principle is that each of these men found a way to illustrate basic principles of behavior in their work.

James McKeen Cattell

James McKeen Cattell was born in 1860 in Harrisburg, PA, the son of the president of Lafayette College. His precollege education was accomplished primarily through private tutoring and instruction from the faculty at Lafayette, but he did formally enroll at Lafayette and receive his undergraduate degree in 1880 (Landy, 1993). While enrolled at Lafayette, he was greatly influenced by the philosophical system of Francis Bacon known as *empiricism*. One interpretation of this system is that through the collection and analysis of empirical data, structure will be liberated and inference will be little more than recognition of obvious principles. In such a system, theory building and hypothesis testing have, at best, a secondary and subsequent role rather than a primary or formative one. This extension of Baconian thought has also been labeled *vulgar utilitarianism* (Sokal, 1982).

In 1881, Cattell had a degree, money, standing, time, and an interest in pursuing intellectual challenges, so he left for Europe to study philosophy in Germany. Had he been born 15 years later, he would most likely have studied philosophy at Harvard with Josiah Royce, George Santayana, William James, and Hugo Münsterberg, but instead, he traveled to Göttingen to study with Rudolf H. Lotze. His plan was to return after a year and complete his studies for the PhD with G. Stanley Hall at Johns Hopkins. Very shortly after Cattell's arrival at Göttingen, Lotze died, and Cattell transferred to Leipzig and spent the year attending Wundt's lectures. Unlike many of his American contemporaries at Leipzig, Cattell mastered German and was able to take full advantage of his year with Wundt. He returned to a fellowship at Johns Hopkins but longed to return to Wundt, and did after a year in Baltimore. In 1886, he received his PhD from the University of Leipzig and moved on to Cambridge University, Cambridge, England, to pursue a doctor of medicine degree.

Shortly after arriving at Cambridge, Cattell was contacted by Francis Galton, a cousin of Charles Darwin who was working out the details and implications of Darwin's notions regarding hereditary transmission and natural selection. Both Darwin and Galton believed that traits, mental and physical, were transmitted from generation to generation along genetic pathways. Galton had established a laboratory to collect data about physical traits but knew little about mental measurement. Cattell, on the other hand, had been developing and refining mental measurement techniques in Wundt's laboratory, and Galton was aware of that work. As a result, when Galton learned that Cattell was at Cambridge, he asked Cattell to advise him on the addition of mental measurements to his collection of physical measurements.

Cattell was greatly influenced by Galton, as most would be. Galton was a significant intellectual figure, conversant with the natural and the physical sciences, inventive, relentlessly curious, and with a penchant for the application of scientific principles to real-world issues. He was also committed to the same brand of Baconian empiricism with which Cattell was familiar. To support Darwin's theory of genetic transmission, it was necessary to observe and measure what was known as "biological variation," or individual differences in traits.

Like others in Wundt's laboratory, Cattell had noticed individual variation in participants. Unlike Münsterberg, who saw these individual variations as rather glaring exceptions to Wundt's attempt to formulate general laws, Cattell simply noted these differences but was neither unduly concerned nor interested in them in his laboratory work. Nevertheless, many of the measurement techniques that he had developed did reveal these differences. This was what Galton needed: a medium for illuminating individual differences in traits beyond the simple physical or anthropometric ones he was using in 1886. Thus, when Cattell arrived in Cambridge at that time, the stage was set for a very useful collaboration between Galton and Cattell. For the next 2 years, Cattell was able to apply the empiricist principles that he had incorporated at Lafayette through the work of Galton. In turn, he was able to provide Galton with a much broader range of traits to measure. He developed measures of reaction time, time estimation, and memory, as well as the more physiologically based measures of the senses (e.g., smell, taste, and touch).

Cattell left Cambridge in 1888 with a strong belief in Darwinist theory and the principles of genetic transmission, as well as an impressive array of measurement techniques for assessing mental characteristics, or traits. Throughout his lifetime, Cattell was an enthusiastic eugenicist, believing that progress in the human condition could be made through control of breeding patterns and the improvement of genetic stock. He made a standing offer to each of his daughters that he would present them with $1,000 if they chose to marry an academic. This was the natural applied extension of his Darwinist beliefs. He was not unusual in that respect. Darwin's propositions were well accepted in many scientific circles, and the behaviorism of John B. Watson was still decades away. In the scientific thinking of the time, nature prevailed over nurture.

Cattell returned to America in 1888 without a medical degree. He was now more interested in the new science of psychology than either medicine or philosophy. He accepted teaching positions at both the University of Pennsylvania and Bryn Mawr College. In 1889, he was offered a professorship at the University of Pennsylvania, which he accepted, and he then set about establishing the psychology laboratory there. His work with Wundt had helped to establish his reputation as one of the leading thinkers of the discipline, and in 1892, he was invited to join a select group of other psychologists who would form the APA.

In 1893, Cattell was offered a position at Columbia University, and he accepted. He held this position until he was fired in 1917. The circumstances of his termination were complicated. He was against the entry of the United States into WWI and, as such, was branded a traitor by many of his Columbia colleagues. Many believe that this was the reason for his dismissal. But Cattell was also a difficult faculty member and had openly challenged and ridiculed the president of Columbia and many of his colleagues for many years preceding his 1917 dismissal. This insubordination was the reason for his dismissal rather than any charges of treason (Gruber, 1972).

During the period 1893 through 1900, Cattell had been given carte blanche to assess incoming freshmen at Columbia with his mental tests. This he did with great enthusiasm. His mental tests were tests of reaction time and sensory abilities and involved little of the higher order mental faculties that were of interest to colleagues such as Alfred Binet, James Jastrow, James Mark Baldwin, and Lewis Terman. Further, he proposed no theory that would unify these measures into a coherent view of a construct such as intelligence. If Cattell had a working theory, it was that some people were suited for postsecondary education and others were not. By eventually comparing his assessments with college success, he hoped to better articulate this proposed relationship. As a corollary, Cattell also believed that students might be given some guidance about avenues, or courses, of study to pursue based on these assessments (e.g., natural sciences vs. physical sciences vs. pedagogy), but again, this was more assumed than proposed. He was confident that from the pattern of associations among the variables (including both the mental measures and grades), he would be able to illustrate both a theory of intelligence and the practical value of *mental testing* (a phrase he had coined in 1890). The data were duly analyzed in 1900, and the results were a disaster. Cattell was not able to demonstrate any coherent or consistent relationship among his various mental measures. Further, there was no relationship between any of these mental measures and college success. Eight years of study had come to nothing.

Fortunately, while gathering his empirical data on college freshmen, Cattell had continued to be active in professional and scientific matters. He had become the owner and editor of several leading journals, including *Psychological Review, Psychological Abstracts,* and *Psychological Bulletin*. In addition, he had begun to identify "eminent men of science" and had assumed the position of arbiter of excellence in psychological accomplishments. Thus, by the time he had analyzed his 8-year collection of data and found little support for his predictions, he was well established as a leader of the science of psychology, and his stature was only minimally affected by this failure.

The period 1900 through 1917 can be characterized as a time of campus activism for Cattell. His professional contributions to psychology were now more in the form of journal editing, advising colleagues in the development of psychology programs, and advocating the application of psychology to everyday problems. But even in this latter arena, he was generally unfocused, arguing in the abstract that psychology was applicable rather than demonstrating its applicability. Thus, Münsterberg could be seen as the advocate of applied psychology through his examples of application, but Cattell was the advocate of applicable psychology.

Because of his opposition to America's entry into WWI, Cattell was isolated from the greatest opportunity to apply psychology that had ever presented itself: the psychological testing of army recruits. This would have been a perfect opportunity to resurrect his belief in the value of mental testing. But this task was left to Walter VanDyke Bingham and Walter Dill Scott. Nevertheless, Cattell was able to take advantage of the newly emerging enthusiasm for mental testing after the war. He founded the Psychological Corporation in 1921 and reintroduced his unique brand of mental testing to industry. For many reasons, some related to his personality and others related to his modest skills as a leader and visionary, the Psychological Corporation floundered badly until he relinquished control of the organization to Bingham in 1926. Cattell continued to contribute to the growth of psychology through his administration of professional journals but had little additional impact on I/O psychology, applied psychology, or general psychology between 1926 and his death in 1944.

How, then, are we to think of Cattell and his contribution to what has become I/O psychology? He was certainly committed to both differential psychology and to application. Those were positive forces in psychology's early development. Further, he understood the centrality of the concept of a scientist–practitioner and developed the Psychological Corporation to demonstrate the value of this model to both the profession and the public. But he failed to grasp the importance of theory building and hypothesis testing while others around him were actively engaged in such pursuits. When his empirical structure collapsed, he had nowhere to turn. As a subdiscipline, I/O psychologists have long had problems with theory development. In an interview several years ago (Landy, 1991b), Morris Viteles spoke disparagingly of I/O psychologists who spent their time in theory building. He considered theory building a luxury that society and the profession could ill afford. I suspect that Cattell would have agreed. If there is a lesson to be taken from these examples, it is that theory turns data from potential to kinetic energy. Without theory, Cattell was mute.

It is worth speculating what Cattell might have done with modern analytic techniques and hardware. Would path analysis or confirmatory factor analysis have changed the outcome of his research? I think not. His analyses were conducted by others. His was not an analytic weakness, it was a failure to appreciate the value of reasoning. He did not understand that data follow thought rather than precede it. His contemporaries in cognitive research—Charles Spearman, Lewis Terman, and Robert Yerkes—were busy building models of the intellect, yet he persisted in believing that the structure would emerge and yield theory.

What then were Cattell's contributions? Like Münsterberg, he was a proselytizer. He took every opportunity to speak for the power of differential psychology to affect lives. Unlike Münsterberg, he gathered a substantial cadre of functionalists, applied psychologists, and applied statisticians around him at Columbia, including E. L. Thorndike and Leon L. Thurstone. In the period after WWI, he devoted his considerable reputation and energies to developing the Psychological Corporation and, in doing so, helped to establish the legitimacy of psychology applied to industry with other nonapplied psychologists. The Psychological Corporation was set up as a nonprofit corporation in which psychologists held shares. The profits from the application of psychology would go toward endowing a research fund for supporting both basic and applied psychological experimentation. In fact, Cattell's administrative skills did not match his vision, and the Psychological Corporation wallowed until Bingham took over in 1926. Nevertheless, Cattell was able to persuade a substantial number of APA members to buy shares in this applied effort. This was no small feat and undoubtedly increased the respect for applied psychology among non-applied colleagues.

Walter Dill Scott

In the year that Münsterberg returned from Harvard to Germany and Cattell finalized his testing program at Columbia, Walter Dill Scott received his undergraduate degree from Northwestern University and entered the Presbyterian seminary with the goal of becoming a missionary in China (Jacobson, 1951). Three years later, in 1898, it became clear to him that his superiors would not give him the assignment that he wanted. Bitterly disappointed, Scott left for Leipzig to study psychology with Wundt. In 1900, he received his PhD. He was one of the last Americans to study with Wundt and completed one of the few nonempirical dissertations to come out of Wundt's program: a consideration of impulses. Scott had a strong interest in motivation, and his dissertation, along with some companion research on suggestion and persuasion, laid the foundation for the expression of this interest over the next 15 years.

On his return trip from Germany, Scott stopped for a year with Edward Bradford Titchener at Cornell, to learn how to assemble and administer a psychological laboratory. He planned to return to Northwestern and teach psychology, so this training would be put to good use. In 1901, he assumed a position as an assistant professor of psychology and pedagogy at Northwestern and settled in for a career of teaching and research.

Even before Scott returned to Northwestern, a group of visionary business leaders glimpsed the advantages of applying psychology to advertising. They tried to interest Hugo Münsterberg first, and then E. L. Thorndike, to explore this possible application of the new science of psychology. Münsterberg was still in his antiapplication phase and would have none of it. Thorndike was still a good deal more interested in animal learning than in human motivation. Recognizing that Chicago now had its own Wundt-trained psychologist in the form of Scott, the advertisers turned to him for help. Scott was anything but enthusiastic. He had just left Titchener, who was a critic of application. His time with Wundt had provided little opportunity for application. And like most new assistant professors, he was anxious to create a good image for himself with his Northwestern colleagues. Nevertheless, he saw advertising as an arena to test out some of his ideas about attention, suggestion, and persuasion. As a result, he agreed to provide a series of lectures in the general area of applying psychology to advertising but kept this activity hidden from his faculty colleagues.

Scott's lectures were very well received and he ended up giving a regular series of these lectures. In addition, he agreed to write a regular column in an advertising publication known as *Mahin's Magazine*. In all, he published 33 columns over an 8-year span. These columns also formed the foundation for two books that Scott published. In 1903, he presented 14 columns in *The Theory of Advertising*. This book is, in all likelihood, the first publication applying psychological principles to the world of business (Kuna, 1974, 1976). In 1908, he published a second book with the original 14 articles and 19 additional ones. Feeling more professionally secure by this time, Scott was emboldened to use the title *The Psychology of Advertising*. Applied psychology was popular in 1908. In that same year, Münsterberg published his first formal foray into the world of the applied with his text on forensic psychology, *On the Witness Stand*.

As a result of his publications, by 1910, Scott's name was well-known in business circles. He had branched out from advertising to consider issues of leadership and supervision, industrial efficiency, selection, and motivation. In 1910, he published a series of essays on the general application of psychological principles to the problems of industry: *Increasing Human Efficiency in Business*. In that same year, Münsterberg began writing his text, *Psychology and Industrial Efficiency*, but it was published only in German. The English edition would not appear until 1913. Thus, Scott was more widely recognized than Münsterberg in industrial circles. In addition, Münsterberg's book was a careful introduction to application only after a solid empirical and theoretical foundation had been laid. The first half of Münsterberg's text could have been considered a book on general psychology. Scott wasted no time on principles. He went immediately to application, which made it the more attractive text for business leaders.

During the period 1901 to 1916, Scott prospered at Northwestern. In 1909, he was given a position as a professor of advertising in the school of commerce, and by 1912, he was holding joint appointments in both psychology and advertising. Scott was more than the equal to Münsterberg in creative application and theoretical thinking. He explored the psychological characteristics of piece-rate payment systems (unlike the more mechanical economic explorations of his contemporary, F. W. Taylor), organizational culture, worker attitudes, and motivation. It is best to think of his contributions as pretheoretical in these areas. Although his innovations neither flowed directly from, nor led directly to, a full-blown theory of behavior, they were based on contemporaneous research and theoretical propositions of people such as Ordway Tead, E. L. Thorndike, and John B. Watson. If I/O psychologists were searching for a role model, Scott would best fit the bill. He was a legitimate bridge between the basic and applied and was widely recognized as such.

In 1916, Carnegie Institute of Technology (now Carnegie Mellon University) embarked on an ambitious effort to build a research institute to serve the business community in Pittsburgh, PA. To lead this effort, the Carnegie Institute chose Walter VanDyke Bingham. Bingham immediately nominated Scott to be his deputy and assist in this pioneering effort. The president of Carnegie Institute persuaded the president of Northwestern University to "loan" Scott to Carnegie for a few years. In 1916, Scott was appointed as a professor of applied psychology and joined Bingham in developing the Division of Applied Psychology. By now, Bingham and Scott were the two most prominent industrial psychologists in the country and commanded both attention and respect. A young Bruce Moore made his way to Pittsburgh to study with them, only to find that they had left to apply their new science to winning WWI. Moore promptly enlisted as well!

Scott was at Carnegie less than 2 years. He and Bingham left in 1917 to assist the adjutant general of the U.S. Army in techniques of selection, training, and performance assessment. Scott had started several testing and performance measurement projects when he arrived at Carnegie. He simply transferred those projects to the military environment and continued his work. More is said about these military years in the notes on Bingham.

When the war ended in 1919, several of Scott's colleagues persuaded him to form a private company that would consult with businesses. This was to be pure application with little formal research and no teaching. He agreed. The Scott Company was formed with headquarters in Philadelphia. The staff was a "who's who" of psychology, including John B. Watson, Bingham, Robert Yerkes, and E. L. Thorndike. Scott was also elected president of APA in 1919. He was the consummate scientist–practitioner. And at the peak of his power and popularity, he left psychology for administration. He was offered the presidency of Northwestern and accepted it. He was an enormously successful president and remained in that office until his retirement in 1939.

Although less the public promoter than Münsterberg or Cattell, Scott had a substantial influence on the increasing public awareness and credibility of industrial psychology. As a result of his efforts, over 1 million men, who might never have encountered a psychologist for the rest of their lives, were tested. This was as powerful a promotional device as any that Cattell or Münsterberg might have proposed. In fact, Münsterberg had already begun such an initiative. As mentioned earlier, at the time of his death, Münsterberg was preparing to expose movie audiences to psychological testing. More than Münsterberg, Cattell, or Bingham, Scott valued theory as much as application.

The record is clear that without Scott, the testing movement launched with the armed forces in WWI would not have occurred. He had the vision, administrative skill, and scientific stature to pull it off.

Yerkes had gone in a very different direction and was more interested in winning an intellectual battle with Terman over the nature of intelligence than he was in winning a war. There is little debate about the effect of WWI testing on the growth of I/O psychology. We can be grateful to Walter Dill Scott for the success of that effort.

Walter VanDyke Bingham

In 1901, at the age of 21, Walter VanDyke Bingham, armed with an undergraduate degree from Beloit College, embarked on a career as a high school mathematics teacher. He had taken courses in psychology at Beloit from a recent PhD student of Wilhelm Wundt but was not immediately attracted to the new science. After 4 years of high school teaching, Bingham was restless and unchallenged and decided to return to study psychology at the University of Chicago. At the time, the University of Chicago had a vibrant and ambitious psychology training program. John Dewey had grafted the pragmatism of William James onto the functionalism of Thorndike and Cattell and created a new generation of functionalism before he left to join Cattell at Columbia in 1905. This new functionalism was appealing to the students looking for opportunities for application. A new assistant professor in the department was John B. Watson, who would soon power a paradigm shift with his introduction to the new model of behaviorism. Watson had received his PhD at Chicago in 1903.

After 2 years of study, Bingham left for Harvard to study philosophy for a year with William James, George Santayana, George Herbert Palmer, and Josiah Royce. Although William James was his Harvard adviser, Bingham was impressed by the new applied psychology of Hugo Münsterberg. After his year of study, Bingham returned to Chicago and received his PhD in 1908 for a dissertation based on the perception of melodies.

Given the links between Chicago and Columbia, it is not surprising that Bingham's first postgraduate job was at Columbia, assisting E. L. Thorndike in research. Although his primary research interest was still the perception of music, Bingham became interested in the differential research at Columbia and was soon an active collaborator in the new mental testing program. He was particularly impressed with Thorndike's emerging theory of intelligence and was fast becoming a critic of Spearman's g theory.

In 1910, Bingham was offered a faculty position at Dartmouth and accepted it. He was to supervise the experimental laboratory. In addition to his teaching and administrative responsibilities, he introduced a student testing program patterned after Cattell's efforts at Columbia. As a result of his time with Thorndike, Bingham's testing program was more sophisticated than Cattell's. It had a heavier flavor of the "higher" mental abilities, particularly reasoning. Nevertheless, the Dartmouth student testing program proved no more useful than the program at Columbia. In 1912, a bright mathematics major took Bingham's psychology course, and because they shared a love of mathematics, Bingham took the student under his wing and suggested that he pursue advanced studies in applied psychology at Harvard, with Hugo Münsterberg. That student was Harold Burtt. He did go to Harvard, he did study under Münsterberg, and he became a leading industrial psychologist during the period between the two world wars.

While attending an APA convention in Philadelphia, Bingham was introduced to the president of the new Carnegie Institute of Technology. He was asked to visit Carnegie and prepare a report outlining what psychology could do for the institute. After a site visit, Bingham suggested that psychology could help students to understand and influence people. Further, he felt that mental testing could identify those applicants most suitable for admission as well as help to direct those students who were accepted to the right curriculum of study. This vision of mental testing was identical to that proposed by Cattell at Columbia 20 years earlier and by Bingham, himself, at Dartmouth.

The president of Carnegie was so impressed with Bingham's report that he offered him the opportunity to head a division at Carnegie that would accomplish the objectives that Bingham had identified. It would be called the Division of Applied Psychology and would have several sections, including the Bureau of Mental Tests, the Department of Training Teachers, and the Department of Psychology and Education. On the basis of that plan, Bingham accepted the position.

Shortly after his arrival, Bingham shifted the thrust of the initiative. As originally conceived, it was to focus inward on the development of students. This focus shifted rapidly toward the development of external consumers—businesses and government agencies (Bingham, 1952; Ferguson, 1965). This was due, at least in part, to the objections of other universities in the area to the training of psychologists at the new institution. As a result, Bingham produced no PhD students, because there was no formal graduate instruction program in the new applied psychology.

Bingham's first "customers" were a group of local business leaders who asked him to develop a program for training sales representatives. To fulfill this request, Bingham introduced the Bureau of Salesmanship Research and persuaded Northwestern University to assign Walter Dill Scott to head the new bureau for its initial period. Bingham was familiar with Scott's writings in advertising and believed that such a background was perfect for directing research on and training of sales personnel. In addition, Scott had recently begun a research project that focused on the selection of sales personnel.

As a result of early successes of the Bureau of Salesmanship Research, a second bureau was formed to concentrate on the training and development of retail personnel. These efforts were well publicized, well funded, and well staffed. During a 9-year period after Bingham's arrival at Carnegie, he supervised the work of Scott, Guy Whipple, Raymond Dodge, L. L. Thurstone, J. B. Miner, Marion Bills, Max Freyd, Beardsley Ruml, Richard Uhrbrock, and Clarence Yoakum. By 1917, the new Division of Applied Psychology was under a full head of steam.

The United States entered WWI in 1917, and the Division of Applied

Psychology offered its services to the government. Simultaneously, APA, through its president, Robert Yerkes, took the lead in the mobilization of psychology in the war effort. Yerkes saw the war as an opportunity to demonstrate the value of psychology and to strengthen the position of the discipline in the scientific community. Scott and Bingham were less ideological; they simply wanted to help. There was considerable tension between Scott and Yerkes on this point, and Bingham was the mediator. A bargain was struck that left Yerkes in charge of recruit selection and classification and Scott in charge of recruit placement. Bingham was interested in the work of both camps, so he continued to support the efforts of each as well as to act as channel of communication between them.

When the war ended in 1919, mental testing was a familiar process. Not only had Yerkes and Scott been successful in publicizing the testing program, but well over a million recruits, many who would return to positions of power in business and government, had undergone testing. Scott never returned to Carnegie. Bingham returned to Carnegie, but the war had derailed the Carnegie program of applied psychology and the new Scott Company was doing much of the work of the Division of Applied Psychology. As a result, Bingham left Carnegie in 1924 to head the Personnel Research Federation and, in 1926, to take over the direction of the Psychological Corporation from Cattell. From 1926 until his death in 1952, Bingham worked to achieve recognition and respectability for I/O psychology. During the period 1926–1940, this caretaker role was an important one because there were no "elder statesmen" left to fill that role. To be sure, there were a number of newer I/O psychologists coming along who would make significant contributions, such as Harold Burtt, Morris Viteles, Robert Hoppock, and E. K. Strong. But none of these individuals were yet well enough known to assume the role of spokesperson. Münsterberg was dead. Scott was devoting all of his energies to the presidency at Northwestern, and Cattell's role had become exclusively that of journal owner–editor. During that period, Bingham represented industrial psychology in the national public forum. He was appointed to commissions, hosted a weekly nationally syndicated radio program devoted to applied psychology (and, in particular, highway safety), and contributed frequently to newspapers and magazines on topics of applied psychology.

Bingham's contribution to the development of I/O psychology was manifold. His vision led to the Division of Applied Psychology. His efforts as a statesman leveraged the considerable egos of Scott and Yerkes to produce a massive mental testing program. His ability to explain the importance of applied psychology to radio audiences, readers of newspapers and magazines, legislators, and business leaders maintained the momentum that had developed during the war.

Discussion

There are some inferences that might be drawn from this review of the leading figures in the development of I/O psychology. With respect to the subdiscipline, the differences between I/O psychology and other branches are rather striking. First, it had had remarkably little internal conflict in its development. During the period from 1880 to 1920, there was little of the rancor that characterized differences between Freudians and non-Freudians or neo-Freudians, or between those who would later follow Clark Hull and Kenneth Spence and the advocates of behaviorism. This may be seen as good or bad. It is good because it has permitted I/O psychologists to work together toward some common goals, such as ability assessment, training models, or organizational design. If there is a downside, it is that many disciplines and subdisciplines have flourished in the context of intellectual conflict. The most striking example of that was the competition between Linus Pauling and the Watson–Crick team for breaking the DNA code. Part of the reason for the absence of conflict may have been the absence of conflicting theories. In fact, with the exception of an emerging classical test theory, there were few theories of any kind. Or the absence of conflict may have been because there was little opportunity for power struggles to occur. Münsterberg died. Cattell withdrew. Scott left the field. Bingham endured. To be sure, these figures were capable of conflict. Münsterberg fought with everyone, as did Cattell, Scott's battle with Yerkes was bitter and long lasting. Bingham, alone, seemed conflict free. For better or worse, during its formative years, I/O psychology had at least few internecine battles.

There were really two generations of I/O psychology represented in the figures we have considered. Münsterberg and Cattell formed the first generation, and Scott and Bingham, the second. The third would include people like Strong, Burtt, and Viteles. There were some commonalities between those first two generations, however. Each of the four were classically trained, three by Wundt directly. They were well trained in the substance of the discipline. This, in turn, afforded them the respectability and tolerance of their less applied colleagues. Further, each of the four had gained considerable respectability for their accomplishments. Three of the four had written landmark texts; three of the four were elected to the presidency of APA. All had received recognition from groups beyond the borders of psychology. All gravitated toward policy formulation. They were driven to change systems of thinking and action, and they sought to influence the well-being of collections of people, whether they be students, soldiers, or employers. Their thoughts were all on a grand scale.

There is little value in singling out one figure as the founder of the subdiscipline. Each had a unique influence in his own way and in his own time. In this case, the whole was greater than its constituent parts. It is relatively easy to trace the path of I/O psychology from the groundwork laid by these four men to the present-day architecture. The commitment to differential psychology is obvious, as is the intricate interplay between practice and science. Although they may not have developed a completely articulated discipline by 1920, many of the tools and the underlying assumptions of current research and practice were anticipated by their collective work.

References

Bingham, W. V. (1952). Walter VanDyke Bingham. In C. Murchison (Ed.), *Psychology in autobiography* (pp. 1–26). Worcester, MA: Clark University Press.

Ferguson, L. (1965). *The heritage of industrial psychology.* Hartford, CT: Finlay Press.

Gruber, C. (1972). Academic freedom at Columbia University, 1917–1918: The case of James McKeen Cattell. *AAUP Bulletin, 58,* 297–305.

Hale, M. (1990). *Human science and social order.* Philadelphia: Temple University Press.

Jacobson, J. Z. (1951). *Scott of Northwestern.* Chicago: Mariano.

Kuna, D. P. (1974). *The psychology of advertising.* Unpublished doctoral dissertation, University of New Hampshire, Durham.

Kuna, D. P. (1976). *The psychology of advertising 1896–1916.* Ann Arbor, MI: Xerox University Microfilms.

Landy, F. J. (1991a). A conversation with Harold Burtt. *The Industrial–Organizational Psychologist, 28,* 73–75.

Landy, F. J. (1991b). The I/O family tree. *The Industrial–Organizational Psychologist, 29,* 31–34.

Landy, F. J. (1992a). Hugo Münsterberg: Visionary or victim? *Journal of Applied Psychology, 77,* 787–802.

Landy, F. J. (1992b, August). *The roots of I/O psychology.* Master Lecture in Psychology presented at the 100th Annual Convention of the American Psychological Association, Washington, DC.

Landy, F. J. (1993). Development of I/O psychology. In T. K. Fagan & G. R. VandenBos (Eds.), *Exploring applied psychology: Origins and critical analyses* (pp. 81–118). Washington, DC: American Psychological Association.

Napoli, D. S. (1975). *The architects of adjustment: The practice and professionalism of American psychology.* Ann Arbor, MI: Xerox University Microfilms.

Sokal, M. M. (1982). James McKeen Cattell and the failure of anthropometric mental testing: 1890–1901. In W. R. Woodward & M. G. Ash (Eds.), *The problematic science: Psychology in nineteenth century thought* (pp. 322–345). New York: Praeger.

Article Review Form at end of book.

What were the unique contributions of the female pioneers of industrial organizational psychology? Was their perspective truly unique?

American Female Pioneers of Industrial and Organizational Psychology during the Early Years

Laura L. Koppes
Tri-State University

However carefully the present is studied and however refined the techniques of analysis, the present is not fully comprehended if the past is ignored or distorted. (Gutman, 1977, p. 259)

This article presents female psychologists who contributed through scholarship, practice, and service to the discipline of industrial psychology (now known as industrial and organizational [I/O] psychology) during its developmental years (1900–1930). Changes in society, generally, and in psychology, particularly, combined with opportunistic approaches and individual characteristics (e.g., intelligence, assertiveness, perseverance) empowered these individuals to research and practice I/O psychology. Their accomplishments illustrate the modern idea of the scientist–practitioner model; they used scientifically rigorous methods to conduct research in applied settings and upheld scientific integrity when implementing the results of their research and when applying psychological principles to solve problems. They shared with male psychologists the experience of being successful pioneers of applied psychology, or the "second" psychology (Cahan & White, 1992). The findings presented in this article contradict published research on the early history of I/O psychology. Existing historical accounts describing the evolution of I/O psychology (e.g., Baritz, 1960; Ferguson, 1952, 1961, 1962–1965; Hilgard, 1987; Katzell & Austin, 1992; Landy, 1992, 1993; Stagner, 1982; Viteles, 1932) give the impression that women did not contribute to the development of I/O psychology during the early years because the authors gave little or no attention to contributions by female psychologists.

Discovering Female I/O Psychologists

Compared with other sciences, women constituted a larger proportion of psychologists during the formative years of psychology (Furumoto, 1987). When the American Psychological Association (APA) observed its 25th anniversary in 1917, women constituted 13% of the membership. Cattell (1917) ascertained from his second edition of *American Men of Science* the following percentages of women among the sciences: psychology, 9.8; zoology, 7.5; chemistry, 2.1; and physics and geology, 1.3. Rossiter (1982) compared 15 sciences and observed that nutrition was the only field other than psychology that had a higher proportion of women. In fact, several historical accounts of early female psychologists have been completed in recent years (e.g., Bernstein & Russo, 1974; Furumoto, 1979, 1987, 1991, 1992; Furumoto & Scarborough, 1986; O'Connell & Russo, 1980, 1983, 1988, 1990; Russo & Denmark, 1987; Scarborough & Furumoto, 1987; Stevens & Gardner, 1982a, 1982b); however, scant attention is given to female I/O psychologists.

Napoli (1981) noted that women constituted the majority of applied psychologists (men constituted the majority in academia). The proportion of women and men in subfields of applied psychology varied. For example, in school psychology, women outnumbered men by 3 to 1 by 1938. Equal numbers of men and women were performing clinical work (Finch & Odoroff, 1939). I/O psychology had the lowest proportion of women in the field

"American Female Pioneers of Industrial and Organizational Psychology during the Early Years," by Laura L. Koppes, *Journal of Applied Psychology*, 82, 1997, pp. 500–515. Copyright © 1997 by the American Psychological Association. Reprinted with permission.

(Furumoto, 1987). One explanation for the low proportion of women in the industry was the difficulty of locating I/O psychologists. Professional positions labeled specifically as "I/O psychologist" were nonexistent. In fact, Napoli (1981) revealed no full-time I/O psychologists from 1913 through 1917; however, there were individuals practicing I/O psychology, although their work was not labeled as such.

The discovery and identification of female I/O psychologists have been complicated and difficult because records of female psychologists were poorly preserved. A reasonable elucidation for inadequate documentation of women's accomplishments is that female professionals were marginalized during the late 19th and early 20th centuries; their employment opportunities were limited and they "were relegated to a distinctly inferior position" (Furumoto, 1987, p. 97) in terms of occupational status. Female psychologists were not located in the high-status branch of the discipline, academic psychology, but rather in applied settings. Their contributions and accomplishments were given second-class status, and were not widely recognized.

Furumoto (1987) observed that, for individuals who worked in applied settings in particular, "a great deal of painstaking work, much of which involves tracking down and collecting material from scattered and obscure sources, remains to be done" (p. 103). Two sources typically consulted by historians of psychology, the *American Psychological APA Directory* and *American Men of Science*, has insufficient information about practitioners. They provide only "the tip of the iceberg" (Furumoto, 1987, p. 103); thus, they cannot be relied upon as the primary sources. For example, individuals working in applied settings typically did not join APA (Finch & Odoroff, 1939). Many sources were examined to discover female I/O psychologists, including I/O psychology-related books (e.g., Burtt, 1926; Scott & Clothier, 1925) and journals, archival materials (institutional records, correspondence, manuscripts) of prominent psychologists (e.g., Bingham, Cattell, Crissey, Münsterberg, Scott, Viteles), and other relevant materials (e.g., Boring & Lindzey, 1952; Kimble, Boneau, & Wertheimer, 1996; Sokal & Rafail, 1982).

Four female psychologists (Marion Almira Bills, Elsie Oschrin Bregman, Lillian Moller Gilbreth, and Mary Holmes Stevens Hayes) who were directly involved with I/O psychology for most of their careers are presented. These individuals are highlighted because information was found for them, their professional activities represent pioneering contributions by women to the field, and they are good examples of individuals who exemplified traits and professional styles representative of current I/O psychologists.

Four Major Contributors
Background

Furumoto and Scarborough (1986) found, when they researched the origins of the first generation of American psychologists, that many of them were born in the northeastern or the midwestern United States before 1900. This is true for three of the four major contributors. The exception is Lillian Moller Gilbreth, who was born in Oakland, California, in 1878. Mary Holmes Stevens Hayes was born in Rochester, New York, in 1884; Marion Almira Bills was born in Allegan, Michigan, in 1889; and Elsie Oschrin Bregman was born in Newark, New Jersey, in 1896.

Furthermore, similar to the first generation of female psychologists (Furumoto & Scarborough, 1986), female pioneers of I/O psychology attended public and private coeducational institutions that were considered leaders for granting degrees to women (see Table 1). During the early 20th century, there was an increase in the number of academic institutions offering undergraduate and graduate education (Sokal, 1992), and additional universities were allowing women to enroll (Rossiter, 1974). These women benefitted from the perseverance of their predecessors (e.g., Mary Whiton Calkins, Christine Ladd-Franklin) who opened the doors for acceptance of women in graduate education and psychology (Stevens & Gardner, 1982a). The first generation (e.g., Kate Gordon, Gertrude Rand) demonstrated that success in higher education and in psychology was attainable despite stereotypes of women's roles in society.

The four women completed their undergraduate studies immediately after completing secondary education. Their mean age at completion of the undergraduate degree was 20.75 years (range = 19–22). Of the first generation of female psychologists, some women completed graduate work immediately after their undergraduate education, and others delayed graduate work (Furumoto & Scarborough, 1986). Three (Bills, Bregman, and Hayes) of the four women completed their doctorates immediately after their undergraduate studies (mean age = 26.67 years; range = 26–28). Gilbreth was awarded her doctorate when she was 37 years old.

All four women enrolled in quality psychology graduate programs, where they studied with distinguished male and female psychologists and were trained in traditional scientific psychology; however, they studied in programs where functionalism was emerging (e.g., University of Chicago, Columbia University; Hilgard, 1987). During the early 20th century, psychological thought moved from structuralism to functionalism, with the latter considering how individuals adapt differently to particular environments (Landy, 1992). Functionalism is viewed as providing the basis for applied psychology, specifically I/O psychology (Katzell & Austin, 1992); so, while these students were being trained in traditional basic and experimental psychology, they were exposed to the idea of applying psychology.

Bills received a Ph.D. from Bryn Mawr College, where she studied with Clarence E. Ferree, a Titchener student and widely published expert on visual perception (Austin & Waung, 1994). Ferree and Gertrude Rand are also noted for their research in visual processes in industrial and applied settings (Zusne, 1975). Bryn Mawr's faculty was largely composed of women, and in addition to Gertrude Rand, Kate Gordon, associate professor in the Education Department from 1912 to 1916, probably served as a role model (Austin & Waung, 1994).

Bregman was awarded a Ph.D. in psychology from Columbia Univer-

Table 1 Four American Female Psychologists Who Contributed to the Development of Industrial and Organizational Psychology: Origins, Education, and Professional Positions

Name	Birth	Year and Location Bachelor's Degree	Doctoral Degree	Institution/Organization	Title	Dates
Marion A. Bills	1889; Allegan, MI	1908; University of Michigan	1917; Bryn Mawr College	Miami University	Professor	1917–1918
				University of Kansas	Assistant professor of psychology	1918–1919
				Bureau of Personnel Research, Division of Applied Psychology, Carnegie Institute of Technology	Research assistant	1919–1920
				Bureau of Personnel Research, Division of Applied Psychology, Carnegie Institute of Technology	Associate director	1920–1923
				Life Insurance Sales Research Bureau	Consultant	1922–1925
				Aetna Life Insurance Company	Assistant secretary	1926–1955
Elsie Oschrin Bregman	1896; Newark, NJ	1918; Barnard College, Columbia University	1922; Columbia University	Guardian Life Insurance Company	Psychologist	1918–1919
				R. H. Macy and Company	Psychologist	1919–1921
				Institute for Educational Research, Teachers College, Columbia University	Research assistant	1922–1927
				The Psychological Corporation	Associate	1924–1925
				The Psychological Corporation	Assistant secretary	1925–1934
				National Research Council	Research fellowship	1929–1930
				Department of Nursing Education, Teachers College, Columbia University	Consultant for psychology	1931
				Institute for Educational Research, Teachers College, Columbia University	Research associate	1931–1934
				Progressive Education Association, Committee on the Study of Adolescents	Research associate	1935
				Private practice	Consultant	1936–1963
				James McKeen Cattell Trust Fund	Secretary/treasurer	1950–1963
				James McKeen Cattell Trust Fund	Trustee	1942–1969
Lillian Moller Gilbreth	1878; Oakland, CA	1900; University of California, Berkeley	1915; Brown University	Frank B. Gilbreth, Inc., Consulting Engineers	Director of Motion Study Institute	1904–1929
				Gilbreth, Inc.	President	1929–1964
				Purdue University	Professor of management	1935–1948
				Newark College of Engineering	Chair, Department of Personnel Relations	1941–1943
				Massachusetts Institute of Technology	Resident Lecturer	1964–1972
Mary H. S. Hayes	1884; Rochester, NY	1904; University of Wisconsin	1910; University of Chicago	Laboratory of Social Hygiene, Bedford Hills, NY	Psychologist	1915–1917
				Pathology Section, U.S. Army Medical School and Surgeon General's Office	Laboratory technician and civilian expert	1919–1920
				The Scott Company	Consultant	1920–1922
				U.S. Children's Bureau	Special agent	1922–1924
				Vocational Service for Juniors	Director	1924–1935
				Division of Guidance and Placement, National Youth Administration	Director	1935–1940
				Division of Youth, National Youth Administration	Director	1940–1943
				War Relocation Authority	Relocation officer	1943–1946
				National Executive Committee, Girl Scouts of America	Chair	1947

sity. She was a student of E. L. Thorndike, an original researcher of employee selection (Sokal, 1981) and proponent of applied psychology. While enrolled at Columbia University, Bregman took several courses with Leta S. Hollingworth (probably a female role model), who was a notable psychologist of the first generation of American female psychologists and was married to an eminent psychologist, Harry Hollingworth.

Hayes's interest in psychology likely began when she took courses with Joseph Jastrow, a student of G. Stanley Hall (Hilgard, 1987), at the University of Wisconsin. She then attended graduate school at the University of Chicago, where she studied with James Rowland Angell, a founder, along with philosopher John Dewey, of the functionalism school of thought and tradition (Hilgard, 1987). She was one of 14 female students during Angell's tenure at the University of Chicago. (Other notable female psychologists include Helen Thompson Woolley, June Downey, Florence Richardson Robinson, and Kate Gordon.) In addition, Hayes was at the University of Chicago when Walter VanDyke Bingham completed his doctorate. Mabel Fernald, later to become an eminent child psychologist, was one of her dissertation subjects.

Gilbreth followed a different path. She developed an interest in psychology when she took undergraduate classes with George Stratton at the University of California, Berkeley. She enrolled in the English doctoral program with a minor in psychology at the University of California, Berkeley, after completing a master's degree in literature in 1902 there. Shortly after marrying, she changed her major to psychology, at the suggestion of her husband, who recognized the value of psychology theory and principles for management (Kelly & Kelly, 1990). She submitted a doctoral dissertation to the University of California, Berkeley, which was accepted; however, the Ph.D. was not conferred because she did not fulfill the requirement of a final year in residence (she did not want to leave her family; Perloff & Naman, 1996).

While working with her husband in engineering, Gilbreth observed that engineers were addressing their technical problems scientifically, but they appeared to be unaware that psychology had much to offer as a science. She and her husband agreed that she should enroll in a doctoral program and study the "newer kind of psychology" (Yost, 1943). They chose Brown University because it was one of the first universities to acknowledge scientific management as a profession; thus, she could receive a Ph.D. in the type of psychology she desired (Yost, 1943). She was awarded a Ph.D. in psychology in 1915. (During this year, she gave birth to her seventh child.) Her research was the application of scientific management principles and psychology to the work of classroom teachers (L. M. Gilbreth, 1914), an integration of I/O psychology and educational psychology. Her dissertation was published as a book entitled *The Psychology of Management* in 1914. Some researchers credit her for completing the first dissertation in I/O psychology (Koppes, Landy, & Perkins, 1993; Landy, 1994; Perloff & Naman, 1996), which may contradict the widespread belief that Bruce V. Moore was the first recipient of a doctorate in I/O psychology in 1921.

In addition to origin of birth and educational background, two aspects of psychologists' lives examined by historians are marital status and family status (e.g., O'Connell, 1983; Russo & O'Connell, 1980). Bryan and Boring (1946) reported that almost all the married men in psychology, but only half the married women, felt that marriage helped their careers. Russo and O'Connell (1980) noted that "having a spouse in psychology enhances the productivity of both women and men psychologists although the men receive a disproportionate benefit from the arrangement" (p. 22). For the first generation of American female psychologists, marriage served as a detriment to their careers, and there was an incompatibility between being a successful mother and having a successful career in academe (Furumoto & Scarborough, 1986).

Of the four major contributors, three married and two had children. While attending the University of Chicago, Mary Holmes Stevens met her husband, Joseph Hayes, who completed his doctorate in psychology there in 1911 and became an industrial psychologist; they did not have children. Elsie Oschrin married Adolph Bregman, a consulting metallurgical engineer, in 1919; they had two daughters. Lillian Moller married Frank Bunker Gilbreth, a contracting engineer and pioneer of time and motion studies, in 1904. They had 12 children, highly unusual for a dual-career couple then and now.

It does not appear that these women's careers were negatively affected by marriage or children; in fact, their careers were enhanced. Their husbands were also professionals who provided support and inspiration. In later years, Gilbreth acknowledged how fortunate she was with her marriage and its importance to her success. According to Yost (1943), Gilbreth noted that her success reveals ". . . proof of what marriage can do for a woman who wants to combine other work with homemaking if her husband believes in his wife's capacities and wants to help her use all of them" (p. 100). Successful portions of both Bregman's and Gilbreth's careers were due to addressing family issues.

From Academicians to Practitioners

Unlike the first generation of female psychologists, in which 55% of the women had regular positions in higher education (Furumoto & Scarborough, 1986), these four women spent substantial portions of their careers in applied settings. They were involved with academic work only on a part-time or short-term basis. Two (Bregman and Bills) attained academic positions immediately after graduate work. Hayes and Gilbreth taught in academic settings after being practitioners for several years. Why did these individuals who received education and training in traditional scientific psychology programs become practitioners of psychology?

One possible explanation is the doctrine of separate spheres (Furumoto, 1992; Russo & Denmark, 1987; Scarborough & Furumoto, 1987) that existed at the turn of the century. This doctrine refers to the distinction between women's work and men's work, with women's work being within the home and men's work being outside the home. Consequently, the formal and institutional challenges faced by women when pursuing an academic career in psychology were substantial during this period. Male psychologists prevailed in universities, whereas female psychologists worked in employment settings that reflected societal stereotypes of the women's sphere (Russo & Denmark, 1987). The four contributors' academic positions were short-term or existed only after they gained experience and proved their competence. Possibly, they experienced similar difficulties faced by the first generation of female psychologists in academic settings (e.g., slow advancement in academic rank and difficulty in showing competence; Scarborough & Furumoto, 1987).

O'Connell and Russo (1988) noted that, despite the doctrine of separate spheres, the early 20th century was positive and productive for female professionals, partly as a result of the women's suffrage movement at the turn of the century. During this time, a particular need surfaced for female psychologists' involvement in work outside the home. Russo (1988) stated, "The goal of melding science and motherhood in the service of child welfare provided a rationale for women's higher education and legitimized women's participation in the world of work" (p. 10). Furthermore, other changes in American society and changes in psychology thought (from structuralism to functionalism) contributed to the creation of the new science, applied psychology (Katzell & Austin, 1992; Napoli, 1981). With the growth of industrialization, organizations expanded in size and complexity, and the need for qualified employees surfaced; consequently, the demand for services offered by applied psychologists increased (Napoli, 1981). The emergence of capitalism and an emphasis on efficiency warranted assistance from I/O psychologists to select hard-working and committed employees (Katzell & Austin, 1992). Experts with scientific credentials were sought to address individual and social problems; academicians' proactive involvement with society opened the doors for opportunities in alternative settings. In fact, the number of APA members in teaching positions increased five times, from 233 to 1,229, between 1916 and 1938; however, the number of members in applied positions grew almost 29 times, from 24 to 694 (Finch & Odoroff, 1939).

Table 1 lists professional positions held by the four women. Their professional paths varied, and no two women followed the same path. They worked in different settings (e.g., private corporations, consulting firms, government agencies), not dissimilar from today's I/O psychologist. In addition, diversity within individual careers was common (e.g., Hayes). As was working in sundry applied settings across time and sometimes in several jobs at the same time (e.g., Bregman). Their careers illustrate how these women had to be opportunistic; they found (and, in some cases, created) opportunities that allowed them to apply psychology. In the following section, professional positions related to the evolution of I/O psychology are highlighted.

Involvement with I/O Psychology

The four pioneers were actively engaged in the field of I/O psychology through scholarship, the practice of psychology, and professional service. In many instances, their scholarship and applications were at the forefront of modern issues of I/O psychology (e.g., use of multiple predictors, training, performance evaluations, hiring individuals with disabilities). In addition, they were groundbreakers for newly formed professional organizations.

Scholarship and Practice

During the early years of I/O psychology, applied psychologists, like members of other occupations, were legitimizing and professionalizing their work by creating ways to address societal concerns (Camfield, 1973). Practitioners of I/O psychology found and initiated work in government, consulting firms, and private industry. These settings also provided opportunities for field research; subsequently, many applied psychologists practiced and researched applied psychology at the same time. The four female psychologists participated in several of these endeavors.

One program that promoted applied psychology was the Division of Applied Psychology at Carnegie Institute of Technology, established in 1915 and organized and directed by Walter VanDyke Bingham. This cooperative venture between industry and a university was important for facilitating the development of I/O psychology and for preparing psychologists, particularly women, for industry (Hilgard, 1987). Its initial purpose was to train applied psychologists (Hilgard, 1987); however, the division evolved into helping businesses and government agencies (Landy, 1993). In 1919, Bills was hired by Bingham as a research assistant for the Bureau of Personnel Research, a component of the Division of Applied Psychology, then directed by C. S. Yoakum, and formerly called the Bureau of Salesmanship Research when headed by W. D. Scott. Bills became the associate director of the Bureau of Personnel Research in 1920 and served in that capacity until 1923. Her activities included consulting for businesses on selection, training, and supervision. Between 1922 and 1925, the Bureau of Personnel Research became the Life Insurance Sales Research Bureau [LISRB] currently known as the Life Insurance Marketing and Research Association [LIMRA]. Bills continued to work for LISRB after it relocated to Hartford, Connecticut, and in doing so, consulted with several companies on personnel issues such as office management. She developed an interest and expertise for personnel selection and specifically conducted research on the analysis of selection techniques for clerical and sales positions (e.g., Bills, 1921b).

Bills conducted predictive validity studies by examining the relationship between selection tests and criteria, including productivity and withdrawal. For example, in a description of a study on the selection of comptometer operators and stenographers (Bills, 1921a), she stated the following:

Both because of the problem presented and because of the methods of attack, which differ from those previously used, the study seems of special interest. The correlation between efficiency in the tests and efficiency in work has been the prime consideration in former studies. In this study, because of the nature of the problem, correlations became merely a by-product, and critical scores the fundamental consideration. Also, a battery of tests has been used rather than a single test, with the idea in mind, that the more measures we could get of a person, the higher would be our ratio of success in selecting promising applicants. (p. 275)

Bills concluded the article by noting, "A battery of tests is more effective both in eliminating failures and picking successes, than any single test" (p. 283).

Psychologists further promoted psychology through their involvement with World War I (Camfield, 1973). Few women were directly involved with the war (Furumoto, 1987), but Hayes was a notable exception. She worked as a laboratory technician and civilian expert, located in the Pathology Section of the U.S. Army Medical School and Surgeon General's Office. In addition, she was associated with the Committee on Classification of Personnel in the Army, a civilian body directed by Walter Dill Scott. The purpose of the committee was to consult and conduct research on personnel problems (Strong, 1918). Other psychologists involved were E. L. Thorndike, W. V. Bingham, R. M. Yerkes, E. K. Strong, L. M. Terman, and J. B. Watson (Strong, 1918).

After the war, opportunities for practicing psychology proliferated because of a heightened awareness of psychological applications and an increased concern by management for personnel issues (Baritz, 1960; Hilgard, 1987; Katzell & Austin, 1992; von Mayrhauser, 1987). Several members and associates of the Committee on Classification and Personnel formed The Scott Company, considered the first applied psychology consulting firm. The purpose of the company was to apply psychology to industry by providing consulting for personnel issues. In addition, the consultants frequently served as mediators for labor disputes (Landy, 1993). Hayes was invited by the organizers to join the firm in 1919 as a professional consultant (The Scott Company Executive Committee, 1919). The Scott Company experienced financial difficulties beginning in 1921. Hayes was laid off with hesitation and regret by the founders in that year. After working with various companies, Hayes left The Scott Company in 1922 (Hopkins, 1921).

While at The Scott Company, Hayes coauthored with W. D. Scott one of the first professional personnel manager books entitled *Science and Common Sense in Working with Men* (Scott & Hayes, 1921). She was identified as M. H. S. Hayes, a common approach used by publishers to conceal an author's gender (Bernstein & Russo, 1974). Although Scott is the first author, the book appears to be written largely by Hayes, revealed by the informal commonsensical writing style. Also, by this time, Scott's efforts were directed toward the responsibilities of being president at Northwestern University rather than toward applying psychology to industry.

Scott and Hayes discussed prevalent issues for current I/O psychologists and suggestions to personnel executives, including the advantages and disadvantages of testing. In addition, they presented benefits of hiring "handicapped" individuals, and to do so, the necessity for identifying the physical requirements of a job. Scott and Hayes (1921) concluded the book by emphasizing the importance of acknowledging individual differences:

When management comes to realize that labor is not a compact mass from which it indiscriminately chips off blocks to fill gaps, but that it is rather an aggregate of disparate, distinct, and ever-changing individuals, it may come to devote the time and effort necessary for an adequate adjustment, and for its own ultimate salvation! (p. 154)

Hayes also developed a graphic rating method with D. G. Paterson while at The Scott Company. They published a frequently cited article entitled "Experimental Development of the Graphic Rating Method" in *Psychological Bulletin* (Hayes & Paterson, 1921). The authors described a new method for obtaining judgments by supervisors on employees, stating that "graphic rating scales are simple, self-explanatory, concrete and definite. The qualities included in the scales are objective, and conceded to be of general importance for success" (p. 99). They administered the scale to several occupational groups such as carpenters, clerks, machine operators, and assemblers, and they found their method to be highly reliable when correlating ratings made by the same supervisors across time.

Many companies, after the war, hired full-time psychologists to handle personnel problems. In 1919, R. H. Macy and Company in New York (Sokal, 1981) hired Bregman as a psychologist to examine the company's personnel processes. During her employment, Bregman conducted research on procedures for recruitment, selection, training, management, and adjustment of sales and clerical positions (Bregman Biography, 1970, March 12). In an article she wrote about her experiences at R. H. Macy and Company, she addressed the dispute over the use of psychological tests for personnel purposes in industry (Bregman, 1922a). In doing so, she described how the company took the lead in researching tests in the field:

At R. H. Macy and Company the possibilities of this field of work had been brought out to the executives, even before the use of the Army tests, by some tests I carried on clerks in the store when I was a student. And so, about three years ago, an almost unprecedented experiment was begun. Almost never before had a psychological laboratory been equipped in an industrial organization, certainly not a department store, and a psychologist commissioned to experiment in his own field of science.

The result of this experimental work was the discovery of tests which could be used in the employment of two kinds of workers, salesclerks and clerical workers. (p. 696)

In a frequently cited publication, Bergman described a study conducted at R. H. Macy and Company for which she applied criteria for selection developed by Thorndike (1916) in his "Fundamental Theorems in Judging Men" (see also Sokal, 1981). She computed correlations, using the Spearman formula, between performance on 13 tests and actual sales ability of retail saleswomen at "one of the largest department stores of New York City" (Oschrin, 1918, p. 148). Additional research at this department store was highly regarded by researchers. One colleague noted, when referring to another study by Bregman (1921). "This appears to be the most important single piece of work done in the department store field so far" (Craig, 1921).

The Psychological Corporation, founded in 1921 by James McKeen Cattell (Cattell, 1923), was formed for the "advancement of psychology and the promotion of the useful applications of psychology" (Cattell, 1923, p. 165). The corporation did not succeed as anticipated during its early years, and beginning in 1923, Cattell used several tactics to save the corporation (Sokal, 1981). One such tactic was hiring Bregman as associate (1924–1925) and later assistant secretary (1925–1934) to develop and publish revisions of the Army Alpha General Intelligence Examinations (initially developed for testing the intelligence of Army recruits during World War I) for use by businesses and educational institutions. The revisions were entitled "Bregman Revision of the Army Alpha Examinations for General Intelligence Forms A and B" (Bregman, 1926, 1935b). These tests were sold and administered by The Psychological Corporation as a means to generate revenue. Unfortunately, there was little net income once royalties and overhead costs were paid (Sokal, 1981). Bregman, however, received royalties (10% of every sale) throughout her lifetime. By receiving these royalties, she is considered to be the only individual to profit from The Psychological Corporation during its early years (Sokal, 1981).

Bregman handled other activities, such as writing articles requested by Cattell and developing the *Bregman Language Completion Scales* (Bregman, 1935a). Over the years, she developed a lifelong professional relationship and friendship with Cattell. From 1942 until her death, she was named a trustee of the James McKeen Cattell Fund, a small foundation that gave grants for applied psychology research. From 1950 until 1963, she was the secretary–treasurer of the fund.

While at The Psychological Corporation, Bregman wrote and published three books with E. L. Thorndike and others: *The Measurement of Intelligence* (Thorndike, Bregman, Cobb, & Woodyard, 1927), *Adult Learning* (Thorndike, Bregman, Tilton, & Woodyard, 1928), and *The Prediction of Vocational Success* (Thorndike, Bregman, & Metcalfe, 1934). In addition, her prolific publishing included 12 scientific articles between 1918 and 1947 in journals such as *Journal of Applied Psychology, Psychological Bulletin,* and *Journal of Education Research.*

Companies continued to hire psychologists during the 1920s. For example, in 1926, Bills agreed to join Aetna Life Insurance Company as an assistant secretary if she were made a voting officer (Patricia Cain Smith, personal communication, June 14, 1996). She implemented personnel procedures and conducted extensive research to answer problems faced by Aetna. For example, she developed a unique wage incentive system for clerical positions, devised a job classification method, instituted a job evaluation program, and served as a consultant to top management (Austin & Waung, 1994).

While at Aetna, Bills published extensively in scientific journals, including *Journal of Applied Psychology, Journal of Personnel Research* (later *Personnel Journal*), *Personnel,* and *Journal of Consulting Psychology.* She also published in practitioner journals read by executives, including *American Management Association Office Executives Series, American Management Association Office Management Series, American Management Association Marketing Series* and *Life Office Management Association.* Topics included measurement of office work, bonus plans, compensation, and the "relative permanency of men and women office workers" (Bills, 1928, p. 207).

An example of a consulting endeavor during the early years of I/O psychology was an industrial management and engineering consulting business established by Frank and Lillian Gilbreth, originally known as Frank B. Gilbreth, Inc., Consulting Engineers. The Gilbreths used time and motion studies to determine how worker efficiency could be enhanced and productivity improved. Clients included Eastman Kodak, Remington Typewriter, and U.S. Rubber. The Gilbreths also developed a time and motion laboratory in their home, where they conducted summer workshops for managers, professors, and others about their system and techniques.

When Gilbreth's husband died in 1924, she continued to operate the consulting business from the home office for the next 40 years. In 1925, Gilbreth reestablished the Institute for Motion Study, for which she recruited students from all over the world to come to her home to learn about time and motion studies. By 1929, Gilbreth quit teaching at home and pursued consulting full-time. The consulting firm was renamed Gilbreth, Inc., and she continued to consult a "humanized version of scientific management" (Kelly & Kelly, 1990, p. 122). One objective of her consulting was to encourage management and labor to discern the benefits of working together (Yost, 1943). She worked with companies such as R. H. Macy and Company and Sears, Roebuck, and Company. When hired by R. H. Macy and Company, she worked as a salesperson in a store to gain a worker's perspective for identifying ways to reduce fatigue and increase job satisfaction. In addition, she trained one executive to conduct motion studies and operational analyses, which led to additional requests for training other executives.

While consulting, Gilbreth published eight books and numerous articles on education, engineering, management, and psychology. The major emphasis of her work was applying psychological principles to scientific management to compensate for Frederick Taylor's omission of human aspects (Kelly & Kelly, 1990). Gilbreth understood the importance of identifying the best motions to improve efficiency, but she also wanted to know if those best motions provided the happiest results to those who used them. She believed "nothing could really be 'best' that did not take into account the way those who used them felt about them" (Yost, 1943, p. 107).

Gilbreth's publication, *The Psychology of Management* (1914), was considered to be one of the most influential textbooks on industrial relations (Stevens & Gardner, 1982a). She presented innovative ideas for the time by asserting that the laws of psychology support the laws of management:

"Management," until recent years, and the emphasis placed on Scientific Management was undoubtedly associated, in the average mind, with the *managing* part of the organization only, neglecting that vital part—the best interests of the managed, almost entirely. Since we have come to realize that management signifies the relationship between the managing and the managed in doing work, a new realization of its importance has come about. (L. M. Gilbreth, 1914, pp. 6–7)

According to Gilbreth, psychology, defined as "the study of the mind," is invaluable to a manager. A manager needs to know how the mind works in order to give and receive information in an efficient and effective manner.

In 1925, Gilbreth published an article entitled "The Present State of Industrial Psychology" (L. M. Gilbreth, 1925), in which she presented current applications of I/O psychology. For the area of selection, Gilbreth noted the value of observing an applicant in the proposed workplace, the notion underlying work sample tests or simulations. She described the utility of a questionnaire for selection, a questionnaire that asks for what is labeled today as biodata. She also emphasized the importance of informing the applicant why questions are being asked and the advantages of answering them correctly and completely. Gilbreth included a discussion of tests in industry by describing advantages and problems and recognizing the lack of criteria for validating them. Furthermore, Gilbreth's (1925) article addressed the issues of gender and selection, in particular, "whether the selection of workers is a job best filled by a man or a woman" (p. 1040). She concluded, "There seems to be no special reason why an industry should not prefer to have a man hire the women, and a woman hire the men. A complete survey of existing practice in this field is lacking" (p. 1040). She also discussed topics such as promotions, job evaluations, training, and group cooperation.

I/O psychologists found work not only through private industry and consulting, but also through government agencies. For example, in 1935, Hayes was hired as a general consultant by the Children's Bureau of the U.S. Department of Labor, a federal personnel agency that addressed employment issues of youths (Thompson, 1921), to conduct a research study (requested by the U.S. Congress) on the problems of unemployed youths. Hayes proposed a program to employ the unemployed, which was accepted and served as the basis for the National Youth Administration (NYA), one of several New Deal programs created within the Works Progress Administration (Cashman, 1989). In September 1935, Hayes was hired to lead the Division of Guidance and Placement, one division of the NYA. In 1940, she was promoted to director of the Division of Youth, when the NYA was placed under the auspices of the Federal Security Agency. While Hayes was the director of this division, she made decisions regarding selection, placement, compensation, and training. She was a member of the Technical Committee on Probation, Parole, and Crime Prevention to help reorganize the Division of Probation, Parole, and Crime Prevention. She was a member of the Advisory Group of the Civil Service Commission and of the Subcommittee of the Committee appointed by the secretary of labor to consider coordinating labor and training facilities of the government. In the latter part of her tenure, Hayes made decisions on how to prepare youths for national defense jobs. She had a substantial and significant impact on the success of NYA and decisions made on Capitol Hill from 1935 to 1942. For example, it was reported in 1939 that 270,000 youths had been employed through the NYA, 115,000 youths were helped through college, and 250,000 received aid for secondary education ("N.Y.A. Leader Finds State Progressive," 1939). While Hayes worked for the NYA, she developed expertise in guidance and placement, and she published articles in journals such as *Personality Journal, Occupations, Personnel Journal,* and *The Psychological Exchange* (a short-lived journal that kept practitioners apprised of research publications and activities).

Professional Service

Similar to individuals in other developing sciences and professions, psychologists convened at meetings to discuss common issues and to become familiar with each other (Hilgard, 1987); consequently, organizations were created. The APA, organized in 1892, was the first professional organization of psychologists; however, the majority of members were male psychologists because of the APA's preference for members who were employed by universities. In 1923, 18% of APA members were women (Bryan & Boring, 1946). It was not until 1926, when the associate category of membership was established, that more women joined. In 1928, 34% of the members were women (Bryan & Boring, 1946). The four women discussed here were members of APA, and Bregman and Gilbreth were fellows. Bills served on the APA Council of Representatives (1945) and was a member of the Policy and Planning Board (1945–1947), the Committee on Academic Freedom and Conditions of Employment (1952), and the Conference of State Psychological Associations. Bills was also on the original committee that structured Division 14 of the APA (now known as the Society for Industrial and Organizational Psychology, Inc.) and served as the seventh President of the Division, the first woman, and one of three women to be elected in 50 years.

In the published version of her Division 14 Presidential Address entitled "Our Expanding Responsibilities," Bills (1953) foresaw the gap between scientists and practitioners. She argued that psychologists working in industry were not given sufficient credit for their contributions to science. She stated,

Perhaps our [psychologists in private industry] real function is that of a liaison officer between our experimental workers and management under which function our chief duty would be to keep them very well informed on both sides, and display the ingenuity to connect them, even when in many cases the connection is far from obvious. (Bills, 1953, p. 145)

In addition to holding memberships in the APA, psychologists joined other organizations supporting applied psychology such as the Association of Consulting Psychologists (ACP; organized in 1930) and the American Association for Applied Psychology (AAAP; organized in 1937). Bregman was vice president (1931), member of the Executive Committee (1935–1937), and chair of the Committee on Constitution and Bylaws (1933) of ACP. Three women were members of AAAP. Bills served on the newly formed Board of Governors of AAAP during 1939, on the conference program committees, and as the recording secretary of the Industrial and

Business Section. Hayes was a member of the Public and Professional Relations Committee, and Bregman was chair of the Committee on Membership. Bregman also was chair of the Legislative Committee (1939) and chair of the Committee on Constitution and Bylaws (1938) of the New York State Association of Applied Psychology.

Bills, Bregman, Gilbreth, and Hayes were members of other organizations relevant to their interests. Bregman and Bills were involved with the American Board of Examiners of Professional Psychology (ABEPP). Bregman was a diplomate in Counseling of the ABEPP, and Bills, in 1947, was a charter trustee for the ABEPP. Bills also was a founder of the Connecticut Valley Association of Psychologists and its successor, the Connecticut State Psychological Society. She facilitated the development of the Certification of Psychologists, serving as secretary from 1945 to 1950. She served as the second president of the Connecticut State Psychological Society in 1945–1946. Hayes was a member of the Personnel Research Federation, the American Statistical Association, and the Voca-tional Guidance Association (as president in 1928).

Gilbreth, in 1921, was elected as a member to the Society of Industrial Engineers (the first woman to become a member). In 1924, she was elected as a member of the American Society of Mechanical Engineers, and she was appointed as chair of the Management's Division meeting on the psychology of management. She was also a member of the American Management Association, and in 1965, she was the first woman elected to the National Academy of Engineering.

Contributions to I/O Psychology

It is apparent from the overview of their involvement with I/O psychology that the four female psychologists contributed to the development of the discipline during the early years. Similar to other early female psychologists who produced scholarship (Furumoto, 1987; Russo & Denmark, 1987), these four psychologists contributed to the literature. They typically published in applied journals introduced during 1900 to 1930 (e.g., *Journal of Applied Psychology, Journal of Personnel Research, Journal of Consulting Psychology*). DeMeuse (1987) found that, in the *Journal of Applied Psychology,* for the years 1917 through 1919, 16.7% of the senior authors were women, and for the years 1920 through 1929, 24.6% of the senior authors were women. In addition, reviews of journal articles by Kornhauser (1922), Moore and Hartmann (1931), and Viteles (1926) revealed some scholarship produced by women.

The four female psychologists used scientifically rigorous methods to conduct research on areas of I/O psychology typically examined by applied psychologists of the time, such as selection, acquisition of skills, and work methods and job design for improving efficiency (Katzell & Austin, 1992). Both Bills and Bregman completed studies on testing for selection purposes. Hayes and Gilbreth discussed in their writings the advantages and disadvantages of testing. Gilbreth conducted extensive time and motion studies to understand methods of work and design of jobs. These research areas are not surprising, because the women's thinking was guided early in their careers by the functionalism school of thought.

Their research studies are pioneering because they were conducted in applied settings. The importance of field research was espoused by Bregman (1922b) in an introduction for a series of studies entitled "Studies in Industrial Psychology":

The studies are not laboratory studies. They come out of the midst of a very busy industry. They were in consequence subject to restrictions, exercised not only by the factors of time and cost, but also certain other factors, inherent in the situation of the youngest of the sciences trying to work out its usefulness in an environment traditionally and actually so foreign to it.

The writer believes that notwithstanding their shortcomings the studies have a certain significance and usefulness, and in this belief they are presented to the reader in this volume. (p. 4)

In addition to conducting field research on topics typical for the time period, these women contributed to the literature by researching uncharted territory. For example, Bills and Bregman investigated the use of multiple predictors for selection purposes, an unusual practice in industry during the time. Bills, Bregman, and Gilbreth recognized the importance of criteria; subsequently, they conducted predictive validity studies. Hayes and Gilbreth advocated and investigated the advantages of hiring individuals with disabilities. Hayes developed a graphic rating scale for performance evaluations and examined issues regarding vocational guidance and the employment of youths. Bills completed research on compensation and bonus plans. Gilbreth professed and studied the application of psychological principles to management work.

Not only did these four women contribute to I/O psychology through research, they also contributed by practicing psychology. They had the foresight to apply psychological principles for solving problems in business and society. In addition, they worked in positions that were stereotypically unacceptable for women. For example, Hayes was involved with World War I and The Scott Company. Both Bills and Bregman worked in private corporations. Gilbreth and Bregman ran consulting businesses from their homes, a woman's work style that was not popular until 70 years later (Perloff & Naman, 1996).

The four individuals worked with several different areas of I/O psychology, but they concentrated primarily on personnel issues, not unusual for the time. Areas of practice included compensation, job classification, job evaluation, labor disputes, management, placement, recruitment, selection, supervision, time and motion studies, training, vocational guidance, and work efficiency. For many of these areas, they implemented new applications of psychology. For example, Gilbreth emphasized the value of gaining the worker's perspective and did so for her consulting. Bills developed a unique wage incentive system as well as created and instituted an innovative job classification method. Bregman revised and distributed intelligence tests for vocational guidance and selection purposes. Hayes participated in labor–management disputes, an atypical consulting activity. These applications of psychology were accomplished without compromising the scientific integrity they learned while in graduate school.

The applied settings provided opportunities to these individuals to research and practice psychology at the same time. In fact, much of their scholarship was directly related to problems they addressed in their employment. For example, Bills completed selection research while consulting for companies on personnel issues at the Division of Applied Psychology. Bregman conducted research on multiple predictors and criteria while improving personnel procedures at R. H. Macy and Company. Hayes, while providing personnel consulting through The Scott Company, wrote about and researched personnel issues. Also, Hayes studied extensively vocational guidance and employment of youths during her time at the NYA. Gilbreth's consulting activities were based on time and motion studies and the application of psychology to management.

Finally, in addition to research and practice, female psychologists contributed to I/O psychology through professional organizations. They were initiators, active members, and officers of newly formed professional organizations during a critical period for the development of the discipline. Their involvement demonstrated dedication, commitment, and willingness to maintain strong links to psychology.

An illuminating observation of these four women is that they simultaneously performed successfully in their work, produced valuable scholarship, and were key players in professional organizations. Although these contributions have been overlooked by historians, their accomplishments were recognized by their contemporaries. Archival materials reveal that these four women were highly regarded and respected by their colleagues. For example, Hayes was invited frequently to speak at professional conferences on work-related issues. When The Psychological Corporation celebrated its 20th anniversary in 1941 and honored its founder James McKeen Cattell, Hayes was invited as a guest to participate on a panel where she was to address the use of psychological tests in the fields of job selection and training.

The following tribute, written when Hayes died in 1962, reveals others' respect for her:

Those of us who worked with Dr. Hayes recall her wit, her quick grasp of the heart of any subject under consideration, and her great intellectual capacity. She was warmly interested in her fellow citizens and deeply devoted to the welfare of children and young people. Her loss will be felt in the many causes she served and among the wide circle of friends she made during a productive life. (Girl Scouts of the United States of America, 1962, May 23, p. 1)

Bregman interacted and corresponded regularly with eminent psychologists; in fact, the correspondence often had an amicable tone. Cattell invited her to lunch, Paul Achilles asked her to "drop in some day," and she received congratulatory letters from colleagues after the birth of her first child. Hollingworth (1921) wrote the following:

Judith, if I estimate correctly, is now 41 days old, she is following a moving light with the eyes, shows pupillary and grasping reflexes, displays occasional strabismus, recognizes the human voice, clasps with four fingers, and makes all but the more difficult consonant sounds. These are her minimum attainments. How far she exceeds them it would be rash to predict.

And no doubt you will insist that the very most important part of her personality is left out of this description. And so it is. But what do you expect from one who has not even seen her? Relying on what biology I know I predict for Judith a brilliant, useful and happy future, and you may tell her so. (Hollingworth, 1921, p. 1)

Bills worked closely with Bingham and others at Carnegie Institute of Technology and continued extensive interactions with contemporaries while working for Aetna. She was the founder of a group called Psychologists Employed Full-Time in Industry, which met at APA meetings. Well-known members of this group included Orlo Crissey, Ed Henry, and Joe Weitz. Colleagues' admiration and respect for Bills are expressed in a letter by Orlo Crissey when she was recognized as the founder of this group:

At Aetna, the impact of your work, as well as your personal charm and understanding counseling, has been tremendous. It should be a source of deep job satisfaction to see the job classification method for clerical jobs still in successful use, not only at Aetna but in other insurance companies as well. Likewise, your clerical wage incentive system is also unique. Your studies in selection for clerical jobs and insurance salesmen, as well as other research, have been frequently quoted.

You can take pride in the many examples of persons trained under you who are now prominent, not only in Aetna, but in other insurance companies across the United States. . . . Your understanding and wise counsel have made you loved and revered by the many, many people with whom you have been associated.

We are all grateful for your contributions to the field of Psychology. You served conscientiously in a variety of important assignments during the formative and trying years of psychological history. (Crissey, 1957)

While Gilbreth worked with Hayes on the Girl Scouts of America movement and collaborated with some psychologists (e.g., Thorndike), much of her recognition came from engineers and scientific management colleagues (e.g., Taylor). Her strong identification with engineering, but her training as a psychologist and her advocacy of psychology for the workplace, raises the question of why Gilbreth did not identify strongly with psychology in general and I/O psychology in particular. One obvious explanation is her partnership with her husband. His work with engineering engendered their identification with the engineering profession. Furthermore, her husband encouraged her to pursue a career, but insisted she focus on "practical work." Although he recognized the value of psychology to engineering, from his perspective, engineering was more practical than psychology. Gilbreth foresaw the practical value of psychology, but accepted that its practicality had not been accepted (L. M. Gilbreth, 1914). Furthermore, as stated earlier, Gilbreth, similar to other psychologists, probably encountered resistance from academic colleagues for applying psychology. Engineers, specifically proponents of scientific management, on the other hand, were open to Gilbreth's ideas. A historical speech by Gilbreth was made at a meeting of scientific management supporters at Dartmouth College in 1908. She was asked for her opinion because she was the only woman attending the meeting. Yost (1943) stated the following:

Lillian Gilbreth rose to her feet and remarked that the human being, of course, was the most important element in industry, and that it seemed to her this element had not been receiving the attention it warranted. The engineer's scientific training, she said, was all for the handling of inanimate objects. She called attention to the fact that psychology was fast becoming a science and that it had much to offer that was being ignored by management engineers. The plea in her impromptu remarks was for the new profession of scientific management to open its eyes to the necessary place psychology had in any program industrial engineers worked out. (pp. 113–114)

Their accomplishments and the respect of their colleagues clearly indicate that these women were successful in applied psychology. Their research contributions, their applications of psychology to solve problems in business and society, and their profound involvement and service in professional organizations warrant placing the four female pioneers in the early history of I/O psychology.

Other Contributions and Recognition

In addition to addressing business and employment-related problems, these women examined other issues, some of which were associated with stereotypes of women's work (e.g., child welfare, homemaker's work). For example, Bregman expanded her interests to child development around the same time she was raising her children. She was awarded a research fellowship in child development from the National Research Council from 1929 to 1930. In 1935, she was hired as a research associate for the Progressive Education Association on the Committee on the Study of Adolescents. She applied her research and measurement skills by designing and conducting a substantial education and vocational test survey in the New York City public schools. In relation to this study, she developed a record blank for maintaining a complete, continual record of a student's progress throughout their primary and secondary education (Bregman, 1936). Also, Bregman was hired as a consultant for psychology in the Department of Nursing Education at Teachers College, Columbia University, in 1931. She created a program for developing vocational tests for nurses, and later published a nationwide survey on the intelligence of nurses (Bregman, 1933).

Hayes in 1924 was employed as director of Vocational Service for Juniors, a private philanthropic organization. The organization was responsible for establishing the position of vocational counselor in the New York school system and creating a junior placement office in the State Department of Labor (Hayes, 1932).

Gilbreth directed her attention to challenges faced by women, including managing homes, raising families, and working in jobs outside the home. Two publications (L. M. Gilbreth, 1927, 1928) contained her view that "every housewife and mother needs to be an effective, efficient manager" (Kelly & Kelly, 1990, p. 123). She professed the following:

Homes should be happy places in which individuals can achieve fulfillment and a degree of freedom: wives and mothers are entitled to share in this freedom and fulfillment, but this happy situation can be attained only if the responsibilities of running the home are shared and efficiently handled. (Kelly & Kelly, 1990, pp. 122–123)

Furthermore, she was hired by General Electric Company and other appliance manufacturing companies to assist in redesigning kitchen and household appliances to match the needs of homemakers and to maximize efficiency and effectiveness. (Two of her most notable inventions were the shelves inside refrigerator doors and the foot-pedal trash can.)

The four pioneers advocated equal employment opportunity for women, which was reflected by their own careers as well as other efforts. For example, Bills promoted equitable and fair treatment of both women and men at Aetna, which was demonstrated by her dedication, persistence, and quiet implementation of fair personnel policies (Austin & Waung, 1994). During World War II, Gilbreth provided consulting services to companies to assist in the employment of women and to heighten management's awareness of women's needs (Russell, 1994). Hayes assisted in developing selection standards for selecting women for industrial war projects (Hayes, 1942). In addition, Gilbreth and Hayes believed in the value of preparing young women for future work. They were involved extensively with the Girl Scout Movement. In 1947, Hayes became chair of the National Executive Committee for Girl Scouts of America, and at the same time, was a member of the legislative policy committee, the board staff planning committee, and the board of directors. When Gilbreth was 73 years old, she was made the chair of the national personnel division committee.

These four individuals have been formally acknowledged elsewhere for their accomplishments. For example, all four were included in Cattell's *American Men of Science*. Bregman and Gilbreth are listed in *Who's Who of American Women*. Hayes was noted by O'Connell and Russo (1980) as having a distinguished career. Bregman is included in *Leaders in Education* and *American Women*. Bills, in 1940, received the Leffingwell Medal from the National Office Management Association for her work with personnel management.

Gilbreth is well known, if not for her husband's and her work with scientific management, then for the notoriety her family received from the popular books written by two of her children. *Cheaper by the Dozen* (F. Gilbreth & Carey, 1949) and *Belles on Their Toes* (F. Gilbreth & Carey, 1950), which were made into popular movies. She has been labeled as the "Mother of Scientific Management," the "First Lady of Management," the "World's Greatest Woman Engineer" (McKenney, 1952), and the "Mother of Industrial Psychology" (Stevens & Gardner, 1982a). She is included in *Notable American Women: The Modern Period* (Sicherman, Green, Kantrov, & Walker, 1980), and several publications of her voluminous accomplishments exist (e.g., F. Gilbreth, 1970; Gotcher, 1992; Kelly & Kelly, 1990; Perloff & Naman, 1996; Spriegel & Myers, 1953; Stevens & Gardner, 1982a; Yost, 1943, 1949). Gilbreth received over 20 honorary degrees and numerous awards, primarily in areas of engineering and management (comprehensive lists can be found in F. Gilbreth, 1970, and Perloff & Naman, 1996). In 1984, a commemorative postage stamp was issued in her honor; she was the only psychologist to receive this honor (Bales, 1984). Interestingly, neither Gilbreth nor the other three women were listed in the study of 538 important contributors to psychology (Watson, 1974).

Lessons for Current and Future I/O Psychologists

What can we learn from the successes of these four pioneers? First, we realize that existing historical accounts of I/O psychology are incomplete and distorted. Thus, additional research on both female and male contributors is needed to have a complete understanding of our past. Second, the value and importance of networking and collaborating with colleagues, as well as maintaining links with the profession, are evident. Furumoto and Scarborough (1986) noted the existence and importance of a network for the first generation of American female psychologists, especially for those working in academia. O'Connell (1983) stated that, for many female psychologists, "the mentors provided professional socialization for these women and formed critical links in the professional and social networks so necessary for reaching eminence in psychology and other fields" (p. 322). Beginning with college and throughout their lives, the careers of the four female I/O psychologists were aided by both eminent male psychologists (e.g., Bingham, Cattell, Ruml, Scott, Thorndike) and prominent female psychologists (e.g., Fernald, Gordon, Hollingworth, Ladd-Franklin, Rand). These colleagues provided guidance, advice, support, and visibility.

Third, these women's accomplishments reveal that both circumstances and individual characteristics can contribute to one's success. Whether these women were forced to pursue applied work or chose to pursue applied work, their success was partly due to changes in American society in general and in psychology in particular. In addition, individual characteristics (e.g., intelligence, perseverance, assertiveness) account for their success. They could take advantage of opportunities because they were creative, flexible, and persistent. Consequently, they had productive, professional, and rewarding careers in psychology.

Finally, we learn of role models who overcame obstacles. Professional advantages of same-sex role models in the lives of prominent women have been well documented (Almquist & Angrist, 1985; Goldstein, 1979). The four women described in this article are role models because they realized their fullest individual potentials despite opposition. They successfully practiced and researched psychology, although they experienced resistance from their academic contemporaries and from society for working outside the home (i.e., doctrine of separate spheres) and for working in positions atypical for women. They maintained a science–practice interface throughout their careers without compromising integrity and quality because of a sound scientific education and training as their foundation. They also demonstrated that success is possible with a supportive spouse or family. Spouses and families of three of the women enhanced their careers. Current and future psychologists can learn from these women's experiences to blend research, practice, service, and a personal life successfully.

Conclusion

This research is a nascent attempt to discover and identify female pioneers of I/O psychology. These four women represent a larger cohort of female psychologists that contributed to the development of I/O psychology during its infancy. Preliminary research reveals at least 15 additional American female psychologists who were involved with I/O psychology during the early years (Koppes, 1997). Recognizing these early women's experiences and accomplishments is an initial step toward placing women in the history of I/O psychology. Incorporating women into that history is imperative in the attainment of a more complete understanding of I/O psychology's past and a fuller comprehension of the present. Acknowledgment of these professionals makes historical accounts of I/O psychology more accurate and complete. My hope is that this overview of four women in I/O psychology during the early years will provoke an interest in the history of I/O psychology and will stimulate historical research needed to identify, understand, and preserve contributions of both female and male I/O psychologists.

References

Almquist, E. M., & Angrist, S. S. (1985). *Careers and contingencies.* Amherst: University of Massachusetts Press.

Austin, J. T., & Waung, M. P. (1994, April). Dr. Marion A. Bills: Allegan to Aetna. In L. Koppes (Chair), *The founding mothers: Female I/O psychologists in the early years.* Symposium conducted at the Ninth Annual Conference of the Society for Industrial and Organizational Psychology, Inc., Nashville, TN.

Bales, J. (1984, February). Lillian Gilbreth honored on U.S. stamp. *APA Monitor,* Vol. 15, No. 2 p. 2.

Baritz, L. (1960). *The servants of power.* New York: Wiley.

Bernstein, M. D., & Russo, N. F. (1974). The history of psychology revisited: Or, up with our foremothers. *American Psychologist, 29,* 130–134.

Bills, M. A. (1921a). Methods for the selection of comptometer operators and stenographers. *Journal of Applied Psychology, 5,* 275–283.

Bills, M. A. (1921b). A test for the selection of stenographers. *Journal of Applied Psychology, 5,* 373–377.

Bills, M. A. (1928). Relative permanency of men and women office workers. *American Management Association, 5,* 207–208.

Bills, M. A. (1953). Our expanding responsibilities. *Journal of Applied Psychology, 37,* 142–145.

Boring, E. G., & Lindzey, G. (Eds.). (1952). *A history of psychology in autobiography* (Vol. 1). Worcester, MA: Clark University Press.

Bregman Biography. (1970, March 12). E. O. Bregman Collection. Akron, OH: University of Akron, Archives of the History of American Psychology.

Bregman, E. O. (1921). A study in industrial psychology—Tests for special abilities. *Journal of Applied Psychology, 5,* 127–151.

Bregman, E. O. (1922a). A scientific plan for sizing up employees. *System,* 696–763.

Bregman, E. O. (1922b). Studies in industrial psychology. *Archives of Psychology, 9,* 1–60.

Bregman, E. O. (1926). *Revision of the Army Alpha Examination. Form A.* New York: Psychological Corporation.

Bregman, E. O. (1933). *The performance of student nurses on tests of intelligence.* New York: Teachers College, Columbia University.

Bregman, E. O. (1935a). *Bregman Language Completion Scales. Forms A and B.* New York: Psychological Corporation.

Bregman, E. O. (1935b). *Revision of the Army Alpha Examination. Form B.* New York: Psychological Corporation.

Bregman, E. O. (1936). *Comprehensive individual history record form and manual: Infancy through high school*. New York: Psychological Corporation.

Bryan, A. I., & Boring, E. G. (1946). Women in American psychology: Statistics from the OPP Questionnaire. *Psychological Bulletin, 41*, 447–454.

Burtt, H. E. (1926). *Principles of employment psychology*. New York: Harper.

Cahan, E. D., & White, S. H. (1992). Proposals for a second psychology. *American Psychologist, 47*, 224–235.

Camfield, T. (1973). The professionalization of American psychology, 1870–1917. *Journal of the History of Behavioral Sciences, 9*, 66–75.

Cashman, S. D. (1989). *America in the twenties and thirties*. New York: New York University Press.

Cattell, J. M. (1917). Our psychological association and research. *Science, 45*, 275–284.

Cattell, J. M. (1923). The Psychological Corporation. *Annals of the American Academy of Political and Social Science, 110*, 2–232.

Craig, D. R. (1921, October 12). [Letter to E. O. Bregman]. E. O. Bregman Collection, Box M296, Folder: Correspondence 1936–1922. Akron, OH: University of Akron, Archives of the History of American Psychology.

Crissey, O. L. (1957, October 19). [Letter to M. A. Bills]. Marie Crissey Collection, Box M2054, Folder 4: Industrial psychologists employed full-time in industry. Akron, OH: University of Akron, Archives of the History of American Psychology.

DeMeuse, K. P. (1987). A historical examination of author sex and research funding in industrial and organizational psychology. *American Psychologist, 42*, 876–879.

Ferguson, L. W. (1952). A look across the years 1920 to 1950. In L. L. Thurstone (Ed.), *Applications of psychology: Essays to honor Walter V. Bingham* (pp. 1–17). New York: Harper.

Ferguson, L. W. (1961). The development of industrial psychology. In B. von H. Gilmer (Ed.), *Industrial psychology* (pp. 18–37). New York: McGraw-Hill.

Ferguson, L. W. (1962–1965). *The heritage of industrial psychology* [14 pamphlets]. Hartford, CT: Finlay Press.

Finch, F. H., & Odoroff, M. E. (1939). Employment trends in applied psychology. *Journal of Consulting Psychology, 3*, 118–122.

Furumoto, L. (1979). Mary Whiton Calkins (1863–1930): Fourteenth president of the American Psychological Association. *Journal of the History of the Behavioral Sciences, 15*, 346–356.

Furumoto, L. (1987). On the margins: Women and the professionalization of psychology in the United States, 1890–1940. In M. G. Ash & W. R. Woodward (Eds.), *Psychology in twentieth-century thought and society* (pp. 93–113). Cambridge, England: Cambridge University Press.

Furumoto, L. (1991). From "paired associates" to a psychology of self: The intellectual odyssey of Mary Whiton Calkins. In G. A. Kimble, M. Wertheimer, & C. L. White (Eds.), *Portraits of pioneers in psychology* (pp. 56–72). Hillsdale, NJ: Erlbaum.

Furumoto, L. (1992). Joining separate spheres—Christine Ladd-Franklin, woman-scientist (1847–1930). *American Psychologist, 47*, 175–182.

Furumoto, L., & Scarborough, E. (1986). Placing women in the history of psychology: The first American women psychologists. *American Psychologist, 41*, 35–42.

Gilbreth, F., Jr. (1970). *Time out for happiness*. New York: Thomas Y. Crowell.

Gilbreth, F., Jr., & Carey, E. G. (1949). *Cheaper by the dozen*. New York: Bantam.

Gilbreth, F., Jr., & Carey, E. G. (1950). *Belles on their toes*. New York: Bantam.

Gilbreth, L. M. (1914). *The psychology of management*. New York: Sturgis & Walton.

Gilbreth, L. M. (1925). The present state of industrial psychology. *Mechanical Engineering, 47*(11a), 1039–1042.

Gilbreth, L. M. (1927). *The homemaker and her job*. New York: Appleton-Century.

Gilbreth, L. M. (1928). *Living with our children*. New York: W. W. Norton.

Girl Scouts of the United States of America, Board of Directors. (1962, May 23). [Tribute to Dr. Mary H. S. Hayes]. New York: Girl Scouts of the United States of America, National Historic Preservation Center.

Goldstein, E. (1979). Effect of same-sex and cross-sex role models on the subsequent academic productivity of scholars. *American Psychologist, 34*, 407–410.

Gotcher, J. M. (1992). Assisting the handicapped: The pioneering efforts of Frank and Lillian Gilbreth. *Journal of Management, 18*, 5–13.

Gutman, H. G. (1977). *Work, culture and society in industrializing America*. New York: Vintage.

Hayes, M. H. S. (1932). The work of the psychologist in the Vocational Service for Juniors. *The Psychological Exchange, 1*, 35–36.

Hayes, M. H. S. (1942). [Memorandum to regional youth representatives]. Washington, DC: National Archives, Division of Youth Personnel, Record Group 119, National Youth Administration Archives.

Hayes, M. H. S., & Paterson, D. G. (1921). Experimental development of the graphic rating method. *Psychological Bulletin, 18*, 98–99.

Hilgard, E. E. (1987). *Psychology in America: A historical survey*. New York: Harcourt Brace Jovanovich.

Hollingworth, H. L. (1921, August 24). [Letter to E. O. Bregman]. Box M296, Folder: Correspondence 1936–1922. Akron, OH: University of Akron, Archives of the History of American Psychology.

Hopkins, L. B. (1921, June 16). [Letter to Active Members of The Scott Company]. The Scott Company Collection, Box 1, Folder 5. Evanston, IL: Northwestern University Archives.

Katzell, R. A., & Austin, J. T. (1992). From then to now: The development of industrial-organizational psychology in the United States. *Journal of Applied Psychology, 77*, 803–835.

Kelly, R. M., & Kelly, V. P. (1990). Lillian Moller Gilbreth. In A. N. O'Connell & N. F. Russo (Eds.), *Women in psychology: A bio-bibliographic sourcebook* (pp. 117–124). New York: Greenwood Press.

Kimble, G. A., Boneau, C. A., & Wertheimer, M. (Eds.). (1996). *Portraits of pioneers in psychology* (Vol. 2). Washington, DC: American Psychological Association.

Koppes, L. L. (1997). *Female pioneers of industrial and organizational psychology*. Manuscript in preparation.

Koppes, L. L., Landy, F. J., & Perkins, K. N. (1993). First American female applied psychologists. *The Industrial-Organizational Psychologist, 31*, 31–33.

Kornhauser, A. W. (1922). The psychology of vocational selection. *Psychological Bulletin, 19*, 192–229.

Landy, F. J. (1992). Hugo Münsterberg: Victim or visionary? *Journal of Applied Psychology, 77*, 787–802.

Landy, F. J. (1993). Early influences on the development of industrial/organizational psychology. In T. K. Fagan & G. R. VandenBos (Eds.), *Exploring applied psychology: Origins and critical analyses* (pp. 83–118). Washington, DC: American Psychological Association.

Landy, F. J. (1994, April). Lillian Gilbreth. In L. Koppes (Chair), *The founding mothers: Female I/O psychologists in the early years*. Symposium conducted at the Ninth Annual Conference of the Society for Industrial and Organizational Psychology Inc., Nashville, TN.

McKenney, J. W. (1952). The world's greatest engineer. *CTA Journal, 48*, 9–10, 20–23.

Moore, B. V., & Hartmann, G. W. (Eds.). (1931). *Readings in industrial psychology*. New York: D. Appleton-Century.

Napoli, D. S. (1981). *Architects of adjustment: The history of the psychological profession in the United States*. Port Washington, NY: Kennibat Press.

N.Y.A. leader finds state progressive. (1939, March 15). *The Courier-Journal*. Washington, DC: National Archives, Division of Youth Personnel, National Youth Administration Archives, Record Group 119.

O'Connell, A. N. (1983). Synthesis: Profiles and patterns of achievement. In A. N. O'Connell, & N. F. Russo (Eds.), *Models of achievement: Reflections of eminent women in psychology* (pp. 299–326). New York: Columbia University Press.

O'Connell, A. N., & Russo, N. F. (Eds.). (1980). Eminent women in psychology [Special issue]. *Psychology of Women Quarterly, 5*(1).

O'Connell, A. N., & Russo, N. F. (Eds.). (1983). *Models of achievement: Reflections of eminent women in psychology*. New York: Columbia University Press.

O'Connell, A. N., & Russo, N. F. (Eds.). (1988). *Models of achievement: Reflections of eminent women in psychology* (Vol. 2). Hillsdale, NJ: Erlbaum.

O'Connell, A. N., & Russo, N. F. (Eds.). (1990). *Women in psychology: A bio-bibliographic sourcebook*. New York: Greenwood Press.

Oschrin, E. (1918). Vocational tests for retail saleswomen. *Journal of Applied Psychology, 2,* 148–155.

Perloff, R., & Naman, J. L. (1996). Lillian Gilbreth: Tireless advocate for a general psychology. In G. A. Kimble, C. A. Boneau, & M. Wertheimer (Eds.), *Portraits of pioneers in psychology* (Vol. 2, pp. 106–116). Washington, DC: American Psychological Association.

Rossiter, M. W. (1974). Women scientists in America before 1920. *American Scientist, 62,* 312–323.

Rossiter, M. W. (1982). *Women scientists in America*. Baltimore: Johns Hopkins University Press.

Russell, D. (1994). *Lillian Gilbreth: Pioneer in the psychology of management*. Unpublished manuscript, Austin Peay State University, Clarksville, TN.

Russo, N. F. (1988). Women's participation in psychology: Reflecting and shaping the social context. In A. N. O'Connell & N. F. Russo (Eds.), *Models of achievement: Reflections of eminent women in psychology* (Vol. 2, pp. 9–27). Hillsdale, NJ: Erlbaum.

Russo, N. F., & Denmark, F. L. (1987). Contributions of women to psychology. *Annual Review of Psychology, 38,* 279–298.

Russo, N. F., & O'Connell, A. N. (1980). Models from our past: Psychology's foremothers. *Psychology of Women Quarterly, 5,* 11–54.

Scarborough, E., & Furumoto, L. (1987). *Untold lives: The first generation of American women psychologists*. New York: Columbia University Press.

The Scott Company Executive Committee. (1919, March 28). [Meeting minutes]. The Scott Company Papers, Box 1, Folder 4. Evanston, IL: Northwestern University Archives.

Scott, W. D., & Clothier, R. C. (1925). *Personnel management*. Chicago: Shaw.

Scott, W. D., & Hayes, M. H. S. (1921). *Science and common sense in working with men*. New York: Ronald Press.

Sicherman, G., Green, C. H., Kantrov, I., & Walker, H. (Eds.). (1980). *Notable American women: The modern period*. Cambridge, MA: Belknap Press.

Sokal, M. M. (1981). The origins of The Psychological Corporation. *Journal of the History of the Behavioral Sciences, 17,* 54–67.

Sokal, M. M. (1992). Origins and early years of the American Psychological Association, 1890–1906. *American Psychologist, 47,* 111–122.

Sokal, M. M., & Rafail, P. A. (1982). *A guide to manuscript collections in the history of psychology and related areas*. Millwood, NY: Kraus International.

Spriegel, W. R., & Myers, C. E. (1953). *The writings of the Gilbreths*. Homewood, IL: Irwin.

Stagner, R. (1982). Past and future of industrial/organizational psychology. *Professional Psychology, 13,* 892–903.

Stevens, G., & Gardner, S. (1982a). *The women of psychology, Vol. 1: Pioneers and innovators*. Cambridge, MA: Schenkman.

Stevens, G., & Gardner, S. (1982b). *The women of psychology, Vol. 2: Expansion and refinement*. Cambridge, MA: Schenkman.

Strong, E. K., Jr. (1918). Work on the committee on classification of personnel. *Journal of Applied Psychology, 2,* 130–139.

Thompson, J. D. (1921). *Personnel research agencies* (Bureau of Labor Statistics Bulletin No. 299). Washington, DC: U.S. Government Printing Office.

Thorndike, E. L. (1916). Fundamental theorems in judging men. *Journal of Applied Psychology, 2,* 67–76.

Thorndike, E. L., Bregman, E. O., Cobb, M. V., & Woodyard, E. (1927). *The measurement of intelligence*. New York: Teachers College, Columbia University.

Thorndike, E. L., Bregman, E. O., & Metcalfe, Z. F. (1934). *The prediction of vocational success*. New York: Commonwealth Fund.

Thorndike, E. L., Bregman, E. O., Tilton, J. W., & Woodyard, E. (1928). *Adult learning*. New York: Macmillan.

Viteles, M. S. (1926). Psychology in industry. *Psychological Bulletin, 23,* 631–680.

Viteles, M. S. (1932). *Industrial psychology*. New York: W. W. Norton.

von Mayrhauser, R. T. (1987). The manager, the medic, and the mediator: The clash of professional psychological styles and the wartime origins of group mental testing. In M. M. Sokal (Ed.), *Psychological testing and American society 1890–1930* (pp. 128–155). New Brunswick, NJ: Rutgers University Press.

Watson, R. I. (1974). *Eminent contributors to psychology, Vol. 1: A bibliography of primary references*. New York: Springer.

Yost, E. (1943). *American women of science*. New York: Stokes.

Yost, E. (1949). *Frank and Lillian Gilbreth: Partners for life*. New Brunswick, NJ: Rutgers University Press.

Zusne, L. (1975). *Names in the history of psychology: A biographical sourcebook*. New York: Halstead.

Article Review Form at end of book.

Try to organize Campion's items into themes or factors. What patterns emerge? Did he miss any items identified by the other authors? Do you see any potential conflicts in what we do?

Why I'm Proud to Be an I/O Psychologist

Mike Campion

I'm Proud to Be an I/O Psychologist Because:

- we strive to do research that is both practically and scientifically meaningful.
- I can tell managers and executives that there is a whole body of science behind my recommendations.
- I can tell students that what we teach is practically useful in the real world.
- we are as much at home in the board room as in the classroom and every room in between.
- we are skeptical of the latest management fads, and we require proof that something works before we believe it.
- our knowledge is built on a foundation of nearly 100 years of research.
- we are idealists. We seek perfection and improvement of the world of work.
- we are pragmatists. We try to have an actual impact on organizations, and we realize the practical constraints of the real world.

I'm Proud to Be an I/O Psychologist Because:

- we collect and analyze data. Our conclusions are based on facts.
- we develop and use theories to summarize our knowledge and generalize them to new situations.
- we make predictions about the future. We don't just seek to explain things after the fact.
- we attempt to change things rather than just explain them.
- we try to prove that our programs and interventions are worthwhile.
- we help enhance the effectiveness of organizations. We try to increase the job performance of individual employees and groups, as well as the efficiency of the organization as a whole.
- we are concerned with the welfare of the worker as well the organization. Consider, for example, all of our research in areas such as job satisfaction and attitudes, career development, work-family issues, fairness and justice, job stress, safety, training, rewards, ethics, and so on.

I'm Proud to Be an I/O Psychologist Because:

- I can tell my kids that I design systems that help ensure that the most capable and motivated people will get the good jobs, and that bias and discrimination are eliminated.
- we develop training programs so that employees can acquire the skills to perform their jobs effectively and feel a sense of accomplishment.
- we develop pay systems that ensure that people are paid fairly and equitably.
- if we want to, we can help design jobs, teams, and organizations to maximize both satisfaction and efficiency.
- we develop performance appraisal systems that ensure that the most meritorious employees are identified and rewarded. Hard work will pay off, if we have anything to do with it.
- I can tell my mother that we make sure workers are happy. We draw management attention to employee morale and help enhance employee job satisfaction, commitment, and the quality of their working life.
- we construct management development programs that help ensure the future leadership of our organizations.
- we design career development systems that help people reach their full potential.

"Why I'm Proud to Be an I/O Psychologist," by Mike Campion, *The Industrial Organizational Psychologist*, 34, (1), 1996, pp. 27–29. Reprinted by permission.

- we are concerned with employee stress, and we try to understand and lessen that stress through our research and our interventions.
- we help develop and transform entire organizations. We will help lead America to a prosperous 21st century.

I'm Proud to Be an I/O Psychologist Because:

- we are highly educated. Most of us have PhDs, which is the highest educational degree offered in our country.
- our education combines the free-thinking of liberal arts and the disciplined-thinking of science.
- we willingly share our knowledge with each other and with those in other organizations and occupations. This is not true of all professions. Most of us do volunteer work for our profession at one point or another in our careers, if not regularly.
- we look for what is of value, not just for what is wrong. We are critical of each others work, but it is for the purpose of the improvement of that work and the improvement of the field. We recognize and reward excellence.
- most of us are very hard working, and our behavior is guided by higher-order principles and standards. Perhaps because we study work motivation and strive to increase the job performance of others, most of us feel compelled to work extremely hard ourselves. That is probably why it seems like an oxymoron to think of a lazy I/O psychologist.

Finally, I'm proud to be an I/O psychologist because of all the wonderful people in this profession. As Ben Schneider said a few years ago in his presidential speech, "the people make the place."

Article Review Form at end of book.

Why are people confused about industrial/organizational psychology? Why is it important for industrial/organizational psychologists to respond to this confusion?

I-O Psychology: What's Your Line?

Michael Gasser, David Whitsett, Neoshon Mosley, Karla Sullivan, Tammy Rogers, and Rowena Tan

As I got on the elevator, another graduate student in the clinical psychology program stepped on as well. We were both going to the top floor, and had some time since this was the slowest elevator on campus. We struck up a conversation and I told her that I was in the I-O psychology program. "What does an Input/Output psychologist do, anyway?" she asked.

I was talking with some people at a party one night. A tall man just beginning to bald came over and we were introduced. He was the president of a local bank that had incidentally just given me a loan for a new car. He asked me what I did and I told him I was an organizational psychologist. "You're an organizational psychologist," he exclaimed. "Boy, I really need to get organized!"

My personnel psychology class was going to start in a week. A young student came to my office and asked me to sign her add slip so she could register for the class. "Why are you taking personnel psychology?" I asked. "I just wanted to know more about myself," she replied (personal psychology—get it?).

"Well, just what does an I-O-U psychiatrist do, dear?"

"Mom, I've already told you a hundred times. Why don't you ask Dad?"

"He fell asleep an hour ago, besides, just last night he told our neighbor—you remember poor Mrs. Jenkins—that after you graduate you could help her with her son—you remember the poor Jenkins boy."

"Mom, I'm not that kind of psychologist."

"I know dear, that's too bad, but we still love you."

These are examples of experiences in which members of the general public (and our families), members of the business community and other psychologists showed that they did not have any idea what someone in our profession does. We suspect that these experiences are not unique to us, but have happened to many others who call themselves I-O psychologists. This problem of recognition has been noted by others concerned with the development of I-O psychology including past SIOP President Wally Borman who would like I-O psychology to be a household word (May, 1995) and past SIOP President James Farr who, in his presidential address reflecting the 50th anniversary of APA Division 14, questioned why there is still "limited acceptance and understanding" of our profession (Farr, 1997).

So what if others do not know who we are or what we do? Is this really a problem? When dealing with the general public, this lack of acceptance and understanding is a problem for clinical psychologists. Many lay persons do not know the difference between a therapist (a generic term which could mean a lot of things) and a professionally trained and licensed psychologist. A similar dilemma exists for I-O psychology. The general public does not know the difference between someone who is an I-O psychologist and a business consultant, which is a generic term that could be used by anyone with any level of training. These individuals may be promoting questionable "pop" management fads that will ultimately do more harm than good and foster distrust of business consultants—I-O psychologists or otherwise.

We see two major benefits if there is generally a clear understanding of who we are.

1. *Who ya gonna call?* The higher-ups in a company with a human resources problem will know who to contact. Why is this important? Consider this analogy. If you had a leaky pipe in your basement and you had never heard of a plumber you might end up calling an electrician or a general contractor. This worker, after seeing your problem, may steer you to a good plumber or maybe not. Perhaps instead they will fix the problem themselves (it's all billable hours after all!). The electrician may wire the lights so you can no longer see the problem. The general contractor may develop an excellent drainage system so the leaking water is transported away. The true problem, however, was not fixed. The higher-ups in a company with a

human resource problem may contact a business consultant who turns out to have a great deal of expertise in financial matters and approaches the problem from this angle. The problem does not get fixed, but becomes harder to see or is moved to another location.

2. *Who ya gonna believe?* If the higher-ups in a company do get someone that specializes in human resource matters, did they get someone with good credentials? We believe that if the business community knows what an I-O psychologist does and knows who they are professionally, then they might increase the utilization of I-O psychologists over generic consultants, reducing the number of workers that have to go through scream therapy with their boss, running around naked in the woods or a seminar on KABLOOY: How to Defuse Your Employees. In addition, the long suffering employee may be more likely to accept the intervention, training or advice put forward by the I-O psychologist if they know more about our credentials.

So how well known are we, anyway? Although the lack of recognition received by I-O psychology has been noted as a problem, we are not aware of any previous surveys that have looked at this subject. Therefore, no baseline information is available to answer the question, "How well are we known?" The purpose of this survey is to ask members of the general community, undergraduate students in the college of business and other psychologists if they have ever heard of I-O psychology or some related titles. In addition, for the participants who answered that they had indeed heard of a particular title, we asked them to provide a self-report estimate of their confidence that they could accurately describe what someone in that profession does.

Method
Participants
Three groups of participants were interviewed over the phone by undergraduate research assistants during the spring semester of 1997. For the sample representing the general community, 259 individuals were randomly selected from the phonebook for Cedar Falls/Waterloo, which has a combined metropolitan area of approximately 100,000 individuals and is located in Iowa. Of the 259 individuals called, 91 were contacted and provided a complete data set. For the business college sample, 380 students in the College of Business at a mid-sized university in Iowa were selected at random from university records. Of the 380 individuals called, 91 were contacted and provided a complete data set. For the sample of psychologists, 324 were randomly selected from the 1996–1997 membership directory of the American Psychological Society. Individuals that were listed as I-O psychologists were not included in the sample. Of the 324 called, 87 were contacted and provided a complete data set.

The average age of the general community sample was 47.89 with a standard deviation of 18.53. The age of the youngest individual contacted was 18 and the age of the oldest individual contacted was 87. For the business college sample, the average age was 20.66 with a standard deviation of 2.39. The age of the youngest business students ranged from 18 to 31. The average age of the sample of psychologists was 49.05 with a standard deviation of 11.80. The psychologists in this sample ranged in age from 30 to 80.

For the general community sample, 37.4% were male and 96.7% reported they were Caucasian. For the business college sample, 52.7% were male and 98.9% reported they were Caucasian. For the sample of psychologists, 63.2% were male and 94.3% reported they were Caucasian.

Survey
Each participant was contacted by telephone and asked to participate in a survey being conducted as part of a research project. Those who agreed to participate were first asked if they had ever heard of each of the following eight professional titles: I-O Psychologist, Industrial Psychologist, Organizational Psychologist, Personnel Psychologist, Consumer Psychologist, Human Factors Psychologist, Human Resource Director and Personnel Director. Participants answered yes or no to each of these questions. Participants that indicated they had previously heard of one of the professional titles were immediately asked how confident they were that they could correctly describe the work someone in that profession does. Participants answered by providing a confidence estimate from 0 "no confidence" to 10 "total confidence." Note that we did not assess actual knowledge of the profession, but only a subjective impression of knowing about the profession.

Results
The results of the initial question that asked if the participant had ever heard of each profession for each sample are presented in Table 1. The results of the follow-up question for each professional title are presented in Table 2. Only those respondents that indicated they had heard of a given professional title were asked to indicate their confidence in explaining the work done in that profession; therefore, the sample sizes will vary for each question.

Conclusions
The results of this survey indicate that not very many people in the general public have ever heard of an I-O psychologist or any of the related professional titles. I-O Psychologist is certainly less than a household name. This is especially noticeable when comparing the various psychological professions to generic terms such as Human Resource Director and Personnel Director. None of the psychological professional titles were recognized by more than 36% of the participants, yet Human Resource Director was recognized by nearly 77% of the respondents and Personnel Director was recognized by 93.4% of the respondents. Furthermore, for those few that did report they recognized one of the psychological professional titles, their confidence ratings that they could accurately describe the work done in that profession were very low. The mean scores for each of the psychological professions, except Consumer Psychologist, were below 4.00.

Table 1 The Percentage of Each Sample That Indicated They Had Heard of Each Given Profession

	Sample		
	General	Business Majors	Psychologists
I-O Psychologist	13.2	06.6	96.6
Industrial Psychologist	35.2	17.6	70.1
Organizational Psychologist	12.1	30.8	73.6
Personnel Psychologist	26.4	35.2	85.1
Consumer Psychologist	28.6	31.9	86.2
Human Factors Psychologist	02.2	06.6	96.6
Human Resource Director	76.9	83.5	92.0
Personnel Director	93.4	91.2	97.7

Table 2 The Mean Confidence Report for the Follow-up Question for Each Professional Title

	Sample					
	General		Business Majors		Psychologists	
	Mean	N	Mean	N	Mean	N
I/O Psychologist	3.33(2.27)	12	6.83(1.72)	6	5.94(2.20)	84
Industrial Psychologist	3.94(2.37)	32	3.25(2.93)	16	5.77(2.02)	61
Organizational Psychologist	2.82(1.78)	11	3.75(2.60)	28	6.03(2.14)	64
Personnel Psychologist	3.67(2.26)	24	3.78(2.46)	32	6.07(1.90)	74
Consumer Psychologist	4.73(1.85)	26	3.66(2.40)	29	5.39(1.99)	75
Human Factors Psychologist	0.00(0.00)	2	3.83(1.94)	6	7.08(1.85)	84
Human Resource Director	4.90(3.23)	70	5.01(2.71)	76	4.48(2.23)	80
Personnel Director	6.53(2.63)	85	5.49(2.78)	83	6.25(2.00)	85

Note: Standard Deviation is given in parentheses following the mean. N = the number of individuals that answered this question for each professional title.

Even more unfortunate for the development of our profession, not many business majors report they have ever heard of an I-O psychologist or any of the related professional titles. Again, none of the psychological professional titles were recognized by more than 36% of the participants, yet Human Resource Director was recognized by over 83% of the participants and Personnel Director was recognized by 91.2% of the participants. Also as occurred in the general sample, of the few that did recognize a psychological profession, their confidence ratings for being able to accurately describe the work done in that profession were very low. The mean scores for each of the psychological professions, except I-O psychologist (which was only recognized by 6 business majors), were below 4.00.

Fortunately, we are recognized by our colleagues in other areas of psychology. The percentage of psychologists in professions other than I-O psychology that had heard of the title I-O Psychologist was an encouraging 96.6%. Furthermore, all of the psychological professions were recognized by at least 70% of the respondents. Human Resource Director was recognized by 92% of the respondents and Personnel Director was recognized by 97.7% of the respondents. Although these results are encouraging, the results of the follow-up question show there is still room for improvement. How confident are you that you could explain what a clinical psychologist does? Probably pretty confident. How confident are other psychologists that they could describe what we do? The mean confidence rating for I-O psychologist was 5.94. Although this is higher than for either the general sample or the business majors, it still represents a moderate level of confidence. An investigation of the frequency distribution of responses for the follow-up question for I-O psychologist indicates that more than 50% of the respondents had confidence levels at or below 6.00 and 25% had confidence levels at or below 4.00. Overall, most of the professional titles received moderate average confidence ratings that were between 5.00 and 6.50.

What to Do

The results of this survey indicate that I-O psychology is not well known in both a sample of the general public and, more importantly for the development of our profession, in a sample of business majors. Furthermore, although there was good general recognition of our profession amongst our colleagues in psychology, there was only a moderate level of confidence that an accurate description of the work we do could be given. Each of these points represents a lack of understanding and recognition of I-O psychology that is detrimental to the development, acceptance and general use of what I-O psychology has to offer. Finally, to improve the level of understanding and recognition of our profession in each of these populations we make the following suggestions.

1. It might be helpful if we collectively picked one name to call ourselves, especially when dealing with the public. Although amongst other psychologists the name I-O Psychologist seems to be recognized, amongst business majors (arguably the future greatest consumers of our services) this title was tied for least-known with Human Factors Psychologist. Business majors recognized the titles

Organizational Psychologist and Personnel Psychologist at much higher levels. Both of these titles include key words that are often found in courses taken by business majors and both of these titles are certainly more succinct than the cumbersome I-O Psychologist. Regardless of the title chosen, using one title allows a simpler message to be conveyed.

2. I-O psychologists (or whatever you call yourself) should make an effort to give guest lectures in the business or management courses of high schools, local colleges, local trade schools, community colleges and chamber of commerce meetings. Be sure to point out the training and credentials of I-O psychologists, as opposed to generic titles such as business consultants or personnel directors. This is a service that is probably not done often enough by I-O types although this is an excellent way to sell the profession (and yourself) to the local business community. We are unaware of any surveys looking at the frequency with which this type of grassroots promotion is done by SIOP members. This would be a valuable piece of information to ascertain in the future.

3. For those of us in academics, or anyone who must deal with other types of psychologists on a regular basis, talk to your colleagues. Tell them who we are and what we do. Be sure to explain the types of research we engage in and the potential for fundamental benefits to individuals and society at large (rather than just the bottom line of a corporation).

References

Farr, J. L. (1997). Organized I-O Psychology: Past, Present, Future. *The Industrial-Organizational Psychologist, 35,* 13–28.

May, K. E. (1995). TIP Profiles: Walter Borman. *The Industrial-Organizational Psychologist, 32,* 52–55.

Article Review Form at end of book.

WiseGuide Wrap-Up

The six readings in this section provide a general overview of the field of industrial/organizational psychology. From a snapshot of our history to a glimpse of our future, it is clear that industrial/organizational psychologists are playing an important role in the development of organizations and in the lives of workers. From these readings, we get a sense of the diversity within the field. We also are presented with the unifying theme of scientific inquiry that ties all industrial/organizational practitioners and researchers together.

R.E.A.L. Sites

This list provides a print preview of typical **Coursewise** R.E.A.L. sites. (There are over 100 such sites at the **Courselinks**™ site.) The danger in printing URLs is that web sites can change overnight. As we went to press, these sites were functional using the URLs provided. If you come across one that isn't, please let us know via email to: webmaster@coursewise.com. Use our Passport to access the most current list of R.E.A.L. sites at the **Courselinks** site.

Site name: Society of Industrial and Organizational Psychology
URL: http://www.siop.org/
Why is it R.E.A.L.? This is the home page for the Society of Industrial/Organizational Psychology and contains information about the field in general, graduate training, and job opportunities.
Key topics: professional organizations, careers, graduate training
Try this: What is the average income for I/O psychologists? Click on the SIOP logo on the left of the screen. Then go to the salary survey. Where are the graduate programs in I/O psychology? Click on the 1998 Graduate Training Programs in industrial and organizational psychology and related fields selection and find alphabetical lists of Doctoral and Masters' programs in the United States.

Site name: Academy of Human Resource Development
URL: http://www.ahrd.org/
Why is it R.E.A.L.? This site provides information about human resource development careers, internships, and academic programs.
Key topics: professional organizations, careers, graduate training, training, employee development
Try this: What do human resource development (HRD) professionals do? Click on Plan a HRD Career and find some general information about the field of HRD. How do you find a graduate program in HRD? Click on HRD Academic Programs in Universities and find a list of colleges and universities offering HRD programs.

Site name: Society for Human Resource Management
URL: http://www.shrm.org/
Why is it R.E.A.L.? This is the home page for the Society for Human Resource Management and provides information about the field in general.
Key topics: professional organizations, careers, graduate training, human resources
Try this: Where are the job openings in human resource management? Click on HR Job Openings and search by geographic location.

section 2

Perspectives on Work

Learning Objectives

- To describe the changes both workers and workplaces are facing today.
- To debate the issues concerning worker/workplace rights and responsibilities.
- To discuss the dynamics of work/family life tension.

WiseGuide Intro

The nature of work has changed dramatically over the past few years. As noted in the previous section, jobs are no longer seen as simply a bundle of tasks—they are more dynamic and varied. Organizations have changed their basic organizational structures by becoming flatter as they have eliminated or changed midlevel management jobs. These changes increase the responsibility of "front-line" workers by including decision-making functions in their jobs. In addition, fewer organizations are providing lifetime employment, thus, workers are changing jobs more frequently, either by choice or by organizational realignments (downsizing, rightsizing, reengineering, or whatever the current term happens to be). As a consequence, for social and economic reasons, workers' expectations have changed in the workplace. We are also seeing more dual-income families placing unique demands on the organization, including childcare and eldercare. We are attending more to gender and racial equality issues. Thus, organizations and individuals are trying to find the optimal balance between the demands of the workplace and family issues, and these constantly evolving forces change the organizations themselves and how we view our work.

In this section, we will examine several current views on how workers and workplaces are responding to the social, political, and economic forces previously noted. We begin by examining Ellig's paper describing the new social contract between employees and employers. He describes the rights and responsibilities of these two groups and offers suggestions on balancing their unique needs and desires. He concludes by arguing that human resource professionals (as noted in the first section, human resource work is directly related to industrial/organizational psychology) are in a unique position to be both an advocate for the employee and a partner with the employer.

In Reading 8, we see that Tucker views work as a moral obligation. He believes that this obligations underlies the essence of a free-market economy. By linking these ideas to both Christian and capitalistic principles, he argues that there are virtues associated with maintaining a proper work ethic. Powell, in Reading 9, takes a different view by suggesting that organizations can become abusive. Powell's paper begins with a case study he describes as a horror story. I imagine Tucker would not view this case as a horror story but one in which the employee freely chose to remain with this organization, despite the demands placed on her.

Reading 10 addresses a related issue—balancing work and family demands. As author Martinez notes, many organizations are currently addressing this issue by developing programs to attract and keep qualified employees. Several magazines (including *Working Mother*, *Business Week*, and *Fortune*) now rate companies on their "family friendly" programs.

Another issue debated in-depth over the past few years involves downsizing. Do corporations have a responsibility to keep individuals employed? It is important to note that often the corporations that downsize are profitable but, by restructuring, they can gain more of a competitive advantage in an increasingly global economy. In Reading 11, Jacoby presents a brief history of welfare capitalism (corporate responsibility to employees) in the United States and describes the current situation.

In Reading 12, the concluding article in this section, discusses the nationally mandated reduction in the work week in France and Italy to thirty-five hours. Although Gumbel does not view this idea with a great deal of favor, it does illustrate the international scope of this topic. Returning to the general theme of this section, how do we balance the rights and responsibilities of employees and employers? Should the government regulate these relationships?

Industrial/organizational psychologists need to understand these debates, because organizations are often turning to them to help resolve workplace dilemmas. As we will see in future sections, these debates will resurface in the areas of selection and recruitment, motivation, leadership, health, and international perspectives.

Questions

Reading 7. According to Ellig, why are workers feeling increasingly disenfranchised, and what can organizations do to address this issue?

Reading 8. Why does Tucker link work to a "moral" topic? Why does he tie this moral obligation to the basis of the free-market system?

Reading 9. What evidence does Powell offer to suggest that workplaces are becoming abusive?

Reading 10. What are some things organizations can do to become more family friendly, and why should organizations want to do these things?

Reading 11. Describe welfare capitalism.

Reading 12. What are some of the costs and benefits of having a federally imposed thirty-five-hour work week?

According to Ellig, why are workers feeling increasingly disenfranchised, and what can organizations do to address this issue?

Employment and Employability:

Foundation of the New Social Contract

Bruce R. Ellig

Bruce R. Ellig graduated Phi Beta Kappa with a B.B.A. and M.B.A. from the University of Wisconsin. Before his retirement he served as Corporate Vice President in charge of worldwide HR for Pfizer.

Introduction

An organization's workforce is its competitive advantage, yet many workers feel disenfranchised, frustrated, and in some cases angry. Lost is the belief that if you work hard, you'll be all right. One no longer has control over one's destiny—if one ever did. Pay for most has not improved (in terms of inflation-adjusted), and in many cases the job itself has disappeared. Since companies are showing no loyalty to their workers, why should the workers show loyalty to the companies?

What are employees—assets or expenses? Companies espouse that employees are their most valuable assets; but rather than develop and nurture these "investments," many companies treat their employees as expenses, quickly reducing head count wherever possible. Simultaneously companies are also hiring but for different skills. This logically raises the question "Why aren't companies doing more training?"

What's the problem? Unfortunately, there is a major gap in mindsets between many employers and their employees. The latter are still grounded in thinking of entitlements while employers have shifted to "opportunities" as the operative word. The former is defined in terms of lifetime employment, good benefits, and advancement by seniority. The latter is represented by training and development programs, pay for performance, and advancement of the most qualified.

One of the greatest injustices done both to the organization and its employees is to tolerate mediocre performance. When "one of the best" brought into the organization turns out to be a mediocre performer, this should be addressed immediately. The person should be counseled, expectations clearly defined, and remedial programs made available. If the person cannot meet the expectations, the individual should be offered an available position for which s/he is qualified. Lacking a suitable position, the person should be graciously and generously exited from the organization. One can afford to be generous as the alternative would be future years still on the payroll.

Such actions mean that mediocre performers do not remain

What are employees—assets or expenses?

in the organization for more than a year or two. Keeping such individuals is inconsistent with an organization's objective of continuous improvement. Furthermore, the mediocre performer is not done any favors by looking past his/her shortcomings. When restructuring is necessary, these "mediocre performer" individuals typically are the ones whose jobs are in jeopardy and who wants to accept the transfer in of a mediocre performer when looking to staff with the best? If only top performers are in the organization, one can always find a place for them. If not, they will be successful elsewhere because they are better than most others in any company.

Respective Wants

To sort this out it is helpful to identify what employers and employees each seek and what each can provide.

What do employees want? They seek job security, interesting work, recognition of results, fair treatment, and work life balance. How many of these can they attain themselves? None of them! Only the employer can provide them—namely, training and development, intrinsic and extrinsic pay, discrimination only on performance, and work/life solutions.

"Employment and Employability: Foundation of the New Social Contract," by Bruce R. Ellig, *Human Resource Management,* Summer 1998, Vol. 37, No. 2, pp. 173–175. Copyright © 1998 by John Wiley & Sons, Inc. Reprinted by permission of John Wiley & Sons, Inc.

What do employers want? Financial success or in a word, "productivity." And although they can invest in the hardware and equipment, they cannot achieve production without the employee.

So what is the result? Mutual dependency! Perhaps a new employment contract or if that is too strong a phrase, a mutual recognition of respective obligations. If either fails to meet its commitment, employment ceases.

Respective Obligations

The employer's commitment to its employees should include the following principles:

- Define challenging but achievable performance objectives and provide reward and recognition that acknowledge the importance of each employee's contribution.

- Encourage initiative and innovation on the part of individuals and work groups: create a work environment in which employees function as a team and assume responsibility for identifying opportunities and solving problems.

- Provide challenging opportunities for individual growth and advancement while ensuring that employment and advancement are based on performance.

- Ensure an ample flow of information and open communication throughout the organization in order to build trust, enhance understanding, and provide for resolution of problems or complaints.

- Provide a work environment that respects the employee as an individual, is sensitive to the needs of employees, and strives to protect employee health and safety.

- Exercise initiative in working with employees in situations when business conditions require expansion and/or contraction of the work force, recognizing the company's responsibility to comply with laws affecting employee relations in each country in which it operates.

In return, the organization's expectations from its employees should include the following:

- Readiness to recognize and adapt to continuous change.

- Commitment to continued work-related learning and mastering new skills needed to meet changing work requirements.

- Continuous improvement in every area of responsibility with an emphasis on working more productively.

- Participation and involvement with others in helping the organization achieve its best.

- Maintaining superior performance and full accountability.

- Strict adherence to workplace safety and environmental health standards.

- Lawful and ethical behavior in every business activity.

Emergence of Employee Resources

Within this setting the roles for Personnel (employee advocate) and Human Re-sources (business partner) have never been greater. The combination of these two responsibilities and the shedding of low-value administrative tasks suggests a new description, "Employee Re-sources." It is a little warmer while still conveying the strategic nature of the function.

The *employee advocate* is focused on values—what one believes is right. The *business partner* deals with goals and objectives needed to be successful. Goals and objectives change with the competitive scene; values do not change. What has an organization achieved if it has attained its goals and objectives but forsaken its values? Is it likely to continue to be successful? Probably not. Its "assets," the employees, are unlikely to have attained their potential, and the company will have lost its real competitive advantage. There is frequent talk of company culture, and many ask how to define it. It is not that difficult: It is the values and beliefs that the company enforces.

If the employer seeks to be the most productive organization within its peer group, it will also have to be the employer of choice enabling it to attract, retain, and motivate the best workers. For many this will mean developing lateral organizations focused on teams that result in the synergy coming from individual contributors. But can one expect teams to recruit, select, train, and reward team members without the appropriate employee resource skills? Obviously not. This is one of the challenges facing the Employee Resource professional.

To meet the challenges, every Employee Resource professional must not only acquire the necessary skills to be both an employee advocate and a business partner, but must then aid managers in the acquisition of these skills, giving them the necessary knowledge to coach and counsel their employees—but it does not end there. The Employee Resource professional must assist the manager in the transfer of the skills to the employees, enabling them to optimize their efforts in teams.

Achieving the vision of most productive organization within one's peer group will also be virtually impossible if employees do not have a shared mindset about organizational values and objectives. In other words, employees not only need the above identified skills, they too must become business partners. If they are not, they will not be focused on outcomes that will help the company achieve its objectives. Shared values are embodied in a corporate culture—for example, how employees should treat each other and provide customer services. Too many companies have found zealous employees who achieved their

> **Within this setting the roles for Personnel (employee advocate) and Human Resources (business partner) have never been greater.**

> **The Employee Resource function is to be the guardian of the company culture, ensuring that it is understood by all and inculcated into the way employees do business.**

objectives in an inappropriate, if not outright illegal manner. Here, too, Employee Re-sources functions in an educational role, teaching and counseling to get "things" back on track. The Employee Resource function is to be the guardian of the company culture, ensuring that it is understood by all and inculcated into the way employees do business.

Some still have difficulty describing company culture; it is not that difficult. It is the values that the company enforces—rewards for accomplishing and penalties for not succeeding.

Conclusion

Some will argue for a return to the old days of lifetime employment. Some want companies to take care of them: others want the freedom of mobility. Given these differences of views, it is hard to argue against a position that says individuals have a responsibility to be the best they can be to improve their employability, and employers have a responsibility to ensure they are getting the best results from each employee before terminating them. This means that the employer has an obligation to coach and counsel as well as to provide appropriate training programs. Career resource centers can be very effective in assisting employees to determine what type of jobs to pursue. Training programs provide the opportunity to improve existing skills and/or acquire new ones. It is the employer's responsibility to make such opportunities available; it is the employee's responsibility to take advantage of them.

This is the new employment/employability model—one that provides a win/win scenario.

Article Review Form at end of book.

Why does Tucker link work to a "moral" topic? Why does he tie this moral obligation to the basis of the free-market system?

The Moral Obligations of Workers

Jeffrey Tucker

Mr. Tucker is director of research at the Ludwig von Mises Institute, Auburn, Alabama.

You hate your boss. Your hours are bad. Your salary is too low, and you haven't been promoted in years. What's a worker to do? If you can't get your way, and just can't take it anymore, you can quit. In a free market for labor, your skills will be better appreciated elsewhere. You gain satisfaction from making this decision on your own. In a free society, no worker is forced to be trapped in a job when there is another that appears more inviting. It's one of the glorious rights a free society offers its members, one that has been unknown to most people during most of human history.

But what happens if you stick around the workplace? What if you choose to continue in your present position on grounds that it's probably the best you can do for yourself right now? The answers to these questions have changed dramatically in the last several decades. There was a time when workers understood their moral obligations to themselves and to the person who signed their checks. It was to fulfill the terms of the contract, and do the best job possible. A productive life requires virtuous work habits and adherence to basic ethical norms; besides, a slothful worker is justly fired at any time.

The right to quit and the right to fire are two sides of the same coin. The boss can't force the worker to stay, and the worker can't force the boss to keep him employed. The beauty is that it depends on voluntarism. No matter how many grievances they may have against each other, if boss and worker choose to continue the economic exchange, they do so by their own free wills. We can assume, in a free market, that all employment contracts work to the mutual advantage of both parties.

Nowadays, the moral code requiring a worker to give a day's work for a day's pay has nearly been shredded. Workers think less and less of production and honest dealing and more and more of rights, protests, strikes, and lawsuits. The best-selling cartoon book of 1996 (featuring the character "Dilbert") is devoted to attacking employers and presenting worklife as a huge ripoff, which is a fundamentally anti-capitalist message. To be sure, this change of attitude toward work began long before the advent of laws allowing employees to sue companies, even bankrupt them, for the slightest grievance. The go-slow, strike-threat strategies of labor unions chipped away at the moral code of workers decades ago.

A union member in the 1950s musical *Pajama Game* sardonically promised his boss "a day's work, for a week's pay." But back then, he could only get it through extreme measures. In the normal course of the workday, only the powerless "grievance committee" lent an ear to the perpetual complainer. Even in this pro-union musical, the fundamental right of the management to hire and fire as it sees fit—and the obligation of workers to do their very best in normal times—was never seriously questioned.

Job Conflict

These are far from normal times. Trouble-makers in the workforce have an exalted status, as well as the legal right to grab whatever they can get from their employers. For those reasons, many employers now fear their employees, and even potential employees in the interview stage of hiring. Anti-discrimination law puts the boss in a double bind. If he hires based only on merit, or on a hunch that the person is a good team player, he must also think of all the people passed by for a job. Are they going to claim to be members of some federally protected victim group (the list of which gets longer every year) and thereby sue on grounds of discrimination? The courts have upheld the rights, for example, of alcohol abusers and convicted felons to have the same "right" to be hired for a job as everyone else.

In practice, this means employers must pad their staffs with officially recognized victims if only to protect themselves from government investigation and class-action lawsuits. This reality has shifted the balance of power in the workplace. Workers no longer view their first obligation as to do their best work for the sake of themselves and the company. Instead, they know that they are potential lawsuit plaintiffs, and hold it over the management and the owners for every slight. A complaining employee can demand pay increases and promotions through a subtle form of legal blackmail, a tactic familiar to most anyone who works in a medium- or large-size

"The Moral Obligations of Workers," by Jeffrey Tucker, *The Freeman*, May 1997, pp. 270–275. Copyright © 1997. Reprinted by permission.

company. Employers now fear using strict standards of merit for promotions and perks. Such evaluations might result in a distribution of wages and salaries that is unequal among the demographic groups represented in the workforce, and therefore draw the attention of government officials or class-action lawyers.

Yet even this type of political padding doesn't always work. Texaco worked for years to keep all types of people represented at all levels of its operations. The company bent over backwards to institute its own private quota system of hiring, if only to keep protesters and trial lawyers at bay. It gave out franchises based on the race of the applicant, and allowed more lenient application standards for groups said to be "underprivileged." Yet when one employee's gripe mushroomed into a class-action lawsuit involving hundreds of workers, Texaco ended up having its good name dragged through the mud, and shelled out $176 million to lawyers and complaining employees, without ever having entered the courtroom.

The sad tale began with an accountant at the company's Denver office who filed an internal complaint of racial discrimination, a powerful weapon in today's workforce. Fearing escalation, supervisors even higher up the management chain did everything possible to make her happy, moving her to a new division with plusher working conditions and assuring her that her job would be secure. It wasn't enough. When a few hotshot lawyers heard of the situation, it was only a matter of time before it became a general lawsuit involving 1,500 people, most of whom had no particular complaints at all! None of this means that the company was necessarily treating anyone poorly on grounds of race. It only means that the money was there for the taking, so who's to say someone shouldn't take it?

Take This Job . . .

In the traditional moral code of work that arose in a free market, the situation would have been handled very differently. If the accountant didn't like her job, she would have quit and gone to work for someone who appreciated her more. If she began to complain too loudly of her plight, undercutting the morale of other employees and creating a hostile work environment, she would have been fired. If she was at fault, she would have learned a valuable lesson in workplace ethics and human relations. If the company was at fault, it would have lost a valuable employee and would learn not to act so hastily next time.

This system of mutual rights creates peaceful cooperation between the employee and the employer. Each understands the obligations he has to the other. The goal, as with any economic exchange, is to better the lot of everyone involved. Contrary to the old Marxian claim that an inherent conflict exists between labor and capital, a free market makes it possible for them to exchange in a mutually advantageous and profitable manner.

The Joys of Work

Ludwig von Mises argues that such a voluntary relationship takes the drudgery (or the "disutility") out of work and can turn it into a genuine joy. The worker can delight that he is achieving personal goals, whether material or spiritual. He gains "self-respect and the consciousness of supporting himself and his family and not being dependent on other people's mercy. In the pursuit of his work the worker enjoys the esthetic appreciation of his skill and its product. This is not merely the contemplative pleasure of the man who views things performed by other people. It is the pride of a man who is in the position to say: `I know how to make such things, this is my work.' "[1] Moreover, "To be joyful in the performance of one's tasks and in overcoming the disutility of labor makes people cheerful and strengthens their energies and vital forces."[2]

It is only legal interventions that tip the balance in favor of either the capitalist or the employee. There can be no doubt that the employee has the upper hand today, much to the detriment of his own ethical well-being. By suing and blackmailing his employers, creating hostile work environments, and threatening to call the government in, the employee is implicitly threatening to take property that is not his to take. That situation is bad for the company, for society at large, and even for the employee in the long run. It is contrary to a market-based work ethic, which is about more than merely working long and hard, but fulfilling the terms of your contract by striving toward excellence in the service of the business's institutional goals.

As Mises points out, when the worker views himself as a "defenseless victim of an absurd and unjust system," he becomes an "ill-humored grumbler, an unbalanced personality, an easy prey to all sorts of quacks and cranks," and even "morose and neurotic." In what appears to be a description of modern-day America, Mises wrote that "A commonwealth in which the tedium of labor prevails is an assemblage of rancorous, quarrelsome and wrathful malcontents."[3]

The Ethics of Work

There is both an economic and moral dimension to the work ethic. The economic side is dictated by the realities of property and contract relations. The employee is not the owner; capitalists and stockholders are. The worker has been hired by these owners to perform a certain function for the good, meaning the profitability, of the company. He is free to choose not to do so, but then he is obligated to do at least what he has agreed to do and then leave the company.

There is a respect in which the employer is an economic benefactor to employees. The capitalist pays out wages to employees before he sees the profits of their current production. He is undertaking a risk in an uncertain economic environment that the employee, the immediate recipient of wages, is not being asked to bear. Moreover, the capitalist cannot merely pay the wage he can afford; he is constantly in a position of having to keep his employees from being bid away by competitive enterprises, even those that take fewer risks in the market.

To accept an employment contract means to agree to provide a certain amount of labor in return for a defined amount of money. To not perform that contract is to violate the terms of the contract and to fail to respect the unique entrepreneurial role of the capitalist. It is also the moral equivalent of stealing property from the capitalist who has employed him.

A system that gives this person legal recourse to turn against his employer-benefactor and loot even more property in a bitter personality struggle is not a system that respects property rights.

On the moral side, we can turn to the brilliant and beautiful writings of Stefan Wyszynski (1901–1981), whom former Polish president Lech Walesa has called "the spiritual leader of Poland." As the teacher of John Paul II, Cardinal Wyszynski was arguably the key intellectual and religious force behind the eventual overthrow of the communist regime, though he did not live to see it. Imprisoned for three years by a totalitarian regime that labeled him one of the "greatest foes of the Polish People's Republic," Wyszynski spent many years reflecting on the nature and morality of work in free and unfree societies. In 1946 he published a full-blown philosophical elucidation of the moral obligations of workers.[4] As a treatise on everyday morality, its power may be unsurpassed.

His views on work were developed in opposition to the pagan view of work, which was to despise labor itself. Pagans "regarded physical work as unworthy of man," Wyszynski writes. "It was the duty of slaves. It could not be reconciled with the sublimity of the free mind, for it limited it too much, and made it dependent both on itself and on others."[5] But the coming of Christianity corrected this error, elevating work to participation in the creative work of God. In this, the Christian view follows the example of Jesus Christ, who said in the Gospel of John, "my Father has never ceased working, and I, too must be at work."

The Christian or Western view of work emphasizes the importance of uniting spiritual and physical work. In early monastic life, sublime contemplation and hard physical labor went hand in hand, and were seen as complementary to the achievement of the sanctity of the individual soul. As the Psalmist says, "For thou shalt eat the labors of thy hands, blessed art thou, and it shall be well with thee."

Putting Talent to Use

Every person has been given gifts that allow for productivity, and they are intended to be used in the service of God and of others. Therefore, man cannot be destined for only prayer or work. Work helps us to become holy, and holiness allows for the inner harmony necessary for productive work. St. John's Gospel uses both images in a passage on salvation: "the wages paid to him who reaps this harvest, the crop he gathers in, is eternal life, in which sower and reaper are to rejoice together." This monastic attitude toward labor spread throughout society as the faith itself did, eventually supplanting both the pagan view that work is only for slaves, and even slavery itself.

As Wyszynski writes of the Christian ideal, "work is the duty of man. This duty arises from the very needs of man's life, as well as from the meaning that work holds for his perfection. Without work it is not possible either to sustain life or to reach the full development of one's personality. Work is the means of God's gift, life, in us, of properly satisfying its needs, and perfecting our rational nature."

Leisure is not the state of nature. Even before the fall, Wyszynski emphasizes in opposition to the pagan view, it was necessary to work. Work is not punishment for sin; it is "closely related to the rational nature of man."[6] In the Genesis narrative, God's commandment to Adam to subdue and rule the earth preceded the first sin and God's judgment. It is only the *burden* of work that is a consequence of sin. "By the sweat of thy brow shalt thou eat bread." This burden should be borne joyously as part of our desire to improve ourselves and our relationship with God.

The implications seen by Wyszynski deserve to be quoted at length. "It is the working man himself who most benefits from work understood in this way. This is not because he gets his wages for his work, but because his work, which is bound inseparably with his person, shapes and develops his mind, will, feelings, and various moral virtues and characteristics, as well as his physical and spiritual skills. . . . Work, based on our reason and freedom, should develop our conscientiousness, our sense of duty, and our responsibility. Only then will it be the work of a rational being. Work, understood in this sense, immediately reveals to us two aims that every man ought to achieve in his personal work: the perfecting of things and the perfecting of the working man. This is the starting point for social-economic progress, for human civilization, for moral religious progress, and indeed for the culture of the world."[7]

Real Social Work

There are many social virtues associated with work. Work creates bonds between people, since it requires that we peacefully associate with others. It calls forth both cooperative behavior and the constant personal improvement needed to compete with our fellows. It makes it possible for families to form and thrive. It allows us to be generous with those who are unable to work for reasons not of their own choosing. Work even generates universal good in that we are participating in the international division of labor and acquire the knowledge of what it requires the world over to bring about a prosperous social order.

Of course, none of this is possible in a collectivist setting, where worker and employer are not free to contract with each other. The institutional setting required to ennoble work is one of markets, competition, and, above all, private property, which Wyszynski calls "the leading principle of a well-regulated society."[8] The true glory of private property is not that it allows personal accumulation. Rather, it allows us to employ others and to be employed in enterprise, with justly given and received wages, and thereby spreads prosperity to more and more members of society in service of the common good.

The Six Virtues of Labor

In addition to the social virtue of work, there are also individual virtues associated with keeping our moral obligations to those who employ us. Quality work requires and encourages them, even as a free market in labor rewards them. Wyszynski lists and discusses these virtues, in this order:

1. *Patience.* The task of patience is to control excessive and undisciplined sadness, and the tendency to complain and strike

out when things do not go our way. We are usually more convinced of our own value to a company than are those who employ us, so it requires patience to put aside resentment and discouragement when we do not get the recognition we think we deserve. Those who do not succeed at this task are "full of complaints, grievances, and lamentations arising out of their state of sadness."[9]

2. *Longanimity.* This is the virtue of forbearance or long-suffering, "a spirit of lasting endeavor in the pursuit of a distant good," writes Wyszynski.[10] Every employer knows the types of workers who "watch the clock" from the beginning to the end of their shifts, who live for the weekend and for vacations, and can't see their way to the end of a major project. They do hasty, shoddy work because they lack longanimity, lost creativity and hope, do not improve as workers, and eventually break their moral obligations to those who employ them.

3. *Perseverance.* This means a "prudent, constant, and continual persistence in a rationally taken decision to strive toward some desired good."[11] Above all, this means the avoidance of emotional outbursts and wild shifts in mood that might cause us to hate our co-workers or employers, and pursue actions that are designed to cause them damage. For example, if a person who is pursuing a discrimination lawsuit against an employer were thinking clearly, he would realize there is much more to be gained over the long haul by perfecting skills, being rational, and working one's way up. Perseverance engenders others to trust us.

4. *Constancy.* This virtue allows us to pursue our goals no matter what obstacles may arise from external causes. Perhaps a worker has an employer who treats people unfairly. Perhaps a person is unjustly passed over for a promotion or a raise. Perhaps he is fired without seeming cause. Constancy allows a person to look past these slights to larger personal goals and do what is necessary to attain them. "Armed with constancy," writes Wyszynski, "we calmly await even the most unpleasant surprises."[12]

5. *Mildness.* This virtue is necessary to maintain concentration in a disorderly setting. "Silence and quietness are the essential conditions for fruitfulness in every type of work," says Wyszynski, "whether we are dealing with supernatural action, the world of science, or just ordinary daily work."[13] Every employer knows of workers who spend more time talking than producing, and generate more noise than thought. But to do truly good work, for the sake of our employers and ourselves, requires that we filter out "superfluous sensations"[14] and exercise control over our mental faculties.

6. *Conscientiousness.* This is the spirit of cooperation that makes the division of labor possible, and turns a workplace into a place of mutual aid. It helps us understand that in any organization, people must take instruction from others. There are structures of authority that must be obeyed. Workers must submit to direction. Wyszynski reminds workers that this is not a power-based relationship but an educational one that aims at perfecting work. To be conscientious is also to be humble, an attitude that drives "out disputes, discord, quarrelsomeness, and division."[15]

What a welcome change that would be in the modern workforce, where everyone seems to be at each other's throats, each demanding his rights or accusing someone of violating his.

If these six virtues are cultivated, writes Wyszynski, then we can enjoy the blessing of leisure and prosperity that follow six days of work, and, he says, fully enjoy the presence of God after a lifetime of toil and struggle, when our sorrow is truly turned to joy.

If these attributes of virtue were once deeply ingrained in our culture, today they seem long gone. We recognize them only when we study the diaries of our great-grandparents, or read older works of pre-New Deal literature, but we don't see these virtues in most co-workers or the high-profile cases of workplace conflict that bombard us every day on the news. These virtues were sustained by a vibrant market economy free of government controls and the conflicts they inevitably engender. It was a system that required personal responsibility, rewarded virtue, and kept the base desire to steal from others at bay.

However, the passing of that system is to excuse for not retaining and obeying the moral obligations inherent in every aspect of work. Virtuous work is the social and cultural foundation of freedom, and we must reclaim the ethics of work if our liberty is to be regained. It will always be true, as Wyszynski says, that "work cannot be carried out with a clenched fist and a shriveled heart."[16] For the "result of all human work should be not merely the perfecting of the thing produced, but also the perfecting of the worker, not merely external order in work, but also inner order in man."[17]

Notes

1. Ludwig von Mises. *Human Action* (Chicago: Regnery [1949] 1963), p. 589.
2. *Ibid.*, p. 591.
3. *Ibid.*, p. 591.
4. Stefan Cardinal Wyszynski. *All You Who Labor* (Sophia Institute Press [1946] 1995).
5. *Ibid.*, p. 21.
6. *Ibid.*, pp. 23–24.
7. *Ibid.*, p. 28.
8. *Ibid.*, p. 42.
9. *Ibid.*, p. 121.
10. *Ibid.*, p. 127.
11. *Ibid.*, p. 137.
12. *Ibid.*, p. 139.
13. *Ibid.*, p. 153.
14. *Ibid.*, p. 155.
15. *Ibid.*, p. 158.
16. *Ibid.*, p. 186.
17. *Ibid.*, p. 151.

Article Review Form at end of book.

What evidence does Powell offer to suggest that workplaces are becoming abusive?

The Abusive Organization

Gary N. Powell

Gary N. Powell is a professor of management at the School of Business Administration, the University of Connecticut.

Ugly things are happening to employees in the business world. Here is an example, as recently related by a student in an evening MBA course that I teach on managing diversity:

A couple of months before, on a Saturday, Jennifer (not her real name) held a fiftieth birthday party for her mother. She worked for several months in arranging the party and in getting her family to agree to the arrangements. She lined up the restaurant at which the party would be held. She arranged the group gifts, prepared for the follow-up party to be held at her house afterwards, the whole works. It was going to be a special day for Jennifer, her mother, and everyone else involved. Early on that Saturday morning, Jennifer received a call from her boss and was told that she had to come to work that day. When she began to describe her plans for the day, she was cut off and told, "The board doesn't want excuses. The board wants work." The fiftieth birthday party was held, but without Jennifer present. She spent the whole Saturday at work. According to Jennifer, it wasn't even an emergency that led her to be called in.

Horror stories like Jennifer's are common these days. It seems that everyone has one to tell or knows someone who has one to tell. Many successful organizations, such as DuPont, GTE, Johnson & Johnson, Merck, Midland Bank (UK), Motorola, and Price Waterhouse have implemented work-family programs that enable workers to have more flexible work schedules or otherwise help them to meet their family-related needs while maintaining high levels of performance.[1] However, Jennifer's story may more accurately describe the typical corporate work-family program as we approach the new millennium. Employees in many organizations are expected to put work first at all times and to have a family life only when granted permission to take time off from work. I regard such organizations as abusive organizations.

The abusive organization operates with callous disregard for its employees, not even displaying what might be considered a minimum amount of concern for their human needs. Abusive organizations have always been with us. However, it seems that their numbers have been increasing lately. How come? Most organizations in the business world are facing increasing pressures from competitors. Downsizing, rightsizing, reengineering, and so on have left many organizations with fewer employees to perform just as much work as before. Even organizations in the public sector are facing increased pressures to cut labor costs to enable tax cuts or to reduce the increase in state or local spending. In fear of further downsizing, the employees who remain in such organizations feel desperate to hold on to their jobs. They are so desperate that they are willing to accept abusive treatment in the short run to increase the chance of holding on to their jobs in the long run. Employers are aware of this. As a result, many of them push their employees, and push them some more, and never stop pushing them to work as long as possible to get as much work done as possible. This has become the price that employees have to pay to keep their jobs these days. And the price is high.

How could Jennifer's employer get away with forcing her to miss her mother's birthday party? When Jennifer was ordered to work that Saturday, she asked herself, "How dependent am I on this job?" The economy has been very slow in the region where Jennifer works, shedding jobs during most of the last decade rather than adding them. As a result, Jennifer saw herself as very dependent on her job. If she had lost it, she most likely would have had to relocate to find a comparable job. In a soft or declining economy, companies are more able to get away with treating their employees in an abusive fashion. If the regional economy had been adding jobs in her field instead, Jennifer might have responded differently and attended her mother's birthday party, even if it meant losing her job, because she would have felt more confident that she could obtain at least a comparable job without

"The board doesn't want excuses. The board wants work."

Reprinted with permission of Academy of Management, PO Box 3020, Briar Cliff Manor, NY 10510–8020. *The Abusive Organization*, Gary N. Powell, Academy of Management Executive 1998, No. 12. Reproduced by permission of the publisher via Copyright Clearance Center, Inc.

relocating. She might have even been able to find employment with an organization that acknowledged that employees have lives outside of work that are important to them.

What can be done about abusive organizations? One can hope for a growing economy that is less of a buyer's market, so that people will be more able to choose their employer rather than have to grab for any job remotely related to their interests and expertise that they can get. In the meantime, other steps might help. For example, someone could start a Business Hall of Shame and nominate employers like Jennifer's for membership. However, the risk is that the nominees might welcome the publicity.

Yes, there are many successful companies with excellent work-family programs. However, there are just as many abusive organizations, perhaps even more. Some abusive organizations even have the gall to brag about their work-family programs, but only pay lip service to the notion and promote such programs just for the public relations value. In my opinion, such organizations deserve to lose business to employers who show greater concern for employees' family lives and are less inclined to make unreasonable demands on a routine basis. Otherwise, things will continue to look grim in many areas of the workplace. We already have programs and facilities to help battered wives and battered children. Unfortunately, given the prevalence of abusive organizations, we also need programs to help battered employees.

Endnote

1. Parasuraman, S. and Greenhaus, J. H. (Eds.) 1997. *Integrating Work and Family: Challenges and Choices for a Changing World*. Westport, CT: Quorum. Lewis, S. and Lewis, J. (Eds.) 1996. *The Work-Family Challenge: Rethinking Employment*. London: Sage.

Article Review Form at end of book.

What are some things organizations can do to become more family friendly, and why should organizations want to do these things?

An Inside Look at Making the Grade

Michelle Neely Martinez

Michelle Neely Martinez is contributing editor to HRMagazine *and managing editor of* Employment Management Today. *She can be reached at MartinezMN@aol.com.*

You receive a call from your boss, the CEO. He just finished reading *Working Mother's* annual "100 Best Companies" list. He wants the company to get a piece of the action, so he tells you to get cracking and find out what it takes to get recognized as a family-friendly/ best-place-to-work employer.

With unemployment at a 25-year low, employers everywhere are searching for ways to rise above their competitors. Appearing on *Working Mother's* list is certainly one way of doing so. In fact, one "best" company told me that it had to revamp its employment office to handle the outpouring of resumes and job inquiries.

Corporate stakeholders are beginning to realize that work-life programs can help boost employee satisfaction, which translates to happier customers and increased profits. Because of that, *Working Mother* magazine is no longer the only publication telling us which companies are the most family friendly or the best to work for. Major business magazines such as *Business Week* and *Fortune*, have recently jumped on the "best company" bandwagon.

First Tennessee Bank, which is ranked on all three lists, operates under the concept that "profit begins with satisfied employees," according to Chief Executive Officer Ralph Horn. The bank's philosophy, says Horn, is "putting employees first versus putting the shareholders first." That formula is working; in the past two years, the bank's overall revenue growth hit 11 percent per year. The industry average is between 6 and 7 percent.

What does it take to get your company on one of these lists? Here's an outside look at how the three most prestigious award programs, *Working Mother, Business Week* and *Fortune* conduct their selection process and what they look for in winners.

Working Mother Magazine's "Best Companies for Working Mothers"

When this contest began 13 years ago, *Working Mother* struggled to find 30 employers willing to participate. Now, a panel of judges reviews close to 500 applications annually from all types and sizes of businesses and industries. In the past several years, more Wall Street firms and fewer hospitals have been recognized, a subtle sign of how sensitivity to work-life issues is spreading. In 1997, a dozen new companies joined the 100 best. New for the 1998 judging is a scoring system that awards points for the various policies and programs entrants have in place. Companies with the highest scores will go on to the final judging phase.

What They're Looking For

Good employee compensation; opportunities for women to advance; child care benefits such as back-up care, on-site child care, or subsidies offered to low- or middle-income employees; flexibility in how work gets done; and other family-friendly benefits such as paid maternity and paternity leave.

"Family friendly involves much more than, `Oh, we have this great policy,' " explains Deputy Editor Deborah Wilburn. "If people are afraid to use the policy or suffer consequences for doing so, then the company efforts are not ideal."

Wilburn says that the questions asked on the lengthy entry form are designed to get at the heart of work and family efforts. "We like to see information that proves employees use the benefits in place and are positively affected by them" says Wilburn. "We also love to hear bottom-line results of how the company benefited from such efforts. We want numbers."

Though the survey is rewritten each year to ensure its clarity, Wilburn says, applicants often find the trickiest question to be the amount of leave allowed new mothers. "We want to know what type of leave time is available that is not part of the Family and Medical Leave Act," she explains. "We are looking for the total amount of time a woman can take off after the birth of a child in uncomplicated cases."

Companies are dropped and added annually to the *Working*

"An Inside Look at Making the Grade," by Michelle Neely Martinez, *HRMagazine*, March 1998. Copyright © 1998. Reprinted with the permission of *HRMagazine* published by the Society for Human Resource Management, Alexandria, Va.

Mother 100 for various reasons, says Wilburn. For example, nine companies that had been on the list in previous years returned in 1997 after strengthening their programs and achieving a better representation of women in management (AT&T, Dayton Hudson, First Chicago NBD, Gallup, MassMutual, NIKE, The St. Paul Companies, the *St. Petersburg Times* and Sequent Computer Systems). "We don't want companies on the list who just reach a status quo and then don't continue to make improvements," says Wilburn.

Milton Moskowitz, a respected workplace critic and co-author of *The 100 Best Companies to Work for in America* (Doubleday), has written *Working Mother*'s annual article on the winning 100 since its inception. He says: "A company where 77 percent of the workforce is female, but only 15 percent of the highest paid employees are women cannot hope to be on the list."

The good news for small employers is that larger companies don't always have the upper hand in this contest. Large companies with well-known programs have been dropped from the list to make room for smaller companies that exhibit outstanding accomplishments in the work-life area. The Benjamin Group is a good example. The California-based 66-person public relations firm appeared on the list for the first time in 1997. The firm is noted for its on-site child care as well as other family-friendly perks.

Business Week's "Best Companies for Work and Family"

First published in September 1996, *Business Week*'s "Best Companies for Work and Family" is a biannual ranking based largely on formal surveys of employees' opinions about their companies. Employers that participate must be willing to have 500 company employees randomly surveyed about work and family activities.

Employees are asked questions, such as, "Can you vary your work hours or schedule to respond to family matters? Is your supervisor flexible when it comes to responding to your work-family needs? Do you feel comfortable taking time off from work to attend to family matters?"

Employers' final scores are based 60 percent on the employee surveys and 40 percent on a four-page survey completed by the management outlining the programs offered, mission statements and results of their efforts.

What They're Looking For

Benefits aren't the most critical criteria. Instead, *Business Week* and its survey partner, Boston College's Center for Work & Family, consider respect for employees more important than innovative programs. The center developed and wrote both the employee surveys, analyzed the data, and chose the finalists.

"Benefits are important for attracting workers, but it's the company's culture that retains them," says Ellen Bankert, director for corporate partnerships at the college's Center for Work & Family. "Programs and policies are increasingly less important than respect."

The best incentive for participating in this survey, as well as *Fortune*'s "The 100 Best Companies to Work for in America," is that applicants receive a confidential analysis of how their workplace culture compares with other participants. Even those not designated a winner obtain some great benchmarking data.

Fortune Magazine's "The 100 Best Companies to Work for in America"

For the first time this year, *Fortune* published a highly competitive list, "The 100 Best Companies to Work for in America," patterned after the book with the same name by co-authors Moskowitz and Robert Levering. To start the survey process, *Fortune* asked Levering and Moskowitz to identify 275 large and medium-sized employers from their Best Places to Work database. These companies were invited to participate by:

- Filling out a 29-page People Practices Inventory, developed and tabulated by Hewitt Associates, covering the organization's practices in areas such as training, teamwork and pay, as well as turnover rates and company demographics.

- Allowing the latest sponsors to survey 225 randomly selected employees. Employees fill out a two-page survey and then complete a section in which they can write their own comments. An e-mail address and toll-free number are also available to employees to voice their opinions about the company.

Despite the survey's huge requests for data and the time demands, 225 companies participated.

What They're Looking For

This list is based on more than work-family issues; its focus is determining companies that, overall, are great places to work. Levering admits that benefits play a big part in how companies are rated. But, he says, what distinguishes the very best is "the kind of relationship management has with employees. Trust and respect are critical to great workplaces," says Levering, and they have a great influence on what companies get ranked in the 100.

Fortune's first winner, Southwest Airlines, insists its unique corporate culture drives its success, according to Libby Sartain, SPHR, Southwest's "vice president of people" and a Society for Human Resource Management board of directors member.

While other companies rely on "canned" workplace programs, the Dallas-based airline has resisted the trends and fads in benefits and practices that many companies have attempted. "We've said 'no' to dry cleaning on-site. We don't need it, because we wear jeans to work," Sartain said. The company has also rejected on-site child care.

"Instead, we're giving employees the freedom to make a contribution. They know that each one of them makes a difference to the company, and can make decisions that will affect our business," she said. "They go to work feeling like they can have a great time every day."

Companies on the *Fortune* 100 list have other traits in common:

- They are run by demanding, visionary leaders; but the leadership styles inspire employees instead of oppressing them.

- Many offer a physical environment and services that employees appreciate, which might include a driving range and fitness center or concierge and dry-cleaning services.

- Work is framed as part of a deeper purpose in society, which is an attitude that employees find rewarding.

- Employees talk about having fun at work.

Tips from Two Winners

First Tennessee Bank's Pat Brown, vice president and manager of family matters, could write a book about how companies can become great workplaces for employees. But, with Levering and other experts, she will tell you that it all starts with the CEO.

"Leadership is the gatekeeper of loyalty," says Brown. "The leader sets the tone for how the workplace is and generates that sense of accomplishment among employees."

In addition to having a great leader, what steps can you take to make your organization stand out in these competitions or ones like them? First Tennessee Bank's Brown and Tony Harris, director of diversity and employee relations for BNA, a Washington, D.C.-based publisher, offer the following pointers:

Share the Workload

The *Fortune* application, by far, was the most comprehensive, says Brown. But no matter what contest or competition you plan to enter, she suggests group involvement. She works with a group of people across the organization to gather input and to collect information.

"The first time, this is an awful lot of work, but after you've done it once, it gets easier," she says. "Even when you are updating and adding information, the process becomes easier because you now know who to go to, to get the best information."

Be Cautious about Consultants

Work-family consultants seem to have cropped up overnight. Of course there are some highly effective and reputable ones but be careful of those who think they can help you win a competition.

"The objective should not be doing well on a survey," says Brown; it should be what works best for employees and the business. "We approach all programs to see what the bank is getting out of it," she says. And the key to integrating family-friendly programs with business operations, Brown says, is to understand the business and how it makes profits.

Be Specific about Results

When possible, quantify your efforts and be very specific about the impact programs or benefits have on employees. *Working Mother*'s Wilburn says that numbers can really bring out the bottom-line perspective, making it easier for the judges to understand the financial impact of what the companies are doing. Here are four examples of how First Tennessee Bank puts numbers to its work-family success story:

1. By surveying employees and customers at each bank location and analyzing the financial performance of each branch, Brown found that employees whose needs are met provide more value to customers. And customers satisfied with the service or product will stay with the company. In fact, business units run by managers who rank highest in the work and family area have a 7 percent higher customer retention rate than other managers. "This may not seem like a lot, but it amounts to millions of dollars," says Brown.

2. Employees with supportive bosses stay employed at the bank 50 percent longer than other employees. By encouraging this supportive behavior, the bank saved more than $1 million in turnover costs in the past three years. "We now have one of the highest customer retention rates of any bank in the country," says Brown.

3. Once reduced-time work with full benefits was instituted, 85 percent of the employees who switched over from full-time hours said they would have quit otherwise. The bank estimates that total replacement costs saved are $5,000 to $10,000 per nonmanagerial employee and $30,000 to $50,000 per executive.

4. The account-processing department instituted longer shifts at the beginning of the month because that is considered a "crunch" period. Employees then took a day off during a slower time of the month. Result: The time it took to reconcile customer accounts was reduced from 10 days to four—thereby increasing customer satisfaction without increasing salary costs.

Don't Leave Any Questions Unanswered

"If there's a reason we don't do something that is mentioned in a question, I explain," says BNA's Harris, even if it means talking about something that is just generally related to the question at hand. "Also, I'm prepared to share annual report information, employee benefit manuals and other materials, such as videos, that might help judges better understand the workplace," Harris says. BNA appears on all three lists.

If You Win an Award, Use It As a Recruitment Tool

Harris says that candidates love to hear about the recognition BNA receives and says it's also a great morale booster for existing employees.

Article Review Form at end of book.

Describe welfare capitalism.

Downsizing in the Past

Corporations have long had a sense of responsibility toward their workers. History can teach us some lessons about today's business environments.

Sanford Jacoby

Sanford Jacoby is a professor of management, history, and policy studies at UCLA.

Recent mass layoffs at Kodak, Pillsbury, and other companies refute the claim that the wave of corporate downsizings has crested. For decades, Kodak was a pioneer of enlightened employer paternalism, so the news is especially sobering and likely to fuel continued unease in the labor market.

Despite the rising stock market and falling unemployment rate, Americans remain deeply anxious about the availability of "good" jobs: career-type positions that offer decent wages and benefits. Pundits regularly pronounce that global competition and information technology are making those kinds of jobs obsolete. Yet many Americans nurse a lingering belief that, if corporate employers were pushed just a little bit harder, they would treat workers better. That, at least, was the public sentiment at the time of last August's Teamsters' strike, which sought to check the proliferation of part-time jobs at UPS.

The topic of employer responsibility became a major issue in the 1996 presidential campaign. Patrick J. Buchanan won the New Hampshire primary on a platform of vilifying corporate America, aiming his rhetoric at top executives such as Robert E. Allen, the head of AT&T, who receive huge salaries while laying off thousands of workers.

Later that year, the White House held a conference attended by the heads of the largest and most progressive companies in the United States. President Bill Clinton told the visiting CEOs, "The most fundamental responsibility of any business in a free-enterprise system is to make a profit. . . . But we must recognize that there are other responsibilities as well."

The notion that corporations have responsibilities to their employees is hardly a new or radical idea. Its roots lie deep in the American past—dating back a century or more—when companies first began systematically to provide for the welfare of their employees. That system was known as "welfare work" or "welfare capitalism." Understanding the history of welfare capitalism is essential to fathoming what's happening in today's labor market.

The Rise of Welfare Capitalism

American welfare capitalism began in the nineteenth century, when the population started moving in large numbers from rural to urban areas. This transformation forced people to seek new ways of dealing with the uncertainties of life. Urban-dwelling workers could not rely on home-grown food to get them through a spell of joblessness. The elderly, who were an important part of rural family life, found that industrial corporations were reluctant to employ them. Young unmarried women began to work outside the home, raising parental concern for their morals. Meanwhile, dangerous factories and crowded cities brought on occasional injuries and other health problems.

One response to these problems was market individualism: Workers saved as best they could while taking fierce pride in the independence that came from having a well-rounded set of skills. Another strategy was to form mutual benefit associations to provide savings funds, health plans, and burial expenses. These associations sometimes grew into trade unions. An alternative to individualism and mutualism was government, which sought to minimize risk through protective legislation or to redistribute risk via social insurance programs. This was the logic of the European welfare state, which pooled risks by providing all citizens with unemployment, sickness, and old-age security. A fourth option was to have corporations reduce risk or protect their employees against it. This, essentially, was welfare capitalism.

By the beginning of the twentieth century, welfare capitalism could be found throughout the industrialized world, including Japan. But it was especially popular in the United States. American employers favored welfare capitalism because they thought that it would inhibit the growth of unions and government. And they saw it as an efficient alternative to market individualism: Training would be cheaper and productivity higher if employees spent their work lives with a single firm instead of seeking their fortunes

"Downsizing in the Past," by Sanford Jacoby, *Challenge,* 41, No. 3, May/June 1998, pp. 100–112. Reprinted by permission of M.E. Sharpe Inc.

Welfare Capitalism at S. C. Johnson & Son

During the early 1900s, one of America's leading employers was S. C. Johnson & Son of Racine, Wisconsin, makers of floor wax and other household products. Samuel C. Johnson, who founded the company in 1886, gave his employees recreational facilities, a profit-sharing plan, paid vacations, group life insurance, and myriad other benefits. Samuel's son, Herbert, followed in his father's footsteps. During World War I he stabilized the company's erratic employment levels. He hired more full-time workers and trained them to perform several jobs so that they could be rotated around the company. In 1922 he started what was to become a highly publicized private unemployment insurance plan. To American reformers concerned about the "labor question" of the early twentieth century, companies like S. C. Johnson offered a distinctively American answer: The business corporation, rather than government or trade unions, would be the source of security and stability in modern society. This approach was dubbed "welfare capitalism."

Today, S. C. Johnson continues to win praise for its progressive employment policies. A leader in the corporate child-care movement, it has a day-care center and a summer camp for children. The manager in charge of the child-care program recently said, "This isn't a benefit—it's a good business decision because we want to attract the best." Although innovative, S. C. Johnson has a strong sense of tradition. The current chairman, who is the great-grandson of the company's founder, said recently, "Our company's social involvement grew out of this early sense of local community involvement. My great-grandfather had a sense that there had to be a fair way to do things." The company provides profit sharing, child care, and other benefits because, says the chairman, they create "a family atmosphere within the company. We all sit on the same side of the table, so to speak, so we don't have a confrontational environment between the various groups of people who work here. As a result, we have very low employee turnover and no unions," just as in the 1920s.

---

on the open market. There also was a moral impulse behind welfare capitalism: Self-made business owners felt a sense of parental obligation to their employees. In short, welfare capitalism was a good fit for a distinctive American environment comprising large firms, weak unions, and small government.

Welfare capitalism was an influential movement for the first three decades of this century. It was embraced by employers as well as by intellectuals, social reformers, and political leaders, all of whom shared the belief that industrial unrest and other problems could best be alleviated by this distinctively American approach: private, not governmental; managerial, not laborist. To put its ideas into practice, employers cleaned up their factories, constructed elaborate recreational facilities, launched "company" unions, and even built housing for their employees. Like S. C. Johnson, they turned casual positions into career jobs offering pensions and other benefits. By the 1920s, welfare capitalism reached millions of workers at thousands of firms. It was an impressive if imperfect system, whose notions of order, community, and paternal responsibility recalled the preindustrial household economy. The firms pursuing welfare capitalism were, in effect, modern manors.

Welfare capitalism, an influential movement for the first three decades of this century, crumbled during the Great Depression.

But the edifice crumbled during the Great Depression. Companies cut wages, instituted massive layoffs, and discontinued most of their welfare programs. Economist William Leiserson, who earlier had been dazzled by welfare capitalism, wrote pessimistically in 1933 that the depression had "undone fifteen years or so of good personnel work." Now workers searched for new alternatives to safeguard their security. They voted for the Democratic party, supported the New Deal, and enthusiastically joined unions. Welfare capitalism appeared to be dead and gone.

Or was it? In fact, welfare capitalism did not die in the 1930s but instead went underground—out of the public eye and beyond academic scrutiny. There it began to reshape itself. Without doubt, welfare capitalism *had* to change if it was to survive what was becoming a hostile climate, in which company unions were unlawful, collective bargaining was public policy, and the new American welfare state promised to shield workers from the uncertainties of industrial life. In response to these challenges, welfare capitalism was gradually modernized by a group of firms that had been spared unionization and the ravages of the depression, exemplified by three companies—Kodak, Sears Roebuck, and Thompson Products. These three companies were exceptions to the "rise and fall" story of welfare capitalism: Each one made major contributions to welfare capitalism's modernization between the 1930s and 1960s, when labor and government activism were at a peak in the United States.

In their attempts to build modern manors, these companies retained many elements of earlier welfare capitalism. Kodak, Sears, and Thompson provided generous benefit plans to their employees, though these plans were redesigned as supplements to social security and other public programs. Moreover, each company still asserted that it was a corporate community whose cohesion stood in opposition to the occupational and industrial solidarity of the labor movement. But employers now had to be more careful to make sure that their attempts to build an industrial community did not violate the new labor laws, such as the Wagner Act, which promoted collective bargaining.

Mixed motives like those represented in modern welfare capitalism have never been well understood by scholars, trade unionists, or employers. Liberals focus on workplace conflict, while conservatives emphasize the harmony between labor and capital. But, in reality, workers and owners simultaneously have opposing *and* shared interests. While they disagree over issues like the split between profits and wages, they depend on each other for their livelihoods, a point that French sociologist Emile Durkheim made a century ago, when he observed that the division of labor creates a shared interest in the enterprise as an economic community.

American workers of the 1930s, 1940s, and 1950s shared skills and technical expertise with their employers. They also shared cultural aspirations. Even the lowliest manual laborer had middle-class yearnings: to own a home, be comfortable, and obtain respect in the community. A sizable portion of the American working class hoped that they would someday have their own businesses or that their children would. Workers believed that it was within their power to succeed, and, in fact, it was not unrealistic for them to expect some advancement in the career-type jobs offered by welfare capitalism. Of course, social class did constitute a cultural divide. But inside the workplace, class barriers could be bridged by common ethnicity, gender, and loyalty to the enterprise.

During the 1930s and 1940s, many American workers joined unions. But it is also true that many workers did *not* believe in unions. At its peak after World War II, the labor movement represented less than a third of nonagricultural workers and its strength was concentrated in only a few regions and industries. Just three sectors—construction, manufacturing, and regulated transport and energy utilities—accounted for more than 80 percent of organized labor at its peak. Although much has been written about recent union losses in representation elections, this trend actually started during World War II.

Even the automobile industry, a hotbed of unionism, was filled with anti-union individualists, many of them skilled workers who boasted of their superior experience, dedication, and loyalty. Then there were groups like African-American workers, who were skeptical of both unions and management but willing to give management the benefit of the doubt so long as it kept its promises, especially about employment security, a critical issue for workers who lived through the Great Depression. Indeed, one important reason that some large companies were able to remain nonunion is that they suffered less from the depression than other firms in their industries.

Modernizing the Manor, 1930–1970

Historians have written prolifically about welfare capitalism during the first three decades of this century, and there are many articles about today's progressive employers. But we know little about welfare capitalism during the crucial period from the 1930s to the 1960s. Explanations for this gap are not hard to find. Industrial relations experts were preoccupied during the 1940s and 1950s with forging a new labor relations system based on collective bargaining. These experts thought that collective bargaining would protect individuals from the political power of business and from the psychological demands of bureaucratic work organizations. They saw unions as a way to preserve independence in the modern world. That is the same message they tried to bring Japan during the postwar occupation. But because these experts gave the labor movement such an important historical function, they viewed nonunion companies as socially retrograde and undeserving of scrutiny.

One result of this blind spot was the erroneous impression that organized labor had achieved greater stability and acceptability than was actually the case. True, it was possible to find managers who gave lip service to the legitimacy of labor unions. John E. Rovensky, a prominent industrialist, said in 1952, "All sound-thinking businessmen today recognize the right of labor to collective bargaining. Unions are an absolute necessity."[1] But Rovensky's words masked a division between management's public pronouncements and its private beliefs. In truth, most American managers intensely disliked unions. As two experts from MIT said in 1957, "If American management, upon retiring for the night, were assured that by the next morning the unions with which they dealt would have disappeared, more management people than not would experience the happiest sleep of their lives."[2]

American managers were deeply shaken by the Great Depression and demoralized by the rise of mass unions and the New Deal. But by the end of World War II, American managers had regained their self-confidence and started to take aggressive steps to contain unionism. The effort to secure passage of the Taft-Hartley Act, which placed new constraints on unions, was one example; another example was the actions of General Electric. Although GE was often cited as a union-friendly firm, in the 1950s it began to move its plants from the unionized North to the nonunion South. It also started to take a more combative approach toward its unions. Finally, it developed a variety of new programs for securing the loyalty and commitment of its employees. Some of these programs were old-fashioned welfare benefits. Others were based in the behavioral sciences, such as attitude surveys and employee counseling. In designing these programs, GE looked for inspiration and ideas to those employers who had modernized welfare capitalism, companies like DuPont, Eli Lilly, IBM, Kodak, Procter & Gamble, S. C. Johnson, Sears Roebuck, Standard Oil, and Thompson Products. Another thing GE learned from these companies was how to aggressively keep unions out of the new plants that GE opened in the South. In this way, modern welfare capitalism spread from a minority of employers who had avoided unionization in the 1930s to a much larger group of companies.

By the 1960s and 1970s modern welfare capitalism began to spread more rapidly because of the shift away from mass production, the growing importance of educated workers, and the greater willingness of American employers to fight aggressively to keep unions out of new

> By the end of World War II, American managers had started to take aggressive steps to contain unionism.

> Modern welfare capitalism's emphasis on commitment proved well-suited to managing college-educated workers.

plants and offices. Modern welfare capitalism's emphasis on commitment proved well suited to managing college-educated workers, who were becoming the dominant group in the labor force. Modern welfare capitalism also meshed neatly with the participative principles that were replacing the scientific management approach to work organization. What management scholars identified in the 1980s as a "new" nonunion model of work organization was, in fact, not especially new. It was simply a variant of modern welfare capitalism.

The Situation Today

Since the late 1980s, however, modern welfare capitalism has been experiencing its most critical test since the Great Depression. Massive layoffs have occurred throughout American industry. Nonunion companies that had never previously experienced a major layoff—firms like IBM, Kodak, and Sears—now began jettisoning thousands of employees.

These layoffs were—and are—a shock to those employees who thought themselves immune from job loss. Middle-level managers found that the elimination of their jobs often was the chief goal of industrial "restructuring." It is important to put these changes in perspective, however. While absolute job security no longer exists, especially in blue-collar employment, not all jobs are in peril, nor is modern welfare capitalism a relic of the past. Despite laying off thousands of workers, large corporations continue to offer career employment. Successful companies still put enormous effort into transforming new recruits into company men and women, both in the way they think and the skills they possess. In fact, economists find that most middle-aged workers currently have jobs that will last for decades. Despite the fashion for restructuring, there is no strong evidence of a secular decline in job stability.

What are the reasons behind this paradox of change amidst continuity? First, the U.S. labor force is huge and highly mobile; the unemployed either retire or get swallowed up in the market's constant churning. Second, the layoffs of the 1990s received enormous publicity because they represented a qualitative transformation: a shift away from high levels of security for previously protected white-collar groups like managers.

But if one looks closely at companies like Kodak or IBM, one finds that modern welfare capitalism remains alive and well. Both companies still spend huge amounts on training, career planning, and fringe benefits. In 1995, IBM and Kodak were two of the twenty major corporations that pledged to invest millions of dollars to make child care and elder care more available for their workers. (The other companies included such paragons of modern welfare capitalism as Hewlett-Packard, Mobil, TRW, and Texas Instruments.) Furthermore, most of these companies remain nonunion strongholds and pride themselves on that fact.

It is important to remember, however, that there is more to the U.S. economy than these giant Fortune 500 companies. Even at the height of the postwar economic boom, there remained areas of the labor market where unions did not reach and where employers were unconcerned with the niceties of employee commitment. In the 1950s and 1960s, it appeared that the number of such firms was shrinking because of pressure from union organizing, federal labor standards, and labor-market competition. Today, however, instead of shrinking, this job market is growing ever larger and wage inequality is steadily widening. Many American workers today hold temporary part-time, or casual jobs. These contingent employees are disproportionately nonwhite and without high school diplomas; their pay is low and they lack pensions and health insurance. These are the people who rooted from the sidelines during the UPS strike.

If these trends continue, modern welfare capitalism will turn back into the elite preserve that it was in the 1920s, when corporate manors housed only salaried employees and a lucky minority of hourly workers. As in the 1920s, the workforce today increasingly is split between the "have-nots" and the "haves," who will spend most of their careers working in paternal companies like S. C. Johnson or Microsoft. True, the have-nots have more options than in the 1920s. The rate of new job creation is high, and there is also the welfare state's safety net to fall back on. But the safety net is tattered, while the quality of those new jobs is debatable. Indeed, it remains to be seen whether the progressive nonunion sector will be able to absorb large numbers of new labor market entrants. While hiring continues—even at companies like AT&T and Sears that recently laid off thousands—anxiety remains widespread. Welfare capitalists of the 1920s had a buoyant optimism that is noticeably missing in American industry today. Welfare capitalism is not about to disappear in the United States, but its future looks less bright now than at any time since its postwar modernization.

This brings us back to the sense of insecurity among American workers and the national debate about corporate responsibility. Clearly, American employers are reluctant to shoulder as much risk as they once did. And some American workers—young and highly educated—are returning to market individualism: taking care of themselves by having a diverse set of skills and purchasing their benefits on the open market. But these workers are an atypical elite. Most Americans still look to their employers as the first line of defense against risk. As that line is pushed back, they question the fairness of today's leaner, meaner arrangements. Moreover, for every Kodak there are dozens of employers unconcerned with any type of commitment to their employees: places where the pay is low, jobs temporary, and benefits shrinking or nonexistent. Layoffs at firms like Kodak give less scrupulous companies a pretext for restructuring the social contract even when their economic situation does not warrant it.

In short, employer paternalism is not dead but its contours are changing and the majority of workers lack the power to strike a deal more to their liking. That is reflected in the current economy's conundrum of wage stagnation despite high productivity and low unemployment. In the 1930s, workers turned to unions and to government in search of a New Deal that would pressure employers to fulfill promises broken during the depression. While the probability of a union resurgence or of new governmental programs seems remote, the issue of employer responsibility will surely resurface in the next presidential campaign. Buchanan-style populist rhetoric is a strong possibility. The Democrats may dust off the Bingaman-Kennedy proposals to give tax and regulatory preferences to companies that train their workers, give them decent benefits, and try to avert layoffs.

In effect, such legislation would penalize employers who fail to establish or maintain commitments to employees. It is not a new idea but, rather, has deep roots in American history, as reflected in the tax treatment of employee benefits and the integration of private pensions with social security. Ironically, it was a farsighted Kodak executive named Marion Folsom who, in the 1930s, helped design these features of the Social Security Act. Above all, what we need today are business leaders who, like Folsom, combine a concern for the commonwealth with the self-interests that limit us all.

Notes

1. Quoted in Herman E. Krooss, *Executive Opinion: What Business Leaders Said and Thought on Economic Issues* (Garden City, NY: Doubleday, 1970), p. 397.
2. Douglass V. Brown and Charles A. Myers, "The Changing Industrial Relations Philosophy of American Management," *Proceedings of the Industrial Relations Research Association* (Madison, WI, 1957), pp. 84–99.

Article Review Form at end of book.

What are some of the costs and benefits of having a federally imposed thirty-five-hour work week?

A Shorter Week? Hell, No

Andrew Gumbel

"Independent on Sunday" (centrist), London, Oct. 26, 1997.

Nothing good ever came from the government," said Mimmo Calabresi, a typesetter in Rome. "A 35-hour week sounds good, but you can be sure that if they're proposing it, it's for their benefit, not for people like me."

The idea Calabresi was complaining about started out as an election slogan by a party that never imagined it would actually win office. Now, it is in danger of turning into a European trend. First France, now Italy: Both are talking in earnest about reducing the working week to a maximum of 35 hours, with no loss of earnings for the employee.

Sounds good, doesn't it? Getting the same but doing less, and all in the name of reducing unemployment. But it is provoking outrage across both countries and causing consternation among their European Union partners.

The idea, in itself, is a perfectly respectable piece of left-wing thinking. Now that computer technology is taking over from industrial mechanization and further reducing the demand for labor, it makes sense to free people up to allow them to spend their time, and their money, more creatively. New jobs will arise from this extended leisure time, especially in the service sector, and the extra costs imposed on employers will soon be absorbed by the general increase in living standards.

The trouble is, the present calls for a 35-hour week seem inspired not by doctrine, but by a kind of political lunacy that even the governments involved have grave doubts about.

In France, Prime Minister Lionel Jospin's Socialist Party was desperate for new proposals in the run up to last spring's general elections. The 35-hour week made a good slogan and best of all did not need to be explained in detail because President Jacques Chirac's center-right coalition was almost certain to return to power. But then the Socialists won, and Jospin was stuck with his glaringly memorable promise.

Over the past few weeks, the head of France's industrial employer's association, Jean Gandois, has resigned in disgust at the idea of a 35-hour week, Jospin himself has looked a little uncertain, and even left-wing theorists have pointed out that a government edict on working hours is against the whole spirit of a more flexible labor market.

But at least in France there is a tradition for such notions. Italy is entirely different: Governments rarely succeed in ordaining anything, while trade unions negotiate labor contracts in detail.

So what on earth made Italy jump on this ill-fated bandwagon? Again, it was crazy politics. Prime Minister Romano Prodi's center-left coalition depends on the far-left Rifondazione Comunista for its majority in the Chamber of Deputies; and Rifondazione decided to provoke a crisis over the government's plans to cut into welfare and pensions for last year's budget—a necessary piece of austerity to get Italy into the single European currency. In a desperate attempt to appease Rifondazione, Prodi decided to join Jospin in the 35-hour stunt. The good news was that his budget was saved at the 11th hour; the bad news is that he now has to come up with a bill to cut working hours by January, or else risk a split with Rifondazione all over again.

There is no end to the absurdity of such legislation in Italy. For a start, almost nobody in fixed employment works more than 35 hours anyway. Civil servants, railwaymen, post-office workers, and journalists enjoy a 36-hour week, policemen a 37-hour week. Only hard-core industrial workers have to work 39 hours, while cinema workers put in the maximum 40. A few people at the top, most with political connections, enjoy extremely high salaries, but most of the lower- and middle-ranking workers can barely survive on their take-home pay. Cutting working hours would only give people more time to do what they already do to make up the shortfall in their living standards: contribute to the thriving black economy.

"The idea seems inspired by a kind of political lunacy."

Article Review Form at end of book.

"Italians smell a rat as they are offered a shorter working week" by Andrew Gumbel, *Independent on Sunday*, October 26, 1997 (published under the headline "A Shorter Week? Hell, No," in *World Press Review*, January 1998, p. 33). Reprinted by permission of Independent Newspapers (UK) Ltd.

WiseGuide Wrap-Up

As we have seen in this section, there are increasing demands placed on workers by organizations and increasing demands placed on organizations by workers. These issues reflect social, economic, and political changes. Socially, we are trying to balance the rights and responsibilities of the worker with those of the workplace. With increasing numbers of dual-income families, how do we balance work and family demands? Politically, to what extent do we want the government intervening in these issues? As a potential employee, how important are these programs to you (now and maybe five to ten years from now)? Would they affect your decision to work for a particular company or stay with a company, once you receive a job? In this section, we have only scratched the surface of the changing nature of work. How many more issues do you see facing workers and organizations today? What are the important issues to you, as you begin or continue your career?

R.E.A.L. Sites

This list provides a print preview of typical **Coursewise** R.E.A.L. sites. (There are over 100 such sites at the **Courselinks**™ site.) The danger in printing URLs is that web sites can change overnight. As we went to press, these sites were functional using the URLs provided. If you come across one that isn't, please let us know via email to: webmaster@coursewise.com. Use your Passport to access the most current list of R.E.A.L. sites at the **Courselinks** site.

Site name: Working Woman Magazine
URL: http://www.workingwomanmag.com/
Why is it R.E.A.L.? This is a web page by the publishers of *Working Woman* magazine that includes databases on salaries and top woman-owned businesses.
Key topics: work and family, gender issues
Try this: Under the special database section, click on *Working Woman 500* and search by state to find the companies near you that received a top 500 award by this organization. Under the special database section, click on Salary Survey, select an interesting occupation, and compare salaries for men and women.

Site name: Working Mother Magazine
URL: http://www.workingmother.com/
Why is it R.E.A.L.? This is a web page by the publisher of *Working Mother* that addresses the concerns of working parents. Topics include careers, family, health, and politics.
Key topics: work and family, gender issues
Try this: Click on the Family icon and find some recent headlines concerning working mothers.

Site name: Work & Family Connection
URL: http://www.workfamily.com/
Why is it R.E.A.L.? This site includes information about a wide variety of work/life issues. It maintains a work/family search service, a collection of important studies in this area, a listing of "model companies," and a newsletter.
Key topics: work and family
Try this: Click on Important Studies to view some recent research projects concerning work/family issues.

section 3

The Legal Environment

Learning Objectives

- To become familiar with the legal environment of the workplace.
- To understand issues related to workplace law.
- To describe the role of regulatory bodies and the enforcement of workplace law.

WiseGuide Intro

It has become vitally important that industrial/organizational psychologists and human resource professionals understand the legal environment of the workplace. It is common that individuals working in these fields must consult with lawyers, corporate executives, union representatives, and individual employees to ensure that the organization follows fundamental legal principles. Some of these principles are broad in scope:

- Equal Pay Act of 1963
- Civil Rights Act of 1964 (amended by the Equal Employment Opportunity Act of 1972)
- Age Discrimination in Employment Act of 1967
- Immigration Reform and Control Act of 1986
- Americans with Disabilities Act of 1990
- Civil Rights Act of 1991
- Family Leave and Medical Act of 1993

In addition, many practitioners must be familiar with more specific legislation and laws concerning sexual and racial harassment, rights to privacy, workplace safety, and rehabilitation services.

Legal regulation of the workplace is sometimes confusing and often controversial, specifically in regard to the rights and responsibilities of the workers and the employers. It seems that every aspect of the employment relationship is legally regulated: recruitment, initial screening, selection, placement, compensation, training, promotion, evaluation, workplace environment, and termination.

One of the agencies charged with regulating and enforcing federal Civil Rights laws is the Equal Employment Opportunity Commission (EEOC). The EEOC is an independent regulatory agency consisting of a chairperson and four commissioners, all appointed by the president of the United States and confirmed by the U.S. Senate. No more than three of the commissioners may be from the same political party. In 1997 this committee saw 80,680 charges filed and, with a 1998 budget appropriation of $242 million, you get the sense that this organization is very large and complex. Reading 13, the first article in this section, addresses the role and procedures of the EEOC by interviewing Gilbert Casellas, who recently stepped down as the agency's chairperson. This reading provides a good overview of some of the issues facing the EEOC.

Reading 14 addresses the question of why we need legal regulation of the workplace and asks if unfair discriminations exist today (but what does unfair mean—unfair to whom?). In his paper, Van Buren poses the question "How is it possible for racist attitudes to exist in U.S. organizations 33 years after the Civil Rights Act of 1964?" Many would argue we subscribe to the goal of equal opportunity, but what does that actually mean? Van Buren believes these are important issues for organizations and our government to address.

Questions

Reading 13. What are some of the issues facing our government that address the conflicting demands of increasing workplace legislation while reducing the size and expense of the federal government?

Reading 14. What are some of the obstacles that inhibit agreement on defining an Equal Opportunity Workplace?

Reading 15. What should you do if you feel you have been a victim of unfair discrimination?

Reading 16. What are the underlying issues that are cause for debate when discussing balance between the rights of the individual and those of the organization?

Reading 17. Who was Franz Kafka? Does the title of the reading seem appropriate for the content?

Reading 18. According to this reading, how are judges interpreting the Americans with Disabilities Act as it pertains to mental illness? Contrast these rulings with rulings related to alcoholism.

Reading 19. According to this reading, how are disabilities being defined? How should courts decide which disabilities are protected by the Americans with Disabilities Act and which are not?

Reading 20. Should organizations develop zero tolerance policies on sexual harassment? What is the estimated legal cost for a sexual harassment trial?

If we agree that there is at least the potential for some individuals to be unfairly harassed or discriminated against at work, we need to address how to handle these situations. For example, in Reading 15, Wallace presents a case study addressing discrimination. What would you do in this situation? Who should be held responsible for such a case—the supervisor or the organization? Organizations often find themselves in a bind, trying to decide what to do to prevent these occurrences.

Another spirited controversy on workplace law addresses the Americans with Disabilities Act of 1990. This act was designed to protect an estimated 43 million Americans with disabilities. The controversy surrounds the definition of a disability and the organization's response. For example, people with walking, seeing, hearing, or talking disabilities are protected, as are individuals with health-related problems, such as diabetes, AIDS, and high blood pressure. The act also protects certain drug and alcohol abusers (all rehabilitated drug users are protected, but current use of illegal drugs is a dismissable offense, whereas current alcoholics must be given opportunities for rehabilitation). The next four readings address whether or not these regulations are fair to organizations. As Price notes in Reading 17, we may be putting ourselves in a double bind. Organizations and legislation must determine where to draw the line and clearly define what disabilities should be protected. This is very tricky when discussing mental disabilities. As Herbert Wray notes in Reading 18, the courts are skeptical about mental disability claims, and it is often difficult to demonstrate mental disability and what is a reasonable accommodation. Shapiro fears in Reading 19 that we may be creating the Americans with Minor Disabilities Act. For example, is an allergy to peanut butter a disability that should cause a school or workplace to forbid the consumption of peanut butter on the organization's premises (as a reasonable accommodation)?

Organizations need to respond to the legal environment of the workplace both in principle and practice. In principle, organizations need to address the spirit of the legislation that should create a workplace free of unfair discrimination or bias. In practice, organizations need to develop policies and guidelines that address these issues. In Reading 20, Garland presents a tip sheet for companies on how to protect themselves against lawsuits as well as how to handle unwanted harassment against workers.

What are some of the issues facing our government that address the conflicting demands of increasing workplace legislation while reducing the size and expense of the federal government?

Life at the EEOC

Bill Leonard

In mid-October, Gilbert Casellas announced that he would step down from his job as chairman of the Equal Employment Opportunity Commission (EEOC) on December 31. After serving as EEOC chairman for three years, he plans to reenter private practice as an attorney. Soon after announcing his resignation, Casellas agreed to talk with HRMagazine *about his tenure as EEOC chairman, recent trends in employment law and how the EEOC is currently positioned to address these issues.*

HRMagazine: You have spent most of your career as an attorney in private practice. What were some of the surprises and challenges you faced when you began working in the public sector?

Casellas: First a little history here. I didn't come directly from private practice to the EEOC. I first came to Washington as general counsel of the Department of the Air Force—which was also a presidential appointment. I was there for just under a year, and then I came to the commission in September of 1994.

I think that several things surprised me when I began working for the federal government. One is the level of professionalism of the staff both here and at the Pentagon. I think that you assume on the outside, particularly if you're not from Washington, that you have folks here who are watching the clock all day and are uncaring bureaucrats. Well, that's not true. The fact is that many of the people here have dedicated much of their professional lives to working for the commission. They are very proud of what they do and try to do a good job every day.

The second big surprise was the extent of the restrictions on the way you do business and your ability to change business methods. Some of these restrictions are personnel rules; others are restrictions on your budget in terms of how you can spend money for your office and your agency.

Third, the role of individual members of Congress was a surprise and definitely a challenge. I discovered there were some members who have a peculiarly narrow and parochial interest. By that I mean the operation of an EEOC office in their district or state is far more important to them than the agency nationally.

I've faced situations where members have tried to push a particular action—not with regard to cases—but in regard to the operation of a particular office or a budgetary issue. And the action that they were pushing would definitely have had a detrimental effect agency-wide. But that's not their concern. They've told me that the concerns in their district are important to them. One other challenge is obviously the scrutiny that comes with appointed positions such as this one. I think it is rare in the private sector to be involved in matters that generate such a high level of corporate scrutiny. In the private sector you just don't spend your days responding to questions as you do in a government position. In the private sector, you have a lot more time to work affirmatively and accomplish particular missions or goals.

HRMagazine: Congress seems interested in enacting more workplace legislation, such as the Workplace Religious Freedom Act and the Employment Non-discrimination Act (ENDA). At the same time there is pressure to reduce the size and expenses of the federal government. Is Congress sending a mixed message by creating more responsibility for the EEOC, while reducing the agency's resources?

Casellas: This certainly appears to be the case with the laws that are being proposed, whether it's the ENDA or the bill that would outlaw genetic discrimination. Presumably, these laws would be enforced by the EEOC. I don't know that for a fact, or how it will ultimately come out. So yes, there seems to be a mixed message here.

A lot of the problems we face at the EEOC are resource-driven. If you can't train people—and if you don't have enough people to do the kind of intake work we face at the agency—then you will run into real problems. We haven't hit that level quite yet, but the commission continues to be strapped for resources. Our field offices and headquarters are much smaller than three years ago, and the EEOC is certainly a lot smaller than it was 20 years ago.

And we have been given more responsibility, such as enforcing the

"Life at the EEOC," by Bill Leonard, *HR Magazine,* January 1998. Reprinted with the permission of *HRMagazine,* published by the Society for Human Resource Management, Alexandria, Va.

ADA and the Civil Rights Act of 1991. If other pending bills should result in enacted legislation and come to the EEOC, the agency is going to be trying—again—to do a lot more with a lot less.

HRMagazine: With the heightened awareness on issues like sexual harassment and age discrimination and the enactment of laws like the ADA and the Civil Rights Act of 1991 it seems that the number of claims filed with the EEOC must be rising dramatically. Is this true?

Casellas: Actually, the number of charges filed with the commission has dropped slightly. This decrease has a lot to do with new intake procedures and efforts to do a better job of screening claims. But, ultimately, we can't stop an individual from filing a complaint. And even if we determine that the complaint has no merit, we can't stop someone from filing suit. But the commission still gets blamed for flooding the courts with lawsuits that we don't file. The EEOC filed half the number of lawsuits last year as we did the year before, and critics still claim that we are flooding the courts. We also get blamed for accepting charges that, by law, we have to accept.

HRMagazine: Does the EEOC get named as a co-litigant because the original discrimination claim was filed with the commission?

Casellas: Yes it happens, but not very often. But even if the commission is not named as a co-litigant, we still receive some blame because it's a civil rights law and involves the workplace. There are certain cases, whether they are filed under the Civil Rights Act or the ADA, where people look at the case and they say, "Well here's this case again, and it's another one of those kooky kinds of cases that the EEOC files." And while we at the commission agree that the case has no merit, we can't stop individuals from filing lawsuits. So the agency faces this spillover effect and gets blamed if somebody wants to take advantage of a statute or try to read the law in a certain way.

HRMagazine: A recent survey of HR professionals conducted by the Society for Human Resource Management found that nearly 60 percent of the respondents said their employers had been named as a defendant in an employment lawsuit within the past five years. But you claim the number of discrimination complaints and lawsuits filed by the EEOC has declined. How do you explain this survey response?

Casellas: There has been an increase in the number of employment-related lawsuits filed. If you look at the statistics of the Administrative Office of the U.S. Courts, they show a large jump in the number of employment-related lawsuits over the past few years. But these aren't lawsuits filed by the EEOC. What I'm saying is that in one breath someone may say there is a spike in the number of lawsuits. Then, in the next breath, they take this leap of logic and blame the EEOC when, in fact, we have filed fewer and fewer lawsuits in the last couple of years.

HRMagazine: Does this increase in the number of lawsuits place any burden on the EEOC?

Casellas: The number of lawsuits pending in court by private parties doesn't really implicate the EEOC or the commission's resources because those are not cases that we need keep track of or follow at all. So those are completely out of our system and out of our control.

To the extent that there is any increased burden on the EEOC—and I use the word burden in quotation marks—it comes from the fact that with additional statutes to enforce there are going to be more people to whom the commission must respond. The agency will have the same number of people responding to claims and questions from more and more members of the public.

HRMagazine: The EEOC made some significant headway in reducing its case backlog over the past three years. Will this remain a top priority for the commission? And how would you grade the EEOC's performance during your tenure as chairman?

Casellas: I think, overall, the record has been excellent when you consider what we were given to work with. The backlog has been eliminated, for all intents and purposes. Let me explain what that means. A backlog is the number of cases you can't get to that are not current. That is, at the end of the year, you are resolving fewer cases than are coming in the door, so you create a backlog. It's the same thing in a business context: There are more orders than you can fill, so you have a backlog.

The commission is now resolving more cases than are coming in the door and has been for the past two years. So the number of cases that are pending has dropped over the last two years to just under 70,000. I think on that we should get a very good grade. Number two, we put in place an alternative dispute resolution (ADR) program that has shown some promising results, although we were able to implement it only on a limited trial basis due to limited commission resources. We had very little money to do it, so we patched the program together with volunteers, colleges and universities, local chambers of commerce, bar associations and money from EEOC headquarters. But the program deserves special mention because there was a great deal of resistance to the idea because some people view strong law enforcement principles as antithetical to the concept of mediation.

And third, we have an excellent record in encouraging voluntary compliance. For example, there are an increased number of policy and enforcement guidances to help explain the law so that people understand their rights and their responsibilities. There was a 50 percent increase in employer participation in technical assistance programs around the country. The response was so great that hundreds of people were turned away last year because we just didn't have the space to accommodate everyone who wanted to learn about preventing workplace discrimination and avoiding liability.

As I mentioned before, we have filed fewer lawsuits. In fact, the agency filed half the number of lawsuits last year as we did the year before but recovered twice the monetary benefits. We have been much more selective in the cases we have chosen to litigate. We have focused on more strategic-type cases that will have a greater impact, either because of the development of the law or a particular employment practice.

HRMagazine: You have said that the agency gets unfairly blamed for spurring workplace litigation when, in fact, the agency filed fewer suits in 1996 than it did in 1995. But the latest EEOC statistics show that in 1997, the number of suits jumped to nearly 300—almost the same number of suits as in 1995. Do those numbers contradict what you have been saying?

Casellas: I think the number went up last year because all the elements of our national enforcement plan were finally in place for all of the EEOC offices around the country. The agency's national enforcement plan was not fully implemented until February 1996, and some offices took longer than others to identify and develop their priority charges for litigation. Because we replaced the old assembly line process, the agency's case work now moves faster, so we must use a more strategic approach to filing suits. The number of lawsuits filed annually will probably not reach the levels of the late 1980s and early '90s, when the agency filed about 600 suits a year.

Assuming that the EEOC's present staffing level is maintained, we believe the number of lawsuits filed every year should settle in around 300 annually and continue to bear a greater yield either in dollar, precedents or deterrent value compared to the number of suits filed prior to implementing the national enforcement plan. But it's really hard to say how many lawsuits will be filed in a year. We are not setting any quotas, although at one time there was a quota system in place. What should be driving the number of lawsuits filed is a strategic and well-defined selective screening process.

But I really want to be careful about just looking at the numbers. The number of lawsuits filed isn't really a meaningful or credible measure of the agency's effectiveness, nor should it be. In any event, if you compare 1997 with where the agency was 8 to 10 years ago, I believe that—given the agency's resources and our new strategic approach—the numbers are about right. No one has a set goal in mind, I certainly don't.

HRMagazine: What has been your proudest achievement as chairman of the EEOC?

Casellas: I have worked to restore the sense of pride in the work among employees of the agency. I have also worked to change the outside perceptions of the agency, not because I wanted to draw attention to the commission, but to put back in the public eye the importance of civil rights and equal opportunity in the workplace.

I say this because when people have attacked our choice of cases, they have done it in a very superficial way. This suggests to me that it is really an attack on the laws that the commission enforces and whether those laws are even needed—whether what we do is worthwhile.

I have tried to change the internal culture of the EEOC so that people work together as a team. It has been a top priority for us in the agency to focus on a common mission. The employees of the agency should recognize that they are here to serve everybody and to be helpful as best they can to both employers and employees.

Finally, I tried to instill the ideal in employees that what we do here is indeed noble and is as worthy of respect as the enforcement of any other federal laws.

I don't know that we've succeeded, and I don't know if we will ever succeed in that. Some people say the only way to succeed in that effort is to bring more lawsuits, to try to draw more attention to the lawsuits that the agency brings and basically to get people to hate you and to hate what you do—in other words, create enemies.

That has not been my style or my approach, but I think in the end the agency has been successful in raising people's consciousness about these issues in a way that is constructive. I think the agency has successfully suggested that there are ways to comply with the law and has encouraged compliance with the law. For those few out there who are either ignorant or just don't care, we have shown them that there are meaningful steps that the commission will take to enforce the law.

HRMagazine: Do you have any regrets in leaving this job? Are there any goals you set but didn't achieve?

Casellas: There are so many things that we could do if we had support in terms of resources and moral support from the public. I don't have any regrets because, given what we started with, I think we have done more than could have been expected. But I think there are still things that need to be looked at. One that is more internal to the EEOC is where the agency has located its offices and whether those locations make sense. The location of offices evolved in a less than scientific way over the years, so this really needs to be examined.

Secondly the relationship and the financial arrangements with state and local agencies really need a fundamental examination, particularly in this time of diminishing resources. Also, I would have liked to have implemented the ADR program a little more quickly and have had a better universe to study its impact and where we are heading.

HRMagazine: How can the EEOC be more effective? Is it through vigorous enforcement, by filing discrimination lawsuits, or is it through education of employers and community outreach programs?

Casellas: I would like to see people focus on the fact that the commission is an integrated system. I think the hardest thing for me to get across to the agency's critics, to the folks on Capitol Hill and to people inside the agency is that the commission is not either/or—it is both. You can be a strong, effective and vigorous enforcer of the laws and at the same time you can educate the public, provide technical assistance to employers, offer mediation, be selective in the charges you investigate and be even more selective in the lawsuits you bring. This whole system must work in harmony. No one thing can take precedence over any other part. I think that it has always been easier to polarize these things and say, "The EEOC is doing nothing but flooding the courts with lawsuits," or say, "The EEOC only cares about mediation," or, "They're only focusing on charge processing." We're trying to do it all, and I think we're doing the best that we can with the resources we've been given. If we had just a few more resources, you would see a lot more in terms of educating employers and educating employees.

HRMagazine: Can you give us an example of the most egregious case of employment discrimination you've seen during your tenure as chairman?

Casellas: I can give you several. The first one to come to mind is an employer who has a "Speak English Only" policy that extends to the sidewalk outside his place of business. That is an actual lawsuit that is pending.

Another that pops to mind is where an employer would not permit an individual in a wheelchair to even apply for a job as a teacher. Another is an employment referral agency that instructed employees to refer blacks and Hispanics only to short-term low-paying jobs, not higher-paying long-term positions. The agency also instructed workers not to refer anyone with a disability for a job.

HRMagazine: Can you give us any examples of frivolous claims filed with the commission?

Casellas: Certainly the frivolous claims are the ones we screen out. But there was one lawsuit recently that just wouldn't die. It kept resurfacing, and every time it surfaced critics of the EEOC and the press pointed to it as a prime example of the laws and legal system gone awry.

The case involved an individual who believed that, because of his significant mental disability, he had the right to bring a gun to work. The EEOC did not find any merit to the case. But just because we said that doesn't mean the individual didn't have a right to file a lawsuit.

So he filed a lawsuit with a federal court in Florida, and for some reason the employer's original motion to dismiss the case was denied. Ultimately, the case was dismissed before it came up for trial. So the system worked in that the EEOC did what it could to screen the case out. But this individual was undeterred, he filed a lawsuit and ultimately lost.

HRMagazine: What's the best piece of advice you can give employers to protect themselves from discrimination claims?

Casellas: Hire me as their attorney! All kidding aside, I would say they need to have in place procedures that follow the law. But they also need to make sure that their people are following those practices and procedures. Just having a policy, isn't enough. You can have a policy that says you will operate a safe workplace but then have a dozen OSHA violations. What good does a safe workplace policy do then? Your conduct has to support your policies.

I would add a second piece of advice and that is to provide as many credible outlets and mechanisms as possible that allow people to file complaints so they don't have to go outside the organization. No internal system, whether its an internal ombudsman or grievance system or whatever it is, is going to capture every possible complaint, but if there's some credible mechanism for doing that—no matter how informal it is—it will go a long way in helping to keep workplace issues from escalating out of your control.

HRMagazine: What's the one change you would like to see made at the EEOC to make the agency more effective?

Casellas: That's tough because I have to pick from my extensive wish list. But I think that money is first. I think having the resources so that the commission could expand its technology is a primary concern. We have a web site now, but 98 percent of the people in the agency can't access it because they don't have the equipment to do it. Because we don't have a computer network in place, we can't communicate effectively among our offices to ensure consistency.

We also have training problems throughout the agency. We need to train people but don't have the money to do it. People are only as good as the training you give them, and when you can't provide adequate training you will ultimately face some bigger problems.

So, the single most important thing is resources. Without a significant infusion of resources, the agency's case backlog will build up again over the long run, the next 10 to 15 years.

And there's the possibility of additional statutes that the agency might have to enforce, whether its the ENDA, religion in the workplace or whatever those laws might be. At some point, the agency may find itself having to choose which statutes it enforces. Now, I won't be around for that, but it won't be a pretty picture. No government agency should be put in the position of having to pick and choose which laws its going to enforce.

HRMagazine: What advice would you give to your successor?

Casellas: I'm going to adopt a line from Sheldon Hackney, who was head of the National Endowment for the Humanities. When someone asked him what he would say to his successor he replied, "Stay home." I think my approach has been to be an ecumenical chairman. That is, in terms of the laws we enforce, to try not to pick favorites. I have tried to focus on the larger mission of the commission without regard to political pressure, pressure from within the agency or pressure from outside advocacy groups—whether they were employer or civil rights groups.

So I guess I would tell my successor that if you maintain your principles and make principled decisions, when you are criticized—as you will be—you will have the solace and satisfaction that you tried to do the right thing.

Article Review Form at end of book.

What are some of the obstacles that inhibit agreement on defining an Equal Opportunity Workplace?

Ending the Culture of Corporate Discrimination

Harry J. Van Buren III

Harry J. Van Buren III is a doctoral student at the University of Pittsburgh's Katz Graduate School of Business.

The well-publicized meeting at which Texaco executives denigrated minority employees and conspired to destroy evidence relating to an equal employment opportunity (EEO) lawsuit shocked people inside and outside corporate America. The language heard on the tape of the meeting seemed like it was from 1956, not 1996. The Texaco case illustrates how far the United States has to go in ensuring equal treatment for all of its citizens—and demonstrates why affirmative action programs are still needed.

But one question has been largely unasked and unanswered in the furor about taped meetings and document destruction: How is it possible for racist attitudes to exist in U.S. organizations 33 years after the Civil Rights Act of 1964? Diversity, after all, has become a cottage industry. Many organizations have held diversity training seminars, established programs, and printed material attesting to their belief that "fair employment is good business." It is hard to imagine how anyone can believe that treating people differently based on their sex or race is morally acceptable or financially responsible and yet the Texaco case indicates that disparate treatment of women and people of color is still widespread. In short, EEO programs are one thing and actual fair treatment of women and members of minority groups quite another.

For people interested in corporate social responsibility, EEO is an interesting test case for how social norms are communicated to and enforced in an organization. Societal expectations of fair employment are codified in law. The penalties for employment discrimination are steep indeed, including both legal judgments and negative publicity. But even despite all of the organizational and social influences that would seem to inhibit discriminatory behavior—employment discrimination happens. Why?

Perhaps the problem is definitional—we can't agree on what an equal opportunity workplace looks like. As a matter of public policy, employers are proscribed from discriminating against protected classes of individuals, like women and African Americans. Fair treatment in employment is also a strong social norm; there is broad agreement that discriminatory behavior is wrong. But despite legal strictures and social norms, there is still much disagreement about what constitutes adherence to equal employment opportunity. Does EEO mean that an organization practices affirmative action? Does it ensure nondiscrimination without overt attempts to increase organizational diversity? Or does equal employment mean a corporation merely issues EEO statements? Shareholder activists, among others, still struggle with the answers to these questions.

But another reason for the persistence of corporate racism and sexism is that EEO programs threaten established patterns of working together in organizations. When organizations seek to create a diverse work force in which fair treatment is the norm, white men often feel like they are under siege. They believe that their organizational culture is under attack by people who are different from them. Diversity is threatening to them because diversity means sharing organizational space with people who are different—even when diversity leads (as it often does) to higher profitability for the company.

If we want to change the way in which fair employment policies and practices are perceived by American managers, we need to understand why they are resistant to diversity initiatives in the first place.

Why Is EEO So Controversial?

Since the Civil Rights Act of 1964 and continuing through subsequent federal government efforts to legislate equal employment opportunity—such as the creation of the Equal Employment Opportunity Commission in 1965—EEO has been a contentious issue in American society. Although there is widespread agreement in principle that enduring fairness in employment is a legitimate public interest, resistance to EEO programs in practice is strong. Analyzing individual and organizational resistance to EEO is difficult because the ethical norm of fair employment is widely shared, but there is little agreement on which policies and programs designed to achieve the norm are appropriate.

There is, for example, some social-acceptability bias when people are asked about EEO; everyone knows that the "right" answer to the question, "Do you believe that employers should not discriminate in employment?" is yes. But many people responding in this way are being less than truthful. A more systematic approach to analyzing resistance to EEO starts with the looking at reasons why EEO programs and policies may be seen as illegitimate. The academic literature on equal employment opportunity programs suggests nine reasons for managerial resistance:

1. Conflict between general proposition and "favoritism" toward certain groups. Some studies indicate that approval for affirmative action as a means of ensuring fairness in employment declines when the targeted groups are blacks or women.

2. Lack of preparation for policies. A fair employment policy that is simply dictated to the organization without an adequate explanation for why the policy is needed will be strongly resisted.

3. Belief that discrimination does not occur in the organization. Although many if not most people agree that employment discrimination occurs, a belief that one's own organization does not discriminate may cause resistance to EEO programs and policies.

4. Individuals' tendencies to overrate their own selection/performance assessment abilities. Unfortunately, individuals tend to overstate their abilities to appraise performance accurately and well. To the degree that there is either latent racism and sexism at work in the selection and performance appraisal processes, resistance to fair employment programs is likely.

5. Belief that disparate outcomes are based on job related criteria. There is still a persistent belief among some people that certain groups in our society do not possess the abilities needed to succeed in particular occupations. Research into sex and race stereotyping indicates that strongly held racial or sexual stereotypes lead to discriminatory outcomes.

6. Low support for EEO on the part of senior management. Many EEO policies may be understood by some employees as merely public relations exercises. Almost every organization of any size has developed some statement about its commitment to fairness in employment. But without senior management support for EEO, employees will be likely to ignore or circumvent such policies.

7. A dearth of powerful stakeholders who can exercise influence over the organization. Organizations that do business with the federal government, for example, will face greater oversight of their EEO programs than those that do not have this kind of relationship. Shareholders and customers can also wield influence and force the organization to undertake actions that it might otherwise avoid.

8. Lack of resources for EEO programs and policies. To the degree that the HRM department has insufficient organizational resources, it will be unable to enforce EEO in the organization. In the EEO area, organizations may decide to allocate enough resources to ensure that their fair employment programs and policies look good in the public square, but not enough on training and monitoring programs to adequately ensure that discrimination does not occur (or more positively, that the work force is diverse).

9. Pursuing diversity is seen as illegitimate. If organizations are judged based on profitability and EEO is not understood to contribute to profit, then EEO programs will be judged illegitimate and not useful to the organization.

All of the factors outlined above contribute to organizational resistance to EEO. But there is yet another dimension to consider: the reasons white males feel threatened by initiatives to increase the numbers of women and people of color in positions of authority.

Suppose we accept that people, at least in the abstract, believe that fair treatment in the workplace is a value to which they subscribe. If fair treatment is the widely held norm, then we should expect little resistance to programs designed to ensure it. Yet we know that people are resistant to programs that seek to implement the value of equal employment opportunity. Why might this be the case?

Some potential reasons may relate to how the programs are administered. But perhaps there's something more pernicious at play. Suppose that people believe in the norm of equal employment, but the practice thereof contradicts other, more submerged beliefs. Suppose managers believe that in addition to qualifications, managers must look and behave the same way as their peers look and appear. Suppose that people believe that equal employment opportunity is acceptable if one woman and/or person of color takes over a position of authority, but not when many women or minorities do so. If any one of these propositions is true, then perhaps it starts to get easier to explain why people are resistant to fair employment initiatives.

In their book *American Apartheid*, Douglas Massey and Nancy Denton discuss how blacks and whites think of "integration." Studying attitudes toward the preferred racial composition of neighborhoods, they found that whites felt most comfortable in neighborhoods that were lightly (or not at all) integrated. More than 70 percent of whites in one study said that they would not move into a neighborhood that was 36 percent black. The point for the many surveys done on housing integration is clear: whites, if they are comfortable with integration in principle, only want so much of it.

This kind of phenomenon, it is proposed, accounts for much of the resistance to equal employment opportunity programs. People do not want to think of themselves as racist and sexist and will say as much if you ask them. Many managers are willing to put up with affirmative action programs if there are only one or two women and/or people of color involved. But once significant numbers of women and members of minority groups start to move up the corporate ladder—which you would expect, after all, in a true meritocracy—the people who have traditionally occupied positions of power start to get nervous. White males interpret equal employment opportunity programs as a threat to their jobs and promotion. The phenomena of "angry white males" can be ascribed to the sense of threat many white men feel when their organizations attempt to diversify.

If you read transcripts of the Texaco meeting, this line of reasoning starts to explain resistance to real diversity in organizations. Not only were the Texaco employees denigrating minority and female employees, they were also protesting the imposition of activities related to Hanukkah and Kwanzaa which they felt were emblematic of how different their new colleagues were from them.

Real diversity means the way people work together in organizations will change. Pictures of a smiling multiracial work force in company-printed equal employment opportunity pamphlets mask the reality of why ending employment discrimination is so difficult—at the core, diversity means that organizational cultures and habits must change, and all too often change is resisted.

The Need for Management Commitment

The problem of resistance to diversity is as much cultural as it is economic. It is true that ensuring equal employment opportunity means that jobs which used to go exclusively to white males will now be increasingly occupied by women and people of color—and we should not underestimate self-interest as a reason for resistance to EEO. But the reason for resistance to organizational diversity that has not been as well examined is cultural in nature: diversity means that the culture of organizations will change. Because change is threatening, it is resisted.

Consider the oil industry. It has been well documented that the oil industry historically has been racist and sexist. Not surprisingly, the executive ranks of oil companies were composed almost exclusively of white males. At one time in American history—long before the civil rights movement won important victories for all of us—this was considered to be acceptable by many. Thankfully, we have started to realize that disparate treatment of people based on sex or race is wrong. But it takes a long time for beliefs about fairness to be reflected in our organizations—and longer still in some industries. Our abstract beliefs about fairness have to be enacted in concrete policies and programs—and therein lies the problem.

So Texaco, like many other companies, had in place the right kinds of programs but did not demonstrate the necessary management commitment to change the culture in which its employees worked. It put a good face on its commitment to fair treatment without matching rhetoric with substance. The lesson is clear—all of the glossy pamphlets and EEO officers in the world cannot make up for a lack of management commitment. Unless executives understand why EEO is both morally right and financially prudent and are willing to change the culture of their company, diversity will be a buzzword rather than a fact of life. The Texaco case has laid bare how far American corporations—and other organizations, including churches—have to go before the culture of racism and sexism is destroyed. In December 1996, Texaco announced a set of initiatives that both demonstrate management's commitment to eradicating a culture of discrimination and ensuring accountability for achieving fair employment goals throughout the organization. Unfortunately, it took a tape recording of a meeting at which illegal activities were being planned for people in the United States to realize that we are far from Martin Luther King's dream of a color-blind society. The nature of the debate about organizational and societal EEO issues, however, can and must change from a discussion of supposed "reverse discrimination" to an examination of the cultural reasons for the persistence of racism and sexism.

What You Can Do

People and organizations interested in corporate social responsibility have a window of opportunity to explain why EEO programs and policies are still desperately needed. We can educate corporations about the continued need to have EEO policies and programs in place that are supported by senior management. Socially responsible shareholders can continue to file resolutions asking companies to diversify their boards of directors and implement strong fair employment programs. Consumers can write to companies to ask how the latter are ensuring that fair treatment is the norm. What is needed now is a concerted effort to change how we think about diversity, fair employment, and institutional racism and sexism.

The Texaco case, in addition to other stories about discrimination in corporate America, shows that barriers to equal employment opportunity still exist. For people who want to effect social change, this issue offers a tremendous opportunity to change our society and its institutions for the better.

Article Review Form at end of book.

What should you do if you feel you have been a victim of unfair discrimination?

What Would *You* Do?

It's (Still) a Man's World

Jack was promoted over Linda, who was more qualified. She protested but was told, "Mind your own business."

Doug Wallace

The Case

Linda had parked the car and turned to the company's human relations consultant. She couldn't believe what she was hearing. "You have three choices: stay angry and continue to cause trouble, let me try to resolve the matter, or contact the EEOC, but I don't advise that because it'll be three to five years before they adjudicate it." She felt pinned to her seat, her mind racing.

Linda had worked for this company—a logging company in the Northwest—for years, first as a clerical worker and now as an accountant. She and many of her co-workers had been irked that Jack was appointed five months ago to a position for which Linda was much better qualified. The job had never been posted. It was suddenly boosted five grades in pay, and Jack was inserted into it, after his previous job as a programmer had been eliminated. He was making more than the other accountants, including Linda. The supervisors of the unit thought Linda should have been first in line for the new position, and they took their case to the comptroller. His response: "Mind your own business, that's the end of it."

That ignited Linda. She applied for the position. Interviews were delayed by the comptroller for weeks. Finally he told her, "You don't want this job. It's not as challenging as what you're doing now." When Linda disagreed, the comptroller put his hand on her shoulder and said, "The decision has already been made. You need to understand it's a man's world. My wife has experienced the same thing." Stunned, Linda went to the general manager. The comptroller didn't represent the company's view, he told her. He said he'd work something out. But when she called him regularly over the next three months, he kept putting her off. Now, fuming, Linda sat in the car wondering what she would do.

Marlene Fondrick, retired VP of Operations, Children's Health Center, St Paul, Minn.

It looks like a given in this case that no one in the company is going to do anything about Linda's situation, unless the human relations consultant is willing to negotiate on her behalf. She has too many things against her in the company.

I think I would first find someone to talk with outside the company—an attorney, for example—who is not already biased in favor of the company. Then I would contact the Equal Employment Opportunity Commission, knowing it might not be able to help me in a timely fashion. Linda certainly has a good case on the face of it, and with legal assistance she may be able to get the help she needs.

Don Conley, former VP of Public Affairs and VP of Human Resources, Honeywell, currently a partner in The Fulcrum Group, Minneapolis

From the sound of it, Linda has had a long-tenured investment in this company, it's probably located in a small town where people know each other outside of work, and the corporate office is remote from her facility. That picture has a bearing on this case.

If I were Linda, I'd do four things: 1) From those who support her, I would get their views in writing. 2) I'd take the consultant up on the offer to handle it, but would place a deadline of 30 days on that option, and ask, "What can you do?" 3) If this didn't resolve the matter, I'd retain an attorney, preparing a letter to the GM to respond within 30 days. Clearly, discrimination has occurred. 4) Failing this, I'd file with the EEOC.

Reprinted with permission from Business Ethics, PO Box 8439, Minneapolis, MN 55408.   612/879-0695.

Doug Wallace's Comments

Businesses are not democratic in nature. As a result, there are always power differentials. Some people have more control over others, and when they abuse that advantage, employees are left dangling in the wind. The ethical principles of respect for human dignity, fairness, and autonomy become casualties, as they are in this case. Companies should learn a lesson from allowing this kind of abusive culture to exist—the consequences eventually are costly in human and financial terms.

Both of our guest commentators eschew passivity, recommending that Linda needs to remain active in bringing her case forward. They also agree she has to get help outside the company, despite the probability of a long struggle. From my experience, you must have a fire that burns inside, to stay the course in a situation like this. It's not for the faint of heart. It requires ethical courage, a willingness to risk a lot to pursue a just cause.

What Actually Happened?

Linda filed her case with the EEOC after being encouraged to do so by an officer of the agency. Three weeks later she had enlisted 100 percent of the office personnel (16 persons) to form a union, presenting its formation as a complete surprise to management. Over a year later, with the matter still pending, the parent company appointed a new president who promptly fired both the comptroller and the GM after looking into their performance. He asked Linda what she wanted. She replied, "All I want is to get the job I applied for, nothing more—no settlement money—just what I wanted from the beginning." She got the job. The company lost at least $200,000 in legal costs, pursuing the matter, plus the challenge of dealing with a new bargaining unit. Sometimes justice does prevail.

Article Review Form at end of book.

What are the underlying issues that are cause for debate when discussing balance between the rights of the individual and those of the organization?

Are the ADA Guidelines on Mental Disabilities Fair to Business?

Tipper Gore

Gore is an advisor on mental health policy to President Clinton and the wife of Vice President Al Gore.

In 1990, Congress clearly sought to eradicate employment discrimination against people with mental, as well as physical disabilities, when it passed the Americans with Disabilities Act (ADA). Although thousands of people with psychiatric disabilities are working successfully in a variety of jobs in this country, many more are denied employment opportunities because of myths, fears and stereotypes. These barriers of attitude often exclude qualified candidates from being considered for a job, and they keep people with mental disabilities from leading productive lives.

Recently, the Employment Opportunity Commission (EEOC) published policy guidance to explain to private employees how they can comply with the ADA's requirements. Like the ADA itself, the EEOC's policy guidance recognizes both the rights of people with psychiatric disabilities to be free from discrimination in the workplace and the legitimate concerns of businesses that are trying to comply with the law. Unfortunately, the reaction of some in the business community to these guidelines makes it clear that the battle against the stigma associated with mental illness has not yet been won. . . .

Contrary to reports, EEOC's guide does not require that employers give special treatment to people with psychiatric disabilities. Rather, the EEOC and the ADA require employers to do for employees with psychiatric disabilities what they must do for employees with physical disabilities—make reasonable accommodations that will enable such employees to do their jobs.

Many employees with psychiatric disabilities are now working successfully without any accommodations. Others require accommodations that are relatively inexpensive and easy to provide. The ADA even provides employers a defense—"undue hardship"—when making an accommodation proves too difficult or too expensive.

Let's be clear. As I understand the rules, the ADA requires that an employee who wants to be accommodated because of his or her psychiatric disability must show that he or she falls within the legal definition of the term "disability." That employee must demonstrate to the employer—with documentation—that he or she has a disability that substantially limits one or more major life activities.

Essentially, the employee must have a serious, definable mental illness. Of course, even then, the employee is not entitled to be excused from relevant standards of conduct or from job performance standards. This is simply an issue of equality of people with mental and physical disabilities. . . .

National Federation of Independent Business

The [EEOC] guidelines send a serious but confusing message from the government to employers, telling them they may not discriminate against qualified workers with mental illness, yet they may not ask job applicants if they have a history of mental illness and they must accommodate employees with psychiatric or emotional problems. . . .

Small-business owners are already overwhelmed with government rules, regulations, paperwork and taxes. The new EEOC guidelines are lengthy, confusing, and dangerously vague. Additionally, they provide provisions that . . . leave them wide open to the risk and cost of frivolous litigation.

From Tipper Gore, "Razing Workplace Barriers," *The Washington Post,* May 12, 1997. © The Washington Post. Reprinted by permission.

For example, the guidelines state, "Expert testimony about substantial limitation is not necessarily required. Credible testimony from the individual with a disability and his/her family members, friends or co-workers may suffice." This phrasing is full of ambiguity—"not necessarily" and "may suffice" leave plenty of room for interpretation. How is an employer to know what to do if an employee's spouse calls the office and says, "John is going through post-traumatic stress and needs a leave of absence." If John does not come to work for a month, he is protected by the ADA because his wife gave "credible testimony."

The guidelines also say that, "Requests [from the employee] for reasonable accommodation [in the workplace] do not necessarily have to be in writing. Employees may request accommodations in conversation or may use any other mode of communication." Without a paper trail, the case becomes the word of the employer against the word of the employee and renders the employer defenseless. This type of guideline is an open invitation to lawsuit abuse. . . .

Mental illness is a type of disability that is still, in many ways, a mystery to the medical community. Yet these guidelines set up an expectation that the average small-business owner should comprehend and act on the needs of the mentally ill. It may be obvious to the small-business owner that someone in a wheelchair needs a ramp to enter the building. . . . But the needs of someone who suffers from major depression or obsessive-compulsive disorder are, unfortunately, difficult to identify and implement.

Small-business owners do not maintain legal counsel or a personnel department to help them decipher their obligations under the ADA. Small-business owners are responsible and thoughtful citizens who want to comply with the law, but without specific guidance, neither Main Street business owners nor people with disabilities know what actions are expected, appropriate or legal.

Article Review Form at end of book.

Who was Franz Kafka? Does the title of the reading seem appropriate for the content?

Kafka Wasn't Kidding

David A. Price

You know the sad story: In the early hours of the morning of March 24, 1989 the tanker Exon Valdez hit a reef in Prince William Sound, Alaska, spilling 11 million gallons of crude oil. Exxon paid billions in fines and cleanup costs. Many people still curse Exxon as a despoiler of the environment.

It is widely believed that the captain of the tanker was drunk. To minimize the chances of another such disaster, Exxon implemented a new policy: While offering employees help in getting treatment for alcohol or drug dependency, the company declared some jobs, where safety is critical—tanker captains, for example-off-limits to anyone who has a history of abuse of alcohol or some other substance.

Now Exxon is in court again. This time the bureaucrats in the U.S. Equal Employment Opportunity Commission are suing the company to protect ships' captains and the like who have had drinking or drug problems.

No, we are not kidding. The feds say Exxon's policy, aimed at minimizing accidents, violates the 1990 Americans with Disabilities Act. The EEOC says that Exxon is illegally discriminating against some 50 employees who have had alcohol or drug problems but have since been rehabilitated.

Chrys Meador, an EEOC trial attorney on the case, defends her agency's kafkaesque action. "Exxon believes they cannot get a guarantee that somebody who's had a substance abuse problem will never relapse," she says. "Well, we can't give them that guarantee. But the experts we have consulted have said that there are very positive employee assistance programs that actively monitor individuals, and there are telltale signs so that you can detect these things before they become a problem."

In other words, it's the company's responsibility to know when an exdrunk is about to slip off the wagon or when a schizophrenic has stopped taking his pills. Only it had better be careful how it monitors these things.

Meador says the agency is just following what Congress said in the 1990 Disabilities Act. Scary thing is, she's right.

Big companies like Exxon can afford to pay these fines and put up with the expensive red tape and legal costs. Owners of small businesses cannot. Talk about discrimination.

Article Review Form at end of book.

Reprinted by permission of *Forbes Magazine* © Forbes Inc., 1997.

According to this reading, how are judges interpreting the Americans with Disabilities Act as it pertains to mental illness? Contrast these rulings with rulings related to alcoholism.

Troubled at Work

Herbert Wray

Marquita Palmer had no blemishes on her performance record—and then Clara Johnson became her supervisor. Suddenly, the Cook County, Ill., caseworker began to unravel. She had a falling out with co-worker Nicki Lazzaro, who she believed had forsaken her friendship for one with Johnson. According to the court's opinion, she threatened Lazzaro, promising to "kick her ass" and "throw her out the window." Palmer was suspended for 10 days.

The time off didn't restore Palmer's equilibrium. Once back at work, she told Johnson to "go to hell" and was sent home for another seven days. Believing that Johnson was conspiring against her, Palmer started calling the office, accusing her supervisor of harassing her and threatening Johnson's life. "I'm ready to kill her," she told one colleague. "I don't know what I'll do. . . . I want Clara bad and I want her dead:' In a call to Johnson, Palmer said: "Your ass is mine, b———." After the phone calls, Palmer was fired.

But she wasn't ready to disappear quietly. Because Palmer had sought psychiatric help in the midst of her conflicts with Johnson—and had been diagnosed with major depression and delusional paranoid disorder—she immediately sued Cook County under the Americans with Disabilities Act (ADA). Her firing, she claimed, was an illegal act of discrimination because of her mental illness; the county was legally bound to make allowances for her disability just as if she had been in a wheelchair or hard of hearing.

The Fine Points

Though Palmer would eventually lose her case, one aspect of her argument is indisputable: The 1990 law was indeed designed to protect the rights of people with psychiatric as well as physical disabilities. But the details of what it means at the office to accommodate those with mental illness are only now being worked out. Since the law went into effect, the federal Equal Employment Opportunity Commission has received more than 10,000 complaints of workplace discrimination against the mentally disabled, second only to the number from people with back injuries. Employers, unsure of their obligations and baffled by how to fulfill them, have implored the EEOC for guidance. It's a simple enough matter to identify the need for ergonomic furniture or wheelchair ramps, but how to handle a manager so depressed that he can't concentrate on a presentation? Or a secretary too anxiety-ridden to handle the phones? Last spring, in an attempt to clarify how the ADA applies to the mentally ill, the commission published guidelines on who typically qualifies for protection and what kinds of workplace modifications might be made to allow people with various disabilities to remain on the job. More flexible scheduling, job coaches, and brighter and quieter work stations, for example, were among the accommodations the EEOC said might "reasonably" be expected of employers under the law.

The reaction to the guidelines was swift and outraged. Editorialists argued that employers would be obliged to put up not only with pesky malingering but with uncooperative, hostile, even violently psychotic workers. Critics also maintained that the need to make allowances for millions of people struggling with life's travails—a failed relationship, for example—would cripple American business. Cultural critics, far more skeptical today than when the first civil rights laws were passed, bemoaned the creation of one more class of victims with special entitlements—and the further undermining of personal responsibility in American society. For some time, there has been a growing perception in the culture that the definitions of mental, emotional, and behavioral abnormality have expanded far beyond the bounds of common sense. Psychiatry's official handbook of mental disorders, the *Diagnostic and Statistical Manual,* has grown bulkier with every new edition; the current volume identifies more than 300 disorders, up from 106 just 18 years ago. Each year, more of what was once considered normal (though not necessarily pleasant) becomes pathological and, in theory at least, excusable under the civil rights laws. The proliferation of diagnosable anxiety and stress disorders has been especially bothersome to critics, who lament that we're creating disease out of everyday life.

Copyright, February 9, 1998, *U.S. News & World Report.*

Course Correction

Given these concerns, it's instructive to examine how complaints under the ADA are playing out in the courts. The case law is not vastly expanding the pool of mentally disabled workers getting special treatment; indeed, the opposite seems to be occurring. From a broad cultural perspective, one could even argue that the courts are correcting course, forcing society back toward a view of behavior that demands more—not less—accountability from citizens.

Marquita Palmer's is a case in point. The court dismissed her claim of discrimination—a ruling that was upheld on appeal. Writing for the federal appeals court, Judge Richard Posner allowed that Palmer might have a disabling mental illness and that her personality conflict with Johnson might well have triggered her psychotic break. Even so, Posner reasoned, Palmer was fired for threatening to kill another employee—behavior that is unacceptable regardless of its cause. Posner cited the false reasoning of Hamlet, who also attempted to shirk responsibility for abusive behavior: "Was't Hamlet wrong'd Laertes? Never Hamlet. / If Hamlet from himself be ta'en away, / And when he's not himself does wrong Laertes, / Then Hamlet does it not; Hamlet denies it. / Who does it then? His madness."

The literary Posner was saying that a psychiatric diagnosis does not justify unacceptable behavior. And judge after judge in court after court has insisted on this distinction. While judges rarely dispute a psychiatric diagnosis, they have generally required workers claiming a right to special treatment to establish two things: that they are persistently unable to perform at least one major life activity—getting enough sleep to be alert on the job, for example—and that they are "otherwise qualified" for the job. Thus a New York judge dismissed a clerical worker's claim that her chronic tardiness should be forgiven because it was caused by depression and antidepressant medication. If you can't get yourself to work, the court argued, you're not "otherwise qualified" for the job. A Maryland judge defended the firing of a typist with bipolar disorder whose bizarre and insubordinate behavior included dumping trash on a conference table; insubordination, regardless of its cause, disqualifies a claim for special protection. And a judge in Maine dismissed a depressed worker's argument that he shouldn't lose his job because his mental disorder made him incapable of interacting with other workers. Since the illness didn't interfere with any "major life activity," the judge ruled, it did not rise to the level of legal disability.

A Rare Win

The courts have held for workers on occasion. For example, a San Francisco attorney with severe depression won an award of $1.26 million when his employer tried to force his resignation and refused to honor his request to work no more than 90 hours in any two-week period. And the 7th Circuit reinstated the claim of an Indiana custodian who was fired; the appeals court said that the lower court had not explored whether the worker's manic depression, anxiety attacks, and paranoid schizophrenia might have been accommodated by rethinking his duties. But these rulings for workers are the exception because of a linguistic paradox written into the law. On the one hand, many legitimate psychiatric impairments that can be treated clinically are not disabling in a legal analysis since they don't persistently interfere with a person's ability to function. In fact, the law explicitly excludes some disorders from protection pyromania, kleptomania, and certain sexual disorders among them. And the EEOC emphasized last spring that common "adjustment disorders" (the melancholy following a marital breakup, for example) would not necessarily qualify someone as disabled under the law, since such disorders are usually temporary. On the other hand, workers who can prove that their disability hinders them from performing a major life function—they can't get up in the morning, say—often establish as well that they're not "otherwise qualified."

Palmer lost her battle on both fronts. Because her performance had not been problematic before Johnson arrived, she wasn't able to convince the court that she suffered from a long-standing impairment. And her abusive, threatening behavior was indisputably insubordinate.

It's clear that judges have allayed fears of some critics that healthy workers—and even mentally impaired workers who are able to function—would flagrantly abuse the ADA's protections. What's less clear (and probably will be so for some time) is whether those who truly deserve protection are getting it. Workplace experts believe that many people with psychiatric disabilities are indeed succeeding because of simple and inexpensive changes such as shorter hours, on-the-job training, and a move to a quiet corner. But the evidence is anecdotal; success stories tend not to appear on the court docket.

Advocates for the mentally ill are divided about the ADA and the EEOC rules. Some, while pessimistic that any law can correct the enduring stigma surrounding mental illness, applaud the effort to clarify employers' duty to help the disabled succeed. Others take issue with the whole notion of accommodation and are heartened by the courts' conservative bent. They argue that the challenge of work—including showing up and acting cooperatively—is empowering and that lowering expectations reinforces dysfunction.

It was certainly not the primary purpose of a law protecting the disabled to nudge the culture back toward self-reliance and personal responsibility. But judges have interpreted the law that way and have allowed few mentally ill workers to gain extra protection. When it comes to most dysfunction, judges are saying, "Deal with it."

Article Review Form at end of book.

According to this reading, how are disabilities being defined? How should courts decide which disabilities are protected by the Americans with Disabilities Act and which are not?

The Americans with Minor Disabilities Act

Joseph P. Shapiro

Jeffrey Ola had never heard of the Americans with Disabilities Act. He certainly didn't consider himself disabled. So it was a shock when the Nashville and Davidson County, Tenn., Fire Department rescinded its offer to him of a paramedic job because of his "disability." A physical exam had turned up that Ola had 80 percent hearing loss in his right ear, the lingering effect of a childhood infection. Ola did not even use a hearing aid. And that hearing loss never kept him from doing anything. Not from studying to be an emergency medical technician. Not from beating out 65 other people for the paramedic's job. But fire department policy was strict that normal hearing was required to perform a paramedic's duties. On the sly, a sympathetic fire captain suggested that Ola file a federal antidiscrimination complaint. After several years, and the eventual intervention of the U.S. Department of Justice using the ADA, Ola got the job last summer.

When Congress passed the ADA in 1990, it was widely seen as a tool for ending discrimination in the workplace and in public accommodations for the paralyzed, the blind, the deaf, and others with severe disabilities, and for delivering independence. Almost every member of Congress got a visit from at least one disabled constituent, usually a war veteran, a mother with a child in a wheelchair, or someone else with a compelling story about discrimination. But it turns out that the clearest beneficiaries have not been the severely disabled but a much larger group of people who, like Ola, have relatively minor impairments. For better or for worse, the ADA has greatly expanded the definition of disability to include chronic and often hidden problems—like bad backs, bad hearts, cancer, diabetes, learning disabilities, arthritis, and epilepsy.

Vast Reach

Some 54 million Americans—20.6 percent of the population are disabled, says the Census Bureau. Slightly under half are counted as having a "severe" impairment. Last week, by a narrow vote of 5 to 4, the Supreme Court approved an expansive definition of disability under the act. A majority of the justices ruled that the law defines the term broadly to protect people with severe and minor disabilities alike. In specific, the ruling allows Sidney Abbott, an active woman with no visible disability, to sue a dentist who refused to treat her in his office because she has HIV.

Whether the public was fully aware or not, Congress intended for the ADA to cover a wide range of people. Lawmakers even allowed the government to protect people with asymptomatic HIV, like Abbott. Similarly, the statute encompasses people who have no disability yet face discrimination because they are "regarded as" disabled (like someone who was assumed to have AIDS though he didn't). But the ADA did not list the disabilities it covers, leaving it to the courts to decide who gets included in many instances.

The case files of the Department of Justice and the Equal Employment Opportunity Commission, the ADA's primary enforcers, are filled with examples of people who received protection even though they do not fit common notions of what a disabled person looks like. Back injuries, for example, are the most common disability cited in ADA complaints lodged with the EEOC, making up 17 percent of cases.

Typical is the case of New York plumber Cosimo Chindemi, who has spent his career surviving off odd jobs. He is shut out of big contracts and unable to start his own company because, with severe dyslexia, he cannot take Rockland County's written licensing exam. The county argues that a plumber needs to read things like the instructions on a boiler. Chindemi says he has 40 years experience and even helped install the pipes in the building that houses the Rockland County Board of Plumbing, Heating, and Cooling Examiners. In the face of Justice Department pressure, the county agreed to modify its exam—although Chindemi and the board are still fighting over how to test him.

Peanut Butter Allergies

The ADA has changed the face of preschool, too—opening up classes to thousands of children often excluded

Copyright, July 6, 1998, *U.S. News & World Report.*

because they had minor disabilities like diabetes and food allergies. The nation's two largest child-care chains had prohibited their employees from using a finger-prick test to monitor the blood-sugar level of children with diabetes or to administer injections to kids suffering from life-threatening allergic reactions—calling for these medical tasks to be done by nurses or paramedics, not child-care workers. Marcia Fisher faced taking her son, who is allergic to peanut butter, out of the preschool he loved, until the Justice Department forced a change in the policy at his school.

Separate legislation passed in 1991 allowed disabled employees to sue bosses for discrimination under the ADA and collect up to $300,000. That meant some lawyers were willing to press inappropriate cases. Courts have thrown out most silly lawsuits, like those of the college professor who was fired for sexual harassment and then blamed his use of antidepressant medications. Still, even winning a suit can be expensive for a company that gets sued.

Critics of the ADA argue that while the law helps people who have gotten a raw deal, it covers too many who do not deserve protection but who get it at great cost to the rest of society. Walter Olson, author of *The Excuse Factory*, argues that the ADA makes employers, fearful of lawsuits, reluctant to fire incompetent or unsafe workers. United Parcel Service, notes Olson, was sued by the EEOC for its policy that delivery-truck drivers must have normal vision in both eyes. Companies like UPS, whose brown delivery trucks travel daily on residential streets, need to set their own safety standards, Olson says, especially when public safety is involved. The ADA, responds EEOC attorney Peggy Mastroianni, requires that applicants be considered for their abilities, not ruled out by blanket restrictions.

Ironically, there is also disappointment with the law among some of its advocates. While the ADA has helped a wide range of people with minor disabilities, the breadth of its impact among the severely disabled is less clear. The law has prompted some notable changes—construction of ramps to building entrances; improvement of urban transit for wheelchair users; and establishment of telephone relay systems for the deaf. But proponents hoped the law would end the 70 percent-plus unemployment rate among the severely disabled and it has not. For the severely disabled, says Sid Wolinsky of Disability Rights Advocates, an Oakland legal center, the ADA has been very much a mixed bag: Supporters of the ADA originally argued that the law would help move many of the 7.5 million Americans who get Social Security disability payments off those rolls, saving billions of dollars. Instead, fewer than 1 percent find permanent work and leave welfare, notes Mitchell LaPlante of the University of California-San Francisco. A sign that the ADA primarily helps the less severely disabled is that 87 percent of complaints to the EEOC come from people already in jobs.

Expecting Too Much

Some experts have concluded that many of the problems faced by the severely disabled cannot be solved by the ADA. "People expect too much of the ADA," says John Lancaster of the President's Committee on Employment of People with Disabilities. "It's just a civil rights law." There are many other barriers to getting a job, like the need for transportation to work, for good vocational rehabilitation and, most important, for access to health care. Severely disabled people on Social Security work disability quickly lose their eligibility for public health insurance once they work full time. Private insurance often will not cover all their needs.

Stephen Olson has the kind of problem that the law alone can't solve. He may soon be forced to quit a job that he loves and go back on welfare. Olson, a 40-year-old quadriplegic, earns $18,000 working 30 hours a week for a Berkeley, Calif., disability group—making him too wealthy to qualify for the state program that pays an attendant to help him dress and bathe. The attendant costs $1,200 a month, but Olson only clears $1,300 after taxes. "The ADA gives me a right to work," says Olson. "But it doesn't protect me as far as keeping my funding." Congress is considering legislation to ease these "work disincentives" by letting disabled people who take jobs buy coverage from Medicaid or Medicare. For the severely disabled who it was widely thought would be the main beneficiaries of the civil rights law, expanding the definition of disability has not been enough to deliver the ADA's promise of independence.

Article Review Form at end of book.

Should organizations develop zero tolerance policies on sexual harassment? What is the estimated legal cost for a sexual harassment trial?

Finally, a Corporate Tip Sheet on Sexual Harassment

Susan B. Garland

Garland covers legal affairs from Washington.

A chill wind ran through corporate boardrooms on June 26 as the Supreme Court handed down two landmark rulings on sexual harassment. The justices ruled that companies can be held liable for a supervisor's sexually harassing behavior even if the offense was never reported to management. And the high court said an employer can be liable when a supervisor threatens to punish a worker for resisting sexual demands—even if such threats aren't carried out.

At first blush, the decisions sound like a prescription for a flood of new lawsuits. But take a deep breath, Corporate America. There's actually some good news for employers in the fine print of the justices' decisions. For the first time, the court is giving companies guidelines on how to protect themselves against sexual-harassment charges. There are no guarantees, of course. But, if companies get serious about stamping out harassment and sustain the efforts, they can be better protected in court—and their employees can feel safer at work.

Affirmative Defense

The court's advice: Develop a zero-tolerance policy on harassment, communicate it to employees, and ensure that victims can report abuses without fear of retaliation. "Employers should feel safe as long as they are vigorous," says Susan R. Meisinger, senior vice president at the Society for Human Resource Management.

So even though the court has broadened the conditions under which suits can be brought, a company can deflect sexual-harassment charges with a two-pronged "affirmative defense," the justices said. First, it must take "reasonable care to prevent and correct promptly any sexually harassing behavior." Then, it must show that an employee failed to use internal procedures for reporting abusive behavior. This defense won't work when a supervisor retaliates against a worker for resisting sexual advances. But it will protect a company from charges that it tolerates a hostile work environment.

That means if a company has a strong antiharassment policy and a worker doesn't report an incident of sexual harassment and later sues, an employer can use that as part of a defense. Says Boston employment lawyer Marilyn D. Stempler: "The court places obligations on employers to set up policies, but it also places an obligation on the victim to come forward."

Not every nuance is spelled out. The court didn't describe, for example, what constitutes "reasonable care" for preventing or halting harassment. But employment consultants say companies should now publicize the policies as aggressively and regularly as possible—in handbooks, on posters, in training sessions, and in reminders in paychecks. Line supervisors and employees should be given real-life examples of what could constitute offensive conduct.

Companies also must ensure that workers won't face reprisals if they report offending behavior. Employment experts say companies should designate several managers to take these complaints, so that employees don't find themselves reporting to their immediate supervisor—very often the abuser. Managers should be trained in sexual-harassment issues. And, experts say, punishment against harassers should be swift and sure.

With legal costs for a jury trail running as high as $200,000 it's cheaper for most companies to put in place a basic sexual-harassment pro-

Reprinted from July 13, 1998 issue of *Business Week* by special permission. Copyright © 1998 by the McGraw-Hill Companies, Inc.

The Court Strikes a Balance

Employees Gained Because They Can:

- File a harassment complaint even if they don't suffer retaliation after resisting a supervisor's sexual advances
- Hold an employer liable for a supervisor's harassment even if top management doesn't know about it

Employers Gained Because They Can:

- Protect against sexual harassment charges if their company has a zero-tolerance policy that is widely observed
- Win a case if the employee does not report the offenses to a supervisor who is responsible under the company program.

gram. Still, none of this is simple. Small companies may not have the expertise to investigate complaints. And for all companies, once a complaint is filed, employers will face increased pressure to sort out who's telling the truth and to mete out serious punishments.

But by both expanding a company's potential liability and offering a valid defense, the Supreme Court noted that it was giving employers "an incentive to prevent and eliminate harassment." That means companies can protect themselves while doing right by their workers. That's an opportunity for Corporate America, not a threat.

Article Review Form at end of book.

WiseGuide Wrap-Up

These are some, but by no means all of the legal issues facing organizations today. The goal of most of this legislation is to balance the rights and needs of the individual with those of the organization. Some would argue that enacting legislation supporting EEO laws or Affirmative Action, may unfairly keep qualified individuals out of jobs. How far should an organization go to achieve the reasonable accommodation standard for the ADA, and who should bear the expense of that accommodation? How does all of this fit within the ethical guidelines for psychologists to respect the dignity and welfare of the individual? Do you see other binds and dilemmas here?

I have ended this section with a lot of questions, because I see questions as the basis of law. Industrial/organizational psychologists should remember that laws are not objective truths. They reflect a social process and provide standards and guidelines. They are meant to be questioned and constantly reevaluated.

R.E.A.L. Sites

This list provides a print preview of typical **Coursewise** R.E.A.L. sites. (There are over 100 such sites at the **Courselinks**™ site.) The danger in printing URLs is that web sites can change overnight. As we went to press, these sites were functional using the URLs provided. If you come across one that isn't, please let us know via email to: webmaster@coursewise.com. Use your Passport to access the most current list of R.E.A.L. sites at the **Courselinks** site.

Site name: Equal Employment Opportunity Commission
URL: http://www.eeoc.gov/
Why is it R.E.A.L.? This is the federal government's web site describing the mission, organization, and power of the EEOC.
Key topics: law, EEOC
Try this: How do you file an EEOC complaint? Click on the Filing a Charge section and follow the directions. Be sure to visit the Fact Sheet on Federal EEOC Complaint Processing.

Site name: Ross Runkel Employment Law Page
URL: http://www.rossrunkel.com/
Why is it R.E.A.L.? This is a service providing a wide range of information on employment and labor law.
Key topics: law, EEOC
Try this: To find out about some current Supreme Court cases addressing Labor Law click on the US SC Docket icon (United States Supreme Court Docket). Click on the Employ Discrimination icon to find some recent decisions on employment discrimination.

Site name: Court TV
URL: http://www.courttv.com/
Why is it R.E.A.L.? This is a commercial site containing information about current and famous court cases.
Key topics: law
Try this: To view some current legal cases concerning sexual harassment, click on the search icon and enter "sexual harassment" in the search area. What does PRIMA FACIE mean? Click on the Legal Terms icon and look it up.

section 4

Recruitment and Selection

Learning Objectives

- To describe the importance of the job–person fit.
- To become aware of hiring trends in organizations.
- To address the strengths and limitations of various selection tools and techniques.

WiseGuide Intro

Finding a job. Finding the right person to fill a job. These are very important considerations for both the job seeker and the organization, but how do you find the job that's right for you, and how does the organization know when it has found an individual who will help the company? As we consider the related topics of recruitment and selection, it is important to remember that any company or organization is a collection of individuals. With the right people in the right places, organizations can excel, but, just as people can make the place, people can also break it. Organizations that fail to recruit or select the appropriate individuals are doomed to failure. Thus, finding the right fit is important for both the individual and the organization.

Industrial/organizational psychologists conduct research and develop programs to help individuals and organizations find the appropriate fit. An early trend in the field of industrial/organizational psychology was the development and use of employee screening tests. For example, during WWI, Robert Yerkes argued that selection tests, such as the Army Alpha or Army Beta tests, could be used to place recruits in the appropriate places in the armed forces, thus making the whole organization more efficient and effective. As organizations bought into this idea, there were increasing demands for the development and validation of selection techniques.

As we explore factors that contribute to making a good fit, we assume that both parties know their needs/skills and goals. When you ask yourself, "What type of job do I want?" you need to be able to identify your abilities and your interests. It is also very helpful to know your options. Industrial/organizational psychologists and others in the career development field have developed a wider variety of assessment tools to help people organize their thinking in this area. Some of these tools are now in the public domain and can be accessed via the Internet (see the R.E.A.L. sites listed at the end of this section and at the **Courselinks**™ web site). These sites provide a good start for helping you develop a realistic and effective career plan.

It is equally important to know what employers want before you begin your job search. As McGuire points out in Reading 21, employers want workers with flexibility. As job stability decreases, organizations need people who can learn new things. They need employees who have the ability and the personality to survive and thrive in an environment where there is constant change and training. They also need individuals who can work with others in an increasingly diverse organizational environment.

These trends suggest that organizations are increasingly focusing on personality characteristics. As Behling notes in Reading 22, managers traditionally have looked for knowledge, ability, and skill profiles that match a specific job. However, some organizations currently lean more toward other factors. For example, the Bill Gates strategy at Microsoft gives preference to "intelligence or smartness over anything else." Other organizations hire for personality characteristics or dispositions, such as motivation or friendliness. Behling argues that no single strategy is universally more effective than any other—organizations must select the strategy which best fits that organization or a particular job.

In Reading 23, Hogan, Hogan, and Roberts make a strong case for the use of personality measures in the selection process. In this article, they address such key areas as the relationship between personality and performance, possible invasions of privacy, and the potential that job seekers will give false information on the tests. All of these represent legitimate questions that employers should consider before using personality tests as selection tools. However, they argue that, when used appropriately, personality tests provide a reliable and valid means for selecting and placing employees.

In Reading 24, Nelson argues that recruitment and selection are tied to organizational structure. Companies are changing their basic organizational structure and are becoming virtual or empowered organizations. This jargon implies that organizations are reducing traditional boundaries, such as access to data, and are increasing the variety of employee tasks. This movement has yielded increased diversity in how workers structure their tasks and organize their time. As noted in the first section, work is no longer a fixed bundle of tasks. Because of this dynamic change in work, specific skills become obsolete quickly, and employers need individuals who can respond to changes and new skills as situations demand.

Questions

Reading 21. According to McGuire, what are the most important trends occurring in the workplace?

Reading 22. What are the primary issues involved in using personality tests in the selection process?

Reading 23. The authors suggest that personality tests are a way to promote social justice and increase organizational effectiveness. How do they defend this position? Do you agree or disagree with this position? What does it mean to match the "whole person" with the "whole job"? What are the big five personality dimensions, and how are they linked to job performance?

Reading 24. According to Nelson, what are the boundaries in organizations?

According to McGuire, what are the most important trends occurring in the workplace?

Wanted:

Workers with Flexibility for 21st Century Jobs

Future workplace changes have businesses looking to psychology for help with its most important commodity.

Patrick A. McGuire
Monitor staff

Like a trailer for a Hollywood film, the 90s have previewed the coming attractions we can expect more of as we merge into the re-engineered fast lane of the 21st-century world of work—blazingly faster information systems, blink-of-an-eye access to a global marketplace, virtual offices, virtual teams, even virtual organizations.

Yet all of those streamlined advances will cough and sputter, say psychologists, unless organizations, large or small, in cyberspace or on terra firma, concentrate in the next century on better understanding and nurturing the human side of business.

In fact, to accomplish that—to be able to regularly recruit and hang onto good employees who will be committed to a job even though it may not be committed to them; to train a new breed of leaders who can hold the center while keeping two increasingly disparate types of employees working together—psychologists and organizations have already put their heads together.

- Psychologists at the Center for Creative Leadership are urging organizations to be prepared to fill the "existential emptiness of workers."

- New research suggests a growing importance for the role of personality in determining job performance.

- Psychologists working with the Hewlett Packard Corporation, are role-playing various scenarios for managing those virtual teams learning to instill isolated team members, scattered across the globe, with a sense of belonging.

"We have gone from an era in which we have tried to get the most out of people, to the soft, touchy-feely age" says Lily Kelly-Radford, PhD, vice president of educational programs at the Center for Creative Leadership, headquartered in Greensboro, N.C. "Now we have to go back and balance the two."

And, says psychologist Seymour Adler, PhD, of Assessment Solutions Inc. in New York, "the real challenge for organizations, that I think psychology is going to be uniquely capable of helping, is creating coordination and commitment."

Less Job Stability

The impetus, of course, is technology. As it streaks into the future, says Kevin Murphy, PhD, president of the Society for Industrial-Organizational Psychology (Div. 14), "organizations are moving toward flatter, more flexible structures with fewer levels of supervision and more wide ranging job descriptions. So there is less likelihood of a very stable structured job where you can write down what you will do for the next 20 years."

There will still be large corporations—just fewer of them, say psychologists, as many organizations will begin decentralizing their operations. And while those large organizations will still need good people, the theory is that they won't need as many of them and, because of the constant change, won't be able to guarantee them long-term job security.

"You'll see a dramatic increase in the use of temps, contractors and outsourcing," says Adler, creating a need for managers who can coordinate two distinct types of employees.

"You're going to need leaders who can manage diversity beyond the traditional sense of race or gender," predicts psychologist Mitchell Marks, PhD, a San Francisco management consultant. "I mean diversity in individuals with different psychological needs, like outsourced contractors or in-house team players. Leaders will have to be driving in two lanes at once."

Road crews are already working on the problem. "Organizations

"Wanted: Workers with Flexibility for 21st Century Jobs. Future workplace changes have businesses looking to psychology for help with its most important commodity," by Patrick A. McGuire, *APA Monitor*, Vol. 29, No. 7, 1998. Copyright © 1998 by the American Psychological Association. Reprinted with permission.

have expanded their scope in areas we never saw before," says Chockalingam Viswesvaran, PhD, a psychologist at Florida International University. "Topics like fairness, and justice and work-family conflicts are being pushed to the forefront" by employers, he says. "No longer can you compartmentalize a person."

What exactly will change with everyday work?

Right now we have work structured so that we leave home at 8 and come home at 6," says Viswesveran. That structure won't be there any more. People will be able to work anytime. Those who have an inner drive will be able to do well. Those who find it difficult to work without a structure will find it hard."

Many jobs once handled by salaried employees will be outsourced, meaning it will become commonplace for future workers to develop careers built around freelance work, perhaps from home or temporary offices, going from project to project, even from company to company. Paychecks will come in piecemeal.

The drawbacks may be outweighed by a hidden plus, says Adler, as new demands "foster a sense of the professional, and you find people taking individual responsibility for themselves, managing their own careers."

Constant Training

Those who do stay in the more traditional jobs will find they are expected to cover more bases, while knowing their job could be eliminated or outsourced at any time. Most likely, say industrial-organizational psychologists, they will be in constant training as technology continuously spawns new products and new markets that expect new and faster ways of doing things. One expert predicts that by 2010 it will take 50 percent of a work day to come up to speed with what's transpired since you left the day before.

"How can we prepare our organizations or our people to function in this environment?" says Adler. "The way you will thrive in the marketplace is by living on chaos. There is the challenge of balancing work and home life when operating globally, 24 hours a day. With digital phones you can be reached any time. E-mail is filling up every hour. new items are coming in 24 hours a day. How do you balance that?"

With flexibility, he says. For example, Adler and his company recently conducted training exercises for computer giant Hewlett Packard. The goal was to assess and train managers of remote workforces. In several three- to four-hour exercises, psychologists role-played the parts of members of a virtual team, while various Hewlett Packard executives practiced coordinating those unseen team members in offices from Singapore to Silicon Valley.

"Solutions [by managers] have to be super creative from a psychological perspective," says Adler, "to create a sense of belongingness and to help people overcome the information deficit that comes from operating in a virtual environment."

"We are still human beings," adds Marks. "We are not drones or clones in our cubicles. We will still have human needs for affiliation and attachment. There will still be a need for interaction."

Even so, the demands of a faster pace of work will require a stable personality. Some psychologists believe this reality breathes new life into the role of personality as a predictor of behavior in the workplace. The standard measurements of work behavior have been skill and knowledge, and in fact, says Murphy, "Industrial/organizational psychology has for a longtime dismissed personality because the quality of research and applications was uneven." But new research, along with the expanding need for multiskilled individuals in the work force, has caused many to "take a second look," he says.

Counterproductive Behaviors

One of those engaged in the personality research is Deniz Ones, PhD, the Hellervik professor of industrial/organizational psychology at the University of Minnesota. She says organizations are interested in personality, not just for ensuring efficiency, but to screen out those prone to "counterproductive behaviors," such as absenteeism. "The idea is, what do we want people to be like when they work in organizations that span the globe? There's not enough research now to say what those characteristics might be, but we no longer are willing to write personality off." Her collaborative work with Viswesvaran into "integrity testing," for instance, measures a combination of "agreeableness, emotional stability and conscientiousness."

A more controversial aspect of personality research has to do with the mapping of the human genome. For a long time psychologists have debated whether or not behaviors and personalities and abilities were a function of the environment or genes, says Ones. Current thought is that genes are the determining factor, and some psychologists, she says, are researching ways of measuring personality characteristics using genetic techniques.

While that raises the specter of employers one day using a blood test to screen out undesirable employees, Ones takes a more hopeful view. "It might mean you would be suited to do this job if you had this kind of training and we'll do this intervention to make sure you succeed in the job."

Many psychologists doubt that genetic determinism will play a role in future work environments and concentrate their efforts on upgrading the more traditional role of leadership.

"It will require a certain kind of human being to be able to manage in the future," predicts Kelly-Radford. While the idea of "coaching" has taken hold in team-based work environments, she says, the new crop of leaders will need to be "master coaches."

They must be adept at interpersonal, on-the-job coaching, she says, sensitive enough to win an individual's loyalty, but skilled at avoiding entanglements as they cross boundaries.

"I might be coaching you and understanding your weaknesses," she explains, "and we may have some emotional periods as I coach you. If you allow me to come into your personal world, I need to have good boundary management to get out of that discussion. Some managers get seduced by that sort of dialogue, and they allow it to affect their decisions."

Future leaders will commonly face this kind of delicate position, she says, because "with everything big and expansive and fast, there is no sense of intimacy. There's almost an existential emptiness that people will experience."

The leader's job will be to "act as the knitting that holds the structure together." That will include filling worker emptiness with high-level discussions that reinforce positive values, she says, "providing ground rules for functional behavior."

Leaders, she adds, "will have to learn how to give coaching and even be vulnerable enough to accept coaching; to not just be the omnipotent leader who knows all."

Not Just Charisma

But, Kelly-Radford warns, being inspirational alone will not cut it. "We are beyond charismatic leadership," she says. "A leader has to have grounding and authenticity, but also a good business understanding and very strong interpersonal skills. Flash with nothing behind it will not work anymore."

At least, says Marks, leaders of tomorrow have already been primed by experience gained today. "You have a generation of executives who grew up with team building," he says. "They have been exposed to psychologists as consultants, so the idea of using them will be less foreign. You'll find people becoming more attuned to team-building efforts, personality assessments and other psychological interventions."

As for Murphy, he regards predictions about work in the next century with a grain of salt. "Whenever a millennia comes around," he jokes "this kind of hype is what happens."

But is all of it hype? "Some of it will happen," he says. "I would bet on it happening slowly. Don't forget. The government and civil service won't change fast, making this a slower revolution."

Article Review Form at end of book.

What are the primary issues involved in using personality tests in the selection process?

Employee Selection:
Will Intelligence and Conscientiousness Do the Job?

Orlando Behling

Orlando Behling is distinguished university professor of management emeritus at Bowling Green State University and a principal of Behling Associates. His current research projects deal with alliances, guan-xi, employee selection and performance improvement, and cross-cultural research methods.

Ask any ten human resource managers how they select employees and you will find that most of them work from the same set of unchallenged, generally unspoken ideas. Their way of thinking and the employee selection procedures that stem from it involve precise matching of knowledge, ability, and skill profiles. They see employee selection as fitting a key—a job candidate—into a lock—the job. The perfect candidate's credentials match the job requirements in all respects. Only an exact fit guarantees top employee performance. Cook, McClelland and Spencer capture the precise matching idea in the AMA's *Handbook for Employee Recruitment and Retention:*

The final selection decision must match the 'whole person' with the 'whole job.' This requires a thorough analysis of both the person and the job; only then can an intelligent decision be made as to how well the two will fit together . . . stress should be placed on matching an applicant to a specific position.[1]

A quick examination of Gatewood and Feild's *Human Resource Selection*[2] illustrates the importance that many human resource managers and industrial psychologists assign to precise matching. The authors devote 576 of the book's 726 text pages to discussions of measuring the characteristics of jobs and the competencies they demand, measuring job candidates' knowledge, skills and abilities, and to the problems involved in matching the two.

A small number of top managers and others now publicly question the precise matching approach. They argue that firms can identify top performers by focusing on key employee characteristics that lead to success in all or almost all jobs. Bill Gates of Microsoft belongs to this group. He is reported to have a bias toward, "intelligence or smartness over anything else, even, in many cases, experience" in judging potential employees.[3] His inclination has been translated into action at Microsoft, whose recruiters seek high-IQ candidates and worry about teaching skills later.[4] Daniel Seligman, a *Fortune* editor, takes Gates's argument a giant step further. He writes, "(1) *all* companies would benefit from hiring smarter people, and (2) IQ matters in *all* jobs, including sweeping up the place after the programmers go home."[5]

Others who depart from precise matching focus less on intelligence than on what they call employee attitude or character. Richard L. Barclay, vice president of Barclay Enterprises, Inc., a small California firm that remanufactures telephone equipment, argues:

For the lower echelon, unskilled positions, companies don't need trained applicants nearly as much as they need people of character. I can train a person to disassemble a phone; I can't train her to not get a bad attitude when she discovers that she's expected to come to work everyday when the rest of us are there. I can train a worker to properly handle a PC board; I can't train him to show up for work sober or to respect authority.[6]

> A small number of top managers and others now publicly question the precise matching approach. They argue that firms can identify top performers by focusing on key employee characteristics that lead to success in all or almost all jobs.

Southwest Airlines, Nucor Steel, and Silicon Graphics Inc. emphasize the importance of character in hiring for a wide range of jobs, not only for the unskilled, entry-level ones that concern Barclay. These companies share an approach to hiring based on the idea that:

What people know is less important than who they are. Hiring, they believe, is not about finding people with the right experience. It's about finding people with the right mindset. These companies hire for attitude and train for skill.[7]

While not everyone accepts the idea that focusing on single key employee characteristics should replace precise matching, some exciting research supports this line of thinking.

Smart People Finish First

Intelligence, the peculiarly human talent for solving problems using words or symbols, has been the source of many acrimonious debates among psychologists, who argue over its very nature. Some hold that intelligence consists of a number of more-or-less independent gifts. Thurstone, one of the pioneers of intelligence research, concluded that each human has his or her own mix of ten different intelligences: deductive, inductive, mechanical, memory, numerical, perceptual, reasoning, spatial, verbal, and vocabulary.[8] Opponents argue that these specific intelligences are merely minor subdimensions of a single human ability that they call "general intelligence," or g.

The available research points strongly to the conclusion that adding measures of specific intelligences like those identified by Thurstone increases g's ability to predict employees' job performance only marginally. Ree and Earles report in the case of US Air Force airmen that considering non-g intelligence scores improved the average correlation coefficient by only .06.[9]

Experts on intelligence have accumulated enough research on the general intelligence-performance relationship to allow us to draw two additional conclusions.

First, g predicts employee performance in job training extremely well. Analyses going back to the early part of the century, when paper-and-pencil tests of intelligence originated, indicate that g predicts classroom performance of students from the early primary grades to the college level quite nicely. Such tests also predict how well men and women do in job training. Ree and Earles studied Air Force enlisted personnel who had participated in 89 different job training programs.[10] They found that g correlated extremely highly (an average correlation coefficient of .76) with training performance. The relationship held for easy courses as well as for difficult ones.

Second, general intelligence does a good job of predicting job performance, though not as good as it does regarding training performance. Hunter and Hunter, for example, performed a meta-analysis of existing studies of the relationship between g and performance in training programs and on the job. (Meta-analysis is a procedure that researchers use to draw general conclusions from a set of existing studies using different subjects, measures, and methods.) The results led them to conclude that if "general cognitive ability alone is used as a predictor, the average validity across all jobs is .54 for a training-success criterion and .45 for a job proficiency criterion."[11]

This does not mean that general intelligence predicts job performance poorly, however. Studies done over the last 85 years indicate that paper-and-pencil tests of g consistently predict job performance well. In fact, much of the early interest in paper-and-pencil measures of intelligence and other human characteristics stemmed from the US Army's success in placing World War I recruits into occupational specialties on the basis of their scores on a primitive intelligence test called army alpha. Over forty years ago, Ghiselli and Brown, concluded that the average correlation between g and job proficiency for managers was .37,[12] a figure Schmidt and Hunter argue actually substantially underestimates the relationship's true strength because of quirks in statistical analysis.[13]

More recent work by Schmidt and his co-workers and by Ree and Earles indicates that g predicts performance well in a wide range of jobs, not just those we normally think of as requiring substantial brain power. For example, Hunter and Hunter analyzed data from 515 studies that the US Employment Service conducted to find out if its measure of general intelligence predicted job performance.[14] The occupations in the USES studies sampled practically the entire range of those described in the *Dictionary of Occupational Titles*, far and away the most complete listing of jobs around. Hunter and Hunter's results indicate that g does a good job of predicting performance for almost all of them. The average of the correlation coefficients obtained was .47, substantially higher than industrial psychologists usually obtain when they try to predict performance on the basis of other human characteristics.

Similarly, Ree and Earles report the results of studies of the relation between general intelligence and job performance in two groups of US Air Force personnel. In the case of college-graduate navigators and pilots, the correlations between g and ten different job performance measures averaged a gratifying .33. In the case of airmen with roughly two years experience in eight different jobs (two administrative, two electronic, two general technical, and two mechanical), the correlations between g and hard measures of their on-the-job performance, their ability to explain key elements of their jobs step-by-step, and ratings by their supervisors, averaged an even more impressive .44. Ree and Earles found the evidence so convincing that they concluded, "If an employer were to use only intelligence tests and select the highest scoring applicant for each job . . . overall performance from the employees selected would be maximized."[15]

Schmidt and his associates suggest that:[16]

- While general intelligence predicts performance well, it predicts employee job knowledge even better.

- The relation between g and performance holds beyond the employee's first weeks or months on the job, when critical job knowledge is learned. General intelligence was found to predict performance five years out, the longest span studied.

- The relationship between g and performance is stronger for supervisors than it is for non-supervisors.

```
[g] → [Training Performance] → [Job Knowledge] → [Job Performance]
```

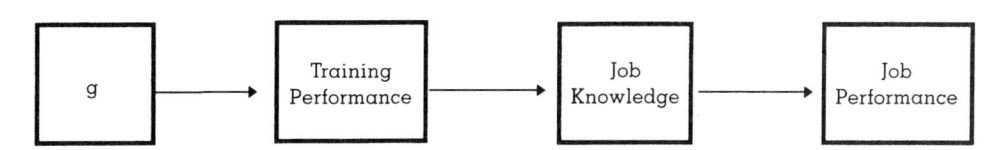

Figure 1. A first cut at modeling the relation between general intelligence and job performance.

```
                    [Problem Solving Requirement]
                              |
          ┌───────────────────┼──────────────────────┐
          ↓                                          ↓
[g] → [Training Performance] → [Job Knowledge] → [Job Performance]
```

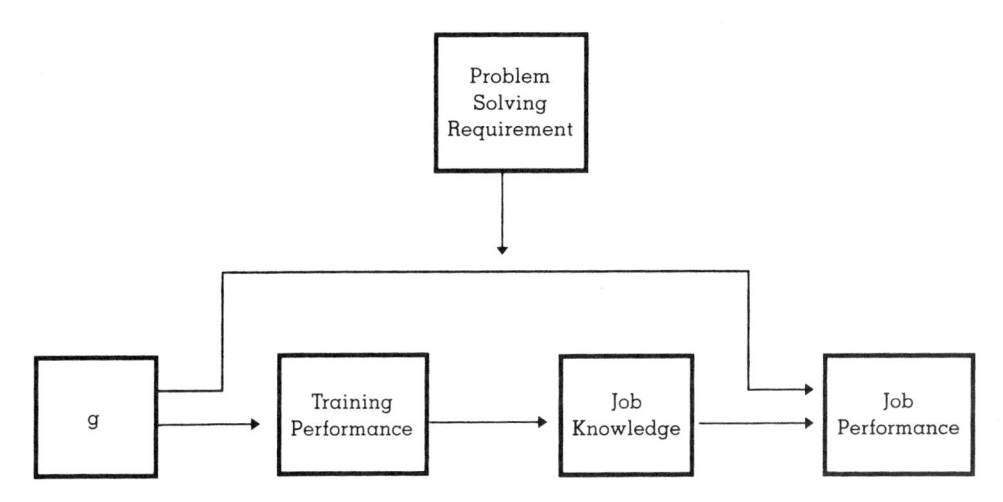

Figure 2. A second cut at modeling the relation between general intelligence and job performance.

On the basis of these research results, we can take a first cut at modeling how general intelligence influences employees' performance. This model is based primarily on the ideas of Schmidt and Hunter, who provide a comprehensive discussion of the relationships involved.[17]

As shown in Figure 1, the simplest interpretation suggests a straightforward pattern in which general intelligence governs how well employees do in training, which affects their job knowledge, which in turn influences their job performance. This relationship is very strong, but additional results suggest that it is not the only way in which intelligence affects job performance.

As shown in Figure 2, certain refinements of the simple model are in order. First, Schmidt and Hunter's analysis indicates that g affects job performance directly, though the relationship is not as strong as the one that goes through training performance and job knowledge. Second, they conclude that the relationship is stronger for some jobs, for example, those of supervisors, than it is for others. Although this fact can be explained in a number of ways, Schmidt and Hunter suggest that the difference lies not in the job of supervisor itself, but in the fact that supervisors are required to improvise solutions to poorly defined problems, something intelligent individuals do especially well. In other words, the more problem solving a position requires, the better the job g does in predicting employee performance.

The "Big Five" Personality Dimensions

A second important body of research has to do with character or employee attitude, with what psychologists are likely to label personality or dispositional factors. These are patterns of behavior that persist across a wide range of situations and over much of a person's lifetime.

The never-ending list of terms invented to designate human traits—dimensions or aspects of personality—has long frustrated psychologists, who hold that a small number of major traits probably underlie all of the labels. While psychologists began to speculate about the nature and number of these underlying dimensions in the 1930s, it was not until the 1960s that a general framework based on solid research began to emerge. This framework captures the key aspects of personality in five primary dimensions. Inevitably, these have become known as "the Big Five."[18] Not every personality expert believes that the big five framework is the best one, but it is more widely accepted than any other. The Big Five are:

Extroversion

Extroversion is the degree to which a person is active, assertive, gregarious, sociable, and talkative. I used to teach management training programs for business firms and trade associations. As a strong introvert, after a long day on the platform I wanted only to go back to my hotel room, lock the door and talk to no one for the rest of the evening. My partner, an extrovert, happily headed for the bar and dinner with a half-dozen program participants in tow.

Emotional Stability

Emotional stability is the opposite of emotional instability, which is the degree to which a person is angry, anxious, depressed, emotional, insecure, and worried. Abraham Lincoln is reported to have said, "Most people are just about as happy as they choose to be," implying that your outlook plays a bigger role in happiness than do things that happen to you. Many psychologists agree with Lincoln, though they probably would add that he should have said, "Most people are just about as happy as their level of emotional stability leads them to be."

Studies by University of Minnesota researchers indicate that people have an emotional "set point" to which they return.[19] The researchers argue that this set point is mainly hereditary. Arvey, Bouchard, Segal, and Abraham indicate that job satisfaction is a function of personality, as well.[20] Their studies of identical twins raised apart indicate that as much as 30 percent of job satisfaction derives from our genes rather than our jobs.

> Emotional stability is the opposite of emotional instability, which is the degree to which a person is angry, anxious, depressed, emotional, insecure, and worried.

Agreeableness

Agreeableness is the degree to which someone is cooperative, courteous, flexible, forgiving, good-natured, soft-hearted, tolerant, and trusting. Many people are easy to be around, but others are thorny, prickly, and hard to get along with. The contrast between the two was driven home to me when I was asked to evaluate two candidates for a key management position. It was not their skills that separated them; both were technically qualified to do the job. However, A was consistently described by colleagues, subordinates and superiors as "a really nice guy," while B was labeled "a pain," among other things. When pressed for concrete examples of what they meant, some people described times when A had gone out of his way to help them. Others cited his consistent concern for coworkers. B was described as tough, abrasive, and focused on getting the job done, with little thought to who might be hurt in the process. While some worried that A might be too soft for the job, my final report pointed out that his agreeableness had allowed him to develop close ties to experts inside and outside the firm whose specialized knowledge would be valuable down the road. He would be able to enlist their help in solving the unknown but inevitable problems the new job promised.

Conscientiousness

Conscientiousness is the degree to which an individual is achievement-oriented, careful, hard-working, organized, planful, persevering, responsible, and thorough. I have supervised both high and low conscientiousness employees over the years. Many of the latter were charming individuals; they were often laid back, relaxed and hard to ruffle. One once told me, "I don't sweat the small stuff." He might have added: "even many of the things that you think are critical!" One highly conscientious subordinate was all business. He arrived at our first meeting with a typed copy of his daily schedule, a sheet bearing his home and office phone numbers and addresses and his e-mail address. At his request, we established a time table for meetings for the next four months. He showed up on time every time, day planner in hand, and carefully listed tasks and due dates. He questioned me exhaustively if he didn't understand an assignment and returned on schedule with the completed work or with a clear explanation as to why it wasn't done.

Openness to Experience

Openness to experience is the degree to which the individual is artistically sensitive, broad-minded, cultured, curious, and original. Obviously, those concerned with success on the job are more interested in the broad-minded-curious-original side of this dimension than they are in the artistically sensitive-cultured side. For those high in this aspect of openness to experience, the old dictum, "If it ain't broke, don't fix it" has little meaning. They embrace change and seek new ways of doing and thinking about things.

A discussion of the Big Five, taken alone, usually generates a "So what?" response from managers. It is only when we begin to discuss a ground-breaking piece of research by Barrick and Mount, that their ears perk up.[21] Barrick and Mount identified 231 studies testing the relationship between various big five personality dimensions and performance. They discarded 114 of them for various technical reasons. From their analysis of the remaining 117 studies, they were able to draw conclusions about the usefulness of the Big Five as predictors of training and of job performance. They were able to draw conclusions for five groups: professionals, police officers, managers, salespersons, and skilled/semiskilled employees in a wide range of occupations.

Barrick and Mount's critical finding is this: In every case where they had enough data to make a judgment, for each one of the five occupations conscientiousness significantly predicted performance. In fact, with the exception of training performance, where the impact of openness to experience and of extroversion were fractionally greater, conscientiousness was the best single predictor in every case in which Barrick and Mount had enough data to draw conclusions.

While Barrick and Mount included only studies performed in North America, Salgado recently performed a similar analysis focusing on studies performed in the European Community.[22] Though his results differ in some respects from those of Barrick and Mount, they clearly support the idea that conscientiousness is a critical predictor of performance across a wide range of jobs.

Obviously, these works suggest further refinements of the model of performance laid out in Figure 2. As shown in Figure 3, conscientiousness affects job performance through two paths. First, it acts by improving performance in training programs, which in turn improves job knowledge, leading eventually to better job performance. Second, it affects job performance directly; conscientious individuals simply are likely to do a better job.

As also shown in Figure 3, the results of a later study by Barrick and Mount[23] indicate that the impact of conscientiousness is not the same from job to job. In this study, they examined the role that an individual's autonomy plays in determining the impact of conscientiousness on the performance ratings received by

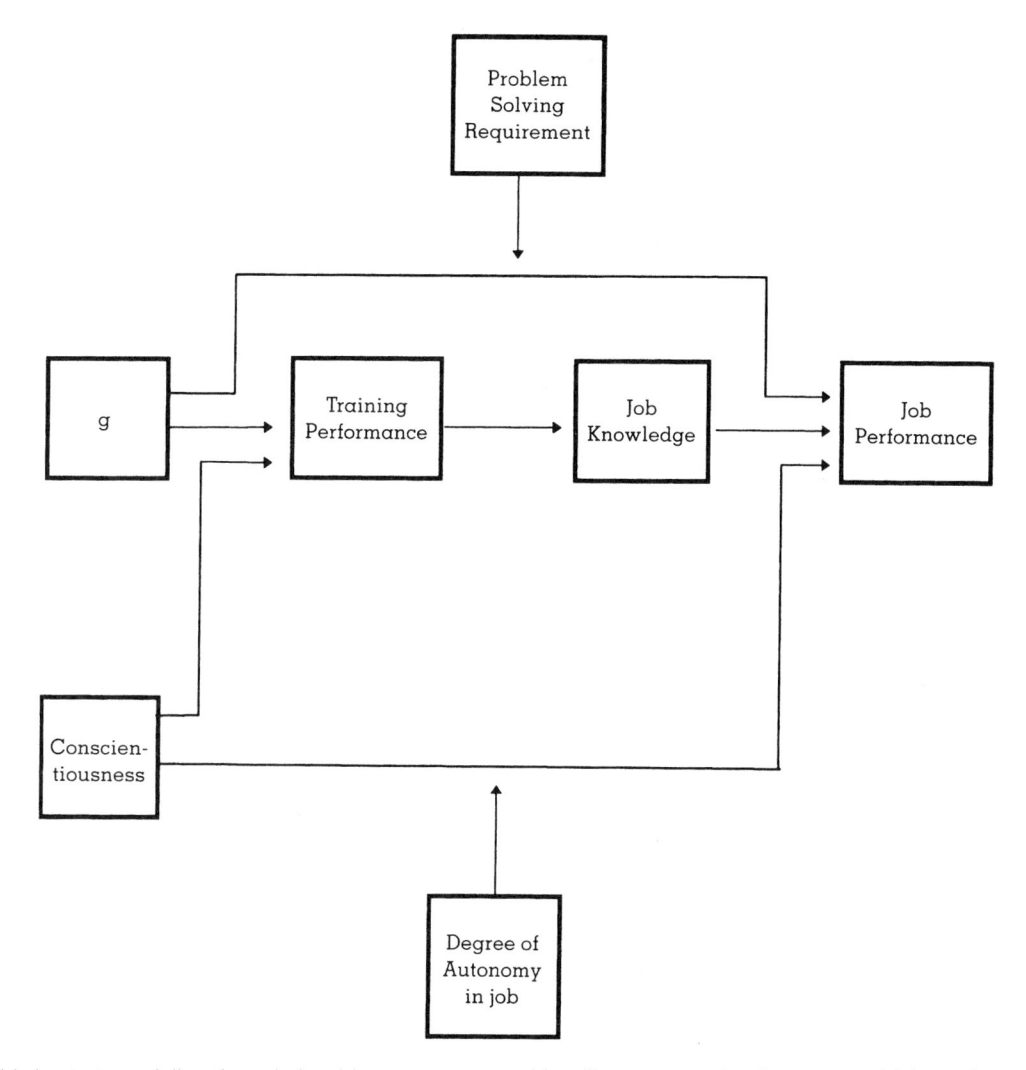

Figure 3. A third cut at modeling the relationships among general intelligence, conscientiousness and job performance.

154 managers. Conscientiousness affected the ratings for managers holding high autonomy jobs more than it did for managers in low autonomy jobs. This makes sense. If an individual is closely supervised or is carefully monitored in other ways, conscientiousness should be less critical.

Putting the Research to Work

The first response of some managers to the facts laid out in the previous paragraphs is, "It's a no-brainer! All we need to do is hire smart, conscientious people!" However, two general cautions are in order.

First, while conscientiousness and general intelligence predict performance well, they do not predict it perfectly. Most of us can think of races in which a persistent tortoise outperformed a brilliant hare and of specific assignments in which agreeableness or some other trait proved more important than conscientiousness. Intelligence and conscientiousness are excellent indicators of potential, not guarantees of success. Second, the evidence is far from complete, but a nagging possibility exists that g and conscientiousness may predict job performance better for yesterday's jobs than they do for today's. The bulk of the research we have considered thus far focuses on individual job proficiency in traditional jobs. Despite the widespread use of work teams in today's businesses, there are no studies that look at how well intelligence predicts performance in teams. Studies of the role conscientiousness plays on work team performance are few in number and yield mixed results. On the one hand, Thoms found that conscientiousness predicts employees' estimates of their own ability to perform well in teams, which has repeatedly been shown to relate to actual performance in teams.[24] On the other hand, Barry and Stewart found no significant relationship between conscientiousness and teammates' perceptions of the

> **Intelligence and conscientiousness are excellent indicators of potential, not guarantees of success.**

Rely Primarily on g and Conscientiousness When . . .	Rely Primarily on Precise Matching When . . .
• The new employee will be called on to do a great deal of problem solving.	• The new employee will be called on to do little or no problem solving.
• The new employee will have a high degree of autonomy; i.e., he or she will work pretty much on her or his own.	• The new employee will be closely monitored or performance problems will be otherwise obvious to his or her superior.
• The skills and abilities the new employee will learn on the job are more important than those he or she brings to the job.	• The skills and abilities that the new employee brings to the job are more important than the things he or she will learn on the job.
• The new employee must learn the job rapidly and adapt equally rapidly to job changes.	• The new employee will have plenty of time to learn the job and can expect to deal with few, gradual changes, if any.
• Two or more top job candidates are practically equal in terms of key skills and abilities.	• One job candidate is clearly superior to the others in terms of key skills and abilities.

Figure 4. When it makes sense to de-emphasize precise matching of knowledge, ability and skill profiles and to focus on general intelligence and conscientiousness.

kinds of contributions individuals made to group functioning or to team performance in graduate student problem-solving teams.[25]

The same kind of uncertainty exists about the role that conscientiousness plays in generating the often-unrewarded "beyond the call of duty" contributions called organizational citizenship behaviors (OCB). Organ's 1994 review of research on the relationship led him to be hopeful, though far from confident: "For now, if we had to stake our hopes on one measurable fact of the person that explains appreciable variance in OCB, the data suggest that it would have something to do with the Big Five's Conscientiousness."[26] However, a later study of factors influencing supervisors' ratings of OCB in a large hospital was able to uncover only a somewhat suspect relationship between conscientiousness and one of five forms of organizational citizenship behavior.[27]

Beyond these two caveats, however, we need to deal with a pair of additional matters that take selecting employees out of the "no brainer" category. First, there are situations where employers must as a matter of necessity use a precise matching approach rather than focus on candidates' general intelligence and conscientiousness. We need to lay out the circumstances under which this is the case. Second, we need to spell out some key ideas having to do with measuring g and conscientiousness.

Choosing Between Precise Matching and a Focus on General Intelligence and Conscientiousness

As Figure 4 indicates, there are at least five circumstances that should lead employers to consider replacing precise matching with a search for employees with a mix of g and conscientiousness. The first two suggestions rest on the results of the research discussed in the preceding pages. The remaining three have not been tested in the laboratory, but make sense logically.

- **When the Job Calls for a Great Deal of Problem Solving.** In this case, g influences the ability of individuals to identify problems and to come up with creative ways to solve them. It appears likely, as well, that conscientious men and women assign high priorities to company concerns and thus look for solutions that benefit their employers, not just themselves.

- **When the New Employee Will Have a High Degree of Autonomy.** Employees in some jobs have little opportunity to show initiative on the one hand or to goof off or goof up on the other. Some of these workers spend the bulk of their day under their supervisor's direct gaze. The pace at which others work and the methods they use are spelled out in excruciating detail and any departure is instantly obvious. The archetypal assembly line job scores high in this respect. Other jobs stand in stark contrast,[28] and require independent initiative. Other things being equal, conscientiousness is more likely to separate high performers from low performers in such low control–low structure jobs than it is in their high control–high structure counterparts.

- **When the Things New Employees Learn on the Job Are More Important Than What They Bring to the Job.** Pilots, surgeons, lawyers, and plumbers bring a well defined set of skills to their jobs. Other jobs are different, however. New employees come to them with little or no direct preparation. They are expected to learn their jobs after they are hired, sometimes with the help of formal training, sometimes without. Sixty or 70 percent of jobs probably fall into this category. For these jobs, the ability and drive to learn the new assignment is paramount, making general intelligence and conscientiousness important keys to success.

- **When the New Employee Must Learn the Job Rapidly and Adapt Equally Rapidly to Job Changes.** High general intelligence is consistently associated with the ability to grasp new information. Conscientious candidates are likely to strive to do so. Thus, both g and conscientiousness probably characterize individuals who will learn new jobs quickly and deal effectively with change.

- **When Two or More Top Job Candidates are Just About Equal in Terms of Knowledge, Skills, and Abilities.** Even in jobs that demand precise matching, the selection process sometimes yields two or more top candidates who are evenly matched in terms of specific requirements. In such cases, the candidate who scores highest in terms of g and conscientiousness is the better choice.

Measuring g and Conscientiousness

If employers are to use conscientiousness and general intelligence in selecting employees, they must be able to measure each.

Using Paper-and-Pencil Instruments

A number of accepted paper-and-pencil tests of general intelligence and conscientiousness are available. For example, one can select from among the numerous measures of g discussed in books such as Aikin's *Assessment of Intellectual Functioning*.[29] The revised NEO-Personality Inventory is widely used to measure conscientiousness and the other four Big Five dimensions.[30]

Industrial/organizational psychologists can help managers find paper-and-pencil measures that may meet their needs. Even more importantly, they can spell out the steps federal and state governments require employers to take to validate these instruments. They also can also explain why the fact that existing paper-and-pencil measures of conscientiousness are, for the most part, easily faked by clever job candidates does not create major problems in using them to select employees.[31] Such questionnaires are not the main focus of this discussion, however.

We concentrate here on a few of the clues candidates high in general intelligence and in conscientiousness leave in their resumes and in job interviews. It is reassuring to learn that managers can and do recognize the importance of g and conscientiousness in choices that they make from among job candidates. Dunn, Mount, Barrick, and Ones asked 84 managers who make hiring decisions to rate 39 hypothetical job applicants in terms of their hirability and counterproductivity. They found that g and conscientiousness were the best predictors of the managers' ratings of hirability and, along with low emotional stability and low agreeableness, of ratings of counterproductivity.[32] Similarly, Mount, Barrick, and Strauss found that supervisor, coworker, and customer ratings of conscientiousness were accurate predictors of sales representatives' performance ratings.[33]

Reading Resumes and Interviewing for Evidence of g

Looking for g is relatively easy, as such things go, since a number of readily observable personal history items correlate highly with general intelligence:

- **School Grades.** School grades do not indicate g perfectly. Individuals may over- or underachieve relative to their intelligence for a variety of reasons. Differences in school quality and in cultural and family emphasis on the importance of academic performance may handicap some students, for example. Such things aside, however, the relationship between school grades and g is very strong.

> School grades do not indicate g perfectly. Individuals may over- or underachieve relative to their intelligence for a variety of reasons.

- **Vocabulary.** Language facility also relates highly to g. Indeed, critics argue that some measures of intelligence are little more than disguised tests of vocabulary and reading ability.

- **Problem-Solving Success.** Many jobs and hobbies involve problem solving. Previous success in such activities suggests that a candidate has a high level of general intelligence.

Reading Resumes and Interviewing for Evidence of Conscientiousness

Psychologists have not studied the clues managers can use in judging candidates' conscientiousness. Anything we say on this issue is therefore highly speculative. However, we can build on the definition of conscientiousness that says that conscientious individuals are achievement-oriented, careful, hardworking, organized, planful, persevering, responsible, and thorough to tentatively suggest that those making hiring decisions should look at nature and quality of the candidates:

- **Preparation for the Interview.** The job candidate who arrives at the interview having carefully researched the firm and the job opening, is probably more conscientious than the one who arrives uninformed.

- **Dress and Self-Presentation.** In the same fashion, the candidate who arrives dressed appropriately shows at least some of the signs of conscientiousness.

- **Career Progression.** Careful career planning, as well as careful planning in other aspects of an individual's life, would appear to be an attribute of those high in conscientiousness. Thus a logical progression as the job candidate moves from position to position would likely indicate a conscientious individual.

Conclusion

The challenge raised by Bill Gates and other managers to the conventional wisdom of precise matching has solid support not only in their experience, but in carefully crafted, widely repeated research. Study after study indicates that general intelligence and conscientiousness relate strongly to performance across a wide range of jobs and situations. Clearly the time has come for those who set hiring policy to raise their own challenge to human resource managers and industrial psychologists who administer their firms' hiring programs:

- To determine exactly what role g and conscientiousness play in success in key jobs in their firms and, where appropriate,
- To find reliable and valid ways of measuring these key variables so that they can be made part of their selection programs.

When these determinations have been made, firms will have taken an important step in assuring that they staff their operations with those who have the highest chance of contributing the most.

Endnotes

1. Cook, M. F., McClelland, D. C. & Spencer, Jr. L. M. 1992. *The AMA handbook for employee recruitment and retention.* New York: AMACOM. 104–105.
2. Gatewood, R. D. & Feild, H. S. 1994. *Human resource selection* (3rd ed.). Fort Worth TX: Dryden Press.
3. *Fortune.* 1996. Microsoft's big advantage—hiring only the supersmart. November 25: 159–162.
4. *Ibid.*
5. *Fortune.* 1997. Brains in the office. January 13: 38.
6. *Wall Street Journal.* 1995. The poor? I hire them. May 24: a14.
7. *World Executive's Digest.* 1997. Hire for attitude, train for skill. January: 44, 46.
8. Thurstone, L. L. 1941. *Factorial studies of intelligence.* Chicago: University of Chicago Press.
9. Ree, M. J., Earles, J. A. & Teachout, M. 1991. *General Cognitive Ability Predicts Job Performance.* TR-1991-0057 (Armstrong Laboratory, Brooks AFB TX) as discussed in Ree, M. J. & Earles, J. A. 1992. Intelligence is the best predictor of job performance. *Psychological Science,* 1: 86–89.
10. Ree, M. J. & Earles, J. A. 1989. *The Differential Validity of a Differential Aptitude Test.* AFHRL-TR-89-59 as discussed in Ree, M. J. & Earles, J. A. 1992. Intelligence is the best predictor of job performance. *Psychological Science,* 1: 86–89.
11. Hunter, J. E. & Hunter, R. F. 1984. Validity and utility of alternate measures of job performance. *Psychological Bulletin,* 96: 72–98.
12. Ghiselli, E. E. & Brown, C. W. 1955. *Personnel and industrial psychology* (2nd ed.) New York: McGraw-Hill.
13. Schmidt, F. L. & Hunter, J. E. 1977. Development of a general solution to the problem of validity generalization. *Journal of Applied Psychology,* 62: 529–540.
14. Hunter, J. E. & Hunter, R. F. 1984. Validity and utility of alternate measures of job performance. *Psychological Bulletin,* 96: 72–98.
15. Ree, M. J. & Earles, J. A. 1992. Intelligence is the best predictor of job performance. *Psychological Science,* 1: 86–89.
16. Schmidt, F. L. & Hunter, J. E. 1992. Development of a causal model of processes determining job performance, *Current Directions in Psychological Science,* 1: 89–92.
17. Schmidt, F. L. & Hunter, J. E. 1992. Development of a causal model of processes determining job performance, *Current Directions in Psychological Science,* 1: 89–92.
18. Digman, J. M. 1990. Personality Structure: Emergence of the five-factor model. Annual Review of Psychology, 41: 417–440 summarizes the nature and development of the Big Five.
19. Tellegen, A., Lykken, D. T., Bouchard, Jr., T. J., Wilcox, K. J., Segal, N. L., & Rich, S. 1988. Personality similarity in twins reared apart and together. *Journal of Personality and Social Psychology,* 54: 1031–1039.
20. Arvey, R. D., Bouchard, T. J., Segal, N. L. & Abraham, N. L. 1989. Job satisfaction: Environmental and genetic components. *Journal of Applied Psychology* 74: 187–192.
21. Barrick, M. R. & Mount, M. K. 1991. The big five personality dimensions and job performance: A meta-analysis. *Personnel Psychology* 44: 1–26.
22. Salgado, J. F. 1997. The five factor model of personality and job performance in the European Community. *Journal of Applied Psychology* 82: 30–43.
23. Barrick, M. R. & Mount, M. K. 1993. Autonomy as a moderator of the relationships between the big five personality dimensions and job performance. *Journal of Applied Psychology.* 78: 111–118.
24. Thoms, P. 1996. The relationship between self-efficacy for participating in self-managed work groups and the big five personality dimensions. *Journal of Applied Psychology.* 81: 474–482.
25. Barry, B. & Stewart, G. L. 1997. Composition, process and performance in self-managed groups: The role of personality. *Journal of Applied Psychology.* 82: 62–78.
26. Organ, D. W. 1994. Personality and organizational citizenship behavior. *Journal of Management.* 20: 465–478.
27. Konovsky, M. A. & Organ, D. W. 1996. Dispositional and contextual determinants of organizational citizenship behavior. *Journal of Organizational Behavior.* 17: 253–266.
28. Mischel, D. refers to these jobs as "weak" situations in his 1977 work: The interaction of the person and the situation. In D. Magnusson & N. S. Miller, (Eds.) *Personality at the crossroads: Current issues in interactional psychology.* Hillsdale NJ: Erlbaum.
29. Aikin, H. R. 1996. *Assessment of intellectual functioning.* New York: Plenum Press.
30. Costa, P. T., Jr. & McCrae, R. R. 1985. *The NEO personality inventory.* Odessa FL: Psychological Assessment Resources.
31. Recent work (Schmit, M. J., Ryan, A. M., Stierwalt, S. L. & Powell, A. B. 1995. Frame-of-reference effects on personality scale scores and criterion-related validity. *Journal of Applied Psychology,* 80: 607–620) indicates that application-related instructions and work-related items led subjects to practice impression management, but this actually led to greater rather than less validity. Studies (Barrick, M. R. & Mount, M. K 1996. Effects of impression management and self-deception on the predictive validity of personality constructs. *Journal of Applied Psychology,* 81: 261–272 and Ones, D. S., Viswesvaran, C. & Reiss, A. D. 1996. Role of social desirability in personality testing for personnel selection: The red herring. *Journal of Applied Psychology,* 81: 660–679) indicate as well that the fact that applicants may slant their answers in socially-desirable directions does not significantly affect the usefulness of personality measures in selecting employees.
32. Dunn, W. S., Mount, M. K., Barrick, M. R. & Ones, D. S. 1995. Relative importance of personality and general mental ability in managers' judgments of applicant qualifications. *Journal of Applied Psychology,* 80: 500–509.
33. Mount, M. K., Barrick, M. R. & Strauss, J. 1994. Validity of observer ratings of the big five personality factors. *Journal of Applied Psychology,* 79: 272–280.

Article Review Form at end of book.

The authors suggest that personality tests are a way to promote social justice and increase organizational effectiveness. How do they defend this position? Do you agree or disagree with this position? What does it mean to match the "whole person" with the "whole job"? What are the big five personality dimensions, and how are they linked to job performance?

Personality Measurement and Employment Decisions:

Questions and Answers

Robert Hogan, Joyce Hogan, and Brent W. Roberts
Department of Psychology, University of Tulsa

The invisible college psychologists who do research with measures of normal personality now largely agrees about the structure of personality; this group also agrees that competently developed personality measures are valid predictors of real world performance. Outside that college however, there is still considerable skepticism regarding the meaning and validity of these measures. This article attempts to summarize the data needed to answer the most frequent questions about the use of personality measures in applied contexts. Our major conclusions are that (a) well-constructed measures of normal personality are valid predictors of performance in virtually all occupations, (b) they do not result in adverse impact for job applicants from minority groups, and (c) using well-developed personality measures for preemployment screening is a way to promote social justice and increase organizational productivity.

Many people agree that intelligence tests predict important practical outcomes (e.g., "Mainstream Science," 1994). In contrast, the conventional wisdom of modern psychology is that personality measures lack validity, are easily faked, and are generally unsuitable for preemployment screening purposes. The preferred answer in response to a question from a study guide for a licensing exam characterizes personality tests as poor predictors of job success and suggests their use in employment settings could be unethical. Similarly, Reilly and Warech (1993), in a review of alternatives to cognitive tests for employment decisions, concluded that, "The generally low validities reported and the problem of faking in operational settings make it difficult to recommend personality measures [sic] as an alternative" (p. 187: see also Blinkhom & Johnson, 1990). On a personal note, hardly a day goes by without our being asked—by a lawyer or human resource specialist—to defend the use of personality measurement in organizational contexts. Although a small group of researchers in personality and industrial–organizational psychology believes personality measures can predict important aspects of occupational performance, the larger psychological community seems unpersuaded. This is unfortunate because the data are reasonably clear that well-constructed personality measures are valid predictors of job performance, and they can enhance fairness in the employment process. This is an important public policy issue and an area in which psychology can contribute to both organizational productivity and social justice. This article presents frequently raised questions about personality measurement in employment and offers some responses.

What Is Personality?

MacKinnon (1944) noted that personality is defined in two ways. On the one hand, personality refers to "factors" inside people that explain their behavior. These factors include *temperaments*—genetically controlled dispositions that determine the fundamental pace and mood of a person's actions (cf. Buss & Plomin, 1975)—and the interpersonal strategies that people have developed to deal with others and find their way in the world. These factors inside people are what drive their social behavior, including their performance in assessment center exercises and their responses to personality questionnaires.

On the other hand, according to MacKinnon (1944), personality refers to a person's distinctive interpersonal characteristics, especially as described by those who have seen that person in a variety of situations. This aspect of personality is functionally equivalent to a person's reputation. It is also the source of the big-five personality factors (cf. Digman, 1990; Goldberg, 1993; McCrae & Costa, 1987) which, at least in the beginning, were discovered in factor analyses of observers' ratings (Norman, 1963; Thurstone, 1934, Tupes & Christal, 1961). Some personality psychologists regard this as the most important aspect of personality; Hofstee (1994), for example, argued that, "The averaged judgment of knowledgeable others provides the best available point of reference for both the definition of personality structure in general and for assessing someone's personality in particular" (p. 149). Moreover, because reputation is built on a person's past behavior, and because past behavior is the best predictor of future behavior, this aspect of personality has important practical use. In addition, the reputational aspect of personality is the most accessible to measurement. And finally, most people care deeply about their reputations and will go to great lengths to preserve them.

Although personality is defined in two very different ways, both definitions are important, and both refer to individual differences in interpersonal style. From a pragmatic perspective, personality is most evident in and consequential for social interaction because people are social animals and it is during interaction that human nature is primarily expressed.

What Is Personality Measurement?

Personality measurement is any procedure that systematically assigns numbers to the characteristic features of a person's interpersonal style according to some explicit rules. These numbers can then be used to make predictions about that person's responses in future settings. This definition includes many different procedures: interviews, in-basket exercises, integrity tests, and the Minnesota Multiphasic Personality Inventory (MMPI; Hathaway & McKinley, 1943). And therein lies the rub. The real issue, in our judgment, is not "What is personality measurement?" but rather "What is a good personality measure?"

A good personality measure will, minimally, have two features. First, scores on the measure should be temporally stable (i.e., scores will be reliable over time). And second, there should be credible evidence that scores on the measure relate to indexes of meaningful nontest behavior (i.e., scores should predict real world performance). Although a very large number of instruments purport to measure personality, only a small subset meets the modest but crucial criteria listed above.

The Scales on the Various Personality Inventories Have Different Names— How Is One to Choose?

Terminological confusion abounds in the practice of personality measurement, and this is a professional embarrassment. But there is at least one answer to the confusion: the Big-Five model mentioned earlier. Many personality researchers now agree that the existing personality inventories all measure essentially the same five broad dimensions with varying degrees of efficiency. Various test authors have favorite dimensions in addition to the standard Big-Five, and legitimately so. Our point is that the Big-Five model is one taxonomic answer to the problem of terminological confusion.

A potential user should examine the test he or she is considering to ensure that it contains reliable and valid scales for at least the standard five dimensions—it is like making sure that the car you want to buy has an engine, brakes, steering system, transmission. and headlights. Any additional scales that the test may have are the optional features. When using an inventory to predict performance in a particular job, some dimensions will be irrelevant on the basis of a prior validity study. But when conducting validity studies, it is useful to begin with an inventory that adequately covers the major dimensions of personality so that one can determine empirically which dimensions are irrelevant.

Why Should an Employer Use a Multidimensional Inventory If Only One Aspect of Personality Is of Interest?

Scores on a single scale are useful when that scale maps a unidimensional domain (i.e., cognitive ability). However, the domains of personality and occupational performance are multifaceted. Many employers want to make personnel decisions that are based on, for example, conscientiousness scores alone. This practice is risky because most performance criteria are best predicted by a combination of scales. For example, persons with high scores on a measure of integrity will follow rules and be easy to supervise, but they may be poor service providers because they tend to be inflexible in following rules. Similarly, persons with high scores on measures of service orientation will be tolerant, patient, and friendly, but they may not work very hard. It is an article of faith in traditional personality assessment that interpreting a single scale in the absence of other information is usually ill advised.

What Do Personality Scales Measure?

Personality scales are typically described as self-report measures. We believe this is misleading. The processes that govern responses to items on personality scales are formally identical to those underlying social interaction in general (cf. R. Hogan, 1991, in press). During interaction, people usually try to control how others perceive them—they try to manage their reputations—so as to maximize positive attention and minimize criticism. Responding to questionnaire items is like talking with an anonymous interviewer. People use their item responses to tell an anonymous interviewer who they are and how they would like to be seen. Thus, item endorsements are self-presentations, not self-reports. This means that personality scales sample a person's typical interpersonal style, and that style is what creates a person's reputation how he or she is perceived by others.

Gough (1965) argued that what personality scales measure is defined by what they predict, and what they predict best is observers' ratings. This means that both personality scale scores and observers' ratings are rough indexes of reputation. And it is the link between scale scores and reputation that explains why well-constructed personality scales predict nontest behavior.

Why Use Personality for Employment Decisions?

During job analysis interviews, if you ask incumbents what is required for effective performance, they typically describe characteristics such as "being a team player," "remaining calm under pressure," "being responsive to the client's needs," "being persistent," and "taking initiative" as crucial for their jobs, and these characteristics are precisely what well-constructed measures of normal personality assess. When incumbents complete structured job analysis questionnaires, they again describe characteristics such as self-control, stress tolerance, leadership, and willingness to listen as essential for job performance (J. Hogan & Stark, 1992). Job analysis instruments are now being developed that focus exclusively on the personality and interpersonal requirements of jobs (Schmit, Guion, & Raymark, 1995); their development will greatly facilitate the use of personality measures in personnel selection.

Do Personality Inventories Predict Job Performance?

As recently as 1990, many academic psychologists would have answered no. Since then, however, estimates of the validity of such measures have steadily inched up. In an important "early" article, Barrick and Mount (1991) studied the relationship between the Big-Five personality dimensions and job criteria across five occupational groups and concluded that, minimally, measures of conscientiousness reliably predict supervisors' ratings of job proficiency and training proficiency (each estimated true validity = .23). Next, Tett, Jackson, and Rothstein (1991) concluded that, when researchers choose tests on the basis of job analysis, conduct confirmatory analyses, and study incumbents with reasonable job tenure, they find validity coefficients even larger than those reported by Barrick and Mount (1991). In fact, validities for the Big-Five dimensions of intellect and agreeableness approach those for cognitive measures in predicting job performance (e.g., corrected mean r's of .27 and .33, respectively).

In addition, McHenry, Hough, Toquam, Hanson, and Ashworth (1990) found that the personality inventory that they developed for the U.S. Army significantly predicted relevant nontechnical performance criteria for enlisted personnel (corrected mean r's ranged from .33 to .37). In the largest meta-analysis of personality measures ever conducted, Ones, Viswesvaran, and Schmidt (1993) found that integrity tests, which are composed of facets of the Big-Five dimensions of conscientiousness and emotional stability, significantly predict supervisors' ratings of job performance in a variety of settings (estimated operational validity = .41). McDaniel and Frei (1994) reported that customer service measures, which contain facets of the Big-Five dimensions of agreeableness and emotional stability, have a mean validity of .50 for predicting rated performance in service jobs.

We are skeptical about the merits of some of the procedures used in some meta-analyses. In particular, we believe that in some cases, corrections for attenuation are used inappropriately and lead to an overestimate of predictor–criterion relationships. Nonetheless, we believe that the meta-analyses described above provide lower bound estimates of the validity of personality measures in predicting job performance. This is so because the researchers had to deal with four difficult, nonstatistical problems that necessarily obscured their results. First, the meta-analyses combined the results of research on the basis of personality scales that were not equivalent in their construction, their measurement goals, or their underlying theory. Second, the researchers sometimes misclassified scales, for example, Barrick and Mount's (1991) raters classified the California Psychological Inventory (CPI; Gough, 1987) Achievement via Independence Scale as a measure of conscientiousness when it should be aligned with openness–intellect. They also classified the CPI Self-Control Scale as emotional stability rather than conscientiousness (Megargee, 1972). Third, the jobs included in the validation studies were not classified in any rational way, for example, results that were based on military enlisted mechanics were combined with results that were based on teachers and social workers. Because effective performance in these jobs is a function of different Big-Five characteristics, aggregating results from jobs with different psychological requirements reduces the resulting validity coefficients.

Finally, when those meta-analyses were conducted, there was no agreed-on rationale or method for classifying the criterion space: Measures were aligned with criteria in an atheoretical manner with predictable results. In our view, the best way to evaluate the validity of personality measures is to study the evidence associated with a single scale on an inventory such as the CPI using a variety of construct-relevant performance criteria, as opposed to combining data across scales and measures. For example, Collins (1995) reviewed the validity data from 24 studies in which the Socialization Scale of the CPI was correlated with a range of social behavior criteria; she estimated that the true score validity for this scale is .56. We believe this is the correct way to estimate the validity of a personality measure. Similar results are available for occupational scales of the Hogan Personality Inventory (HPI; R. Hogan & J. Hogan, 1995, pp. 66–67).

Are Personality Measures Valid Predictors of Performance in All Jobs?

When compared with studies evaluating cognitive abilities (cf Hunter, 1983), the absolute number of job titles that have been studied using personality measures is small. In our research, however, we find that good truck drivers are pretty much the same, regardless of where they work and what they are transporting. Recent meta-analytic research suggests that performance in many jobs should, in principle, be predictable using good measures of normal personality. Negative cases include highly scripted jobs in which there is little room for personality to take effect (Barrick & Mount, 1993).

Employers, however, typically do not find meta-analytic studies very helpful. When employers ask if a test works, they want to know: (a) Has this test been used in our industry?; (b) has it been used for Job X?; (c) can it identify persons who will perform well in Job X?; and (d) will it work in our (unique) company? Psychologists need to present their research results differently to communicate with employers.

We use the Big-Five model combined with the insights of Ghiselli and Barthol (1953) and Holland (1985) to organize this information. We first classify a job into its major Holland code, then we examine the validity coefficients of personality measures, classified in terms of the Big-Five model, for that job. We call our approach the 5 × 6 Model (J. Hogan & R. Hogan, 1993) because it considers the Big-Five personality requirements of the six Holland occupational-type categories.

Consider, for example, the job of truck driver. In Holland terms, this is a realistic-conventional occupational type, in which the average incumbent should be conforming and introverted. Campbell's (1990) "universal dimensions of job performance" (pp. 708–710) suggest that high-performing people in realistic–conventional jobs are hard working and good organizational citizens; on the other hand, they are not good communicators, leaders, or administrators, nor do they need the ability to work well in a team. The Big-Five dimensions associated with hard work and organizational citizenship are conscientiousness and emotional stability; the other dimensions are much less important. And this is exactly what we find using the HPI (R. Hogan & J. Hogan, 1995); truck driver performance is predicted by high scores for prudence and adjustment and low scores for sociability, because high sociability is associated with impulsivity, and impulsive truck drivers get in trouble on the job (J. Hogan & R. Hogan, 1989).

Our point is that if researchers classify jobs by occupational type and then consider the Big-Five dimensional requirements and performance criteria relevant to that occupational type, the predicted relationships between personality and job performance will increase.

Is Much of the Research Relating Personality Measures to Job Performance Methodologically Flawed?

The answer to this question is yes. It is also true that most of the people who play the piano do not play it very well, but that does not mean we should ban piano playing. It means, rather, that we should judge an activity in terms of the performance of the best players in it. And in these terms, there is some impressive research available (cf. Gough, 1975; Hall & MacKinnon, 1969; Ones et al., 1993).

Were Not Most Personality Inventories Developed for Clinical Settings and, Therefore, Are They Appropriate for Preemployment Screening?

Historically this statement was true. But since World War II, a small number of tests have been developed explicitly to assess normal personality. To avoid using a measure of psychopathology, the test user need only examine the item content of the test being considered and consult the test manual to understand the purpose of the test.

Is Behavior Not More Important Than Personality?

Describing jobs in terms of behaviors (e.g., the President of the United States shakes hands, signs documents, reads prepared statements, etc.) focuses attention on simple manifestations of more complex underlying processes. The more significant tasks of a President include providing leadership, inspiring followers, motivating subordinates, and persuading Congress—activities that are hard to reduce to a list of behaviors. As noted above, it is not *what* a person does but *how* he or she does it (e.g., calmly, creatively, attentively, etc.) that determines effective performance.

In our view, what people do—their behavior—is a function of the kind of people they are—their personalities. We use behavior to interpret and evaluate other peoples' personalities. Although we need contextual information to interpret their behavior and we need many contexts to make reliable judgments, any single behavior is a high fidelity, narrow bandwidth expression of a personality disposition (J. Hogan & R. Hogan, 1994). We rarely want to predict how late an employee will be next Tuesday; rather, we are interested in a person's punctuality. To predict punctuality—a broad bandwidth behavioral characteristic—we need constructs of the same bandwidth (i.e., personality dispositions).

People's Behavior Constantly Changes: Does This Not Invalidate Personality Measures?

It is difficult, if not impossible, to predict the weather in any city more than a few days in advance. However, we can predict seasonal and regional climates. For example, although we cannot predict well the weather in Miami on a particular day in January, we know that Florida will be warmer on that day than New Jersey.

Behavior is like the weather, it changes from moment to moment and from context to context. The personality differences that characterize people are like seasonal and regional climate differences. Personality attributions reflect judgments about others' behavior averaged over many contexts and times; they are patterns, not specifics. Nonetheless, when properly assessed, these patterns are consistent and, over time, people differ from one another in ways that are important to employers. Are there any empirical data to support this weather analogy?

Beginning about 1980, a series of studies showed that personality is consistent across adulthood. For example, Costa and McCrae (1988) presented correlations between personality traits over a six-year period that averaged .83. Similarly, Helson and Wink (1992) reported correlations between scores on the CPI and the Adjective Checklist (Gough & Heilbrun. 1983) across 10 years averaging close to .70.

The most impressive evidence for personality consistency comes from truly longitudinal studies. In a 45-year follow-up of the sample originally studied by Kelly (1955), Conley (1984, 1985) found that personality was not only quite consistent (r's averaged about .34), but it was consistent across both self-reports and observers' ratings. Finn (1986) found, across 30 years, that the scores on the first two factors of the MMPI, Negative Affectivity and Constraint, had retest correlations averaging about .53. Using CPI scales, Helson and Moane (1987) reported 20-year correlations averaging .50 in the Mills Longitudinal Study. Stevens and Truss (1985) presented stability coefficients on the Edwards Personal Preference Schedule over 20 years ranging from .20 to .40, with some as high as .70. Finally, Haan, Milsap, and Hartka (1986) found personality correlations across a 50-year period from early childhood to late adulthood averaging around .25 (for reviews & other examples, see Conley, 1984; Heatherton & Weinberger, 1994; Kogan, 1990; McGue, Bacon, & Lykken, 1993).

Recent research also demonstrates the longitudinal predictive power of personality: Who you were 20 years ago predicts your performance now. For example, Caspi, Bern, and Elder (1989) found that middle-class boys who were ill-tempered as children tended to leave school early, achieve less occupational status than their better-natured peers, and experience downward mobility. In a 25-year follow-up of the architects studied at the Institute of Personality Assessment and Research (see MacKinnon, 1962), Dudek and Hall (1991) found that those who were more creative when they were young were more productive, less likely to retire, and still winning awards for their work in late adulthood. In a study of creativity in women, Helson, Roberts, and Agronick (in press) reported that measures of creativity gathered in college correlated .48 with occupational creativity assessed 30 years later. In the same sample, Roberts (1994) found that traits similar to the Big-Five dimensions of extraversion and conscientiousness measured in college predicted successful participation in the paid labor force 20 years later.

We are not suggesting that personality is destiny. Nor are we saying that personality never changes. But from the data, it appears that when personality changes, it changes gradually; meanwhile, the stable components affect our lives in important ways. This means, in particular, that it is highly useful for individual careers to know where our potential problems are, so that we can take steps to mitigate them.

Do Personality Measures Discriminate Against Protected Classes of Job Seekers and Violate the Terms of the Americans With Disabilities Act?

There are three parts to the answer to this question. First, there is no evidence whatsoever that well-constructed personality inventories systematically discriminate against any ethnic or national group (cf. R. Hogan & J. Hogan, 1995).

Moreover, the evidence suggests persons with disabilities receive, on average, the same scores as nondisabled persons (Hayes, 1996); thus, measures of normal personality could be useful in allowing persons with disabilities to demonstrate their qualifications. In addition, normative data from the HPI indicate that persons over 40 years, as a group, receive slightly higher or more positive scale scores than the under 40 group (R. Hogan & J. Hogan, 1995), probably because they are, in fact, more mature. Finally, there are gender differences in mean scale scores. As a group, men have somewhat higher scores on measures of emotional stability; as a group, women have somewhat higher scores on measures of conscientiousness (R. Hogan & J. Hogan, 1995). However, these differences seem not to translate into differential selection rates for men and women applying for jobs.

Second, measures of normal personality are not medical examinations and, therefore, do not fall under the purview of the Americans with Disabilities Act (ADA). For example, Howell and Newman (personal communication, May 11, 1994) from APAs Science and Practice Directorates, in a letter to the chairman of the Equal Employment Opportunity Commission (EEOC), noted that personality tests are not medical examinations and are appropriate for preemployment inquiries when they assess job-relevant abilities, skills, or traits. Moreover, the October 10th, 1995, EEOC final enforcement guidance on Preemployment Disability-Related Questions and Medical Examinations under ADA (EEOC, 1995a), which replaced the May 1994 EEOC guidance (EEOC, 1994), defined a medical examination as one that is designed to "provide evidence that would lead to identifying a mental disorder or impairment (for example, those listed in the American Psychiatric Association's most recent *Diagnostic and Statistical Manual of Mental Disorders*) . . . [I]f a test is designed and used to measure only things such as honesty, tastes, and habits, it is not *medical*" (p. 16).

Third, the intent of the policy set forth in Volume 2 of the *EEOC Compliance Manual* (see EEOC, 1994) is to proscribe questions that are likely to lead to an inference that a person has a disability; the intent is not to proscribe questions that might lead to such an inference. A positive answer to an item such as "I have trouble sleeping" might lead a clinician to infer depression, but it is equally reasonable to infer that the person is very energetic; in principle, therefore, this item can be used to screen job applicants.

Moreover, Section 902 of the 1992 EEOC (EEOC, 1995b) issuance 915.002, dated March 14, 1995, which defined the term *disability*, noted that (a) "Like physical characteristics, common personality traits also are not impairments"; (b) "a psychological profile of an applicant for a police officer position determined that the applicant 'showed poor judgment, irresponsible behavior and poor impulse control. . . . The court ruled that the applicant's personality traits do not constitute an impairment'"; (c) "Example 1—CP [complaining party] is a lawyer who is impatient with her boss. She often loses her temper, frequently shouts at her subordinates, and publicly questions her boss's directions. Her colleagues think she is rude and arrogant, and they find it difficult to get along with her. CP does not have an impairment. Personality traits, such as impatience, a quick temper, and arrogance, in and of themselves are not impairments"; and (d) "Note, however, that CP's employer does not have to excuse CP's misconduct, even if the misconduct results from an impairment that rises to the level of a disability, if it does not excuse similar misconduct from its other employees. See 56 Fed. Reg. 35, 733 (1990) (referring to revisions that 'clarify that employers may hold all employees, disabled . . . and nondisabled, to the same performance and conduct standards')". (EEOC, 1995b, pp. 902–910)

Do Personality Measures Invade Privacy?

Measures of psychiatric disorders and many commercially available integrity tests contain items that may be offensive or invasive; items concerning religious preferences or sexual orientations are invasive. Nonetheless, it is possible, even easy, to measure normal personality well and avoid using these kinds of items. But some people want to define invasion of privacy so broadly that it can preclude any attempt to understand the causes of behavior. We agree that people should be evaluated exclusively on their actual job performance, but by definition we have no performance data for job applicants. Employers are increasingly reluctant to comment on the performance of former employees. Moreover, a person's right to privacy is balanced against an employer's (a) right not to hire incompetent, insubordinate, or lazy people and (b) obligation not to hire someone who is a threat to the safety and security of other employees.

Are Not Many Items on Personality Inventories Unrelated to Job Requirements—Do They Not Lack Face Validity?

The topic of face validity has always been a problem for personality assessment, especially for tests developed in the MMPI tradition of empirical keying, with which tradition we identify. Cronbach (1960) defined *face validity* as "a test which looks good for a particular purpose" (p. 143), and he noted that many good-looking tests fail as predictors of job performance. He concluded that if one must choose between a test with face validity, but no empirical validity, or one with empirical validity and no appeal to the layman, "he had better choose the latter" (p. 144). We agree. Nonetheless, there are circumstances in which face validity is important: A simulation used in a selection battery should resemble the relevant components of the job as closely as possible (this is an issue of fidelity and adequate sampling of the construct domain). Moreover, face validity normally enhances applicants' acceptance of a testing procedure, and that is always desirable. On the other hand, a face-valid measure that fails to predict nontest behavior is useless for decision making.

Personality measures are in a somewhat awkward position because they are often strong on empirical validity and often weak on face validity. Moreover, personality test authors have paid little attention to developing items with occupationally oriented item content. More effort has been directed toward eliminating items with unusual content rather than developing new ones that "look good" in an employment context. The degree to which future test developers will attend to the face validity of their items is an open question. In the meantime, the problem for personality assessment becomes one of educating the public about the difference between empirical and face validity while continuing to demonstrate the job relatedness of personality measures.

Are Not Personality Measures Easily Faked?

The items on many commercially available integrity tests are transparent and therefore easily faked. Many items on empirically keyed measures such as the CPI are not transparent and are therefore hard to fake, but this leads to complaints about lack of face validity. This is an issue on which the critics are allowed to have it both ways—in other words, items that are face valid are transparent and easy to fake; items that are not transparent and are, therefore, hard to fake also lack face validity. But there are some additional responses to this criticism. First, when asked, some people can intentionally raise some of their scores on measures of normal personality. Second, the base rate of deliberate faking in applicant populations is low (cf. Hough, Eaton, Dunnette, Kamp, & McCloy, 1990). Third, the consensus among researchers who have studied the problem is that correcting for faking seems to reduce the validity of the scales that are corrected (cf Barrick & Mount, 1995; McCrae & Costa, 1983). Fourth, efforts to enhance one's scores artificially are usually detected by special scales measuring social desirability or "unlikely virtues." And finally, in a careful review of the empirical data on this issue, Hough and Schneider (in press) concluded that "intentional distortion does not appear to affect criterion-related validity negatively, as is often assumed." Although the data needed to resolve this issue are clear, the issue seems somehow unlikely to go away.

What Is the Best Way to Use Personality Measures for Preemployment Selection?

The answer to this question depends on the hiring strategy being used; these strategies fall into two major categories, although there will always be mixed cases. In the first case, an organization has many applicants for a large number of openings, and positions are filled on a continuous basis. Because the applicant pool is large, processing costs are an issue, and the goal will normally be to screen out potentially unsuitable employees. To avoid hiring mistakes, one should use broad measures of integrity and the capacity to handle the pressure of a heavy work load because these measures predict accidents, absenteeism, turnover, and other undesirable behavior patterns. To ensure adequate applicant flow, it is necessary to use moderate test cutoff scores. Typically, the personality measures (integrity and stress tolerance) are supported by criterion-related validity.

In the second case, an organization has few applicants and few openings. The goal normally will be to identify excellent applicants as opposed to screening out marginal ones. Here, one should use an inventory of normal personality to match the applicant with the psychological requirements of the job. For example, potential sales personnel should have high scores on measures of extraversion and ambition. Again, the scales used should be identified on the basis of a criterion-related validity study.

In our view, an inventory of normal personality, supported by the proper validity evidence, is an essential part of any preemployment screening process. Although such measures provide information about the personal characteristics of the applicant, they cannot assess technical skills, experience, and ability to learn.

Conclusions

This article can be summarized in terms of four points. First, a surprising number of people still believe that personality measures are unsuitable for use in preemployment screening, and a variety of reasons are given to support this judgment; we have tried to show that these criticisms are less serious than is generally believed. Second, we present data showing that scores on well-developed measures of normal personality are (a) stable over reasonably long periods of time and (b) predict important occupational outcomes. Third, we want to suggest in the strongest possible terms that the use of well-constructed measures of normal personality in preemployment screening will be a force for equal employment opportunity, social justice, and increased productivity. Finally, although we believe that personality measurement is appropriate for most preemployment decisions, it should always be used in conjunction with other information, particularly in regards to the applicant's technical skills, job experience, and ability to learn.

References

Barrick, M. R., & Mount, M. K. (1991). The Big-Five personality dimensions in job performance: A meta-analysis. *Personnel Psychology, 44,* 1–26.

Barrick, M. R., & Mount, M. K. (1993). Autonomy as a moderator of the relationship between the Big-Five personality dimensions and job performance. *Journal of Applied Psychology, 78,* 111–118.

Barrick, M. R., & Mount, M. K. (1995, May). *Does response distortion influence the validity of Big-Five personality constructs?* Paper presented at the 10th Annual Conference of the Society for Industrial and Organizational Psychology, Inc., Orlando, FL.

Blinkhorn, S., & Johnson, C. (1990). The insignificance of personality testing. *Nature, 348,* 671–672.

Buss, A. M., & Plomin, R. (1975). *A temperamental theory of personality development.* New York: Wiley-Interscience.

Campbell, J. P. (1990). Modeling the performance prediction problem in industrial and organizational psychology. In M. D. Dunnette & L. M. Hough (Eds.). *Handbook of industrial and organizational psychology* (Vol. 2, pp. 687–732). Palo Alto, CA: Consulting Psychologists Press.

Caspi, A., Bem, D. J., & Elder, G. H. (1989). Continuities and consequences of interactional styles across the life course. *Journal of Personality, 57,* 375–405.

Collins. J. M. (1995, May). *Socialization: The "highest good."* Paper presented at 10th Annual Conference of the Society for Industrial and Organizational Psychology, Inc., Orlando, FL.

Conley, J. J. (1984). Longitudinal consistency of adult personality: Self-reported psychological characteristics across 45 years. *Journal of Personal and Social Psychology, 47,* 1325–1333.

Conley, J. J. (1985). Longitudinal stability of personality traits: A multi-trait-multi-method-multioccation analysis. *Journal of Personality and Social Psychology, 49,* 1266–1282.

Costa, P. T., Jr., & McCrae, R. R. (1988). Personality in adulthood: A six-year longitudinal study of self-reports and spouse ratings on the NEO personality inventory. *Journal of Personality and Social Psychology, 54,* 853–863.

Cronbach, L. J. (1960). *Essentials of psychological testing* (2nd ed.). New York: Harper & Row.

Digman, J. M. (1990). Personality structure: Emergence of the five-factor model. In M. R. Rosenweig & L. W. Porter (Eds.), *Annual review of psychology* (Vol. 41, pp. 417–440). Palo Alto, CA: Annual Reviews.

Dudek, S. Z., & Hall, W. B. (1991). Personality consistency: Eminent architects 25 years later. *Creativity Research Journal, 4,* 213–231.

Equal Employment Opportunity Commission, (1994). *Enforcement guidance: Preemployment disability-related inquiries and medical examinations under the Americans with Disabilities Act of 1990.* Washington, DC: Author.

Equal Employment Opportunity Commission. (1995a). *ADA enforcement guidance: Preemployment disability-related questions and medical examinations.* Washington, DC: Author.

Equal Employment Opportunity Commission. (1995b). *Definition of the term disability* (Order 915–002, Section 902). Washington, DC: Author.

Finn, S. E. (1996). Stability of personality self-ratings over 30 years: Evidence for an age/cohort interaction. *Journal of Personality and Social Psychology 50,* 813–818.

Ghiselli, E. E., & Barthol, R. P. (1953). The validity of personality inventories in the selection of employees. *Journal of Applied Psychology, 37,* 18–20.

Goldberg, L. R. (1993). The structure of phenotypic personality traits. *American Psychologist, 48,* 26–34.

Gough, H. G. (1965). Conceptual analysis of psychological test scores and other diagnostic variables. *Journal of Abnormal Psychology, 70,* 294–320.

Gough, H. G. (1975). *Manual for the California Psychological Inventory.* Palo Alto, CA: Consulting Psychologists Press.

Gough, H. G. (1987). *Manual for the California Psychological Inventory.* Palo Alto, CA: Consulting Psychologists Press.

Gough, H. G., & Heilbrun, A. B., Jr. (1983). *The Adjective Checklist manual: 1983 edition.* Palo Alto, CA: Consulting Psychologists Press.

Haan, N., Millsap, R., & Hartka, E. (1986). As time goes by: Change and stability in personality over fifty years. *Psychology and Aging, 1,* 220–232.

Hall, W. B., & MacKinnon, D. W. (1969). Personality inventory correlates of creativity among architects. *Journal of Applied Psychology, 54,* 322–326.

Hathaway. S. R., & McKinley, J. C. (1943). *Manual for the Minnesota Multiphasic Personality Inventory.* New York: Psychological Corporation.

Hayes, T. L. (1996). Personality correlates of performance: Does disability make a difference? *Human Performance, 9,* 121–140.

Heatherton, T, & Weinberger, J. L. (1994). *Can personality change?* Washington, DC: American Psychological Association,

Helson, R., & Moane, G. (1987). Personality change in women from college to midlife. *Journal of Personality and Social Psychology, 53,* 176–186.

Helson, R., Roberts, B. W., & Agronick, G. (1995). Enduringness and change in creative personality and the prediction of occupational creativity. *Journal of Personality and Social Psychology, 69,* 1173–1183.

Helson. R., & Wink, P. (1992). Personality change in women from early 40s to early 50s. *Psychology and Aging. 7,* 46–55.

Hofstee, W. K. B. (1994). Who should own the definition of personality? *European Journal of Personality, 8,* 149–162.

Hogan, J., & Hogan, R. (1989). How to measure employee reliability. *Journal of Applied Psychology, 74,* 273–279.

Hogan, J., & Hogan, R. (1993, April). *The ambiguities of conscientiousness.* Paper presented at the 8th Annual Conference of the Society for Industrial and Organizational Psychologists, Inc., San Francisco.

Hogan, J., & Hogan, R. (1994, April). *Fidelity and bandwidth: Personality assessment and job performance.* Paper presented at the 9th Annual Conference of the Society for Industrial and Organizational Psychologists, Inc., Nashville, TN.

Hogan, J., & Stark, D. (1992, June). *Using personality measures to select firefighters.* Paper presented at the 16th Annual Meeting of the International Personnel Management Association Assessment Council, Baltimore.

Hogan, R. (1991). Personality and personality measurement. In M. D. Dunnette & L. M. Hough (Eds.), *Handbook of industrial and organizational psychology* (Vol. 2, pp. 327–396). Palo Alto, CA: Consulting Psychologists Press.

Hogan, R. (in press). A socioanalytic perspective on the Five Factor Model. In J. S. Wiggins (Ed.), *Theories of the Five Factor Model.* Now York: Guilford.

Hogan, R., & Hogan, J. (1995). *Hogan Personality Inventory manual* (2nd ed.). Tulsa, OK: Hogan Assessment Systems.

Holland, J. L. (1985). Making vocational choices., A theory of careers. Englewood Cliffs, NJ: Prentice-Hall.

Hough, L. M., Eaton, N. K., Dunnette, M. D., Kamp, J. D., & McCloy, R. A. (1990). Criterion-related validities of personality constructs and the effect of response distortion on those validities. *Journal of Applied Psychology, 75,* 581–595.

Hough, L. M., & Schneider, R. J. (in press). The frontiers of I/O psychology personality research. In K. R. Murphy (Ed.), *Individual differences and behavior in organizations.* San Francisco: Jossey-Bass.

Hunter, J. E. (1983). *Test validation for 12,000 jobs: An application of job classification and validity generalization analysis to the General Aptitude Test Battery* (USES Test Research Report No. 43). Washington, DC: U.S. Employment Service, U.S. Department of Labor.

Kelly, E. L. (1955). Consistency of the adult personality. *American Psychologist, 10,* 659–681.

Kogan, M. (1990). Personality and aging. In J. E. Birren & S. W. Schaie (Eds.), *Handbook of the psychology of aging* (pp. 330–346). San Diego, CA: Academic Press.

MacKinnon, D. W. (1944). The structure of personality. In J. McVicker Hunt (Ed.), *Personality and the behavior disorders* (Vol. 1, pp. 3–48). New York: Ronald Press.

MacKinnon, D. W. (1962). The nature and nurture of creative talent. *American Psychologist, 17,* 484–495.

Mainstream science on intelligence. (1994, December 13). *The Wall Street Journal,* p. A18.

McCrae, R. R., & Costa, P. T., Jr. (1983). Social desirability: More substance than style. *Journal of Consulting and Clinical Psychology, 51,* 882–888.

McCrae, R. R., & Costa, P. T., Jr. (1987). Validation of the five-factor model of personality across instruments and observers. *Journal of Personality and Social Psychology, 52,* 81–90.

McDaniel, M. A., & Frei, R. L. (1994). *Validity of customer service measures in personnel selection: A review of criterion and construct evidence.* Manuscript submitted for publication.

McGue, M., Bacon, S., & Lykken, D. T. (1993). Personality stability and change in early adulthood: A behavioral genetic analysis. *Developmental Psychology 29,* 96–109.

McHenry, J. J., Hough, L. M., Toquam, J. L., Hanson, M. A., & Ashworth, S. (1990). Project A validity results: The relationship between predictor and criterion domains. *Personnel Psychology, 43,* 335–354.

Megargee, E. I. (1972). *The California Psychological Inventory handbook.* San Francisco: Jossey-Bass.

Norman, W. T. (1963). Toward an adequate taxonomy of personality attributes: Replicated factor structure in peer nomination personality ratings. *Journal of Abnormal and Social Psychology: 66,* 574–583.

Ones, D. S., Viswesvaran, C., & Schmidt, F. L. (1993). Comprehensive meta-analysis of integrity test validation: Findings and implications for personnel selection and theories of job performance. *Journal of Applied Psychology, 78,* 679–703.

Reilly, R. R., & Warech, M. A. (1993). The validity and fairness of alternatives to cognitive tests. In L. C. Wing & B. R. Gifford (Eds.), *Policy issues in employment testing* (pp. 131–224). Norwell, MA: Kluwer Academic.

Roberts, B. W. (1994). *A longitudinal study of the reciprocal relation between women's personality and occupational experience.* Unpublished doctoral dissertation, University of California, Berkeley.

Schmit, M. J., Guion, R. M., & Raymark, P. H. (1995). *Personality-related position requirements: Matching people and jobs.* Unpublished manuscript, Bowling Green State University, Ohio.

Stevens, D. P., & Truss, C. V. (1985). Stability and change in adult personality over 12 and 20 years. *Developmental Psychology, 21,* 568–584.

Tett, R. P., Jackson, D. N., & Rothstein, M. (1991). Personality measures as predictors of job performance: A meta-analytic review. *Personnel Psychology, 44,* 703–742.

Thurstone, L. L. (1934). The vectors of the mind. *Psychological Review, 41,* 1–32.

Tupes, E. C., & Christal, R. E. (1961). *Recurrent personality factors based on trait ratings* (ASD-TR-61-97). Lackland Air Force Base, TX: Aeronautical Systems Division, Personnel Laboratory.

Article Review Form at end of book.

According to Nelson, what are the boundaries in organizations?

The Boundaryless Organization:

Implications for Job Analysis, Recruitment, and Selection

Jodi Barnes Nelson

Jodi Barnes Nelson is a Human Resource Management Ph.D. candidate at The University of Georgia. She currently teaches labor relations and organizational behavior at North Carolina State University.

The boundaryless organization is a paradigm shift that recognizes the limitations inherent in separating people, tasks, processes, and places, and emphasizes the benefits of moving ideas, information, decisions, talent, and actions where they are most needed (Ashkenas, Ulrich, Jick, & Kerr, 1995). This article proposes that some job analysis techniques and recruitment and selection practices are incongruous with the principles of the boundaryless organization. However, existing worker-oriented approaches to job analysis, recruitment based on person-organization value congruence, and selection based on both skills and traits are consistent with the tenets of the boundaryless organization. Limitations of workforce homogeneity are also discussed. Finally, recommendations for researchers and practitioners are offered.

Reengineering, restructuring, even rethinking approaches to organizational design have proliferated in recent management literature (Keidel, 1994). Purported to underlie hundreds of these and other innovative approaches is a fundamental paradigmatic shift called the boundaryless organization. A boundaryless organization is one that focuses on permeating all internal and external boundaries (e.g., those between functions, the organization and its suppliers, even between nations) with free movement of ideas, information, decisions, talent, rewards, and action (Ashkenas et al., 1995).

At the same time, cogent arguments have been made to bury our long-standing conceptualization of the job and, instead, to recognize a post-job society where the norm of payrolled, full-time employees performing narrow duties in particular departments is history (Bridges, 1994). In fact, "work" has been described as undergoing such a fundamental transformation that we must necessarily question and perhaps replace the body of knowledge underlying the psychology of work behavior (Howard, 1995). This literature advocates radical departures from the ways in which we view what are organizations' most important tasks; where, when, and how work is done; and who decides these issues.

While organizational design and strategic management solutions have been proposed for the boundaryless organization (e.g., Ashkenas et. al, 1995; Davis, 1995), relatively little has been discussed in terms of the human resource practices and processes to best support it. In other words, how specific human resources practices "fit" or become consonant with boundaryless organizational principles is not clear.

One reason for the lack of clarity surrounding human resources' role in the context of the boundaryless organization is due to the field's traditional dependence on the job as the fundamental unit of the organization. Indeed, job analysis provides the basis for virtually all human resource functions (i.e., recruitment, selection, compensation, training); thus, much of human resource technology is grounded in the notion of individuals holding jobs (Lawler, 1994). However, viewing the job as the fundamental organizational unit has been criticized as outmoded and ineffective (Bridges, 1994; Lawler, 1994). This apparent conflict between the idea of jobs being the central focus of human resources and recent literature proposing that the job is no longer a useful way to organize and manage work is the motivation behind this research.

The purpose of this paper is to examine implications of the boundaryless paradigm for three areas of human resources: job analysis, recruitment, and selection. Due to its centrality to both recruitment and selection, job analysis will be examined first. Two major approaches to job analysis will be evaluated based on boundaryless principles. Recruitment and selection practices will then be similarly evaluated.

The intended goal of this paper is to challenge human resource practitioners and researchers to view job analysis, recruitment, and selection as boundaryless functions. Specifically, it will be argued that one major job analysis method, as well as some existing recruitment and selection practices, can benefit the boundaryless organization. Because one of human resource management's strategic roles is to find the best potential match between the organization and the individual, the importance of organizational culture, and person–organization value congruence in particular, is discussed. Finally, general propositions for both practitioners and researchers are provided.

The Boundaryless Paradigm

Underlying the rise of various forms of "new organization" to which have been ascribed the terms virtual organization, empowered organization, high-performing work teams, and process reengineered organization is "a single, deeper paradigm shift that we call the emergence of the boundaryless organization," (p. 2; Ashkenas et al., 1995). This shift recognizes the limitations of the following four types of organizational boundaries: vertical (between levels and ranks of people), horizontal (between functions and disciplines), external (between the organization and its suppliers, customers, and regulators), and geographic (between nations, cultures, and markets). In the boundaryless organization, these boundaries are not used to separate people, tasks, processes, and places; rather, the focus is on how to move ideas, information, talent, and decisions where they are most necessary (Ashkenas et al., 1995). Somewhat similarly, Miner and Robinson (1994) define a boundaryless organization as one in which rules regarding membership, departmental identity, and job responsibility are ambiguous. Organization membership rules refer to the blurring of organizational boundaries (e.g., increases in outsourcing of activities, contingent employment arrangements); department identity rules refer to decentralization, cross-functional coordination, and teams which blur functional boundaries; and job responsibility rules refer to a movement toward more general job descriptions, emphasizing important values instead of specific, predetermined duties (Miner & Robinson, 1994; Souder, 1987). Indeed, other researchers have noted increased organizational fluidity over the past decade, particularly in the area of jobs (Belous, 1989).

Conversely, a boundary mindset assumption is that knowledge, skills, and abilities (KSAs) are found in abundance at the top of the organizational pyramid, whereas lower-level workers have narrow technical skills, mostly used to produce services or products (Ashkenas et al., 1995). Thus, every worker in a boundary mindset hierarchy has a clearly defined role. In the boundaryless organization, competencies reside and are recognized throughout the workplace. When an individual has the skill to do a task, he or she is encouraged to do it, regardless of title or position (Ashkenas et al., 1995). Similarly, Lawler (1994) challenges what he calls the job-based approach to organizing and managing (i.e., jobs are the basic building blocks of complex organizations) and calls for a paradigmatic shift to the competency-based organization, which focuses on the individual's needed skills to accomplish organizational goals.

> The reality is that the "post-job" worker will be far more independent and self-directed than was the job-based worker (Bridges, 1994).

Although virtually all human resource technology is grounded in the notion of individuals holding jobs, there is evidence to suggest that this notion is no longer the best way to think about organizing and managing individuals (Lawler, 1994). In fact, Bridges (1994) posits that while the amount of work in organizations continues to grow, the "familiar envelopes" we call jobs are becoming extinct. First, an increasing number of jobs is in constant flux and job descriptions cannot be rewritten every week. Further, when organizations reduce head count, the very jobs that are represented by boxes on an organizational chart encourage hiring because managers are bestowed power according to the number of turf areas they oversee. Finally, jobs are rewarded on the basis of doing the jobs, not for accomplishing the necessary work. Thus, personal accountability for the work is discouraged at the expense of accountability for the job (Bridges, 1994; Bowen & Lawler, 1992).

Bridges (1994) further asserts that most organizations lack effective ways to manage in "de-jobbed" environments which consist of significant numbers of temporary workers, part-timers, consultants, and contract workers. His solution, in part, is a project-based organizational structure whereby job descriptions and supervisors' orders are replaced by evolving demands of a project. The reality is that the "post-job" worker will be far more independent and self-directed than was the job-based worker (Bridges, 1994).

Boundaryless Employment Arrangements

An increase in nontraditional employment contracts between the worker and the organization is cited as an example of blurred organizational boundaries (Miner & Robinson, 1994), as well as evidence of a post-job society (Bridges, 1994). The term contract denotes the different forms employment is taking in the 1990s: temporary, part-time, job-sharing, consulting, contracting, and leasing. Although some employees have little choice but to accept one of these forms of employment, many employees welcome these options for more flexible hours and more control over where they work, how they work, and which projects they would most prefer (Belous, 1989).

The collective contingency of non-traditional U.S. workers numbered over 30 million in 1988—about one-quarter of the workforce (Belous, 1989). It is now estimated that this contingency represents almost one-half (Halal, 1994) of all employed U.S. workers. Moreover, many companies are not only accepting but encouraging telecommuting among their employees (Charbuck & Young, 1992). Escalating overhead costs coupled with technological advancements such as workflow systems, teleconferencing, videoconferencing, and electronic mail have made working off-site a mutually beneficial option for many workers and organizations.

In sum, boundaryless organization research prescribes permeable structures at all organizational levels. In addition, the growth of diverse employment arrangements provides information about worker mobility and the increasingly flexible nature of employment. Given what we know about the boundaryless organization and the boundaryless worker, what are the important implications for human resources? What, for instance, constitutes effective employee recruitment and selection in such an environment? Because effective recruitment and selection practices are based on some form of job analysis (Gatewood & Feild, 1994), a discussion of analysis and an examination of its role in the boundaryless organization follows.

Boundaryless Job Analysis

Given that the job itself may be an increasingly unreliable way to characterize what workers do (Bridges, 1994; Lawler, 1994; Ashkenas et al., 1995), where, if anywhere, does job analysis fit in the boundaryless organization? Job analysis is the measurement of tasks and/or worker attributes for a given job; thus, job analysis techniques can be classified as work-oriented or worker-oriented (Gatewood & Feild, 1994). Work-oriented methods involve specific descriptions of the various tasks performed on a job, whereas worker-oriented methods examine broad human behaviors involved in work activities.

Whether work- or worker-oriented, job analysis methods allow for the inference of worker KSAs and other characteristics (Gatewood & Feild, 1994). KSAs include job-related information and the necessary human abilities to perform certain job activities. The importance of valid KSAs cannot be overstated, as the relationship between them and individual performance in the organization is well-established (Davis, 1995; Gatewood & Feild, 1994).

Although job analysis is considered the virtual cornerstone of human resources practices, it has recently been criticized as inflexible and legalistic (Drucker, 1987); its traditional conception has been called obsolete (Sanchez, 1994). These criticisms parallel other arguments that focus on creating boundaryless conditions between functions, disciplines, and levels of workers (Ashkenas et al., 1995) and those aimed at thriving in a de-jobbed society (Bridges, 1994). In essence, these arguments posit that the job is too myopic, too restrictive, and too inflexible for the success of both the organization and its workers.

The "job" in job analysis, however, need not imply that this systematic process of discovering work-related information is merely useful for a narrow scope of tasks or easily defined duties. Job analysis is a tool to systematically gather data (i.e., tasks and behaviors leading to KSAs) about virtually any kind of work activity (Gatewood & Feild, 1994). Thus, a plausible argument can be made that job analysis would be more important in the boundaryless organization, where work activities are created and evolve more quickly, than in more traditionally structured organizations, where jobs are static for longer time periods.

Job analysis is the measurement of tasks and/or worker attributes for a given job; thus, job analysis techniques can be classified as work-oriented or worker-oriented.

Contrary to criticisms of the inadequacies of job analysis, it is proposed here that job analysis is capable of examining both diverse and changing occupations. Not all job analysis approaches are equal, however. In general, the worker-oriented approach is proposed as more appropriate than the work-oriented approach because the former possesses the flexibility needed in the boundaryless organization.

Consider a work-oriented method such as the Functional Job Analysis, or FJA (Fine & Wiley, 1977). The FJA assesses specific job outputs, identifies job tasks in terms of task statements (e.g., who does the task, what action is performed, immediate result, tools/equipment used, instructions followed), measures worker involvement with people, data, and things (worker functions scales), and also measures numerous other qualifications and specifications. The main problem with the FJA, and the work approach in general (e.g., identifying what a worker does and how each task is performed), is that it provides limited utility due to the changing nature of the job.

The Position Analysis Questionnaire, or PAQ (McCormick, Jeanneret, & Mecham, 1972), on the other hand, focuses on general worker behaviors instead of tasks. This worker-oriented method includes information about worker input, mental processes, work output, and relationships with others. Worker-oriented methods provide a standardized means for collecting quantitative data across a wide spectrum of jobs and yield helpful information in formulating employee specifications (Gatewood & Feild, 1994). Further, the worker-oriented approach has been called one of the most useful methods of work description developed to date, one that allows "meaningful comparisons" to be made between jobs that are highly dissimilar at the task level (Harvey, Friedman, Hakel, & Cornelius, 1988, p. 639).

Whereas some worker-oriented methods have been criticized for their lack of structure and absence of task data (Gatewood & Feild, 1994), these "limitations" may become less important or even prove useful in the boundaryless organization. For instance, worker-oriented methods do not cover actual task activities, a requirement for job description development. Given that job descriptions are becoming less important for boundaryless organizations (Ashkenas et al., 1995; Miner & Robinson, 1994), however, the worker-oriented approach may have few, if any, limitations.

One criticism that has been aimed specifically at the PAQ is its required reading level, estimated at post-college or higher (Ash & Edgell, 1975). However, another worker-oriented job analysis method modeled after the PAQ, the Job Element Inventory, or JEI (Cornelius & Hakel, 1978), requires a 10th-grade reading level. The JEI has been found to possess a factor analytic structure parallel to that of the PAQ (Harvey et al., 1988). Thus, the JEI's use poses few problems for job incumbents and supervisors who may serve as job analysis raters.

While work- and worker-oriented job analysis methods have not been directly compared by incumbent workers, research shows that workers have criticized the use of a point-factor job analysis questionnaire based on widely used job evaluation scales (Taber & Peters, 1991). Taber and Peters (1991) found the most frequent comment made by hundreds of administrative, technical, and clerical workers was that their jobs could not be described by the job analysis questionnaire. The next most frequent comment was that the questionnaire did not assess some personal attributes brought by the employee to the job (e.g., "Personality, attitude are very important," and "Creativity is not mentioned"). Other comments included (in order): "Interpersonal contacts are inadequately assessed;" "The job has been revised or is evolving;" and "Job tasks are too diverse to be captured in questionnaire form."

According to Taber and Peters (1991), it is likely that any existing job evaluation procedure cannot comprehensively evaluate jobs which are highly interdependent, continuously evolving, unpredictable, or that involve a diverse set of important but infrequent tasks. Indeed, these very types of "jobs" describe what workers do in a boundaryless organization. Although job analysis and job evaluation serve different (yet related) functions, the Taber and Peters (1991) study implies that workers who are only asked work-oriented information such as major tasks, how much time they spend performing each one, the importance of each task, its complexity, equipment used, etc., perceive these data as inadequate measures of what they do.

Skills Emphasis and Work Analysis

Given that functional boundaries will continue to blur (Ashkenas, 1995; Miner & Robinson, 1994), boundaryless organizations may eventually collapse "jobs" into more comprehensive skill- or work-related categories. Not only would this type of integration make the administrative task of job analysis less cumbersome; it could contribute to a culture wherein workers are afforded more freedom and opportunity to engage in different work activities.

For example, Woodsworth, Maylone, and Sywak (1992) found a sufficiently strong relationship between some computing and library jobs to warrant the creation of a single information job family in classification systems. The commonality between jobs was attributed to the jobs' reliance on various information technologies. As information technologies become more interconnected between jobs, functions, and departments, it is plausible that the KSAs which relate to these technologies will become more transferable and less job-specific.

However, a big question is which KSAs will be required for future technologies, and thus, future jobs. Arvey, Salas, and Gialluca (1992) have demonstrated that some existing tasks and skills-abilities correlations can help predict future skill requirements for jobs when only a limited number of tasks is known. The authors caution, however, that this technique assumes current tasks and abilities are representative and inclusive of the kinds of skills and abilities that would be forecasted. Moreover, any changes in job structures that would affect existing covariance patterns would diminish the accuracy of skills forecasting results (Arvey et al., 1992).

Recently, work analysis has been advocated to replace the traditional notion of job analysis (Sanchez, 1994). Few guidelines exist as to how to combine tasks into broader units, but Sanchez (1994) proposes that both employees and management examine tasks and KSAs "to group previous job titles into cross-functional, challenging occupational classifications." Although the idea of work analysis may be intuitively appealing, concrete procedures for work analysis are missing. Only general propositions and recommendations (e.g., "analyze work activities to identify workflow, so that new occupational classifications can be based on workflow rather than functional area," Sanchez, 1994) have been stated.

An important question for practitioners and researchers alike is whether existing job analysis methods such as the PAQ and the JEI, or a broader notion such as work analysis, can be used to capture the flexibility, interdependency, and diversity of work in the boundaryless organization. Because the boundaryless organization does not accommodate stable tasks, work-oriented approaches to job analysis may be both cumbersome and ineffective. On the other hand, gathering information about KSAs which ultimately encompass what workers can do, their values, and how these match the organization's culture and operational needs seems the niche that job (or work) analysis should be filling.

Somewhat along these lines, Davis (1995) has called for adequate methods to determine "organizational KSAs," a term he likens to unique organizational competencies and assumedly different from a compilation of individual worker KSAs. A job or work analysis method that taps organizational KSAs, work-relevant KSAs, and other worker characteristics that can be tied to the organization, the work, or both, would seem to enhance the success of several human resource functions, especially recruitment and selection.

> It is likely that any existing job evaluation procedure cannot comprehensively evaluate jobs which are highly interdependent, continuously evolving, unpredictable, or that involve a diverse set of important but infrequent tasks.

Boundaryless Recruitment

Gaining competent employees at all levels of the organization is more than a matter of training; it stems from changes in recruitment and selection philosophy (Ashkenas et al., 1995). Specifically, the boundaryless organization emphasizes the development of a shared mindset among all of its employees and the continuous support of this collective culture. Although Ashkenas et al. (1995) don't describe specific recruiting approaches that aid in achieving this cohesive culture, they state the importance of thoroughly screening applicants, sometimes with the help of customers, based on skills and personality traits that match the technical and cultural needs of the organization.

It makes sense that an organization's culture would be reflected, to some degree, in its recruitment efforts. However, most research suggests that this is not the case. Bretz, Rynes, and Gerhart (1993) found that despite the recent emphasis on unique organizational values, strategies, or cultures in the person-organization fit literature, recruiters continue to emphasize job-related course work or experience and broad personal characteristics (e.g., articulation, personal appearance, general communication skills). In other words, the immediate job fit dominated the recruiting exchange, whereas the organization's culture and values were relatively absent. Similarly, Adkins, Russell, and Werbel (1994) found that recruiters' perceptions of congruence between the applicant and the organization were not related to the recruiters' judgments of employability.

There may be several reasons why person-organization fit is not assessed or emphasized during recruitment. First, many organizations may be unaware of their cultures (Schein, 1985) despite the recent emphasis on unique organizational values, strategies, or cultures in discussions of fit (Bretz et al., 1993). Second, recruiters may not utilize person-organization fit information for different reasons. For instance, recruiters may lack knowledge about the organization's culture, or they may not have the ability to process knowledge about organizational culture into questions intended to measure person-organization fit. Furthermore, they may not know how to weigh person-organization fit measures with traditional job-related KSAs.

Moving toward Realistic Work Cultures

A recruitment technique that is theoretically derived from an individual need-organization culture matching process is the realistic job preview, or RJP (Wanous, 1992). An RJP presents the candidate with negative and positive aspects about a particular job so that the degree of match between the candidate's wants (derived from individual needs) and the organization's climate (derived from its culture) can be assessed (Wanous, 1992). The more positive and negative information a candidate receives about the job, the more realistic the individual's expectations, and the less likely voluntary turnover is to happen within the first stages of socialization (Meglino, DeNisi, Youngblood, & Williams, 1988). Lawler (1994) notes that RJPs are likely the best approach to selection in the competency-based organization versus the job-based organization.

Given, however, the boundaryless organization's de-emphasis on both hierarchical structure and the job itself, an RJP may not provide enough information to determine the most valid individual-organization match. Specifically, it is suggested that recruiters attempt to communicate, as directly as possible, the culture of their organizations—not just a particular job and its immediate environment—to candidates. Recruiters should provide candidates with previews of organizational culture for several reasons. First, the traditional job description (i.e., thorough listing of specific duties and responsibilities) will become less used by organizations due to the blurring of job rules and functional domains. Instead of workers focusing on "who does what," the values, norms, and beliefs which underlie all of the work in the organization will become increasingly salient to workers. Indeed, many firms have moved to more general job descriptions, emphasizing important values instead of precise, predetermined duties (Miner & Robinson, 1994; Souder, 1987).

Second, because work is becoming "structured" in a less hierarchical fashion and more according to the requirements of the project (Bridges, 1994; Lawler, 1994), the nature of coworker interactions and communicating different work processes will play more vital roles in the boundaryless organization. Devanna and Tichy (1990) describe creating a culture that allows all levels of the workforce to contribute to business strategy formulation, resulting in a fluid power structure. In fact, it has been proposed that every challenge facing the boundaryless organization deals with people management, "with issues of how things get done, not what gets done" (Devanna & Tichy, 1990).

Third, an inferred temporal distinction exists between organizational culture and organizational climate. Traditional RJPs tend to mirror organizational climate. Climate refers to currently shared perceptions of "the way things are around here" (Wanous, 1992), and many times has a specific referent such as a safety climate (Zohar, 1980), a sexual harassment climate (Bill, 1994), or service, cooperation, or rewards/punishments climates (Schneider, 1975).

Culture, on the other hand, refers to subconscious assumptions, shared meanings, and ways of interpreting things that pervade the whole organization (Reichers & Schneider, 1990). Because culture is more fundamental than climate (Wanous, 1992) and less transient than specific work environments (i.e., climates) which are subject to change, it is proposed that applicants and organizations alike would benefit from the exchange of information about the assumptions and values underlying these particular work environments. Whereas "the way things are around here" will change within the organization over time, the assumptions, values, and beliefs that are shared among organizational members are more stable, yet not static

(Schein, 1985), organizational attributes. These assumptions, values and beliefs can then be used by the candidate to make a relatively stable assessment regarding how well his or her wants and needs can be matched by those of the organization.

Finally, the use of values to convey cultural information is consonant with the person-organization fit literature. The degree of cultural (i.e. values) fit between workers and their organizations has been shown to significantly affect several important work outcomes, including organizational commitment, job satisfaction, and employee turnover (O'Reilly, Chatman, & Caldwell, 1991). The O'Reilly et al. (1991) study demonstrated that the factor analytic structure underlying individual cultural preferences was comparable to the structure underlying organizational culture in several firms. Also, individual variations in preferences for different organizational cultures were associated with interpretable differences in personality characteristics. Thus, the organization may benefit from selecting people who fit a given situation given some combination of task and cultural (values) requirements (O'Reilly et al., 1991; Ashkenas, 1995).

Sources of Cultural Information

In addition to revealing a deeper layer of organizational information to the candidate, it is proposed that the source of this information will become an increasingly important consideration. Communicating a realistic work culture should include the shared mindsets (Phillips, 1994) of organizational members. As Wanous (1992) advocates, candidates greatly benefit from conversations with incumbent employees. It is further proposed, however, that whenever possible, candidates receive information from employees who share similar group memberships (e.g., race, gender, age, family responsibilities, employment arrangements). This communication exchange should serve to optimize the matching process. If a candidate volunteers information about his single-father role, for example, conversational opportunities with other single fathers or mothers in the organization should be offered to the candidate. Similarly, those who speak English as a second language or have cultural backgrounds that differ from most coworkers should have commensurate opportunities.

In summary, instead of RJPs that focus virtually all of the candidate's attention on the current job and its immediate climate, we need to broaden the RJP, in practice, to encompass realistic work cultures. In addition, the source of this information should ideally include at least one organizational member who shares one or more of the candidate's cultural and/or social group characteristics. Because there are fewer skilled workers (Kessler, 1990) and yet their diversity continues to increase, tomorrow's employees will be able to choose the environments which appear to suit them best (Thomas, 1991).

Boundaryless Selection

As discussed earlier, the importance of job analysis and derived KSAs for the purpose of valid selection practices has been well-established (Gatewood & Feild, 1994). Within the boundaryless organization, however, it is proposed that managers may more effectively attract, select, and retain qualified workers by looking for broad sets of KSAs that may encompass several "jobs," and personality traits reflective of the organization's culture (e.g., O'Reilly et. al, 1991; Devanna & Tichy, 1990).

Generally, cognitive ability tests have the reputation as the best predictors of job performance across virtually all types of jobs (Schmidt & Hunter, 1981). Thus, there is no reason to assume that cognitive ability will not continue to be a valid predictor of performance within a boundaryless context. However, it is proposed that increased emphasis will be placed on traits such as adaptability and flexibility (Ashkenas et al., 1995). Indeed, Devanna and Tichy (1990) state that while the boundaryless organization will continue to select workers with the appropriate technical mix, selection will also depend on facilitation skills to create and maintain social networks, the ability to motivate with influence versus power, and the ability as well as willingness to teach others what they have learned.

The main idea here is that predicting individual performance in a boundaryless organization will no longer be a matter of studying the same particulars within a job content domain. For most jobs, the domain will change too quickly (Bridges, 1994). However, as long as the individual's aptitude (e.g., cognitive ability) and/or other validated KSAs exist, increasingly important predictors of performance will include traits such as flexibility, adaptability, or attitude toward training and learning in this changing environment.

A number of studies on personality and job performance have demonstrated personality measures' incremental validity over cognitive ability tests (Gellatly, Paunonen, Meyer, Jackson, & Goffin, 1991; Ferris, Bergin, & Gilmore 1986). Moreover, Day and Silverman (1989) found that personality variables can account for more job performance variance than that predicted by cognitive ability.

The Big Five personality dimensions, which include emotional stability, extroversion, openness to experience, agreeableness, and conscientiousness, are widely used in organizational behavior literature (Wagner & Hollenbeck, 1995), have good psychometric qualities, and are especially attractive due to their demonstrated relationship with job performance (Barrick & Mount, 1991). For instance, conscientiousness has been related to both hirability and counterproductivity (Dunn, Mount, Barrick, & Ones, 1995), as well as several job performance criteria for five occupational groups (Barrick & Mount, 1991).

The Big Five could be especially useful in boundaryless selection. Some research indicates that certain personality dimensions are related to worker traits and ways of working that seem characteristic of the boundaryless organization. For instance, extroversion, agreeableness, and conscientiousness have been reported as significantly related to self-efficacy for self-managed work group participation (Thoms, Moore, & Scott, 1996). Also, the predictive validity of conscientiousness and extroversion is greater for managers in jobs high in autonomy compared with those in jobs low in autonomy (Barrick & Mount, 1993). Expectations of self-management and autonomy are increasing for tomorrow's worker (e.g., Ashkenas et al., 1995; Bridges, 1994).

Another potentially helpful selection tool in the boundary organization is biodata. Biodata is the use of life history data that entails a sophisticated understanding of values, attitudes, motivational forces, and experiential bases (Landy, Shankster-Cawley, & Moran, 1995). Theoretically, people seek opportunities and experiences to maximize long-term adaptation to their environment; and given satisfactory outcomes, people will actively seek out similar situations in the future, resulting in coherent patterns of behavior (Mumford, Stokes, & Owens, 1990). Evidence of construct validity and theory underlying biodata predictors has proliferated in the last decade (Landy et al., 1995).

Dilemma of Boundaryless Recruitment and Selection: Too Much of a Good Thing

Ashkenas et al. (1995) emphasize the importance of achieving a shared mindset among employees as early as possible or hiring individuals with shared values. A dilemma regarding a high degree of person-organization culture fit surfaces: What about the potentially negative consequences of attracting and selecting too many like-minded individuals? For instance, Schneider (1987) has suggested that organizational dysfunction and eventual demise can be traced to an overabundance of homogeneous worker characteristics. As a corollary, some diversity of worker attributes may be necessary to respond to environmental threats and opportunities, ultimately ensuring the viability of the organization.

Another caveat to consider is the possibility of adverse impact. Any employment test which results in different acceptance/pass rates for individuals belonging to different groups must be validated and its continued use demonstrated as necessary (e.g., no other test possesses its prediction power). If a disproportionate number of females, for instance, are judged to be a good fit for the organization based on the Big Five, male candidates may have cause for grievance or litigation.

Thus, the very homogeneity of employee values proposed as necessary for the success of the boundaryless organization may lead to two serious problems: decreased organizational performance and adverse impact. Approximately how much and what kinds of cultural parity between worker and organization are necessary for a productive mindset? Approximately how much and what kinds of cultural (i.e., values) similarity between worker and organization lead to litigation and/or poor organizational adaptability?

Because the work and how it is accomplished are based on flexibility to move ideas, information, talent, and decisions where they are most necessary (Ashkenas et al., 1995), the boundaryless organization may be less likely to realize organizational adaptability and performance problems compared to other organizations. The possibility of adverse impact seems a more likely threat. However, if employees are chosen on the basis of the organization's core values which reflect pivotal norms (Shein, 1980), and not on the basis of all possible organizational values and norms, the chance for worker trait homogeneity is lessened.

It may be that just as the organization needs different skill sets to accomplish a unified performance goal, organizations need different traits and worker characteristics to accomplish the longer-term goal of survival (Schneider, 1987). However, worker heterogeneity does not necessarily preclude the selection of homogeneous traits that primarily serve to reinforce core values and pivotal norms. More research is needed to build theory and enhance practitioner success in recruiting and selecting workers for boundaryless organizations.

Summary and Recommendations

A boundaryless organization presents a challenge to some forms of job analysis, and traditional recruitment and selection practices that center around a job to be analyzed in terms of relatively stable tasks. There now exists evidence to suggest the job, as a structure within the organization, is no longer stable enough to use as a basis for making strategic human resources decisions. Although the scope of this paper was limited to job analysis, recruitment, and selection, boundaryless implications for compensation, training and performance management are certainly as important (Lawler, 1994).

The importance of rethinking and developing job analysis and recruitment and selection strategies which consider the realities of the boundaryless organization, contemporary employment arrangements, and the importance of person–organization fit has been the focus of this paper. Recent work in the area of person-organization fit suggests that value congruency may significantly affect employment satisfaction, organizational commitment, likelihood to quit, and actual turnover (O'Reilly et al., 1991). Thus, value congruency might also be used to help predict employee performance across jobs within an organization. On the other hand, a perfectly value-congruent workforce may present a different set of problems, namely poor adaptability to change (Schneider, 1987) and adverse impact. The boundaryless organization's focus is on reducing unnecessary structures so it can be highly adaptable to change. More research is needed to determine how much value congruence is necessary for optimal organizational adaptability and performance without adverse impact.

Recommendations

1. Some method of analyzing what workers do (i.e., job analysis) is necessary in the boundaryless organization. Worker-oriented job analysis approaches such as the PAQ and the JEI allow more flexibility in the boundaryless organization because they focus on worker behaviors instead of specific tasks. Additionally, worker-oriented approaches provide a standardized way of collecting data across many "jobs." Newer approaches like work analysis, based on workflow, should be pursued.

2. An organization's understanding of its culture and its ability to communicate its cultural attributes (i.e., organizational values) to recruits will benefit both the organization and the recruit more than the conveyance of a job and its immediate climate, leading to a better person-organization match.

3. Recruits who receive cultural information from those employees who share similar group memberships (e.g., race, gender, age, family responsibilities) will be able to make better "matches" between themselves and the organization.

4. Understanding its own culture will enable the organization to articulate core values which can then be translated into traits and nontechnical abilities to be validated as selection measures, ultimately enhancing organizational and individual outcomes (e.g., commitment, satisfaction, turnover).

5. Attracting and selecting candidates whose traits highly "match" the organization's cultural profile may result in two problems: organizational dysfunction and adverse impact on different social groups. It is possible that if the boundaryless organization selects employees based on its core values, and affords employees creative individualism in the area of its peripheral values, adverse impact and poor organizational adaptability will be less likely. Research is needed to determine the relationship between worker trait homogeneity and these potential threats.

Rethinking the role of the job in a boundaryless organizational context has tremendous implications for human resource researchers and practitioners alike. Such implications necessitate an examination of how human resources can best fulfill its strategic roles in an environment of fewer vertical, functional, external, and geographical boundaries.

> Recent work in the area of person-organization fit suggests that value congruency may significantly affect employment satisfaction, organizational commitment, likelihood to quit, and actual turnover.

References

Adkins, C. L., Russell, C. J., and Werbel, J. D. "Judgments of Fit in the Selection Process: The Role of Work Value Congruence." *Personnel Psychology*, 47 (1994): 605–623.

Arvey, R. D., Salas, E., and Gialluca, K. A. "Using Task Inventories to Forecast Skills and Abilities." *Human Performance*, 5 (1992): 171–190.

Ash, R. A. and Edgell, S. L. "A Note on the Readability of the Position Analysis Questionnaire (PAQ)." *Journal of Applied Psychology*, 60 (1975): 765–766.

Ashkenas, R., Ulrich, D., Jick, T., and Kerr, S. *The Boundaryless Organization: Breaking the Chains of Organizational Structure.* San Francisco: Jossey-Bass, 1995.

Barrick, M. R. and Mount, M. K. "The Big Five Personality Dimensions: A Meta-analysis." *Personnel Psychology*, 44 (1991): 1–26.

Barrick, M. R. and Mount, M. K. "Autonomy as a Moderator of the Relationships Between the Big Five Personality Dimensions and Job Performance." *Journal of Applied Psychology*, 78 (1993): 111–118.

Belous, R. S. *The Contingent Economy: The Growth of the Temporary, Part-time and Subcontracted Workforce (Report No. 239).* Washington, D.C.: National Planning Association, 1989.

Bill, J. B. "Sexual Harassment as a Work Climate: Moving Beyond the Reasonable Gender Approach." Paper presented at the annual meeting of the Academy of Management, Dallas. 1994 (August).

Bowen, D. E. and Lawler, E. E., III. "Total Quality-oriented Human Resources Management." *Organizational Dynamics*, 20 (1992): 29–41.

Bretz, R. D. Jr., Rynes, S. L., and Gerhart, B. "Recruiter Perceptions of Applicant Fit: Implications for Individual Career Preparation and Job Search Behavior." *Journal of Vocational Behavior*, 43 (1993): 310–327.

Bridges, W. *JobShift.* Reading, MA: Addison-Wesley, 1994.

Charbuck, D. C. and Young, J. S. *The Virtual Workplace.* Forbes, 1992 (November): 184–190.

Cornelius, E. T. and Hakel, M. D. "A Study to Develop an Improved Enlisted Performance Evaluation System for the U.S. Coast Guard." Washington, DC: Department of Transportation, United States Coast Guard, 1978.

Davis, D. D. "Form, Function, and Strategy in Boundaryless Organizations." In A. Howard, (ed.), *The Changing Nature of Work.* San Francisco: Jossey-Bass, 1995.

Day, D. V. and Silverman, S. B. "Personality and Job Performance: Evidence of Incremental Validity." *Personnel Psychology*, 42 (1989): 25–36.

Devanna, M. A. and Tichy, N. "Creating the Competitive Organization of the 21st Century: The Boundaryless Corporation." *Human Resource Management*, 29 (1990): 455–471.

Drucker, P. F. "Workers' Hands Bound by Tradition." *Wall Street Journal* (August 2) (1987): 18.

Dunn, W. S., Mount, M. K., Barrick, M. R., and Ones, D. S. "Relative Importance of Personality and General Mental Ability in Managers' Judgments of Applicant Qualifications." *Journal of Applied Psychology*, 80 (1995): 500–509.

Ferris, G. R., Bergin, T. G., and Gilmore, D. C. "Personality and Ability Predictors of Training Performance for Flight Attendants." *Group and Organization Studies*, 11 (1986): 419–435.

Fine, S. A. and Wiley, W. W. *An Introduction to Functional Job Analysis: A Scaling of Selected Tasks from the Social Welfare Field.* Kalamazoo, MI: W. E. Upjohn Institute for Employment Research, 1977.

Gatewood, R. D. and Feild, H. *Human Resource Selection (3rd ed.).* Fort Worth: Harcourt Brace, 1994.

Gellatly, I. R., Paunonen, S. V., Meyer, J. P. Jackson, D. N., and Goffin, R. D. "Personality, Vocational Interest, and Cognitive Predictors of Managerial Job Performance and Satisfaction." *Personality and Individual Differences*, 12 (1991): 221–231.

Halal, W. E. "From Hierarchy to Enterprise: Internal Markets Are the New Foundation of Management." *The Academy of Management Executive*, 8 (1994): 69–83.

Harvey, R. J., Freidman, L., Hakel, M. D., and Cornelius, E. T. "Dimensionality of the Job Element Inventory, a Simplified

Worker-oriented Job Analysis Questionnaire." *Journal of Applied Psychology,* 73 (1988): 639–646.

Howard, A. *The Changing Nature of Work.* A. Howard (Ed.) San Francisco: Jossey-Bass, 1995.

Keidel, R. W. "Rethinking Organizational Design." *The Academy of Management Executive,* 8 (1994): 12–30.

Kessler, L. L. *Managing Diversity in an Equal Opportunity, Workplace: A Primer for Today's Manager.* Washington D.C.: National Foundation for the Study of Employment Policy, 1990.

Landy, F. J., Shankster-Cawley, L., and Moran, S. K. "Advancing Personnel Selection and Placement Methods." In A. Howard (ed.) *The Changing Nature of Work.* San Francisco: Jossey-Bass. 1995.

Lawler, E. E. III. "From Job-based to Competency-based Organizations." *Journal of Organizational Behavior,* 15 (1994): 3–15.

McCormick, E. J., Jeanneret, P. R., and Mecham, R. C. "A Study of Characteristics and Job Dimensions as Based on the Position Analysis Questionnaire (PAQ)." *Journal of Applied Psychology,* 56 (1972): 347–368.

Meglino, B. M., DeNisi, A. S., Youngblood, S. A., and Williams, K. J. "Effects of Realistic Job Previews: A Comparison Using an Enhancement and a Reduction Preview." *Journal of Applied Psychology,* 73 (1988): 259–266.

Miner, A. S. and Robinson, D. F. "Organizational and Population Level Learning as Engines for Career Transitions." *Journal of Organizational Behavior,* 15 (1994): 345–364.

Mumford, M. D., Stokes, G. S., and Owens, W. A. *Patterns of Life Adaptation: The Ecology of Human Individuality.* Hillsdale. NJ: Erlbaum, 1990.

O'Reilly, C. A. III, Chatman, J., and Caldwell, D. F. "People and Organizational Culture: A Profile Comparison Approach to Assessing Person-organization Fit." *Academy of Management Journal,* 34 (1991): 487–516.

Phillips, M. E. "Industry Mindsets: Exploring the Cultures of Two Macro-organizational Settings." *Organization Science,* 5 (1994): 384–402.

Reichers, A. E. and Schneider, B. "Climate and Culture: An Evolution of Concepts." In B. Schneider (ed.). *Organizational Climate and Culture.* San Francisco: Jossey-Bass, 1990.

Sanchez, J. I. "From Documentation to Innovation: Reshaping Job Analysis to Meet Emerging Business Needs. *Human Resource Management Review,* 4 (1994): 51–74.

Schein. E. H. *Organizational Psychology, (3rd ed.).* Englewood Cliffs, NJ: Prentice Hall. 1980.

Schein, E. H. *Organizational Culture and Leadership: A Dynamic View.* San Francisco: Jossey-Bass, 1985.

Schmidt, F. L. and Hunter, J. E. "Employment Testing: Old Theories and New Research Findings." *American Psychologist,* 36 (1981): 1128–1137.

Schneider, B. "The People Make the Place." *Personnel Psychology,* 40 (1987): 437–454.

Schneider, B. "Organizational Climates: An Essay." *Personnel Psychology,* 28 (1975): 447–481.

Souder, W. E. *Managing New Product Innovations.* Massachusetts: D.C. Heath and Co., 1987.

Taber, T. D. and Peters, T. D. "Assessing the Completeness of a Job Analysis Procedure." *Journal of Organizational Behavior,* 12 (1991): 581–593.

Thomas, R. R., Jr., *Beyond Race and Gender: Unleashing the Power of Your Total Workforce by Managing Diversity.* New York: American Management Association, 1991.

Thoms, P., Moore, K. S., and Scott, K. S. "The Relationship Between Self-efficacy for Participating in Self-managed Work Groups and the Big Five Personality Dimensions." *Journal of Organizational Behavior,* 17 (1996): 349–362.

Wagner, J. A. and Hollenbeck, J. R. *Management of Organizational Behavior, (2nd ed.).* Englewood Cliffs. NJ: Prentice Hall, 1995.

Wanous, J. P. *Organizational Entry (2nd ed.).* Reading, MA: Addison Wesley, 1992.

Woodsworth, A., Maylone, T., and Sywak, M. "The Information Job Family: Results of an Exploratory Study." *Library Trends,* 41 (1992): 250–268.

Zohar, D. "Safety Climate in Industrial Organizations: Theoretical and Applied Implications." *Journal of Applied Psychology,* 65 (1980): 96–102.

Article Review Form at end of book.

WiseGuide Wrap-Up

As we have seen in this section, organizational structures are changing—traditional boundaries are fading, and jobs are becoming increasingly dynamic. These changes have led both job seekers and employers to change their job search strategies. Organizations are increasingly focusing on such factors as personality and values when making hiring decisions. This trend suggests that job seekers need to be aware of their own personality and value system to find an appropriate person/organization match.

R.E.A.L. Sites

This list provides a print preview of typical **Coursewise** R.E.A.L. sites. (There are over 100 such sites at the **Courselinks**™ site.) The danger in printing URLs is that web sites can change overnight. As we went to press, these sites were functional using the URLs provided. If you come across one that isn't, please let us know via email to: webmaster@coursewise.com. Use your Passport to access the most current list of R.E.A.L. sites at the **Courselinks** site.

Site name: College Board Online: Career Search
URL: http://www.collegeboard.com/career/bin/career.pl
Why is it R.E.A.L.? This site provides interesting and useful information about a wide variety of careers.
Key topics: career development, selection
Try this: Need help deciding on a career? Click on the questionnaire link and answer the questions. Any surprises?
Want to know how much I/O psychologists earn? Click on the Social Scientists and Urban Planners Folder, then on Psychologists, then on Earnings.

Site name: Interviewing for Employment
URL: http://minerva.acc.virginia.edu/~career/handouts/interviewing.html
Why is it R.E.A.L.? This site contains information on the structure, organization, and content of job interviews. It contains helpful information on what to expect during an interview.
Key topics: selection, interviewing
Try this: To see some questions you should ask during an interview, click on the Questions link, then on You Ask Employers.

Site name: Monster.com
URL: http://www.monster.com/
Why is it R.E.A.L.? This is a resource for both employers and job seekers. It provides lists of job openings in a variety of areas, including human resources and health care.
Key topics: selection, recruitment
Try this: Click on Browse Jobs by U.S. City/State and find some job openings near you.

section 5

Learning Objectives

- To understand why companies need training and development programs.
- To realize training is not always limited to specific job skills.
- To view training as a process that begins with needs and ends with evaluation.
- To consider the unique contributions psychologists can make to the training process.

Training and Development

WiseGuide Intro

A recurring theme you may have noticed is that jobs are no longer static. Organizations and employees face challenges to keep up with constant changes in technology, to understand different cultures (as the economy becomes more global and the workplace becomes more diverse), to respond to rapid changes in the marketplace, and to be aware of the social and economic forces that affect workers and companies. It is not surprising that organizations want individuals who are flexible, who are capable of learning new skills, and who can adapt to a workplace in flux. This implies that organizations must provide opportunities for employees to develop. Just as with recruitment and selection, industrial/organizational psychologists are in a strong position to help organizations create and implement training and development programs. In Reading 25, Murray provides an interesting overview of some of the areas in which industrial/organizational psychologists can help organizations.

Two of the challenges facing individuals working in this area are the identification of training needs and the determination of how to best accomplish organizational goals. Increasingly, organizations are viewing training as an ongoing process, addressing the person as a whole. When we consider the history of psychology—specifically, the work of Frederick Taylor and his time motion studies—we see that training has focused on developing highly specific work skills. For example, how can we get this worker to shovel more coal in an hour? More recently, organizations have begun addressing employee needs, which sometimes can extend beyond the job or organization. For example, if you review some organizational training programs listed on the Internet (see the R.E.A.L. sites listed at the end of this section and at the **Courselinks**™ web site), you will find that several organizations offer training in personal money management, time management, and even exercise and health. Companies also offer such programs as diversity management and sensitivity training to improve understanding in an increasingly diverse workplace and community. Thus, organizations are increasingly viewing the employee as a whole—not simply someone who performs a specific task while on the job. In some ways, it makes sense for the organization to assist its employees in money management if it can make them more efficient in the long run.

Since organizations have broadened the scope of training, one of the areas that has been growing is ethics training. As a society, we claim to value ethical decision making, but, in business, it is often difficult to clearly define morally responsible decisions. For example, if you are a manager and you know that three of your staff are going to be laid off in the next six months, what should you tell them? Can you imagine other situations which pose ethical dilemmas in business? In Reading 26, Knouse and Giacalone present a case for providing training in ethical decision making at work. They argue that there are significant moral dilemmas we face at work, and, since the workplace is so busy, we often do not have the time to fully contemplate each situation; thus, we may fail to account for individual and organizational values. In this article, they present six components of developing a successful ethics training program for industry. The technique they describe uses case studies as a vehicle for identifying areas of ethical concerns.

It should be noted that training does not need to be limited to the classroom or to reading manuals. The next two articles identify some new and creative ways organizations are using training to develop employees. In Reading 27, McEvoy, Cragun, and Appleby present a case study of outdoor training techniques. They argue that these techniques convey that the organization is interested in the employees as individuals and as team players. Those who participated in this program showed higher levels of self-esteem and organizational commitment. In Reading 28, Salopek describes how organizations can use new technologies to train employees. Specifically, she presents several applications for computer simulation training.

Reading 29, the final article in this section, suggests that training is not limited to people who have jobs. In addition to developing specific skills, people seeking employment need to be trained in how to persist in finding a job and how to cope with rejection. Proudfoot, Guest, Carson, Dunn, and Gray present a cognitive-behavioral training program to assist long-term unemployed people find work.

Finally, a theme throughout each of these readings is outcome evaluation. Simply providing training is not sufficient, because organizations and employees need to know if the training is effectively accomplishing its goals, or if it has become a waste of time and money. Thus, there must be some assessment following training. This assessment may be direct in terms of what people have learned or indirect in terms of how employees feel about the organization or their jobs.

Questions

Reading 25. According to Murray, what are some of the areas in which psychologists are in a good position to help train individuals in industry?

Reading 26. Why should organizations be concerned with ethics training? What are some ethical dilemmas that may face workers?

Reading 27. What is the point of using an outdoor training technique similar to the one presented in this article? What are some ways to measure the effectiveness of these techniques?

Reading 28. What are the advantages and disadvantages of using simulators in training? Does this reduce the importance of a human trainer?

Reading 29. Describe cognitive-behavioral training. Apart from addressing the needs of long-term unemployed people, are there other applications for this technique in industry?

According to Murray, what are some of the areas in which psychologists are in a good position to help train individuals in industry?

Psychologists Needed to Retain Employees

Downsizing and on-the-job training are made easier with psychologist's expertise.

Bridget Murray
Monitor staff

As businesses undergo a fast-paced evolution in their technology use, corporate structure and demographic makeup, employees need ongoing training just to keep up with those changes. And psychology can make a considerable contribution to that training process, said Jill Reich, PhD, APA's executive director for education and the senior staff liaison for the Roundtable group.

Psychology tends to concentrate its efforts on educating and training its own students, and overlooks what it pedagogy offers to industry, notes Reich.

Equipped with knowledge of human relations and cognitive processes that can help companies improve services and adjust to corporate change, psychologists are uniquely positioned to assist industry, especially during this time of organizational upheaval, she said. A 1993 survey by Gateway Management Consulting indicates that 88 percent of senior executives seek to re-engineer, or redesign their companies, a process that requires considerable retraining of employees by business experts, including industrial/organizational (I/O) psychologists. "When we consider the amount of education and training being done in industry, we've got a whole 'new' group of students to consider," said Reich.

Training for Transitions

Organizational change has become the fastest growing area of I/O psychology, says Ann Howard, PhD, a senior consultant at Pittsburgh-based Development Dimensions International (DDI), a human resources consulting firm serving 400 of the Fortune 500 companies. During the often-tumultuous process of corporate restructuring, psychologists can help organizations re-engineer their work structure and retrain their employees, she says.

They might, for example, devise a plan to reduce the hierarchy within an organization, and train managers within the organization to carry out the plan. Howard's firm, DDI, helps companies (particularly start-up auto plants) empower their workers by organizing them into teams. They train the workers teams to handle new job tasks and take over responsibilities formerly held by supervisors. The team structure increases workers' involvement in the company, which boosts their morale and the company's efficiency, says Howard.

In cases of downsizing and outsourcing, psychologists can provide needed support to both employer and employee, says James Farr, PhD, a psychology professor at Pennsylvania State University and the president of APA's Div. 14 (Industrial and Organizational). Some I/O psychologists work to boost the sagging morale and productivity of employees who remain after a company outsources or cuts jobs, he notes.

Still a larger number provide training on problem-solving and effective management of workplace change to the corporate leaders who administer job restructuring and downsizing programs. In a former job at Bell Atlantic, for example, I/O psychologist Nancy Tippins, PhD, helped managers effectively collapse tasks from five jobs into one new job.

In many situations, the psychologist's task is reconciling the company's restructuring needs with employees' interests, says Farr. Downsizing plans, especially, must be free of favoritism and clearly explained. "There needs to be fairness in decision-making and open communication of procedures," said Farr.

"Psychologists Needed to Retain Employees," by Bridget Murray, *APA Monitor*, March 1997. Copyright © 1997 by the American Psychological Association. Reprinted with permission.

Technology As Trainer

Also new on the horizon for I/O psychologists is the integration of technology in to employee's jobs, says Howard. As corporations expand their operations and start offices overseas, many favor training delivered via computer over training delivered in the classroom. Howard is helping companies develop computer software that teaches interpersonal and leadership skills. And psychologist Ray Noe, PhD, a management professor at the Eli Broad Graduate School of Business at Michigan State University, is helping to fine-tune workplace training over the Internet.

Noe is consulting on a project by software company Strategic Interactive that will allow employees of auto companies to access Internet job training 24 hours a day, from any location. Using self-paced training modules posted online, employees study aspects of their jobs, including job policies and procedures, customer-service etiquette, basics of financial analysis, and car repair and maintenance duties. The learners test themselves and receive feedback on their progress. They also use chat rooms offered by the service to share job knowledge and problems, and give one another advice, says Noe.

The service unites employees scattered throughout the country and the world, and saves corporations the expense of flying in employees for job training, he says. Companies who use the service track students' training progress and reward them with coupons once they've finished the training. The coupons qualify them to buy toaster ovens, golf clubs and other merchandise.

Ongoing Demand for Training

In other training arenas such as improving employee's on-the-job performance, there has historically been—and continues to be—demand for psychologists as well, says Tippins. For example, in her present job at General Electric in Dallas, she is helping to improve training programs for GE phone representatives who take customer orders for GE telephone and Internet services and answer customers' questions. Tippins is working with the representatives' trainers to hone and test their handling of customer accounts and their finesse with callers.

In other traditional I/O areas, such as hiring, psychologists help businesses choose screening tests for job applicants, and train them to use tests reliably and interpret the results accurately.

And, says Farr, psychologists are increasingly involved in developing employee evaluation systems—which help employers gauge and manage employee productivity—and employee assistance programs—which involve workshops on stress reduction, conflict management, sensitivity to diversity and interpersonal skills.

Farr notes that teaching in an industrial setting is both similar to, and different from, teaching younger students at a school or university. The function of teaching—transmitting skills and knowledge—stays the same but the teaching approach is considerably more interactive, he and other psychologists acknowledge.

Adult learners ask more questions and demand more justifications and examples, so I/O psychologists must "do their homework" on an organization before conducting training with its employees, says Farr. Trainers need a thorough understanding of the company's history, mission and work force, he said.

Article Review Form at end of book.

Why should organizations be concerned with ethics training? What are some ethical dilemmas that may face workers?

The Six Components of Successful Ethics Training

Stephen B. Knouse and Robert A. Giacalone

Stephen B. Knouse is the Alvin and Patricia Smith Professor of Management at the University of Louisiana at Lafayette. Robert A. Giacalone is a professor at the School of Business Administration at the University of North Carolina at Charlotte.

Ethics training in business represents an earnest attempt on the part of organizations to train employees to engage in morally proper behavior in a business setting. The goal of ethics training is not to teach morality, but rather to help employees make the right decision from a position which is morally comfortable to both the company and the employee. Thus, the company needs to judge the success of its ethics training not by how many questions employees answer correctly in workshops, but by how many questions the training has forced them to ask about their past and future ethical decisions and about the consistency of these decisions with the values of the employee and the organization.

The common excuse that is often heard around business circles is that business persons seldom have well-formed ideas regarding the morality of their decisions. The lack of these ideas often cause them to relinquish any responsibility for ethical actions, thereby inviting amorality and even immorality into the workplace. It is the organization's responsibility, therefore, to structure ethics training so as to help employees clarify both their own expectations and the expectations of the organization, while at the same time examining both sets of expectations within a larger moral framework.

The Six Components

If we want realistically to prepare employees to deal with the ethical problems they will encounter at work, an ethics training program must not dwell on esoteric philosophical approaches. Rather it must deliver a practical understanding to employees of the ethical issues they face. In this light, we propose that the structure of ethics training should consist of six components. We lay out each of these components in turn along with examples of how they may be carried out.

Component 1: Provide Trainees with an Understanding of Ethical Judgment Philosophies and Heuristics

Most trainers wish that they could tell you that there are right and wrong answers to ethical problems. In essence, they realize that finding an answer to ethical problems is like trying to describe a natural shade of grey. It is very difficult to say how dark or light it is; people would prefer to describe it in terms of how it relates to black and white. Indeed, most employees would be surprised about what people (both in and out of the organization) disagree on as being ethically acceptable or unacceptable. Although it is probably presumptuous to think that we can (or should) train employees in the appropriate philosophical approaches that they should take, we would argue that a crucial aspect of training employees to use their critical thinking skills effectively is to help them determine the consistency of their actions with their values and those of the organization.

Training in Component 1 involves a search for common ethical values among employees and between employees and the organization, as well as a respect for various ways these values might be interpreted. Workshops can explore these common threads to discover core values. For example, employees may see the core value of freedom in many different forms: freedom of choice in career matters (choosing to accept or reject a transfer), freedom of choice in personal benefits (choice of medical plans), freedom to make decisions about work (empowerment), and freedom of access to important information about their work, jobs, and careers.

Managers, on the other hand, may see freedom as the operation of

Stephen B. Knouse and Robert A. Giacalone, "The Six Components of Successful Ethics Training," *Business and Society Review,* No. 98, pp. 10–13. Copyright © by Blackwell Publishers. Reprinted by permission of Blackwell Publishers.

the free market in the business environment: freedom from government restriction on business operations, freedom of the company to follow new business opportunities, and freedom of customers to choose among products and services.

In the area of heuristics, organizations can provide trainees with critical thinking strategies for approaching ethical situations. In particular, clear, analytically based questions may help trainees to think about issues. Moreover, a series of critical questions can more clearly elucidate the issues and point out alternative avenues for resolving the problem.

For example, an employee can be asked to describe an ethical dilemma that he or she experienced or witnessed. Other participants in the training session can then be given questions that they ask the employee, which are designed to allow them to evaluate critically the information about the dilemma, the ethical goals and assumptions of the people involved, and the values that could be applied to the dilemma. A discussion among the participants of different ethical alternatives would follow:

Component 2: Provide Industry/Profession-Specific Areas of Ethical Concern

Many ethics trainers emphasize a broad brush stroke of the endless stream of ethically problematic areas: workers relations, discipline and discharge, and consumer concerns. What they fail to see is that most industries and professions have a host of ethical issues and dilemmas that are peculiar to them alone.

For example, human resources managers face unique ethical problems with job applicants. How much truth should be involved in the hiring process? Should you tell an applicant that he or she does not come across well in the employment interview? Human resources managers also face ethical dilemmas with being honest with employees. Should you tell employees as soon as possible that their jobs may be eliminated by planned downsizing?

Another example can be found in the securities industry. The peculiarities of insider trading and churning of client accounts may render general ethics training of little use. Instead, ethics training in the securities area must carefully delineate the specific aspects of a problem, such as insider trading—how to identify it, what to do if one suspects it is occurring, and how to use personal records to identify insider trading trends.

In order to deal with these specific issues, ethics training should include specific training modules for a particular profession or industry. Whereas combining different types of employees is beneficial for Component 1, trainers should divide out similar groups of employees for modular training and specific discussion in Component 2.

Component 3: Provide Trainees with Organizational Ethical Expectations and Rules

Company expectations about ethical behavior usually are contained in employee handbooks and codes of ethics—two documents that are among the least read in the organization. Training usually involves a short introduction during the indoctrination of new hires, which is quickly forgotten in the rush of newcomers to learn what they should be doing.

A more workable solution is ongoing training with more extensive (and readable) documents. For example, an effective code of ethics should not read like a legal book of statutes. Rather it should give a definition of the ethical problem in plain English and numerous examples of what is described. The training session should then focus on hypothetical situations that trainees can discuss and evaluate against the standards in the code.

For example, in dealing with sexual harassment, trainees are instructed that harassment is unethical because it robs employees of dignity, creates fear, creates dishonesty, and restricts their freedom to work as an effective employee. Harassment can be in the form of an overt request for sex in return for favors, such as a promotion or raise. Harassment can also include telling off-color jokes, the display of offensive pictures, undue staring, and touching.

Hypothetical situations may include an employee being asked for sex by a boss who offers to transfer her (or him) to a better job. This is obviously wrong, but why? At this point, trainees should have an opportunity to apply the critical thinking skills they learned in Component 1. Trainees could discuss how this situation creates long-term bad feelings, mistrust, and even fear, possible coworker suspicions, and a tarnished company image.

Component 4: Provide Trainees with an Understanding of Their Own Ethical Tendencies

People differ in terms of how they perceive and react to ethical issues. The reason for this is that they not only have different perspectives on what is right and wrong, but also that they have different personalities which guide them. Thus, while much work has focused on the more philosophical aspects of ethical behavior at work, individual differences or personality traits may also impact the choice of ethical action. Measures of individual differences and characteristics related to an employee's morality can provide an employee with an understanding of his or her proclivities toward particular ethical judgments, both in terms of deficits and strengths.

For example, Machiavellian personality types believe that any means justifies an end they seek. They see no problem with lying to customers, being dishonest with coworkers, and manipulating those under them, if their end goal is better performance for the company. The upshot is that ethics training should include means of dealing with Machiavellian types, such as building a paper trail in dealings with them (it is harder to lie and be dishonest if others have the evidence) and ensuring that you deal with them in public meetings (it is harder to manipulate people in front of others than in private one-on-one meetings).

> "Should you tell employees as soon as possible that their jobs may be eliminated by planned downsizing?"

Component 5: Take a Realistic View—Elaborate on the Monkey Wrenches in Ethical Decisions

Unfortunately, what one does about an unethical behavior may go well beyond any guidelines or personality trait. Even employees with best intentions sometimes go awry, often because other factors enter the ethics picture. This is especially true of managers who are asked to evaluate whether an employee's action was unethical and then having to respond to the action. Such managers are often influenced by a variety of other causes, which we call biasing factors. Indeed, most ethical training does not help trainees deal with these factors.

In some cases, these causes are a result of the attributes of the manager himself. For example, differences as a result of socialized gender roles (e.g., belief that males are more objective, females more emotional), philosophies of punishment (punishment as deterrence of future unethical actions, retribution for past actions, or rehabilitation of the individual), or the impact of the unethical behavior on the manager himself may hamper an objective assessment of and a reaction to the unethical behavior.

For example, a sales manager may complain that he is unable to do anything about a renegade salesperson who steals thousands of dollars of merchandise a year from the company. The sales manager explains that because this salesperson is his top producer taking action against him would reduce the overall department performance and thus ultimately impact the evaluation (and subsequent raises) of the sales manager. In this case, the manager cannot be objective because he perceives the solution to the unethical actions only in terms of how it adversely affects him.

Evaluators of the behavior may also take other things into account that bias the evaluation of ethical performance. For example, the unethical behavior may be considered within the context of the attributes of the offender, including membership in racial, ethnic, and gender groups, the rarity of the offender's skills (highly marketable employees may be forgiven more easily than those with few important skills), the importance of the person to organization (key people may have more latitude to sin than those on the periphery), political connections, the offender's ethical work history, and the offender's likability (we are more forgiving of nice people than nasty people). Perhaps most important, managers are often duped by the ability of ethical offenders to create the right impression of the unethical event (it wasn't my fault, or, if it was, there were extenuating circumstances).

Sometimes, it is the attributes of the offense that are taken into account and create bias. For example, a manger may take into account the magnitude of the offense (were people actually hurt?), the characteristics of the offense (was the action violent?), who was hurt by the action (were the victims nice, likable people?), and the specificity of codes related to the action (was it clearly prohibited by ethical guidelines?).

Other times an apparently insignificant unethical behavior may pervade the entire organization and establish a low ethical standard. We recall one company that, during a holiday season, it had so much masking tape taken home by employees to wrap presents that the replacement cost for the disappearing tape reached into the thousands of dollars. Instead of enforcing company rules on theft, executives stated that it was an "annoyance" and put together a creative solution for the next season. The company gave each employee a gift box of tape with a note asking them to please leave the company tape on the premises. Whereas the executives came off looking generous in keeping with the season, they did implicitly tolerate the theft and offered a "payoff" to solve the problem. The unintended consequence is that employees may now be tempted to take more expensive items from the company, because they believe that the company will condone theft.

There are three basic problems here that can cause bias. First, people are fairly easily deluded by appearances and good image management for actions. Second, the perceivers of unethical actions filter their perceptions through their personalities, biases, and past experiences. And third, people look at immediate effects and do not take long-term consequences into account. Ethics training therefore should not only focus on improving the situation but should realistically explore the many ways people can cloak unethical actions in appearances, the various influences on people's perceptual filters, and the importance of examining long-term effects of actions.

> "Simply training employees to 'do the right thing' in today's complex, changing situations will not work."

> "A manager cannot be objective if he perceives the solution to unethical actions only in terms of how it adversely affects him."

Component 6: Get the Trainees to Practice and Return

Trainees need time to absorb the concepts. Trainers should allow employees to go back to the organization and spend time trying to understand the material in the context of daily work life. Then employees should be brought back to another session with questions to ask and specific case situations to examine. Only then can it be certain that the concepts have been applied and employees are well into the process of internalizing the ideas.

This process can be enhanced by having employees keep a journal of both their work activities and how they and others react to their actions. After they describe their activities, they could write whether they believe these actions are ethical, unethical, or if they are unsure. In addition, they should identify the short-term and long-term consequences, consider how good they felt about their actions, describe how others responded to their actions, and consider if they had it to do over again, would they do the same thing. Armed with a critical analytic understanding of ethics, employees could meet periodically in discussion workshops and share their journal entries.

Coworkers could provide feedback on how they perceived the actions. Together employees could then explore commonalities in values and identify areas where the company could provide further guidance about ethical conduct.

Conclusion

These six components are designed to reveal common core ethical values shared among employees, managers, and the organization that may provide overall direction about ethical behavior. At the same time, these components help employees to be flexible, to recognize that various situations may require unique responses, and to evaluate realistically the ethical dilemmas they face. If we expect to refine ethical decision making as new contingencies arise in coworker interactions, to improve dealings between management and workers and to better meet customer demand in an ever increasingly competitive marketplace, we need to offer employees a holistic training approach to help them solve these issues. Simply training them to "do the right thing" in these complex, changing situations will not work.

Article Review Form at end of book.

What is the point of using an outdoor training technique similar to the one presented in this article? What are some ways to measure the effectiveness of these techniques?

Using Outdoor Training to Develop and Accomplish Organizational Vision

Glenn M. McEvoy and John R. Cragun
Department of Management and Human Resources, Utah State University

Mike Appleby
Information Processing Center–Ogden

This article presents a detailed case study relating training and organizational strategy. It provides an example of how the human resources process of training and development can add value when it is tied explicitly to the future direction of the organization. In this case, outdoor training provided the context for the initial development of a strategic vision by the top management group, as well as a means of eliciting support from the remainder of the organization's members. The article describes the process used as well as the results achieved with this approach.

Outdoor Training Overview

The use of an outdoor setting in the training of managers is a rapidly growing phenomenon (Burnett, 1994; Wagner, Baldwin, & Roland, 1991). Most commonly, this type of training is used to develop teamwork and team skills such as interpersonal communication, trust, leadership, group problem solving, and the ability to work effectively with others. Outdoor training is also frequently used to encourage participants to expand their own horizons by taking risks and accomplishing things they never believed they were capable of doing. Such personal growth and development is believed to have significant organizational payoffs by companies, such as Federal Express, DuPont, and Martin Marietta, that have utilized such training (Gall, 1987; Wagel, 1986).

In general, there are two overall types of outdoor training programs (Wagner et al., 1991). One is "wilderness-centered." Such training frequently involves white-water rafting or canoeing, or exercises in the wilderness where a team works and lives together outdoors for up to a week at a time. Typically, wilderness programs do not use a particular home camp or training facility.

Outdoor training programs can have an even greater organizational impact if they are tied more explicitly to the direction in which the organization is heading—

The other general category of outdoor training can be called "outdoor-centered." Here, a base camp is used and participants live and eat indoors, but specific outdoor events or initiatives are available for use depending on program goals. Participants go through events in small groups followed by a discussion or "debriefing" to bring out the learnings from each of the events and to tie those learnings back to the workplace. In such a configuration, it is quite common for outdoor training camps to include events such as a high ropes course, a rock climb and/or rappel, and a series of group problem-solving activities. See Bank (1985) or Cacioppe and Adamson (1988) for the details of such initiatives.

While these types of programs may improve participants' team and interpersonal skills (Bronson, Gibson, Kichar, & Priest, 1992; McEvoy & Buller, 1991), it is possible that such outdoor training programs can have an even greater organizational impact if they are tied more explicitly to the direction in which the organization is heading—that is, to its strategic vision (Bechet & Walker, 1993; Ulrich, 1992). This article presents a case study of an organization that used outdoor-centered training as a vehicle for the development of a vision and future direction, as well as the first steps in the implementation of that vision. We first provide some background on the organization and then discuss the five phases of the program. Last, we review some of the results that have accrued to the organization from the training.

Organizational Background

The Information Processing Center-Ogden (IPCO) is a Defense Logistics Agency (DLA) activity located in Ogden, Utah. While the IPCO is an activity of the Department of Defense (DoD), all but two employees are civilians. One of the two military employees is the Commander of the IPCO, and the third author of this article.

The IPCO was formed in 1991 as part of a DLA plan to consolidate data processing services from 23 to six sites across the country. The nucleus of the IPCO came from an existing data processing organization at the Defense Depot-Ogden, which consisted of 65 people in 1991. Because of the consolidation, the IPCO grew to over 150 people in the 1991–1992 time period. Not only did this change represent a rapid increase in the size of the operation (about 250%), but it also represented a significant change in scope of the mission. Before the change, the 65 people provided data processing support for only one co-located defense supply operation. After the change, the 150 people provided data processing services for numerous DoD supply depots throughout the country.

This significant and rapid growth in a short period of time brought together a group of people who had never worked with each other, and who had differing levels of competence and skill in teamwork. This situation convinced the Commander that something new had to be done to quickly bring the diverse group of new employees together as a team. That "something new" is the subject of this case study.

Phase I: Outdoor Training with the Management Team and the Development of an Organizational Vision

The first step in the process began when the IPCO Commander attended a "sampler" of outdoor training at the Logan Canyon Outdoor Learning Center at Utah State University (USU). Through this one-day sampler, combined with exposure to the benefits of a "ropes course" experience on a previous job, he became convinced that the kinds of insights and learnings that could accrue from outdoor-centered training had value for the people at the IPCO by moving the group quickly toward a team environment.

Specifically, the Commander believed that an outdoor experience—contrasted with an indoor one—provided a venue that allowed the perception of risk to both, on a personal level, help individuals "stretch and grow" and, on a group level, ensure that the need to work together was real. He believed that a simulated exercise in an indoor setting would not provide the same feeling of risk and accomplishment as being placed in a situation where the result of failure is a dip in a cold lake for either the individual or a member of the team.

As it happened, along with the major reorganization and expansion in 1991, the Commander was given a budget that could be used for training and developing his new team. He believed that in order to ensure that the team was focused on customer service and quality improvement, he had to first build teamwork, communication, and commitment within the new organization. With these goals in mind, he approached two senior facilitators at USU's Management Institute (the first two authors of this article), and asked them to develop a program of outdoor training which would get the new management team working together quickly and point them in the right direction.

Through preliminary discussions with the 16 members of this management team, an initial agenda was developed. The plan was to use outdoor training to: a) help the manager become better acquainted with each other; b) help meld them into an effectively functioning team; and c) help develop a sense of direction and vision for themselves and the rest of the IPCO.

The specific program that evolved included a program of seven days, the first four of which were spent primarily outdoors. The fifth day was indoors and was focused on the initial development of a vision statement for the IPCO. The sixth and seventh days, one and two months later respectively, were designed to help fine-tune the strategic vision and think through the process of communicating this vision to the rest of the organization. These last two days were also designed to help develop the initial steps of an action plan to help move the IPCO in the direction of its vision.

The four-day outdoor training segment of this phase consisted of activities designed to remove the managers from their "comfort zones," help them get to know themselves and each other better, and begin to understand on both cognitive and emotional levels what the characteristics of an effective management team were. Events included a high ropes course, a rock climb and rappel, a "triangular partnership," several trust-building and group problem-solving activities, a wilderness trek, and others. The concluding event was "The Wall," where team members worked together to get each other safely over the top of a 14-foot-high-wall

At the end of this four-day outdoor program, participants had a better understanding of themselves—including a sense of enhanced personal self-efficacy—and greater confidence that the management team could accomplish difficult challenges if its members worked to-

> Participants had a better understanding of themselves—including a sense of enhanced personal self-efficacy—and greater confidence that the management team could accomplish difficult challenges if its members worked together effectively.

Figure 1 IPCO (Information Processing Center–Ogden) Strategic Vision Statement

IPCO accepting the challenge... reflects our vision of going the extra mile in becoming a world class information processing organization. We are committed to delighting our customers. This is accomplished in a supportive and innovative environment which encourages all members of the IPCO team to contribute, grow, and stretch to reach their full potential.

Figure 2 Critical Training Attributes

I. Fostering a Caring Learning Environment

Description: Creates an environment where the learner can explore and express feelings without fear of judgment, where the learner will be comfortable to experiment with behavior change, and where the learner feels the warmth and friendship of others.

II. Interpersonal Communication Skills

Description: Demonstrates ability to focus on the person and listen for the meaning underlying each interpersonal interchange, to interpret accurately non-verbal communication, to respond to and reflect feelings, to be precise in communicating personal feelings, and to maintain ownership of personal feelings.

III. Program Design Skills

Description: Ability to develop training programs designed to achieve the organization's vision/mission. Clear expression of ideas in writing and use of good grammatical form. Ability to articulate goals for training, organize effort to attain those goals, and develop an internally consistent approach to training. Adept at preparing ahead of time and anticipating problems that may arise with a particular training approach.

IV. Creativity and Problem Solving Skills

Description: Seeing transfer possibilities for training. Generating and/or recognizing imaginative solutions and innovations in training-related situations. Ability to assist others to see the relevance of training activities, events, and learning to back home work environment. Behavior indicating a lack of rigidity, being open to the ideas and learning of others (even if different from own).

V. Personal Traits/Characteristics/Temperaments

Description: A variety of psychological traits relevant to success as a trainer, as well as ethical and career issues.

---

gether effectively. With this as a background, participants engaged in a process of discovering the importance of strategic vision, studied the vision statements of other successful organizations, visualized the possibilities for the IPCO, and used an iterative process to arrive at a final vision statement upon which all could agree. This vision statement is provided in Figure 1.

It should be pointed out that several parts of this vision statement came directly from the learnings and insights gained by the management team in the outdoor training. "Accepting the challenge" and "going the extra mile" reflect the learning that many of the outdoor initiatives, while at first glance seemingly impossible, are in fact feasible if individuals and the team commit to them. The "supportive and innovative environment" refers to the learning that organization goals cannot be accomplished in an environment where managers and employees fail to support each other and where risk-taking is discouraged through assignment of blame for failures. "Contribute, grow, and stretch" refers to the learning that there is no personal growth without risk and that the organization has to encourage such growth if it is to succeed in adapting to the significant changes coming in the near future.

Phase II: Selecting Internal Trainers

At this point, the management team decided that the best way to communicate the new vision and build support for it would be to provide all IPCO employees with a similar experience. Further, in order to save money, the management team decided that this training should be done using in-house resources. Phase II, therefore, was designed to help IPCO select six individuals who had the potential to be successful outdoor training facilitators. The organization used its own screening process to develop a candidate list of 16 potential facilitators.

The candidate group then went through a four-day outdoor training program that was similar in some respects to the training that the management team had received. However, prior to the training, the two USU facilitators developed a checklist of facilitator qualities and capabilities that were to be assessed during the outdoor training program. This list was eventually whittled to five major categories referred to as Critical Training Attributes (CTAs), a summary of which is provided in Figure 2.

From six to 19 relevant behaviors were identified for each of the five CTAs, and these behaviors were placed on an observation form. Candidate behaviors were observed and recorded during outdoor training. The observers included the two USU facilitators, two experienced safety technicians, one outsider with a Ph.D. in Psychology, and three IPCO managers. At the end of the training program this group of eight pooled their observations and identified six individuals who seemed to have the greatest potential to become successful outdoor training facilitators.

Phase III: Training the Trainers

Phase II was completed in the fall of 1991. Over the course of the next four months the six selected internal facilitators did some independent readings on related topics and became involved with the ongoing training agenda of the IPCO. The general objective of the facilitator training which then began in the spring of 1992 was to develop the capacity of the six selected trainers so that they could conduct portions of the outdoor experience to foster the accomplishment of the vision and long-range strategy for the IPCO.

More specifically, the purposes included: a) understanding the various initiatives/events which could be conducted outdoors and how they might be modified to accomplish organizational and team objectives; b) establishing a working relationship with the safety technicians; c) achieving a level of comfort in using outdoor initiatives; d) developing general facilitation skills; and e) developing facilitation skills specific to outdoor initiatives. These objectives were accomplished through the following process.

First, a needs analysis was conducted. It resulted in 113 questions about facilitation which needed to be addressed. These were clustered into the following categories:

- Avoiding misunderstandings
- Communication
- Maintaining group cooperation
- Maintaining trust
- Dealing with hurt feelings
- Managing anger
- Management of resources
- Management of time
- Stimulating personal and group development
- Self-management and self-worth
- Enthusiasm and excitement
- Working with other facilitators and with safety technicians
- Turning failure into success
- Understanding the needs of the group
- Maintaining control of the group
- Managing the learning environment

- Coping with the elements (e.g., weather)
- Understanding and managing group membership
- Setting up the events/initiatives

The first step in the training itself consisted of reviewing videotapes of the earlier outdoor experience which was the backdrop for selecting the trainers. During this review each event was discussed at length. Reviewing the videos helped reestablish the feelings and emotions associated with each event. An extensive facilitator training manual which had been prepared provided for a discussion of the anticipated learnings associated with each event, fundamental concepts and questions about facilitation generally and outdoor training specifically. CTAs, terms and definitions, the scope of outdoor initiatives available, and an extensive set of readings. The readings and discussion covered many of the topics identified in the needs analysis.

The next step in the training process was to "pass the torch" from the USU facilitators to the IPCO facilitation team. This was done in two back-to-back outdoor training programs. The first program was led by the USU facilitators. The IPCO facilitators observed and co-facilitated as appropriate. Questions were noted and subsequently discussed. The second program was facilitated by the IPCO trainers with the USU facilitators serving as coaches and mentors. For all subsequent programs, the USU facilitators were available for consultation and mentoring as requested.

Phase IV: Training the Troops

At this stage of the process, IPCO had its strategic vision which, in part, indicated that the organization wanted to develop a culture in which all individuals could "grow and stretch to reach their full potential." Part of the achievement of this portion of the vision statement was to be an opportunity for all 150 or so individuals at all levels of the organization to go through a four-day outdoor training experience.

As was the case with the prior outdoor training programs, this one included a mixture of personal stretching and risk-taking exercises in combination with a variety of team-based problem-solving activities. A hallmark of the program was that it always ended its outdoor segment with "The Wall" exercise, in which team members worked together to get each other from one side of a wall to the other in a short period of time. This event invariably created a considerable amount of enthusiasm and camaraderie among the participants.

Three of the four days of the program were primarily outdoors. The fourth and final day was indoors. The purpose of the fourth day of the program was to take the enthusiasm, excitement, energy, and insight that had been developed from three outdoor days and make commitments both as individuals and as a group in terms of what they would do to help the organization accomplish its vision. Each individual made commitments to himself or herself and publicized those to the rest of the participants in the training group. These commitments were personal changes to be made based upon insights gleaned from the program. Figure 3 provides a sampling of the commitments made.

Additionally, each training group as a whole chose a specific project it would work on which would help IPCO move in the direction of its vision. A senior manager was appointed to each training group to help accomplish the chosen project. His or her role was to knock down organizational roadblocks and provide needed resources to help the group accomplish its goal. Examples of the kinds of tasks that were chosen by these groups based upon their outdoor training experiences included:

- Establishment of an employee forum where employees could bring problems and have them discussed by other employees;
- Development of a functional cross-reference by employees that would

> IPCO had its strategic vision which, in part, indicated that the organization wanted to develop a culture in which all individuals could "grow and stretch to reach their full potential."

Figure 3 — IPCO Team Member Commitments

- Become a more active team member, learning more about the others and how I can relate to their problems and help resolve them.
- Treat each member of the IPCO team as if they were scaling the rock wall and were dependent on me for minding their rope. Conversely, depend on each member of the team as if they were minding my rope.
- Promote team effectiveness by providing "positive" support to each of my customers so that our vision statement will be realized.
- Work wholeheartedly working towards the accomplishment of the IPCO vision.
- Learn all I can about my job and how I can better serve my customers. To be able to answer the challenge and give the service needed.
- Inspire others to accept the challenge of the IPCO vision.
- Provide an environment that allows us to openly deal with problems and organizational relationships.
- Give my best effort to becoming a good example of the vision statement by: a) becoming more competent on my job; b) helping division members gain a better understanding of the vision, and c) providing to the best of my ability those things which are requested by other divisions.
- Communicate thoroughly with IPCO personnel to help alleviate possible problem areas and work to comprehend other viewpoints in an effort to contribute to the success of the team.

---

allow responsibility to be quickly established to resolve information processing problems;

- Development of a new employee handbook that included a brief description of the mission of each subunit at the IPCO;
- Establishment of procedures for voice mail use that ensured all IPCO customers, both internal and external, were responded to promptly;
- Establishment of community service projects to improve the relationship between the IPCO and the local community;
- Identification of a nucleus of people who would promote the IPCO externally within DLA by taking courses in how to set up conferences and how to communicate effectively.

Clearly, all these tasks were helpful in moving the IPCO in the direction of its vision statement.

Phase V: Follow-up with the Management Team

Within a year after the initial training session and the development of the strategic vision, all of the employees at the IPCO had been through the four-day outdoor training experience. At this point, they had a much better understanding of the vision and what it meant for them and their organization. They also had considerable enthusiasm and energy which needed to be focused on specific strategies for accomplishing the IPCO's vision.

At the same time, the management team felt that some of the commitments they had made to working effectively in a team had begun to disintegrate and that their own unity as a team had begun to splinter. Many of these managers were concerned that at just the time that the non-management employees seemed to have enthusiasm for a team-based, high-trust organization, the managers as a group were exhibiting behaviors that were not supportive of either a team organization or high trust within themselves. Therefore, the management team decided to go off-site for a four-day "refresher" training program.

This training was not duplicative of the outdoor program in which they had participated a year before. Rather this training was designed to build on the foundation established earlier and re-energize and refocus the management team so that they could serve as role models for the rest of the organization.

Taking the strategic vision as a given, the USU facilitators gathered some data from the rest of the IPCO on its present status and found that: a) considerable learning had taken place at lower levels in the IPCO as a result of the outdoor training experiences; b) there was a higher level of motivation and enthusiasm, as well as commitment to the IPCO vision, than prior to the training; and c) employees were waiting to see what the management team wanted to do next in terms of specific approaches to accomplishment of the vision.

As a result of this diagnosis, the management team follow-up program had two objectives: to help the group improve its internal functioning, including personal insights into the effects of some dysfunctional behaviors that individuals were engaging in on the team; and to help the management team develop an empowerment action plan which would help employees who had been through the outdoor training to take the next step in the direction of the IPCO vision.

The design of this follow-up program used primarily indoor activities but included at least one outdoor activity per day. Each outdoor activity was designed to give participants insight into their own individual behaviors and the impact that those behaviors had on everyone else. The outdoor activities included such events as a raft building, orienteering, and a team rappel. The primary focus of the indoor activities was on giving and receiving feedback about individual behaviors on the job and how those behaviors either positively or negatively affected the functioning of the team. Through several activities, individuals were able to get specific feedback (both anonymous and direct) about their behavior and the impact it had on others. In the end, each participant developed a personal action plan designed to help overcome any weaknesses or deficiencies in their behaviors while operating in the management team.

> "The Wall" event invariably created a considerable amount of enthusiasm and camaraderie among the participants.

Managers also worked in subgroups to develop the next steps in terms of empowering the employees who worked for them. Examples of some of the action steps that were developed for empowering employees included:

- Conduct a roundtable discussion with employees on the meaning of "empowerment" for them;

- Provide each employee with a copy of a short book on the topic of empowerment to provide a common framework throughout the IPCO for identification of actions that help and hinder empowerment;

- Conduct role clarification sessions between employees and their managers so both could understand the present level of empowerment;

- Develop team and individual visions, under the assumption that empowerment requires direction;

- Initiate mini-training days in which outdoor events are used as a vehicle for helping both mangers and employees understand what empowerment means for them and their organization.

Reactions to this follow-up phase of the program were very positive. A number of individuals were able to use the time off-site to work through interpersonal problems that they had been having with particular individuals on the management team. In addition, departments were able to hammer out working agreements with other departments where there had been inefficiencies and poor information flow in the past.

Upon returning to the work site, the staff meeting that the management team had the following week was the "best they had ever had," with a lot of participation and good ideas for next steps in the empowerment process. Some managers who had identified themselves as "control freaks" knew that to empower their employees they would need to learn how to "let go," regardless of how difficult that might be. But the first steps had been taken and a public commitment to change had been made.

The top team set itself a goal of having all departments renegotiate working relationships with every other department within a two-month time frame. One management team member who had initially been a reluctant participant in the follow-up phase of the outdoor training wrote an insightful editorial for the internal organization newsletter. Excerpts from this editorial are given in Figure 4.

Results

The direct costs for this training program were approximately $255,000. This included USU facilitator and safety technician time, meals and lodging, transportation, training materials, equipment and camp rental, construction and maintenance of some training facilities on IPCO property, and so forth. Indirect costs were the four days of time away from the job for each of 150 IPCO employees (approximately $110,000 in salary and benefit costs).

What is the payoff from this type of investment in outdoor training and organizational visioning?

Figure 4 Excerpts from Participant Editorial in IPCO Newsletter "The Wall"

I have just returned from four days among the forests and cliffs of Logan Canyon. Along with fifteen other managers I made a journey into self-discovery. Our purpose was to develop a team spirit as real as the rocks and pines that surrounded us. I think we succeeded. On the last day each of us wrote on ribbons what we had come to value most about the team. I wrote several, but on reflection the one I think is most basic and broadest is faith.

From what I saw and heard on those four days, I have come to believe that a team—a true team—is founded on each member's faith in the other and in the cause they are dedicated to. At the outset I felt estranged from this group. But the events of the succeeding days melted my reservation toward them. I saw their courage and compassion in action toward me and toward the others. Again and again we wrestled with the challenges of miscommunication and mistrust. Much soul searching and self-discovery occurred, in both the indoor and outdoor activities. Only in a team where all have mutual faith in each other could such openness have taken place.

Our vision statement at IPCO says nothing about eliminating people; it speaks of service to others. It does not stress profit making; it calls for a quality product. It does not demand adoration of the IPCO leaders; it advocates each member realizing his or her full potential. Rather than stressing separation, it promotes cooperation. Instead of a narrow view of our capabilities, it encourages a wider, loftier outlook.

I have come to you with a message. An opportunity has been given to us to better our lives through overcoming our doubts about ourselves and our fellow workers. Such opportunities do not often come to us. Success is not a golden promise but I think the venture is worth the effort. To fail in a good cause is better than to succeed in an evil one. My message has no official sanction. It is not a message from top management or from the developers of the outdoor training program. It is a message from the heart.

Clearly this organization has only begun its journey towards accomplishing its vision. However, a number of positive outcomes have already been obtained.

First of all, most employees were extremely appreciative of the opportunity to engage in this type of training. The reactions of training participants were very positive as measured both immediately after the program and in interviews conducted four to eight weeks after the outdoor training took place. One participant said simply, "This is the most amazing thing that's ever happened to me." While not all participants were that positive, there was strong evidence from the interviews that individuals felt the organization had shown it really cared about them and their development as individuals and as team players. The investment of time and money in the program clearly played an important symbolic role in communicating to employees that they were valued.

Second, a learning assessment was undertaken to see if individuals learned and retained key concepts from outdoor training such as the importance of reflective listening, the effective utilization of all group resources when solving problems, and so forth. This learnings assessment demonstrated conclusively that a considerable amount of conceptual material was learned and retained by the participants in the outdoor training program.

Third, measures of self-esteem and organizational commitment were taken before and after the training and showed significant increases due to participation in the program. Both the learnings assessment and the assessment of changes in self-esteem and organizational commitment were conducted using a true experimental design with random assignment to experimental (trained before the measurements) and control (trained after the measurements) groups. Thus, considerable confidence can be placed in attributing the outdoor training as the source of these improvements. Details of this evaluation are provided in the Appendix.

Fourth, like many government organizations, the IPCO operates within a "Total Quality Management" (TQM) paradigm. Part of the TQM philosophy is to measure on a regular basis employee perceptions of teamwork, customer focus, the quality of management and leadership, and so forth. The IPCO has implemented such surveys, and, over the period in which the organizational vision and outdoor training steps above were implemented, these surveys clearly demonstrated considerable improvements on these measures.

Fifth, as one hard indicator of increases in employee commitment and motivation, the organization tracked the use of sick leave before and after the training program. The result: roughly a 50 percent decrease in sick leave usage (from 5.8 hours per month per employee to 3.3 hours per month).

Finally, as another hard indicator of employee commitment and productivity, the final IPCO staffing level of 150 employees was 90 fewer than originally forecast and budgeted for by the DLA during this consolidation of information processing centers.

There was strong evidence from the interviews that individuals felt the organization had shown it really cared about them and their development as individuals and as team players.

Had all 240 been hired, the salary and benefit costs for the IPCO would have been approximately $4 million greater each year of operation.

While these results are preliminary, and the organization is only in the early stages of accomplishing its vision, it is also clear from these indicators that the IPCO is on the move and heading in the right direction. Would outdoor training work in all settings? Probably not. Here, there was a strong, unambiguous commitment from the top to make this approach work. There was also pressure from the environment to do things differently, stimulated by rapid expansion of workload and workforce. The organization had the resources to "do it right" in terms of putting everyone through the training and providing for transfer and follow-up to keep the spirit of the training alive. Lastly, the outdoor training had a specific focus—the new vision—that provided the "why" for the program.

Conclusion

In summary, outdoor training was used successfully by the IPCO to quickly bring together a new management group, form them into a true team, and allow them to develop a strategic organizational vision. This vision was then used as the focus of the outdoor training for the rest of the IPCO thereby giving employees a strong sense of purpose and an understanding of why the training was being done. Without this focus, the outdoor training would have been simply "fun in the sun," rather than a powerful experience in pointing the organization toward a new vision of its own future.

References

Bank, J. 1985. Outdoor Development for Managers. Brookfield, VT: Gower.

Bechet, T., & Walker, J. 1993. "Aligning Staffing with Business Strategy." *Human Resource Planning*, 16(2):1–16.

Bronson, J., Gibson, S., Kichar, R., & Priest, S. 1992. "Evaluation of Team Development in a Corporate Adventure Program." *The Journal of Experiential Education*, 15(2):50–53.

Burnett, D. 1994. "Exercising Better Management Skills." *Personnel Management*, January: 42–46.

Cacioppe, R., & Adamson, P. 1988. "Stepping Over the Edge: Outdoor Development Programs for Management and Staff." *Human Resource Management Australia*, 26(4):77–95.

Gall, A. L. 1987. "You Can Take the Manager Out of the Woods, but. . . ." *Training & Development Journal*, 41(3):54–58.

McEvoy, G. M., & Buller, P. F. 1991. "Evaluation of an Outdoor Management Skills Development Program." Paper presented at the Western Academy of Management meeting. March 22–24: Santa Barbara, CA.

Mowday, R. T., Porter, L. W., & Steers, R. M. 1982. Employee-organization Linkages: The Psychology of Commitment, Absenteeism, and Turnover. New York: Academic Press.

Pierce, J. L., Gardner, D. G., Cummings, L. L., & Dunham, R. B. 1989. "Organization-based Self-esteem: Construct Definition, Measurement, and Validation." *Academy of Management Journal*, 32: 622–648.

Ulrich, D. 1992. "Strategic and Human Resource Planning: Linking Customers and Employees." *Human Resource Planning*, 15(2): 47–62.

Wagel, W. H. 1986. "An Unorthodox Approach to Leadership Development." *Personnel*, 63(7): 4–6.

Wagner R. J., Baldwin, T. T., & Roland, C. C. 1991. "Outdoor Training: Revolution or Fad?" *Training & Development Journal*, 45(3):50–56.

Appendix—Evaluation Details

IPCO employees were randomly assigned to groups to undergo the training. We administered a questionnaire at the point at which 70 had been trained and 59 had not. There were no significant differences in the demographic characteristics of these two groups (experimental and control, respectively).

Learning was assessed through evaluation of answers to three open-ended questions about teamwork. The questions sampled key learnings in areas such as active listening, use of resources in group problem solving, and the importance of trust, communication, feedback, leadership, and conflict resolution in effective team functioning.

Answers to these three questions were scored by two university professors blind to experimental assignment. Interrater agreement was high (r = .89) so the two sets of scores were combined. Those who had received the training scored significantly higher on this learning measure than those who had not (9.06 vs. 6.51, p < .01).

Self-esteem was assessed using the construct organization-based self-esteem (OBSE) as developed by Pierce, Gardner, Cummings, and Dunham (1989). The coefficient alpha reliability we achieved for this 10-item scale was .93. Those who had received the training scored significantly higher on this measure than those who had not (40.73 vs. 38.69, p < .05).

Organizational commitment was assessed using the short, 10-item version of the Organizational Commitment Questionnaire (Mowday, Porter, & Steers, 1982). Coefficient alpha was .92. The trained group scored 57.60 while the untrained group scored 54.63 (p < .05).

Article Review Form at end of book.

What are the advantages and disadvantages of using simulators in training? Does this reduce the importance of a human trainer?

Workstation Meets Playstation

New kinds of training enter the realm of the flight simulator.

Jennifer J. Salopek

Jennifer J. Salopek is associate editor of Training & Development.

Teenagers learning to drive a car. Bank employees learning coaching skills. Amoco Corporation clerks learning to package hazardous materials. Dentists brushing up on their patient-evaluation skills. Pharmaceutical reps reviewing best practices for a new product launch.

What do all of those learners have in common? They are all being taught by simulation, a form of interactive multimedia training that recreates the work environment (or the behavior being modeled) to a degree of near-realism. The teenagers can see in the rear view mirror. The dentist can examine a mouth, order x-rays, prescribe medication. All of those skills can be practiced in a safe environment with no safety risks and less fear of failure—right at the learner's PC.

"What I hear, I forget; what I see, I remember; what I do, I understand." That quote from Confucius (451 B.C.) is a simulation developer's mantra. Simulation is a teaching method solidly rooted in statistical evidence that learners retain more information by doing rather than by just reading or listening. According to Debra Lavender, business development manager of Strat*X International in Cambridge, Massachusetts. "Simulations link learning and action to deliver applications know how that delivers return on training investment."

A 1996 *McKinsey Quarterly* states that more than 60 percent of U.S. corporations have used some sort of simulation. As technology advances and becomes cheaper, that figure is sure to increase. "This is a great time to be considering simulation," says Suzanne Biegel, president of Internal & External Communication of Marina del Ray, California. "There is much more to see; simulation has been effectively demonstrated across categories of content, and major corporations can attest to simulation's effectiveness and worth as a training mechanism."

When most people think of simulation, what they are really envisioning is a simulator—an inhabitable environment such as the flight simulators used to train pilots. Simulators are used to train other types of operators, such as the simulator built by EBIM S.A. of Manosque, France, to train conductors operating the trains that run through the channel tunnel connecting England and France. Another example is the Center for Maritime Education, part of the Seamen's Church Institute of New York, which operates a computer simulation training facility in Kentucky to train commercial barge and tugboat crews.

A new entry into the simulation training environment is a simulator-PC hybrid, such as the one developed for Amoco Corporation by Bravo multimedia of Chicago. Although the program runs on an Intergraph PC, it is contained within a driving pod that includes an actual truck steering wheel, accelerator, and brake. The complete system is housed in four cases and is easily portable. Called *truck driVR*, the program trains Amoco truck divers how to handle road emergencies and other hazardous driving situations better.

PC-based simulations aren't just computer games. IEC's Biegel notes that a game structure is not always appropriate. When it is, however, she says it builds motivation and provides an extra indicator of progress, unlike role play.

Says Deborah Blank, director of interactive multimedia at Electronic Learning Facilitators in Bethesda, Maryland, "Every trainer's favorite activity is role play, because it uses the desired skills. A simulation puts the learner in an environment that has the characteristics of the actual work environment, where he or she can perform tasks and receive feedback. It's a holdover from the days of apprenticeships."

Bells and Whistles

Simulations have the following elements:

- a precipitating event or key task (examples: performance review, selling a car)

- well-defined participant roles (examples: the manager, the sales consultant)

- an underlying model of effective performance (examples: five principles of successful

Copyright August 1998, *Training & Development,* American Society for Training and Development. Reprinted with permission. All rights reserved.

performance counseling, an eight-step professional sales process)

- complicating factors and unexpected events (examples: accusations of bias from an employee, late arrival of an additional buyer who is the real decision maker)

- realistic interaction context (examples: a manager's office, the automotive showroom)

- outcomes that reinforce the desired performance (examples: successful review acknowledged by both parties, sales made).

Some simulations incorporate virtual reality—a three-dimensional, computer-generated environment that is produced in real time. Unlike animation, which permits the user to replay only set sequences, virtual reality allows complete freedom of movement within a lifelike world. For examples, Bravo Multimedia's *truck driVR* features a head-mount display that immerses the user in the virtual environment.

A simulation developed for Motorola by Adams Consulting Group (now Asymetrix Learning Systems) of Western Spring, Illinois, features PC-based technology coupled with a head mount and tracker. The simulation trains Motorola associates to run the manufacturing equipment that produces pagers. The computer model replicates the actual assembly line, including a conveyor system, robotic work cells, a machine-vision inspection system, and a laser-making system that etches an identification number on each product.

Simulations can be team-based or self-paced. Each approach has its proponents and detractors. Team-based simulations can address many organizational issues by

- recognizing the value of individual differences

- breaking down functional and cross-cultural barriers to communication

- building relationships through shared insight and experience

- developing a common language and understanding

- improving effectiveness, productivity, and performance back on the job.

Robert Brodo, vice president of marketing at Strategic Management Group in Philadelphia, says, "We have found that a group of 25 to 30 people creates a more dynamic learning environment. We typically divide a group of 30 into six teams of five. Each team is in direct competition with the others, fighting for market share or playing out a strategy. The more teams, the more strategy is involved to find the segment of customers that can benefit from your product or service."

Although most simulations are delivered via CD-ROM, Internet delivery or some sort of CD-ROM/Internet or intranet hybrid are becoming popular options. Blank notes

Simulation Development: Problems and Solutions

Phase Analysis:		Phase Design:	
Potential Problem	**Implication**	**Potential Problem**	**Implication**
Subject matter experts are unavailable to clarify content or answer questions.	A lack of access to SMEs (or the same SMEs) may cause schedules to slip and budgets to increase. If the vendor tries to move ahead without SMEs' help (not recommended), the content may be incorrect and/or improperly weighted as to importance.	Lack of communication about wants, needs, likes, dislikes.	Problems that could have been caught now aren't caught until later when they're more costly to fix.

Solution: Client

- To avoid this, carefully select SMEs who are able to commit the time necessary to answer questions and clarify content for the life of the project.

Solution: Vendor

- Give the client a heads-up in your proposal that you will need SME involvement. Describe how much and when.
- Be firm about this as it could make or break your project.

Solution: Client

- Be completely honest about what you like and don't like, and remember that changes can be made fairly easily at this phase.

Solution: Vendor

- Solicit client feedback often; really listen to what is said or not said.
- Remember that what you want is not always what the client wants. Your goal is to give clients what they want.

Courtesy of Andrea David, used by permission of Electronic Learning Facilitators, Inc.

that some Electronic Learning Facilitators clients have chosen the hybrid option, with the audiovisual material residing on CD-ROM and the program itself on the company intranet. "It's seamless to the user," she points out. SMG of Philadelphia is delivering simulations over the Internet as part of its Business IQnets—online business resource centers. Says Brodo, "It provides a continuous learning environment that allows employees to access the training they need—whenever and wherever they need it." SMG recently provided simulation over the Internet for employees of a high-tech firm at its locations in San Francisco, Hong Kong, and Munich.

Gearing Up for the Game

"Trainers currently have two preoccupations," says Blank, "With technical training, especially IT, it's 'How do we get over the learning curve?' With training in general, the preoccupation is 'How do we cut training costs?'"

To maximize return-on-investment, Blank suggests the following guidelines to consider when contemplating whether to use simulation.

Content

Examine the content of the material you will be teaching. Does it lend itself to any particular type of presentation? For example, are there a lot of visuals associated with the information? How important is simulation to the learning experience? Does the content require frequent revision?

Audience

Where are they located? How well do they read? How much information is it reasonable for them to remember without support tools? Are they comfortable with computers?

Environment

Where does the training have to take place? Is there access to computers? What kind of computers, and are they part of a local area network?

Implementation

Will learners have time to study? Where? How will their progress be measured and recorded? Is there enough hardware available? How will course updates be distributed?

Biegel agrees that content should be your first consideration. Are the competencies appropriate for simulation? Simulation is best at teaching competencies in which the desired behavior requires seeing other people interact. Simulation is also effective in teaching a process that is blended with interpersonal skills. This hard skill-soft skill mix was integrated in a simulation developed by Internal and External Communication for FedEx, which trains new couriers in services and communications and in using computer tracking systems and hand-held scanners. Biegel advises that conveying pure knowledge, such as product information, is not an appropriate use of simulation.

Many trainers wonder whether simulation can teach soft skills as effectively as it can teach hard or technical skills. The answer was a

---

Phase Development and Programming:

Potential Problem	Implication
Assumption that each side understands clearly what the program will look like and how it will function.	The program may not be what is expected. Better to find that out as soon as possible.

Solution: Client
- Participate in the process as much as possible. It takes time to learn how to think interactively and visually. At a minimum, look at the program in progress at least once.

Solution: Vendor
- Budget for and create a robust prototype.
- Show clients a lot of multimedia programs so they can learn to visualize concepts.
- Have the client view and sign-off on graphics and other audiovisual components.
- Develop your program in modules; have the client review each module in progress and when completed.

Phase Implementation:

Potential Problem	Implication
The platform selected to deliver the multimedia application has changed and shifted. Multimedia technology is evolving and improving at a rapid rate. It's likely that a better platform exists by the time the application is ready to be implemented.	The thought of switching platforms or technologies will occur.

Solution: Client
- Don't look back. Remember that you made the best decision you could at the time.
- Before considering the new platform, weigh the benefits of the improved technology versus the cost to you (in time and money), and whether end users will have access to the new technology

Solution: Vendor
- Educate your clients about the rapid pace of technology and "technopeer pressure."
- Discuss current and future hardware and software needs during the analysis phase. Discuss pros and cons for each potential platform, and determine the best overall solution.
- Once a mutual decision is made, stick to it.

resounding "yes" from everyone interviewed for this article.

Example: Royal Bank Financial Group of Canada determined that coaching skills were a key competency it wanted to address. Why coaching skills? According to Nancy Milne, then project manager for the bank and now an independent consultant, "As organizations flatten, as more employees work from remote locations, as people get busier, managers have to be more effective." The bank wanted to teach not only top-down coaching skills, but also peer coaching, "Peer coaching is more likely on a daily basis," notes Milne.

The resulting product, developed by IEC, is called *The Royal Coaching Journey*—a three-phase learning experience that features DOS-based CBT, a Coaching Resource Kit, and a CD-ROM with the simulation. The training, developed for all 58,000 employees, addresses a broad range of professional roles. The CD-ROM's five-hour training program teaches RBFG employees how to provide, understand, and respond effectively to coaching feedback in the workplace. The program teaches users the coaching skills associated with active listening, questioning, and giving and receiving feedback.

Special features include a "learn by example" model, in which video and audio exercises help users experience effective and ineffective coaching techniques. Learners interact with the scenarios provided, by selecting appropriate courses of action and identifying less-effective approaches. The video branching model in the exercises challenges users to select the desired path from three distinct choices, based on one common coaching scenario. Users can then see the outcomes of three different coaching sessions, and learn the pros and cons of each.

Astra Merck Pharmaceuticals would agree that simulation is appropriate for soft-skills training. In contemplating the launch of a new product, senior management became concerned that there were deficiencies in marketing, strategic thinking, and leading the launch process. Working with Strategic Management Group of Philadelphia, Astra Merck created a simulation to develop the skills necessary for supporting the launch of the new product. According to SMG's Brodo, "As part of the experience, we gathered information about the different markets and competitors in order to explore business issues and values." The simulation was rolled out to senior management as a planning and learning tool, and then to the rest of the organization.

Says Blank, "Simulation can teach a mental model, not just a discrete skill. It is best used when you want someone to practice a behavior that involves decision making or a routine sequence of actions."

Can you anticipate all possible outcomes and scenarios in planning a simulation? "You can't," says IEC's Biegel, "but there is usually a set of possible outcomes. You can get the learner thinking about things in the right way. The overarching benefits of simulation are consistency, control, and interactivity. You can use the other components of the training to address other nuances."

RBFG's Milne agrees. "You don't have to anticipate all possible outcomes," she says. "Most behaviors that we're training are going to have some gray areas. We just give a range of choices to make."

Simulation Development: Problems and Solutions

Phase Evaluation:		Phase Overall:	
Potential Problem	**Implication**	**Potential Problem**	**Implication**
No evaluation is done after delivery of the program.	If you don't evaluate, you'll never really know whether the program achieved its goals. Worse, all of your hard work could be for naught in six months because the program becomes out of date. Even worse, you're afraid of what you might find out.	Both vendor and client underestimate the amount of time required to complete a project successfully.	Both schedule and budget can be adversely affected.

Solution: Client

- Budget for periodic evaluations and subsequent maintenance of your investment.
- Express worries and concerns up-front so that evaluation seems less daunting.

Solution: Vendor

- Encourage clients to evaluate their programs after delivery, by discussing the importance of evaluation up-front and including summative evaluation in your proposals.

Solution: Client

- Set aside time to be an integral part of the process.
- Make an extra effort when necessary.
- Don't balk at the vendor's projected staff hours and dollars (particularly for project management) as they're rarely underestimated.

Solution: Vendor

- Include clients in your staffing plans, and communicate the level of effort required at the beginning and throughout the project.
- Put money in the budget for extra meetings, project documentation, staff, and emergencies.

Arm Yourself with Advantages

PC-based simulations allow trainers to address a number of issues that often make training costly and difficult. Here are a few.

Geographic Disparity

CD-ROMs, the most common form of simulation delivery, can be sent to employees at remote locations. If desired, the program can then be loaded onto a user's hard drive. With Internet and intranet delivery, location becomes even less of an issue.

Classroom training just wasn't an option for GE Supply's inside salesforce, says Dan Castro, manager of field sales development. His 650 employees to be trained were nonexempt, meaning they would have to be paid for the overtime spent in training. Travel and lodging costs were prohibitive, not to mention lost productivity due to removing trainees from their actual work. "We have to keep our people at their workstations," he explains. With the targeted employees spread over 130 locations, traditional stand-up training would have required too many instructors and too much time to roll out.

A Large Number of Trainees

Large populations can be trained simultaneously with Internet delivery or CD-ROM. SMG's Brodo says his company has recently signed an agreement to deliver simulation over the Internet to more than 22,000 managers at a manufacturing company.

Idle Equipment

Some organizations prefer giving learners a hands-on experience as part of new equipment training. Because it is too costly in most situations to have a separate manufacturing line reserved for training, some companies shut down the line for a specific time to conduct training. That approach allows each learner to operate the actual equipment without breaking it or risking ruining a production run. But it is very costly to shut down a line.

Motorola University had invested a significant amount of money to duplicate its automated machinery in classroom facilities, says Nina Adams of Asymetrix. Trainees learn to set up, start, and shut down the line. Motorola's approach provides learners with a safe environment in which to practice, before they have to operate the real equipment. Adams does say that the separate facilities are expensive, require trainees to travel to the site, and command resources to maintain.

Safety

As with the Motorola assembly-line equipment, safety was also a factor at Amoco Corporation. It needed to train its employees on packaging and shipping hazardous materials in accordance with U.S. Department of Transportation requirements. The training simulation, developed by Bravo Multimedia and called *By the Book,* satisfies DOT certification requirements in an entertaining, safe environment.

The simulation lets employees practice skills right before they have to use them; course information acts as a reference tool.

Bravo's *truck driVR* simulation for Amoco also had safety as a major objective. "In the real world, road emergencies can't be called up on demand," explains project manager Ginny Towbin. "But in the virtual world we've created, drivers can interact with speeding motorists, careless cyclists, and ambulances. Poor judgment in this virtual world can result in a fatality."

A simulation developed by ELF for the American Automobile Association Foundation for Traffic Safety, *driver-ZED*, presents teen drivers with unexpected road conditions and trains them to anticipate and avoid such hazards (ZED stands for "zero-errors driving"). The product literature states: "Statistics show that not only are an extraordinary 40 percent of all 16-year-olds involved in automobile crashes, but the number of teen drivers on the road is rapidly increasing, while at the same time public funding for driver education is decreasing." The program has a dual objective: to provide safe training while training about safety. AAA members can purchase *driver-ZED* on CD-ROM.

Just-in-Time Learning

ELF developed a simulation for GE Supply, called *Inside Edge,* for assisting inside salespeople in sales, negotiation, and product knowledge. A self-paced program of 20 hours of learning broken into 15-minute modules, the simulation lets employees practice skills right before they have to use them. They use course information in the simulation as a reference tool.

Compressed Learning Time

In the case of the GE Supply simulation, what would have taken 40 hours of classroom instruction requires half that time—and it doesn't have to be consecutive time. RBFG's *Royal Coaching Journey* takes about four hours to complete, versus 10 hours in the classroom. "It's an excellent compression of learning time," says Biegel.

Chemical Engineering magazine reports that a simulator developed to train refinery operators at Conoco in England has substantially reduced training time for new employees: "Previously, a typical operator required 12 to 18 months of conventional training before assuming full production responsibility. With the customized simulator, new operators are now able to take over full responsibilities after only six months."

Literacy

ELF developed a simulation for the U.S. Department of Agriculture to train school cafeteria workers in safe food handling. The developers faced a dual challenge: a wide range among trainees in reading and language skills, as well as a low level of computer literacy. To address those challenges, ELF developed a simulation that features more narration than onscreen text and provides "tools" for food handling, such as a thermometer, that are used in real cafeterias. The simulation, which requires only basic mouse skills, cost $170,000 to develop and is now used in 30,000 schools.

Consistency

There are a number of variations of on-the-job training, but almost all involve an employee teaching a trainee. "The employee doing the training may be a supervisor, a team leader, an outstanding performer, or just the person most readily available," says Adams. On-the-job training addresses questions quickly and allows each training situation to be customized for the learner. However, notes Adams, the training is inconsistent and costly because the trainer is less productive while training. It also may not cover all of the required steps.

GE Supply's Castro agrees. Before the development of *Inside Edge*, new employees were seated next to seasoned ones. "We just hoped for osmosis," he says. "It diluted the effort of senior employees. Knowledge is only as good as the person transferring it."

Strategic Knowledge

Castro thinks that another benefit of simulation is the ability to teach strategic, as well as tactical, knowledge. He says, "It's proactive, instead of reactive. The simulation causes trainees to experience all types of possible events, instead of waiting until they actually happen."

GuSS (Guided Social Simulation) is a tool developed by the Institute for the Learning Sciences at Northwestern University in Evanston, Illinois. GuSS teaches complex social tasks. The systems contain teaching modules that monitor the simulation and, via video, provide stories, commentary, and guidance to users. One application of the GuSS tool is *Yello*, a simulation built by ILS to teach account executives at Ameritech Publishing how to sell Yellow pages advertising. Trainees must get to know each client's business, come to understand the business's market and advertising needs, construct a proposal geared to those needs, and present the proposal in a convincing way.

Control of the Message

RBFG's Milne emphasizes that, with simulation, an organization can tightly control the message and model the behavior being taught. Although many simulation exercises feature only good/better/best answers as possibilities, Milne notes that *Journey* has built-in wrong answers for the behaviors RPFG is interested in eliminating.

Social Issues

There are also social issues to consider. Says Milne, "When you get to a certain level, such as senior managers and vice presidents, those people are reluctant to complete training in public and often refuse to attend traditional classroom training." She emphasizes that the PC-based simulation is accessible to everyone, often in the privacy of their own workspaces.

Freedom to Fail

Simulation also provides learners with an atmosphere in which it is safe to fail and they aren't embarrassed by that failure. Product literature for ILS's *Yello* notes that "failing is a key element in *Yello*. Students realize what they need to learn in a very direct way. They fail at a task and become interested in discovering what they need to know to succeed."

Supporting Resources

"Other kinds of resources are built in," says IEC's Biegel, such as pop-up references, cue cards, and customers' voices. She urges clients to consider what will surround the simulation and emphasizes that managers must support the transfer of learning: "You can't assume that the simulation will exist in a vacuum." Many of IEC's clients are using simulations as pre-work, introducing skills in a safe environment, then using workshops to practice and provide feedback.

Power Play

Once you've decided that simulation is the way to go, follow these guidelines:

Be Aware of All Possible Audiences

Biegel recommends that you ask yourself whether there is a common set of things you want people to learn, or different perspectives. Simulation can be quite effective in teaching the same material to different audiences, such as line employees and managers. "We can write paths for different audiences quite easily," she says.

Know the Subject Matter's Life Span

If your content is likely to change more than once a year, cautions Milne, simulation via CD-ROM might not be for you. Although updates are relatively simple and pressing a new CD-ROM costs only about a dollar these days, it's still a large investment when there are 58,000 employees to be trained.

Strive for Realism

"You must put people as close to the real work as possible," says Biegel. Production values count, such as the background and environment of the simulation, the quality of the acting, the lighting, and the music. Cheapness and cheesiness are distracting and lack credibility.

Consult the Owner of the Training Need

GE Supply's Castro urges you to identify what should be trained, from the people who have responsibility for it as well as from the trainees (in other words, trainees' managers). He also suggests surveying customers. "It's a good benchmark for what's right with your industry, and it helps you set a minimum standard to train to."

Choosing Your Teammates

Next, you must select a contractor to develop your custom simulation. Brodo suggests the following criteria when selecting a simulation development supplier:

Ability to Gain Credibility with Senior Management

"Any computer geek with a textbook can build a computer-based simulation in his garage." Brodo says. "Interviewing senior managers and probing the business issues are skills that are very important to the process. The ability to ask the right questions and know what to do with the answers is the difference between

Benefits of Multimedia Training

For the Organization	For the Learner
Reduces training delivery time by 30 to 50 percent.	Reduces learning time up to 50 percent.
Increases productivity through cross-training, efficient retraining, less time away from job.	Increases retention by 25 to 50 percent.
Reduces training costs; once break-even point is reached, training is free.	Evaluates existing knowledge to avoid unnecessary training.
Ensures every trainee reaches a level of mastery.	Provides individualized, self-paced instruction.
Reduces the need for a dedicated training facility.	Allows flexible time, place, and privacy for training.
Requires fewer trainers and subject matter experts.	Provides unlimited practice and remediation.
Delivers standardized, consistent instruction.	Delivers consistent, nonjudgmental instruction.
Relates directly to job skills and performance, through customized course materials.	Relates directly to job skills and performance through customized course materials.

Used by permission of Electronic Learning Facilitators, Inc.

toys like Nintendo games and tools for sophisticated business planning and education."

Experience

No matter what you plan for, something is always going to happen that you didn't expect—changes in the business, changes in staff, delays, not getting the right information, and so forth. "If the vendor doesn't have the experience to plan for the unexpected and be flexible, the project will be late, of poor quality, and won't achieve the desired results," warns Brodo. The supplier should also have experience in the actual learning environment, whether it is over the Internet or in the classroom.

Content Expertise

Potential clients should make sure that the supplier is well-grounded in the content the simulation is built around. "If not," says Brodo, "there will be mistakes that are apparent and, worse, not apparent until a participant challenges a result."

Instructional Design

Simulations are designed to teach people to do something. "If you don't carefully craft the simulation around achieving learning results, then you are simply playing a game," says Brodo. "It is critical that the instructional design synthesize content and learning into the solution."

Technology

Make sure that you are using the technology that best accomplishes the learning results and provides the flexibility to make the solution cost-effective. Smart vendors will develop platforms that are easily tailored, as opposed to building from scratch every time. "Clients should feel comfortable 'looking under the hood' and asking questions about modeling techniques and the guts of the simulation," says Brodo. The technology should also be easy to use and understand.

However, don't let technology worries give you fits. "The hardware platform you select will probably be outmoded by the time your project is completed," says Karen Taylor, systems manager for ELF Interactive. "Never look back." She adds, "Your next PC will be a multimedia delivery platform. The possibilities are endless."

Results and Feedback

Ask where the reports and feedback will come from. How will they be developed? Do they agree or conflict with your corporate strategy and culture?

Castro urges clients to make their suppliers part of the team. Don't hold back," he says. "The supplier is a special type of partner. You don't have to be a filter."

As a client, you also have a job. Andrea David, operations manager for ELF Interactive, suggests these client responsibilities:

- Designate one point of contact for the project.

- Plan to spend a lot of time working on the project—especially up-front.

- Provide access to the target audience.

- Provide timely and complete access to all documentation, systems, and other information requested by a vendor.

- Dedicate the appropriate number of subject matter experts for the life of the project and make sure they're given the time to participate fully.

- Set aside time to review all deliverables thoroughly.

- Give only specific constructive feedback.

- Give timely sign-offs.

- Be flexible as things change frequently and rapidly on multimedia projects.

- Avoid scope creep—allowing the project to grow uncontrolled. Stick to your original mission.

- Alert your vendor immediately to any new developments that may affect the completion of the project—such as work stoppages, delays, or cancellations. Be prepared for internal upheavals that may affect your project.

- Understand that in most cases the vendor is working on a fixed budget based on hours per task. Overages on tasks mean loss of revenue to the vendor.

- Be sympathetic. Multimedia professionals routinely endure long hours and tight deadlines to make you, the client, happy.

Most simulations take six months to a year to develop. Although the traditional ISD process has only five stages, multimedia production has many more. Here they are, courtesy of ELF's Taylor.

1. **Analysis.** Determining the goals, audience, needs, content, task, performance, environment, media, cost-benefit, potential problems and risk, and technical needs.

2. **Preliminary design and prototyping.** After a thorough analysis, the high-level design for the application will be perfected and documented in a preliminary design document. The document includes creative approaches, artwork, visuals, teaching strategies, layout, concept visualization, and production schedules. Next, a functional prototype is developed to demonstrate the concepts described in the preliminary design. Because it's difficult to visualize a multimedia application on paper, the overall look and feel and major interactions will be developed. The prototype gives a client the opportunity to see an example of how the final program will look and function.

3. **Client review and sign-off.**

4. **Storyboarding.** Storyboards provide a paper-based representation of the final program and serve as the blueprint team members will follow during production. Everything you see, hear, or do in the entire simulation is documented in this stage. If you don't see it in the storyboards, you won't see it in the program.

5. **Client review and sign-off.**

6. **Programming, authoring, and media production (simultaneous).** During media production, assets are developed. Assets are the individual pieces (graphics, animation, video, audio, photographs, text) that are combined using a programming language or authoring package to create the final application.

7. **Testing.** All elements of the program are tested to ensure that they match what is specified in the storyboards. The look and feel are evaluated. A near simulation is carried out to test program performance under "real-life" circumstances. Needed revisions are identified, documented, fixed, and checked again.

8. **Client review and sign-off.**

9. **Implementation and evaluation.** The multimedia application is implemented first in a test environment at the client site. The supplier evaluates test results, conducts interviews with participants and observers, and assembles the data in an evaluation report. Then, revisions are made to create a final version of the application.

    Evaluation ensures the effectiveness of the instruction by subjecting deliverables to rigorous procedures. Prototyping, pilot testing, and client review and input at key points in the process help produce programs that will fully meet your needs.

10. **Support and maintenance.**

The Price of the Game

"There can be a really high development cost," says Blank candidly. "However, very few companies add up what training really costs, including all the various areas of the budget such as salaries, travel, lodging, room rental, and so forth. Often, they only compare the program development costs. When contemplating a simulation, you must keep a broader budget perspective."

Biegel says that simulation quickly becomes cost-effective in either of two scenarios: when you have a small group of trainees whose behavior of skills have a great affect on the organization and can't be ignored, or when you have an exceptionally large number of people to train. IEC's FedEx simulations have targeted 10,000 to 35,000 employees.

"The magic number seems to be about 300 people to be trained," says Blank. "At that point, the cost-benefit gets very clear." GE Supply's Castro estimates the cost of developing *Inside Edge* at approximately $1,500 per person. "And that's just for our current population. New people coming in are free." Castro finds it easy to justify the expense. *Inside Edge* is an up-front investment in a permanent product, modifications are inexpensive, and tracking and assessment are built in.

Brodo says, "When we first started to talk with senior managers at Astra Merck, they guessed it would cost millions of dollars to develop. Because SMG had developed a flexible simulation authoring tool, we were able to deliver the project in less than six months and at a cost of about $400,000. Typically, a custom simulation costs between $100,000 and $500,000 to fully develop and implement."

Blank shares the following list of variables that can affect the cost of multimedia training:

- **Audiences.** How many and how different are their needs?

- **Technology.** Is it in place? Is it standard? Will you need to buy services, licenses?

- **Content.** How much is there? Shorter courses cost more per hour. Does the content exist in some other form? Will content elements be disputed? Is content changing, and do you have to accommodate frequent changes?

- **Prototype.** Don't cut here; it saves money in the long run.

- **Record-keeping.** How much is required? What kind of analysis is needed to be useful for HR purposes?

- **Asset production.** How many graphics and what type? Animation costs more. How much audiovisual material is needed for instruction? How much for motivation?

- **Programming.** Allow money for testing, especially for an off-the-shelf product.

- **Other factors.** Who is doing the work? In-house staff? A contractor? Consider travel and phone interviews. If contracting, expect to allocate 10 to 20 percent of total budget for project management.

Biegel at IEC offers these guidelines to production budgeting:

- High production values, high design complexity. That includes full-motion video, professional talent and crew, realistic sets, complex graphics and animation, elaborate tree structure, varied feedback strategies, multiple multimedia learning resources, and a complex gaming and scoring structure.

- Medium production values, medium design complexity. That means lower frame-count video, fewer actors and simpler sets, more bounded design with fewer branches, targeted learning resources, and a simpler scoring strategy.

- Basic production values, low to medium design complexity. Photographs plus audio, professional or nonprofessional voice talent, text-based choice points, and text or audio performance feedback.

Game Over for Stand-Up Trainers?

Trainers may fear that simulation will obviate their jobs. Not so, say simulation developers and clients. "The true ISD trainer plays a large role in the development of a simulation," says RBFG's Milne. She notes that a background in classroom facilitation is helpful and that expertise in adult learning is important: "You don't sublimate the learning to the technology design," she says. She urges simulation clients to really think about the learning and keep coming back to the learner.

Biegel emphasizes that the trainer is her partner. "The role of the trainer is to do the instructional design," she says, "to think through the performance support mechanisms to surround the simulation. It's an opportunity to use new media. "Says Biegel, "Training in the classroom is always going to make sense."

Brodo says, "One of the most interesting parts of the Astra Merck project was the one that the trainer played. Instead of her job going away because of simulation, it was enhanced. She was looked at as a critical resource and an internal superstar. She became a key facilitator during the deliveries and discovered that there is a strong need for additional modules that reflect new challenges of the process."

Article Review Form at end of book.

Describe cognitive-behavioral training. Apart from addressing the needs of long-term unemployed people, are there other applications for this technique in industry?

Effect of Cognitive-Behavioural Training on Job-Finding among Long-Term Unemployed People

Judith Proudfoot, David Guest, Jerome Carson, Graham Dunn, and Jeffrey Gray

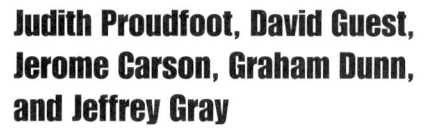

Departments of Psychology (J. Proudfoot, Ph.D., J. Carson, M.Sc., Prof. J. Gray, Ph.D.) and Biostatistics and Computing (G. Dunn, Ph.D.), Institute of Psychiatry, University of London, DeCrespigny Park, London SE5 8AF, UK; and Department of Organisational Psychology, Birkbeck College, University of London (Prof. D. Guest, Ph.D.)

Summary

Background

The principles of cognitive-behavioural therapy (CBT) have been applied successfully through individual psychotherapy to several psychiatric disorders. We adapted these principles to create a group-training programme for a non-psychiatric group—long-term (>12 months) unemployed people. The aim was to investigate the effects of the programme on measures of mental health, job-seeking, and job-finding.

Methods

289 volunteers (of standard occupational classification professional groups) were randomly assigned to a CBT or control programme, matched for all variables other than specific content, that emphasised social support. 244 (134 CBT, 110 control) people started the programmes and 199 (109 CBT, 90 control) completed the whole 7 weeks of weekly 3 h sessions (including three CBT, seven control participants who withdrew because they obtained employment or full-time training). Questionnaires completed before training, on completion, and 3–4 months later (follow-up data available for 94 CBT, 89 control) assessed mental health, job seeking activities, and success in job-finding. Analyses were based on those who completed the programmes. Participants were not aware that two interventions were being used. Investigators were aware of group allocation, but were accompanied in all programmes by co-trainers who were non-investigators.

Findings

Before training, 80 (59%) CBT-group participants and 59 (54%) controls scored 5 or more on the general health questionnaire (GHQ; taken to define psychiatric caseness). After training, 29 (21%) and 25 (23%), respectively, scored 5 or more ($p < 0.001$ for both decreases). Improvements in mean scores with training on the GHQ (between-group difference 3.91, $p = 0.05$) and in other measures of mental health were significantly greater in the CBT group than in the control group. There were no significant differences between the groups in job-seeking activity during or after training, but significantly more of the CBT group than of the control group had been successful in finding full-time work (38 [34%] vs. 13 [13%], $p < 0.001$), by 4 months after completion of training.

"Effect of Cognitive-Behavioural Training on Job-Finding among Long-Term Unemployed People," by Judith Proudfoot, David Guest, Jerome Carson, Graham Dunn, and Jeffrey Gray, *The Lancet*, July 12, 1997, v. 350. no. 9071, pp. 96–100. Reprinted by permission of the authors.

Interpretation

These results suggest that group CBT training can improve mental health and produce tangible benefits in job-finding. Application of CBT among the unemployed is likely to benefit both individuals and society in general.

Introduction

People attribute events, particularly success and failures, to causes, whether they are real or imagined.[1] Such causal attributions may be classified in several dimensions, such as internality (due to oneself or to external factors), stability, pervasiveness, and controllability.[2] These dimensions can be used to measure, by questionnaire,[3] or content analysis,[4] an individual's characteristic attributional style, which correlates with susceptibility to clinical depression[5] and physical illness,[6] risk of relapse in depression,[7] low motivation and poor achievement in education and athletics,[8] job satisfaction,[9] and sales performance.[10,11] Individuals who typically attribute their failures to internal, stable, and global factors, and their successes to external, temporary, and specific causes, are most vulnerable to poor persistence, impaired performance and depression.[12] Clinically, cognitive-behavioural therapy (CBT) can modify attributional style,[7] and can have beneficial effects in depression[13] and other psychiatric disorders.[14]

Unemployment is associated with personal, financial, and social restrictions, which can affect psychological health.[15] The proportion of unemployed people who score above the cut-off point for "psychiatric caseness" on the general health questionnaire (GHQ)[16] is typically 60%, compared with 20% among employed groups.[17] Long-term unemployment typically brings further difficulties, such as psychological changes that can prevent re-employment.[18] Reduced self-esteem, self-efficacy, and expectations of success all decrease the likelihood of a successful outcome in job-seeking, or may reduce the motivation to seek work at all. Many long-term unemployed people cease to believe in their ability to regain employment.[19] The personal cost of unemployment can, therefore, be substantial. There are also, of course, substantial costs to society.

There is a clear need for interventions to assist unemployed people to reduce the negative psychological impacts of unemployment and to help them back into work. However, little psychological assistance is given. Most re-employment programmes aim to clarify job goals, to provide job-seeking or job-related skills, or to resocialise unemployed people to the work environment. There have been few empirically assessed interventions, and those assessed so far have proved to be of little use.[20] Three studies that described psychological interventions, however, have reported encouraging results.

The programme to improve self-efficacy in job-seeking led to higher rates of re-employment; job-search behaviour was the major mediator through which high self-efficacy was converted into re-employment.[19] A social-support and problem-solving intervention resulted in increases in quantity and quality of re-employment, but no difference in job-seeking behaviour.[21] Expressive writing by job-seekers about the thoughts and feelings surrounding job loss increased re-employment success, but did not change job-seeking behaviour.[22] To date, however, no psychological intervention derived from an empirically validated psychotherapy technique has been formally investigated.

Our occupational training programme, based on the principles of CBT (table 1), aims to help people identify and modify their attributional style. We assessed the effectiveness of the programme in a group of long-term unemployed professional people, who were likely to experience repeated failure in job-finding. We compared the effects on mental health, job-seeking activities, and success in job-finding with those of a social-support programme in a similar control group. The primary outcome measure of the study was obtaining full-time employment.

Methods

Professional people of standard occupational classification[23] groups 1, 2, 3, and 7 (managerial, administrative, professional, technical, and sales) who had been unemployed for longer than 12 months were recruited via newspaper advertisements, mail shots, the UK Employment Service, and a major out-placement company (Sanders & Sidney). Calculations to ascertain the sample size needed for sufficient statistical power were based on the endpoint of change in attributional style (effect size calculated by subtracting mean attributional style in control group from that in CBT group, divided by 1 SD); the calculations were based on a previous study.[24] We found that 70 participants per group were needed (effect size 0.6, significance level 0.05, power 80%). To allow for attrition and to ensure sufficient power by the follow-up phase of the experiment, a sample size of 95 people per group was set. We used a controlled, experimental, two-group design.

We initially planned to have an additional no-training control group. However, recruitment was unexpectedly difficult, perhaps because of the very psychological sequelae of long-term unemployment that our programme was targeting. To maintain sufficient statistical power in the study we therefore dispensed with this control group. The CBT programme had been previously compared with a wait-list control condition in our study of insurance sales personnel, among whom there is also a high rate of rejection and failure.[24] To compensate for the lack of a no-treatment control group, outcome figures from the UK Department of Employment programmes, attendance at which is a standard requirement for all people registered as unemployed, were used as a baseline comparison.

289 people volunteered to take part in the study (figure 1). They were randomly assigned to two groups: the CBT group (n = 145) or, to control for the Hawthorne effect,[25] the control group, which undertook a programme that emphasised social support[26] (n = 144). Social support has been shown to moderate the negative psychological consequences of unemployment[27] and was, therefore, thought to be a suitable control for the CBT programme. Allocation was generated by a random numbers table.

Table 1 Structure of CBT and Control Programmes

	CBT Programme	Control Programme
Structure	Seven 3 h seminars, one per week. Assignments between sessions to assist experimentation with and application of strategies	Seven 3 h seminars, one per week. Assignments between sessions to extend each topic
Content		
Seminar 1	Introduction to cognitive model	Concept of social support, health, and unemployment
Seminar 2	Automatic thoughts, goal-setting, time management, task breakdown	Life satisfaction graphs, peaks and troughs, importance of people
Seminar 3	Thought-recording and common thinking errors, planning	Role-mapping, satisfying relationships, personal support networks
Seminar 4	Techniques to change unhelpful thinking	Social awareness, how to create a positive impression, rules of relationships
Seminar 5	Gaining access to deeper beliefs, dimensions of attributional thinking	Listening and conversation skills
Seminar 6	Specific applications to personal and work situations	People as resources, individual presentations
Seminar 7	Integration of strategies, action planning, and relapse prevention	Goal-setting, course summary
Training Processes	Socratic questioning, group discussions, self-observation, experimentation, individual and group activities, homework assignments	Small group activities, group discussions, individual presentations
Session Format	Review of previous seminar	Review of previous seminar
	Discussion of homework assignments	Discussion of homework assignments
	Introduction of seminar topic	Introduction of seminar topic
	Individual or group activities	Discussion
	Feedback and discussion	Individual or group activities
	Suggestion of weekly homework tasks	Feedback
	Summary of session	Outline of homework task
	Survey of participants' response to session	Summary of session

Throughout the study, participants were not aware that two different interventions were being used. Investigators were aware of group allocation, but were accompanied in all programmes by co-trainers who were non-investigators. 244 people started the programmes (CBT n=134), control n=110). The mean age was 43 years in both groups (ranges 23–62 CBT, 23–61 control). The mean duration of unemployment was 25.8 months in the CBT group, and 23.1 months in the control group (range 12 months to < 12 years). 83% of participants were male.

The two programmes (table 1) were based on widely accepted principles of training[28] and matched for all variables (e.g., format, structure, inclusion of "homework") except detailed content and specific strategies.

Both programmes targeted professional people (although the techniques are equally suitable for manual workers) to enable specific job-seeking issues and activities to be addressed. The CBT programme included techniques such as eliciting, recording, and testing the validity of thoughts, reattribution, behavioural monitoring, and experimentation. Weekly homework projects between the sessions helped participants to apply the techniques to their job-seeking activities. In the final session, participants were taught how to use the programmed strategies to maintain the changes they had made to their thinking and behaviour, and to overcome future difficulties they might encounter. The social support programme focused on helping participants to explore and strengthen their social and professional networks, with related activities to complete between sessions. (Full details of the programmes are available from the authors.) Both groups attended 3 h sessions once a week for 7 weeks in subgroups of between ten and 15 people. Each session was run by two psychologists, one of whom, in most cases, was JP. 209 participants completed the training and were included in the analyses. This total includes ten (three CBT, seven control; p = 0.23) who obtained jobs or went on full-time courses during the training period. 31 (20 CBT, 11 control; p = 0.34) withdrew from the study, mostly after the first and third sessions. The data were incomplete for a further four participants.

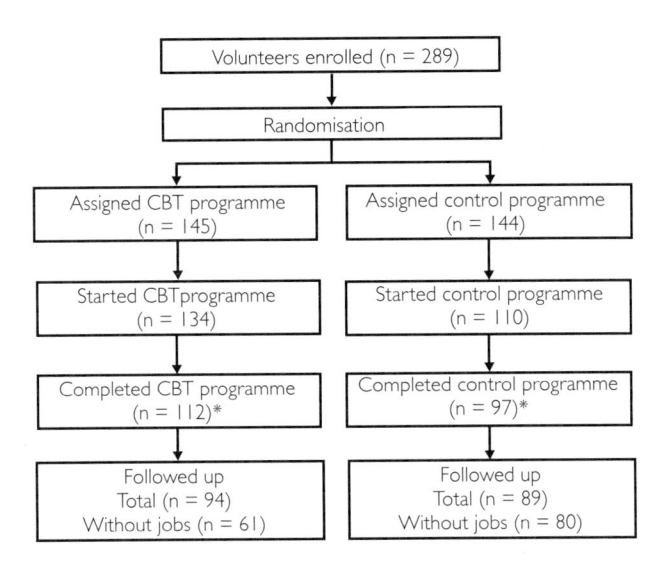

Figure 1. Trial profile.

*Includes participants who withdrew from the programme because they gained employment or full-time training; CBT, n=3; control, n=7.

Table 2	Summary of Psychological Tests Used	
Questionnaire	**Scale**	**High Score Indicates**
Professional self-esteem scale[29]*	0 to 6	Strong self-esteem
Job-seeking self-efficacy scale[21]	1 to 6	Strong self-efficacy
GHQ 30[16]	0 to 30	High mental strain
Attributional style questionnaire[3]	–21 to 21	Strong attributional style for positive and negative events
Motivation for work[30]†	1 to 50	Strong motivation to find work
Life satisfaction[31]	1 to 7	Highly satisfied

*Plus three additional items: capable/not capable; effective/not effective; confident/not confident.

†Composite of value of work and expectation of re-employment.

Before training started, all participants completed several questionnaires to assess psychological characteristics relevant to job-seeking (table 2). The questionnaires were administered again after the final session and 3–4 months later. Analysis of covariance (ANCOVA), with pretest scores as covariates and posttest or follow-up scores as dependent variables, was used to test for differences between the groups resulting from the intervention. Data were analysed with SPSS/PC version 4.

We collected data on jobseeking activity from daily entries by each participant into a log-book to record the number of different jobseeking activities (e.g., seeking information about an advertised job, making a speculative approach to a potential employer, attending an interview, making telephone calls, completing a job application) and the number of hours spent each day in job-seeking. We collected information on job-finding success 4 months after course completion by means of a questionnaire. Differences between the two groups in measures of jobseeking activity were assessed by ANCOVA. Where the assumptions underlying ANCOVA were not met, the data were plotted to ascertain the exact nature of the slopes and converted to change scores (before to after intervention; before intervention to follow-up), and an analysis of the change scores was done by t tests. This method for testing group differences is less satisfactory than ANCOVA, but it does provide a way of taking into account the effect of preintervention scores on outcomes. Differences between the two groups in job-finding success were assessed by χ^2 tests or, for smaller frequencies, by Fisher's exact test.

Results

A score on the GHQ of 5 or above is taken to indicate "psychiatric caseness." At entry to the trial 80 (59%) of CBT-assigned participants and 59 (54%) control-assigned participants scored 5 or higher (p = 0.42). The overall proportion (57%) is similar to that in previous reports on unemployed people.[17] After training, the proportion scoring 5 or higher on the GHQ was significantly reduced in both the CBT group (to 29 [21%], p<0.001) and the control group (to 25 [23%], p<0.001), but again the difference between the groups was not significant (p = 0.78). The post-training proportions are similar to those of people in employment.[17] There was, however, a significant difference between the groups in mean GHQ score after training, with a greater improvement in the CBT group (figure 2, table 3, p=0.05).

After training, there were also significant differences between the groups in self-esteem, job-seeking and self-efficacy, attributional style, motivation for work, and life satisfaction (table 3). The greater improvement in the CBT group persisted until the 3-month follow-up in jobseeking self-efficacy, mental strain, attributional style, and motivation for work. At this point, 38 (34%) of the CBT group and 13 (13%) of the control group had full-time jobs; when the data for these participants were excluded from the analyses, the only significant group difference at follow-up was in attributional style. There were no significant differences between the groups in job-seeking activity (tables 4 and 5), except among participants who, before therapy, had spent little time job-seeking (less than 8 h per week); in this subgroup there was a significantly greater improvement among those in the CBT group ($F = 14.17$, df = 1, 61, p < 0.001). However, significant differences were found in the outcome variables for success in job-finding (table 6). In the control group, 13 (13%) people had found full-time jobs by 4 months

Table 3 Group Differences in Psychological Variables Measured by χ^2 Analysis at Postcourse and Follow-Up

	Group Differences in Mean Score (F df1, df2)			
	Before vs. after training	p	Before training vs. follow-up	p
Self-esteem	6.25 (1,187)	0.01	1.60 (1,178)	0.2
Job-seeking/self-efficacy	11.20 (1,183)	0.001	4.62 (1,175)	0.03
Mental strain (GHQ)	3.91 (1,172)	0.05	3.85 (1,166)	0.05
Attributional style (composite)	18.11 (1,169)	0.001	11.12 (1,154)	0.001
Motivation for work	3.83 (1,179)	0.05	5.86 (1,170)	0.02
Life satisfaction	4.71 (1,184)	0.05	0.99 (1,176)	0.32

GHQ=general health questionnaire.

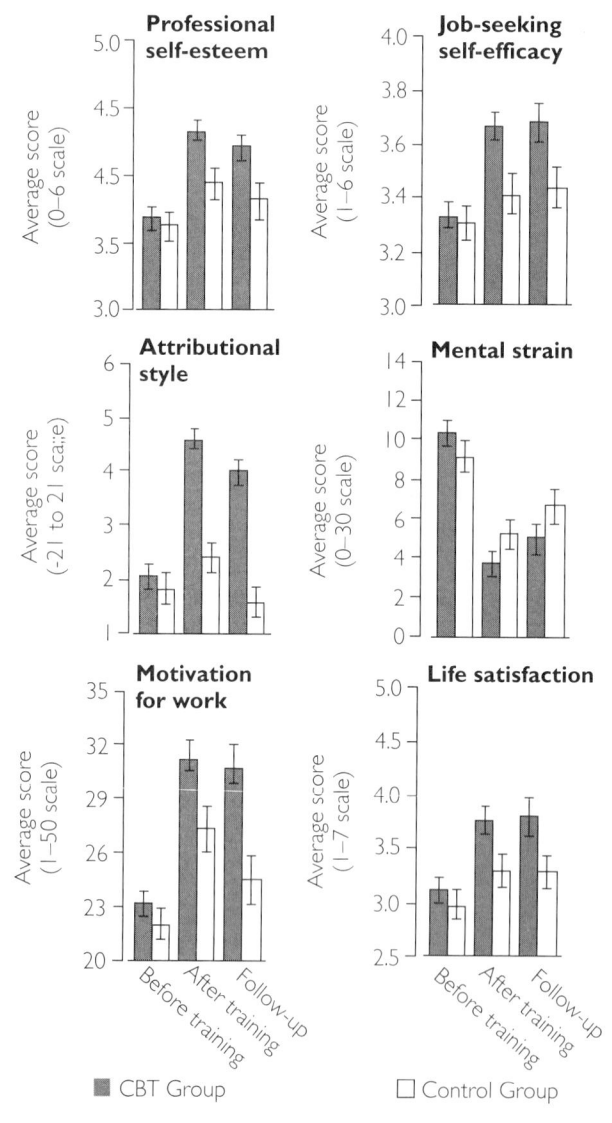

Figure 2. Mean (SE) scores before training, after training, and at follow-up for CBT and control groups.

after the end of training compared with 38 (34%) in the CBT group (p = 0.0006). If part-time and temporary employment is included, the numbers successful were 27 (28%) in the control group and 55 (49%) in the CBT group (p=0.0016).

Discussion

Our results show that the principles of CBT can be applied in disciplines other than psychiatry, in which they were first developed. There were greater improvements in the CBT than in the control group on several measures of mental health, though the controls also improved (figure 2). Participation in the CBT programme produced substantial changes in job-finding, a good measure of real-life performance. Compared with participants assigned to the social-support programme, almost three times as many CBT participants successfully found full-time employment. No data are available from which to estimate the rate of job-finding in this population if they are given no training at all. However, data from a 6-month Employment Department course for professional people, the "Open Learning" scheme, suggest that 27% of 2900 learners obtained full-time, part-time, or temporary employment[32] the same proportion as in our control group. Therefore, the high proportion who found jobs after CBT probably represents a real effect from our programme.

Participants on the CBT course benefited from improvements in psychological well-being, as well as finding a job. For those who did not find employment, however, the benefits had dissipated by the 3-month follow-up in all variables except attributional style, which suggests a need for regular "top-up" seminars once the programme has finished. Nevertheless, for nearly half of the CBT group, the psychological effects were accompanied by success in job-finding. 15% of the CBT group gained part-time or temporary work. Although these people may become unemployed again in the future, part-time or temporary work is recognised as an effective way to re-socialise unemployed people back

Table 4 Job-Seeking Activities

	CBT Group			Control Group		
	Before training (n = 85)	During training (n = 82)	After training (n = 57)	Before training (n = 104)	During training (n = 104)	After training (n = 87)
Job information	1.25 (2.4)	1.28 (2.56)	1.61 (4.23)	0.99 (2.79)	0.94 (2.29)	0.89 (2.58)
Speculative calls	2.61 (6.52)	1.31 (3.66)	1.69 (6.26)	0.74 (2.72)	0.88 (3.22)	0.60 (1.66)
Job applications	1.63 (2.74)	1.45 (2.06)	0.91 (1.76)	1.34 (3.42)	1.28 (3.05)	0.87 (2.37)
Interviews	0.17 (0.33)	0.35 (0.48)	0.35 (0.48)	0.25 (0.48)	0.27 (0.41)	0.33 (0.83)
Follow-up/contacts	3.08 (5.28)	2.44 (4.25)	2.27 (3.81)	1.20 (2.92)	1.17 (2.68)	0.96 (2.86)
Total hours	15.02 (10.36)	18.01 (9.29)	15.41 (10.07)	12.18 (10.32)	14.89 (9.98)	12.83 (9.68)

Table 5 Between-Group Differences in Job-Seeking Activities

	Before vs During Training		Before vs After Training	
	t or F* (df1, df2)	95% CI	F or t† (df1, df2)	95% CI
Job Information	0.48 (1, 135)	−0.47 to 0.49	1.2 (1, 130)	−1.42 to 0.41
Speculative calls	−1.81 (1, 105)	−1.16 to 0.94	0.15 (1, 130)	−1.73 to 1.16
Job applications	0.01 (1,173)*	−0.59 to 0.64	−0.95 (1, 125)†	−0.31 to 0.61
Interviews	3.27 (1, 173)*	−0.21 to 0.009	0.21 (1, 130)	−0.28 to 0.18
Follow-up/contacts	1.76 (1, 92)	−0.58 to 0.69	0.07 (1, 130)	−1.02 to 0.77
Total hours	0.08 (1, 128)	−2.71 to 0.76	0.42 (1, 130)	−3.38 to 1.71

Table 6 Job-Seeking Outcomes for CBT and Control Groups

Job-Seeking Outcomes	CBT Participants (n = 112)	Control Participants (n = 97)	p for Differences
Full-time job	38 (34%)	13 (13%)	0.0006
Part-time job	7 (6%)	4 (4%)	0.49
Contact/temporary work	10 (9%)	10 (10%)	0.73
Work placement/training for work	10 (9%)	6 (6%)	0.46
Further education, full-time	6 (5%)	7 (7%)	0.58
Further education, part-time*	4 (4%)	1 (1%)	0.38
Voluntary work/community action*	4 (4%)	4 (4%)	1.0
Set up own business	5 (4%)	6 (6%)	0.57
Unemployed	28 (25%)	46 (47%)	0.0007

*Fisher's exact test, others by χ^2 test.

into the world of work, and to improve full-time job prospects. 34% of the CBT group gained full-time employment. Each long-term unemployed professional who gains a full-time job saves the UK welfare budget about £14 700 a year and generates at least £5000 a year revenue in tax paid. Therefore, the application of CBT to the employment sector has potential benefits for individuals and society at large. The estimated cost of the CBT programme is £400 per person, largely owing to trainers' fees; however, we are developing a multimedia computerised version of the programme, which will substantially reduce the cost.

Of course, this is only one approach to helping unemployed individuals. Job creation and other policy issues in the labour market (such as "social guarantees" of employment and training), and the individual job-related and job-seeking skills need to be addressed. Nevertheless, our results show the value of psychological interventions such as our CBT programme in reducing negative effects of long-term unemployment and helping the unemployed to gain jobs.

Contributors
This research was carried out by Judith Proudfoot as part of her Ph.D. project. Jeffrey Gray and David Guest supervised the research project. Graham Dunn provided advice on the research design and data analysis. Jerome Carson developed the social skills training programme against which the CBT programme was compared.

References

1. Wong P, Weiner B. When people ask "why" questions, and the heuristics of attributional search. *F. Per Soc Psychol* 1981; **40**: 650–63.
2. Weiner B. An attributional theory of achievement motivation and emotion. *Psychol Rev* 1985: **92**: 548–73.
3. Peterson C, Semmel A, von Baeyer C, Abramson L, Metalsky G, Seligman M. The attributional style questionnaire. *Cog Ther Res* 1982; **6**: 287–300.

4. Stratton P, Munton T, Hanks H, Heard D, Davidson C. Leeds attributional coding system manual. Leeds: Leeds Family Therapy & Research Centre, University of Leeds, 1988.
5. Sweeney PD, Anderson K, Bailey S. Attributional style in depression: a meta-analytic review. *F Pers Soc Psychol* 1986; **50;** 974–91.
6. Peterson C, Seligman MEP, Vaillant GE, Pessimistic style is a risk factor for physical illness: a 35 year longitudinal study. *F Pers Soc Psychol* 1988; **55;** 23–27.
7. Seligman MEP, Castellon C, Cacciola J, et al. Explanatory style change during cognitive therapy for unipolar depression. *J Abnorm Psychol* 1988; **97:** 13–18.
8. Seligman M. Learned optimism. New York: Alfred A. Knopf, 1991.
9. Furnham A, Sadka V, Brewin C. The development of an occupational attributional style questionnaire. *J Organ Behav* 1992; **13;** 27–39.
10. Seligman MEP, Schulman P. Explanatory style as a predictor of productivity and quitting among life insurance sales agents. *F Pers Soc Psychol* 1986; **50;** 832–38.
11. Corr P, Gray J. Attributional style, socialisation and cognitive ability as predictors of sales success. *Pers Indiv Diff* 1955; **18;** 241–52.
12. Abramson L., Seligman MEP, Teasdale J. Learned helplessness in humans. *F Abnorm Psychol* 1978; 87: 49–74.
13. Hollon S. Cognitive therapy and pharmacotherapy for depression. *Psychiatr Ann* 1990; **20:** 249–58.
14. Hawton K, Salkovskis PM, Kirk J, Clark DM, eds. Cognitive behaviour therapy for psychiatric problems. Oxford: Oxford Medical Press, 1989.
15. Feather NT. The psychological impact of unemployment. New York: Springer-Verlag, 1990.
16. Goldberg D. The detection of psychiatric illness by questionnaire. In: Maudsley monograph no 21. London: Oxford University Press, 1972.
17. Warr P. Job loss, unemployment and psychological well-being. In: Allen V, Van de Vliert E, eds. Role transition. New York: Plenum, 1984.
18. Warr P, Jackson P, Banks M. Unemployment and mental health: some British studies. *J Soc Issues* 1988, **44:** 47–68.
19. Eden D, Aviram A. Self-efficacy training to speed reemployment: helping people to help themselves. *F Apply Psychol* 1993; **78:** 352–60.
20. Goldstein IL. Training in organisations, 3rd edn. Pacific Grove: Brooks Cole Publishing, 1993.
21. Caplan RD, Vinokur AD, Price RH, VanRyn M. Job-seeking, reemployment and mental health: a randomised field experiment in coping with job loss. *F Appl Psychol* 1989, **74:** 759–69.
22. Spera SP, Buhrfeind ED, Pennebaker JW. Expressive writing and coping with job loss. *Acad Manage F* 1994, **37:** 722–33.
23. Office of Population Censuses and Surveys. Standard occupational classification. London: HMSO, 1990.
24. Proudfoot J. The application of attributional training and cognitive therapy to occupational settings: PhD thesis. London: University of London, 1996.
25. Roethlisberger FJ, Dickson WJ. Industrial jobs and the worker. Boston: Harvard University Press, 1939.
26. Brugha T. Support and personal relationships. In: Bennett D, Freeman H, eds. Community psychiatry. Edinburgh: Churchill Livingstone, 1991: 115–61.
27. Ullah P, Banks MH, Warr PB. Social support, social pressures and psychological distress during unemployment. *Psychol Med* 1985, **15;** 283–95.
28. Tannenbaum SI, Yukl G. Training and development in work organisations. *Annu Rev Psychol* 1992; **43;** 399–441.
29. Beehr TA. Perceived situational moderators of the relationship between subjective role ambiguity and role strain. *F Appl Psychol* 1976; **61:** 35–40.
30. Vinokur A, Caplan R. Attitudes and social support: determinants of job-seeking behaviour and well-being among the unemployed. *F Appl Soc Psychol* 1987; **17:** 1007–24.
31. Kinicki A, Latack J. Explication of the concept of coping with involuntary job loss. *F Vocat Behav* 1990; **36:** 399–60.
32. Crowley-Bainton T. Evaluation of the open learning credits pilot programme. Sheffield: Employment Department, 1955.

Article Review Form at end of book.

WiseGuide Wrap-Up

Should training programs be considered an investment or an expense? As we have seen in this section, many organizations have moved away from simply training basic skills to developing the person as a whole. It should be noted that employee development is expensive, and organizations legitimately question the value of training programs not directly associated with the company's goals. Why should a company spend money to help employees manage personal issues? Could treating the person as a whole become too invasive? Where do we draw the line?

However we answer these questions, training and development will continue to play an increasingly significant role in the workplace. Industrial/organizational psychologists will be called on to assist organizations, employees, and society to achieve their goals.

R.E.A.L. Sites

This list provides a print preview of typical **Coursewise** R.E.A.L. sites. (There are over 100 such sites at the **Courselinks**™ site.) The danger in printing URLs is that web sites can change overnight. As we went to press, these sites were functional using the URLs provided. If you come across one that isn't, please let us know via email to: webmaster@coursewise.com. Use your Passport to access the most current list of R.E.A.L. sites at the **Courselinks** site.

Site name: American Society for Training and Development

URL: http://www.astd.org/

Why is it R.E.A.L.? This site, designed as a virtual community for training and development specialists, provides information and resources about this field.

Key topics: training, development, professional organizations

Try this: Does spending money on training actually translate to improved employee performance? Click on the Library link, then scroll down to the Training Statistics Link. Then select the Training-Performance link. How do you interpret this graph? To find out some of the trends in the training/development area, click on the Communities link, then on the Trends link to find out some of the directions in which this area is heading.

Site name: The Alliance for Employee Growth and Development

URL: http://www.employeegrowth.com/

Why is it R.E.A.L.? The Alliance for Employee Growth and Development is a nonprofit organization created by CWA, IBEW, AT&T, and Lucent Technologies to foster continuous learning experiences and growth for employees.

Key topics: training, development

Try this: What are some of the training opportunities available to individuals in this organization? Select the Training & Services option, then Training Your Way. Note the variety of programs available in this organization.

section 6

Evaluation and Compensation

Learning Objectives

- To explain the reasons for conducting performance evaluations.
- To define a job competency.
- To summarize the process of 360 feedback and to describe the strengths and limitations of this approach.
- To summarize compensation trends in the United States and to describe some of the factors that contribute to income inequality.

WiseGuide Intro

Most organizations continually monitor and evaluate employee performance. For many managers, the evaluation process represents an important and difficult part of their job. For example, in Reading 30, Jaffe states that he actually hates doing performance reviews. An effective performance evaluation requires constant attention (not just attention during the week of the review), and he presents some "preparation rules" for making performance evaluations less problematic for both the reviewer and the employee. In this section, we will review the rationale behind employee evaluation and describe several techniques for assessing performance. At the end of this section, we will link this discussion to compensation and reward systems.

When we think of evaluations, it is common to think of tests or examinations. As you may have experienced, some tests are good; they provide you with realistic and reasonable feedback about what you have accomplished. Others are not so good; they do not seem to relate to the tasks you engage in. As we develop and use appraisal systems in organizations, we need to make sure they are effective. That is to say, they should meet several important criteria. First, the appraisal must be relevant to the employee's work and must contain clear examples of performance. For example, it is not sufficient to say to an employee, "Your performance rating was a 3 on a scale of 5." The evaluator and the employee should know the behavioral criteria that would receive a 4 or 5 rating. Second, this process should provide specific feedback to the employee. It is not sufficient to tell an employee, "You need to do better," but the process should include specific steps or objectives for improvement. Third, the results of the evaluation should be used in organizational decision making (salary increases, promotion, termination, or training), since there is no reason for conducting an appraisal unless there is a consequence of performance.

Industrial/organizational psychologists are involved in all aspects of the performance evaluation process—from developing the assessment tools to providing feedback to the employee. Typically, performance evaluations begin with identifying the criteria of or goals related to the job. Psychologists often refer to this process as operationally defining the constructs (an operational definition is simply a construct made observable and measurable). How do we know when someone is doing an outstanding job, or when they are not doing his or her job? In academia, for example, faculty often operationally define "outstanding performance" (a letter grade of *A*) as answering 90 percent of the questions correctly on a test, thus making the construct (outstanding performance) observable and measurable.

Organizations follow a similar process. In order to determine the outstanding performers, they operationally define performance in terms of behaviors and outcomes. One perspective on this process is the identification of job competencies. In Reading 31, Parry states that competencies (a cluster of related knowledge, skills, and attitudes correlated with performance) provide important insights into understanding job outcomes. He suggests that, in order to improve overall employee effectiveness, organizations should identify, train, and assess competencies.

However the performance criteria are defined, someone must then supply the information and evaluate it. Traditionally, this role has fallen to the manager or supervisor. However, as organizations have restructured, other sources of information have become critical to this process. Now commonly referred to as "360-degree feedback," the evaluation process includes self-assessments, peer/subordinate appraisal, and customer/client reviews. The idea underlying this process is that, by including more sources of information, we can see converging (consistent) and diverging (inconsistent) performance patterns. Readings 32 and 33 suggest technological procedure for conducting a 360-degree performance appraisal and who should be held accountable for the overall process.

Questions

Reading 30. Why is doing a performance review stressful for the evaluator? Are there any rules you would add to those listed in this reading?

Reading 31. According to Parry, what is a job competency? How is a job competency different from traits, skills, or values?

Reading 32. Define 360-degree feedback systems.

Reading 33. According to Atwater and Waldman, how should this process be introduced into an organization? How can organizations use technology to improve the quality of performance evaluations? What are some of the problems in using technology during this process?

Why is doing a performance review stressful for the evaluator? Are there any rules you would add to those listed in this reading?

Following a Few Simple Rules Can Ease the Pain of Employee Reviews

Brian D. Jaffe

Brian D. Jaffe is an IT director in New York and a member of the Info World Corporate Advisory Board.

I hate doing performance reviews. There, I said it! I know it's part of being a manager, and it helps employee development, but that doesn't mean I have to like it. As I send last year's completed reviews to the human resources department, and begin to note employee activities for this year, let me heed my own advice and write down some lessons learned about the process that I have found valuable over the years:

Rule No. 1: No surprises. A performance review is not the time for employees to learn you are disappointed in their performance. That dialog should have started long ago. That is your job as manager.

Rule No. 2: Be prepared. I start by combing my files for status reports (theirs and mine), memos, and e-mails for items to include in the evaluation. Not only does this help fill all the white space on those forms from HR, but it also gives me specifics to buttress the points I'm trying to make.

I also encourage employees to make their own lists of accomplishments for the past year. I admit to them that, although I try to keep thorough notes, I may have missed some items. Their input gives me more information to include, and knowing their perception of things gives me a broader perspective. It virtually eliminates my fear of failing to recognize something that meant a great deal to the employee.

Rule No. 3: Don't treat your employees like children. Reviews should not be used as verbal spankings. I'll give employees a copy of their evaluation the day before I meet with them. Seeing it in advance means that they can discuss it more knowledgeably when we meet. It also means that I don't have to sit there and watch them read it for the first time.

Rule No. 4: Feedback should be constructive. Identifying performance deficiencies is easy, but being a manager means figuring out how to work with the employee to address them. When I had to tell one employee that his project-management skills were lacking, I included that he seemed to be having too frequent project meetings, which was a poor partner to his difficulty in delegating tasks. Coaching opportunities almost always benefit the manager as well as the employee.

Rule No. 5: Performance reviews are a time for discussion, not for negotiation. Admittedly, reviews are a pretty subjective process, which makes the quantitative aspects of ratings and merit increase amounts difficult issues to tackle and present. HR policies often leave the manager with little leeway in determining the size of salary increases. Regardless, it is important to speak with conviction and to resist the urge to point fingers at HR. I will tell disappointed employees that I'll work with them over the next year to realize their full potential, so hopefully we'll be able to justify more next time. I will have failed if, at the end of the discussion, he or she doesn't feel opportunity and motivation to improve.

Copyright 1998, by InfoWorld Media Group, Inc., a subsidiary of IDG Communications, Inc. Reprinted from InfoWorld, 155 Bovet Road, San Mateo, CA 94402. Further reproduction is prohibited.

Rule No. 6: Don't expect total agreement. Not every employee agrees with every word. And some can be emphatic about it. If an employee refuses to sign the review, I'll indicate that on the form, and place it in his or her personnel file. If an employee wants to add his or her own comments, I will review and attach them to the evaluation forms, all the while remembering Rule No. 5.

Rule No. 7: Be clear. Performance reviews should not meander like a tumbleweed blowing around a ghost town. You can't say you have done a proper evaluation if, at the end of the process, the employee does not know what was done well, what was done poorly, and what needs to be done to improve and grow.

Between preparation, writing, and discussion I spend about eight hours on each review. As much as I hate doing them, I consider it time very well spent.

Article Review Form at end of book.

According to Parry, what is a job competency? How is a job competency different from traits, skills, or values?

Just What Is a Competency?
(And Why Should You Care?)

Competency studies are hot, but be careful out there. You could end up with a long list of "competencies" that are really skills, values or personality traits.

Scott B. Parry

Scott B. Parry is chairman of Training House Inc., a Princeton, NJ, consulting company.

Recently, a client told me with pride that she had just completed a six-month survey of her company's managers, asking them what competencies were "core" or essential to world-class performance. She planned to use this list as a guideline for recruitment and training. She gave me a copy of her list of 78 competencies and asked if I could suggest any obvious omissions—as if 78 weren't enough.

Thousands of organizations have conducted studies to identify the competencies that are important to success in a given job or cluster of jobs. They apply the results of these studies to recruiting, training, counseling and evaluating employees. Unfortunately, few agree about what constitutes a "competency" in the first place.

A number of people in the business world lately have taken to saying "competency" when they mean nothing other than "skill." They evidently believe that because the former has four syllables, this makes them sound more professional. And when competencies aren't being mixed up with skills, they're being confused with personality traits.

Since most managers (and many trainers) don't know what a competency is, an organization that asks its managers to come up with a list of desired competencies will get a laundry list that mixes competencies with skills, personality traits and other attributes.

Managers' suggestions may not correlate with performance on the job, so the lists they generate may not be very useful to trainers. And attempting to refine such a list becomes a political exercise; that might be one reason my client ended up with 78 core competencies—far too many. Most companies have identified between 10 and 14.

Here are some sample entries from my client's list:

1. Initiative
2. Self-esteem
3. Decisiveness
4. Negotiation
5. Counseling
6. Interviewing
7. Analytical
8. Intuitive
9. Action-oriented
10. Time management
11. Listening
12. Problem-solving

The first three entries are *traits and characteristics*. The next three are *skills or abilities* ("how-to-do-it"). the next three are *styles and values* of the fundamental sort that Carl Jung described as "psychological types" (Intuitor, Thinker, Feeler, Sensor). Only the last three are *competencies*.

What's the difference? And is it important? Absolutely.

To sort out the mess, it's easiest to start with traits, then define competencies, then distinguish the latter from skills and styles/values.

Traits and Characteristics

This category consists of personality descriptors and distinguishing qualities. Gray-haired readers will recall that grade school report cards and performance-appraisal forms used to contain lists of traits and characteristics. Here are some common ones:

Reprinted with permission from the June 1998 issue of *Training* Magazine. Copyright 1998. Lakewood Publications, Minneapolis, MN. All rights reserved. Not for resale.

cooperative	assertive
steadfast	decisive
creative	humble
independent	conforming
ambitious	to policies
committed	initiative
flexible	team player
disciplined	self-esteem

Psychologists know that personality traits are formed early in life; some may even be inherited. Thus, they resist change—that is, training is unlikely to alter them much. In addition, the role of training professionals is to deal with performance, not with personality. Managers are taught that appraisals should focus on performance, not on psychoanalytic explanations of why a person's behavior is what it is. If certain traits and characteristics are important to a job, then recruiters and interviewers might look for these qualities among job candidates during the selection process. But it is not the trainer's job to assess or develop them.

Another problem: There are likely to be contradictions in any lengthy list of traits. It's questionable, for instance, whether a person can be both creative and conforming. Or independent and a team player. Or committed and flexible.

Competencies

So what *is* a competency? It's a cluster of related knowledge, attitudes and skills that affects a major part of one's job (i.e., one or more key roles or responsibilities); that correlates with performance on the job; that can be measured against well-accepted standards; and that can be improved via training and development.

Consider time management, for example. This competency meets all four criteria. But most courses on time management teach it as a *skill*, concentrating on such things as how to delegate, prioritize, negotiate, say "No" gracefully, make daily "to do" lists and so on. The *knowledge* and attitude dimensions are neglected. This is a major reason why time management courses often don't make much difference in the performance of their graduates.

> **By teaching underlying competencies first, you can lay a solid foundation that will enable you to get far more mileage from skills instruction.**

Many erroneous *attitudes* get in the way of effective time management and should be addressed: "Well, it's all got to be done sooner or later." "I can't say no to the boss or a client." "I have no one to whom I can delegate this. . . . Besides, it's quicker if I do it myself." "I shouldn't give anyone an assignment I'm not willing to do myself." All of these beliefs or attitudes are usually false.

Similarly, *knowledge* relating to time management should be addressed. If employees realize they are costing the organization at least twice their salary (factoring in benefits and overhead), they are more likely to look for ways to invest their time wisely.

If a manager understands that the real value of his time is, say, $120 an hour, he has a basis for making assignments and for deciding what should and shouldn't be done. The question is "Would I pay someone $120 per hour to do this assignment?" If the answer is "No," don't do it. Find someone whose meter is running at a lower rate, one you would be willing to pay to get the work done.

Another example of a competency is the ability to get unbiased information. Many skills rely on this underlying competency: interviewing, teaching, researching, running meetings, giving appraisals and so on. Any one of these activities probably doesn't take more than 20 to 30 hours per year of the average manager's time. But that same manager probably spends more than 1,000 hours per year in interpersonal communications. You have at least a 30-to-1 advantage in developing the generic competency of getting unbiased information rather than the specific skills of interviewing or giving appraisals.

I'm not suggesting you do away with the teaching of specific skills. These are also important. But by teaching the underlying competencies first, you can lay a solid foundation that will enable you to get far more mileage from skills instruction . . . more depth of understanding and transfer of training by your learners.

I would argue that most core *management* competencies are generic and apply to most managers, regardless of function or type of organization. If you look at studies conducted by organizations that know the difference between a competency and a personality trait, the same competencies tend to be mentioned again and again, although the descriptive language may vary.

I believe the most common core competencies for managers can be grouped into four clusters, as follows:

Administrative
Time management and prioritizing
Setting goals and standards
Planning and scheduling work

Communication
Listening and organizing
Giving clear information
Getting unbiased information

Supervisory
Training, coaching and delegating
Appraising people and performance
Disciplining and counseling

Cognitive
Identifying and solving problems
Making decisions, weighing risks
Thinking clearly and analytically

Skills/Abilities

Some skills—welding, computing, writing—can be acquired. Others—musical talent or artistic ability—are inborn. And perhaps all skills are some combination of both nature and nurture.

Skills courses often deal with the behavior needed in specific situations: how to run an effective meeting, make a winning presentation, negotiate a win-win outcome, write memos and reports, interview a job applicant, prioritize work.

Skills tend to be situational and specific, whereas competencies are generic and universal. Consider the six skills listed previously. They all depend upon a number of universal competencies:

- Listen, summarize what was said, clarify, restate key points.

- Ask questions that will elicit complete, clear, unbiased responses.
- Evaluate, categorize, problem-solve.
- Give concise, compelling information that achieves its objective.
- Win agreement on goals, standards, expectations and time frames.

These competencies are generic; they apply in many interpersonal situations, not just the six skills listed. In virtually all aspects of face-to-face communication—selling, teaching, disciplining, briefing the boss or client—they would come into play. In other words, there is much more opportunity to apply generic competencies than specific skills—and training in competencies provides for better odds on transfer of learning and better return on the training investment.

Of course, teaching a competency often means focusing on specific skills to illustrate the learning points. For example, consider the competency of eliciting unbiased information. It relies largely on one's ability to use nondirective, open-ended questions. Role-plays might be drawn from many how-to-do-it skills courses—selection interviewing, performance appraisal, coaching and counseling, and so on. But the emphasis is on a generic competency and not on the specific skills used to illustrate it.

Similarly, if you are teaching the competency of setting goals and standards, you may draw from such applied areas as project management, sales forecasting, setting training objectives and so on. Again, these are skills courses, but they illustrate and give learners practice in applying a competency (the goal-setting process) to a variety of situations.

Styles/Values

The ancients believed that "to name it is to know it"—an urge manifested in the seemingly universal need to categorize people. Hippocrates labeled the four personality types Sanguine, Phlegmatic, Choleric and Melancholic, based on biological functions. Carl Jung identified the four types as Intuitor, Thinker, Feeler and Sensor. Larry Wilson's Social Styles Profile described these four as Driver, Expressive, Analytical and Amiable. Ned Herrmann bases his Brain Dominance Assessment on quadrants of the brain: upper left (analytical, problem-solver), lower left (planner, organizer), upper right (imaginative, holistic), lower right (interpersonal, emotional). Douglas McGregor offered his Theory X (Parent-Child) and Theory Y (Adult-Adult) as two sets of assumptions that influence one's management style.

According to Jung, our styles and values are formulated early in life (by age 10), shaped by the environment and authority figures who served as role models, good or bad. Styles and values are often confused with competencies because the two are intertwined: Your proficiency level on different competencies reveals the relative strength of the cards in your hand—the combination of knowledge, attitudes and skills on each competency. Your styles and values predict how you are likely to play the cards that you hold.

For example, Jennifer and Bill score high (in the 80th percentile on nationwide norms) when assessed on listening. Both are strong in this competency. However, looking at their styles, Jennifer is high in empathy and strong in Theory Y (Adult-Adult) orientation, while Bill is low in empathy and strong in Theory X (Parent-Child). Who do you think is likely to listen more effectively?

Another example: Joe scores low on Jung's Thinker (analytical, left brain) and high on Intuitor (creative, right brain). This might explain his low score on analytical thinking, his weakest competency. Joe has relied on his intuition and "gut reactions" rather than having to apply logic and think things through in a linear, analytical manner. Here is a case in which a person's style or values influenced the development (or lack of development) of his competencies.

In short, your style will influence the way you *use* your competencies. People who are assessed and trained on the basis of competencies should be helped to understand the relationship between styles and competencies. But the two things should not be confused.

Assessing Competencies

If we want to target our training and development efforts on competencies that are weaker than desired, we need a way to assess an individual's competencies that is valid, reliable, and relatively easy to administer Three methods are commonly used:

- 360-degree feedback, with ratings by the individual's peers, manager, work group (if a team leader)—in short, anyone who knows the person well.
- Assessment labs, in which the individual being assessed fills a role (a newly appointed supervisor, for instance) and interacts with trained evaluators who fill other roles—bosses, subordinates and so on.
- Interactive multimedia, where individuals view a series of video episodes, respond to dozens of situations, and are assessed based on their responses.

Until recently, management development programs were typically a patchwork quilt of topics with little relevance and less impact on job performance. Thanks to dozens of competency studies and refinements in assessment and validation techniques, companies can now evaluate a manager's performance by analyzing his or her competencies . . . and then do something about it.

Article Review Form at end of book.

Define 360-degree feedback systems.

High-Tech 360

Here's a technology solution for conducting 360-degree feedback—and a way to determine whether your organization is ready.

David W. Bracken, Lynn Summers, and John Fleenor

David W. Bracken is president of dwb assessments, Dunwoody, GA.
Lynn Summers is vice president of research and development at Mediappraise Corporation, Raleigh, NC.
John Fleenor is a research scientist at Mediappraise Corporation.

There's a strong move beyond the traditional use of 360 feedback only for development to link it instead to an organization's performance management system. Because such programs are complex, labor intense, and expensive, it's difficult to imagine expanding one to cover an entire workforce. But information technology is making that more practical. Can it make 360 easier? Is your organization ready for high-tech 360?

In its simplest form, an Internet-based 360 process consists of a survey loaded at a Website. Most service providers (vendors that offer the online feedback) build into the engine that runs a Website many of the administrative steps involved in conducting 360—from start to finish. Within an organization, an administrator (usually an HR professional) is responsible for setting up and maintaining the Internet-based process. The administrator interacts with the service provider over the phone or online at the administrator's page on the Website and sets the parameters for the company's application of the 360 process by "flipping" a series of switches at the Website.

Let us assume that a 360 process has been set up by your organization to be conducted over the Internet. Here's how your own personal 360 evaluation might work.

You receive an email from the service provider giving you instructions and timeframes for the assessment. Next, using your PC's standard browser, you access the service provider's Website on the Internet and key in your personal ID and password. Then, you create a list of raters who will be asked to provide feedback about you. As you build your rater list, you can select names from a drop-down menu of company employees or enter other names and email addresses. Some raters might already have been preloaded onto your list—such as your boss, your staff, and yourself. Usually, your boss or an HR representative reviews the selections.

Next, raters are sent an email message requesting them to go to the Website and complete an assessment. At the end of the time window, feedback on you and other participants is collected, collated, and assembled into feedback reports. The administrator sets all of the parameters up-front, including timeframe, deadlines, content, email wording, identification of rater groups, and provisions for anonymity, such as how and to whom feedback reports will be routed.

An Internet-based system runs on the service provider's computer system. Employees of the client organization access the Website through their browsers the same way they would access the *New York Times* or ESPN Websites. In contrast, an intranet process is delivered on a company's LAN (local area network) and is owned, operated, and maintained by the company rather than a service provider.

Here are several ways an Internet-based solution can improve the 360-degree feedback process.

Logistics

In an Internet-based process, email replaces paper communication. The forms are not distributed but are filled out at the Website and collected electronically as raters complete them. The administrator doesn't have to initiate each communication or touch each form because distribution and collection are automatic. Raters don't receive separate communications from all of the feedback recipients. The information is collated, and one email is sent to each rater regardless of the number of assessments that a rater has been requested to do. So, with most systems, you aren't trading a paper logjam for an electronic one. Thus, things are easier logistically for participants, raters, and administrators.

If an assessment is being used for administrative rather than development purposes, a participant can ask her supervisor to check her rater list online to make sure there's a fair representation of raters. In fact, that request can be made via email from the service provider as part of the administrative automation.

Copyright August 1998, *Training & Development*, American Society for Training and Development. Reprinted with permission. All rights reserved.

To reduce the chances of someone being rated by bogus raters, security provisions can block raters without valid IDs and passwords from gaining access to the Website. If a rater list is preloaded from the employee database, a participant's supervisor and staff are already known by the system. Raters can receive training through an interactive online module before they do any rating. That feature alone can save a bundle in terms of time and resources and can produce more accurate ratings.

During the time window for completing assessments, it's recommended to send reminder emails to raters who haven't done their ratings. Some still might not respond. In such cases, their supervisors should be notified by email. That can also be handled automatically by the service provider's system.

Rater Overload

An interesting technological solution to rater overload is to set a cap on the number of assessments any one rater can be asked to complete—for example, a limit of 15 assessments. As participants build their rater lists, the system keeps track of how many participants each rater is being asked to assess. If a participant enters a 16th name on a list, he will get a notice onscreen saying that rater is "booked up."

There will always be an overload problem, however, for supervisors who have to evaluate a large number of staff, all by the same due date. Even a high-tech system can't reduce the number of staff. But what it can do is shield a supervisor from having to rate an excessive number of non-staff people in addition to direct reports. Another thing it can do is make the process of completing an assessment less onerous than filling out and mailing a paper form. That's due partly to Web design, and we'll see improvements in that as providers gain experience conducting online assessments. Regardless of the technology, the questionnaire has to be concise—that is, no more than 60 items.

Rater Reliability

Some technical steps can improve the quality of rater-provided data. Because raters interact directly with the system as they make their ratings, the system can respond directly when their responses fall outside predefined limits. For example, a system can look for instances in which a rater gives the same rating on all assessment items—such as, all 5s. Such "straight ticket" scoring is most likely due to the rater rushing through the assessment without carefully reading the items. In such cases, the system can issue a friendly warning and suggest that the rater go back and find some items that might rate other than a 5. Some systems can prevent invalid input from being submitted.

Insulating Layer of Comfort

One reason companies often use an outside provider to conduct 360 feedback is that raters are more likely to be candid when they know that the data is being collected by an independent firm. Intranet administration of 360 programs in which data is collected on a company's LAN doesn't provide raters with an insulating layer of comfort.

One way to increase rater accountability with technology-based systems is to give raters feedback reports on how closely they agree with others' ratings of the same participants. That gives raters a frame of reference: Are their ratings more severe or more lenient? You can do that with an Internet-based system because the raters' identities are known to the system, and it's important to ensure their confidentiality. In a paper-based approach, typically the raters' identities are not captured.

Creating Behavior Change

Before participants read their feedback, they can complete an online training module that prepares them to accept the feedback. In feedback workshops we've conducted, we have seen that a similar exercise helps reduce participants' defensiveness. An online program is especially effective when used as a prerequisite to working with a feedback coach.

In addition, participants can work with a virtual feedback coach online to help prepare their development plans. At the conclusion of the assessment process, they go to the Website and read their feedback reports. The site links to an interactive development-planning system that guides them through steps to identify key development needs and design an individual development plan to address those needs. Periodically, the site should be updated to reflect participants' progress.

Such online modules aren't meant to substitute for face-to-face discussion with a supervisor or feedback consultant. The intent of hooking up 360 feedback to Internet technology isn't to remove all human interaction; it's to cut down on the resources your company has to expend on the administrative aspects of 360 so that those resources can be redirected towards such value-adding activities as feedback and development planning, whether with a coach or supervisor. Online modules help optimize face-to-face discussions.

Cost

Internet applications are designed to handle volume, and much of the administrative labor is automated. Consequently, the price per participant is usually considerably less than with traditional methods, and administrative work is reduced substantially.

One distinction between Internet and intranet solutions is that intranet applications require the installation of software programs. Your organization pays for the software and each upgrade—a substantial investment. With an Internet system, there's nothing to install. Standard Internet browsers get you to the Website. Some service providers have a "pay as you go" cost structure: you pay on a per-participant basis whenever the service is used. The cost of startup is low; when the service provider upgrades the system, the new features are available to all users immediately.

Look Before You Leap

Before you try to use an Internet-based 360 system, you should evaluate your organization's readiness. Here are several factors to consider.

Prior 360-Feedback Experience

If employees are accustomed to a traditional 360-feedback process, the transition to Internet-based 360

Traditional 360 Feedback

If you work with a large organization, most of the employees probably know what 360 feedback is from their experience either as a participant or a rater. Such programs share these characteristics:

- **Multiple people rate you.** You and your supervisor, peers, direct reports, and others (including customers) complete surveys that assess your behavior on the job. Usually, everyone's but the supervisor's and your own ratings are collected anonymously.

- **You get feedback.** You receive a feedback report detailing the results of the assessment. You look for high points, low points, and gaps between your own and others' perception of your behavior. You can do that with the assistance of a professional feedback consultant.

- **You plan your development.** Either the feedback consultant or your supervisor works with you to identify ways you can change your behavior to become more effective.

It's increasingly common for a company to use employees' feedback results to make such decisions as pay increase and promotions. Originally, 360 feedback was meant to be a development tool only, but it's being more widely used for appraisal because it tends to be more accurate than traditional, top-down appraisal. Often, a boss sees only one side of an employee's performance, usually the side the employee wants the boss to see. A supervisor might not be aware of many other aspects of an employee's performance or might show favoritism towards some employees because of factors unrelated to job performance. Also, many bosses have trouble giving honest performance appraisals if they're negative. So in many organizations, everyone gets good reviews regardless of actual performance.

Another problem with traditional 360 feedback is that the participants pick the raters. People can stack the deck with cronies or even complete all of the forms themselves. Also problematic is that raters sometimes check the wrong box indicating their relationship to the feedback recipient. That's why participants sometimes receive ratings from two "bosses."

Some traditional 360-feedback programs provide training for the raters to help them avoid such common rating errors as the halo effect, in which one very positive characteristic unduly influences the ratings on all behaviors—for example, rating someone as a good decision maker because he is an effective speaker. Another purpose of training raters is to calibrate them so that they understand clearly what they're supposed to be rating and so that they use a similar metric in making their ratings. Because training a lot of raters can drain resources, many companies skip that important step.

After raters complete their assessments, they typically mail the forms to a central service bureau for scoring. Feedback recipients receive reports mailed directly to them, a feedback specialist, or their supervisors, depending on company policy. Then, their supervisors schedule a session to review the results. As you can imagine (and perhaps have experienced), that can take weeks or even months. The process can be especially drawn out when the response rate is low and raters have to be cajoled into completing the assessments.

One reason some raters are late returning their forms is that they've been overloaded with requests from many participants. Supervisors can be especially overloaded. When 360 feedback is used for appraisal purposes, supervisors are generally required to rate each member of their staffs. Sometimes, a rater may make a heroic attempt to complete a lot of forms but succumbs to "rater fatigue." Unable to concentrate on the task at hand, the rater produces inaccurate and unreliable ratings, or may not return the form at all.

Although psychologists debate the meaning of reliability in 360-feedback applications, for all practical purposes it means accuracy. A participant wants raters to rate her accurately so that she can identify strengths and areas for improvement, and initiate appropriate development actions. If the 360 feedback is used for appraisal purposes, participants' companies want them to be rated accurately so that employee decisions will be based on valid information and be seen as fair.

Typically, traditional 360 does little to hold raters accountable for the accuracy of their ratings. That raises concerns about whether raters take their task seriously. Most approaches for holding raters accountable entail removing their anonymity—for example, giving face-to-face feedback in a group meeting. With their cover blown, they're likely to be less candid. The dilemma is that not holding raters accountable may make them take their task less seriously; holding them accountable may cause them to be too lenient in their ratings.

The aim of most 360-feedback programs is to get people to change their behavior on the job. In effect, a company is betting that participants will use their feedback to figure out how to become better-performing employees.

Participants receive feedback training more often than raters do. The training for participants emphasizes how to accept and act constructively on feedback. Sometimes, the feedback can come as a shock and be difficult to deal with. That's especially true if someone thinks of a characteristic or behavior as a strength and learns that others see it as a development need.

We've found that most people don't prepare a development plan after receiving feedback. Those that do typically focus on completing activities. For example, if the primary development need is to manage one's time more effectively, the development plan might be to attend a time-management seminar. Behaviorally oriented plans and accountability for acting on feedback are more likely to produce behavior changes. That usually involves sharing development plans with one's boss.

All of that is time-consuming and costly, especially the training in development planning. Though those are excellent investments, there is a more efficient way to conduct 360—through technology.

A Readiness Worksheet

Factor	Low	Medium	High
Prior 360 experience	No prior 360 experience	1–2 administrations and/or only for part of the company	2 or more administrations involving the entire company
Commitment to ongoing use	No plans beyond current administration	Plans for at least one more cycle	Integrated into HR systems requiring its ongoing use
Accessibility	Little or no access to Internet from inside the company	About 50% of employees have some access to Internet	More than 80% of employees can access Internet
Familiarity	Employees have little reason to use Internet	Company allows and encourages use of Internet	Many systems require employees to access Internet
Culture supports technology	Significant resistance to using technology	Some new technologies recently introduced	Technology advances seen as competitive advantage
Organizational demand	No demand for the service	Able to recruit a group for pilot program	High demand for the service from the entire organization
Technical sophistication	Perception that someone could hack into data	Perception that Internet is reasonably secure	Perception that Internet is more secure than other media
Adequate IT resources	No commitment from IT	IT availability on as-needed basis	Full-time, dedicated IT resources
Geography	Single location	Multiple U.S. locations	Multiple worldwide locations
HRIS data	No HRIS database	HRIS database is often unreliable	HRIS database is comprehensive, well-maintained

should be welcome—for two reasons. One, users will find that an Internet application alleviates such administrative burdens as rater nomination, survey administration, and reporting. Two, the Internet is a secure, confidential medium; that could be especially attractive to raters who might have felt exposed in prior 360 approaches when the data was collected and stored in-house.

Accessibility

Access to the Internet is a key factor in technology-based 360. So when employees don't have direct Internet access through their PCs, the benefits of an Internet solution can dissipate. One solution is to provide computer kiosks that nonconnected employees can use. Another option is to use multiple media—for example, the Internet for connected employees and paper forms for those who aren't. That can, however, increase the cost and logistical complexity. And it may raise the question whether different technologies produce different ratings.

Familiarity

Though completing a questionnaire using the Internet may not sound particularly challenging, it can be daunting for new Internet or intranet users. Even experienced users can become frustrated if the process isn't clear, easy to navigate, and tolerant of mistakes and lost connections. If your organization already uses the Internet for other applications, such as benefits enrollment or job postings, it's an ideal candidate because employees are likely to be comfortable online—making the addition of 360 feedback a minor step.

A Technology-Supportive Culture

Companies that embrace technology in general are quicker to welcome an Internet 360 process. In those that view technology as a way to achieve competitive advantage, there's an expectation that all work processes should apply the latest technology: Enter 360. Companies at the other end of the continuum are technology-averse or have senior management teams that resist change. An ideal situation is when a company has used other technologies that have been less efficacious than the Internet so they are aware of the benefits of putting processes online.

Technical Sophistication

Technical savvy can be a double-edged sword. Security issues arise as organizations and their employees become more educated and aware of the pros and cons of different technologies. The designers of 360-feedback systems must ensure full security and confidentiality for users, and they should communicate the system's features that protect it from unauthorized access. We know of one organization that hired an outside security firm to try to gain unauthorized access to its 360-feedback system. The security firm reported to employees that the data was secure. But most companies don't need to take such dramatic measures.

Adequate IT Resources

The amount of internal IT assistance will vary from project to project. The good news about using the Internet, compared with some internally installed software, is that the Internet provider bears most of the burden for implementation. IT support will probably be most crucial during the early phases of a project when the system is being accessed for the first time. For example, employees with old versions of standard browsers may need to upgrade them.

One critical need is an accurate list of email addresses for all feedback recipients and for as many potential raters as possible. It's not unusual for 10 percent of a company's employee email addresses to be incorrect. The IT group should work with the service provider on firewall issues and security interfaces.

Geography

One compelling benefit of an Internet solution is transnational data access that's cost-effective and instantaneous. Companies with global sites will see a substantial advantage to an Internet application.

HRIS Database

An advantage already discussed is that participants can easily and accurately select their raters, and the system can identify raters who have been selected too frequently. Depending on the way the administrator implements a 360 program, it may be necessary to access the HRIS database to identify participants; their demographics (such as department, location, and so forth); and, ideally, the reporting relationships (such as supervisor, staff, or peer). Having a reliable, up-to-date HRIS database is invaluable.

Not every company is ready to embrace an Internet 360-feedback application. Don't plunge into the high-tech waters without first investigating your company's readiness carefully. On the other hand, your competitors may already be making the move. There's evidence that companies that embrace such progressive HR practices as using 360 feedback for administrative purposes are more successful in terms of productivity, profitability, and market value than those that don't.

Article Review Form at end of book.

According to Atwater and Waldman, how should this process be introduced into an organization? How can organizations use technology to improve the quality of performance evaluations? What are some of the problems in using technology during this process?

Accountability in 360-Degree Feedback

Is it time to take the 360-degree feedback method to its next step?

Leanne Atwater and David Waldman

Leanne Atwater, Ph.D., is an associate professor of HRM at Arizona State University West. She is a member of SHRM and the faculty adviser for the student chapter. David Waldman, Ph.D, is a professor of HRM at Arizona State University West. Atwater and Waldman perform consulting and research in the area of 360-degree feedback. Their book, The Power of 360 Degree Feedback, *was scheduled for release in early 1998.*

An estimated 90 percent of *Fortune* 1000 firms use some form of multisource assessment. These assessments are known as 360-degree feedback because managers are rated by a whole circle of people—including supervisors, subordinates, peers and even customers.

In the majority of organizations, 360-degree feedback is used developmentally: Ratings are collected anonymously and fed back to managers in the aggregate. Usually, only the managers being rated see the feedback. The ratings are not included in the managers' formal performance appraisal.

Increasingly, however, management is asking, "How do we hold individuals accountable for making improvements if they are the only ones who see the data? If the individual needs development and chooses to ignore the feedback, we can't remedy the situation." This is certainly a reasonable question, particularly when companies are spending a good deal of time and money on the 360-degree feedback process.

There are valid reasons for limiting the use of 360-degree feedback to developmental purposes and separating it from the formal appraisal process. First, researchers have demonstrated that when individuals believe the ratings will be used for performance appraisals, they may alter their ratings. Generally, the ratings are more favorable; but occasionally employees see this as a chance for retribution, so they lower their ratings.

Second, if the ratings are used as part of the individual's appraisal, game playing may occur. Supervisors may try to get higher ratings by catering to subordinates—at the expense of meeting organizational goals. Or supervisors may implicitly or explicitly indicate that "if you give me good ratings, I'll give you good ratings."

Third, in some companies, the idea of subordinate or peer ratings as part of one's appraisal is so taboo that many individuals boycott the process and refuse to participate. When participation rates decline, feedback becomes less useful for both development and evaluation.

So, how do companies make the most of the 360-degree feedback process? Are there ways to increase accountability? Are there conditions under which 360-degree feedback can be successfully included in the appraisal process?

Based on our research experience, as well as our experiences implementing 360-degree feedback in a number of organizations, the following recommendations are provided for companies that want to include 360-degree feedback in their performance-management system and add accountability to development.

Taking the First Step

During initiation, 360-degree feedback should be introduced solely for development. Ratings should be collected anonymously and provided confidentially only to the managers who were rated.

Beginning with a confidential process is important for several reasons.

First, in many organizations this inversion of the pyramid (followers rating leaders) is a novel idea.

"Accountability in 360-Degree Feedback," by Leanne Atwater and David Waldman, *HRMagazine*, May 1998, pp. 96–104. Reprinted with the permission of *HRMagazine*, published by the Society for Human Resource Management, Alexandria, Va.

Supervisors and managers may fear that this inversion will threaten their power as "bosses." Individuals at all levels need time to adjust to the idea that managers will receive feedback from a number of individuals, including subordinates.

A number of companies, including McDonnell-Douglas, AT&T, Allied Signal, Dupont, Honeywell, Boeing and Intel, have successfully adapted their 360-degree feedback systems to provide evaluations. Each, however, began using the process strictly for development.

Second, many supervisors and managers have received formal feedback only from their superiors. They are skeptical about how they will be rated by others and whether the ratings will be valid. After experiencing the rating process, most managers recognize the value of the feedback and discover that it was not as negative as they might have feared. However, in every organization, a few managers are very surprised with the negative feedback they receive. For these managers, exposure to the feedback in a confidential manner gives them an opportunity to make changes without revealing their weaknesses to others.

Thoughtful Introduction

The 360-degree feedback process needs to be thoughtfully and carefully introduced. Managers and employees need to understand the rules about anonymity and confidentiality, be fully informed about how the process works, and buy into the fact that the process is a helpful exercise. If individuals perceive that the process is intended to be potentially punitive, there will be resistance to its use.

Introductory sessions should be conducted with all employees who will be involved in the process. Ample time should be given for employees and managers to ask questions about the process, its implementation and the uses of the feedback. Introductory sessions can be conducted in groups, but they should include a thorough description of the process including its goals and who will see the data and reports.

Raters should then be trained about the process. Studies have shown that even a 30-minute training session instructing potential raters on how to avoid possible rating errors can be useful. For example, raters can be encouraged to avoid the "central tendency error" where only the middle values of the scale are used. The tendency of some to rate very leniently also can be curbed with a short training session. If open-ended comments will be included as part of the 360-degree process, rater training becomes even more important.

Raters should learn that comments about an individual's developmental needs should be constructive and behaviorally oriented. For example, a comment such as "Fred has no supervisory skills and shouldn't be a supervisor" provides little constructive value for the individual who is looking for suggestions for improvement.

Comments should be geared to specific weaknesses and suggested methods of improvement. For example, a comment such as, "Fred dominates the conversation in meetings and doesn't give others the opportunity to share their ideas," gives Fred specific information and a specific challenge.

Assessing Readiness

Before 360-degree feedback can be successfully incorporated into appraisals, individuals need to feel comfortable with the process; they need to believe they will be rated honestly and treated fairly.

If these assurances are missing, implementation problems may occur. Managers may attempt to sabotage the process by pressuring their peers and subordinates into refusing to participate in the rating process. Grievances (or even lawsuits) may be filed if ratings are used for decisions about raises or promotions. Dissatisfaction with the process may be so great that it takes a toll on morale.

To avoid these problems, an organization should assess its readiness to include 360-degree feedback in appraisals. The survey shown on this page offers one way to assess organizational readiness. Once individuals at all levels have experienced the 360-degree feedback process, they could be surveyed about the organization's readiness for incorporating its ratings into the appraisal process. An additional issue involves layoffs and reductions in force. Any organization that has recently experienced a layoff or reduction in force is not a good candidate for incorporating 360-degree feedback into appraisals. Even if every assurance has been made to employees that the layoff was a one-time occurrence, skepticism will be rampant. Individuals will fear that

---

Getting Feedback on 360 Feedback

Here is a readiness questionnaire that employers can use to help determine whether or not their organizations are prepared to use 360-degree feedback for evaluations. Questionnaire respondents should be asked if they "mostly agree" or "mostly disagree" with the questions posed.

If more than 70 percent of respondents provide "mostly agree" answers to at least eight of the questions, the organization can consider itself ready to introduce 360-degree feedback into appraisals. If these goals are not met, more work needs to be done to develop trust and confidence and to improve the culture.

Readiness Questionnaire

1. Input and participation in decision making is valued in this organization.
2. Cooperation is evident among employees from different units or departments.
3. There is little fear of speaking up.
4. Generally, employee attitudes in this organization are quite positive about working here.
5. High ethical standards are evident among employees at all levels.
6. Favoritism in reward and promotion decisions is rarely evident.
7. I believe my peers have valuable information about my performance.
8. I believe my subordinates have valuable information about my performance.
9. Decisions in this organization are rarely based on hearsay.
10. Employees are trusted to get the job done.

360-degree ratings will be used to identify the next set of individuals who will be cut.

Even if this is not the case, verbal assurances will not suffice. In this scenario, 360-degree feedback should be used only for developmental purposes until employees' comfort level and feelings of stability return.

Take It Slow

If the organization "passes" the readiness test, introducing 360-degree ratings into the formal appraisal process needs to proceed slowly. A first step could have managers share developmental areas or action plans suggested by the feedback with their superiors—without sharing specific ratings or comments.

A number of companies, such as NORTEL and Texaco, use this process to promote accountability. Managers then are encouraged to work with their superiors to set development goals and to chart progress.

UPS, on the other hand, began its 360-degree program by sharing feedback with the recipient's boss. The company has since decided that this was a mistake because its purpose was developmental. Managers realized that individuals completing evaluations were influenced by the feedback results, and thus, the process was not strictly developmental.

Many companies believe that sharing development goals is sufficient and inclusion of actual 360-degree ratings into appraisals is unnecessary. Others contend that appraisal is "where the rubber meets the road." If ratings are not ultimately tied to rewards, they will not be taken seriously.

Sharing ratings with one's superior is a major step in making ratings a part of evaluation. Some companies require managers to share their feedback results with their respective superiors, but they do not view such practices as equivalent to including 360-degree ratings in formal appraisal. Clearly, it is difficult (and perhaps not even advisable) for a superior conducting a formal appraisal to ignore all information that was available in the feedback if it is relevant to the criteria being evaluated.

Requiring managers to share feedback with their bosses has great potential to influence subsequent appraisals. If ratings—rather than development areas and goals—are to be shared with superiors, superiors need to receive clear direction about how 360-degree ratings are to be included.

For example, ratings could be used as input into some appraisal criteria but not others. NORTEL, for example, gave managers the opportunity to use their 360-degree ratings and improvement scores as indications of improvement in the area of employee development, one of the three critical areas evaluated.

> **Requiring managers to share feedback with their bosses has great potential to influence subsequent appraisals.**

The Final Step

Formally including 360-degree feedback numeric ratings into appraisals is the final step in implementation. A great deal of thought needs to go into this process, and certain questions need to be answered:

a) Which criteria in our appraisal will be addressed with the 360-degree feedback ratings?

b) Which rater group is in the best position to provide accurate feedback on each criterion?

c) How will we handle the situation of a manager receiving conflicting ratings from different rater groups?

d) How will ratings from various groups be weighted? For example, will ratings from superiors carry more weight than ratings from peers? Or will all ratings be averaged across groups for one score?

e) How will managers be evaluated if they do not have 360-degree feedback (perhaps because they had too few subordinates or peers to preserve their anonymity, or perhaps because their raters did not return their surveys)?

f) What are the potential legal ramifications when a negative decision concerning a manager was influenced in whole, or in part, by a 360-degree feedback rating?

g) Will extreme scores or "outliers" be dropped before averages are computed? This method, like that used in the Olympic games, tends to eliminate strong minority opinions from affecting average scores.

Some employers may decide that including numeric ratings is too risky, cumbersome or time-consuming. As an alternative, they may use the ratings only to identify those with dramatic development needs. For example, we provided 360-degree feedback to a small company that employed five division supervisors. All supervisors were rated by four peers, four managers, and between five and 10 subordinates. One supervisor received exceptionally poor ratings from every individual who rated him.

At first, we were shocked that this supervisor was still employed. However, we realized that the managers were unaware of how poorly this manager had been rated by others. They knew their rating of this individual was low, but they did not know their feelings were shared by all. In this case, ratings were being done for the first time and were confidential; the manager himself was the only one who ever knew how poorly he was rated by all raters.

This clearly demonstrates how individuals who have severe development needs could be identified by 360-degree ratings. If suitable training and time failed to improve the ratings, the person could be reassigned or released. In other words, the 360-degree ratings are used to identify those at the extremes, rather than to attempt to discriminate among the many in the middle.

FedEx used such a process whereby any manager who received scores below a cutoff number in two consecutive rating processes was relieved of supervisory responsibilities. This strategy may be somewhat severe, but it could be considered if the cutoff was only at the tail end of the distribution, i.e., the individual's scores were very low.

Options for Making It Work

Companies such as Trompeter Electronics and Xerox include 360-degree ratings in the appraisal process, but they are not a critical component. At Xerox, for example, feedback results are a very small part of the formal review and are used with a focus on continuous development. Trompeter Electronics includes ratings in the review, but they do not affect decisions about raises or promotions.

Many individuals involved in the 360-degree feedback implementation process strongly discourage its use for evaluation. Others, such as the Center for Creative Leadership in Greensboro, N.C., even restrict the use of their published instrument to development purposes only.

We recognize that some organizations are ready and able to successfully make the transition. As one client stated, "How could having more raters than merely one's superior make the appraisal process any worse?"

Superiors—often the sole evaluators in the traditional appraisal process—generally welcome the additional input and shared responsibility for evaluations. If handled properly, 360-degree feedback can broaden the perspective of performance appraisals and be a useful addition to the traditional performance-appraisal process. But, it may not be right for everyone.

Article Review Form at end of book.

WiseGuide Wrap-Up

In this section, we have examined the related topics of performance evaluation and compensation. These are topics that are very important to organizations and employees. An effective performance evaluation provides the organization with important information that can be directly linked to all aspects of organizational life. For example, performance evaluations can be used in selection procedures, training needs identification, and even the restructuring of organizations. For the employee, the performance evaluation can serve as a marker of self-worth. The evaluations (good or bad) can affect our sense of self, both in and outside the organization. Thus, it is important to develop, collect, and use this information carefully.

Just as organizations should attend to evaluation procedures, they should also carefully develop pay systems that reward employees based on their knowledge, skills, abilities, and performance. These procedures raise many issues related to salary inequities and present one of the great challenges organizations will continue to face in the upcoming years.

R.E.A.L. Sites

This list provides a print preview of typical **Coursewise** R.E.A.L. sites. (There are over 100 such sites at the **Courselinks**™ site.) The danger in printing URLs is that web sites can change overnight. As we went to press, these sites were functional using the URLs provided. If you come across one that isn't, please let us know via email to: webmaster@coursewise.com. Use your Passport to access the most current list of R.E.A.L. sites at the **Courselinks** site.

Site name: American Enterprise Institute for Public Policy Research
URL: http://www.aei.org/
Why is it R.E.A.L.? This site examines U.S. trends in employment and income.
Key topics: wages, salary

Site name: Executive PayWatch
URL: http://www.paywatch.org/paywatch/index.htm
Why is it R.E.A.L.? This site is maintained by the AFL-CIO and keeps records on executive pay and bonuses. It also provides information on how executive pay is determined.
Key topics: wages, salary
Try this: Select the CEO and YOU; then select Executive PayWatch Database and pick a company you are interested in.

Site name: American Compensation Association
URL: http://www.acaonline.org/
Why is it R.E.A.L.? The American Compensation Association (ACA) is a not-for-profit association of human resource practitioners who design and manage employee compensation and benefit programs in their respective organizations. In association with the Canadian Compensation Association (CCA) and the Global Remuneration Organization (GRO), ACA serves the worldwide needs for information, training, networking, and research in various professions.
Key topics: wages, salary
Try this: Select Newsline to find some current news and issues related to compensation. Also try the Government Updates link to find some recent legislation and court rulings pertaining to compensation.

section 7

Motivation

WiseGuide Intro

Organizations need and want a motivated workforce. This statement represents a commonly held belief in organizations but does not address the complexity of the construct. It is easy to say we want workers to be motivated or to believe that motivated workers are more productive than unmotivated ones, yet the task facing us is how to create a motivated workplace.

Psychologists begin understanding a phenomenon by defining the construct of interest. Although psychologists do not universally agree on a single definition, most psychologists would agree that motivation involves interrelationships among energy, direction, and persistence. For example, consider the course you are currently taking; there likely exists individual differences in motivation among the students in the class. Some students devote more energy to studying and preparing. This statement suggests that motivation is not reducible simply to energy, because motivation requires goals. We could provide some students with caffeine (a stimulant which activates the body), which would give them energy, but they still may not become more motivated to study. Finally, motivation involves persistence. Highly motivated workers (or students) persist in working on a task until the goal is achieved. Even when they encounter a difficult problem or another option is presented (watching a movie, going out to dinner) they stay on the task. Thus, motivation includes physiological (energy), cognitive (goals, choices), and external (options, rewards) components.

Given this general definition of the construct, there are many theories explaining individual differences in motivation by emphasizing the various components. Some are dispositional, arguing that motivation is a stable and enduring property of the personality—some people are simply more motivated or easy to motivate than others. If this belief is correct, organizations must rely on appropriate selection strategies to hire motivated workers. Behavioral or environmental theories suggest we motivate individuals by controlling external contingencies. Thus, they would conclude that organizations need to make workplaces physically appealing and to provide suitable rewards or punishers on appropriate schedules. Cognitive theories place the responsibility of motivation on how the individual constructs his or her world. This is, motivated individuals maintain motivational schemas by setting goals and developing plans. Whatever theory you favor, the truth is probably a combination of all three perspectives, but psychologists disagree as to which one exerts the most influence on behavior.

Understanding the complexity of motivation is important for industrial/organizational psychologists, because it is common for organizations to request assistance in this area. When you visit some of the **Courselinks**™ web sites, you will find a number of organizations that focus almost exclusively on employee motivation. These organizations provide a multitude of items that purport to motivate workers. Many of these items provide information to the workers about motivation. Certainly, there is some value in reminding workers about organizational goals and the importance of motivation, but as Laurinaitis states in Reading 34, this complex task cannot be accomplished by posters or slogans alone. Simply telling someone to be motivated is ineffective without appropriate organizational supports. If organizations want to maintain a motivated

Learning Objectives

- To define *motivation*.
- To appreciate the complexity of the construct by understanding several motivational perspectives.
- To summarize several techniques to enhance worker motivation.

> ## Questions
>
> **Reading 34.** The author suggests that posters "talk the talk," but managers must "walk the walk." What does this mean? Does this statement imply that motivational posters are ineffective?
>
> **Reading 35.** What are two reasons given by McNerney that motivating employees is more crucial and complex now than it was in the recent past? Do you agree with these conclusions? According to McNerney, what are some of the common themes for successfully motivating workers?
>
> **Reading 36.** What are some of the costs and benefits of the Starbucks motivation approach? Should all companies adopt this strategy?
>
> **Reading 37.** Define *future time perspective*. Seijts states that a future time perspective may lead to some undesirable short-term outcomes but will create a more desirable future state. What does he mean by this statement, and how does he support it? Compare and contrast several ways for assessing time perspective. What are some things organizations can do to motivate workers by using time perspective research?

workforce, there must be a convergence of policies consistent with the overall objectives. In Reading 35, McNerney suggests several common themes that organizations need to address to motivate workers—and money (pay) is not the primary one. He then presents three organizations that address these themes in different ways. In Reading 36, Weiss illustrates how Starbucks has developed a logically consistent set of programs that is congruent with their organizational objectives.

Reading 37 takes a strong cognitive bias by linking motivation with time perception. Specifically, Seijts argues that the way in which people perceive the future directly affects their motivation. By taking a future time perspective, we are able to effectively set long-term and short-term goals and then to plan activities to achieve these goals. As you read this review article, consider some specific applications of this research in organizations, including how teachers can motivate students.

The author suggests that posters "talk the talk," but managers must "walk the walk." What does this mean? Does this statement imply that motivational posters are ineffective?

Actions Speak Louder Than Posters

Jill Laurinaitis

They're both a new accessory in office decor and an attempt to enhance corporate culture. Either way, motivational posters are finding their way onto workplace walls. And most of the managers who put them there hope the posters will create a pleasant atmosphere, change employees' behavior, and ultimately boost productivity.

But do these posters really motivate? If they're perceived as a flavor-of-the-month management tactic, employees may scoff, warns Samuel Culbert, Ph.D., professor of management at UCLA. "Unless they're depressed, people are already motivated to succeed," Culbert notes. "Managers should be trying to remove obstacles to productivity, and they need to ask their people how to do this. By putting up these signs, managers are showing that they don't care about the answers."

Another potential danger is that employees may become confused or cynical if the posters relay messages that contradict the behavior the company actually rewards. Still, it's possible that the posters can have positive effects if they're part of a plan that teaches a company's values and priorities. The problem comes when managers rely on posters to do their work for them. "We don't guarantee anything," says Mac Anderson, chairman of Successories Direct Marketing, a leading motivational-products firm. "We don't think people will change unless management walks the walk."

Article Review Form at end of book.

Reprinted with permission from *Psychology Today* Magazine, Copyright © 1997 (Sussex Publishers, Inc.).

What are two reasons given by McNerney that motivating employees is more crucial and complex now than it was in the recent past? Do you agree with these conclusions? According to McNerney, what are some of the common themes for successfully motivating workers?

Employee Motivation:

Creating a Motivated Workforce

Donald J. McNerney

How do you create a motivated workforce? This question has bedeviled managers and HR professionals for decades.

Some say money is the answer—"Pay 'em more and they'll be motivated." Others say recognition is the key—"Give 'em pats on the back, awards and gifts when they achieve business objectives, and they'll be motivated."

Those with a more Machiavellian view of human nature believe that people are motivated not so much by material rewards but by a desire to increase their power and prestige in the corporate hierarchy. Still others say that the work environment is critical—that providing employees with interesting work and treating them with respect will motivate them.

Each of these theories has some truth to it, of course. But no single theory adequately explains all human motivation. The fact is, human beings are complex creatures. They are not purely economic animals. Nor are they purely political or psychological beings. Most people have a complex set of needs and desires—part material, part social, part emotional—that must be met if they are to be motivated. The answer is never as simple as, "Give them more money" or "Give them more interesting work."

An Urgent Question

The question of what motivates workers is more urgent today than ever before, for at least two reasons.

First, workforce morale is at a low ebb. Rocked by downsizings and job instability, American workers are in a funk. According to a recent survey of 905 workers by Kepner Tregoe Inc., a Princeton, N.J.-based management consulting firm, only one third (37%) feel that their bosses know what motivates them. "We would guess that these individuals are probably less motivated than they were in the past," says T. Quinn Spitzer, CEO of Kepner Tregoe. "They're more concerned, more apprehensive."

Secondly, the old methods of motivating people—through command-and-control—are no longer viable options. Organizations no longer have layers of management to hover over workers and push them. If companies are to succeed today—in the de-layered, service-oriented economy—they must have motivated workers. "We need to motivate, people to want to satisfy customers and solve problems, and use more of themselves, which is not just performing a task, but actually being motivated to care about the business and its success," says Michael Maccoby, author of *Why Work? Motivating the New Workforce*.

The Real World

Given the limits of the various theories of human motivation, it is useful to turn our attention to the real world and some examples of what is working. Southwest Airlines Co., AptarGroup Inc., and Chick-fil-A Inc. are three companies known to have highly motivated workforces, evidenced by their low turnover rates, high employee productivity and consistent profitability. Each, it should be noted, puts a high priority on selecting motivated people to begin with.

Chick-Fil-A

In an industry where turnover rates of 300 percent are the norm—the fast food industry—Chick-fil-A Inc., the Atlanta-based chicken chain, enjoys a turnover rate of 40 percent. Why so low? According to Huie Woods, vice president for human resources, the following factors make Chick-fil-A a very pleasant place to work.

Reprinted from *HRFocus*, August 1996. Copyright © 1996 American Management Association International. Reprinted by permission of American Management Association International, New York, NY. All rights reserved. http://www.ansnet.org.

Strong Corporate Culture

Chick-fil-A's corporate culture is rooted in the biblical principles of its founder. "That doesn't mean we cater to any one class of people or denomination," says Woods. "We just emphasize certain general business practices—fair play, pleasing the customer, a willingness to go the extra mile, hard work. . . . Things you would find in a lot of different places."

Trust is a critical part of the culture. Employees and store operators are not closely supervised at Chick-fil-A. "As long as you do your job, they're going to leave you alone," says Woods. This lack of "bossy bosses," as Woods calls them, motivates people.

A Stable Work Environment

Chick-fil-A has never laid anyone off. It has been able to avoid furloughs because it has successfully pursued a strategy of gradual growth. "We don't grow that fast," says Woods. "We don't add a bunch of employees and then cut back a bunch." Providing a stable work environment has helped Chick-fil-A rid its workplace of one of the worst demotivators: employment insecurity.

Good Pay

Employees at the home office of Chick-fil-A earn competitive salaries and enjoy company-paid benefits, a pension plan and profit sharing. Notable but unremarkable: The most interesting aspect of the compensation system—in terms of motivation—is the arrangement with operators. Under the arrangement, the company builds the store for the operator, leases it to her and then splits the profits with her. All that is required financially of the operator is $5,000 in startup capital. "The $5,000 is a token amount," says Woods. "We'll put them in business and split the profits with them. What a tremendous incentive that is!" This pay structure has allowed Chick-fil-A operators to earn twice as much income as operators at some other fast-food establishments.

Good Perqs

As a private company, Chick-fil-A can offer some perquisites to its employees that would be difficult for a public company to offer. Every year, for instance, the company takes its entire 225-person home office staff—plus their spouses—to the company convention, free of charge. Last year the event was in Bermuda. Next year it will be in Orlando, Fla.

Chick-fil-A also gives away cars to store operators who increase sales by 20 percent in one year. Last year the firm gave away 18 cars. And store employees—most of whom are high school or college students—can get $1,000 scholarships from the parent company. To qualify, all they need is a recommendation from the store operator and proof of their enrollment in an accredited institution.

Southwest Airlines

Southwest Airlines, Dallas, prides itself on being a fun place to work, having an "amazingly low" turnover rate (7.5 percent) and a highly productive workforce. "We have the most productive workforce in the industry," boasts Sherry Phelps, director of corporate employment. The reason: its workers are highly motivated. And here's why, according to Phelps.

Strong Company Culture

Southwest is a company that encourages its people to express their individuality. "We don't tell anyone: 'You have to be an entertainer in your job' but, if that is your natural bent, then you can use any creativity and talent that you have to get your job done," says Phelps.

That is why flight attendants at Southwest have been known to sing the safety instructions and why pilots have been known to tell jokes over the PA system. "Every time that happens, the crowd loves it," says Phelps.

Southwest's culture also deemphasizes hierarchy. "Elitism isn't looked upon very highly here," says Phelps. "Titles are not that important." She adds, "If somebody in the field has a great idea for something, they can go directly to that department head and say: 'Have you ever thought about this?' "

Job Stability

Like Chick-fil-A, Southwest Airlines has pursued a strategy of steady growth. "We've never wanted to be the biggest," says Phelps. "We just want to be the best, in the markets we serve."

And also like Chick-fil-A, that strategy has allowed the company to offer job security. In its 25-year history, Southwest Airlines has never furloughed anyone. "We won't staff up for peak, and then furlough people once the peak season is over," says Phelps. Employees have been known to forego higher pay at other airlines in exchange for more security and a better work environment at Southwest.

Opportunities for Growth

Because employment at Southwest Airlines is relatively stable, employees can be reasonably sure that they will have the time—and the opportunities—to grow at the firm. Pilots, for instance, can look forward to a steady stream of promotions over the years—from flight engineer to first officer to captain—provided they acquire the requisite skills and flying experience.

Other employees, likewise, can advance their careers by attending classes at the "university for people," run by Southwest's "people department." The university offers a wide variety of classes designed to "help people reach their personal best," according to Phelps.

Incentives

Because Southwest is an airline, it can offer employees one particularly attractive incentive: discounted or free travel.

Those employees with no absences or late arrivals over a three-month period, for instance, receive two free, space-available airline tickets from the company. They can use these tickets any way they wish; even give them away to a friend. "That is a very valuable incentive," says Phelps. "It costs us nothing, because it's space available. But the value to our people is enormous."

Compensation

Southwest Airlines is 83 percent union, so most of its salary and wage structure is determined by union contract. In that respect it is quite similar to the pay structures of other airlines and therefore unremarkable.

What is unique about Southwest is its profit sharing plan. When the company is profitable, as it has been in each of the past 24 years, a certain percentage of that profit is put into the company's profit sharing and that money is initially invested in Southwest stock but, after five years of service, each employee of the company is fully vested and many direct the money into several different funds.

As a result of the investments—and Southwest's excellent financial performance over the years—a number of employees have become millionaires after 18 or 20 years of service.

Aptargroup Inc.

Few employees leave AptarGroup Inc., the Crystal Lake, Ill.-based manufacturer of aerosol valves, finger pumps and other caps for shampoo and suntan lotion bottles. The turnover rate at the firm is about 10 percent, half the local average, a clear indication of a highly motivated workforce.

What's more, many of those individuals who do leave the firm actually return fairly quickly. "It is very common to see people reapplying to the firm within a year," says Rob Revak, director of human resources at Seaquist Perfect Dispensing, one of Aptar's divisions. Why do they return? Well, there are many reasons, some of which are outlined below.

Employment Security

While it does not have a formal policy on job security—doing so could "get us into difficulties," according to Larry Lowrimore, vice president, HR—it does have a long track record of providing steady employment.

When business slows down, as it does from time to time. Aptar prefers to ask people to voluntarily take time off rather than cut jobs. Generally, enough people opt for voluntary time off to tide the company over until business picks up again.

Communication and Employee Involvement

Aptar management believes that open communication and employee involvement in the workplace are central to motivating its workforce. The efforts to achieve these goals occur regularly.

Each quarter, for instance, the president of each division holds a staff meeting to which all division employees are invited. At the meeting, the president discusses the financial state of the division and assesses how much progress has been made toward business goals. He or she also presents customer feedback that has been collected and asks for employee feedback on business issues. "Our employees know what's going on," says Revak.

Aptar employees also participate in work teams. "Each team sets its own goals and reports on its progress to senior management," says Revak.

"That, I think, has helped to motivate the workforce," he adds, "because they set their goals, strive toward them, and are very proud when they achieve them and can present their accomplishments to top management."

Recognition

The quarterly staff meetings at AptarGroup also provide an arena for publicly recognizing outstanding employee performance. At each meeting, one "quality employee of the quarter" is selected. The winner receives a couple of awards and some words of congratulation from his or her manager.

While awards of this kind might not motivate all workers, they certainly do motivate some. "I've seen employees stand up and say, 'Thank you, this is the greatest award I've won in my life,'" recalls Lowrimore. "So, it means something to these people."

Aptar also offers less formal perqs like pizza parties, extended lunch hours and brief work shutdowns to show that it appreciates outstanding work.

Compensation

Aptar pays competitive salaries and offers a competitive benefits package. "We do an annual salary survey, and we are usually right near the top in terms of average wage," says Revak.

But in addition to paying good wages, AptarGroup allows employees—all employees—to earn bonuses as well. The formulas used to calculate the bonuses vary from division to division, of course. Some are based on financial results, some on quality measures, and some on safety measures. But they all send the same message, namely: when the company does well, the workers also do well. This is motivating.

Opportunities for Advancement

In addition to offering above-average compensation, Aptar also offers people opportunities to advance within the company. "I once did a little study of how many people had been promoted in the preceding three years," says Revak. "And although I can't remember the exact percentage, it was an amazing number. So, there is a great deal of opportunity within our company, and I think people realize that."

Conclusion

It is interesting to note that none of these companies rely heavily on elaborate new incentive plans or high base salaries to motivate employees. Pay is competitive at all the firms—and there are opportunities for individuals to augment their salaries with bonuses, stock and profit sharing—but money is not at the center of the motivation strategy.

Rob Revak of AptarGroup may have come the closest summarizing the consensus of these companies on the issue of motivating when he said, "Money is important, but if I had to rate it on a list of ten items that motivate people, I would put it somewhere in the middle. . . . Once pay is at a respectable level, then I think those other things, like a good work environment, a safe place to work, a feeling of security, opportunities to progress in the company and how management treats employees, would be weighed by the average person much more than money."

Article Review Form at end of book.

What are some of the costs and benefits of the Starbucks motivation approach? Should all companies adopt this strategy?

How Starbucks Impassions Workers to Drive Growth

With a special blend of employee benefits and a work/life program, one company has elevated a routine cuppa-joe to a supreme business entity.

Naomi Weiss
Naomi Weiss is a freelance journalist based in Seattle, Washington.

You can't help but appreciate a company that routinely begins meetings with a coffee tasting. Or a corporate work setting where traditional conference rooms are replaced by parks resembling contemporary Euro-style cafès, where associates pour themselves a double tall latte, easy on the foam, and sit on a cozy couch alongside their "partners" and colleagues.

Welcome to the Starbucks Support Center. Starbucks Coffee Co.'s headquarters in Seattle. There's an energy here—not induced by a caffeine rush—but from associates drinking up a robust blend of teamwork, sense of mission and challenge. As one of *Fortune* magazine's 1997 "100 Best Companies to Work For in America," not to mention one of the world's fastest growing purveyors of indulgence, Starbucks has been giving its employees a daily lift since 1971.

Woven into the company's Mission Statement is the objective to "Provide a great work environment and treat each other with respect and dignity." But it takes more than company declarations to motivate and inspire people. So how does a young, developing company on an aggressive growth track motivate more than 27,000 people and inspire balance and camaraderie?

The answer is what Starbucks refers to as "a special blend of employee benefits" and a work/life program that focuses on the physical, mental, emotional and creative aspects of each person. This dynamic company developed an innovative work/life program to brew a committed coffee culture—and a passionate partnership.

Starbucks Coffee Co. provides even part-time employees with health coverage, dental and vision plans, disability and life insurance. And those are just a few of the perks.

Everywhere You Look, There's Starbucks

Since Starbucks arrived on the scene, coffee isn't just a morning ritual. The ubiquitous Starbucks Coffee Co. brew has defined a fast-spreading trend from North America to Asia and beyond. Starbucks has met its goal of becoming a $1 billion company by the turn of the century. Its stock is up more than 800 percent since going public in 1992. And there's no question the company is one of the more phenomenal success stories.

Indeed, the Starbucks philosophy and the loyalty of its people have built a company with more than 1,700 stores worldwide, including a recent unveiling in the United Kingdom. The Starbucks blend can be found in restaurants, hotels, offices and airlines. The company also operates a mail-order business worldwide. Its retail sales exceeded $966 million in the 1997 fiscal year.

In little more than a decade, Starbucks elevated a routine "cuppa-joe" to its current supreme status. It operates in nearly every major U.S. metropolitan area, serving more than 5 million coffee lovers each week. Starbucks opens virtually a store a day. Turn on the television and witness "Frazier," "Seinfeld" and medics on "ER" sipping Starbucks in the course of their prime-time adventures.

A global player, the company plans to continue expanding at 35

At a Glance

Organization
Starbucks Coffee Company

Industry
Service

Employees
27,000

HR Employees
112 Worldwide

Challenge
Protect the unified and innovative company culture in the wake of global expansion. Ensure that people feel valued, inspired and serve as a vital link in the growth process, while maintaining the highest commitment to quality coffee and service.

Solution
"A special blend of employee benefits" and an innovative work/life program.

Results
Turnover rate is 60 percent, versus 300 percent industry-wide; company's sales and stock performance—attributed to a dedicated and effective "partnership"—are at their peak. Employees value the benefits and work/life perks that come with the job.

---

to 40 percent in coming years—an achievement possible only with committed, stake-holding associates. But Starbucks isn't just about a great cup of coffee. It's about people—and a humanistic approach to doing business that produces bottom-line results.

Ask Joan Moffat, the Starbucks manager of partner relations and work/life. A member of the HR team, she's responsible for the company's work/life program, which includes on-site fitness services, referral and educational support for childcare and elder-care issues, an Info-line for convenient information and the "Partner Connection"—a program that links employees with shared interests and hobbies.

Moffat, who worked in part with a benefits management organization, Portland-based Working Solutions Inc., says the investment pays for itself, and that many of the programs cost very little to implement. Starbucks has comparatively low health-care costs, reduced absenteeism and one of the strongest retention rates in the industry. "Our turnover rate is 60 percent, which is excellent as compared to the restaurant and retail industry," says Moffat. Moreover, employees reap the benefits of the company's ongoing success.

A Shot of Equity in Every Cup

"Seize the day" is a perfect motto for Starbucks. The company empowers its employees—or *partners* as they're regarded—to do just that. Starbucks is committed to providing an atmosphere that breeds respect and values the contribution people make each day, regardless of who they are or where they are within the company. All partners who work a minimum 20 hours a week receive full medical and dental coverage, vacation days and stock options as part of Starbucks *BEAN STOCK* program. The awarding of stock options to every level of the organization was unprecedented in the service industry a few years ago.

"We established *BEAN STOCK* in 1991 as a way of investing in our partners and creating ownership across the company," explains Bradley Honeycutt, vice president of human resource services. "It's been a key to retaining good people and building loyalty. Naturally, the level of our customer service is favorably impacted, as a result," she adds.

For those involved early on, the rewards have been especially generous as the company has grown and the price of Starbucks stock jumped from $17 to $46. In the process, the term "partner" was introduced through-out the company.

Just as with the *BEAN STOCK* program, all employees who work 20 hours or more are eligible for a universal benefits program. It's not just reserved for the corporate or managerial level. Eligible partners can choose health coverage from two managed care plans or a catastrophic plan. They also can select between two dental plans and a vision plan. Because of the young, healthy workforce, Starbucks has low health benefit costs. According to Annette King, HR benefits manager, the company's health-care costs are approximately 20 percent lower than the national average.

The company also provides disability and life insurance, a discounted stock-purchase plan, and a retirement savings plan with company matching contributions. The benefits provide a powerful incentive to stay with the company, particularly among part-timers, thus reducing Starbucks recruiting and training costs. "We have historically had low turnover, most of which can be attributed to the culture and a sense of community," says Moffat.

As anyone in the service industry realizes, finding and keeping good people is more difficult than ever before—and more important. Much of the company's ambiance—what makes its coffee experience particularly special—is its enthusiastic staff. Starbucks has discovered that when partners are actively involved in the company, the customer benefits and the bottom-line grows.

That's why the statement "Bring ideas to the table" has real meaning at Starbucks. For example, the idea of a cold, coffee blended beverage, such as a Frappuccino® blended drink, was the collective brainchild of a few partners. And when one of the store managers began experimenting with customized in-store music tapes, the idea evolved into Starbucks-branded CDs, explains Moffat. That sense of contribution has translated into retention.

Some "baristas," or espresso drink makers, have been with Starbucks seven or more years, which is particularly unusual for part-timers whose ranks annually turn over 300 percent at more conventional restaurants.

> **We have historically had low turnover; most of which can be attributed to the culture and sense of community.**
> Joan Moffat, Manager of Partner Relations and Work/Life

HR's Challenge into the Next Millennium

Like many other U.S. Companies, Starbucks is expanding in an era of corporate downsizing and economic belt-tightening. Its challenge is to meet customer expectations, while not diluting the company's culture and the contribution of every person.

Human resources' challenge is to ensure that the company's partner-based values survive its ambitious expansion into the new millennium. Therefore, HR takes stock in being a democratic operation, inviting ideas and solutions, and sharing in the rewards. To nurture open communications and innovative thinking, several Partner Relations mechanisms exist:

- *Mission Review* is a forum that encourages partners to tell the company how they're feeling and ask any questions. "Promote a very open environment . . . here's what you've told us and here's what we've done," says Moffat. "We provide supportive action out of their comments." Partners always receive a response to their inquiries within two weeks. The goal of such openness: a feeling of internal respect.

- *Open Forums* are regularly held to examine performance, recognize achievements, plus look at the future. It's also another opportunity for partners to freely question upper management.

- The *Warm Regards* recognition program was developed to spotlight outstanding achievement that embodies the guiding principles, mission and goals of Starbucks. Specific awards include "The MUG (Moves of Uncommon Greatness) Award," "BRAVO!," which recognizes partner achievements and also "The Spirit of Starbucks," which honors passion and action.

None of these initiatives, of course, could gain hold without support from the top. Heading the java empire since 1987 is chairman and CEO Howard Schultz. What Wall Street and stockholders view simply as business acumen, Schultz sees as building a solid business with heart and soul. "We're profitable because of the value system of our company," says Schultz. "American companies have failed to realize that there's tremendous value in inspiring people to share a common purpose of self-esteem, self-respect and appreciation," he says.

He draws on his own personal experiences growing up in a rough, blue-collar neighborhood of Brooklyn, New York. The title of Schultz's best-selling book about the company, *Pour Your Heart Into It*, is no accident. It's an article of faith at Starbucks: How people are treated motivates a unified and committed operation.

Work/Life Benefits Are Part of the Blend

Providing balance only makes sense to Schultz. To do so, the company must constantly evaluate employees' needs and wants by using opinion surveys and maintaining an open ear to partners. Such diligence is an intrinsic part of the culture Starbucks seeks to create.

Three years ago, human resources began examining how it could become more attuned to its partners. For instance, some employees who started with the company when they were in college are now buying homes and managing the realities of child-care and elder-care issues. Starbucks has responded by providing flexible work schedules as part of the work/life program. "Our environment lends itself to meet multiple life demands. By virtue of our strong sales and accelerated growth, flex schedules have not hurt productivity in the least," says Moffat. "Flexibility is particularly inherent in our stores because of our extended hours of operation and the diversity of our workforce—from students to parents—who need to work alternative hours."

HR also has engaged Working Solutions to offer a range of integrated benefit services that address the modern climate and culture of corporations—referred to as "non-traditional" benefits, or emerging needs. Working Solutions has trained life-event specialists who can help solve issues that require health, social, educational and counseling resources. In addition, Working Solutions offers online employee support anywhere in the world, 24-hours a day.

Recent studies have shown that 60 percent of American workers have child- or elder-care responsibilities. Starbucks recognized—as many other companies have—that partners less encumbered by personal stress and obligations are more innovative and productive. Working Solutions helped Starbucks implement several programs that specifically address the life stages and personal needs of its workforce. "Working Solutions' style of caring and support complements our work/life program, and helps ensure the quality our partners deserve," says Moffat. "And, as a company, we see a high rate of return."

Help Juggle Life Demands

To help deal with the fast-paced and demanding environment at Starbucks, Working Solutions also provides referral services for partners and eligible dependents enrolled in the medical plan. It connects them with information that helps make extraordinary life issues more manageable. Moffat recently put the program to use when she needed elder-care advice for her grandmother. In another case, a partner needed emergency child care for his ill son. Working Solutions made prompt arrangements for a certified in-home caretaker, no work was missed, and Starbucks covered half of the cost.

Another example of Starbucks corporate caring: Three years ago, a Starbucks partner suggested a company-sponsored soccer team. The recommendation inspired *Partner Connection,* a program designed to link partners with similar interests, whether they be social, recreational, art and leisure, parenting or volunteerism. The Wonderful World of Food—a group that shares a common interest in great food and dining out—produced "The Partners Table," a cookbook whose sale benefits Fare Start (formerly Common Meals), a non-profit program that provides skills training to the homeless. A surge of interest in baseball resulted in a Starbucks softball league. Now, there's even a Starbucks choir. The

New Parent Network, which offers such activities as CPR training for new parents, is especially active, given the significant number of Starbucks partners who are first-time parents.

As part of the New Parenting Network, Anne Rauh, Starbucks administrative assistant for Learning and Partner Development, feels a special kinship with other Starbucks partners. "It's great to network on a consistent basis and share parenting issues with my colleagues," says Rauh. "Parenting isn't just something you do after 5 p.m., when you go home; you think about the things that are important to you—like your family—during the course of your workday. We're parents 24-hours a day."

The *Partner Connection* program, which requires little company cost, has flourished because the partners run it, and it stays responsive to their interests, company officials say. After partners were initially queried, it didn't take long for the program to gain popularity—almost immediately, 25 groups formed in Seattle. Similar partner programs operate throughout the company's regions.

Encourage a Passionate Partnership

As Starbucks pursues its coffee quest, the social and personal climate of the company continues to evolve. HR strives to stay abreast of its partners' needs and life-stages by periodically conducting opinion surveys. Its mission is to respond accordingly with effective work/life solutions. Starbucks provides on-site services that motivate a healthy mentality and allow for management of daily and extraordinary life demands. The company invites creative and innovative thinking through open communications, as well as established criteria for awards and recognition.

These elements, combined with a comprehensive benefits package, make for a passionate partnership between the company and its most vital resource. Being at the forefront among U.S. company benefits is central to Moffat. "We have the best and the brightest, and our success in the marketplace is directly related to our people," says Moffat. "We will ask our partners constantly what's important to them and consider these things as we plan into the year 2000 and beyond."

CEO Schultz had a mission since day one. "I wanted to establish the kind of company that gave people an opportunity for equity (ownership) and for comprehensive health insurance, among other things. . . . You can empower people with money and responsibility, but what about the person?" asks Schultz.

Starbucks answers that question.

Article Review Form at end of book.

Seijts states that a future time perspective may lead to some undesirable short-term outcomes but will create a more desirable future state. What does he mean by this statement, and how does he support it? Define *future time perspective*. Compare and contrast several ways for assessing time perspective. What are some things organizations can do to motivate workers by using time perspective research?

The Importance of Future Time Perspective in Theories of Work Motivation

Gerard H. Seijts
Faculty of Management
University of Manitoba, Canada

Abstract

The ability to foresee and anticipate, to make plans for and organize future possibilities, represents one of the most outstanding traits of individuals. Theories of work motivation, however, appear to have ignored the construct of future time perspective. In this article, the relationships between future time perspective, the capacity to plan activities, and proximate goals that intervene between one's present state and the desired ultimate, distant goal are explored. Several methodological concerns pertaining to the study of future time perspective are discussed.

The possible time span across which individuals project actions and their consequences ranges from zero to a lifetime. Knowledge about the time span a person considers when making decisions is important in predicting how he or she will act, that is, what goals will be pursued. The ability to foresee and anticipate, to make plans for and organize future possibilities, represents one of the most outstanding traits of individuals (Fraisse, 1963; Gjesme, 1983; Locke, 1975). Theories of work motivation, however, appear to have ignored the construct of future time perspective or future orientation.[1]

Goal-setting theory, for example, has been recognized as a major accomplishment of organizational psychology (Dunnette, 1976; Latham, 1996). The overall validity and usefulness of goal-setting theory have been demonstrated in several reviews (Latham & Locke, 1991; Locke & Latham, 1990; Locke, Shaw, Saari, & Latham, 1981), in meta-analyses (Mento, Steel, & Karren, 1987; O'Leary-Kelly, Martocchio, & Frink, 1994; Wood, Mento, & Locke, 1987), and in comparative assessments of goal-setting theory relative to other theories of work motivation (Kanfer, 1990; Pinder, 1984). However, we know little about how future time perspective affects goal choice and, eventually, behavior. Locke and Latham (1990) acknowledged that future time perspective is a disposition that has not been studied very much and yet shows promise with respect to its relationship to goal setting.

Given the amount of speculation concerning the role of future time perspective in theories of human motivation and behavior, it is useful to consider what is known about the construct and to identify avenues for future research. In this article, I review the core findings of research on future time perspective, and I make testable propositions.

Most, if not all, research on future time perspective has been guided by clinical interest, following the general assumption that an extended future time perspective leads to a well-adapted and psychologically healthy personality. To bring the future into the present, the individual has to have, or develop, the capacity to plan his or her activities. Planning is facilitated by developing proximate goals that intervene between one's present state and the desired ultimate, distant goal. In this article, I briefly review the literature on planning and proximate goals, because both constructs are intimately intertwined with future time perspective.

"The Importance of Future Time Perspective in Theories of Work Motivation," by Gerard H. Seijts, *Journal of Psychology*, v. 132, n. 2, 1998, pp. 154–168. Reprinted with permission of the Helen Dwight Reid Educational Foundation. Published by Heldref Publications, 1319 Eighteenth St. NW., Washington, D.C. 20036-1802.

I also discuss several methodological issues pertaining to the study of future time perspective. I am convinced that a multidimensional model of the construct is the appropriate form. A major conclusion that I draw, however, is that currently developed scales do not adequately measure the multidimensionality of future time perspective. Therefore, I offer suggestions for improving the operationalization of future time perspective and scale development.

Future Time Perspective: Definition and Measurement of a Construct

There are striking differences in the extent to which individuals are inclined to consider distant outcomes in choosing present behaviors. In other words, people differ in the consistency and persistence with which they project the future (Locke, 1975). People with remorse, for example, often think about the past. Others think little about the future and the future consequences of their behavior. These individuals are more concerned with maximizing immediate benefits, and they prefer to take each day as it comes. Finally, some individuals are so preoccupied with their own future expectations and intentions that the past and even the present are disregarded. These individuals "live for the moment in preparation for the future."

People who are more oriented toward the future place a great value on doing future-oriented tasks. Such tasks or actions (e.g., devoting considerable financial resources to education and professional training) will often lead to immediate outcomes that are relatively undesirable (e.g., substantial loans and a high demand on personal time), but ultimately a more desirable future state will be achieved (e.g., outstanding training as a surgeon or commercial pilot). Because most human motivation is future oriented, I focus here on people who live in the "here and now" versus those who are more oriented toward the future. The past provides important lessons but, for most of us, has little interest in itself for everyday life.[2]

In a review of the future orientation literature, Gjesme (1983) concluded that "empirical studies have revealed contradictory results concerning future time orientation and various other factors" (p. 443), and that "the inconclusiveness of empirical findings is almost complete" (p. 445). An important reason for the diversity of results is the variability in definitions of the construct and in the measurement instruments used.

Definition of the Construct

The conceptualization of future time perspective has been of great concern to both theoretical and empirical investigators of human motivation and behavior. Future time perspective is a measure of an individual's ability to conceptualize the future and has vaguely been defined as "the totality of the individual's views of his psychological future and psychological past existing at a given time" (Lewin, 1951, p. 75), "the timing and ordering of personalized future events" (Wallace, 1956, p. 240), "a general concern for future events" (Kastenbaum, 1961, p. 204), and "a general capacity to anticipate, shed light on and structure the future" (Gjesme, 1983, p. 452).

Gjesme (1983) suggested that the function of future time perspective is analogous to a searchlight, which helps to illuminate events ahead. To paraphrase Gjesme, an individual's future orientation highlights objectives not yet in the present. The stronger the searchlight, the farther individuals see, the more objects they discover, the brighter and clearer these objects appear, and the nearer and more real individuals perceive them. As a consequence, individuals are better able to structure and plan future actions and to take precautions against future events.

Based on my review of the literature, I have concluded that there is no clear and precise definition of future time perspective that researchers agree on. As a consequence, we do not have a good idea of the boundaries of future time perspective or reasonable knowledge about the nature of its properties. Two issues in particular need additional clarification: whether future time perspective is a stable disposition or a cognitive structure that is flexible and capable of modification, and whether future time perspective is a unitary or a multidimensional construct.

Empirical evidence suggests that future time perspective is a cognitive structure rather than a stable disposition. First, the capacity to experience time, and estimate it, has been found to be a gradually developing characteristic. The ability to extend the idea of time into both the past and the future continues to develop with age (Green, Fry, & Myerson, 1994; Klineberg, 1967), and both children and adolescents become more realistic in their expectations (Klineberg, 1967). Second, treatment programs for drug addicts (Alvos, Gregson, & Ross, 1993; Henik & Domino, 1975) have influenced the length of future time perspective, suggesting that perceived life circumstances are an important determinant of future time perspective.

Third, there is evidence that future time perspective is an outcome of the socialization process (Lamm, Schmidt, & Trommsdorff, 1976; Stein & Craik, 1965; Stein, Sarbin, & Kulik, 1968). Individuals learn that society as a whole, as well as the specific social class and groups to which they belong, provide an organized array of future events and goals, some of which are more time specific than others. According to Stein and his colleagues, more socialized individuals (e.g., nondelinquents versus delinquents) have not only learned about these goals, but have also integrated them into their cognitive time structure, and these have become part of a series of proximate goals toward which progressive movement occurs.

Cross-cultural differences in future time perspective further support the proposition that the construct is, in part, an outcome of socialization processes. Researchers (Levine & Bartlett, 1984; Levine, West, & Reid, 1980; Meade, 1971; Sundberg, Poole, & Tyler, 1983) have found striking differences in the future orientations of both students and adults in Australia, Brazil, India, and the United States. Based on these four pieces of research evidence, I have concluded that future time perspective is a flexible construct and is capable of modification.[3]

Adding to the lack of understanding of future time perspective is the issue as to whether it is a unitary or a multidimensional construct. Researchers (de Volder, 1979; Trommsdorff, 1983; Wallace, 1956; see Daltry & Langer, 1984, for an exception) have suggested as many as five dimensions of future time perspective: (a) extension, the length of the future time span that is conceptualized; (b) coherence, the degree of organization of the events in the future time span; (c) density, the number of events expected in one's future, that is, one's goals, hopes, fears, and wishes; (d) directionality, the extent to which one perceives oneself as moving forward from the present moment into the future; and (e) affectivity, the extent to which a person is gratified or pleased by anticipated events.

Extension and coherence are the cognitive aspects of future time perspective. Future orientation as a cognitive schema means the structuring of future events in terms of their temporal sequence and causal order (Trommsdorff, 1983). A cognitive schema can be more or less extended, coherent, differentiated, precise, and realistic. Conversely, density, directionality, and affectivity are the affective and motivational aspects of the construct. The future can be experienced as more optimistic or pessimistic (affect), which in turn will influence behavior (motivation) (Trommsdorff, 1983).

A person who is well-adapted to his or her environment integrates future orientation with a present orientation. This is because future orientation leads to further attainment of clarity abut the self (e.g., "How far can I go?") and the environment (e.g., "What will happen?"), whereas situations without future orientation and future goals are more likely to maintain clarity about the self (e.g., "This is what I am") and the environment (e.g., "I know what should happen") (Sorrentino & Short, 1986). This leads to another question that has to be resolved, namely, whether individuals differ along an underlying dimension from present to future or whether there exist two orthogonal dimensions: concern for present (low to high) and concern for future (low to high).

Because researchers have identified different dimensions of future time perspective, it seems plausible to suggest that each of these dimensions develops somewhat independently of the others as a function of different antecedents. Moreover, the functional consequences or manifestations of each of these components may differ. For example, an extended future orientation as such does not by definition indicate a well-adapted and psychologically healthy personality. Older people, for example, may have a shorter extension of future time perspective than adolescents simply because their life expectancy is shorter. Similarly, older people being asked to complete a future time perspective instrument may select the past more than the present because they have lived longer. Also, although most individuals may have an extended future orientation, for some people, hopes may be dominating, whereas for others, fears may be prevailing.

Most of the work on future time perspective, however, has been correlational with little theoretical rationale for relating variables to (dimensions of) future time perspective. For example, Henik and Domino (1975) examined the effects of methadone treatment for narcotic addicts on five dimensions of future time perspective, namely, extension, coherence, density, directionality, and affectivity. They were unable to explain differential effects of the treatment on the separate dimensions of the construct. Unless the dimensions of future time perspective are demonstrated to differentially influence, or be influenced by, other variables of interest, there seems little to be gained from working at a more micro level.

In past research, I elaborate on how future time perspective has been measured not only because the construct is the focus of the present article but also because it is the most ambiguous of the constructs dealt with in the current article. Future time perspective has most often been measured using a projective test. For example, the Future Events Test (Kastenbaum, 1961; Wallace, 1956) requires the person to list events he or she believes will occur in his or her future (e.g., "I get married"), including the age at which the person thinks the event may occur. This test measures the dimensions of density, extension, affectivity, and coherence.

Similarly, a person can be asked to record up to 25 (life) events he or she had thought about during the past 2 weeks. Individuals are asked to rate each item according to whether, at the time they had thought or talked about it, they referred to something in the past, present, or future (Eson, 1951; Roos & Albers, 1965; Strumpf, 1987). This test provides an indication of directionality. The Story Completion Test (Barndt & Johnson, 1955) requires the person to complete story roots (e.g., "About 4 o'clock one bright sunny afternoon in May, two boys [girls] are walking together down on 39th street . . ."). This test provides a measure of extension.

Using the technique of Time Metaphors (Knapp & Garbutt, 1958), some that reflect a dynamic–hasty orientation to time (e.g., a speeding train), some that indicate a passive approach (e.g., drifting clouds), the person indicates whether the metaphor reflects his or her own sense of time. This test provides an indication of directionality. Finally, the Incomplete Sentences Test (Lessing, 1968) involves asking individuals to choose a number of events they think about now, or for which they have started to plan, and to estimate the number of years that will elapse before they expect each event to occur (e.g., "I like best thinking about _____ when I will be _____ years old"). This test measures the dimensions of extension, coherence, density, and affectivity.

In addition to projective measures, questionnaires have been used to measure time orientation (Gonzalez & Zimbardo, 1985; Murrel & Mingrone, 1994; Stewart & Ahmed, 1984; Strathman, Gleicher, Boninger, & Edwards, 1994). For example, based on a *Psychology Today* reader survey involving 11,982 respondents from 50 states and Canada, Mexico, Puerto Rico, and the Virgin Islands, Gonzalez and Zimbardo identified two scales, namely Goal Seeking and Planning (e.g., "When I want to achieve something, I set subgoals and consider specific means for reaching those goals") and Pragmatic Action for Later Gain (e.g., "I believe that 'a bird in the hand is worth two in the bush'") that correspond to what researchers consider to be future time perspective.

A problem with most of these measures is that they do not provide consistent results. Specifically, the test–retest coefficients of the measurement instruments are low, and different tests of the construct have been found to have low convergent validity. Lessing (1968), for example, compared three measures of future time perspective: the Future Events Test, the Incomplete Sentences Test, and the Story Completion Test. She found that the reliability of the scales assessed by test–retest coefficients ranged from –.07 (Story Completion Test) to .73 (Incomplete Sentences Test). The intercorrelations between these measures ranged from a nonsignificant value of .06 (Incomplete Sentences Test–Story Completion Test) to .37 (Incomplete Sentences Test–Future Events Test). Furthermore, Lessing reported that, for students in Grades 5, 8, and 11, the three measures had different correlations with intelligence, sex, academic achievement, social class, and traits such as personal control.

Lessing (1968) offered two explanations for these findings: (a) the reliability and validity of instruments measuring future time perspective differ, and (b) the exercise and expression of the cognitive capacity to anticipate the future is strongly influenced by situational and specific instrumental determinants. For example, story completion stems, which often mention an hour in the morning or early afternoon, elicit a powerful set toward using a day as the temporal unit.

Additional conceptual and methodological problems associated with the construct of future time perspective will be addressed in more detail in the discussion. It should be clear, however, that we will not have a full understanding concerning the relationships between future time perspective and other constructs unless a valid and reliable measure of future time perspective is developed—one that is free from bias.

Behavioral Consequences of a Truncated Future Time Perspective

Despite conceptual and measurement problems, research indicates that future time perspective may have a profound effect on human motivation and behavior. This research, however, is mainly from the field of clinical and abnormal psychology. For example, researchers (Barndt & Johnson, 1955; Davids, Kidder, & Reich, 1962; Stein et al., 1968) have found evidence that delinquents have a shorter time perspective than nondelinquents (after controlling for intelligence, sex, age, academic achievement, and socioeconomic status). Delinquents seem to live in the "here and now," unconcerned about rewards and punishments in the near future.

Manganiello (1978) contrasted opiate addicts from five residential therapeutic communities with controls. Scores on the Future Events Test indicated that opiate addicts had a significantly foreshortened future time perspective. Specifically, for about 70% of the addicts, anticipation of future events was restricted to the relatively immediate future, that is, between 0 and 1 year, whereas the scores for the control group indicated a more extended anticipation, that is, between 6 and 10 years. Manganiello suggested that a foreshortened future time perspective may be an expression of two personality variables, namely locus of control and self-esteem. Addicts may not be inclined to anticipate and plan for the future because they do not believe in instrumental relationships between their behavior and future events. Similarly, for individuals who are pessimistic abut their current life and who feel incompetent and inadequate, the future holds the prospect of failure (including death) and, consequently, it is not to be anticipated.

Alvos, Gregson, and Ross (1993) compared future time perspective, as measured by the Future Events Test, in both previous and current drug users. Results indicated that those currently using drugs had a more truncated future time perspective as well as a greater number of non-answers on the Life Events Scale, which, according to Alvos et al., further supports the view that those individuals have a lower degree of future time extension and contact with reality.

Additional studies in clinical psychology have found a restricted future time perspective in alcoholics (Smart, 1968) and poor contraceptors (Mindick, Oskamp, & Berger, 1977). Statistically significant but weak correlations (.18–.28) were found between length of future time perspective and the practice of positive health behaviors including good nutrition, relaxation, safety, and limited substance use (Mahon & Yarcheski, 1994).

Whenever a potential relationship between future time perspective and maladjustment, including delinquent behavior and drug use, is examined, there is an inevitable question of causal direction. It may be argued that the socioeconomic background and an erratic upbringing of delinquents and drug addicts result in a restricted concern for and conceptualization of the future. Furthermore, once one has become a delinquent or addict, the environment may reinforce and further restrict the already limited future time perspective. Because of the correlational nature of most of the studies, the interpretation in terms of a cause–effect relationship is ambiguous.

In one of the few field experiments that have been conducted, Henik and Domino (1975) reported that a treatment program for narcotic addicts resulted in a significant change in the dimension of extension for the experimental group from pre- to post-methadone treatment. However, the dimensions of coherence, density, directionality, and affectivity did not show significant changes between pre- and post-methadone treatment of the experimental group. The researchers concluded that methadone treatment can make a number of desired goals available to the addict, and "consequently, an increase in the conceptualization of his future follows" (p. 562).

It has also been argued that future time perspective is tantamount to having a high achievement orientation. Research has shown that future time perspective is related too school performance (Klineberg, 1967; Lessing, 1968; Murrell & Mingrone, 1994; Nuttin, 1985; Raynor, Atkinson, & Brown, 1974; see Dickstein, 1969, for an exception). For example, Volder and Lens (1982) found evidence that an extended future time perspective is an influential factor in academic performance improvement.

They explained this relationship as follows: (a) High-achieving students ascribe a higher valence to general goals in the distant future than low-achieving students do; and (b) high-achieving students grasp the long-term consequences of behavioral acts better than low-achieving students do. Therefore, high-achieving students put in more effort and are more persistent in their daily study activities and obtain better academic results than low-achieving students do.

Proposition 1. Individuals with an extended future time perspective will set goals that are distant in nature more often than individuals with a truncated future time perspective.

This proposition is based on the premise that future time perspective refers to the degree of involvement in the future. Individuals with an extended future time perspective are more involved in the future, either in the thought level or on the action level, than individuals with a foreshortened future time perspective.

In a review of the goal-setting literature, Locke and his colleagues (1981) concluded that "the only consistent thing about the studies of individual differences in goal setting is their inconsistency" (p. 412). Most of the goal-setting studies have focused on goals that were assigned to individuals and, almost universally, individual differences have been treated as a moderator variable. The issue as to whether individual differences, such as future time perspective, influence the level at which individuals set goals for themselves has been largely unexplored.

Planning for Goal Attainment

Complex or difficult tasks that lie in the future need careful planning. For example, specific strategies have to be developed for earning tenure, for being promoted to full professor, or for starting up a private business and making it profitable. Thus, a major process involved in orientation to the future concerns how individuals plan to realize the goals they have adopted.

Pearlson and Raynor (1982) demonstrated how individuals engage in planning and develop strategies to attain a distant goal. They asked students to write down a future goal, then to write down the steps that would lead to that goal, the activity that constituted each step, the positive and negative outcomes that might result from each activity, the chances of succeeding at each activity, and the importance of the future goal to them. Results indicated that those students high in achievement orientation had a more differentiated cognitive map of how to get from where they were to where they wanted to be than students low in achievement orientation, and this was particularly true if the goal was of great importance to them.

Proposition 2. Individuals who have attained their goal will have developed and implemented (a) a broader range of strategies and (b) a superior set of strategies than individuals who have not set themselves a goal (or individuals who have failed to reach the goal).

This proposition is based on Trommsdorff's (1983) argument that future orientation needs less complex structuring in the near or immediate future. This is because fewer instrumental activities are necessary to reach a less distant goal. Conversely, extensive cognitive structuring, including evaluation of future problems and planning for possible future behavior, should be adequate if a more distant goal is to be attained.

Choosing realistic proximate goals help individuals to reach their distant goal. For example, a large number of individuals look for a new direction in their career (Foord Kirk, 1996). A change in career, however, needs to be part of a well thought out career plan rather than an escape hatch. There are a number of things an individual can do. For example, if a person wants to cross over to a high-technology industry, he or she can ask senior people in the industry for their advice and guidance, tell them about his or her background and accomplishments, and add that he or she wants to move into the high-technology field but lacks the necessary technological background. Senior people can be asked how to overcome this obstacle. What training to undertake? What reading to do? What associations to join to increase a successful and speedy transition into a new career? These (and other) small, tentative steps are necessary to attain the distant goal of a successful change in career.

Bandura (1982) argued that self-motivation is best summoned and sustained by adopting attainable proximate goals that lead to large future goals. Whereas proximate goals provide immediate incentives and guides for action, distant goals are too far removed in time to effectively mobilize effort or to direct what one does in the "here and now." That is, proximate goals provide clear markers of progress toward a distant goal (Bandura, 1986). Remedial action can be taken when there is a discrepancy between the goal that is set and actual performance. Individuals may try harder for the goal, identify and implement better strategies to attain the goal, or both.

Proximate goals may also serve as a vehicle for the development of high self-efficacy through enactive mastery. For example, Bandura and Schunk (1981) found that setting proximate goals had a greater positive effect on school children's self-efficacy, persistence, and performance in a math course than did setting a distant goal or setting no goals. On a complex task, high self-efficacy is necessary for the ongoing search for effective strategies. The development of appropriate strategies, in turn, will further increase self-efficacy regarding task mastery and performance. Perceived self-efficacy and the development of appropriate strategies have thus a reciprocal effect on each other (Wood & Bandura, 1989).

Weick (1984) argued that setting proximate goals allows individuals to recast a distant goal regarding a task that is relatively complex for them into a smaller, more workable task. Setting a proximate goal facilitates the identification of a series of controllable opportunities of modest size that produce visible results. When a solution is put in place, the next solvable problem allowing proximate goal attainment usually becomes visible, leading to the attainment of the distant goal.

Small wins are more structurally sound than focusing solely on a large win, because small wins are stable building blocks for increasing self-efficacy. For example, a distant goal can be to increase one's work attendance within a specific time frame. Proximate goals are specific behaviors that the individual has to engage in to attain the distant goal. Examples include solving difficulties with co-workers, overcoming alcohol and drug-related issues, and coping with family demands.

In conclusion, setting proximate goals facilitates self-regulation, which is helpful in remaining oriented toward the future (Bandura, 1986; Bandura & Simon, 1977; Seijts & Latham, 1995).

Proposition 3a. Individuals who have set themselves proximate goals in addition to a distant goal will (a) pursue their distant goal in a disciplined manner, and (b) will experience success at a faster rate than individuals who have not formulated proximate goals.

Proposition 3b. This effect (Proposition 3a) is mediated through self-efficacy and strategies. There exists a reciprocal relationship between these two constructs.

Conclusion

Despite strong individual differences in future time perspective, no theory of work motivation explicitly addresses this construct. This is unfortunate because knowledge about the time span an individual is considering when making decisions is important for predicting how the individual will act. In other words, future time perspective determines, to a large extent, the kind of goals that are set or accepted, and whether goal conflict is likely to occur (e.g., short-term gratifications versus long-term planning and orientation). I have outlined several mechanisms that explain how future time perspective is related to human motivation and performance.

Although much has been written about future time perspective and many studies have been conducted, several conceptual and methodological problems can be identified. First, there does not appear to be a clear and precise definition of the construct. The lack of a clear definition increases the likelihood that measurement instruments are both contaminated (i.e., variance in the measure that is not present in the construct) and deficient (i.e., variance in the construct that is not captured by the measure) (Schwab, 1980). Researchers have long neglected this issue. More important, what is currently lacking is an understanding of the antecedents of future time perspective and how each of the dimensions of the construct develops as a function of different antecedents. Thus, a strong theory-based model of how the antecedents of future time perspective combine and jointly influence its development is needed.

Second, the lack of consensus between the theoretical construct and the measures intended to assess the construct is an important explanation for the inconclusiveness of empirical findings (Gjesme, 1983). Little, if any, systematic exploration of the psychometric properties of the various measurement instruments has been conducted. Information regarding the reliability and validity of the instruments used to measure future time perspective is often not provided in research reports. Face validity appears to have been the major criterion to justify several quite dissimilar measures. A study that examines the convergent and discriminant validity of the several measurement instruments seems long overdue.

Furthermore, future time perspective is often measured by a single instrument. Ideally, researchers should gather information about a construct with multiple measures using different formats of each (Mitchell, 1985; Schwab, 1980). The reliance on a single measure is especially problematic as there is little information concerning both the reliability and validity of the instruments that are intended to measure future time perspective.

Third, as Weiss and Adler (1984) argued, linkages between dispositional variables and components of theories have often been given insufficient theoretical specification. In other words, a nomological network, guided by theory, should be developed that indicates how the construct of future time perspective (as well as its dimensions) is related to other relevant constructs. Dispositional variables (including future time perspective itself) are often treated in isolation from the theoretical context. If one is truly interested in the construct of future time perspective and wishes to understand its antecedents and consequences, then much more attention should be devoted to theory and causality as opposed to simple correlational research designs.

Fourth, most of the research on future time perspective has been correlational in nature. Such correlational studies often lead to ambiguous results, in particular when future time perspective and its correlates are obtained from self-reports. What is needed now are longitudinal studies as opposed to cross-sectional studies that are correlational in nature. Longitudinal studies conducted over a sufficiently long time designed to examine changes in future time perspective would be helpful to test causal hypotheses more directly. In addition, researchers should examine how future time perspective develops over time and consider how the processes linking future time perspective with other variables including proximate goals and planning also change over time.

Notes

1. Though future orientation and future time perspective are often used interchangeably, the two constructs should be distinguished. Future orientation is defined as a person's preferred mode of thought and behavior (Nuttin, 1985). Future time perspective refers to a person's cognitive understanding of the relationship between large blocks of time (e.g., days, weeks, months, and years) and past events or expectations of the future. Thus, future time perspective is the ability to plan and organize activities beyond the present moment (Suto & Frank, 1994). In this paper, I primarily focus on future time perspective.
2. In a series of studies, however, Staw and Ross (Ross & Staw, 1986, 1993; Staw & Hoang, 1995) have shown that decisions of the past can create new valences for the future.
3. Because there is a kind of self-reinforcement inherent in future orientation (e.g., the more satisfaction it gives, the more it is stimulated and developed), it may gradually develop into a stable dispositional characteristic (Gjesme, 1983).

References

Alvos, L., Gregson, R. A. M., & Ross, M. W. (1993). Future time perspective in current and previous injecting drug users. *Drug and Alcohol Dependence, 31,* 193–197.

Bandura, A. (1982). Self-efficacy mechanism in human agency. *American Psychologist, 37*, 122–147.

Bandura, A. (1986). *Social foundations of thought and action: A social-cognitive view.* Englewood Cliffs, NJ: Prentice-Hall.

Bandura, A., & Schunk, D. H. (1981). Cultivating competence, self-efficacy, and intrinsic interest through proximal self-motivation. *Journal on Personality and Social Psychology, 41*, 586–598.

Bandura, A., & Simon, K. M. (1977). The role of proximal intentions in self regulation of refractory behavior. *Cognitive Therapy and Research, 1*, 177–193.

Barndt, R. J., & Johnson, D.M. (1955). Time orientation in delinquents. *Journal of Abnormal and Social Psychology, 51*, 343–345.

Daltry, M. H., & Langer, P. (1984). Development and evaluation of a measure of future time perspective. *Perceptual and Motor Skills, 58*, 719–725.

Davids, A., Kidder, C., & Reich, M. (1962). Time orientation in male and female juvenile delinquents. *Journal of Abnormal and Social Psychology, 64*, 239–240.

Dickstein, L. S. (1969). Prospective span as a cognitive ability. *Journal of Consulting and Clinical Psychology, 33*, 757–760.

Dunnette, M. D. (1976). Mish-mash, mush, and milestones in organizational psychology. In H. Meltzer & F. R. Wickert (Eds.), *Humanizing organizational behavior.* Springfield, IL: Charles C. Thomas.

Eson, M. E. (1951). *Analysis of time perspective at five age levels.* Unpublished doctoral dissertation, University of Chicago.

Foord, Kirk, J. (1996, August 24). Set realistic goals if you plan to change careers. *The Toronto Star*, p. L1.

Fraisse, P. (1963). *The psychology of time.* London: Eyre & Spottiswoode.

Gjesme, T. (1983). On the concept of future orientation: Considerations of some functions and measurements implications. *International Journal of Psychology, 18*, 443–461.

Gonzalez, A., & Zimbardo, P. G. (1985). Time in perspective. *Psychology Today, 19*, 21–26.

Green, L., Fry, A. F., & Myerson, J. (1994). Discounting of delayed rewards: A life-span comparison. *Psychological Science, 5*, 33–36.

Henik, W., & Domino, G. (1975). Alterations in future time perspective in heroin addicts. *Journal of Clinical Psychology, 31*, 557–564.

Kanfer, R. (1990). Motivation theory in industrial and organizational psychology. In M. D. Dunnette & L. M. Hough (Eds.), *Handbook of industrial and organizational psychology.* Chicago, IL: Rand McNally.

Kastenbaum, R. J. (1961). The dimensions of future time perspective: An experimental analysis. *The Journal of General Psychology, 65*, 203–218.

Klineberg, S. L. (1967). Changes in outlook on the future between childhood and adolescence. *Journal of Personality and Social Psychology, 7*, 185–193.

Knapp, R. H., & Garbutt, J. T. (1958). Time imagery and the achievement motive. *Journal of Personality, 26*, 425–434.

Lamm, H., Schmidt, R. W., & Trommsdorff, G. (1976). Sex and social class as determinants of future orientation in adolescents. *Journal of Personality and Social Psychology, 34*, 317–326.

Latham, G. P. (1996, August 9–14). *Critical issues in goal setting research: Moving beyond 1990.* Invited address at the annual meeting of the American Psychological Association, Toronto, Canada.

Latham, G. P., & Locke, E. A. (1991). Self-regulation through goal setting. *Organizational Behavior and Human Decision Processes, 50*, 212–247.

Lessing, E. E. (1968). Demographic, developmental, and personality correlates of length of future time perspective. *Journal of Personality, 36*, 183–201.

Levine, R. V., & Bartlett, K. (1984). Pace of life, punctuality, and coronary heart disease in six countries. *Journal of Cross-Cultural Psychology, 28*, 129–137.

Levine, R. V., West, L., & Reid, H. (1980). Perceptions of time and punctuality in the United States and Brazil. *Journal of Personality and Social Psychology, 38*, 541–550.

Lewin, K. (1951). *Field theory in social science.* New York: Harper and Row.

Locke, E. A. (1975). Personnel attitudes and motivation. *Annual Review of Psychology, 26*, 457–480.

Locke, E. A., & Latham, G. P. (1990). *A theory of goal setting and task performance.* Englewood Cliffs, NJ: Prentice-Hall.

Locke, E. A., Shaw, K. N., Saari, L. M., & Latham, G. P. (1981). Goal setting and task performance: 1969–1980. *Psychological Bulletin, 90*, 125–152.

Mahon, N. E., & Yarcheski, T. J. (1994). Future time perspective and positive health practices in adolescents. *Perceptual and Motor Skills, 79*, 395–398.

Manganiello, J. A. (1978). Opiate addiction: A study identifying three systematically related psychological correlates. *International Journal of the Addictions, 131*, 839–847.

Meade, R. D. (1971). Future time perspective of college students in America and in India. *The Journal of Social Psychology, 83*, 175–182.

Mento, A. J., Steel, R. P., & Karren, R. J. (1987). A meta-analytic study of the effects of goal setting on task performance: 1966–1984. *Organizational Behavior and Human Decision Processes, 39*, 52–83.

Mindick, B., Oskamp, S., & Berger, D. E. (1977). Prediction of success or failure in birth planning: An approach to prevention of individual and family stress. *American Journal of Community Psychology, 5*, 447–459.

Mitchell, T. R. (1985). An evaluation of the validity of correlational research conducted in organizations, *Academy of Management Review, 10*, 192–205.

Murrell, A. J., & Mingrone, M. (1994). Correlates of temporal perspective. *Perceptual and Motor Skills, 78*, 1331–1334.

Nuttin, J. R. (1985). *Future time perspective and motivation.* Hillsdale, NJ: Erlbaum.

O'Leary-Kelly, A. M., Martocchio, J. J., & Frink, D. D. (1994). A review of the influence of group goals on group performance. *Academy of Management Journal, 37*, 1285–1301.

Pearlson, H. B., & Raynor, J. O. (1982). Motivational analysis of the future plans of college men: Imagery used to describe future plans and goals. In J. O. Raynor & E. E. Entin (Eds.), *Motivation, career striving, and aging.* New York: Hemisphere Publishing Corporation.

Pinder, C. C. (1984). *Work Motivation.* Glenview, IL: Scott Foresman.

Raynor, J. O., Atkinson, J. W., & Brown, M. (1974). Subjective aspects of achievement motivation immediately before an examination. In J. W. Atkinson & J. O. Raynor (Eds.), *Motivation and achievement.* Washington, DC: Winston & Sons.

Roos, P., & Albers, R. (1965). Performance of alcoholics and normals on a measure of temporal orientation. *Journal of Clinical Psychology, 21*, 34–36.

Ross, J., & Staw, B. M. (1986). Expo 1986: An escalation prototype. *Administrative Science Quarterly, 32*, 274–297.

Ross, J., & Staw, B. M. (1993). Organizational escalation and exit: The case of the Shoreham nuclear power plant. *Academy of Management Journal, 36*, 701–732.

Schwab, D. P. (1980). Construct validity in organizational behavior. In L. L. Cummings & B. Staw (Eds.), *Research in organizational behavior* (Vol. 2). Greenwich, CT: JAI Press.

Seijts, G. H., & Latham, G. P. (1995, June 15–17). *The effects of proximal and distant goals on a complex task.* Paper presented at the annual meeting of the Canadian Psychological Association, Charlottetown, Prince Edward Island, Canada.

Smart, R. G. (1968). Future time perspective in alcoholics and social drinkers. *Journal of Abnormal and Social Psychology, 73*, 81–83.

Sorrentino, R. M., & Short, J. A. C. (1986). Uncertainty orientation, motivation, and cognition. In R. M. Sorrentino & T. E. Higgins (Eds.), *Handbook of motivation and cognition: Foundations of social behavior.* New York: Guilford Press.

Staw, B. M., & Hoang, H. (1995). Sunk costs in the NBA: Why draft order affects playing time and survival in professional basketball. *Administrative Science Quarterly, 40*, 474–494.

Stein, K. B., & Craik, K. H. (1965). Relationship between motoric and ideational activity preference and time perspective in neurotics and schizophrenics. *Journal of Consulting Psychology, 29*, 460–467.

Stein, K. B., Sarbin, T. R., & Kulik, J. A. (1968). Future time perspective: Its relation to the socialization process and the delinquent role. *Journal of Consulting and Clinical Psychology, 32*, 257–264.

Stewart, R. A. C., & Ahmed, S. M. S. (1984). Factor analysis of the Stewart personality inventory research form and its correlates with some other personality instruments. *Social Behavior and Personality, 12,* 143–151.

Strathman, A., Gleicher, F., Boninger, D. S., & Edwards, C. S. (1994). The consideration of future consequences: Weighing immediate and distant outcomes of behavior. *Journal of Personality and Social Psychology, 66,* 742–752.

Strumpf, N. E. (1987). Probing the temporal world of the elderly. *International Journal of Nursing Studies, 24,* 201–214.

Sundberg, N. O., Poole, M. E., & Tyler, L. E. (1983). Adolescents' expectations of future events: A cross-cultural study of Australians, Americans, and Indians. *International Journal of Psychology, 18,* 415–417.

Suto, M., & Frank, G. (1994). Future time perspective and daily occupations of persons with chronic schizophrenia in a board and care home. *American Journal of Occupational Therapy, 48,* 7–18.

Trommsdorff, G. (1983). Future orientation and socialization. *International Journal of Psychology, 18,* 381–406.

Volder, M. M. de (1979). Time orientation: A review. *Psychologica Belgica, 19,* 61–79.

Volder, M. M. de, & Lens, W. (1982). Academic achievement and future time perspective as a cognitive-motivational concept. *Journal of Personality and Social Psychology, 42,* 566–571.

Wallace, M. (1956). Future time perspective in schizophrenia. *Journal of Abnormal and Social Psychology, 52,* 240–245.

Weick, K. E. (1984). Small wins: Redefining the scale of social problems. *American Psychologist, 39,* 40–49.

Weiss, H. M., & Adler, S. (1984). Personality and organizational behavior. In B. M. Staw & L. L. Cummings (Eds.), *Research in organizational behavior* (Vol. 6). Greenwich, CT: JAI Press.

Wood, R. E., & Bandura, A. (1989). The impact of conceptions of ability on self-regulatory mechanisms and complex decision-making. *Journal of Personality and Social Psychology, 56,* 407–415.

Wood, R. E., Mento, A. J., & Locke, E. A. (1987). Task complexity as a moderator of goal effects: A meta-analysis. *Journal of Applied Psychology, 72,* 416–425.

Article Review Form at end of book.

WiseGuide Wrap-Up

As we have seen in this section, motivation can be considered a hot topic in industrial/organizational psychology. A variety of theories explain the construct and a number of corresponding interventions. The common theme is that all define *motivation* by including energy, direction, and persistence. They differ in explanation and application, because they contain different components. Also, the motivational strategies an organization chooses to use must be congruent with the overall ortgeist (spirit of the place). Not all organizations can or should follow the Starbucks example; each needs to develop systems that are appropriate for the organization and its workers.

R.E.A.L. Sites

This list provides a print preview of typical **Coursewise** R.E.A.L. sites. (There are over 100 such sites at the **Courselinks**™ site.) The danger in printing URLs is that web sites can change overnight. As we went to press, these sites were functional using the URLs provided. If you come across one that isn't, please let us know via email to: webmaster@coursewise.com. Use your Passport to access the most current list of R.E.A.L. sites at the **Courselinks** site.

Site name: The Economic Press: Motivation and Inspiration
URL: http://www.epinc.com/MOTIV/MOTIVATE.HTM
Why is it R.E.A.L.? This site contains techniques, strategies, publications, and products concerning motivation.
Key topic: motivation
Try this: Click on the Techniques and Strategies link to see some ideas about how to motivate yourself and employees.

Site name: Towards a Better Future: The Works of Manfred Davidmann
URL: http://www.solbaram.org/
Why is it R.E.A.L.? England's Manfred Davidmann examines the science of management around the world.
Key topic: motivation
Try this: To read his papers on motivation, simply click on the Motivation link.

Site name: How to Motivate Employees without Using Money!
URL: http://www.employer-employee.com/motivat.htm
Why is it R.E.A.L.? This is a commercial site offering some statistics and suggestions about employee motivation.
Key topic: motivation
Try this: As you read this section, click on the links to answer the questions.

Site name: Nelson Motivation, Inc.
URL: http://www.nelson-motivation.com/
Why is it R.E.A.L.? Author and business consultant Bob Nelson reviews some of his ideas about business motivation.
Key topic: motivation
Try this: Click on the Resources link, then articles by Bob Nelson to read some of his ideas on motivating employees.

section 8

Satisfaction and Attitudes

Learning Objectives

- To understand the complex relationship between job satisfaction and performance.

- To understand the relationship between job satisfaction and other performance areas, including absenteeism and turnover.

- To appreciate why organizations would want to monitor and increase job satisfaction.

- To discuss several strategies for improving employee job satisfaction.

WiseGuide Intro

People who like their jobs (have high job satisfaction) work harder and are more productive than those who do not. Most people would probably agree with this statement. Some would say it is obvious. Others would say that this represents another example that psychological research simply supports common sense. Still others would say the statement is inaccurate.

The assumption behind this statement is that job satisfaction is correlated with job performance. As you may have heard from other sources, we must be very careful in interpreting correlations, because correlation does not imply causation. For example, imagine that research in this area reports a strong positive correlation (let's say +0.90 or above) between job satisfaction and performance (the higher the satisfaction, the higher the performance). Would this evidence be compelling enough for organizations to invest time and money to improve worker job satisfaction (a directional prediction: increasing satisfaction increases productivity)? If workers are more satisfied, will they be more productive and lead the company toward more profitability, or are there other possible interpretations of these data? For example, is it equally likely that high-performing workers receive more rewards and therefore like their jobs more (another directional prediction: increasing performance increases satisfaction)? The idea is that, if you want to be satisfied with your job, be a good performer. Or there could be a third (*intervening*) variable affecting both performance and job satisfaction. For example, maybe people who come from a happy, secure, loving home environment like their jobs (because they are generally happy) and perform well, because they are secure and confident in themselves. Thus, to create a happy and productive workforce, we should focus on developing healthy homes for our employees. Even with strong correlations, the interpretation of the data can be extremely complex.

Reading 38 suggests that the important component in job satisfaction is how we live, not just how we work. We should not completely divorce our work from our outside lives; these two aspects of how we spend our time form an intricate, interrelated bond. Newman suggests that organizations should look to sabbaticals and flexible work schedules to revitalize and energize the workplace. (Individuals may be happier and more productive when they are on the job less but work more.) This argument assumes that there is a strong relationship between job satisfaction and performance. The research, however, is not even clear about the strength of this relationship. In a review of 217 research articles on job satisfaction and performance, Iaffaldano and Muchinsky (1985) found that the average correlation was +0.146. This finding directly challenges the idea that job satisfaction and performance are directly related. However, it does not suggest that job satisfaction or other work attitudes are unimportant. Although job satisfaction may not be a direct link to performance, it may be an important component in a more complex system. For example, job satisfaction seems to play an important role in absenteeism and turnover. In Reading 39, Bernstein states that organizations need to consider job satisfaction for temporary workers, as well as for full-time employees.

Particularly in good economic times or when specific worker skills are in demand, employees have the freedom to change jobs. One of the most frequently cited reasons for leaving a position is job dissatisfaction, not salary level, as some would believe, although pay may fit in with the complex definition of *job satisfaction*. If organizations want to retain workers in order to keep their skills or to avoid the costly expense of selection, they must address such issues as morale and satisfaction. How can they do that? Readings 40 and 41 discuss several techniques for building community and increasing employee satisfaction.

Just as with motivation (discussed in the previous section), there are many techniques and strategies that organizations can use to increase job satisfaction. As you visit some of the **Courselinks**™ sites, you will see several consulting organizations which address this issue.

Iaffaldano, M. T., and Muchinsky, P. M. (1985). Job satisfaction and job performance: A meta-analysis. *Psychological Bulletin* 97, 251–273.

Questions

Reading 38. What is job satisfaction? Discuss problems in interpreting correlation data. Provide examples to illustrate directional predictions and intervening variables. What does the following statement suggest: "The right kind of work—as opposed to jobs—gives people more energy instead of draining it"? What are the implications for organizations?

Reading 39. According to Bernstein, why should organizations be concerned with job satisfaction levels for temporary workers?

Reading 40. What are some general themes that make companies well-loved?

Reading 41. Define the term *community*. What are some costs and benefits for organizations trying to foster a sense of community in the workplace? Why is it important to identify common values to create community? Provide some examples of common values.

What is job satisfaction? Discuss problems in interpreting correlation data. Provide examples to illustrate directional predictions and intervening variables. What does the following statement suggest: "The right kind of work—as opposed to jobs—gives people more energy instead of draining it"? What are the implications for organizations?

A Philosopher's Dream of Making Work Fun

Peter C. Newman

As more and more jobs disappear along with the companies that once provided them, the idea of being employed by a large organization suddenly seems risky, if not obsolete. The alternative—working at home for yourself—is an attractive choice for those who can master the prevailing technologies.

But the majority of Canada's three million-plus unemployed and underemployed fit neither category, and it's that group that finds itself not knowing where to turn, or how to help itself. Now, an Austrian-born American philosophy professor named Frithjof Bergmann has come up with a practical notion of how to reduce our reliance on the overly politicized concept of jobs and extend and inspire our biological need to work.

"People have become so desperate that they're even willing to listen to a philosopher," he quips, his accent a mixture of Sigmund Freud and Brooklyn twang. Bergmann opened his Center for New Work in Flint, Mich., where he did most of his research in the early 1980s, after he began helping General Motors deal with the thousands of laid-off workers from 1981 to 1986. He now runs the Center for New Work in nearby Ann Arbor, and his timely gospel has spread to Wolfen, East Germany, where Bergmann is advising Gos, a large film manufacturing company, on the most humane way to displace 15,000 workers so that they will be able to keep some part-time employment and also have time to pursue a "calling" of their choice. And in Canada, he is working with inner-city youth in downtown Vancouver, where his progressive ideas are being implemented on an experimental basis.

Bergmann resembles a mad scientist in a Mel Brooks movie who has discovered electricity, but can't quite master it. But the intensity of his discourse somehow discharges through his theatrical mannerisms. "The job system is just that: a system—we invented it, we can change it," he told me during a recent Vancouver interview. "With wisdom and foresight, we can fashion from the historic disintegration of the jobs culture a more cheerful, humane, vigorous and hopeful approach that will combine material abundance with human fulfillment. For more than two centuries, The Job has been a kind of tyrant that has reduced human beings, curtailed their potential, exhausted and discouraged them. Now, thanks to advancing technology, we stand on the threshold of being liberated from that tyranny and, instead of fearing it, we should be dancing in the streets and celebrating."

That's easier said than done, but Bergmann advocates a revolutionary new approach that reaches far beyond the standard work-sharing and work-extending remedies. He believes that what ultimately counts is how we live, not how we work. He advocates periodical sabbaticals tied to specific plans for personal and professional growth. These intermissions throughout workers' careers would be tied to both the prevailing job market and the stage of each individual's development and financed through direct corporate contributions, taxes, and quasi-public foundations.

At GM in Flint 15 years ago, his innovative idea of allowing some of the laid-off workers to be put on a six months on, six months off schedule, receiving nine months' pay a year—was accepted by the company on an experimental basis. Most of the men and women who went on these paid sabbaticals started up small businesses, returned to school or grew their own vegetables. "Given the chance," the professor concludes, "people work hard and happily at things they deeply, passionately want to do. The right kind of work—as opposed to jobs—gives people more energy, instead of draining it."

Bergmann is convinced that his new approach is the wave of the

"A Philosopher's Dream of Making Work Fun," by Peter C. Newman, *Maclean's,* Vol. 109, October 7, 1996, p. 56. Reprinted by permission of *Maclean's.*

future. He sees workers and employers co-operating in mutually beneficial pursuits. The bosses will be free to use cost-saving, productivity-boosting automation techniques to their maximum. In return, they will agree to parcel out the remaining jobs on a rotating basis and encourage, and sometimes help finance, their employees to follow meaningful activities of their own choosing.

Interestingly, this would be a return to some of Henry Ford's initiatives when he first invented the mass production line to build his Model-T cars in 1913. During some of the next decade's down sales cycles, the workers he temporarily laid off were offered free farm lands to help feed themselves. Whenever he needed them again, Ford had a trained workforce at his disposal. (Bergmann's urban version is having people plant roof gardens and other self-sufficiency activities.).

The New Work approach doesn't fit all problem areas, but whatever its shortcomings, Bergmann is convinced that the alternatives are much worse. "If we don't make some fundamental adjustments in the work scene," he predicts, "the prospect is for an increasingly wealthy elite oppressing a growing, embittered mass of impoverished workers fighting like dogs over fewer, increasingly unrewarding jobs. We face the prospect of a rapid increase in violence that could easily escalate into some apocalyptic confrontation between the rich and poor. Fortunately, the corporate world has come to see it cannot go on like this. If they lay everybody off, they'll lose their own markets. There won't be anyone left to sell to."

Bergmann freely admits that his scheme for a new, enlightened work ethic will come true only gradually, with people slowly opening themselves up on a million different fronts to being liberated from their "job servitude." His line in the sand is simple and persuasive. The only sure way to make the job market even worse is not to try your damnedest to improve it.

Article Review Form at end of book.

According to Bernstein, why should organizations be concerned with job satisfaction levels for temporary workers?

We Want You to Stay. Really

With labor tight, employers are starting to do more to keep workers

Aaron Bernstein
In Washington

Last year, Harry Cedarbaum was caught in a classic baby-boomer crunch. His parents, who live in Europe, developed health problems and needed help closing the family business. But Cedarbaum, a father of three with a demanding job as a management consultant at Booz, Allen & Hamilton Inc. in New York, simply had no time to help. So he signed up for a job-rotation plan Booz Allen had recently started, and in August, he was assigned to a stint as a recruiter at Columbia University, his alma mater. That has allowed Cedarbaum, 38, to work fewer hours and squeeze in trips to Europe to help his parents. "I get several headhunter calls a week, but I made a commitment to the firm, and they made a commitment to me," says a grateful Cedarbaum. "This loyalty is an incredible thing."

Winning such loyalty is exactly why Booz Allen started the rotation program and other initiatives to help employees cope with a consultant's grueling schedule. With unemployment at a 25-year low and salaries rising in related fields such as banking, all consulting firms are having a tough time hanging on to people. So Booz is hustling to cultivate employee loyalty and retain valuable talent, says Joni Bessler, vice-president for human resources for the company's 2,000-employee commercial consulting business. Quips Bessler: "We'd also like to put chains on the door."

No Bond

Booz Allen is among hundreds of U.S. companies undergoing a sea change in relations between employer and employee. For most of the 1990s, downsizing set the tone for the modern employment contract. As companies frantically restructured to cope with slipping market share or heightened competition, they tore up old notions of paternalism. Don't expect to spend your life at one company anymore, they told employees. You're responsible for your own career, so get all the skills you can and prepare to change jobs, employers, even industries. As for the implicit bond of loyalty that might have existed before—well, forget it, said employers. It's an unaffordable luxury in these days of fierce global competition.

After several years of tight labor markets, though, business is rediscovering the value of corporate loyalty. It's retooled this time—no one is even pretending to offer lifelong employment. But with turnover rates running at a 10-year high of 1.1% a month, executives are trying to send a new message to employees: Don't leave. We need you. Work for us—you can build a career here. Employers are going to great lengths to persuade employees that they want them to stay for years.

The new notion of loyalty is more arms-length than the old 30-years-and-a-watch mentality. It's more like a mutual commitment between employer and employee. "The company is responsible for providing the environment in which people can achieve their full potential, and employees are responsible for developing their skills," says Raymond V. Gilmartin, CEO of Merck & Co. "That's the key to our ability to 'attract and retain talent, and it defines the new employment relationship as I see it today."

Shift Strategy

Employers are trying all sorts of strategies to cement this new relationship. They're revamping rigid pay systems to make it easier for employees to move laterally to enhance their skills. Others even seek the loyalty of that archetypal footloose employee of the 1990s, the temp. And instead of just dumping excess workers when they downsize, some companies are moving skilled employees around in response to market shifts. Raytheon Co., which is slashing thousands of defense jobs, hopes to redeploy many engineers to its booming commercial units.

Companies also are installing new career-development programs to help employees plan their next moves up the ladder. The goal, says Carol Roberts, vice-president for people development at International Paper Co., is to let employees know that IP cares about their long-term future. "If a rival company is going to have that discussion with our employees, we better be willing to have it, too," she says.

Reprinted from the June 22, 1998 issue of *Business Week* by special permission, copyright © 1998 by The McGraw-Hill Companies, Inc.

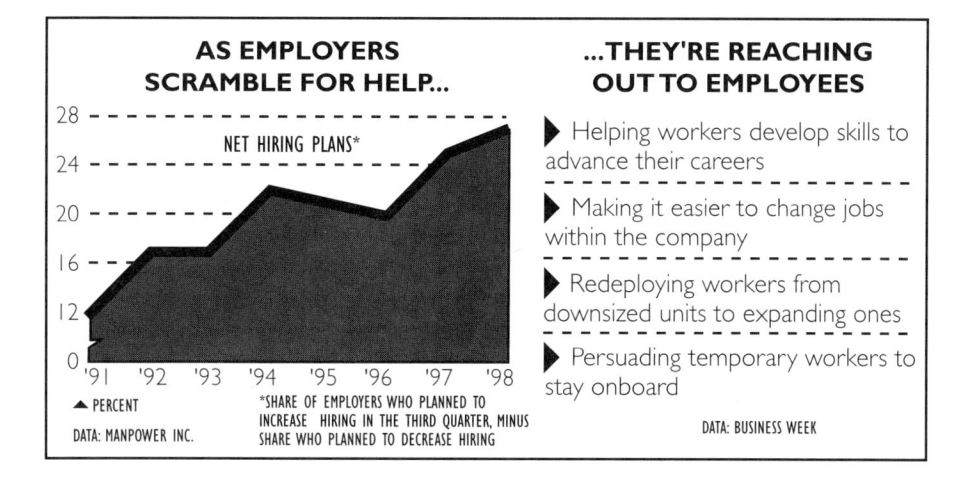

AS EMPLOYERS SCRAMBLE FOR HELP...

NET HIRING PLANS*

'91 '92 '93 '94 '95 '96 '97 '98

▲ PERCENT
*SHARE OF EMPLOYERS WHO PLANNED TO INCREASE HIRING IN THE THIRD QUARTER, MINUS SHARE WHO PLANNED TO DECREASE HIRING
DATA: MANPOWER INC.

...THEY'RE REACHING OUT TO EMPLOYEES

▶ Helping workers develop skills to advance their careers

▶ Making it easier to change jobs within the company

▶ Redeploying workers from downsized units to expanding ones

▶ Persuading temporary workers to stay onboard

DATA: BUSINESS WEEK

Companies may not be moving fast enough, though, to counter deep skepticism among employees who fear employers will toss them out with the next shift in corporate strategy. Indeed, more employees have negative views of their companies today, according to annual surveys of 450,000 employees, mostly at large companies, by Chicago-based International Survey Research Corp. (ISR). Wages finally are beating inflation, according to the Bureau of Labor Statistics, but they have barely made up ground lost over the decade. So when employees see companies raking in record profits, the decent raise they finally got seems inadequate, says ISR CEO John R. Stanek.

Continual restructurings, even in boom times, sap morale. And layoff announcements—and the fear they generate among employees—have abated only slightly in recent years. So employees figure that the company luring them with the promise of a bright career still may dump them down the road. Worse, top executives think they're doing a better job of dealing with employees than in the early 1990s, even as employees' views of them deteriorate, ISR's surveys show (charts, page 200).

Quality Dive

The danger for Corporate America is that the disconnect may sap productivity. If employees feel left behind by today's flush times, they may be less willing to put in the extra effort needed to keep customers happy, say execs and experts. "Employers can't let employees' anger fester, or it hurts your quality," says Kaiser Permanente CEO David M. Lawrence. The healthcare turmoil of recent years has generated tremendous anger among his 100,000 employees, he says. Kaiser is trying to cope by creating new career opportunities and forming partnerships with unions. "But it's not getting better yet," says Lawrence. "We see these efforts as a 10-year investment to turn around employee attitudes."

Companies still haven't been able to overcome deep skepticism among employees, who fear they'll be tossed out with the next shift in strategy.

Corporate efforts to nurture loyalty focus mostly on professionals, whose skills are most in demand. Many employers are dusting off long-ago-shelved training and career-development programs, hoping to reassure skittish employees about their futures. Citibank, for instance, restructured throughout the 1990s and announced 9,000 additional job cuts last fall. But even before its recent merger with Travelers Group Inc. was announced, Citi expected its net employment to grow beyond today's 90,000, says Human Resources Senior Vice-President Marcela Perez De Alonso. Partly to offset anxiety, Citi set up a formal career-development program for 10,000 managers. Twice a year, they're reviewed to see what their next step should be, given what jobs are open. Up to 3,000 managers move in a typical year. "We want to make people feel that they have a long-term career with us," says Perez.

Such efforts often require fundamental shifts in how career decisions are made. Instead of simply allowing managers to decide when to promote their staff, human-resource departments are trying to set up formal procedures to make sure valued employees get attention. Last year, International Paper rolled out a new program for its 13,000 white-collar workers. Managers must sit down with employees every year, says Roberts, and discuss their career desires, separate from the annual performance review. Last year, about half of IP's managers followed the new plan, and CEO John T. Dillon wants the rest to follow suit this year.

Opportunity Knocks

If all this sounds vague and fuzzy, just ask Gerry Miovski how much difference long-term growth prospects make. Miovski, an architect in his late 20s, was promoted rapidly to head of commercial business development for the Northeast in the New Jersey office of Kagima, a huge Japanese contractor with many U.S. contracts. With commercial real estate booming, headhunters called all the time, but Miovski was happy in his job. Then, last fall, he got a call from HLW International, a large New York architectural firm setting up a new commercial-design unit. Miovski agreed to become the unit's business-development director, at no salary increase, because of the chance it offered to build an organization from the ground up. "The decision to move was more about where I'll be five or 10 years from now," says Miovski.

Companies also are trying to open opportunities for employees to broaden their skills. Last year, after a test run in Atlanta, Marriott International Inc. began expanding a new program to lump its 14,500 managers into four broad salary bands. Instead of assigning every job a grade level with a narrow salary range, managers now have wide latitude to get more pay or experience without a formal grade increase. The bands allow managers to seek broader opportunities across Marriott's 10 hotel chains.

Loren M. Nalewanski is reaping the benefits. He recently moved from general manager at a low-end Fairfield Inns in Peoria to human-resources director for a high-end Marriott Resorts hotel at Chicago's O'Hare airport. "I couldn't even have applied for the job under the old system, because this job was three salary grades higher than the old one," says Nalewanski. Adds Steve Bauman, Marriott's head of career management: "The point is to attract and retain people by providing a broader vision for career opportunities."

Employers are trying to make their cultures more employee-friendly, too. Like Booz Allen, they're putting more emphasis than ever on programs to balance work and family life and create more flexible workdays. Some also are training execs to be less hierarchical. Last year, Merck set up a leadership program to teach managers to "balance getting results with how people are treated on the job," says Howard Levine, the company's vice-president for employment issues. Managers' bonuses are now linked to their leadership ability as well as the performance they deliver. And execs use "360-degree" reviews, in which underlings, peers, and bosses assess them anonymously.

CEO Gilmartin set the tone by doing a 360 himself last fall. He used an outside firm to collect and summarize opinions about him from the dozen people on his management committee as well as from Merck's board of directors. "You learn your strengths and where you need to improve," says Gilmartin.

Tight labor markets are even changing the way employers approach restructurings. Layoff announcements in the first five months are running 26% above the same period last year, according to Challenger, Gray & Christmas Inc., a Chicago outplacement firm. But with today's job shortages, some companies try to retain employees who would have been cast aside before.

In January, defense-electronics giant Raytheon said it planned to slice 8,700 jobs, or 10% of its workforce, to consolidate recent acquisitions of Hughes Aircraft Co. and the military business of Texas Instruments Inc. In the process, the Lexington (Mass.) company is cutting the jobs of 2,700 engineers, mostly in defense. Meanwhile, Raytheon's commercial side, which makes everything from aircraft parts to power plants, is booming. Those units need to hire as many as 5,000 engineers this year alone, officials say. The matchup of skills and slots isn't always exact, but Raytheon is doing all it can to redeploy engineers whose jobs are being cut. The company expects virtually all 2,700 to receive at least one job offer from another Raytheon unit.

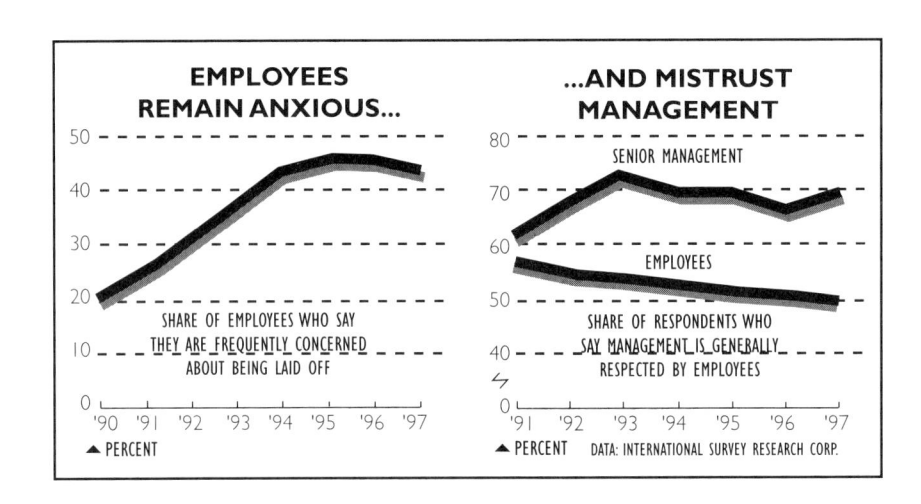

Temp Ties

Some employers are even bidding for the loyalty of contingent workers. Most large companies routinely use temporary-help agencies to fill jobs they don't want to make into permanent posts. But nowadays, companies must hustle just to keep their temps from jumping ship. Xerox Corp. employs 80 phone operators in the Denver suburb of Englewood to provide dispatching services for its repair technicians. Xerox subcontracts to Olsten Corp., a temp agency, for 60 of the operators, who work side by side with Xerox employees. They earn about one-third less, mostly because of fewer benefits, says site manager Steven M. Orton.

But unemployment in Denver, where many companies have call centers, is running at 2% or less. To reduce turnover, Orton has had to jack up hourly pay rates several times, and he also tries hard to make the Olsten workers feel like they're Xerox employees. The two groups have company picnics together, work in teams, and "are called special-assignment representatives, not temps," says Orton. Last year, Xerox began paying a $300 bonus to Olsten workers who rejoin Xerox. Orton started the bonus after Xerox lawyers advised him that temps employed for more than 18 months might be considered permanent Xerox employees. To avoid a legal problem, Olsten agreed to find other temp jobs for the Xerox staff every 18 months. But once operators left for elsewhere, some didn't come back.

To build loyalty and entice more back, Orton now pays every returnee $100 a month for up to three months (which is how long the lawyers say temps have to be off the payroll). They also get a bigger title, a better desk, and a sweatshirt that says: "I'm back." Says Orton: "You can't just treat temps as temps anymore, or you'll lose them. We tell people we want them to work here for years." His approach seems to be working. "MCI called me for an interview the other day, but I probably won't leave here," says Ray Van Allen, an Olsten worker who left Xerox for a three-month stint at U S West inc. last fall and is now back at the Englewood center.

If employers are so eager to please employees, why do surveys show rising negative attitudes? One reason is the uncertainty that remains even as the economy booms, say human-resource experts. Some workers will still lose their jobs at Citi and Raytheon, for example, despite the companies' effort. And Xerox is mulling whether to shrink or close the Englewood unit in a few years, Orton says. Employees are quick to pick up on the mixed messages.

Employees are also smarting at cost-cutting efforts, which continue at many companies. Even as Boeing hustled to hire 1,000 engineers in the past year, it is also cutting benefits. Execs said in March that they will put nonunion employees on a common benefits plan after last year's merger with McDonnell Douglas Corp. The problem is, say officials of the Seattle Professional Engineering Employees Assn. (SPEEA), that Boeing decided to use MD's inferior benefits as the benchmark. SPEEA represents 20,000 Boeing engineers who fear the company will demand that they adopt the new plan, too. Boeing denies that the new plan reduces benefits. SPEEA, which has held protest rallies, says such cost-cutting tactics explain why Boeing employee surveys show slipping morale in recent years.

Employers' traditional response to labor shortfalls is to buy employee loyalty with fatter paychecks and job-security promises. But today's no-price-hikes economy forces companies to find new ways to balance labor needs and cost pressures. The question executives now face is how far they may have to go to win over workers who remain scarred by the turmoil of the past decade.

Article Review Form at end of book.

What are some general themes that make companies well-loved?

What Makes Companies Well-Loved?

Ann Perle

Ann Perle is the director of human resources for Leica, GPS; Torrance, California; and the founder of Pathways Spiritual Foundation, Newport Beach, California.

Abstract

Employees agree that companies with inspiring leadership, sense of purpose and great facilities are ideal organizations to work for. Human resources managers play a central role in instituting these corporate traits that endear organizations to their employees. Dallas, TX-based Mary Kay Inc. demonstrates inspiring leadership by empowering its employees and recognizing good performance. Medtronic Inc. of Minneapolis, MN, gives employees a sense of purpose by allowing them to enhance and improve people's health and lives. The company sponsors a holiday party every December where patients, their families and physicians gather to share to Medtronic employees and officials how their health improved. Northern Telecom Ltd., on the other hand, created a work environment that enabled employees to reach their full productivity potential.

A few months ago, *Fortune* featured its inaugural The 100 Best Companies to Work For in America. The list was based on more than 20,000 questionnaires filled out by employees at 238 companies. Authors Milton Moskowitz and Robert Levering, who have been tracking the most-favored companies since 1981, compiled the *Fortune* list. What intrigued me was a companion piece entitled "Why Employees Love These Companies" by Ronald Lieber. It described the three key corporate traits employees identify as qualities that make their companies so great. These traits are: Inspiring Leadership, Sense of Purpose and Knockout Facilities. In contemplating how HR could directly benefit from this information, the following questions arose: How well does your company perform in these areas? And, in carrying that thought further and deeper, how do you measure and assess yourself and your HR department?

To illustrate this human resources perspective, *Workforce* interviewed two HR executives who work for companies that appeared on the *Fortune* list and that are known for inspirational leadership and sense of purpose (Mary Kay Inc. and Medtronic Inc.). The third interview focused on knockout facilities and was conducted with Northern Telecom Ltd. (Nortel).

Inspiring Leadership

Riz Chand, senior vice president of HR and administration at Dallas-based Mary Kay Inc. (No. 82 on *Fortune*'s list) spoke about his company's inspiring leadership. The company, he explained, was founded essentially on the principle of empowerment. According to legend, Mary Kay Ash was pushed to the sidelines by her male superiors in the 1950s. Undaunted, she quit her job as a saleswoman and went on to build a sales organization that today boasts 475,000 women who sell her products. The company's human resources department comprises 47 employees. One of the best examples of inspired leadership is the company's CEO, who first joined the company as the senior vice president of human resources before rising to her current executive position.

Chand says that HR also inspires leadership by frequently recognizing employees' good work and deeds. For example, at Mary Kay Inc., employees convene periodically at a central location where individuals are publicly recognized for their good deeds. "One security employee was driving home one evening and noticed a sales rep's car on the side of the road. He stopped, took her back to the office, went back to her car, changed the tire and got the leaking one repaired. Then, he went back to the office, picked her up and drove the coworker home." Going that extra mile, he says, exemplifies the notion of leading by inspiration.

Another example of how HR inspires leadership is Chand's commitment to review any case of an employee forced to leave the company. If he and the CEO can turn an employee around, they'll try to place him or her in a different job before considering termination.

"What Makes Companies Well-Loved?" by Ann Perle, copyright April 1998. Used with permission of ACC Communications Inc./*Workforce*, Costa Mesa, CA. All rights reserved.

Handwritten notes of praise also go a long way in inspiring employees to keep up the good work, he says.

Sense of Purpose

Janet Fiola is senior vice president of human resources at Medtronic Inc. (No. 47 on the *Fortune* list), a medical products company based in Minneapolis. Every December, her company sponsors a holiday party where patients, their families and doctors are flown in to tell their survival stories. Improving human health gives Medtronic's employees a deep sense of purpose, says Fiola. "We enhance and improve people's lives." That mission, she adds, was articulated by the company's founder 40 years ago in a statement called "Toward Full Life."

How this quality translates into human resources, she says, is that her department consciously tries to attract candidates who have a strong sense of purpose or value system aligned with the company's mission. It begins in the interview process. And all of the company's recruitment material is geared to attract those believing in full life and good health.

HR staff reinforce the company's mission in several ways—at employee orientations and week-long leadership courses for the company's vice presidents and directors. And how do they measure HR's impact? They conduct a biennial employee-attitude survey called "Global Voices" in which employees answer questions pertaining to job satisfaction. "In the last survey, 94 percent of employees said they understood the company's mission," says Fiola.

Knockout Facilities

Inspiration and purpose are clearly the foundation upon which employees chart their course. But working at a cool facility can't hurt.

At Northern Telecom Ltd.'s Brampton Center in Brampton, Ontario, the senior vice president of HR worked with the chief architect and planner to move 3,000 employees from office towers into a single-floor retrofitted factory. "We took an old manufacturing facility (one million square feet) and turned it into corporate headquarters," says Rosemary McCarney, vice president of employee value research and strategy. "There are no elevators. It feels like a city, so there's lots of opportunity to bump into people and have quick meetings over coffee."

In the past, Nortel's employees were compartmentalized by floors. But with a team-based philosophy, the physical environment had to be an enabler of the process. "A great workplace should honor the workforce and create conditions for full potential performance," she says.

According to an article that appeared in *Business Week* last year, Nortel turned to Houston's Hellmuth, Obata & Kassabaum (HOK) to transform the factory into a horizontal 50-story office building. HOK analysts studied how the work units functioned—the levels and kinds of interaction, mobility, travel and tools used by employees. Today, there are "neighborhoods" for different operations connected by designated boulevards, streets and alleys marked by color-coded signs and banners.

McCarney admits being a disbeliever early on. She couldn't envision how several thousand employees could work on one floor and not become discontented. "I was wrong. The facility is fantastic and

---

Do You Have Purpose?

Bringing meaning to our work, and inspiring others to find meaning, starts with solitude and contemplation. We find it from the inside out. We sense that there's something unique and special that we can contribute and that the kind of work we do should relate to these contributions.

Take a moment to assess your consciousness about purpose. What are the signs in your work that indicate "Yes, my work is on purpose?" What are the signs that indicate "No, my work isn't as joyful and fulfilling as I might wish?" Think of this questionnaire as you would think of taking a periodic physical examination:

- Do I wake up most Mondays feeling energized to go to work?
- Do I have deep energy—feel a personal calling—for my work?
- Am I clear about how I measure my success as a person?
- Do I use my gifts to add real value to people's lives?
- Do I work with people who honor the values I value?
- Can I speak my truth in my work?
- Am I experiencing true joy in my work?
- Am I making a living doing what I most love to do?
- Can I speak my purpose in one clear sentence?
- Do I go to sleep most nights feeling "this was a well-lived day"?

Total "Yes" Responses _____

Check either "yes" or "no" according to how you feel about each question today. The total number of yes responses to the questionnaire provides a general idea of your power of purpose at work. If you have many "yes" responses, you're obviously intent on making a difference through your work. You probably have a sense of purpose or direction, but you might consider further clarifying your gifts, passions and values.

Source: Excerpt from "The Power of Purpose—Creating Meaning In Your Life and Work," by Richard J. Leider. Published by Berrett-Koehler Publishers Inc., San Francisco, 1997. Reprinted with permission of the publisher. From *The Power of Purpose*, copyright © 1997 by Richard J. Leider, Berrett-Koehler Publishers, Inc., San Francisco, CA. All rights reserved. 1–800–929–2929.

there's a strong sense of team mixed with high industry—all at once."

And how about you? After looking at one's HR department, the next step is to look within oneself, which is where the deepest level of understanding can be developed. Ask yourself: Do I inspire me? Am I willing to be inspired? Have I developed a sense of passion around my work that engulfs me so others want to be around me and to follow my lead? After all, the true key to one's happiness and security is understanding oneself. If you're willing to review your company, HR department and your own actions and beliefs, perhaps the *Fortune* article will inspire you to become the best you can be. It's nice to know it's all within your power to make it so.

Article Review Form at end of book.

Define the term *community*. What are some costs and benefits for organizations trying to foster a sense of community in the workplace? Why is it important to identify common values to create community? Provide some examples of common values.

The Search for Community in the Workplace

Thomas H. Naylor, William H. Willimon, and Rolf Osterberg

Duke University professors Thomas H. Naylor and William H. Willimon and Swedish businessman Rolf Osterberg are coauthors of The Search for Meaning in the Workplace *(Nashville: Abingdon Press, 1996).*

No word appears more often today in the literature on corporate human resources and organizational development than community. Everyone seems to be talking about the possibility and desirability of creating community in the workplace, but few have ever experienced real community or have any clue about how to go about building a community. What is a community? Is it possible to create a community in a private profitmaking business, a government bureaucracy, or a nonprofit school, college, hospital, or charitable organization? How do we know whether a particular business or enterprise is a community or not? How does one go about building community in the workplace?

A community is a partnership of free people committed to the care and nurturing of each other's mind, body, heart, and soul through participatory means. Despite all of the hype about community in the workplace, the gap between managers, who may also be the owners of a business, and the employees is often so great as to preclude the possibility of community. Confrontational labor-management relations do little to establish the kind of trust required to build community in the workplace.

However, in spite of our skepticism about the practical possibilities of achieving community in the workplace, we believe that community is an important goal for those seeking meaning there. About community building in the workplace, M. Scott Peck once said, "If Utopia is to emerge, it will do so primarily from the world of business." Not unlike the search for meaning, community building is a slow and arduous process. Many are the obstacles to community—unabashed individuals, narcissism, authoritarianism, excessive inequality, distrust, alienation, competing interests, dependency, and size. Few have succeeded at it, but the potential rewards in the workplace are substantial. Community is about cooperation, sharing, commitment, communication, trust, justice, empowerment, adaptability, and tension reduction—values acclaimed by many but achieved by few.

We now turn our attention to 10 defining characteristics of community building in the workplace:

1. Shared vision—commitment to a shared vision of the future;

2. Common values—identification of common values and objectives;

3. Boundaries—definition of the community's boundaries;

4. Empowerment—creation of a system of governance and a community decision-making process which empowers all community members;

5. Responsibility sharing—implementation of a communitywide responsibility sharing system;

6. Growth and development—formulation of strategies for spiritual, intellectual, and emotional growth and development as well as physiological well-being;

7. Tension reduction—development of a conflict resolution mechanism to reduce tension among community members and between the community and those outside community boundaries;

8. Education—provision of members with education and training on community values, decision making, governance, responsibility, growth and development, and tension reduction;

9. Feedback—implementation of an adaptive feedback control system which monitors community performance against objectives and adjusts community strategies accordingly; and

10. Friendship—creation of an environment which encourages friendships to develop among managers, among employees, and between employees and managers.

Among the examples we shall consider to illustrate the characteristics of community are small Vermont towns and Rhino Foods. Rhino Foods is a small specialty frozen dessert, ice cream novelty, and ice cream ingredient manufacturer located in Burlington, Vermont, whose 60 employees enjoy a strong sense of community. Rhino promotes a so-called "dual bottom line" of profitability and social responsibility and has received national attention for its innovative employee exchange program—Rhino's alternative to market-driven employee layoffs.

1. Shared Vision

Perhaps the single most important element in a real community is a commitment by its members to a shared vision of the future. There must be a consensus among members on the answer to the question, What does the community want to be when it grows up? It may be one thing for Tom Chappell, founder and CEO of the natural toothpaste company Tom's of Maine, to say "We believe our company can be financially successful while behaving in a socially responsible and environmentally sensitive manner," but it is quite another thing for the hundred or so employees of the company to be committed to the same vision of the future.

The failure to reach agreement on the group's mission has led to the demise of many a would-be community. If management's vision of the future is grounded entirely on profits, stock options, executive bonuses, and special privileges, then community is impossible to achieve with a group of employees in search of job security, higher wages, and increased fringe benefits. Management and labor do not even speak the same language. The most clever organizational development consultant could not create community in such a divisive, zero-sum (my gain is your loss) environment. Community is about cooperation, not the achievement of mutually incompatible, unachievable wish lists.

In the words of Ted Castle, president and founder of Rhino Foods, "Community is never easy. It has to come from the heart. We struggle with it constantly—we live and breathe community."

At Rhino the employees are organized in teams that play work-based games for which there are prizes and awards for "winning." Successes and team victories are always "celebrated."

2. Common Values

Shared common values are another important characteristic of community. In workplace communities employees and managers alike view themselves as parts of an integrated whole pursuing a common mission which is consistent with their own personal values. If there is nothing more to the business or the organization than each individual looking out only for his or her self-interest, then community will never be.

Cooperation, trust, and human empathy are among the shared values which are vital to the formation and survival of communities. But the integration of such values into the workplace may be a slow and arduous process. Swiss and Austrian Alpine villages which embrace these values did not become communities overnight. Rather, they have evolved over hundreds of years. Many small New England towns and villages which are committed to individualism, hard work, resourcefulness, versatility, and inventiveness are more than 200 years old. Places such as Middlebury, Brattleboro, and Woodstock in Vermont and New London, New Hampshire, possess many of the characteristics we associate with real communities.

We are skeptical of organizational development consultants and "I'm okay, you're okay" spiritual swamis who claim they can lead groups of 30 to 60 people into community through weekend community-building workshops. We believe that the results of such attempts at instant community building are more likely to be pseudocommunity—pretend community—rather than enduring community. There are no shortcuts to community. We all say we want community, but do we want to risk the time and energy that community requires? Are we prepared to pay the price in terms of our cherished individualism necessary to sustain community?

The typical New England town has a town hall, a school, a church, a post office, a general store or two, a country inn, and possibly a country fair or a summer festival. More often than not, the school, the church, and the traditional town meeting provide the spiritual glue which holds the community together. Where is the spiritual glue which binds a workplace community? Is it money, job security, the workplace environment, personal relationships, or the work itself?

Jerry Greenfield, cofounder of Ben & Jerry's Homemade, Inc., created a new employee committee known as the Joy Gang reflecting Greenfield's philosophy: "If it's not fun, why do it?" The Joy Gang meets periodically to come up with innovative ways to instill more joy into the workplace at Ben & Jerry's. The Joy Gang has been responsible for introducing a stereo system to provide rock music for production workers, a company song, costume contests, frequent employee celebrations, lunch-hour cookouts, and periodic visits of a masseuse to provide free massages.

3. Boundaries

In every community there is an ongoing tension between the group's need for exclusivity on the one hand and the desire for inclusiveness on the other hand. Just as a village with no entry restrictions soon becomes a town and a town without real estate zoning laws evolves into a sprawling metropolis, so too may a small business evolve into a large company and eventually become an unmanageable behemoth such as General Motors or IBM—neither of which is likely to be viewed as a community. A workplace without boundaries will not remain a community very long.

At Rhino Foods, Ted Castle feels that team membership should not be cost-free—easy come, easy go. Associated with participation on a team should be responsibility sharing and well-defined performance expectations. Teams, too, require limits and boundaries.

Kirkpatrick Sale, in his book *Human Scale,* has compiled considerable evidence to suggest that sheer size alone is a very important determinant of the long-term viability of a human community. Sale believes there is a size limit beyond which a community should not be allowed to grow if it is to survive. Indeed, it is hard to imagine a workplace community consisting of more than a few hundred employees. Obviously, it is much easier to control the growth of a privately owned business rather than that of a large publicly held enterprise.

Exclusivity is particularly important during the early stages of development of a community to assure commitment to shared vision, values, and objectives. Rapid organizational growth is incompatible with a stable, enduring workplace community. Mature communities often impose boundaries to limit community growth while simultaneously helping nonmembers organize similar communities.

One of the reasons the state of Vermont with its 250 or so small towns works so well is that it is tiny—not unlike Austria, Denmark, Finland, Norway, Sweden, and Switzerland. With only 58,000 inhabitants, most of whom live either in the countryside or in small towns, Vermont is ranked 49th among the 50 states in population—one fiftieth the size of California.

Some organizations create artificial barriers to community based on race, religion, or national origin. Others use titles and labels to separate the management class from the working class: manager/employee, nonunion/union, exempt/nonexempt, and salaried/hourly. Boundaries of this type are hardly conducive to community building.

Whether or not a workplace community survives may depend on how it balances its mutually contradictory dual needs for exclusivity and inclusiveness. One without the other will surely result in failure.

4. Empowerment

Perhaps the most troublesome attribute of a workplace community is empowerment—the right of each employee to share equally the ability to influence and shape the direction of the organization. Every community member is a leader.

Unfortunately, many corporate managers are into having—owning, manipulating, and controlling money, power, people, and things. In response to their insatiable psychological need to be in control, those who are into having often exhibit behavioral patterns which are aggressive, competitive, and antagonistic. To have someone is to take charge of that person—to control him or her. Those in the having mode are afraid of losing what they have to someone else.

Power sharing may be very threatening to corporate managers, union leaders, and leaders of organizations aspiring to become workplace communities. For an organization to have the possibility of becoming a true community, its leaders must be prepared to risk the total loss of control. This is a higher price than most corporate executives are prepared to pay. This also gets to the crux of why there are precious few workplace communities. As former Soviet Union leader Mikhail S. Gorbachev learned the hard way, power sharing is very risky business.

When its principal business, chocolate chip cookie dough, took an unexpected dip in 1993, Ted Castle turned to the employees at Rhino Foods with the question, "Which do you prefer—layoffs, reduced hours and reduced pay, or temporary job sharing with another firm?" They opted for job sharing. The approach of Rhino's management was that this was the employees' issue and that they should play a major role in deciding what should be done in response to the temporary crisis.

Some company CEOs naively believe that community can be mandated by executive fiat. Community cannot be ordered from above. Top-down community-building initiatives are perceived by employees as deceptive attempts by management to manipulate them. The primary reason that Soviet-style communism failed was that it tried unsuccessfully to impose community on the Soviet people against their will. That affirmation action has met such strong resistance in the United States is hardly surprising as it represents an overt attempt by the U.S. government to impose community in the workplace.

Workplace communities must also be grounded on a foundation of equality and justice. We are not suggesting that all community members must think and act alike. Honest differences of opinion can energize the community and provide a source of creative tension. Members need not have the same level of income or wealth either. But there cannot be huge disparities among members with regard to the fundamental criteria on which the community is based whether they be economic, professional, craftsmanship, artistic talent, or technical proficiency. A workplace community will not flourish if it is dominated by a handful of people possessing a disproportionate amount of power and influence.

For those who choose to avail themselves of the opportunity, New England town meetings are a form of community power sharing. Unfortunately, attendance at Vermont town meetings has been on the wane in recent years, thus providing increased power to a disproportionate few.

5. Responsibility Sharing

The flip side of power sharing in the workplace is responsibility sharing. Community members should be prepared to share the responsibility and accountability for achieving the community's goals and objectives. Responsibility sharing implies a very strong commitment to workplace cooperation, participation, and team building. The group takes on more importance than the individual manager or employee in workplace communities.

The very essence of our free enterprise capitalistic system involves promoting the virtues of individualism—often subordinating the interests of the community to those of the individual. The Japanese, on the other hand, take a quite different view of the relationship between the individual and the community. In Japanese companies, for example, the interests of the CEO are subordinated to those of the employees and the customers. The well-being of the group or the community always takes precedence over individual self-interest.

Several years ago, after the crash of a Nippon Air Lines Boeing 747 which killed several hundred passengers, the CEO of Nippon took personal responsibility for the crash, apologized to the families of those who had been killed, and resigned. One could not even conceive of the possibility of such an act of contrition on the part of the president of an American airline under similar circumstances. In a typical airline crash in America, the airline, the aircraft manufacturer, the pilots, and the FAA each point the finger of blame at someone other than themselves.

Rhino Foods has an employees' "wants program." Employees help each other get what each wants through responsibility sharing. Both the employees and the company benefit from the results.

6. Growth and Development

The primary purpose of a company—its meaning—is to serve as an arena or vehicle for the personal and human development of those who are working in the company. The production of goods and services and the profit which results from the work are byproducts of the process, not ends unto themselves. Because none of us live by bread alone, a viable workplace community must embrace strategies for spiritual, intellectual, and emotional growth and development as well as physiological well-being.

Alienation and distrust are obviously major obstacles to community in the workplace. Competing interests among members can also lead to a breakdown of community. If the real agenda of members is increased personal power and prosperity rather than the well-being of the community, the group will not remain a community for very long. Sustaining the interest and commitment of members, when they are constantly bombarded by external stimuli provided by politicians, the media, peers, and the like, is a formidable challenge to any community.

Excessive psychological dependency on the group leader or guru can also precipitate the premature death of a community. To launch a workplace community often requires a charismatic leader. When members become so attached to the leader that they cannot let go—community degenerates into cult of personality.

7. Tension Reduction

Two other interrelated features of communities are adaptability and conflict resolution. An enduring workplace community might be able to adapt to a rapidly changing economic, social, and political environment. Individual community members must be consulted before any significant changes are made in business policies or strategies. However, when policy changes do occur, they often benefit from consultation with the entire group rather than being based on the shoot-from-the-hip macho opinion of an isolated, traditional autocratic leader. Community decision making is deliberate and time consuming but it allows members to process critical factors affecting the business in a carefully thought-out manner.

Just as communities must adapt to environmental changes, so too must they resolve their own internal conflicts as well as with those outside the community. Each workplace community needs some sort of conflict resolution mechanism to reduce tension when internal disputes arise among individual community members as well as when disputes occur with those outside of the workplace—customers, investors, suppliers, competitors, and government. In all too many American companies, management has consistently taken an adversarial stance against competitors, government, and employees—particularly employees belonging to a labor union. And labor leaders have engaged in similar behavior themselves. There is no place for this type of destructive thinking in a workplace community. A zero-sum mindset soon gives way to a "win-win" approach to problem solving and conflict resolution.

8. Education

Notwithstanding the many virtues of community, life in a workplace community is not without blemishes. Although a small factory or a workplace may be homogeneous and close-knit, it may also be parochial, conservative, resistant to change, and suspicious of outsiders. There is often a low tolerance for nonconformity and opinions which differ from the community norm. Invasion of privacy and nosiness are not uncommon in workplace communities. Rarely are envy, greed, and competitiveness absent from such groups. Even though one may work in a community, one may still find oneself detached and estranged from other community members. Such experiences may evoke feelings of "If community life is so great, then why do I feel so bad?"

For all of these reasons, it behooves the community to have an effective education and training program to teach members community values, decision making, governance, responsibility, growth and development, power sharing, and tension reduction.

9. Feedback

Finally, a viable workplace community needs some type of adaptive feedback control system which monitors community performance against objectives and adjusts community strategies accordingly. Community building is very tough business. It requires constant feedback and evaluation. It should come as no surprise that power sharing, responsibility sharing, team building, and participatory management must be continuously sold and resold. In most firms neither labor nor management is accustomed to this type of thinking. Both require considerable training, coaching, and monitoring.

Any business or organization contemplating the creation of a workplace community should be fully aware of the endless perils of workplace democracy. Participatory management is a much more difficult form of management than authoritarian management. If management can get by with it, ordering someone to do something is much easier than trying to have a group of employees reach a consensus on a particular action. The only problem is that well-educated, affluent employees resent being told what to do by anyone. Therein lies the rub.

To add insult to injury, some employees react negatively to their newfound options in the workplace. They simply do not want the additional responsibility. They would rather be told what to do than to get involved in the decision-making process.

10. Friendship

Spiritual guru Thomas Moore, author of *Care of the Soul* and *Soul Mates,* has some cogent advice for those seeking meaningful work. Moore suggests asking a prospective employer, "How easy is it to make friends in your company?"

Community is about personal relationships. The workplace should foster friendship among employees, among managers, and between managers and employees. Rhino Foods' relationship with its employees is "founded upon a climate of mutual trust and respect within an environment for listening and personal expression." It claims that it is a vehicle for its people to become friends and get what they want. Without friendship there can be little joy and little meaning in the workplace.

Under the most ideal circumstances, community building in the workplace is a slow and tedious process. The risk of failure is substantial. But the possible benefits include improved morale, reduced absenteeism, increased productivity, and more meaningful lives for all concerned.

Article Review Form at end of book.

WiseGuide Wrap-Up

As we have seen from the readings in this section and some of the Internet sites, job satisfaction and work attitudes are important to organizations. Industrial psychologists, relying on research, have helped diffuse the "commonsense" assumption that happy workers are productive workers. This simplistic idea has been replaced with the theory that job satisfaction and other work attitudes form a complex relationship with performance and other aspects of people's lives. Although not directly affecting performance, it benefits the organization to increase employee satisfaction in order to reduce turnover and absenteeism for full-, part-time, and even temporary workers.

R.E.A.L. Sites

This list provides a print preview of typical **Coursewise** R.E.A.L. sites. (There are over 100 such sites at the **Courselinks**™ site.) The danger in printing URLs is that web sites can change overnight. As we went to press, these sites were functional using the URLs provided. If you come across one that isn't, please let us know via email to: webmaster@coursewise.com. Use your Passport to access the most current list of R.E.A.L. sites at the **Courselinks** site.

Site name: CCH Business Owner's Toolkit
URL: http://www.toolkit.cch.com/
Why is it R.E.A.L.? CCH is a provider of business and legal information to the general business community. This site includes a wide variety of helpful business tools and documents. Of particular interest for this section is the "Comprehensive Job Satisfaction Survey." This site also contains documents on compensation, selection, termination, safety, and a number of other topics.
Key topics: job satisfaction, compensation, recruitment and hiring, legal policies, termination, worker safety
Try this: Select the Business Tools link; then scroll down to Employee Management to find the "Comprehensive Job Satisfaction Survey."

Site name: Worker Satisfaction, Motivation and Commitment
URL: http://www.oval.lib.oh.us/ce/wkshpdoc/worker/index.htm
Why is it R.E.A.L.? This is an Internet slide show on job satisfaction and motivation. It provides an overview of the area and suggestions for motivating staff and increasing job satisfaction.
Key topics: job satisfaction, motivation
Try this: Start the slide show.

Site name: The Personality, Job Satisfaction and Turnover Intentions of African-American Male and Female Accountants
URL: http://les.man.ac.uk/cpa96/txt/glover.txt
Why is it R.E.A.L.? This site summarizes a series of studies examining job satisfaction and turnover for African American accountants. These results suggests that African American accountants are less satisfied with their job than are people of other ethnic groups. The site offers some suggestions for addressing this problem.
Key topics: job satisfaction

section 9

Leadership

Learning Objectives

- To understand the concept of leadership.
- To discuss the relationship between leadership and values.
- To appreciate the challenges facing leaders in an increasingly diverse work environment.
- To describe the intellectual procedure for training leaders.

WiseGuide Intro

On a visit to any bookstore, you will find a plethoroa of books on leadership, ranging from case histories of great leaders to practical rules anyone can use to become a great leader. Just for fun, visit an Internet book seller, such as Amazon.com (www.amazon.com) or Barnes & Noble (www.barnesandnoble.com) and do a book search on the subject of leadership. On a recent visit to Amazon.com, I found 3,805 titles directly related to leadership, including

Dubrin, A.J. (1997). *10 Minute Guide to Effective Leadership (10 Minute Guides).* Macmillan.

Hayward, S.F. (1998). *Churchill on Leadership: Executive Success in the Face of Adversity.* Prima.

Kaltman, A. (1988). *Cigars, Whiskey & Winning: Leadership Lessons from Ulysses S. Grant.* Prentice Hall.

Maxwell, J.C. (1988). *The 21 Irrefutable Laws of Leadership: Follow Them and People Will Follow You.* Thomas Nelson.

Pearman, R.R. (1998). *Hardwired Leadership: Unleashing the Power of Personality to Become a New Millennium Leader.* Davies-Black.

Examining these titles and thousands of similar ones, we can conclude that leadership issues engage many people. In business, politics, education, communities, and other groups, we want strong, ethical leaders, but the concept of leadershp raises many questions for psychologists, primarily the very definition of a leader. No single definition of *leadership* has received universal support. Yukl and Van Fleet (1992) state that "leadership has been defined in terms of individual traits, leader behavior, interaction patterns, role relationships, follower perceptions, influence over followers, influence over task goals, and influence on organizational culture" (p. 147). Thus, while we have no clear definition of *leadership,* we agree that it is important.

Just as we have had trouble defining *leadership,* we have had an equally difficult time determining the factors that make a leader effective. Are leaders born, or are they made? Are there some situations in which a particular leader would be effective and other situations in which the same person doing the same things would be ineffective? These are the types of questions with which industrial organizational psychologists wrestle on a regular basis.

However the definition of *leadership* and the determination of the factors that make an effective leader are addressed, formal leader roles in organizations are changing. In Reading 42, Houghton begins addressing leadership by focusing on the changing nature of organizations. As organizations restructure, leadership responsibilities are spread throughout the organization such that we see fewer centralized command and control organizations. However, the expectations for executive leaders are different from those for other organizational leaders; Houghton argues that executive leadership is responsible for setting and maintaining the values, visions, and performance standards for an organization.

Questions

Reading 42. According to Houghton, what are the seven important behaviors for executive leaders? Why are values such an important component of effective leadership?

Reading 43. How does Fraser view the relationship among affirmative action, performance standards, and employment barriers?

Reading 44. Describe the intellectual procedure for developing leaders at West Point. How is this process similar to the scientific method?

In Reading 43, Fraser suggests that understanding and fostering organizational diversity are two of the greatest challenges facing organizational leaders. We need to encourage this diversity, because it is morally and economically the right thing to do. He argues that organizational leaders need to remove employment barriers for all individuals while maintaining professional standards. He likens this to Branch Rickey's integration of professional baseball by hiring Jackie Robinson. He states that this difficult move not only increased the overall quality of the sport, but it also increased its profitability by addressing a new market segment. Overall, developing an organization that truly appreciates and values diversity operates outside the normal business comfort zone but will create the successful organization of tomorrow.

Readings 42 and 43 address the challenges and issues facing organizational leaders, and they offer some suggestions for addressing them. Reading 44 focuses on how we build leaders. McNally, Gerras, and Bullis are faculty members at the U.S. Military Academy at West Point. As they state in the abstract, their job is to teach and train leaders. To accomplish this goal, they present a three-step *intellectual procedure.* As the name suggests, this process is based on inquiry—asking appropriate questions (identification phase), finding relevant information (accounting phase), and taking necessary actions (formulate and apply phase). They argue that an effective leader is a scientist, developing and testing theoretically relevant hypotheses. In this case, the theory represents core organizational goals and values. Thus, leadership is a constantly evolving process.

According to Houghton, what are the seven important behaviors for executive leaders?

Leadership:

Seven Behaviors for Muddling Through

James R. Houghton

James Houghton, Chairman and CEO, Corning Incorporated. Speech delivered to the Senior Leadership/Corporate Transformation Conference, Harriman, New York, April 11, 1996.

Good morning ladies and gentleman. I'm delighted to be here. This meeting is organized around a particularly vital and exciting topic—senior leadership and corporate transformation. I'm going to transpose those topics, however. First, I'll discuss my views on the transformation of corporations. Then, I'll talk about my vision of what it takes to senior leader in today's corporate environment.

As we stand at the door to a new century, it's useful to look back and check the century we're leaving. One hundred years ago, the United States was primarily rural and agrarian. People lived on farms. They worked the fields or toiled in small workshops. Markets were local and the workforce was largely homogenous. Formal education was pretty informal. It usually ended at an early age.

By the start of the 1900s, the Industrial Revolution had changed all that. The body and the soul of America were transformed. Millions of workers and their families migrated to our shores—attracted by opportunity, by jobs. These workers brought a tremendous capacity for work. They helped this country grow great. However, many of them did not know the language; few had any education. These factors—combined with the prevailing psychology of the day—resulted in the creation of large, hierarchical organizations. Workers were consider little more than cogs. Leaders were expected to be commanding and authoritative, armed with all the answers.

But of course, all of that has changed with the advent of the Information Age. In fact, it's my belief that the world's new emphasis on information has caused two major paradigm shifts in the business area.

The first is globalization. Access to information has made national borders meaningless. Meanwhile, this shrinking of the world has increased, by orders of magnitude, the competitive stakes for which we play. No market is protected anymore. Competitive threats appear daily in the form of new technologies and new global contenders. Today, firms in every region of the globe can access any market. They can bring to bear the power of new technologies; of low-paid, highly skilled workers; and large amounts of capital.

How can we respond? With a continuing thrust toward world-class quality. Now a lot of people have written about quality and frankly I wish I could use a different word. People's eyes glaze over when they hear the word *quality*.

You know the story about the Frenchman and the Japanese and the American who were all captured by hijackers. They were asked what they would like as a last wish before they were killed. The Frenchman says, "I want to hear the Marseillaise one more time." The Japanese says, "I would like to make a speech on quality." The American says, "Please shoot me before I have to hear one more speech on quality." So, although we are all veterans of quality, and we're dealing with error rates in the parts per million, I think it is important to keep looking to get more from quality.

Beyond production of perfect products and services, what else can quality give us? Well, I believe quality will allow us to meet customers' needs even before they know they have them. I believe quality will lead to higher levels of employee involvement and training. I believe quality will allow us to fully develop the potential skills and talents of all our employees. There will be no more "check your brains at the door" as you come to work. I love the phrase I heard once, "When you hire a pair of hands, you get a head for free. Use it."

At Corning Incorporated, quality has led to goal sharing and profit sharing. Everybody from senior leaders to the shop floor participates. We've achieved flatter organizations with fewer bosses, more teammates. Our plant in Blacksburg, VA, for example, that has two levels of employment. It has the plant manager and it has teams. It's a very different way of operating.

That leads me to the second paradigm shift occurring in business today. Simply put, in addition to globalization, businesses are facing an unprecedented emphasis on the

"Leadership: Seven Behaviors for Muddling Through," by James R. Houghton, *Vital Speeches of the Day,* July 1, 1996, pp. 571–574. Used by permission.

importance of highly skilled labor. Lester Thurow of MIT has published a book called *Head to Head.* In it, he writes:

> The skills of the workforce are going to be the key competitive weapon in the twenty-first century. Brain power will create new technologies, but skilled labor will be the arms and legs that allow one to employ the new product and process technologies that are being generated. Skilled people become the only sustainable competitive advantage.

Products can be made and shipped from almost anywhere. This can be advantageous for business. However, just as capital and technology flow around the world at lightning speed, conceptual workers—those people who primarily use their heads to get a job done—are mobile and enjoy ever increasing choices as to where they live and work. These conceptual workers are ones who have doctorates in highly specialized fields, or they're talented or trained in marketing, finance, information services, or production management.

At Corning, conceptual workers form a growing percentage of our workforce. For example, in 1972 one-third of our workforce was made up of conceptual workers while two-thirds were people who basically used their hands. Today, that is completely reversed. Two-thirds are conceptual workers and one-third uses mainly physical skills.

Conceptual workers have many opportunities and can sell their skills to the highest bidder, either in money or in the intangibles of the workplace, or both. If we're honest with ourselves, individual businesses need this group of mobile workers more than they need us, so we had better pay attention and prove our worth.

Moreover, if you look at the demographics of the year 2000, it is no surprise that an increasing number of people entering the workforce are going to be women and people of color. To avail ourselves, therefore, of the entire pool of talent out there, we cannot rely only on white males. To attract the best talent we must demonstrate that we really believe in and practice diversity in the workplace.

Now, if you buy the fact that knowledge or skills may be, ultimately, the only competitive advantage, then you must intensify your efforts to truly value "the individual."

Talented individuals will choose a friendly environment where everyone has a chance to succeed to her or his highest potential. Conceptual workers will be drawn to a company that makes them feel appreciated and gives them the independence and flexibility to make decisions at the level where the work is being done. They will not be attracted by hierarchy, but by horizontal structure. They will not be attracted by security, but by the opportunity for personal growth. They wiil not be attracted by homogeneity, but by cultural diversity. Also, they will not be attracted by work alone, but by a perceived balance between work and leisure.

How will traditional businesses need to change in order to keep pace with these challenges? I believe we'll need to adopt a new concept of loyalty and obligation. Companies can no longer guarantee job security—if, in fact, they ever could. What they can and should guarantee is the provision of opportunities for personal and professional growth. In addition, companies must provide the tools by which each individual can attain life-long training, so that his or her skills are constantly upgraded to meet the requirements of the job at hand.

Ultimately, companies should strive to make employees eager to stay, but ready to go. This is a big shift. It moves responsibility from the company to the individual to take advantage of opportunities.

In the *Harvard Business Review,* Chris Bartlett describes it as a shift from "guarantee of employment to commitment to employability." This will not be easy because it flies in the face of the old paternalistic, controlling, "cradle-to-grave" thinking.

We must increasingly think of all employees as professionals. With high performance work teams in both manufacturing and administrative settings, we need to entrust employees with strategic ownership of the business. Without question, this makes for a more inventive company, one that is able to respond to the requirements of a diverse global clientele. Even investors are beginning to appreciate that a company's real investment today is no longer in machines, but in the knowledge of the worker.

Workers today—whether they are equipped with "conceptual" or "physical" skills—must be capable of thinking for themselves. They must be able to make critical decisions about their customers and their immediate work environment. They must possess "transferable" skills and be able to apply knowledge gained in one situation to very different situations. All of this behooves us to make life-long training of each and every employee a priority—and not just for basic skills. The new way of working will require new skills such as empathy and listening. These skills can and must be learned with the same level of priority we put on technical skills.

Perhaps most important, as we turn the corner on the next millennium, companies need to own up to their social obligations and responsibilities to workers. If we ignore this responsibility, it may be taken away.

There is a great euphoria about "market economies" and "globalization." Corporate strategists proclaim the wisdom of comparative advantage, of leanness and meanness. If one can get software development done as well and cheaper in Bangladesh than in Silicon Valley, so be it. If one has to announce a massive layoff as earnings are rising, well, that's good for shareholders—almost always the stock price goes up with such an announcement. However, that kind of game cannot go on forever. Society will not stand for it.

I am all for bolstering the economy of India or China, or wherever—but we cannot forever neglect or ignore our own infrastructure, or our own people. If we take a totally free market view, over time our political institutions will inject themselves into the process, more than they already have—and that would be the worst outcome imaginable.

Already there are questions being raised in this country about why the real income of average Americans is shrinking when corporate earnings, the stock market, and CEO salaries are all growing. If we in business do not show a sensitivity to this issue, and to the fate of our current workforce—whether it be in France, the U.S., or Japan—then someone is going to make some rules we don't like. Jobs will be protected, borders will be closed, and we'll be back in the

Economic Dark Ages. Thus, companies face the difficult, but necessary, task of balancing the need to be global players and the need to ensure a healthy workforce where we operate.

Regarding a healthy workforce, the sorts of changes I'm talking about invariably are accompanied by stress at every level of the organization. Even though employees will have to take a much more proactive role in their own careers through constant renewal and life-long education, this does not lessen the organization's role. Companies will have to apply resources to deal with stress. Leaders will need to be sensitive and sympathetic, and help their people through it. Companies will also have to show responsiveness to employees' needs outside the workplace. This means ongoing support for work-family balance, for flexibility in dealing with individual needs and concerns, and even for continued financial support of the infrastructure in communities where we operate.

Does this sound soft? Too humanistic and liberal? Believe me, it is not. Valuing the individual and a continuing focus on people is a hard-nosed strategy that leads to a competitive advantage and long-term shareholder value.

So far, I hope most of what I've said has elicited a nod of recognition and the thought, "That's right. That's how it is." Now let's take a look at ourselves, as leaders, and see how well equipped we are to manage these new organizations we're creating.

We have traditionally viewed leaders as "heroes" who come forward in a time of crisis to resolve a problem. If we are lucky, we get a Cincinnatus or a Washington, who uses power wisely and lays it down when the job is done. If we are unlucky, we get a Hitler, a Stalin or a Mao. In between are those who can lead only through hierarchical rigidity.

By focusing on the leader as hero, we stress the short term, and we assume the powerlessness of those being led. We also ignore the many other positive examples of leadership history has to offer.

What if we look at leaders like Pericles and Lincoln, Pope John XXIII and Gandhi, Corozon Aquino and Mother Theresa, Hesburgh and Conant, Watson and Sloan? What do these people have in common? What can we learn from their leadership model? I think I can boil it down to seven leadership behaviors. Of course my original list was a lot longer, but we humans can't seem to remember lists of more than seven things, so I've made it easier on myself and on you by categorizing. Let me go through each behavior.

The first one is an adaptation of justice Learned Hand's wonderful description of liberty. He said, "The spirit of liberty is that spirit which is not too sure it is right." I would say that the spirit of true leadership is the spirit that is not too sure it is right—all the time. I like the ring of that because I believe leaders who are not sure they are right are leaders who listen.

History tells us that those in positions of leadership who do not listen, fail. Being a good listener is no guarantee of success, but I believe lack of this characteristic is a fatal flaw. Not being too sure you are right all the time also frees you to take risks, and to take the heat gracefully when things go wrong—as they inevitably will sometimes when you're dealing with ambiguous situations.

In fact, it's important to understand that compromise and "muddling through" are acceptable as long as your basic values and goals are not compromised. As a leader, you need to model this behavior, and become a catalyst for change, a champion of new ideas, a supporter of unconventional thinking. When you don't have to be right all the time, you can also teach your people to ask for help when needed and shamelessly accept it. You can also encourage them to ask, "What needs to be accomplished here?" rather than "Who's in charge?"

That brings us to the second critical leadership behavior: Be a team player—and pay attention to the bench. Of course there is an inherent paradox in being a leader in a non-hierarchical organization. While your relationships with others must be as egalitarian as possible, you'll also be held to higher standards than anyone else.

As you establish the values, create the vision and set the standards for performance. You'll be judged not by your talk, but by your walk. So you better put the best interests of the company and its people above yourself. Sure, I grew up in an age where protection of turf was the bottom line. I know that's a hard habit to break. But turf wars only divert your resources from the real war zone: the marketplace. So, as a leader, you have to demonstrate that personal success comes only from group success.

You also have to keep an eye on the future and develop strong subordinates for succession. Any winning team has a bunch of strong players waiting on the bench. So watch for people smarter than you—these may be your future leaders—coach them, mentor them. Take chances, especially with young people. You can often get uncommon results from common people, but only if you believe that developing people is one of the most important jobs you have.

If you really want to be successful in this ambiguous world we live in, you'll develop this third critical leadership behavior in yourself. Namely—balance deliberation with action.

Yes, you have to be a strategic thinker. Yes, you have to use your intelligence and experience to make good judgments. Yes, you have to think always of the vision and communicate it in a way that people will understand. But in addition to conceptualizing, deliberating, and communicating, you must be swift to action.

Hold yourself and others accountable for great performance over time. Concentrate on high impact opportunities and be oriented at all times towards achievement. Demonstrate your beliefs through your actions. In a word, commit.

Okay. So far I've told you that as a good leader, you must not be too sure you are right all the time. You must be a team player and pay attention to your bench. You must balance deliberation with action. What else makes a good leader?

Filtering everything through a broad-minded widely experienced world view.

This fourth leadership behavior accounts for the fact that you don't see too many 20-somethings running large corporations. It takes time to rack up experience in both line and staff positions, to gain exposure to various disciplines, to develop an appreciation of different cultures, and to be comfortable traveling and working in the "global village."

These are all prerequisites for leading a multifaceted, global enterprise. How else will you gain international experience to apply to business dealings? How else will you practice true diversity as a real competitive advantage? How else will you develop the skills it takes to manage alliances, joint ventures, trading partnerships and all the other forms that business relationships take these days?

In fact, these days there is one dimension of society and business that Cincinnatus and Washington and Lincoln never had to deal with. That is, of course, technology. To be a leader today, you better make technology your friend. That's the fifth leadership behavior we need to cultivate, because whoever "obsoletes the existing," wins.

How do you "obsolete the existing"? You understand and know how to deploy technology. You believe in innovation as a way of life, and you think big. But you also don't innovate for innovation's sake. You make the critical linkage between technology and the marketplace, and you use technology to become the low cost producer.

Because ultimately, you have to adopt the sixth leadership behavior, and that is: Don't forget the bottom line. Be financially adept.

Develop good analytical skills, get comfortable using basic financial tools; understand financial markets; and use economic data and trends to your advantage. But in addition to seeing the big picture from 10,000 feet up, you also need to be able to zero in on the details. Counting your pennies is a good place to start. You'll have to be comfortable with P&L and balance sheet management.

Now, what did I leave for last? What's the final advice I have for anyone interested in being a great leader? It's this: Leave your office once in a while.

Sure, hard work never killed anyone, but why take a chance? Create a balanced, healthy lifestyle. Take care of your physical condition. Pick up a hobby or two. Of course, if it makes you feel better, you can always tell yourself that these other interests give you new perspectives to apply at work.

Also, don't forget the community. Be a good corporate citizen. Contribute your time and your money to some worthy cause. Share your management expertise with a educational or cultural institution. If nothing else, they usually appreciate you more than your business associates. You might even consider running for elective office.

Finally, learn to laugh at life's quirks, and especially at yourself. Be always an optimist, especially in the darkest hour. And show your appreciation, especially for any luck that comes your way.

So what can we conclude about all this. For one thing, as good leaders we should not be too sure it's right. Or maybe we should not be too sure that, even if it is right, that it will stay that way.

Leaders, especially in transformed organizations of the future, will undoubtedly require other behaviors we haven't even considered yet. It's at times like these that I realize how important corporate values are. The leadership behaviors I've suggested or any future behaviors, should always be tested against your corporate values.

I'm fond of saying that our values are the buoys in an everchanging sea of commerce. If you value quality, if you value the individual, and if you value performance, I believe you'll be able to achieve the great feats of leadership that I've been able to achieve. In other words you'll muddle through somehow.

Article Review Form at end of book.

How does Fraser view the relationship among affirmative action, performance standards, and employment barriers?

The Slight Edge:
Valuing and Managing Diversity

George Fraser

Address delivered to The Commonwealth Club of California, San Francisco, California, December 12, 1997.

Good evening and thank you so much for taking some time to be here, and inviting me to speak. Yes I'm Black, in case you were not entirely sure. In fact, that is the beauty of our race, we come in all shapes and sizes, skin tones and hair textures; lots of options. It's important for you to understand my ethnicity because I will be speaking to you out of my cultural paradigm.

Congratulation to our awardees tonight. . . excellence defined.

In the text of my talk tonight, I promise you three things:

- I promise you what Elizabeth Taylor promised her 8 husbands—that is, I will not be keeping you long.

- Second, I will address several questions, they are: what are the new models for transformational leadership today and why they are important? How does one find value in human differences when for years those differences have been overlooked, stereotyped and devalued? What are successful organizations doing to truly value diversity and then manage it effectively as an edge in a globally competitive marketplace?

- Third, I promise you I will leave time for questions. You noticed I said I will address several questions, not provide answers! I'm too old and much wiser than that.

I come at these complex and delicate issues from the perspective of a trend tracker, a watcher of people and events, a ferocious reader and a world traveler (350,000 miles per year, over 100 different cities).

To that end, I am simply reporting to you and giving you my opinion. It is based on what I have observed from my vantage point. The answers lie within your own souls, hearts and minds.

Perhaps something I might say today may shed a little light or add a shade or two of coloring to your ideas. If I do, let me know, if I don't, I hope you enjoyed your meal.

Let me start with what I see as the driving forces shaping new leadership in the workplace.

As I see it, global telecommunications, corporate restructuring and this extraordinary change that we are going through, have repealed every traditional law of leadership and management.

A new generation of men and women are longing to create a fresh approach to leadership that is as radical, and as productive as the technological revolution that we have experienced in the last few years.

What is the new model of leadership all about? I don't think we quite know yet. It is a shifting mosaic that is changing everyday, and there is a powerful lineup of social, political and economic forces that are systematically shattering these traditional notions of leadership.

Patricia Aburdene, co-author with John Nesbitt of several important books including *MegaTrends*, has done a lot of good thinking and writing on these trends. She and a number of think-tank groups have spoken on and published a number of excellent papers articulating several trends that give us a sense of these forces.

I've added to these new trends my own trends, my own analysis, interpretation and observations:

Simply stated they are:

1. Technology has smashed the corporate pyramid thus freeing companies to shift from hierarchies to networks. Technology has linked and liberated everyone in the organization and is now channeling power and information from the system to the individual.

Megatrends' prediction of "those with the best information first, wins" was correct. Except technology has now made the possibility of winning available to everyone.

2. The end of the superpower conflict further discredits the military myths of leadership that was already weakened by the advent and shift in technology.

So long as the U.S. and Russia had military weapons pointed at each other and were ready to use them, most people envisioned the leader (even if only subconsciously) as a military leader. Now all over the world the leadership model is

"The Slight Edge: Valuing and Managing Diversity," by George Fraser, *Vital Speeches of the Day*, February 1, 1998, v. 64, n. 8 (delivered to the Commonwealth Club of California. San Francisco, CA. December 12, 1997). Used by permission.

shifting from "command and control" to the "inspire and communicate" model of leadership; and that now changes everything.

3. Entrepreneurship has been a powerful trend for change. In a good year Americans create one-million new businesses. Entrepreneurs operate (by definition) outside the traditional corporate model. They import innovative and streamlined models of organizational structure in business. This influences mainstream business.

Women start new businesses at twice the rate of men. Women of color start new businesses at 3X the rate of the market overall.

Women-owned businesses as of today employ 35% more people than the Fortune 500. It is expected that will continue until women employ twice as many as the Fortune 500.

The reason for this could be that women were not raised by the traditional military model, or by some of the sports metaphors of leadership; they have brought their own approach to leadership into their businesses.

Judith Posner a professor at the University of California at Irvine, studied 400 male and female executives, and the women that she studied tended to be more open and share more information with the people they worked with. They felt the most important job of leadership is to get people excited about their work and to enhance their sense of self and self-worth.

4. Demographics of the baby boom is changing everything. But the last crust of the old power structure is still stubbornly hanging on. It is a very thin crust, but it's there.

In a recent survey of 75 CEOs of Fortune 500 companies, 95% of these CEOs had wives who stayed home, not one of these CEOs had ever placed their child in daycare, and 87% of these CEOs never experienced a family hardship.

As many now see it, when we think of this thin crust, the leadership gap between a 50-year-old baby boomer and a 60-year-old CEO is about 30 years. So don't give up 10 minutes before the miracle; the baby boomers are coming and so is retirement.

New types of leaders are coming, women entrepreneurs, people of color, techno-wizards and generation Xers, all have come of age and are determined to reject the worn-out language of military management models and metaphors with their implicit message of force and violence. Not necessarily violence in the workplace, but the threat of unemployment at the very least.

The new challenge is to explore new metaphors of leadership, to shift away from the military notions, move more to ideas like creativity, inclusiveness, healing, and morality.

Yes the workplace will be more spiritually-centered. This spiritual movement will be challenged by cynics.

Yes, Dilbert will have a lot of fun with these concepts, but a more spiritual, ethical and moral workplace will prevail over time, just as America is moving toward spirituality.

5. Downsizing has hurt a lot of people; God willing, those people will recover. From my perspective the system will not. If there is a silver lining in all of that painful downsizing, it is that this is the "coup de gras" for "command and control" leadership. Why? Because there are not that many people to boss around anymore. After the layoff mania, whole chunks of the organization chart was AWOL.

But the survivors of downsizing, powered by the internet and e-mail, grew more autonomous, more self-starting, they managed themselves, now everyone is a leader, at least potentially.

The hidden cost of downsizing is that flat organizations crush autocracies and authoritarian tendencies, inviting corporate pioneers to exercise power in fresh new ways. That is an opportunity for all of us.

"An explosion of change has robbed the system of a good deal of power."

Megatrends

6. Changing demographics of the workplace. The Workforce 2000 study published several years ago tells us very clearly that the makeup of America's workforce is dramatically changing.

More women and people of color are entering one of the greatest workforces in the history of the world.

Today, so called minorities represent 25% of the workforce; by the year 2000, they will be 34% and by year 2004 only 57% of people who enter America's workforce are going to be native-born White Americans.

That means the economic future of the children of White Americans will increasingly depend on the talents of non-White Americans. This is not ideology. This is demographics and basic economics; it's also called self-interest!

This will also have a dramatic impact on retail buying decisions, vendor pools, hiring practices, the legal system and corporate culture. In other words, the very fabric of this great nation will be tried and tested.

For example:

In a recent *USA Today* poll over 40% of African Americans polled stated that "Black employment" was an important factor in their buying decision!

Therefore my question to you is . . . does your vendor and hiring practices look like America? If not, it should begin to.

We cannot survive into the twenty-first century as a healthy, vibrant, growing economy if we have 30% of our people with high skills, 40% with low skills and 30% with no skills. We can't do it!

New leaders and managers know that providing opportunity to everyone is not only morally right, it's good business . . . because whenever you are negatively impacting a person's ability to compete, to earn a living, to find meaning, and purpose in their life and/or to feed their family, you are in for a fight.

We've seen this at Texaco, Avis, Dennys, and many more. Within the last 12 months they have paid out nearly 1/2 billion dollars in discrimination suits. Said another way, it is now a bottom-line issue and leaders will be held accountable. Because if you believe you are your brothers keeper, you've got to walk your talk. You can't say one thing and do another!

The trend of changing demographics in the workplace is clear, our choice must be to make this change constructive, not destructive.

To that end, I would like to focus for a few minutes on what an entire industry did to value, then manage diversity to make a quantum leap.

It started with one person. Fifty years ago a visionary and transformational leader named Branch Rickey thought it was time to integrate team sports in America. There were economic and moral reasons driving his decision but none the less Jackie Robinson was selected to break the color barrier.

He was selected because of his skills, character and temperament. Branch Rickey saw the real value of Jackie Robinson's talent to his team and the appeal he would have in attracting large crowds of Black baseball fans to his ballpark! He was right on both counts. It was a painful process but very successful.

That soon led to other sports teams breaking the color barrier. It wasn't easy for anyone, but it was an important start . . . 50 years ago!

Now, 50 years later, having managed diversity and having leveraged the dynamics of a changing marketplace, all the major sports teams in America have increased their business twenty fold, and the new creativity brought to the culture of the game has made baseball, basketball and football far more exciting.

Look what's happening to golf and tennis now that women are involved. Even greater interest will be generated in golf now that Tiger Woods is a professional. It was recently estimated, that after just one year in pro-golf, Tiger brought in $653 million to the PGA Tour, which has pushed up revenues 18%.

What we have learned from this example is that when people are given equal opportunity to grow, and contribute their talents, they can and they do, but it requires a change in attitude and culture.

But for a moment could you imagine if team sports in America had maintained its hard-core racial line or set a quota of only 10% minorities on each team?

We would certainly be watching second-rate sports in America and the industry would not have experienced the incredible growth that it did.

Isn't it silly to have not valued America's greatest strength: its diversity?

So why are whole industries (i.e., oil companies) and companies still not doing it? The reason is because it won't destroy the company today or impact their bottom line right now, therefore valuing diversity is easy not to do. This has proven to be a serious error in judgment, because . . .

As predicted, slowly but surely, the marketplace and workplace are beginning to change. To that end, "newcomers" expect to be treated fairly, if not, they are fighting back, and creating a non-productive workplace steeped in hatred, anger and fear.

If these companies do not correct their course of action, they are destined to become second-rate companies because they were selecting from only part of America's talent great pool.

How then is it possible for a company to be competitive when smart companies are selecting from 100% of America's talent pool?

How is it possible to achieve recruitment or business objectives when disgruntled employees are making a noise loud enough that your customers and shareholders can hear it? No one wins, and it doesn't have to be that way.

The point is, leading edge companies like AT&T and Coke started 20 years ago, valuing and managing a diverse workforce and then, for example, sent African Americans to Africa and the Caribbean to be Presidents of their companies. Each now controls the lion's share of their product category in major global markets.

Recently White employees from these companies who have demonstrated the skills necessary to function effectively within other cultures have also had the opportunity to run these businesses.

Companies like American Express and Kraft General Foods have promoted "home-grown" minorities and women to CEO positions. We know the mind power is there.

Today our workplace, our customers and our suppliers are far more diverse than ever before. You know the statistics.

The role of leadership today is to align themselves with principles that will enable their organizations to truly value America's diversity and then manage it in such a way that it helps to achieve their organizational objectives. When I say valuing diversity I don't mean affirmative action.

Affirmative action puts into place specific goals and objectives in an attempt to include minorities and women. This is important, but there are still many who resent it and certainly place no value in it. They are misinformed and out of touch with a people who had no opportunity for 350 years, but served its country in every war and did its hard and dirty work to see it through its toughest of times.

Blacks only want America to lower barriers, not standards. Did you lower your standards for Colin Powell, Ron Brown, Reginald Lewis, Toni Morrison, Maya Angelou, Alice Walker? All were beneficiaries of affirmative action!

My father, a well-educated Black man from Guyana and England had to drive a New York cab for 30 years, because he could not get a decent opportunity in the public or private sector.

I'm also not talking about understand differences either, which attempts to ensure harmony among the dominant culture of the organization and the different "newcomers" on the belief that improved interpersonal skills will address diversity adequately.

In other words, there are those who may understand culture or gender differences, but for various reasons place no value in it. They, too, are misinformed.

Additionally, I'm not talking about inclusion either because inclusion may mean opportunity but not equal opportunity.

Organizations that include women and minorities, but maintain the culture and systems created by and for the upward mobility of white males, set themselves and the new employees up for failure.

Inclusion often means the person that is different must become like those in the organizational culture, that's assimilation.

Said another way, it requires that "newcomers" suppress their individuality in the interest of fitting in. People today are weary of assimilation.

The most popular analogy is: if elephant built a house for himself and then invited a giraffe to live with him, would the giraffe be comfortable and stay?

The answer is yes, but only if the elephant changed the structure of the house! But if he didn't, after the giraffe bumped his head a few times, got no support, and lived through a few giraffe jokes, he would eventually get frustrated and leave.

This is something that happens quite frequently in the public and private sector.

Managing diversity requires valuing differences first, and then creating structural or cultural changes that empower all members of the workforce to achieve meaning in their work and maximized their full human potential in pursuit of organizational objectives.

Therefore a corporate vision statement for diversity could read: "to confirm the value of diversity within the company by creating an atmosphere that encourages respect for all differences and recognizes our common corporate purpose."

I believe the emphasis in the vision statement is on confirm the value and creating an atmosphere.

That means changing your thinking and the structure; that alone, ladies and gentleman is a steep mountain to climb.

Managing diversity is a process, it requires a long-term commitment to achieve meaningful change. A commitment too many companies either underestimate or are unwilling to make because it brings complexity, some unpredictability, conflict and confusion in the short term.

No change is easy, but the slight edge, the competitive advantage managing diversity can give you in a global marketplace is an important new business tool.

The ability to climb steep mountains using the right tools and a slow but methodical pace will give you the slight edge, not only at work but in life.

Have you ever watched a team climb Mt. Everest, watched the amount of work and preparation that is required first, then the slow zigzag up the side of the mountain, and still only a small percentage ever reach the top, because only the most committed have closed the gap between success and failure; I believe those who get to the top were flexible, intuitive, creative and committed.

To truly value differences and to change one's structure is like climbing a steep mountain; you must be flexible, creative, tolerant and committed, because you must overcome years of stereotypes and programming.

In many cases you must completely change the way you see certain things. We know life change does not start with inspiration, it starts with education.

Educating yourself is an important ingredient.

There are only four ways for you to get this knowledge; please remember them:

1. Studied knowledge

2. Activity knowledge

3. Modeled knowledge

4. Teaching knowledge

I want to spend a few minutes on them.

Let me talk about studied knowledge first.

What I'm referring to is going to lectures and getting specialized training and reading books.

First of all, people in America are not reading. The average American reads only one book per year.

So if you commit to read just one book per month, in 5 years, you will you will have read 60 books and the average American will have only read 5. Who's going to be better prepared for the future and have a slight edge? You will.

Eighty percent of Americans haven't visited a bookstore in the last 5 years. Less than 3% of all Americans own a library card.

So if we are not reading, not going to the library or bookstores, and are not sharing good information through open and honest discussion with each other, where are we getting our information from?

We are getting it from the media, mostly TV. Please help me understand how you can do anything significant with your life based on information from the media?

Forty-eight percent of the stories in *The New York Times* about young people are about violent young people. But are we really to believe that 48% of our kids are violent?

I think that the media's focus on the sensational and the personal peccadillo does not create the space for high-quality dialogue. It profoundly affects the way we view our prospects. It stunts our capacity for racial reconciliation, healing and progress.

Bill Bradley
Restoring Hope: Come West

If you based your beliefs on television programs, you too would believe the two dominant stereotypes of African Americans:

One is the negative image of poverty, crime and drugs, and the other is the stereotypical positive images of singing, dancing, playing football, baseball or basketball.

When in fact, statistics do not support either one. Statistics support the fact that less than 5000 African Americans earn $100,000/year singing, dancing, playing football, baseball, or basketball.

And less than 4% of the African America population is involved in drugs and the criminal justice system in any way! Therefore less than 4% of America's Black population is driving the image of 33.5 million Black people. There's something wrong with the picture, this stereotype!

By the way there are 36 million people in poverty in America: 10 million are Blacks. 26 million non-Blacks, largely Whites.

Poverty is not a Black issue. Forget percentages. In raw numbers Whites have 26 million more. This is a common problem, not a Black problem. Shame on the media!

The media overlooks the fact that 70% of the African American workforce (8 million workers) are in executive, managerial, supervisory, professional specialty, administrative, technical, vocational and business ownership positions; that African Americans represent a $400 billion economy in America, the 10th richest in the world; that African Americans bring to the table of America over 500 billion hours of formal education and professional training, which means our collective intellectual capital base is worth $5 trillion (at $10 per hour) within just the last 30 years alone.

All of these facts are regularly touted and quoted in Black-authored books, magazines and newspapers.

The same could be said for other minorities and women. But we seem to be the only ones writing it and reading it.

When was the last time you read something that a minority or woman wrote telling their side of the story?

If you haven't read anything lately then you are operating based on a philosophy steeped in misinformation and stereotypes.

It would be difficult to find real value in a group if your beliefs are dominated by stereotypes.

In an era of "relationship selling," it would also be difficult for you to bridge the gap with minority customers, all of which now requires sensitivity, trust and problem solving ability.

Intelligent people read, they step outside the stereotypes so often portrayed on television and the front pages of America's newspapers. They seek a deeper and broader understanding of the world around them.

They use this new knowledge to improve themselves and to make greater contributions in the community, at home and at work.

This change will require new paradigms, and that will come in part through new knowledge/programming, which will provide a deeper understanding of the people around you.

Studied knowledge is the first step in that process. No amount of diversity training can equal the "power and elegance of a developed mind." (Dr. Samuel Proctor)

My advice to each of you is to read a few books, magazines and newspapers a year written by Blacks and women.

Take some diversity training each year, and . . . make sure that each activity improves and expands your knowledge about the diverse world we live in.

Most of us are stifled by fear . . . fear is driven only by ignorance. Most people really want to do the right thing, they just don't know what to do.

Is it easy to do? Of course.

Is it easy not to do? Absolutely.

And if you don't do it, will it ruin your life now? No.

But that simple error in judgment, compounded over time, will seriously damage you and America in the long run.

You'll end up a willing participant in the "conspiracy of mediocrity," narrow minded and driven by "isms and blame." That's what's destroying 95% of the people in this country! That's also what destroys companies and organizations.

Activity, modeling and teaching knowledge are also important factors in effecting change in our lives.

Did you know that the quality of your life (work, beliefs, values, education etc.) will tend to be the average of your ten best friends.

Do you know why birds of a feather flock together? Because they're all going in the same direction! They share a common vision; they are modeling and teaching each other.

It's called the law of association, it's a law because it always works.

Let me give you a dramatic example of the power and importance of activity, modeling and teaching knowledge at work.

It is believed by many that the key is overcoming racial hatred and prejudice is education. It is not! Education is very important but it's not the key. The key is close personal friendships.

You see, you as an individual, you cannot solve racism in America; the only thing you can really do is solve it in your own life. So you can read every book written on the subject, but if you don't have a close personal friend that doesn't look like you, you're part of the problem, not part of the solution.

When I say a close personal friend, I mean someone you break bread with occasionally, someone you may even go to church with occasionally. Someone that over time you have built a comfortable, open and honest relationship with, so that when you sit around the table together and talk about the sensitive and tough issues of the day, each will walk away with a better and deeper understanding of each other and their culture.

This will help greatly when each goes back to their respective friends and family and neighborhood and when someone says something "out of line," each person can then honestly respond with remarks and insights that do not reinforce stereotypes or bad feelings thus breaking the chain of ignorance that fuels racism and hatred.

So as trite as this next quote is, it's really true: "I hope that some of your best friends are Black, White, Latino, Asian, women, men etc." You can start right here in the workplace, where we spend a third of our time together.

Here's the point: it is that kind of behavior and friendship that each of us can engage in, then model, and teach our children, and colleagues and friends, and family. If they truly love you and respect you, they too will begin to engage and teach the same kinds of behavior. Then one at a time, over time, little by little, we will fix this insidious problem.

Remember racism is learned and then modeled and taught; it usually begins at home, then is brought into our schools and the workplace, where it has festered and now seriously threatens to erode America's productivity, as well as its moral and spiritual fabric. Don't contribute to it.

Are activity, modeled and teaching knowledge easy to do? Yes, there are good people everywhere.

But it's just as easy not to do because we each believe that we are not guilty of racism.

It is this single error in judgment by each of us, when compounded over time that will prevent America's companies from:

creating better communities and organizations;

moving towards full-utilization of all employees;

improving morale and commitment;

competing more effectively globally, and thus . . .

increasing market share and shareholder value.

With or without diversity training, we must each take personal responsibility for modeling, not just talking diversity, it is in the best interest of ourselves, our company and our country.

We can change America one relationship at a time!

It is not someone else's job; it's your job! Take it personally, it's your slight edge. The final point I would like to make is that . . .

The reality of modern business is that power is shifting and in many cases has already shifted from the system to the individual. Who you are as an individual really matters today, if you know how to find and derive the power from within yourself and bring it into your organization, your community.

Each person has to stand out today, but how can you stand out if you have checked your values and principles, your individuality, your passion, your color and culture, and your ethics, your convictions at the company door, in the company parking lot as you and I were all trained to do in the industrial period. We have entered the age of personal power, and that power comes from within not from the system.

You the individual are the powers and the glory, the wealth and the source; you're what's happening and you're what makes it happen.

The trends I talked about earlier are setting the stage, but we must still operate in the real world; the material world, the marketplace, the third dimension. After all, stockholders want their profit, voters want easy answers and the media complains about the lack of strong (read macho) leaders.

"Where is the modern-day Churchills, or Henry Fords, the media keeps asking again and again." Why stop there, why not Genghis Khan or Attilla the Hun?

But, you can't lead with yesterday's leadership skills.

Forbes magazine asked eight leading CEOs and educators questions about the characteristics of leadership; the response was predictable: intelligence, judgment, character, and knowledge of the industry. There is nothing wrong with these traits, but for me they vividly describe the 1950s conformist captains of industry. You can just see the graying temple, wing tips and pinstripe suit. These traits describe a lot of people, but they are too general for today's fragmented and diverse marketplace.

Patricia Aburdene writes in her forthcoming book, *The Spiritual Path to Leadership:*

Characteristics of the twenty-first century leader will be a lot spicier and sexier, they will be creative, fun-loving, flexible, tolerant of ambiguity, convention busting, cheerleading, great communicators, spiritual, conflict masters, ritual staging, rebellious, healing, storytellers, improvisational, intuitive and entrepreneurial.

These are the characteristics of leadership that will effectively deal with America's greatest strengths.

Whatever your corporate vision, you will need transformational leadership. Not one, but scores of new leaders, perhaps thousands from the bottom up throughout your organization.

A true leader is not the one with the most followers, but the one who creates the most leaders. (*Conversations with God*)

Look at the opportunity that America has in the post cold war world, to lead by the "power of our example." We are the only society that is sufficiently multiracial and multiethnic to be a world society. And if we intend to lead the world by the power of the example of our pluralism then we've got to do a better job here at home.

None of this will be easy, but it has never been easy. New life and change can only come from labor and pain.

To sum all of this up:

Successful companies do what unsuccessful companies are not willing to do.

Successful companies live outside of their comfort zone.

Successful companies go where the opportunity is.

We can also say the same for successful people and leaders, can't we?

Organizations and leaders that focus on fulfilling real human need, and helping people to find meaningful and productive work, are without question living outside their comfort zone, but they are positioning themselves to seize new opportunities and create a brave new world.

This is a process not a program, this process is evolutionary not revolutionary.

This will not happen overnight; it is a slow but steady process, and every single person sitting in this room is an important part.

It comes from the head and the heart, it comes from inside, it requires a personal commitment to a new set of principles, morally grounded and spiritually rooted, if for no other reason than to help make our communities and workplace the best, and most fulfilling and most competitive in the world. Our jobs, our lives and our country are depending on it.

In that context we each need to think about how we feel about each other. This is the really big one.

You can't succeed by yourself, believe me. We all need each other, we're in this together. We may have come over here on different ships but we're in the same boat now!

We're a people united going forward. We need each other's ideas.

We need each other's strengths, we need each other's encouragement, we need each other's gifts.

Each of us must understand how valuable all of us are, and all of us must understand how valuable each of us are.

It was the award winning author John Williams who wrote; "whatever future America will have, will be directly related to solving our racial dilemma, which is a human dilemma."

If our kids can't see the future, they won't pay the price, therefore . . .

The promise of the future is an awesome force.

We each must set our sails on this course toward the future, then we must stay the course.

In closing, I would like to read a short poem I wrote entitled "Stay the Course."

Stay the Course

The ship of life sails at Sea in search of life

As captains of our fate, we must steer the course confident our inner compass will always be true

The Seas will be stormy, but stay the course

Your scope will view danger, but stay the course

You will be tempted to change direction, but stay the course

Your crew may threaten mutiny, but stay the course

Stay the course, and you will land on an island where no one else has landed

It is there you will build your paradise.

Thank you, and may God continue to bless you.

Article Review Form at end of book.

Describe the intellectual procedure for developing leaders at West Point. How is this process similar to the scientific method?

Teaching Leadership at the U.S. Military Academy at West Point

Jeffrey A. McNally
Stephen J. Gerras
R. Craig Bullis

U.S. Military Academy at West Point

The late Jeffrey A. McNally was professor of Leadership and Organizational Studies at the U.S. Military Academy.

Stephen J. Gerras is assistant professor in the Department of Behavioral Sciences and Leadership, U.S. Military Academy.

R. Craig Bullis is assistant professor in the Department of Behavioral Sciences and Leadership, U.S. Military Academy.

The authors present a description and analysis of how they teach leadership to more than 1,000 cadets each year at the U.S. Military Academy at West Point. These cadets, upon graduation and commissioning as second lieutenants, are the future leaders of the U.S. Army. The organizational and institutional context of this work has contributed to the authors' development of a unique methodology for teaching organizational leadership. The authors recently have extended this methodology to the development of leaders in the Los Angeles Police Department and in various police departments throughout New Jersey. The success of this experience over several years has convinced the authors of the merit of their approach for teaching leadership to both aspiring and practicing leaders across military and civilian organizational contexts.

The purpose of the U.S. Military Academy (USMA, or West Point) is "to provide the nation with leaders of character who serve the common defense" (USMA, 1993, p. 6).

The mission of the Academy is "to educate and train the Corps of Cadets so that each graduate shall have the attributes essential to professional growth throughout a career as an officer of the Regular Army and to inspire each to a lifetime of service to the nation" (USMA, 1993, p. 7). One of the central components of the institutional vision of the Military Academy is to be the premier leader development institution in the world. To achieve this vision, every aspect of cadets' lives at West Point is designed to contribute to their development as *leaders of character* in each of three distinct pillars: intellectual, military, and physical development. In this sense, the U.S. Military Academy is not a value-free institution. West Point is interested in developing leaders of character who not only do things right, but who also do the right things under conditions of intense pressure and frequent scrutiny (Bennis, 1989). The role of USMA's Department of Behavioral Sciences and Leadership in this leader development process is to offer a required course in organizational leadership that applies the scientific method, using concepts from the behavioral and social sciences, to the study of leadership within an organizational context. The title of the course is Military Leadership; it is taught to all cadets in their junior year. The present authors have taught this course for a combined 17 years.

Although classroom experience is not the sole source of West Point's success in developing leaders of character, this course is an important component of an overall leader development program that spans a cadet's entire 4-year undergraduate experience. Other aspects of this program include exposure to the experience of followership (beginning most intensively in a cadet's freshman year during the rigors of Cadet Basic Training), hands-on leadership experiences (through cadet chain of command leadership positions and summer military training), analysis of past and present leaders (history and military sciences courses), and exposure to role models (professors, company tactical officers, military mentors, etc.). The Department of Behavioral Sciences and Leadership focuses on scholarly and self-reflective perspectives of leadership by exposing cadets to a theory-based, systemic leadership model that they use as a framework for analyzing complex but realistic leadership situations.

By design, this 40-hour course is taught only to West Point juniors. The intent is to capitalize on the concrete experience, reflective observation, abstract conceptualization, and active experimentation model of learning (Kolb, 1984). During freshman and sophomore years, cadets experience a myriad of firsthand leadership challenges that they often meet with less success than they anticipated. Thus, they are ripe for an intellectually challenging and academically rigorous course of reflection. By junior year, cadets have experienced enough subordinate and leader positions both at West Point and in the field Army to establish a context for the theories and intellectual process taught in the course. In addition, the preponderance of cadets' leadership responsibilities at the Academy comes during their senior year. Consequently, the leadership taught in the classroom can be applied and practiced by the senior student leaders within the leadership laboratory that is the U.S. Military Academy. The opportunity to practice and apply what is learned in the classroom reinforces cadets' desires to thoughtfully analyze leadership situations while cadets and also as junior officers and leaders for the nation.

Methods for Teaching Leadership

To be effective in the 21st century, leaders must possess critical thinking skills (e.g., Hunt & Blair, 1985). Therefore, the instructional strategies used in the West Point leadership course focus on development of these thinking skills while employing relevant subject matter content. The purpose of this course is to illustrate the importance of being a smart, thoughtful, and reflective leader. Cadets are taught numerous behavioral science theories and then required to apply these theories to a case that illustrates a situation they might face as a military leader. In other words, the development of cognitive skills is preeminent over the mere acquisition of knowledge. For example, a student could recite the key points of various theories of leadership without demonstrating *how* these concepts compare and contrast with each other. It is in the comparing, contrasting, and applying of these concepts that students are required to perform at a higher cognitive level (Bloom, 1956). This method of moving students to higher cognitive levels in their scientific study of leadership distinguishes this course from other leader development activities at West Point. The process requires cadets to use higher order cognitive skills such as the identification of ambiguity, the discovery of assumptions and value conflicts, the evaluation of evidence, the application of logic, the generation of alternative inferences, and development of reasoned judgement (e.g., Jacobs & Jaques, 1987).

We call the approach we use to stress the integration of these cognitive skills the Intellectual Procedure (Figure 1). This model, we believe, is simply the application of the scientific method of inquiry to leadership situations. In other words, we integrate within the scientific method the application of a variety of behavioral science theories and concepts in order to enrich the cadets' ability to understand the subtleties and ambiguities they will face in complex leadership situations in the future. Our experience has convinced us that this is a powerful framework for developing thoughtful and reflective leaders.

The application of the Intellectual Procedure (IP) to realistic leadership situations requires cadets to perform three primary intellectual tasks: *identify* what is happening, *account* for what is happening, and then *formulate* and apply leader actions to the situation. Cadets perform these intellectual tasks as they encounter leadership situations in case studies written by department faculty. Cases are based upon actual leadership experiences that the military faculty have encountered in their careers. Having faculty members who are experienced in dealing with the situations represented in the case studies is a side benefit of this approach and a unique aspect of department faculty. The military faculty members are selected based on evaluations of their practical leadership in the military. Consequently, all faculty can discuss the posed situations in light of their own leadership experiences. In addition, our Computer Assisted Instruction (CAI) presents and applies the IP to *cadet* scenarios. While not only reinforcing the structure and requirements of the IP, the CAI also demonstrates the applicability of the course concepts to students' current leadership experiences.

For example, instructors often begin class by describing an incident they actually faced that demonstrates the relevance of the theory. In addition, during classroom discussion of leader actions to solve the problem, faculty can share their actions in a similar situation. Often these examples provide not only scenarios of successful leadership actions, but also illustrate mistakes resulting from *failure* to use a concept correctly. Both are equally valuable in communicating the instructor's leadership experiences to cadets. In addition, instructors often ask cadets to describe a situation they faced (potentially reflected in the CAI) that further underscores the applicability of the concept to their current position in the cadet leadership hierarchy. Although these examples can greatly increase student interest in the subject, there also are potential problems. Cadets may leave class believing that there is a single solution for every case. Other cadets may be discouraged because they recognize their limited experience; consequently, they may believe that they can never reach an adequate standard of performance. The instructor's role is then to show students that their current experiences in the Corps of Cadets, with adequate reflection, can indeed be transferred to the "real Army." Although this initially may appear to be a unique benefit of teaching leadership at West Point, we have found that the same potential exists for the police departments with which we have worked.

Identify What   **Account for What**   **Formulate**
Is Happening   **Is Happening**   **Leader Actions**

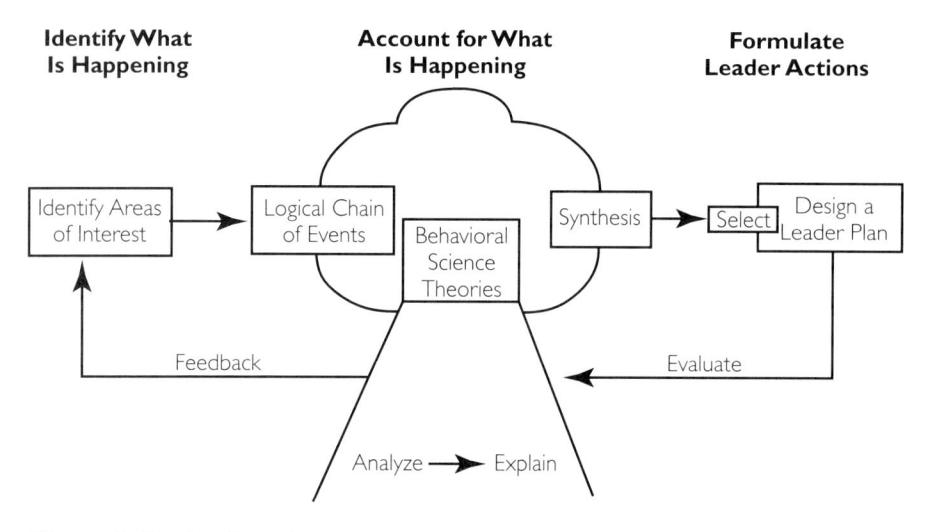

Figure 1. The intellectual procedure.

Identify. For the first IP task—identify what is happening—cadets are expected to detect issues in a leadership situation that compel them to act to resolve organizational problems. Cadets identify these as *areas of interest.* The issues cadets identify may be reactive in nature, for example, "Sergeant Smith failed to prepare his crew for tank gunnery;" or they may be proactive, for example, "We are expecting a new weapons system to be delivered to our unit in 2 months." It is clear that effective leaders not only need to respond to the immediate problems they experience in their organizations, but they also need to anticipate future leadership challenges (Yukl, 1994). We emphasize that effective leaders need to be able to sort through the myriad of daily happenings to focus on those issues that compel action.

Account. The second IP step is to account for what is happening in the situation. This step is the theoretical heart of the intellectual process and the step that contributes most to the development of critical thinking skills. Cadets are expected to use behavioral science theories and concepts to account for why the areas of interest occur. At present, cadets are exposed to 22 leadership-relevant theories and concepts (more than half of course content). However, this number has varied as instructors annually evaluate the course content (see later discussion). Typically, a single theory or concept, such as organizational socialization (Van Maanen & Schein, 1979), is addressed in a 1-hour class, with most time spent processing a relatively simple case study. In addition to these content lessons, 10 of the 40 lessons are devoted to analytical integration and synthesis. Here, cadets use the same intellectual procedure but with the additional requirement to *integrate* multiple theories to enhance their understanding of a more complex case. We have included a complete listing of the course sequence in Appendix 1.

When cadets account for what is happening in a situation, they must ask themselves which theory or theories best account for the occurrence of these events. This is a two-stage intellectual process. The first stage, the *analyze* step, involves the determination of whether a particular theory is applicable to the situation. Cadets must ask themselves, Does sufficient information exist in the case study to distinguish the relevant variables of any particular theory? For example, a cadet determining the relevance of path goal theory (House, 1971; House & Mitchell, 1974) would first ascertain if the case study presented sufficient information to assess characteristics of the task and the subordinates. If it did not, then path-goal theory would be bypassed in favor of a more applicable theory. If sufficient information is available, cadets classify the relevant variables and move to the second stage.

The second stage, the *explain* step, asks students to create an intellectual link between a theory and an area of interest. In other words, this process involves determination of a cause-effect relationship between what has occurred and why it occurred. An example of the explain step might be, "The leader's achievement-oriented behaviors in this case are inappropriate for the characteristics of the task and of the subordinates. This accounts for why Sergeant Smith is dissatisfied with his job."

Because numerous theories could be used to account for the same area of interest, the account portion requires cadets to evaluate evidence and then to select one of several theories that are potentially applicable to the complicated case study. The selection of multiple theories to account for the complexity of the case is practiced during the analytical integration periods that are scheduled at the end of the presentation of each block of theories. The analytical integration case studies parallel our exams in terms of their difficulty. Our intent is for the cadets to understand that there are multiple ways to make sense of the many ambiguous situations they will encounter in organizational life.

In addition to recognizing how relevant theories inform the leader, in the account step, cadets are asked to develop a *logical chain of events* and to *synthesize* the case. The logical chain of events involves organizing the case in a chronological and causal chain. This exercise develops cadets' ability to make decisions such as, Did the organizational culture *cause* the leader to use a poor decision-making style, or vice versa, or are they related at all? This logical chain of events focuses on the higher order cognitive task of logic assessment.

The synthesis requirement asks cadets to examine the case study as a coherent whole. Cadets are asked to perform several tasks. First, they must answer the question, Does a root cause exist that serves as the underlying explanation for the issues present in the situation? If there is an underlying or main cause for a series of issues, effective leaders generally address this first. This becomes the starting point later in the

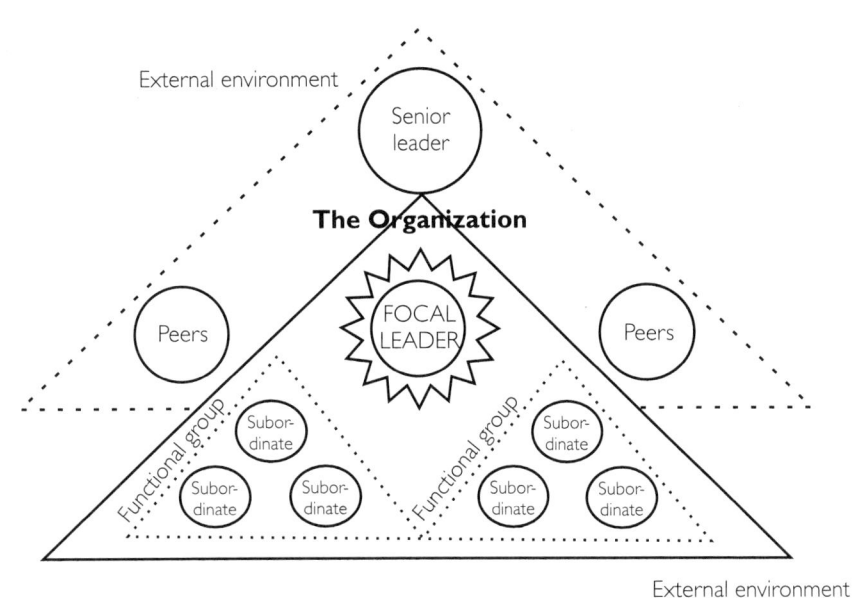

Figure 2. The model of organizational leadership.

IP when cadets formulate leader plans. Synthesis also requires cadets to conduct an assessment of interactions between theories and events. An example of this might be, "Sergeant Johnson's equity issue was amplified by the poor cohesion existing in the unit." Synthesis also involves the search for a common thread—a unifying element throughout the case—such as, "In numerous instances, this unit failed to focus on the long-term results of its actions and instead was only concerned with immediate problems." The synthesis forces cadets to sort through the ambiguity of the case and focus on central issues.

Formulate. The third step in the IP is to formulate leader actions. This provides an applied focus to the department's teaching of leadership. The theoretical prescriptions of the theories used to account for areas of interest are the criteria for this step. Obviously, this theoretical link influences which theories are emphasized in the course. Descriptive theories are taught, but they carry less weight than do prescriptive theories, both in time devoted in the classroom and in evaluation. This formulation step emphasizes again the fact that there are multiple ways to view a situation. In other words, we move from the science to the art of leadership (Csoka, 1985). There clearly is no single approach, for instance, to how a leader can be transformational in moving an organization beyond mediocrity. As cadets increase in sophistication, they recognize that multiple "correct" leader actions are feasible as long as they are organizationally realistic and do not create additional problems. We believe this contributes significantly to cadet intellectual development.

Theoretical Base

Theoretical course content takes a systems approach and is divided into four areas. Similar to many organizational behavior courses, these areas are the individual, group, leadership, and organizational systems. This organization is based on a Model of Organizational Leadership (Figure 2), which places the focal leader at the center of an organization's structure. Our approach to teaching leadership consistently puts the student in the role of the leader rather than in that of an interested observer not ultimately responsible for organizational outcomes. The Model of Organizational Leadership illustrates the importance of the focal leader's understanding of subordinates, peers, superiors, and the immediate group (direct leadership), as well as of the larger organization and the environment in which it exists (indirect leadership) (Pfeffer, 1981).

The individual system starts with theories that account for individual differences, such as attribution theory (e.g., Kelly, 1955) and a general theory of adult development (e.g., Levinson, 1978). Subsequently, it moves to multiple theoretical approaches that help students understand the principles of human motivation (e.g., Steers & Porter, 1991).

The group system focuses on differences between leading individuals and leading groups. Organizational socialization (e.g., VanMaanen & Schein, 1979), group development (e.g., Bennis & Shepard, 1965), cohesion (e.g., Cartwright, 1965), and group decision making (e.g., Vroom & Yetton, 1974) are key topics in this area. The entire course is cumulative, and at this point in the course, cadets are expected to apply the IP to case studies using both individual and group theories.

The leadership system focuses on differences between transactional and transformational approaches to leadership (Bass, 1985). As we move through the course, we expect cadets to shift their perspective from solving problems as they arise to anticipating problems and being proactive to prevent or minimize them. In a lesson on transformational leadership (e.g., Bass, 1985), for instance, the case study describes an average organization featuring general satisfaction yet unremarkable performance. Although there is nothing apparently "wrong" with this organization, it is important for students to understand the leaders' responsibility to move their organizations beyond mediocrity. This is a further illustration of the value-laden nature of our approach to leader development.

The final area in the course, the organizational system, requires cadets, as focal leaders, to examine the "big picture." Organizational culture (e.g., Schein, 1985), managing the environment (e.g., Thompson, 1967), organizational change (e.g., Kotter, 1990), and ethics (e.g., Bandura, 1977) are major topics in this area. The focal leader, at this point, is also the subordinate leader who attempts to understand why things are the way they are in the organization. Because cadets will someday be platoon leaders (an entry-level leadership position), it is important for them to understand why things are happening in their larger organization and the impact of such events on their embedded organization. This focus on the difference between direct and indirect leadership (Pfeffer, 1981) is a major transition in the course, but one that is important for students to understand.

What Is Different about the Department of Behavioral Sciences and Leadership?

West Point's Department of Behavioral Sciences and Leadership includes two categories of military instructors: academy professors and rotating faculty members. Academy professors are senior military officers who have earned a doctorate in an appropriate discipline (e.g., industrial/organizational psychology, social psychology, counseling psychology, and organizational sociology). These professors provide consistency to the department. The remaining department members are rotating faculty. Rotating faculty members have recently completed a graduate degree in a related discipline. They complete a 3-year teaching assignment at West Point before returning to the field Army. This type of faculty member (who put into service both their relevant experience and their formal education) makes West Point unique among management or psychology departments. In fact, these rotating faculty have been highlighted as a benefit for the institution because they bring both youthful enthusiasm and current academic qualifications to their classrooms (Commission on Higher Education, 1989). Moreover, as these faculty bring both practical experience and formal knowledge to the complexities of a case study, they are able to resolve the unique struggle between soldier and scholar that plagues West Point (Lovell, 1979).

West Point, like the other service academies, exhibits a unique friction that separates it from civilian counterparts. Lovell's (1979) book *Neither Athens nor Sparta?* details the struggle between the Athenian values of a liberal education curriculum (that emphasizes academic excellence while promoting innovative and independent thinkers) with the Spartan values of the professional military officer (values of discipline and "duty, honor, country"). This struggle represents the contrast between education (teaching students to think and reason for themselves) and training (teaching students a finite set of knowledge necessary in the performance of a task). It is this fine line that department instructors attempt to negotiate in the leadership course. Having military experience allows them to bring to bear the Spartan characteristics of the military professional. Having an advanced degree provides the faculty with appreciation for the Athenian value of academic excellence. Developing this balance between training and education is reflected in the IP, as it explicitly includes both academic and applied components in the students' requirements.

To develop thoughtful and reflective leaders, the department expects faculty members to create a classroom environment that develops critical thinking and fosters intellectual development. In such a climate, the professor is not the only authority figure; open-ended questions are encouraged and solicited; students are motivated to discuss relevant issues among themselves; and multiple perspectives to account for or resolve a single issue are highlighted as equally feasible. These expectations are supported by a classroom size that does not exceed 18 students.

The department also has created a parallel culture that emphasizes the same qualities faculty are expected to encourage in the classroom. The result of this parallelism is that department faculty interact among themselves in the same informal and developmental way that they interact with students in the classroom. This consistency is important in ensuring that the culture both in classrooms and in the work of the department faculty facilitates the development of critical thinking. The primary means to develop, nurture, and sustain this culture is the department's Faculty Development Workshop.

Prior to their first semester of teaching, all new faculty members (including both rotating and permanent faculty) spend 7 intense weeks in the workshop preparing to teach Military Leadership. They observe experienced faculty members teaching classes and receiving feedback, and in turn, they teach numerous lessons and receive feedback. All instruction is videotaped and then reviewed and critiqued in faculty teams working together to improve the overall quality of instruction. The primary purpose of this workshop is to socialize new faculty members into the culture of the department. Because the departmental culture is more collegial and less hierarchical than most new faculty have encountered in their previous military experiences, the workshop usually is a significant change experience for new organizational members. The workshop is attended by the most senior members of the department to deliberately demonstrate the interaction that is desired in this culture (Schein, 1985). Collegiality is reinforced by referring to one another, regardless of military rank, by first names. Development is enhanced by open and often emotional discussion of teaching style and/or strategy among faculty of all ranks. For example, when providing feedback to a senior faculty member (Academy Professor) who presented an example class in the Faculty Development Workshop, some of the more experienced rotating faculty members may openly debate the validity of the chosen teaching strategy. Alternative strategies are offered and discussed in the presence of the entire group. Early in the workshop, incoming faculty are told that this type of collegial interaction and discussion is desired in all faculty members. However, it is not until a Captain with an M.B.A. openly challenges the teaching strategy of a Colonel with a Doctorate (who also happens to be the officer's immediate rater for annual evaluation purposes) that the reality of this departmental culture is realized. This interaction has a secondary purpose as well, in that it demonstrates to all faculty members (regardless of tenure) that each can further develop (and be developed by) other members of the faculty team.

A major strength of the department lies in the background of its faculty. First, all leadership professors at West Point have been successful commanders in the Army. They have demonstrated their proficiency as soldiers in many varied and difficult military assignments. As discussed earlier, the faculty know the context of the cases used in the course and "have been there," thus providing significant credibility in the classroom. In addition to their military backgrounds, they have received advanced degrees in disciplines such as industrial-organizational psychology, social psychology, organizational behavior, business, and sociology. The interdisciplinary nature of the faculty (and hence, the course) provides multiple perspectives for many of the topics in the course. The group literature has long recognized that, for a complex task, a more heterogeneous group is desired (Steiner, 1972). The following illustration highlights the benefits of this conglomerate of educational backgrounds. When department faculty discuss lesson strategies to teach the unit on organizational culture (Schein, 1985), the psychologist generally focuses on the effects of the culture at the individual level, the sociologist argues for the interactive effects of the organization with the larger environment, and the instructor with the business background focuses on the effects of the culture on organizational productivity. The final outcome of this discussion (which is sometimes documented in the form of a supplemental reading that augments the text) usually includes the most current information from each of the represented disciplines. Consequently, the department seeks to provide an education that is less parochial than that which would otherwise occur with a more homogeneous group.

This multidisciplinary approach is a unique situation, not usually found in academia, that greatly enhances the quality of the course in several ways. First, faculty members are exposed to paradigms that they may have not studied in their education, thereby expanding their appreciation for the weaknesses as well as the strengths of particular theories. In addition, cadets are exposed to the power of the concept in dealing with issues at multiple levels of analysis: individual, group, and organizational.

Evaluation

Cadet Evaluation

Cadet evaluation consists of three examinations during the semester and a comprehensive final examination. The format for all exams consists of a two- to five-page case study requiring cadets to apply the IP. Evaluation is criteria based; therefore, cadets do not compete against one another. Grading facilitates critical thinking skills in several ways. First, the essay format of the exam allows cadets to structure their answers and define problems and issues on their own. Second, noncompetitive grading facilitates classroom discussion during nonexam periods. Because all cadets can benefit from the good ideas that emerge from class discussions, an interactive sharing and discussion of ideas among cadets occurs that might not transpire in a more competitive atmosphere.

The exam itself is often difficult for the cadets, and the evaluation of the cadets' analyses of a case study is likewise not an easy task for the instructors. Cadets are required to think and communicate at the application and possibly even the analysis and synthesis levels of Bloom's (1956) Cognitive Learning Objective Classification. Consequently, instructors grading the exams must be comfortable operating in the evaluation category. Because most graduate school experience has focused on learning at the application and analysis levels, moving to the higher levels requires formal and informal mentoring and coaching among the senior and junior faculty members. These discussions, which occur not only in the Faculty Development Workshop but also throughout the course of the semester, reinforce the interactive culture desired in the department.

Course Evaluation

Course evaluation is conducted both by the cadets and by the instructors. Formal evaluation by the cadets occurs toward the end of the course. The cadets are afforded the opportunity to are evaluate the course and the instructor with a standardize evaluation developed and instituted by the Academy. This form of evaluation consists of a series of questions regarding the course and the instructor that the cadets rate using a 5-point Likert-style response. In addition to the quantitative feedback, most instructors solicit qualitative feedback on their performance as well as on the course in general. As an example, the instructor may ask what issues should change for the next year and what should remain the same. In addition to this end-of-course feedback, many instructors add mid-course evaluations that ask the cadet to comment on issues that the instructor can control immediately to facilitate student learning (e.g., Angelo & Cross, 1993).

Department faculty formally evaluate the leadership course every spring semester. During the Course Development Workshop, instructors meet to discuss any issue that an individual member feels pertinent to making the course better. These issues are discussed and prioritized by all instructors. Subgroup work then develops specific proposals to enact the faculty's wishes. Finally, these proposals are returned to the larger group for review, modification, and acceptance. Among the issues included in recent workshops are: adding or deleting a particular theory from the course, developing or rewriting the written explanation of the IP, rewriting a supplemental reader for an particular theory, modifying or developing individual theory and exam case studies, or modification of the CAI.

It is important to recognize that every cadet at West Point must take this course. Cadets' grades in this course affect their class standing, which further affects their choice of military specialty, first assignment location, and even future promotion dates. Consequently, the Course Development Workshop is the only opportunity for an instructor to change the content of the course. An individual instructor has no autonomy or authority to change course content during the academic year. First-year faculty are expected to trust those who have gone before

Appendix—Course Sequence

Lesson/Topic

1. Course Overview
2. Learning Leadership

The Individual System

3. Understanding Individual Behavior
4. Equity Theory of Motivation
5. Expectancy Theory of Motivation
6. Cognitive Evaluation Theory of Motivation
7. Motivation Through Job Redesign
8. Individual Communication and Counseling
9. The Intellectual Procedure Revisited
10. Analytical Integration IA
11. Analytical Integration IB
12. Exam 1

The Group System

13. Understanding Groups as Open Systems
14. Socialization
15. Cohesion
16. Intergroup Conflict Management
17. Decision Making in Groups
18. Analytical integration IIA
19. Analytical Integration II

The Leadership System

20. Leadership as Interpersonal influence
21. Vertical Dyad Linkage Theory
22. Path-Goal Theory
23. Transformational Leadership
24. Personality and Leadership Effectiveness
25. Analytical Integration IIIA
26. Analytical Integration IIIB
27. Exam 2

The Organizational System

28. The Organization as an Open System
29. The Organizational Environment
30. The Organizational Culture
31. Overcoming Resistance to Change
32. Total Quality Management
33. The Ethical Dimension of Leadership
34. Analytical Integration IVA
35. Analytical Integration IVB
36. Exam 3

Course Integration

37. Counseling Applications
38. Putting It All Together A
39. Putting it All Together B
40. Learning Leadership: *The Journey Continues*

them that the content of the course is the best that the experienced faculty could make it. Nevertheless, academic freedom is evident in the execution of each lesson. With the exception of the exams (which are standardized), faculty are free to teach a particular lesson in any manner that they wish.

Leadership Education for the Future

Over the past 2 years, members of the department's leadership faculty have been involved in outreach programs to teach this leadership course to other organizations. For example, we assisted in designing and implementing a leadership training program for the New Jersey Association of Chiefs of Police. These police department leaders wanted to develop a training course for their officers that focused on the leadership challenges that faced their officers. Professional police organizations could send their officers to several schools that focus on the technical aspects of their police work, but none that deal with the interpersonal skills required of the police officers as they are promoted to positions of responsibility within their department. Consequently, we worked with representatives of statewide police departments in proposing a training course that paralleled our course. Departmental faculty assisted their new instructors in determining theories and concepts to include in the class, writing case studies (using their expertise and experience as a base), and finally developing their faculty by including their primary instructors in our Faculty Development Workshop. The New Jersey leadership education program, which has trained 72 police department leaders during its 2-year existence, has received very positive reviews (Zajac, 1995). This experience is one of several that has convinced us of the generalizability of our course.

Conclusion

The West Point course in leadership provides an example of incorporating the rigor of the scientific method to the behavioral sciences. Our identify, account, and formulate model attempts to develop the critical thinking skills of our students. Evidence indicates that these methods work, not only with West Point cadets, but also with leaders in other contexts. Hopefully, future leadership training will incorporate the notion of a theoretically informed, process-oriented approach to the development of thoughtful, reflective leaders who can play a vital leadership role in the 21st century.

References

Angelo, T.A., & Cross, K.P. (1993). *Classroom assessment techniques: A handbook for college teachers* (2nd ed.). San Francisco: Jossey-Bass.

Bandura, A. (1977). *Social learning theory.* Englewood Cliffs, NJ: Prentice Hall.

Bass, B.M. (1985). *Leadership and performance beyond expectations.* New York: Free Press.

Bennis, W. (1989). *Why leaders can't lead: The unconscious conspiracy continues.* San Francisco: Jossey-Bass.

Bennis, W.G., & Shepard, H.A. (1965). A theory of group development. *Human Relations, 9,* 415–457.

Bloom, B.S. (Ed.). (1956). *Taxonomy of educational objectives.* New York: Longman.

Cartwright, D. (1965). Influence, leadership, control. In J.G. March (Ed.), *Handbook of organizations.* Chicago: Rand McNally.

Commission on Higher Education of the Middle States Association of Colleges and Schools. (1989). *Report to the faculty, administration, superintendent, corps of cadets of U.S. Military Academy.* West Point, NY: U.S. Military Academy.

Csoka, L.S. (1985, December). Why study leadership? *Military Review,* pp. 44–47.

House, R.J. (1971). A path-goal theory of leadership effectiveness. *Administrative Science Quarterly, 16,* 321–338.

House, R.J., & Mitchell, T.R. (1974). Path-goal theory of leadership. *Journal of Contempory Business, 3,* 81–97.

Hunt, J.G., & Blair, J.D. (Eds.). (1985). *Leadership on the future battlefield.* New York: Pergamon-Brassey.

Jacobs, T.O., & Jaques, E. (1987). Leadership in complex systems. In J.A. Zeidner (Ed.), *Human productivity enhancement* (Vol.2, pp. 7–65). New York: Praeger.

Kelly, E.L. (1955). Consistency of the adult personality. *American Psychologist, 10,* 659–681.

Kolb, D.A. (1984). *Experiential learning: Experience as the source of learning and development.* Englewood Cliffs, NJ: Prentice Hall.

Kotter, J.P (1990). *A force for change.* New York: Free Press.

Levinson, D.J. (1978). *The seasons of a man's life.* New York: Ballantine.

Lovell, J.P. (1979). *Neither Athens nor Sparta?* Bloomington: Indiana University Press.

Pfeffer:, J. (1981). Management as symbolic action: The creation and maintenance of organizational paradigms. In L.L. Cummings & B.M. Staw (Eds.) *Research in organizational behavior* (Vol. 3, pp. 1–52). Greenwich, CT: JAI.

Schein, E.H. (1985). *Organizational culture and leadership.* San Francisco: Jossey-Bass.

Steers, R.M., & Porter, L.W. (1991). *Motivation and work behavior* (5th ed.). New York: McGraw-Hill.

Steiner, I.D. (1972). *Group process and productivity.* New York: Academic Press.

Thompson, J.D. (1967). *Organizations in action.* New York: McGraw-Hill.

U.S. Military Academy. (1993, October). *West Point 2002 and beyond: Strategic guidance for the U.S. Military Academy* (pamphlet). West Point, NY: Author.

Van Maanen, J., & Schein, E.H. (1979). Toward a theory of organizational socialization. In B.M. Staw (Ed.) *Research in organizational behavior* (Vol.1, pp. 209–264). Greenwich, CT: JAI.

Vroom, V.H., & Yetton, P.W. (1974). *Leadership and decision making.* New York: John Wiley.

Yukl, G.A. (1994). *Leadership in organizations* (3rd ed.). Englewood Cliffs, NJ: Prentice Hall.

Zajac, M.N. (1995). New Jersey State Association of Chiefs of Police assessment of training, Unpublished raw data.

Article Review Form at end of book.

WiseGuide Wrap-Up

In this section, we have reviewed some of the basic issues concerning leadership and have examined some perspectives on how to be an effective leader. Unfortunately, there are no simple answers to some of the key leadership questions. Although there is truth in each of the perspectives presented here, accomplishing the goals are difficult. It is easy to say that it is important to value diversity, but what does a leader need to do to make that a reality? It seems easy to say that an effective leader must stay true to his or her core values, but that can be a difficult task, both in defining and in maintaining those values. This text is not the last word on leadership, and these important issues will be debated in academia, in industry, and around the world for many years to come. It is important, however, that you participate in this debate.

R.E.A.L. Sites

This list provides a print preview of typical **Coursewise** R.E.A.L. sites. (There are over 100 such sites at the **Courselinks**™ site.) The danger in printing URLs is that web sites can change overnight. As we went to press, these sites were functional using the URLs provided. If you come across one that isn't, please let us know via email to webmaster@coursewise.com. Use your Passport to access the most current list of R.E.A.L. sites at the **Courselinks** site.

Site name: The Center for Innovative Leadership
URL: http://www.cfil.com/indexframenew.html
Why is it R.E.A.L.? The center was formed in the belief that there is a better way to organize human effort. People want to organize, even need to organize, in order to accomplish goals that they deem important. It is not only possible but imperative that we find a way to combine our efforts if we hope to meet the challenges of a more complex, technologically advanced, competitive environment, in which the differences in the human side of enterprise will determine an organization's success or failure.
Key topic: leadership
Try this: Visit the Articles page to read some current perspectives on leadership.

Site name: The Ron Brown Award for Corporate Leadership
URL: http://www.ron-brown-award.org/
Why is it R.E.A.L.? This presidential award honors companies for the exemplary quality of their relationships with employees and communities. The annual award is presented to companies that have demonstrated a deep commitment to innovative initiatives that not only empower employees and communities but also advance strategic business interests. The president of the United States presents The Ron Brown Award for Corporate Leadership at an annual White House ceremony.
Key topics: leadership, awards
Try this: Select the Recent Winners link to see what some companies are doing.

Site name: The Institute for Global Ethics
URL: http://www.globalethics.org/
Why is it R.E.A.L.? The Institute for Global Ethics is an independent, nonprofit, nonsectarian, and nonpartisan organization dedicated to elevating public awareness and promoting the discussion of ethics in a global context. It is an international, membership-based think tank focusing on ethical activities in education, the corporate sector, and public policy.
Key topics: leadership, ethics
Try this: Select the Dilemma: Right vs. Right link and read some of the ethical and leadership dilemmas. What would you do in these cases? Sample resolutions for recent case studies are posted.

# section 10

Stress, Health, and Safety

WiseGuide Intro

Work is stressful. This statement probably does not surprise anyone, but it is commonly misinterpreted to mean that work is bad. Stress is often portrayed as a negative event, something to eliminated; however, we must carefully define our terms. *Stress* refers to the body's nonspecific response to any demand placed on it. These demands, or stressors, can be physical (lifting heavy objects, receiving a tetanus shot, getting into a fight, enjoying a roller coaster ride) or psychological (taking a final exam in industrial/organizational psychology, interviewing for a job, receiving a good job offer, trying to balance the demands of work and home). Note that experiencing stress does not mean that something negative is happening—positive events also cause stress. Interestingly, the body does not completely distinguish between types of stress and, thus, reacts in similar ways to positive and negative events. Basically, the body mobilizes its defenses. Sometimes referred to as the fight or flight syndrome, the stress response consists of physical changes, such as increases in heart and breathing rates. Less noticeable chemical changes in the body include the release of adrenaline, to help the body use its energy stores more rapidly, and hormones, some of which suppress the immune system and increase clotting agents in the blood. These changes are beneficial for dealing with short-term stress. However, if the stressors persist, the body becomes exhausted and begins to break down. Thus, the problem is not with stress (in fact, stress gives us energy to do things) but with chronic and unabated stress that does not allow the body to recuperate.

In this section, we will address the problem of job stress and its effects on our health. Specifically, we will explore some of the chronic stressors in organizations, their effects on our health, and some strategies that companies can use to address these problems.

The first two readings in this section describe some of the chronic stressors of working life. A common theme in these readings is time management. As you may recall from Section 2, people are increasingly reporting conflicts in managing work and home demands. In the first article, Bing reports he feels he is constantly running away from some things and toward others. His running even pervades his sleep, with dreams of work and time. This theme is echoed in Cottle's article, in which she describes *family friendly* time-saving policies that may not be so friendly to the family. Are we experiencing what *Fortune Magazine* refers to as the "Age of Overwork."

How should organizations respond? In Reading 47, Veninga suggests that the responsibility for reducing chronic stress and its accompanying negative effects is the responsibility of both the organization and the employee. He argues that organizations need to preserve jobs while keeping expectations reasonable. Workers, on the other hand, must effectively prioritize their activities and set reasonable goals. By doing these things, we can unleash the organization's greatest asset—employee creativity.

Learning Objectives

- To define stress.
- To discuss sources of chronic stress and some physiological effects.
- To describe some strategies that workers and organizations can use to reduce the debilitating effects of chronic stress.

Questions

Reading 45. Why do you think this person is having these thoughts and feelings? Is it the nature of the job that is so stressful or how he is coping with his work?

Reading 46. According to Cottle, how have communication technologies created more stress on employees? Cottle describes several "family friendly" organizational policies that may increase employee stress or disrupt families. What are the policies and their potential effects?

Reading 47. According to Veninga, what are three strategies organizations can use to help create a productive and healthy workplace? How does effective goal setting help employees reduce job stress?

Why do you think this person is having these thoughts and feelings? Is it the nature of the job that is so stressful or how he is coping with his work?

Running from the Wolves

Stanley Bing

By day, Stanley Bing is a real executive at a real Fortune 500 company he'd rather not name.

Hey! No! Don't eat me!
. . . Wow. What time is it? Three in the morning—again. Be still, heart. No point in bursting a ventricle. It was only a dream. The same dream for two nights in a row, maybe more. Who knows, with dreams?

I am running, running. Something is pursuing me. I look around and realize I am at the zoo—a zoo a bit like the Central Park Zoo in New York City, which is about half a mile from my office. Say, I wonder if that means anything. At this zoo, however, it seems none of the animals are in cages. That's fine when it comes to the zebras, tripping gaily by in the middle distance. And I don't mind the odd gibbon gamboling in the bushes near that fire hydrant, scratching him- or herself.

But right behind me are what I think are wolves. I can feel the moist heat of their breath wilting the back of my summer-weight, pinstriped suit jacket, smell the rotting meat of previous victims on their teeth. They are chasing me quite seriously. If I slow down for even a nanosecond, they will pounce on me and bite me very hard, and it won't be nice at all. I am terrified. My heart pounds and every extremity in my body is seized with a massive weakness. And yet I continue to run, run. Because I am not only running away from the wolves . . . I'm also running toward something, looking for someone . . . very important. I know, it's my kids! They're at the zoo too! Animals are out that might eat them! Help! Help!

And then I woke up. And here we are. Enough of this foolishness! I have three meetings before lunch, and a really bad lunch too . . . with Milton Lassiter. Why did I agree to this? Milton Lassiter is going to wear me out with his industry-nabob routine. I won't be able to drink, even, because there's a two o'clock with Don, Bob, Ed, Ned, and Toby. Bad lunch . . . what a horrible concept. It should be the ultimate oxymoron. Still, there is veal. What am I yammering about? I've got to get back to sleep! Have to relax. Think relaxing thoughts.

I wonder if Grabowski likes me. Sometimes I think he might not. Why not? I'm a likable guy. I'm affable. But is affable a good thing? Of how many really successful guys do you say, "Boy, is he affable!"? You don't. You think other things: "Boy, is he brilliant!" Or "Boy, is he vain!" Or a host of other enormous, dynamic personal qualities that help to define the intransigent self that lies at the core of true business genius. So what does affable buy you? Nothing. I'm wasting my time with it. It's not impactful in the near term. What the hell am I talking about? I'm daydreaming, that's what, instead of . . . going to sleep!

Got to calm down. Almost without volition, my body gets up. I've got to break the grips this obsessive night-brain munching. There is nothing worse than being awake in bed for more than five minutes in the middle of the night. So I'm not in bed anymore. I'm downstairs.

My, how dark the street is at this hour. There is nobody out there at all. Why should there be? Anyone sane is sleeping now. The house is very quiet. The children are asleep in their little beds. They look so peaceful and secure, their hands folded underneath their tiny cheeks, visions of material acquisitions dancing in their heads. I hate it when I don't get to spend enough time with them. I've only got a couple of more years before they won't be caught dead in my company. That's why the next two months are going to be so hard. First Phoenix, for the Marketing meeting with Beiber and his crew, one complete Saturday shot to hell. Why does he always have these things on the weekend? Saves a couple of bucks on the room rates and airfares. Suppose that's laudable. Phooey on it anyway. Then three separate major gatherings in Los Angeles, one right after the other. All the money saved in Phoenix spent on travel to someplace 95% of those attending have no desire to see ever again, and aren't anywhere near. One of these meetings is right on my son's birthday. That will go over really big with the little fellow. Maybe I don't have to go. I'll ask Bob. Bob's a nice guy. Bob will understand.

I wonder if Bob likes me. Of course Bob likes me! What kind of thoughts are these? Three-in-the-morning kind of thoughts, that's what. I'm going to go upstairs and get back into bed . . . and just lie there. No. Not yet. Fred the cocker spaniel is sitting next to me while I stand by the window regarding the street lamps. He is staring at me, his

"Running from the Wolves," by Stanley Bing, *Fortune,* May 27, 1996. Reprinted by permission of Gil Schwartz.

head slightly cocked to one side. He is hoping for a biscuit at this odd, alternative hour. Will he like me if I don't give him one? Man. How far gone am I? I'm wondering if my own dog likes me. I want everyone to like me, that's the thing. Sometimes money will do it. But you can't give a dog money. You have to give a dog love. People like love too. But money is easier to give sometimes.

Except I can't give Kroger that raise she wants. She just had a review four months ago, and HR is beginning to think I spend money like a drunken sailor. I have to be restrained. What if I lose her? That would be terrible. I'd have to manage the entire Summer Bratwurst Festival myself! I can't do that. I don't know the first thing about it. Did I say bratwurst? It's not bratwurst . . . it's . . . something else . . . can't think what. Can't . . . think at all.

I'm on the couch now. That must mean I'm going to read for a little while. Here is my book. It's a good book. I wonder whodunit. Actually, who cares whodunit? I don't. As long as I didn't do it, I'm okay with whatever happens. Maybe that's why I like it. What happens if we acquire BXR in August, when my vacation is scheduled? That would be a disaster. My wife is really looking forward to that trip to Montana. I wonder if while we're there we'll be held hostage by neofascist militarists. At the very least, I wonder if we'll fit in. They don't necessarily take to corporate senior vice presidents in the Old West where the outdoors is as big as all outdoors. I hope we have fun. I hope it costs less than $10,000. Why is my office smaller than Mulroney's? I report to the big guy. He doesn't.

I notice I'm not reading. This is ridiculous. I should get off this couch and go upstairs to sleep. It's 4 a.m. What is that I hear? Birds? Shut up, birds!

Okay—I'm back in bed now. Tomorrow morning I'm going to be a blob of burbling protoplasm. Tricks I plan to implement to stay viable: Get up and rub my face to keep from nodding off; walk around the room, looking extraordinarily serious during meetings; draw portraits of Coogan, who has one of those faces. Faces. Many faces to see in the next 48 hours. Big faces. Little faces. Faces in between. Faces with huge skulls and no hair. Huge protuberances of bone where their foreheads used to be. Big, mean faces on all fours and massive racks of horns leveled at anyone who comes in their path. They're pawing the ground! They're putting down their heads! They're chasing me around the zoo!

Hey! No! Don't butt my butt!

Oh, well. I guess it beats being awake.

Article Review Form at end of book.

According to Cottle, how have communication technologies created more stress on employees? Cottle describes several "family friendly" organizational policies that may increase employee stress or disrupt families. What are the policies and their potential effects?

Working 5 to 9:

All Work and No Play Doesn't Just Make You Dull—It Can Also Drive You Crazy

Michelle Cottle

One enchanted evening last March, I found myself hurtling through the darkened sky in a Boeing 747, suspended 30,000 feet above the still-frozen midwest. I was on the red-eye, the only travel option that would permit me to make a late afternoon meeting in San Francisco and my morning appointment in Boston. The in-flight movie had played itself out, and I'd flipped through the stack of memos and journal articles in my shoulder bag. Now all I wanted to do was sleep.

But I could not drift off. My eyes were glued to one of those individual video screens airlines are now installing on the backs of passenger seats. In between invitations to play video games (for a nominal fee) or peruse the entertainment and sports news of the day, the screen kept flashing a warning at me: "You can't afford to be out of touch. Use the Airfone to contact your office or clients right now."

I was overcome with panic. Should I call the office and check my voice-mail? What if a crisis were erupting that very minute that I wouldn't know about until we landed in another two hours? What if my boss needed to reach me but couldn't because I was busy dragging my carcass across the continent on a bit of company business?

What if, indeed.

The American worker is doomed. Not only do we have to worry about downsizing and stagnant wages and increased productivity demands, we have become the target of a movement, led by shrewd entrepreneurs and by our own employers, to help us minimize the number of seconds we are not actively engaged in job-related activities. What's worse, their efforts are being aided by the unwitting victims themselves, pathologically ambitious worker bees who wear their beepers during sex and develop a nervous tic if they go more than 10 minutes without checking voice-mail.

The Airfone is a prime example of the key role technology plays in this absurd crusade. I don't care if you are the chairman of Philip Morris, chances are there is nothing going down with the Marlboro man that can't be put on hold until you've deplaned. But thanks to the wonders of modem telecommunications (and clever marketing), business travelers have been made to feel we're doing our companies a disservice by being out of touch for the duration of a domestic flight. God forbid we should read a book, write our congressman, meditate, or fritter away our time with some other non-work-oriented pursuit for a few hours. As for travelers so career-crazed they get the shakes at the mere thought of missing a client call: You don't need an Airfone. You need a tranquilizer.

Back on terra firma the situation is even uglier, with faxes, cellular phones, and modems making it possible for us to work anytime, anyplace. No longer does leaving the office signal the end of the work day. People can now send us voice mail and e-mail at 8:00 p.m. on Christmas Eve. And since we can access these systems remotely, there's the constant pressure to respond promptly or have our work ethic questioned. Fortunately, also thanks to cell phones and beepers, a busy parent can easily set up a conference call from the middle of his third-grader's ballet recital. One well-adjusted executive at my old company even managed to conduct sales calls from her hospital bed just hours after delivering her first child. Now that's time well spent.

Recognizing that a workaholic culture might clash with the current hooplah over family values, computer and telecommunications companies have begun marketing their

Reprinted with permission from *The Washington Monthly*. Copyright by The Washington Monthly Company, 1611 Connecticut Ave. N.W., Washington, D.C. 20009, (202) 462-0128.

products and services as "family friendly" conveniences that help employees balance work and personal obligations. Just recently GTE aired a commercial asking if you'd ever tucked your child into bed from 1,000 miles away. Presumably, viewers were supposed to send up a great cheer when the ad assured us that someday soon we'd be able to do just that thanks to video hookups on our home computers. What an ingenious breakthrough in work/child management: remote parenting. Just log on at night for a quick bedtime story, then log off for eight hours of restful, guiltless sleep. As for the kids, what six-year-old wouldn't want a parent that came with an on/off switch?

Already these inspirational child-rearing techniques are gaining popularity. *U.S. News & World Report* recently ran a heart-warming piece about the rise of "virtual parents," who, while working late at the office or away on business, correct their children's homework by fax, oversee their dating life by phone, and keep track of their whereabouts by beeper. Forget all that messy personal interaction. Here's a system in which everyone prospers: Companies don't need to fret about employees being distracted by nonwork issues. Parents don't have to feel guilty about not being there for their kids. And children get to have that great latchkey-kid freedom, but with the security that, if they hear a strange noise outside or feel the urge to begin a life of crime because of parental neglect, they can just beep Mom or Dad for a little electronic emotional support. With any luck, in another five or six years we'll have successfully eliminated the need for all physical contact whatsoever with our offspring—maybe even our spouses. Forget Windows 97; Bill Gates should perfect the cyberhug.

Kill Them with Kindness

Still, it would be too easy to blame technology for our inability to disengage from work. Many of the developments blurring the line between our professional and private lives are decidedly low-tech. Among the hottest is the new breed of employment benefits thoughtfully designed to help stressed-out workers "balance" their personal lives right out of existence:

- Since 1987, the Washington, D.C.-based Arnold & Porter law firm has run an emergency back-up child care center that operates at night and on weekends, for use solely when parents are working overtime. The firm estimates that this family-friendly center clears the way for an additional $800,000 in billable hours a year.

- The Principal Financial Group in Des Moines, Iowa, has established an onsite "lactation center" where new mothers can go to express breast milk. According to a Principal spokesperson, this helps speed women's return to work following childbirth. It's essential not to let newborns get too accustomed to parental affection, lest they develop a sense of entitlement.

- At the Milwaukee headquarters of Northwestern Mutual Life Insurance, employees can enjoy free lunch in the company cafeteria—the company having calculated the money and time lost by people leaving the premises to eat.

Quick to spot a profitable trend, the market has come up with an offering that makes it even easier for companies to provide time-saving benefits: corporate concierge service. Typically managed by an outside contractor, a company's concierge can handle employees' every need—from standing in line at the DMV to retrieving clean dress socks from someone's home (or delivering expressed breast milk).

Now, granted, we'd all love to have someone fluff and fold our underwear and cook dinner for us every night, but these perks aren't about achieving balance so much as about making it easier, and more acceptable, for people to work nonstop. After all, if your company provides after-hours daycare, it suddenly becomes much more reasonable for an employer to expect you to work overtime. And if one phone call to the office concierge can take care of your automotive, grocery, and home-furnishing needs, as well as organize your four-year-old's birthday party, why would you ever need to leave your desk? As one systems analyst whose firm offers such benefits told the *Indianapolis Star*, "I can concentrate on my work and do a good job without having to worry about my personal obligations."

Companies insist (and may even believe) that their goal is not to chain workers to their desks, but the reality is that these programs are being provided within the framework of a business culture that still equates job commitment with hours spent at the office. Even with benefits like flex-time and paternity leave now available in many companies, the unspoken rule remains: He who stays the latest gets the promotion—or at least doesn't get canned. Notes Boston University researcher Laura Nash, "Companies seem willing to do anything for people—except for the employee who says, 'I just want to go home at 5:00 p.m. and have dinner with my family.' That's unheard of."

Employees know this, and the uncertain job market makes them wary of testing employers' humanity. All those media stories about the GM engineer "let go" after 15 years and the UCLA grad forced to shovel fries at Jack-in-the-Box have made people too afraid to leave their desks. We are convinced that, were we to sneak out of the office before 9:00 p.m., we'd find a hungrier, "more dedicated" employee entrenched in our cubicle by morning.

Noses to the Grindstone

So if most people are going to work all night regardless of who's cooking dinner, what's wrong with at least providing them the conveniences?

For starters, these arrangements allow both employers and employees to avoid confronting the true costs involved in achieving a real balance of work and personal demands. We have a desperate desire to believe that what works is the same as what's good. For example, reports show that more and more companies are providing sick/emergency child care. This magnanimous effort to save parents the hassle of scrambling for a sitter when junior is too contagious to be around other children has led to much back-slapping and self-congratulations throughout Corporate America. Well, this is super news, because four out of five pediatricians surveyed say the best possible treatment for a sick toddler is to be handed off to a bunch of strangers as quickly as possible so as not to interrupt Mommy and Daddy's work day.

Quick reality check: Complicated problems rarely have simple solutions. In reality, hiring someone to videotape your child's Little League game does not make working all weekend okay. Similarly, while paying someone to fetch employees' dry cleaning is a nice gesture, it does not counterbalance the increased productivity demands feeding their anxieties and driving them to put in such long hours. In a 1996 Gallup poll, one quarter of employees surveyed said they feel "stressed out" at work every single day. While great news for the makers of Maalox, this bodes ill for our society's overall mental health.

Americans claim they are ready for a change. A 1994 Gallup poll showed that approximately one third of those surveyed would take a 20 percent pay cut in exchange for fewer work hours for them or their spouse. But it will take more than a few office errand boys to effect the required change. At this point, most Americans don't need any help in obsessing over work. By and large, we're a culture that has taken the Protestant work ethic one step too far, gauging people's worth by their professional (and financial) status. Even as we bemoan our chaotic schedules, we're suspicious of those who aren't on the fast track. Twenty-somethings who don't come flying out of college ready to beg, borrow or commit investor fraud to make company VP within five years are labeled "slackers" and expected to move to Seattle and serve up espressos at Starbucks.

No one is looking to undermine America's global competitiveness. We simply need to accept that the law of diminishing returns applies to workloads, and we need to start formulating workplace policy based on that understanding. But don't look for Uncle Sam to lead the way: Executing a bold move in exactly the wrong direction, the IRS ruled in December that companies can now give employees the option to, instead of taking their allotted vacation days, have a percentage of their vacation pay placed into tax-deferred 401k retirement accounts. (Just think of what a nice funeral that fund will provide for when you drop dead from exhaustion at age 45.)

Reform-minded employers may have to take the first step, making better use of part-time work arrangements, and setting limits on the hours people work and the vacation days they must take. Otherwise, we'll continue to learn the hard way about the ugly results of all work and no play. My former employer certainly did: Just a few weeks into my job, I discovered that the woman who'd previously held my position had been wheeled away on a stretcher one afternoon after a small "stress attack" she'd had in front of the elevators.

Needless to say, no one there pushed me to work weekends.

Article Review Form at end of book.

According to Veninga, what are three strategies organizations can use to help create a productive and healthy workplace? How does effective goal setting help employees reduce job stress?

Stress in the Workplace:

How to Create a Productive and Healthy Work Environment

Robert L. Veninga

Professor, University of Minnesota

Address delivered to the Tenth World Productivity Congress, Santiago, Chile, October 14, 1997.

Thank you for the opportunity to speak to the Tenth World Productivity Congress. It is fitting that this conference is held in Santiago, Chile—a city and country which has made significant progress in improving the productivity and living standards of its people.

I have been asked to speak on a topic that is dear to my heart and that is how to create a healthy, productive work-force. It is a pertinent topic, because occupational stress can reduce the vitality of even the most upbeat worker.

Today, stress and its resulting illnesses impact workers in almost every corner of the world. In Australia, stress claims by government workers increased by 90% between 1990 and 1993. A French survey showed 64% of nurses and 61% of teachers were upset over the stresses associated with their jobs. Another study found that stress-related diseases such as high blood pressure and heart attacks cost the U.S. economy $200 billion a year in absenteeism, compensation claims and medical expenses.

The central problem according to the 1993 World Labor Report by the United Nation's International Labor Organization, is that stress stems from impersonal, ever-changing, and often hostile workplaces. In analyzing 100 of America's largest corporations, Natin Noria, a professor at Harvard University found that three million workers in these companies were laid off since 1978. The impact on displaced workers is significant. In a study of 900 Canadian families that had experienced job loss, researchers discovered high levels of psychological problems among the unemployed—55% to 75% greater then those who hold steady jobs.

Workers who survive corporate downsizing also find their lives impacted by the vast changes sweeping their work environments. *The Lancet*, a British medical journal, recently reported increased illness among employees who survive job reductions. States Mark Braverman, founder of Crisis Management Group in Newton, Massachusetts, "Often times, the people who remain after the cuts are made, wind up feeling demoralized, overworked, stressed, and fearful that they will be targeted the next time around."

Now the questions I would like to address are these: What can be done to diminish stress in the workplace? How can the health and vitality of workers be preserved in an era of rapid change? Here are five suggestions.

Strategy One: If in a leadership position, carefully determine whether organization restructuring is in the best interests of your company—and your employees. As indicated earlier, there has been a wave of job layoffs in American corporations. In some cases the layoffs have helped improve the financial health of the organization. But in many instances the restructuring did little to improve productivity. A review of 52 studies of corporate restructuring involving several thousand companies found that on an average, organizational downsizing had little if any positive impact on earnings or stock market performance. And regrettably, 70% of U.S. companies report serious morale problems caused by years of upheaval and restructuring.

The impact on the lives of employees who have lost their jobs is considerable. A 42-year-old manager who lost a valued job when his employer restructured operation said: "You are never the same. Panic sets in. You wonder how you are going to pay the mortgage and meet your obligations. You worry about health insurance. And you always wonder if the loss of a job was somehow your fault."

"Stress in the Workplace" by Robert L. Veninga, *Vital Speeches of the Day*, January 15, 1998, v. 64, n. 7. Used by permission.

What if a corporation has no choice but to down-size operations? It is important to provide severance packages and career counseling services to terminated employees. It is helpful to let workers know that positive letters of recommendation can be written to prospective employers. But it is also important to provide support to the "survivors"—those employees whose have been preserved. The reason? Often there is resentment towards cost-cutting administrators even if their job has been protected. Said one manager: "If I'm cynical, it's for a good reason. I have seen too many people thrown out on the street. And yet the same basic management team that got us in the predicament . . . was still there. You try to be objective. You say there are too many layers of management. There's too much redundancy. It's too difficult to get things done. Then you see lots of people getting hit for little or no reason. If it's someone in your area who is being cut you momentarily think: 'Thank God it wasn't me.' Then you become very bitter about it. Especially if you know that it's somebody who has worked hard, has done a good job and taken their responsibilities seriously."

How best to retain the loyalty of survivors? It is crucial for employees to understand the financial and operational reasons for "right-sizing" an organization. But it is equally important for survivors to understand why their jobs were preserved. They need to believe that their contributions are vital to the future of the enterprise. In brief, they need to see a new challenge, a challenge which when realized will be rewarded by their employer.

Strategy Two: Reexamine work loads. Today there is a tacit expectation in many companies: you cannot work too hard or too long. A new corporate model dubbed "High Commitment" has sprung up that suggests your life should resolve around work and not much else. Said a former executive at Bankers Trust: "Nobody ever got up on a desk and said, 'Work harder,' but somebody would call an occasional meeting at 8 A.M. Then it became the regular 8 o'clock meeting. Then there was the occasional 7 A.M. meeting. And the dinner meetings. It just kept spreading."

According to *Fortune* magazine, "At many companies the kind of punishing hours once reserved for crises have become the standard drill. A whole generation of managers has grown up who never had a 40 hour work week; it appears that some never will. Or will they? With their personal and family lives in smithereens or a state of perpetual postponement, what seems a substantial contingent of the formerly ambitious have begun harboring seditious thoughts about the work ethic and the all-importance of a dazzling career. Exhaustion and disillusion are setting in."

There is growing evidence that employees are less willing to tolerate long work hours. Marilyn Moats Kennedy, managing partner of Career Strategies in Wilmette, Ill., says she sees more people in job interviews stating clearly the number of hours they are willing to work. "I know of one young software engineer who told every employer he interviewed with, that he would give them 40 spectacular hours a week and nothing more," she states. Nonetheless, he received two job offers.

Fortunately, shortening the work-week can be a win-win situation for both employer and employee. According to the U.S. News/Bozell poll, 62% of the managers surveyed indicated that shorter work hours will give employees an incentive to be more productive and would have little impact on the country's overall standard of living. What about companies that have reduced the number of hours employees work? Productivity is strengthened. Morale improves. And stress is diminished. For example, when Metro Plastics Technologies in Columbus, Indiana diminished the number of hours worked by employees, customer returns in the second half of the year dropped 72% compared to the first half—an indication of an improved product. Costs for parts in need of additional work also fell. At a company where job openings stood unfilled for months, hundreds of highly qualified applicants now regularly submit their resumes.

I cannot emphasize this point enough: if work forces are to be skillfully managed so that productivity and morale are heighten, sensitivity to the workloads of employees must be carefully addressed. Fortunately there are executives who understand this issue. David R. Carpenter, CEO of Transamerica states the issue succinctly: "We can't beat people into the ground anymore." States Patrick Price, CEO of San Francisco Federal Savings, "We must recognize the signs when managers are being pushed too hard (we must) help out with people, systems—whatever it takes."

Strategy Three: Unleash employee creativity. Over the past two decades, I and several colleagues have interviewed hundreds of workers in an attempt to understand how stress impacts mental and physical health. We have concluded that many workers feel disillusioned because they feel that their talents are not being adequately recognized.

It is a fact: the talents of employees are not adequately utilized in most organizations. In a study of 1,400 employees by the consulting firm Kepner-Tregoe, two-thirds of the workers stated that their employer was operating with less than half the brain power available. Even worse: 58% of workers and 49% of managers polled stated that they didn't understand decisions made by top management. 39% of workers and 29% of managers indicated that they weren't clear about their roles and responsibilities in solving organizational problems. In short, there were major communication problems in most organizations that keep employees from working to full capacity.

How best to encourage creativity? It is important to understand that creativity is almost universally present in people, at least in childhood. As documented by Laurie Broedling, Senior Vice President, McDonnell Douglas Corporation, the preschool years represent a golden age of creativity in which "every child sparkles with artistry and innovative problem-solving skills. Young children paint in bold and daring strokes. They are able to master two or more languages with little difficulty. After that however, with exposure to more structure and discipline, and with more peer group pressure, a kind of rot sets in, and most of us grow into artistically stunted adults.

It starts with school and it gets a whole lot worse as one enters corporate life."

How do you encourage creativity? The starting point is to ask employees if their talents are being adequately utilized. The answers might surprise you, for managers are often unaware of the creative potential within their staff. In Robert Blake and Jane Mouton's pioneering work on leadership, it was discovered that many workers were perceived to be unproductive at work, yet were highly productive in their personal lives. Many were deeply involved in their communities, providing leadership to schools, churches, and civic organizations. But at work, their talents often went unnoticed.

If you want to energize your workforce, tap into the creativity of your employees. And when new ideas begin to transform your organization, acknowledge employee contributions. As author Morty Lefkoe notes: "Executives assume employees want more money and more benefits. But in my experience with more than 10,000 workers, they say they want some chance to be acknowledged."

We now come to a fourth strategy for reducing stress and that is to keep your goals sharply focused. Is stress really reduced by establishing meaningful goals? Does higher productivity result when priorities are sharpened? Consider a twenty-year study at Yale University in which researchers asked graduates whether they had committed themselves in writing to what they wanted to accomplish in life. Only 3% had taken the time to establish their goals. The class was again surveyed twenty years later. The 3% who had established their goals were more satisfied with their lives then those who had not. And 97% of the wealth of the class was in the hands of the same 3%.

In interviewing hundreds of employees about occupational stress, I ask: "What are your goals? What are you seeking to accomplish?" Those who report low job satisfaction and high stress usually have difficulty verbalizing priorities. While those who report high job satisfaction and low stress are able to articulate their objectives.

When individuals are committed to reaching a goal, optimism resurfaces. This is true both professional and personally. Raymond Flannery, Jr., an Assistant Professor of Psychology at Harvard University studied 1,200 individuals who weathered tough times—from divorce to the death of a loved one to job loss. Those who were able to survive life's insults were committed to reaching a goal. In addition, the survivors ("stress-tolerant people") had the benefit of strong, caring friendships.

It is difficult to overemphasize the empowerment that comes when employees establish meaningful priorities. I think for example, of a nurse manager who can barely contain her excitement about an innovative staffing plan that will improve quality of care while reducing costs. Or I think of an occupational physician who smiled broadly as he described a new chair that he designed to eliminate back problems and reduce worker's compensation costs. Or I think of a high school teacher who discovered that Hollywood films can keep restless teenagers involved in classroom deliberations. If you want to manage stress and reclaim optimism, refocus your goals.

Now we come to a final strategy by which to manage stress and that is to stay open to new ideas—ideas which have the power to alter your outlook on life. In T.H. White's wonderful novel, *The Once and Future King*, Merlyn states. "The best thing for being sad is to learn something. That is the only thing that never fails. You may grow old and tremble in your anatomies, you may lie awake at night listening to the disorders of your veins, you may miss your only love, you may see the world around you devastated by evil lunatics or you know your honor trampled in the sewers of base minds. There is only one thing for it then—to learn. Learn why the world wags and what wags it. That is the only thing which the mind can ever exhaust, never alienate, never be tortured by, never fear of distrust and never dream of regretting. Learning is the thing for you."

Despite the problems associated with many work environments, it is a fact that we live in an incredible age in which new knowledge is produced daily. Eighty-five percent of all scientists who have ever lived are alive today. The time interval between the realization of an idea and its arrival in the marketplace is now the shortest in history, usually but a few months. From the time of Christ's birth to the middle of the 18th century, knowledge doubled. 150 years later it doubled again and then again in only 50 years. Today it doubles every four or five years.

The significance? This is an exciting era in which to live and in which to work. But for workers to catch this excitement, they need to learn, grow and increase their knowledge. This implies that employers must invest in the development of employees. But it also suggests that workers be willing to learn, expand their frame of reference and discover new ways to utilize their talents in an ever changing workplace.

How then can stress be managed in the workplace? Part of the responsibility lies with the employers in preserving jobs and keeping workloads manageable. But a large share of the responsibility rests with each of us as we refocus our goals, prioritize our activities and discover new ideas which transforms our lives. Thank you.

Article Review Form at end of book.

WiseGuide Wrap-Up

In this section, we have reviewed the meaning and consequences of stress. As some of the readings suggest, chronic organizational stressors, including time and security issues in organizations, seem to be increasing. Organizations, employees, and families will pay a high price if these issues are not effectively addressed. Organizations face the possibility of losing employees reducing job effectiveness, and seeing increased health costs. Employees and their families face health problems and threats to the security of the family unit. Answers to combating stress rest with the reciprocal interaction between the organization and the employee; this works for their mutual benefit.

R.E.A.L. Site

This list provides a print preview of typical **Coursewise** R.E.A.L. sites. (There are over 100 such sites at the **Courselinks**™ site.) The danger in printing URLs is that web sites can change overnight. As we went to press, these sites were functional using the URLs provided. If you come across one that isn't, please let us know via email to: webmaster@coursewise.com. Use your Passport to access the most current list of R.E.A.L. sites at the **Courselinks** site.

Site name: Occupational Safety & Health Administration
URL: http://www.osha.gov/
Why is it R.E.A.L.? Established by the Occupational Safety and Health Act of 1970, OSHA is a federal agency charged with protecting the health of America's workers. This site presents the OSHA mission and provides information on regulations, programs, and enforcement policies.
Key topics: safety, health
Try this: What are some of the most hazardous occupations? To find out, select the Library link, then Workplace Injury and Illness Statistics. Compare several interesting occupations. Be sure to visit Hot Topics to find some of the current issues facing OSHA. What are some of the hazards connected with dry cleaning? Select Hot Topics, then Subject Index. Scroll down to then select Dry Cleaning.

Site name: Go Ask Alice!
URL: http://www.goaskalice.columbia.edu/index.html
Why is it R.E.A.L.? This site provides some basic information about stress, health, and a variety of other topics.
Key topics: stress, health
Try this: Do pets really reduce stress levels? Select Emotional Health and then scroll down to Pets and Stress Management. Are you surprised?

Site name: The American Institute of Stress
URL: http://www.stress.org/
Why is it R.E.A.L.? This nonprofit organization serves as a clearinghouse for stress-related information. It was founded by Hans Selye, Norman Cousins, and Linus Pauling. It maintains a large library of information on all stress-related topics and is constantly updated from both scientific and lay publications.
Key topics: stress, health
Try this: Is stress America's number 1 health problem? Scroll down to America's #1 Health Problem and Job Stress and decide for yourself.

Index

Names and page numbers in **bold** type indicate authors and their articles; page numbers in italics indicate illustrations; page numbers followed by *t* indicate tables; page numbers followed by *n* indicate notes.

A

AAA (American Automobile Association) Foundation for Traffic Safety, 145
AAAP (American Association for Applied Psychology), 38
ABEPP (American Board of Examiners of Professional Psychology), 39
Abraham, N. L., 102
Aburdene, Patricia, 217, 222
abusive organization, 61–62
The Abusive Organization (Powell), 61*n*
academic psychologists, women as, 31
Academy of Human Resource Development (R.E.A.L. Site), 51
Achievement via Independence, 109
Achilles, Paul, 40
ACP (Association of Consulting Psychologists), 38
activity, modeling, and teaching knowledge, 221
ADA. *See* Americans with Disabilities Act (ADA)
Adams, Nina, 144, 145
Adams, Scott, 18
Adams Consulting Group, 142
Adamson, P., 133
Adjective Checklist, 111
Adkins, C. L., 119
Adler, Seymour, 96, 97, 190
ADR (alternative dispute resolution) program, 76
Adult Learning (Bregman and Thorndike), 37
Aetna Life Insurance Company, 37, 40
affirmative action, 79, 81, 219–20
African Americans, economics of, 218–20
age discrimination, 76
Age Discrimination in Employment Act (1967), 73
agreeableness, 102
Agriculture, U.S. Department of (USDA), 145
Agronick, G., 111
Aiken, H. R., 105
Allen, Robert E., 67
The Alliance for Employee Growth and Development (R.E.A.L. Site), 157
Allied Signal, 171
alternative dispute resolution (ADR) program, 76
Alvos, L., 188
AMA (American Management Association), 4
Amazon.com, 211
American Apartheid (Massey), 80
American Association for Applied Psychology (AAAP), 38
American Automobile Association (AAA) Foundation for Traffic Safety, 145

American Board of Examiners of Professional Psychology (ABEPP), 39
American Compensation Association (R.E.A.L. Site), 174
American Enterprise Institute for Public Policy Research (R.E.A.L. Site), 174
American Express, 219
The American Institutue of Stress (R.E.A.L. Site), 242
American Management Association (AMA), 4, 37
American Management Marketing Series, 37
American Men of Science (Cattell), 31, 32, 41
American Psychological APA Directory, 32
American Psychological Association (APA), 21, 25, 27, 28, 31, 38
American Psychological Society, 48
The American Psychologist, 3*n*, 107*n*
American Society for Training and Development (R.E.A.L. Site), 157
American Society of Mechanical Engineers, 39
American Statistical Association, 39
American Steel & Wire, 11
American Women, 41
Americans with Disabilities Act (ADA)
  and EEOC, 76
  mental illness, 73, 74, 84–85, 87–88
  and personality measure, 111–12
Ameritech Publishing, 146
Amoco Corporation, 141, 145
Angell, James Rowland, 34
"angry white males," 81
Anheuser-Busch, 11
anti-discrimination law, 57–58
APA (American Psychological Association), 21, 25, 27, 28, 31, 38
APA Monitor, 96*n*
Appleby, Mike, 126, **133**
applied psychology, 21–22, 31, 40
AptarGroup Inc., 178, 180
Army Alpha General Intelligence Examinations, 37
Arnold & Porter law firm, 237
Arthur D. Little survey, 12
Arvey, R. D., 102, 118
Ash, Mary Kay, 202
Ashkenas, R., 119, 121
Ashworth, S., 109
Assessment of Intellectual Functioning (Aiken), 105
Association of Consulting Psychologists (ACP), 38
Astra Merck Pharmaceuticals, 144, 148
Asymetrix Learning Systems, 142
AT&T, 67, 69, 171, 219
Atwater, Leanne, 170
Avis, 219

B

baby boom demographics, 218
Bacon, Francis, 24, 25
Baldwin, James Mark, 25
Bandura, A., 189
Bank, J., 133
Bankert, Ellen, 64
Barclay, Richard L., 99
Barclay Enterprises, Inc., 99
Barnes & Noble, 211
Barrick, M. R., 102–3, 105, 109
Barry, B., 103–4
Barthol, R. P., 110
Bartlett, Chris, 214
Bauman, Steve, 200
behavior, 110–11, 188–90
behaviorism, 28, 29
Behling, Orlando, 94, **99**
Bell Atlantic, 7, 127
Bells on Their Toes (Gilbreth and Carey), 41
Beloit College, 28
Ben & Jerry's Homemade, Inc., 206
The Benjamin Group, 64
Bergmann, Frithjof, 196–97
Bern, D. J., 111
Bernstein, Aaron, 194, **198**
Bessler, Joni, 198
Biegel, Suzanne, 141, 146, 148–49
Big Five personality dimensions, 100–103, 108, 109, 110, 120
Bills, Marion Almira, 28, 32, 33*t*, 35–42
Binet, Alfred, 25
Bing, Stanley, 233, **234**
Bingham, Walter VanDyke
  and female I/O pioneers, 34, 35
  as I/O pioneer, 2, 21, 22–23, 26, 27, 28–29
biodata, 121
Blank, Deborah, 141, 142–43, 144, 148
Bloom, B. S., 229
BNA Publishing, 65
Boeing, 171, 201
Booz, Allen & Hamilton, 198, 200
Borman, Wally, 47
Boston College's Center for Work & Family, 64
Bouchard, T. J., 102
boundaries, organizational, 116
boundaryless organization, 115–23
boundaryless work, 5
Bracken, David W., 165
Bradley, Bill, 220
Brain Dominance Assessment, 164
Braverman, Mark, 239
Bravo Multimedia, 15, 141, 142
Bregman, Adolph, 34
Bregman, Elsie Oschrin, 32, 33*t*, 34, 36–42

243

Bregman Language Completion Scales (Bregman), 37
Bretz, R. D., 119
Bridges, W., 116
Brodeling, Laurie, 240
Brodo, Robert, 142–43, 145, 146, 147, 149
Brown, C. W., 100
Brown, Pat, 65
Brown University, 34
Bryn Mawr College, 25, 32
Buchanan, Patrick J., 67
Bullis, R. Craig, 212, **224**
Bureau of Labor Statistics, 199
Burtt, Harold, 21, 24, 29
Business and Society Review, 79*n,* 129*n,* 205*n*
Business Ethics, 82*n*
Business Week, 63, 64–65, 198*n,* 203
By The Book (simulation program), 145

C

Cacioppe, R., 133
Cadet Uniform Services, 5–6
CAI (Computer Assisted Instruction), 225
Cambridge University, 24
Campbell, D. T., 8
Campbell, J. P., 110
Campion, Mike, 2, **45–46**
Care of the Soul (Moore), 209
Career Strategies, 240
Carey, E. G., 41
Carnegie Institute of Technology, 27, 29, 35, 40
Carnegie Mellon University, 27
Carpenter, David R., 240
Carson, Jerome, 126, **150**
Cascio, Wayne F., 2, **3**
Casellas, Gilbert
Caspi, A., 111
Castel, Ted, 206
Castro, Dan, 144, 146, 147
Catbert, 18
Cattell, James McKeen
    and female pioneers, 31, 37, 40
    as I/O pioneer, 2, 21, 22, 24–26, 27, 28, 29
CBT (cognitive-behavioral training), 150–56
CCH Business Owners Toolkit (R.E.A.L. Site), 210
Center for Creative Leadership, 96, 173
The Center for Innovative Leadership (R.E.A.L. Site), 232
Center for Maritime Education, Seaman's Church Institute, 141
Center for New Work, 196
CEOs (chief executive officers), attention to human resources, 16, 17–18
Challenge, 66*n*
Challenger, Gray & Christmas Inc., 200
Chappell, Tom, 206
character, 99–100, 224
Cheaper by the Dozen (Gilbreth and Carey), 41
Chemical Engineering, 145
Chick-Fil-A Inc., 178–79
chief executive officers (CEOs), attention to HR, 16, 17–18
child development, 41

childcare, 183, 237–38
Children's Health Center, 82
Chirac, Jacques, 71
Christianity and work, 59
Citibank, 199
Civil Rights Act (1964 and1991), 73, 76, 79
climate, work, 119
clinical psychologists, women as, 31
Clinton, Bill, 67
coaches, 5
Coca-Cola, 219
cognitive abilities testing, 7–8, 120
Cognitive Learning Objective Classification, 229
cognitive-behavioral training (CBT), 150–56
collective bargaining, 68
College Board Online: Career Search (R.E.A.L. Site), 124
Collins, J. M., 109
Columbia University, 25, 26, 28, 32–33, 41
communication technologies and stress, 236–38
community, in workplace, 205–9
compensation and changing work world, 10–11
competition, 3–6, 29
Computer Assisted Instruction (CAI), 225
conflict
    on the job, 57–58
    in workplace, 234–35
Confucious, 141
Conley, Don, 82–83
Conley, J. J., 111
Connecticut State Psycholgical Society, 39
Connecticutt Valley Association of Psychologists, 39
Conoco, 145
conscientiousness, 102, 103*t,* 104–5
Continental Bank Corporation, 5
contingency theories of leadership, 5
contingent workers, 69
contract employment, 116–17
Cook, M. F., 99
Cornell University, 26
Corning Incorporated, 213, 214
corporate discrimination, 79–81
correlation data, job satisfaction, 196–97
Costa, P. T., Jr., 111
costs and benefits
    community in workplace, 205–9
    shorter work week, 71
    Starbucks, 181–84
Cottle, Michelle, 233, **236**
Court TV (R.E.A.L. Site), 93
CPI Self-Control Scale, 109, 110
Cragun, John R., 133
creativity, employee, 240–41
crisis management and HR professionals, 15–16
Crissey, Orlo, 40
Critical Training Attributes (CTAs), 135
Cronbach, L. J., 112
cross-cultural differences in future time perspective, 186
CSR (customer service representative), 6
CTAs (Critical Training Attributes), 135

cultures, workplace, 119–20, 122, 236–37
customer service representative (CSR), 6

D

Dartmouth College, 24, 40
Darwin, Charles, 23, 24
David, Andrea, 147
Day, D. V., 120
DDI (Developmental Dimensions International), 127
De Alonso, Marcela Perez, 199
Defense, U.S. Department of (DOD), 134
Defense Logistics Agency (DLA), 134
DeMeuse, K. P., 39
Deming, W. Edwards, 10
democracy, workplace as, 5
Denny's, 219
Department of Behavioral Sciences and Leadership, West Point, 227–29
Devanna, M. A., 119, 120
Developmental Dimensions International (DDI), 127
Dewey, John, 28
Diagnostic and Statistical Manual (DSM), 87
Diasability Rights of Advocates, 90
DILBERT™, 18
Dillon, John T., 199
disabled individuals, 36, 89, 112
    See also Americans with Disabilities Act (ADA)
discrimination
    affirmative action, 79, 81, 219–20
    anti-discrimination law, 57–58
    corporate, 79–81
    and EEOC, 76, 77–78
    gender based, 82–83
    and personality measures, 111–12
disenfranchisement, employee feeling of, 54–56
Disney, 8
diversity, managing and valuing, 217–23
Division of Applied Psychology, 28–29
DLA (Defense Logistics Agency), 134
DOD (U. S. Department of Defense), 134
Dodge, Raymond, 28
Domino, G., 187, 188
DOT (U.S. Department of Transportation), 145
Downey, June, 34
downsizing, 4, 67, 69, 199, 218, 239–40
downward mobility, 4
"The Drew Carey Show" (TV show), 18
driver-ZED (simulation program), 145
Dunn, Graham, 126, **150**
Dunn, W. S., 105
DuPont, 61, 68, 133, 171
Durkheim, Emile, 68

E

Earles, J. A., 100
Eastman Kodak, 37
EBIM S.A., 141
Economic Policy Institute (R.E.A.L. Site), 174

The Economic Press: Motivation and Inspiration (R.E.A.L. Site), 193
economics
   of African Americans, 218–20
   competition, changing nature of, 3–6
   globalization, 214–15
education
   and diversity, 220
   leadership, 229–30
   and prejudice, 221
educational psychologists, women as, 31, 34
Edwards Personal Preference Schedule, 111
EEO (Equal Employment Opportunity Act), 73, 79–81
EEOC. *See* Equal Employment Opportunity Commission (EEOC)
Einstein, Albert, 6
Elder, G. H., 111
elder-care, 183
ELF Interactive, 145, 147
Eli Lilly, 68
Ellig, Bruce R., 52, **54**
emotional stability, 101–2
empiricism, 24, 25
Employee Resources, 55–56
Employee Selection: Will Intelligence and Conscientiousness Do the Job? (Behling), 99n
employment
   best companies, 63–65, 181, 202
   boundaryless organization, 115–23
   employee selection, 7–8, 99–106, 120–21
   employment-related lawsuits and EEOC, 76–78
   and motivation, 178–80
   needs for next century, 96–98
   performance reviews, 160–61
   and personality measurement, 108–13
   recruitment and boundaryless organization, 118–19
   training and development, 8–10
   unemployment and cognitive-behavioral training (CBT), 150–56
   and welfare capitalism, 66–70
   See also jobs; work; workers; workplace
Employment Non-discrimination Act, 75
empowered workers, 5–6
entrepreneurship, 218
Equal Employment Opportunity Act (EEO), 73, 79–81
Equal Employment Opportunity Commission (EEOC)
   corporate discrimination, 80
   Exxon *Valdez*, 86
   life at, 75–78
   personality measurement, 111–12
   R.E.A.L. Site, 93
   United Parcel Service (UPS), 90
   See also Americans with Disabilities Act (ADA)
Equal Pay Act (1963), 73
ethics training, 129–32
eugenics, 25
The Exclusive Factory (Olson), 90
Executive Pay Watch (R.E.A.L. Site), 174
extraversion, 101
Exxon *Valdez*, 86

F

facilitators, 5
Family and Medical Leave Act, 63
family friendly organizations, 63–65, 237–38
Family Leave and Medical Act (1993), 73
Fare Start, 183
Farr, James, 47, 127, 128
Federal Express (Fed Ex), 133, 143, 148, 172
federal government and workplace legislation, 75–78
Feild, H. S., 99
female entrepreneurship, 218
female psychologists
   career settings, 31–32, 35
   I/O pioneers, 31–32, 33t, 34–42
   university enrollment, 32
Fernald, Mabel, 34
Ferree, Clarence E., 32
field studies, importance of, 39
Finn, S. E., 111
Fiola, Janet, 203
First Tennessee Bank, 63, 65
Fiske, D. W., 8
5 x 6 Model, 110
FJA (Functional Job Analysis), 117
Flannery, Raymond, Jr., 241
flattened hierarchies and economic competitiveness, 5
Fleenor, John, 165
flexibility, workplace, 5, 61, 96–97, 183, 237
Florida International University, 97
Folsom, Marion, 70
Fondrick, Marlene, 82
Forbes Magazine ©, 86n, 222
Ford, Henry, 8, 196
Fortune, 63, 64, 65, 99, 165, 181, 202, 234n, 240
France, shorter work-week for, 71
Frank B. Gilbreth, Inc., Consulting Engineers, 37
Fraser, George, 212, **217**
The Freeman, 57n
free-market system and morality, 57–60
Frei, R. L., 109
Freud, Sigmund, 24
Freudians, 29
Freyd, Max, 28
The Fulcrum Group, 82–83
Functional Job Analysis (FJA), 117
functionalism, 22, 23, 32, 34, 39
Furomoto, L., 32, 42
Future Events Test, 187, 188
future time perspective, 185–92

G

gain-sharing *vs.* profit sharing, 11
Gallup poll, 238
Galton, Sir Francis, 23, 24, 25
Gandois, Jean, 71
Garland, Susan B., 91
Gasser, Michael, 2, **47**
Gates, Bill, 99, 106
Gateway Management Consulting, 127
Gatewood, R. D., 99
GE (General Electric), 7, 10, 41, 68

GE Supply, 144, 145, 146, 148
gender differences
   discrimination based on, 82–83
   early career settings, 31–32, 35
   entrepreneurship, 218
   and personality measures, 111
General Electric (GE), 7, 10, 41, 68
General Electric (GE) Supply, 144, 145, 146, 148
General Foods, 11
general health questionnaire (GHQ), 151
general intelligence (g) and employee selection, 100–101, 104–6
General Motors (GM), 11, 196, 206
Genesis, 59
Gerhart, B., 119
Germany and development of psychology, 22
Gerras, Stephen J., 212, **224**
Ghiselli, E. E., 100, 110
GHQ (general health questionnaire), 151
Giacalone, Robert A., 125, **129**
Gialluca, K. A., 118
Gilbreth, F., Jr., 41
Gilbreth, Frank Bunker, 34, 37
Gilbreth, Inc., 37
Gilbreth, Lillian Moller, 32, 33t, 34, 37–42
Giles, Harold, 7
Gilmartin, Raymond V., 198, 200
Girl Scouts of America, 40, 41
Gjesme, T., 186
globalization, 3–4, 214–15
GM (General Motors), 11, 196, 206
Go Ask Alice (R.E.A.L. Site), 242
goal attainment, planning for, 189–90
goal-setting theory, 185
Gonzalez, A., 187
Gorbachev, Mikhail S., 207
Gordon, Kate, 32, 34
Gore, Tipper, 84
Gos, 196
Gospel of John, 59
Gough, H. G., 109
Gray, Jeffrey, 126, **150**
Greenfield, Jerry, 206
Gregson, R. A. M., 188
group-based situational tests, 8
GTE, 61
Guest, David, 126, **150**
Guided Social Simulation (GuSS) program, 146
Gumbel, Andrew, 53, **71**
GuSS (Guided Social Simulation) program, 146

H

Haan, N., 111
Halcrow, Allan, 15
Hall, G. Stanley, 24, 34
Hand, Learned, 215
Handbook for Employee Recruitment and Retention (AMA), 99
Harris, Tom, 65
Hartka, E., 111
Hartmann, G. W., 39
Harvard Business Review, 214

Index   245

Harvard University, 22, 23–24, 28, 241
Hayes, Joseph, 34
Hayes, Mary Holmes Stevens, 32, 33t, 34–36, 38–42
Head to Head (Thorow), 214
Hellmuth, Obata & Kassabaum (HOK), 203
Helson, R., 111
Henik, W., 187, 188
Henry, Ed, 40
Herrmann, Ned, 164
heuristics, training for, 129
Hewitt Associates, 64
Hewlett Packard Corporation, 96, 97
high-performance work practices (HPWP), 9
Hippocrates, 164
HIV and ADA, 88
HLW International, 199
Hofstee, W. K. B., 108
Hogan, Joyce, 95, **107**
Hogan, Robert, 95, **107**
Hogan Personality Inventory, 110
HOK (Hellmuth, Obata & Kassabaum), 203
Holland, J. L., 110
Hollingworth, Harry L., 34, 40
Hollingworth, Leta S., 34
Honeycutt, Bradley, 182
Honeywell, 82–83, 171
Hoppock, Robert, 29
Horn, Ralph, 63
Hough, L. M., 109, 112
Houghton, James R., 212, **213**
Howard, Ann, 127, 128
HPWP (high-performance work practices), 9
HR (human resource) professionals, 16, 17–20, 182–83
HR Magazine, 63n, 75n, 170n
HRFocus, 178n
Hughes Aircraft Co., 200
Hull, Clark, 29
Human Resource Director as recognized profession, 48
human resource (HR) professionals, 16, 17–20, 182–83
Human Resource Management, 54n
Human Resource Planning, 115n, 133n
Human Resource Selection (Gatewood and Feild), 99
Human Scale (Sale), 206–7
humor and human resource workers, 16
Hunter, J. E., 100
Hunter, R. F., 100

I

IBM, 68, 69, 206
IEC (Internal & External Communication), 141, 144, 146, 148
ILS, 146
Immigration Reform and Control Act (1986), 73
incentives and changing work world, 10–11
inclusion, 220
Incomplete Sentences Test, 187, 188
Increasing Human Efficiency in Business (Scott), 27
Independent on Sunday, 71n

Indianapolis Star, 237
individual, value of, 215
individual variation, 25
industrial and organizational (I/O) psychology
  in changing work world, 3–14
  early influences on development of, 21–30
  historical records of, 42
  motivation, 175
  performance/evaluation process, 158
  pride in, 46–47
  recognition of profession, 47–50
  research agenda for, 6–12
  women pioneers in, 31–32, 35–39
The Industrial-Organizational Psychologist, 22, 47n
Information Processing Center - Ogden (IPCO), 134–39
InfoWorld, 160n
Inside Edge (simulation program), 145, 146, 148
Institute for Motion Study, 37
Institute of Personality Assessment and Research, 111
The Institutue for Global Ethics (R.E.A.L. Site), 232
integration issue, 80–81
Intel, 171
Intellectual Procedure (IP) model, 225
intelligence
  general (g), 100–101, 104–6
  as selection criteria, 99–101
  theory of, 25
Internal & External Communication (IEC), 141, 144, 146, 148
international competition, 3–4, 214–15
International Paper Co., 198, 199
International Survey Research Corp., 199
Internet, 360-degree feedback based system, 165
Interviewing for Employment (R.E.A.L. Site), 124
interviews and employee selection, 8
intraversion, 101
I/O psychology. *See* industrial and organizational (I/O) psychology
IP (Intellectual Procedure) model, 225
IPCO (Information Processing Center - Ogden), 134–39
IQ. *See* intelligence
Italy, shorter work-week for, 71

J

Jacoby, Stanford, 52, **66**
Jaffe, Brian D., 160
James, Henry, 24
James, William, 21, 22–23, 24, 28
James McKeen Cattell Fund, 37
Jastrow, James, 25
Jastrow, Joseph, 34
JEI (Job Element Inventory), 117–18
Jesus Christ, 59
Job Element Inventory (JEI), 117–18
jobs
  American, and economic competition, 3–4
  analysis of, 6–7, 116, 117–18, 121–22

  competency, 162–64
  job-based pay system, 10
  satisfaction with, 194, 196–97, 198–201
  stability and welfare capitalism, 69
  See also employment
John, Gospel of, 59
Johns Hopkins University, 24
Johnson, Herbert, 67
Johnson & Johnson, 61
Johnson, Samuel C., 67
S. C. Johnson & Son, 67, 68
Jones, R. G., 7
Jospin, Lionel, 71
Journal of Applied Psychology, 21n, 31n, 37
Journal of Consulting Psychology, 37
Journal of Educational Research, 37
Journal of Personnel Research, 37
Journal of Psychology, 185n
Jung, Carl, 162, 164
Justice, U.S. Department of, 89–90

K

Kaiser Permanente, 199
Kelly, E. L., 111
Kelly-Radford, Lily, 96, 97, 98
Kennedy, Marilyn Moats, 240
Kepner Tregoe Inc., 178, 240
King, Annett, 182
Klimoski, R., 7
Knouse, Stephen B., 125, **129**
knowledge, activity, modeling, and teaching of, 221
knowledge, skills and abilities (KSAs), 116, 117, 118, 120
knowledge-based pay system, 11
Kodak, 67, 68, 69
Koppes, Laura L., 2, **31**
Kornhauser, A. W., 39
Kraft General Foods, 219
KSAs (knowledge, skills and abilities), 116, 117, 118, 120

L

Labor, U.S. Department of, 38
labor laws, 67
labor relations, 68–69
Lafayette College, 24
Lancaster, John, 90
The Lancet, 150n, 239
Landy, Frank J., 2, **21**
LaPlante, Mitchell, 90
Latham, G. P., 185
Laurinaitis, Jill, 175, **177**
Lavender, Debra, 141
law of association, 221
Lawler, E. E., III, 116, 119
Lawrence, David M., 199
layoffs, 4, 67, 69, 199, 218, 239–40
Leaders in Education, 41
leadership
  behaviors for, 213–16
  and best companies to work for, 65, 202
  characteristics of twenty-first century, 222
  defined, 211

needs for next century, 98
training at West Point, 224–31
in well-loved company, 202
least-preferred coworker (LPC) contingency theory, 5
Leffingwell Medal, 41
Lefkoe, Morty, 241
legal issues, 58–59, 73, 76–78, 84–85
Leiseson, William, 66
Lens, W., 188
Leonard, Bill, 75
Lessing, E. E., 188
Levering, Robert, 64, 202
Levine, Howard, 200
Lieber, Ronald, 202
Life Events Scale, 188
Life Insurance Marketing and Research Association (LIMRA), 35
Life Insurance Sales Bureau (LISRB), 35
Life Office Management Association, 37
LIMRA (Life Insurance Marketing and Research Association), 35
Lincoln, Abraham, 101–2
LISRB (Life Insurance Sales Bureau), 35
Locke, E. A., 185, 189
Logan Canyon Outdoor Learning Center, 134
Lotze, Rudolf H., 24
Lovell, J. P., 228
Lowrimore, Larry, 180
loyalty, 198, 240
LPC (least-preferred coworker) contingency theory, 5

M

Maccoby, Michael, 178
MacKinnon, D. W., 107–8
Maclean's, 196n
R. H. Macy and Company, 36, 37, 40
Mahin's Magazine, 27
male entrepreneurship, 218
male psychologists, career settings for, 35
management
changing role of, 5
EEO resistance, 80
motivational posters, 177
outdoor training, 134–35, 137–38
unions, 68
Manganiello, J. A., 188
market individualism, 66, 69
Marks, Mitchell, 96, 97, 98
Marriott International Inc., 8, 199, 200
Martin Marietta, 133
Martinez, Michelle Neely, 52, 63
Mary Kay Inc., 202
Massey, Douglas, 80
Mastroianni, Peggy, 90
Maylone, T., 118
McCarney, Rosemary, 203, 204
McClelland, D. C., 99
McCrae, R. R., 111
McDaniel, M. A., 109
McDonnell Douglas Corp., 171, 201, 240
McEvoy, Glenn M., 126, 133
McGregor, Douglas, 164
McGuire, Patrick A., 94, 96
McHenry, J. J., 109

MCI, 200
McIntyre, R. M., 10
McKinsey Quarterly, 141
McNally, Jeffrey A., 212, 224
McNerney, Donald J., 176, 178
Meador, Chrys, 86
The Measurement of Intelligence (Bregman and Thorndike), 37
Medtronic, Inc., 203
Megatrends (Aburdene and Nesbitt), 217, 218
mental disabilities and ADA, 84–85, 87–88
mental testing, 25
mentors, 5
Merck & Co., 61, 198, 200
Metro Plastics Technology, 240
Microsoft, 69, 94, 99
Midland Bank (UK), 61
Military leadership, West Point, 224–31
Mills Longitudinal Study, 111
Milne, Nancy, 143, 146, 149
Milsap, R., 111
Miner, A. S., 116
Miner, J. B., 28
Minnesota Multiphasic Personality Inventory (MMPI), 108, 110
Miovski, Gerry, 199
MMPI (Minnesota Multiphasic Personality Inventory), 108, 110
mobility, downward, 4
Model of Organizational Leadership, West Point, 227
Moffat, Joan, 182, 183, 184
Moller, Lillian, 32, 33t, 34, 37–42
Monitor, 127n
Moore, Bruce V., 21, 27, 34, 39
Moore, Thomas, 209
moral obligation and work, 57–60
Moskowitz, Milton, 64, 202
Mosley, Neoshon, 2, 47
Motivating Employees (R.E.A.L. Site), 193
motivation
early study of, 22–23
employee, 178–80, 181–84
future time perspective, 185–92
posters and management, 177
Starbucks, 181–84
Motorola, 61, 142, 145
Mount, M. K., 102–3, 105, 109
Münsterberg, Hugo, 2, 21, 22, 23–24, 26, 27, 28, 29
Murphy, Kevin, 96, 98
Murray, Bridget, 127
mutual benefit associations, 66

N

Nalewanski, Loren M., 199–200
Napoli, D. S., 31, 32
Nash, Laura, 237
National Academy of Engineering, 39
National Association of Manufacturers, 9
National Institutue of Industrial Psychology, 24
National Office Management Association, 41
National Research Council, 41
National Youth Administration (NYA), 38, 40
Naylor, Thomas H., 205

Neither Athens nor Sparta? (Lovell), 228
Nelson, Jodi Barnes, 95, 115
Nelson Motivation Inc. (R.E.A.L. Site), 193
NEO-Personality Inventory, 105
Nesbitt, John, 217
New Deal programs, 38, 67
New Jersey leadership education program, 230
New York Times, 220
Newman, Peter C., 196
Nippon Air Lines, 207
Noe, Ray, 128
Noria, Natin, 239
normative decision theory, 5
Nortel, 172, 203
Northern Telecom Ltd., 203
Northwestern Mutual Life Insurance, 237
Northwestern University, 26, 27, 28, 146
Notable American Women: The Modern Period (Sicherman et al), 41
Nucor Steel, 99
(NYA) National Youth Administration, 38, 40

O

OCB (organizational citizenship behaviors), 104
Occupational Safety and Health Administration (OSHA) (R.E.A.L. Site), 242
occupational training programming, 151
Occupations, 38
O'Connell, A. N., 34, 35, 42
OD (organizational development), 11–12
oil industry and discrimination, 81
Olson, Walter, 90
Olsten Corp., 200
On the Witness Stand (Scott), 27
Once and Future King (White), 241
The 100 Best Companies to Work for in America (Moskowitz and Levering), 64
Ones, Deniz S., 97, 105, 109
The Online Career Center (R.E.A.L. Site), 124
openness to experience, 102–3
Ordway, Tead, 27
O'Reilly, C. A., III, 120
Organ, D. W., 104
organizational citizenship behaviors (OCB), 104
organizational development (OD), 11–12
organizational effectiveness and personality tests, 107–14
organizational vision and outdoor training, 134–35
Orton, Steven M., 200
Oschrin, Elsie, 32, 33t, 34, 36–42
OSHA (Occupational Safety and Health Administration) (R.E.A.L. Site), 242
Osterberg, Rolf, 205
outdoor training techniques, 133–40

P

Paganism and work, 59
Pajama Game, 57
Palmer, George Herbert, 28

PAQ (Position Analysis Questionnaire), 117, 118
parenting, 183, 237–38
Parry, Scott B., 158, **162**
part-time workers, 69
Paterson, Donald G., 21, 36
path-goal theory, 5
patterned behavior description interviews, 8
Pauling, Linus, 29
Pearlson, H. B., 189–90
Peck, M. Scott, 205
peer advice to human resource professionals, 17–18
performance
    appraisal of, 10
    attitudes and, 9–10
    cognitive abilities as predictive of, 7, 120
    personality measures as predictive, 110
    reviews of, 160–61
    360-degree feedback system, 165–69, 170–73
Perle, Ann, 202
Perrin, Towers, 9
personal characteristics and workplace changes, 6–7
personality
    vs. behavior, 110–11
    Big Five personality dimensions, 100–103, 108, 109, 110, 120–21
    boundaryless organization, 120–21
    competencies, 162–64
    defined, 107–8
    discrimination, 111–12
    employment decisions, 8, 109–10, 113
    I/O psychology, 97–98
    measurement, 108–9
    types, 164
The Personality, Job Satisfaction and Turnover Intentions of African-American Male and Female Accountants (R.E.A.L. Site), 210
Personality Journal, 38
personality types (Hippocrates), 164
personnel. *See* human resource (HR) professionals
Personnel, 37
Personnel Director as recognized profession, 48
Personnel Journal 37, 38
Personnel Research Federation, 29, 39
Peters, T. D., 118
Pferrer, J., 4
Phelps, Sherry, 178
Pillsbury, 67
poaching trained workers, 9
Position Analysis Questionnaire (PAQ), 117, 118
Posner, Judith, 218
Posner, Richard, 88
Pour Your Heart Into It (Schultz), 183
Powell, Gary N., 52, **61**
power, business, shift in, 222
pragmatism, 22
precise matching, 104–5
The Prediction of Vocational Success (Bregman and Thorndike), 37

President's Committee on Employment of People with Disabilities, 90
Price, David, A., 74, **86**
Price, Patrick, 240
Price Waterhouse, 61
The Principal Financial Group, 237
privacy and personality measures, 112
problem solving skills, 100
process-based organizations, 6–7
Procter & Gamble, 11, 68
Prodi, Romano, 71
productivity, 11, 199
profit sharing *vs.* gain-sharing, 11
Progressive Education Association on the Committee on the Study of Adolescents, 41
project-based work, 7
Proudfoot, Judith, 150
psychiatric disabilities and ADA, 84–85, 87–88
Psychological Abstracts, 25
Psychological Bulletin, 25, 36, 37
Psychological Corporation, 26, 29, 37
The Psychological Exchange, 38
Psychological Review, 25
psychological types (Jung), 162
Psychologists Employed Full-Time in Industry, 40
Psychology and Industrial Efficiency (Münsterberg), 24, 27
The Psychology of Advertising (Scott), 27
The Psychology of Management (Gilbreth, L.), 34, 37–38
Psychology Today, 177n, 187
purpose, sense of, 203

R

Rand, Gertrude, 32
Rauh, Anne, 183–84
Raynor, J. O., 189
Raytheon Co., 198, 200
RBFG (Royal Bank Financial Group), 143, 145, 146, 149
reading, importance of, 220
R.E.A.L. Sites, 51, 72, 93, 124, 157, 174, 193, 210, 232, 242
realistic job preview (RJP), 119, 120
realistic work cultures, 119–20, 122
recruitment and boundaryless organization, 118–19
Ree, M. J., 100
Reich, Jill, 127
Reilly, R. R., 107
relapse prevention model, 10
Remington Typewriter, 37
resumes, 105–6
Revak, Rob, 180
Rhino Foods, 206, 209
Rickey, Branch, 219
RJP (realistic job preview), 119, 120
RJR Nabisco, 4
Roberts, Brent W., 95, **107,** 111
Roberts, Carol, 198, 199
Robinson, D. E., 116
Robinson, Florence Richardson, 34
Robinson, Jackie, 219

Rogers, Tammy, 2, **47**
The Ron Brown Award for Corporate Leadership (R.E.A.L. Site), 232
Ross, M. W., 188
Rossiter, M. W., 31
Rovensky, John E., 68
The Royal Coaching Journey (simulation program), 144, 145, 146
Royce, Josiah, 24, 28
Ruml, Beardsley, 284
Russell, C. J., 119
Russo, N. F., 34, 35
Rynes, S. L., 119

S

salary and performance appraisal, 10
Salas, E., 10, 118
Sale, Kirkpatrick, 206–7
Salgado, J. F., 102
Salopek, Jennifer J., 141
Sanchez, J. I., 118
Santayana, George, 24, 28
Sartain, Libby, 64
Scarborough, E., 32, 34, 42
Schmidt, F. L., 100
Schneider, B., 121
Schneider, R. J., 112
school psychologists, women as, 31
Schultz, Howard, 183, 184
Schunk, D. H., 189
Science and Common Sense in Working with Men (Hayes, M.), 36
Scott, Walter Dill
    and female pioneers, 35, 36
    as I/O pioneer, 2, 21, 22–23, 26–28
The Scott Company, 27, 29, 36, 40
Seaman's Church Institute of New York, 141
Seaquist Perfect Dispensing, 180
Sears, Roebuck and Company, 37, 67, 68, 69
Seattle Professional Engineering Employees Association (SPEEA), 201
second-hour confirmatory factor analysis, 8
Segal, N. L., 102
Seijts, Gerard H., 176, **185**
selection process, personality tests, 99–106
self-esteem and outdoor training, 140
Seligman, Daniel, 99
service industry and employee selection, 8
sexual harassment, 76, 91–92
Shapiro, Joseph P., 89
Sicherman, G., 41
Silicon Graphics Inc., 99
Silverman, S. B., 120
simulator training, 141–49
six virtues of labor, 59–60
skill issues, 9, 11, 118, 163–64
The Skill Standards Network (R.E.A.L. Site), 157
Skinner, B. F., 24
SMG (Strategic Management Group), 142, 143, 144, 148
social justice and personality tests, 107–14
Social Security and disability, 90
Social Styles Profiles (Wilson), 164

social virtues and work, 59
socialization and future time perspective, 186–87
Society for Human Resource Management (R.E.A.L. Site), 51
Society for Human Resource Managment, 76
Society for Industrial-Organizational Psychology, 96
Society of Industrial Engineers, 39
Society of Industrial/Organizational Psychology (R.E.A.L. Site), 51
Soul Mates (Moore), 209
Southwest Airlines Co., 64, 99, 178, 179–80
Spearman, Charles, 26
Spearman formula, 36
SPEEA (Seattle Professional Engineering Employees Association), 201
Spence, Kenneth, 29
Spencer, L. M., Jr., 99
The Spiritual Path to Leadership (Aburdene), 222
Spitzer, T. Quinn, 178
sports and diversity, 219
Srat*X International, 141
Stanek, John R., 199
Starbucks, 181–84
Stein, K. B., 186
Stempler, Marilyn D., 91
Stevens, D. P., 111
Stevens, Mary Holmes, 32, 33*t*, 34–36, 38–42
   See also Hayes, Mary Holmes Stevens
Stewart, G. L., 103–4
Story Completion Test, 187, 188
Strategic Interactive, 128
Strategic Management Group (SMG), 142, 143, 144, 148
strategic planning and consulting, 17
Stratton, George, 34
Strauss, J., 105
stress in workplace, 239–40
Strong, E. K., 21, 29, 36
structuralism, 22, 32
Sullivan, Karla, 2, 47
Summers, Lynn, 165
Sun Microsystems, 8
Sywak, M., 118

T

Taber, T. D., 118
Taft-Hartley Act, 68
Tan, Rowena, 2, **47**
task-based to process-based organizations, 6–7
Taylor, Frederick, 37, 125
Taylor, Karen, 147
Teamsters, 67
teamwork and changing workplace, 7
technology, 4
   and corporate organization, 217–18
   360-degree feedback system, 10, 165–69, 170–73
   and training, 127
   workplace flexibility, 96–97
temporary workers, 69, 198–201
Terman, Lewis, 25, 26, 36

testing
   cognitive abilities testing, 7–8, 120
   for intelligence and conscientiousness, 105
   mental testing, 25
   personality, 99–106, 107–14
   and WWI, 27–28, 29, 36, 37, 94, 100
Texaco, 58, 79, 81, 172, 219
Texas Instuments Inc., 200
The Theory of Advertising (Scott), 27
Theory X, 164
Theory Y, 164
Thompson Products, 67, 68
Thorndike, E. L., 26, 27, 28, 34, 36
Thorow, Lester, 214
360-degree feedback system, 10, 165–69, 170–73
Thurstone, Leon L., 26, 28
Tichy, N., 119, 120
Time Metaphors, 187
time-motion studies, 37, 125
Tippins, Nancy, 127, 128
Titchener, Edward Bradford, 26
Tom's of Maine, 206
Toquam, J. L., 109
total quality management (TQM), 10, 139
Towards a Better Future: The Works of Manfred Davidmann (R.E.A.L. Site), 193
Towbin, Ginny, 145
TQM (total quality management), 10, 139
trade unions, 66, 68
training
   in changing workplace, 8–10
   cognitive-behavioral training (CBT), 150–56
   diversity, 221
   ethics, 129–32
   evaluations, 9
   interactive technology, 128
   need for constant, 97
   outdoor techniques, 133–40
   psychologists' contributions to, 127–28
   simulator use, 141–49
Training, 162*n*
Training & Development, 141*n*, 165*n*
trait-method unit, 8
Tranportation, U.S. Department of (DOT), 145
Transamerica, 240
Travelers Group Inc., 199
trends, workplace, 4–6, 96–98
Trommsdorff, G., 189
Trompter Electronics, 173
truck driVR (simulation program), 141, 145
Truss, C. V, 111
Tucker, Jeffrey, 52, **57**

U

Uhrbrock, Richard, 28
unemployment and cognitive-behavioral training (CBT), 150–56
United Nation's International Labor Organization, 239
United Parcel Service (UPS), 67, 90, 172
University of California, 34, 90
University of Chicago, 23, 28, 34
University of Minnesota, 97, 102

University of Pennsylvania, 25
University of Wisconsin, 34
U.N.'s International Labor Organization, 239
UPS (United Parcel Service), 67, 90, 172
U.S. Air Force, 100
U.S. Army, 109
U.S. Bureau of Labor Statistics, 199
U.S. Department of Agriculture (USDA), 145
U.S. Department of Defense (DOD), 134
U.S. Department of Justice and ADA, 89–90
U.S. Department of Labor, 38
U.S. Department of Transportation (DOT), 145
U.S. Employment Service (USES), 100
U.S. Military Academy (USMA). *See* West Point
U.S. News & World Report, 87*n*, 89*n*, 237
U.S. News/ Bozell poll, 240
U.S. Rubber, 37
U.S. Supreme Court, 91
USA Today, 218
USDA (U.S. Department of Agriculture), 145
USES (U.S. Employment Service), 100
Utah State University, 134

V

Van Allen, Ray, 200
Van Buren, Harry J., III, 73, **79**
Veninga, Robert L., 239
virtual parenting, 237
virtual training with simulators, 141–49
virtual work, 5
Viswesvaran, Chockalingam, 97, 109
Vital Speeches of the Day, 213*n*, 217*n*, 239*n*
Viteles, Morris S., 24, 26, 29, 39
Vocational Guidance Association, 39
Vocational Service for Juniors, 41
de Volder, M. M., 188
von Mises, Ludwig, 58
vulgar utilitarianism, 24

W

Wagner Act, 67
Wahl, Quentin, 6
Waldman, David, 170
Wallace, Doug, 74, **82**
Wanous, J. P., 120
Warech, M. A., 107
The Washington Monthly, 236*n*
The Washington Post, 84*n*
Waterman, Robert, 9
Watson, John B., 25, 27, 28, 36
Watson-Crick team, 29
Weick, K. E., 189
Weiss, H. M., 190
Weiss, Naomi, 181
Weitz, Joe, 40
welfare capitalism, 66–70
Werbel, J. D., 119
West Point, leadership training at, 224–31
Whipple, Guy, 28
White, T. H., 241
Whitsett, David, 2, **47**

Index   249

Who's Who of American Women, 41
Why Work? Motivating the New Workforce (Maccoby), 178
Wilamette Law On-Line: Labor and Employment (R.E.A.L. Site), 93
Wilburn, Deborah, 63, 64, 65
"wilderness centered" training, 133
Williams, John, 222
Willimon, William H., 205
Wilson, Larry, 164
Wink, P., 111
Wolinsky, Sid, 90
women-owned businesses, 218
Woods, Huie, 178–79
Woods, Tiger, 219
Woodsworth, A., 118
Woolley, Helen Thompson, 34
work
    abusive organization, 61–62
    changes in, 5–6
    joy and ethics of, 58–59
    and life balance, 183
    realistic work cultures, 119–20, 122
    shorter work-week, 71
    six virtues of labor, 59–60
    See also employment; jobs; workers; workplace
Work Family Connection (R.E.A.L. Site), 72
work loads, examination of, 240

work performance. *See* performance
workaholic culture, 236–37
Worker Satisfaction, Motivation and Commitment (R.E.A.L. Site), 210
workers
    as empowered, 5–6
    moral obligations of, 57–60, 129–32
    part-time and temporary, 69, 198–201
    poaching trained, 9
work-family programs, 61, 65
Workforce, 15*n,* 181*n,* 202
Workforce 2000, 218
Working Mother, 63–64, 65
Working Mother/Woman (R.E.A.L. Site), 72
Working Solutions, 183
workplace
    community in, 205–9
    conflicts in, 234–35
    as democracy, 5
    employee selection and, 7–8
    flexibility in, 5, 61, 96–97, 183, 237
    inhibitions of equal opportunity in, 79–81
    job analysis and changes in, 6–7
    job tasks in changing, 3–14
    legislation for, 75–78
    and parenting, 183, 237–38
    personal characteristics in, 6–7
    principles and legal issues, 73
    research and I/O psychology on, 6–12

    stress in, 239–40
    technology in, 96–97
    trends, 96–98
Workplace Religious Freedom Act, 75
Works Progress Administration (WPA), 38
The World Competitiveness Report, 4
World Labor Report (1993), 239
World War I, testing movement in, 27–28, 29, 36, 37, 94, 100
WPA (Works Progress Administration), 38
Wray, Herbert, 74, **87**
Wundt, Wilhelm, 21, 22, 26, 28
Wyszsnki, Stefan, 59, 60

X

Xerox Corp., 7, 173, 200

Y

Yello (simulation program), 146
Yerkes, Robert, 26, 27, 28, 29, 36, 94
Yoakum, Clarence S., 28, 35
Yost, E., 34

Z

Zimbardo, P. G., 187

Putting it in *Perspectives*
-Review Form-

Your name:_____ Date: _____

Reading title: _____

Summarize: Provide a one-sentence summary of this reading: _____

_____
_____
_____

Follow the Thinking: How does the author back the main premise of the reading? Are the facts/opinions appropriately supported by research or available data? Is the author's thinking logical?

_____
_____
_____
_____
_____

Develop a Context (answer one or both questions): How does this reading contrast or compliment your professor's lecture treatment of the subject matter? How does this reading compare to your textbook's coverage?

_____
_____
_____
_____
_____

Question Authority: Explain why you agree/disagree with the author's main premise.

_____
_____
_____
_____
_____

COPY ME! Copy this form as needed. This form is also available at http://www.coursewise.com
Click on: *Perspectives*.